NON-V
RESISTANCE
(SATYAGRAHA)

M. K. GANDHI

DOVER PUBLICATIONS, INC.
Mineola, New York

Bibliographical Note

This Dover edition, first published in 2001, is an unabridged republication of the edition published by Schocken Books, New York, in 1961. (Following that edition, there are no pages 1 and 2. Text begins on page 3.)

Library of Congress Cataloging-in-Publication Data

Gandhi, Mahatma, 1869–1948.
   [Satyagraha (non-violent resistance)]
   Non-violent resistance (Satyagraha) / M.K. Gandhi.
      p. cm.
   Originally published: New York : Schocken Books, 1961.
   Includes index.
   ISBN-13: 978-0-486-41606-9 (pbk.)
   ISBN-10: 0-486-41606-2 (pbk.)
   1. Passive resistance. 2. India–Politics and government–1919–1947.
I. Title.

HM1281 .G35 2001
322.4–dc21

                                          2001017199

Manufactured in the United States by LSC Communications
41606210   2018
www.doverpublications.com

EDITOR'S NOTE

Satyagraha means literally 'clinging to truth', and as Truth for Gandhiji was God, Satyagraha in the general sense of the word means the way of life of one who holds steadfastly to God and dedicates his life to Him. The true Satyagrahi is, accordingly, a man of God.

Such an individual in this world finds himself up against evil, which he cannot but resist. He comes across injustice, cruelty, exploitation and oppression. These he has to oppose with all the resources at his command. In his crusade his reliance is on Truth or God; and since the greatest truth is the unity of all life, Truth can be attained only by loving service of all, i.e. by non-violence. The weapon of the Satyagrahi is therefore non-violence. Satyagraha, in the narrower sense in which it is ordinarily understood, accordingly means resisting evil through soul-force or non-violence.

For the required soul-force the individual has to discipline himself in self-control, simplicity of life, suffering without fear or hatred, recognition of the unity of all living beings, and whole-hearted and disinterested service of one's neighbours. The vows which Gandhiji elaborated for members of his Satyagraha Ashram at Sabarmati are of interest from this point of view. They were truth, non-violence, *brahmacharya*, fearlessness, control of the palate, non-possession, non-stealing, bread-labour, equality of religions, anti-untouchability and *swadeshi*.

Gandhiji derived his doctrine of Satyagraha from many sources. It can be traced essentially to the *Gita* ideal of the *karmayogin*, and also to Jesus' Sermon on the Mount; and recently to the writings of Thoreau, Ruskin and more especially Tolstoy. But his practical application of it in the social and political spheres was entirely his own.

Satyagraha, in the narrower sense, takes many forms. Primarily it is a case of appealing to the reason and conscience of the opponent by inviting suffering on oneself. The motive is to convert the opponent and make him one's willing ally and friend. It is based on the idea that the moral appeal to the heart and conscience is, in the case of human beings, more effective than an appeal based on threat of bodily pain or violence. Indeed violence, according to Gandhiji, does not ever overcome evil; it suppresses it for the time being to rise later with redoubled vigour. Non-violence, on the other hand, puts an end to evil, for it converts the evil-doer.

But the non-violence which thus overcomes evil is not the passive resistance of the weak. The non-violence of a Satyagrahi is unflinching. It is the non-violence of the brave. It will lead the Satyagrahi to die with a smile on his lips and with no trace of hatred in his heart.

It presupposes a disciplined character, selflessness and unswerving devotion to duty. The passive resister, or the one who adopts non-violence as policy, on the other hand, is really not non-violent, for he would be violent if he could, and is nonviolent only because he does not for the time being have the means or the capacity for violence. It is a far cry, therefore, from passive resistance to Satyagraha.

Satyagraha may take the form of non-cooperation. When it does, it is not non-cooperation with the evil-doer but with his evil deed. This is an important distinction. The Satyagrahi cooperates with the evil-doer in what is good, for he has no hatred for him. On the contrary, he has nothing but friendship for him. Through cooperating with him in what is not evil, the Satyagrahi wins him over from evil.

Satyagraha may at times take the form of fasting. When it does, there is to be no trace of self in the motive. The fast should be prompted by the highest devotion to duty and love for the opponent. It should aim at purifying oneself, for lack of capacity to convince the opponent shows defect in oneself. It should seek to influence the opponent by converting him, not by coercing him to do something against his conviction. Fasting should be undertaken, according to Gandhiji, only when one is thoroughly convinced of the rightness of one's stand, when all other methods have failed, and as a last resort, and never for personal gain. It should be in the nature of prayer for purity and strength and power from God.

Satyagraha in the political sphere assumes the form of Civil Disobedience. It is for this form of Satyagraha that Gandhiji came to be most reputed. It means mass resistance on a non-violent basis against the Government when negotiations and constitutional methods have failed. It is called 'civil' because it is non-violent resistance by people who are ordinarily law-abiding citizens; also because the laws which they choose to disobey are not moral laws but only such as are harmful to the people. It is civil also in the sense that those who break the law are to observe the greatest courtesy and gentleness in regard to those who enforce the law. They are even to seek not to embarrass the opponent if possible.

Gandhiji organized such Satyagraha for the first time in South Africa against humiliating laws enforced by the South African Government on Indians in that country. With the experience so gained, he organized successfully peasant Satyagraha in Champaran, Kheda, and Bardoli to remove specific local grievances.

But Satyagraha can also be on a nation-wide scale to resist an entire Government when that Government is corrupt and demoralizes the people. It may then take the form of non-cooperation with the Government, as it did in Gandhiji's Civil Disobedience movements of 1920-22, 1930-34 and 1940-44 in India. Non-cooperation may express itself in giving up titles and honours bestowed by the Government, resignation from Government service, withdrawal from the police and military, non-payment of taxes, boycott of courts, schools and legislatures, and running parallel institutions to perform these functions. Gandhiji, however, was very cautious in regard to some of these forms of non-cooperation, as they were likely to bring down on the people the wrath of an indignant Government, and he did not want the people to suffer more than was necessary from Government repression.

Such Civil Disobedience demands on the part of the people disciplined group action, infinite capacity for suffering without retaliation, and strict obedience to leaders. As this discipline and obedience are not, as in the case of the military, based on force, the leaders have to be men of character and public service, whom the people respect and willingly obey. This implies that the leaders are men who generally carry on various forms of constructive service for the people. Gandhiji, therefore, emphasized working of his Constructive Programme as essential for Satyagraha; and not only for this reason, but also because discipline and group action need to be built up steadily among the people. They have to be taught, for example, cooperation, communal unity, fearlessness, consideration for the social good, self-help and resourcefulness, and have to have physical, mental and moral strength. All this can be done only through various forms of constructive endeavour advocated by Gandhiji, such as working for economic self-sufficiency in villages; education, abolition of drink and untouchability, communal concord, uplift of women, sanitation, hygiene, improved diet, child welfare, and so on. Satyagraha in the political sphere is not, therefore, a plan of action adopted merely for a time, wound up thereafter, and requiring no further effort; it presupposes day to day non-political constructive work aiming at the all-around development of the individual from the cradle to the grave.

In this respect Satyagraha or non-violent resistance, as conceived by Gandhiji, has an important lesson for pacifists and war-resisters of the West. Western pacifists have so far proved ineffective because they have thought that war can be resisted by mere propaganda, conscientious objection, and organization for settling disputes. Gandhiji showed that non-violence to be effective requires constructive effort in every sphere of life, individual, social, economic and political. These spheres have to be organized and refashioned in such a way that the people will have learnt to be non-violent in their daily lives, manage their affairs on a cooperative and non-violent basis, and thus have acquired sufficient strength and resourcefulness to be able to offer non-violent resistance against organized violence. The practice of non-violence in the political sphere is not, therefore, a mere matter of preaching or even of establishing arbitration courts or Leagues of Nations, but involves building up brick by brick with patience and industry a new non-violent social and economic order. It depends ultimately on banishing violence from the heart of the individual, and making of him a transformed disciplined person. Gandhiji's contribution lay in evolving the necessary technique and showing by example how all this can be done.

There can be no doubt that in developing Satyagraha in its various forms as a practical means of overcoming violence, more especially in group life, Gandhiji established a new mile-stone in the history of the human race in its march towards peace on earth and goodwill among men. He himself did not claim finality for his methods, as after all he was a pioneer in the field and a humble experimenter. The science of Satyagraha is therefore still in the making. But his teachings and experience are invaluable for all future students and makers of this science. The purpose of this volume is to help in the process by making available for the reader Gandhiji's findings in his own words and in as comprehensive a form as possible.

Bombay, August, 1950   BHARATAN KUMARAPPA

From my introductory note to Section Eighth the impression is created that the *Harijan* after its suspension in November 1940 was permitted to be published again only in February, 1946. This is wrong. As a matter of fact it was restarted in January, 1942, after a lapse of about 14 months. It was published in three separate languages (English, Gujarati and Hindi) by the Navajivan Press from Ahmedabad till August of that year when the press was confiscated by the Government after the arrest of Gandhiji and other leaders. Since that time the press remained in the custody of the Government and the publication of the *Harijan* weeklies could be resumed only in February, 1946.

NON-ENGLISH WORDS WITH THEIR MEANINGS

Abkari : a tax on spirituous liquors and narcotics

Anand : bliss

Abhyasa : repetition, study

Ahimsa : non-violence

Bhajan : a religious song

Bhang : an intoxicant drink made from a kind of hemp

Brahmachari : a celibate

Brahmacharya : celibacy, continence

Bhakti : devotion

Brahma : the Divine Reality

Brahmavidya : knowledge of the Divine Reality, the Upanishads

Charkha : a spinning wheel

Chit : knowledge

Diva-dandi : a light-house

Dhurana : mode of extorting compliance to any demand

Dukkha : misery

Duragraha : foolish obstinacy

Ganja : a kind of hemp

Goonda : a ruffian

Goondaism : reign of ruffians

Gumasta : a shop-assistant

Guru : a teacher

Hai Hai : shame, shame

Harijans : literally, the people of Hari, i.e. God; the name which Gandhiji gave to untouchables

Harijan, Harijanbandhu, Harijansevak : names of weekly journals in English Gujarati and Hindi respectively, conducted by Mahatma Gandhi

Hartal : cessation of work; a strike

Hathayoga : a rigorous mode of religious meditation

Hijrat : exodus or going away from one's native land

Himsa : violence

Jam-i-Jam : universal provider

Kalpadruma : a tree supposed to grant all desires

Khaddar, Khadi : hand-spun and hand-woven cloth

Lathi : a long stick

Lotaful : potful (*lota*, a metal pot)

Mahajan : a trade guild, elders of a trade guild

Mahatma : a high-souled man

Mahayajna : a great sacrifice

Mantra : a sacred incantation meant for recitation and meditation

Mukti : emancipation

Navajivan : literally new life; name of a weekly journal in Gujarati edited by Mahatma Gandhi

Neti, Neti : not this, not this

Nirvana : extinction

Panchama : a fifth-caste man, an outcaste

Pan : a kind of leaf chewed with lime and betel nut

Pardanashin : sitting behind a purdah (veil), veiled

Purna Swaraj : complete independence

Raj : a kingdom

Rishi : a seer

Salaam : a salute

Sanatani : orthodox

Sangha : a commune, an association

Sarkari : governmental

Sat, Satya : Truth

Satyagraha : clinging to truth; civil or non-violent disobedience or resistance

Satyagrahashram : Ashram founded by Gandhi at Ahmedabad in 1915

Satyagrahi : a follower of Satyagraha

Savarna : belonging to one of the four castes

Sena : an army

Shastra : a scripture

Shethia : a merchant, a wealthy man

Shraddha : ceremony in honour of departed spirits of dead relatives

Swadeshi : of indigenous or native make; the principle of using goods made locally or in one's own country

Swaraj : self-government, home-rule

Tahsil : a district

Takli : a wooden or metal device for spinning

Talati : a village revenue officer

Tapa, Tapasya : penance, religious austerity

Thana : a police station

Tonga : horse-carriage

Vairagya : aversion or indifference to worldly interests, desirelessness

Varnashrama : the four castes and stages in life

Yajna : a sacrifice

Young India : name of a weekly journal in English edited by Gandhi

Zoolum : oppression

CONTENTS

Chapter   Page

EDITOR'S NOTE iii

NON-ENGLISH WORDS WITH THEIR MEANINGS . vii

SECTION FIRST : WHAT SATYAGRAHA IS

1 SATYAGRAHA, CIVIL DISOBEDIENCE, PASSIVE RESISTANCE, NON-CO-OPERATION . . 3

2 DOMESTIC SATYAGRAHA 4

3 SATYAGRAHA 6

4 MEANS AND ENDS 9

5 SATYAGRAHA OR PASSIVE RESISTANCE . . 15

6 EVIDENCE BEFORE THE HUNTER COMMITTEE . 19

7 THE THEORY AND PRACTICE OF SATYAGRAHA . 34

SECTION SECOND : DISCIPLINE FOR SATYAGRAHA

8 SATYAGRAHA ASHRAM VOWS . . . 37

    I TRUTH 38

    II AHIMSA OR LOVE . . . 40

    III BRAHMACHARYA OR CHASTITY . 42

    IV NON-POSSESSION . . . 45

9 YAJNA OR SACRIFICE 47

10 PROTECTING HINDUISM 50

11 MORAL REQUIREMENTS FOR SATYAGRAHA . 51

12 CONDITIONS FOR SUCCESSFUL SATYAGRAHA . 56

13 NON-RETALIATION 56

14 COURAGE AND DISCIPLINE NECESSARY . . 57

15 THE NEED FOR HUMILITY . . . 58

16 WORK IN JAILS 60

17 A MODEL PRISONER 62

18 SATYAGRAHI PRISONER'S CONDUCT . . 64

19 PRE-REQUISITES FOR SATYAGRAHA . . 66

20 MY POLITICAL PROGRAMME . . . 68

21 LIMITATIONS OF SATYAGRAHA . . 69

22 A GREAT SATYAGRAHI 72

23 NEILL STATUE SATYAGRAHA . . . 73
24 A HIMALAYAN MISCALCULATION . . 74
25 QUALIFICATIONS FOR SATYAGRAHA . . 77
26 SOME RULES OF SATYAGRAHA . . . 78
27 FULL SURRENDER 81
28 TO WEAKEN COMMUNALISM . . . 82
29 POLITICAL POWER *v.* SATYAGRAHA . . 82
30 FOR 'FOLLOWERS' 83
31 MAINTENANCE ALLOWANCE . . . 84
32 A NON-VIOLENT ARMY 86
33 TO VOLUNTEERS 87
34 REQUISITE QUALIFICATIONS . . . 87
35 QUALIFICATIONS OF A PEACE BRIGADE . . 88
36 THE NECESSITY OF TRAINING . . . 91
37 PHYSICAL TRAINING FOR THE SATYAGRAHI . 92
38 BRAHMACHARYA FOR SATYAGRAHA . . 97
39 DISCIPLINE — SATYAGRAHI AND MILITARY . 98
40 SCORCHED EARTH 99
41 TRAINING FOR A NON-VIOLENT ARMY . . 100
42 CONSTRUCTIVE PREPARATION . . . 100

SECTION THIRD : NON-CO-OPERATION AND CIVIL DISOBEDIENCE

43 THE NATIONAL WEEK 102
44 THE SATYAGRAHA WEEK 104
45 JALIANWALA BAGH 105
46 NEITHER A SAINT NOR A POLITICIAN . . 108
47 THE LAW OF SUFFERING . . . 112
48 HOW TO WORK NON-CO-OPERATION . . 115
49 HOW AND WHEN TO ACT . . . 117
50 AT THE CALL OF THE COUNTRY . . . 119
51 THE FIRST OF AUGUST 122
52 WHO IS DISLOYAL ? 124
53 NON-VIOLENCE AND SWADESHI . . . 126
54 PROGRAMME FOR SATYAGRAHA . . . 128
55 THE DOCTRINE OF THE SWORD . . . 132
56 RENUNCIATION OF MEDALS . . . 136
57 NON-PAYMENT OF FINES 138
58 NON-PAYMENT OF TAXES . . . 139

59 NON-PAYMENT OF TAXES . . . 140
60 BOYCOTT OF COURTS AND SCHOOLS . . 142
61 EMPIRE GOODS BOYCOTT . . . 145
62 SOCIAL BOYCOTT 147
63 SOCIAL BOYCOTT 148
64 SYMPATHETIC STRIKES 149
65 MORE OBJECTIONS ANSWERED . . . 151
66 ANSWERS TO QUESTIONS 153
67 NON-CO-OPERATION EXPLAINED . . . 156
68 LOVE 161
69 THE POET'S ANXIETY 162
70 WHAT IT IS NOT 166
71 THE NON-CO-OPERATION OF A SATYAGRAHI . 169
72 CIVIL DISOBEDIENCE 170
73 CIVIL DISOBEDIENCE 173
74 THE RIGHT OF CIVIL DISOBEDIENCE . . 174
75 AGGRESSIVE *v.* DEFENSIVE . . . 175
76 MY FAITH 176

SECTION FOURTH : VYKOM SATYAGRAHA

77 VYKOM 177
78 VYKOM SATYAGRAHA 180
79 VYKOM SATYAGRAHA 185
80 VYKOM 187
81 VYKOM SATYAGRAHA 188
82 VYKOM SATYAGRAHA 189
83 VYKOM SATYAGRAHA 191
84 SATYAGRAHI'S DUTY 192
85 VYKOM 196
86 TRUE SATYAGRAHA 198
87 VYKOM SATYAGRAHA 200
88 SATYAGRAHA *v.* COMPULSION . . . 201
89 RELIGIOUS SATYAGRAHA 203

SECTION FIFTH : KHEDA AND BARDOLI SATYAGRAHAS

90 THE KHEDA SATYAGRAHA . . . 204
91 BARDOLI'S DECISION 209
92 BARDOLI ON TRIAL 212
93 NON-CO-OPERATION OR CIVIL RESISTANCE ? . 214
94 LIMITATIONS OF SATYAGRAHA . . . 215

95 ALL'S WELL 217
96 A SIGN OF THE TIMES 218

SECTION SIXTH : SALT SATYAGRAHA

97 "NEVER FAILETH" 220
98 TO ENGLISH FRIENDS 222
99 WHEN I AM ARRESTED 223
100 LETTER TO THE VICEROY . . . 226
101 SOME QUESTIONS AND ANSWERS . . 229
102 ON THE EVE OF THE MARCH . . . 233
103 ASHRAM DISCIPLINE DURING THE MARCH . 236
104 DUTY OF DISLOYALTY 238
105 SOME SUGGESTIONS 239
106 TURNING THE SEARCHLIGHT INWARD . . 242
107 NOTES ON THE WAY TO DANDI . . . 246
108 REMEMBER 6TH APRIL 249
109 HINDU-MUSLIM QUESTION . . . 250
110 BARBAROUS 254
111 THE INHUMAN TAX 256
112 A SURVEY 258
113 THE BLACK REGIME 261
114 PURITY IN ACCOUNT-KEEPING . . . 264
115 CALM HEROISM 265
116 MAHADEV DESAI AND HIS SUCCESSOR . . 265
117 GOONDA RAJ 267
118 MESSAGE TO THE NATION . . . 270
119 THE SECOND LETTER 272
120 THE GREAT ARREST 276
121 MORE ABOUT THE SETTLEMENT . . 278
122 THE CONGRESS 280
123 LET US REPENT 282
124 POWER OF AHIMSA 285
125 GOONDAISM WITHIN THE CONGRESS . . 287
126 CONQUEST OVER BODY 289

SECTION SEVENTH : INDIAN STATES SATYAGRAHA

127 SUSPEND CIVIL DISOBEDIENCE . . . 291
128 RAJKOT SATYAGRAHA 292
129 ABOUT THE RAJKOT AWARD . . . 293

130 SUSPENSION OF CIVIL DISOBEDIENCE . . 293
131 ITS IMPLICATIONS 295
132 NON-VIOLENCE *v.* VIOLENCE . . . 297

SECTION EIGHTH : INDIVIDUAL SATYAGRAHA AGAINST WAR

133 NO SUPPRESSION 300
134 EVERY CONGRESS COMMITTEE A SATYAGRAHA
    COMMITTEE 302
135 THE CHARKHA AND SATYAGRAHA . . 304
136 CIVIL DISOBEDIENCE 306
137 NOT YET 307
138 TO THE READER 308

SECTION NINTH : MISCELLANEOUS

I. Fast as an Element in Satyagraha

139 FASTING AS PENANCE 310
140 THE SATYAGRAHA WAY WITH CHILDREN . 311
141 SATYAGRAHA — TRUE AND FALSE. . . 313
142 FAST AS AN ELEMENT IN SATYAGRAHA . . 314
143 FAST AS PRAYER 315
144 IS FAST COERCION ? 316
145 FAST AS THE LAST RESORT . . . 317
146 FAST AS SELF-SURRENDER. . . . 318
147 REQUIREMENTS FOR SATYAGRAHA FAST. . 319
148 COERCIVE FASTS 319
149 FASTING 320
150 FASTING IN SATYAGRAHA . . . 321
151 FASTING IN THE AIR 323

II. Women and Picketing

152 TO THE WOMEN OF INDIA . . . 325
153 WOMEN IN CONFERENCE 328
154 MEN'S PART 330
155 NOTES 333
156 HOW TO DO THE PICKETING . . . 334
157 SOME PICKETING RULES 336
158 A STERN REPROOF. 337
159 PICKETING 338
160 WHEN IS PICKETING PEACEFUL ? . . 340
161 PICKETING AND LOVE 341

III. Satyagraha in Social Reform

162 STUDENTS' NOBLE SATYAGRAHA . . . 342
163 LIMITS OF SATYAGRAHA 344
164 SATYAGRAHA AGAINST THE COLOUR BAR BILL . 347
165 THE JEWS 348
166 THE SATYAGRAHA WAY WITH CRIME . . 350
167 SOCIALISM AND SATYAGRAHA . . . 352

SECTION TENTH : QUESTIONS AND ANSWERS

168 SOME QUESTIONS 354
169 ON NON-VIOLENCE· 358
170 WHAT ARE BASIC ASSUMPTIONS . . 362
171 BELIEF IN GOD 364
172 NOT GUILTY 367
173 QUESTION BOX 370
174 QUESTION BOX 372
175 FIVE QUESTIONS 374
176 THE SERMON ON THE MOUNT . . . 375
177 WHAT CAN A SOLITARY SATYAGRAHI DO ? . 376
178 NON-VIOLENT NON-CO-OPERATION . . 377
179 SABOTAGE AND SECRECY 378
180 SATYAGRAHA IN FACE OF HOOLIGANISM . 380
181 THE NON-VIOLENT SANCTION . . . 382

SECTION ELEVENTH : CONCLUSION

182 MY FAITH IN NON-VIOLENCE . . . 383
183 THE FUTURE 385
     INDEX 389

SATYAGRAHA

SECTION FIRST : WHAT SATYAGRAHA IS

1

SATYAGRAHA, CIVIL DISOBEDIENCE
PASSIVE RESISTANCE, NON-CO-OPERATION

Satyagraha is literally holding on to Truth and it means, therefore, Truth-force. Truth is soul or spirit. It is, therefore, known as soul-force. It excludes the use of violence because man is not capable of knowing the absolute truth and, therefore, not competent to punish. The word was coined in South Africa to distinguish the non-violent resistance of the Indians of South Africa from the contemporary ' passive resistance ' of the suffragettes and others. It is not conceived as a weapon of the weak.

Passive resistance is used in the orthodox English sense and covers the suffragette movement as well as the resistance of the Non-conformists. Passive resistance has been conceived and is regarded as a weapon of the weak. Whilst it avoids violence, being not open to the weak, it does not exclude its use if, in the opinion of a passive resister, the occasion demands it. However, it has always been distinguished from armed resistance and its applica-tion was at one time confined to Christian martyrs.

Civil Disobedience is civil breach of unmoral statutory enactments. The expression was, so far as I am aware, coined by Thoreau to signify his own resistance to the laws of a slave State. He has left a masterly treatise on the duty of Civil Disobedience. But Thoreau was not perhaps an out and out champion of non-violence. Proba-bly, also, Thoreau limited his breach of statutory laws to the revenue law, i.e. payment of taxes. Whereas the term Civil Disobedience as practised in 1919 covered a breach of any statutory and unmoral law. It signified the resister's outlawry in a civil, i.e., non-violent manner. He invoked the sanctions of the law and cheerfully suffered imprisonment. It is a branch of Satyagraha.

Non-co-operation predominantly implies withdrawing of co-operation from the State that in the non-co-operator's view has become corrupt and excludes Civil Disobedience of the fierce type described above. By its very nature, non-co-operation is even open to children of understanding and can be safely practised by the masses. Civil Disobedience presupposes the habit of willing obedience to laws without fear of their sanctions. It can, therefore, be practised only as a last resort and by a select few in the first instance at any rate. Non-co-operation, too, like Civil Disobedience is a branch of Satyagraha which includes all non-violent resistance for the vindication of Truth.

Young India, 23-3-'21

2

DOMESTIC SATYAGRAHA

I had read in some books on vegetarianism that salt was not a necessary article of diet for man, that on the contrary saltless diet was better for health. I had deduced that a *brahmachari* benefited by a saltless diet. I had read and realized that the weak-bodied should avoid pulses. I was very fond of them. Now it happened that Kasturba,* who had a brief respite after that operation, had again begun getting hemorrhage and the malady seemed to be obstinate. Hydropathic treatment by itself did not answer. Kasturba had not much faith in my remedies though she did not resist them. She certainly did not ask for outside help. So when all my remedies had failed, I entreated her to give up salt and pulses. She would not agree, however much I pleaded with her,

---

* Gandhiji's wife.

supporting myself with authorities. At last she challenged me saying that even I could not give up these articles if I was advised to do so. I was pained and equally delighted, — delighted in that I got an opportunity to shower my love on her. I said to her : " You are mistaken. If I was ailing and the doctor advised me to give up these or any other articles I should unhesitatingly do so. But there ! Without any medical advice, I give up salt and pulses for one year, whether you do so or not."

She was rudely shocked and exclaimed in deep sorrow : " Pray forgive me. Knowing you, I should not have provoked you. I promise to abstain from these things, but for heaven's sake take back your vow. This is too hard on me."

" It is very good for you to give up these articles. I have not the slightest doubt that you will be all the better without them. As for me, I cannot retract a vow seriously taken. And it is sure to benefit me, for all restraint, whatever prompts it, is wholesome for man. You will therefore leave me alone. It will be a test for me, and a moral support to you in carrying out your resolve."

So she gave me up. " You are too obstinate. You will listen to none," she said, and sought relief in tears.

I would like to count this incident as an instance of Satyagraha and as one of the sweetest recollections of my life.

Medically there may be two opinions as to the value of a saltless and pulseless diet, but morally I have no doubt that all self-denial is good for the soul. The diet of a man of self-restraint must be different from that of a man of pleasure just as their ways of life are different.

The Story of My Experiments with Truth, Part IV — Chapter XXIX

3

SATYAGRAHA *

For the past thirty years I have been preaching and practising Satyagraha. The principles of Satyagraha, as I know it today, constitute a gradual evolution.

Satyagraha differs from Passive Resistance as the North Pole from the South. The latter has been conceived as a weapon of the weak and does not exclude the use of physical force or violence for the purpose of gaining one's end, whereas the former has been conceived as a weapon of the strongest and excludes the use of violence in any shape or form.

The term *Satyagraha* was coined by me in South Africa to express the force that the Indians there used for full eight years and it was coined in order to distinguish it from the movement then going on in the United Kingdom and South Africa under the name of Passive Resistance.

Its root meaning is holding on to truth, hence truth-force. I have also called it Love-force or Soul-force. In the application of Satyagraha I discovered in the earliest stages that pursuit of truth did not admit of violence being inflicted on one's opponent but that he must be weaned from error by patience and sympathy. For what appears to be truth to the one may appear to be error to the other. And patience means self-suffering. So the doctrine came to mean vindication of truth not by infliction of suffering on the opponent but on one's self.

But on the political field the struggle on behalf of the people mostly consists in opposing error in the shape of unjust laws. When you have failed to bring the error home to the lawgiver by way of petitions and the like, the only remedy open to you, if you do not wish to submit to error, is to compel him by physical force to yield to you or by suffering in your own person by inviting the penalty for the breach of the law. Hence Satyagraha largely

---

* Extract from a Statement by Gandhiji to the Hunter Committee.

appears to the public as Civil Disobedience or Civil Resistance. It is civil in the sense that it is not criminal.

The lawbreaker breaks the law surreptitiously and tries to avoid the penalty, not so the civil resister. He ever obeys the laws of the State to which he belongs, not out of fear of the sanctions but because he considers them to be good for the welfare of society. But there come occasions, generally rare, when he considers certain laws to be so unjust as to render obedience to them a dishonour. He then openly and civilly breaks them and quietly suffers the penalty for their breach. And in order to register his protest against the action of the law givers, it is open to him to withdraw his co-operation from the State by disobeying such other laws whose breach does not involve moral turpitude.

In my opinion, the beauty and efficacy of Satyagraha are so great and the doctrine so simple that it can be preached even to children. It was preached by me to thousands of men, women and children commonly called indentured Indians with excellent results.

Rowlatt Bills *

When the Rowlatt Bills were published I felt that they were so restrictive of human liberty that they must be resisted to the utmost. I observed too that the opposition to them was universal among Indians. I submit that no State however despotic has the right to enact laws which are repugnant to the whole body of the people, much less a Government guided by constitutional usage and precedent such as the Indian Government. I felt too that the oncoming agitation needed a definite direction if it was neither to collapse nor to run into violent channels.

The Sixth April

I ventured therefore to present Satyagraha to the country emphasizing its civil-resistance aspect. And as

* For information about the Rowlatt Act see Editor's introductory notes to III Non-co-operation and Civil Disobedience, at the commencement of Chapter 43 below.

it is purely an inward and purifying movement I suggested the observance of fast, prayer and suspension of all work for one day — the 6th of April. There was a magnificent response throughout the length and breadth of India even in little villages although there was no organization and no great previous preparation. The idea was given to the public as soon as it was conceived. On the 6th April there was no violence used by the people and no collision with the police worth naming. The *hartal* was purely voluntary and spontaneous. I attach hereto the letter in which the idea was announced.

My Arrest

The observance of the 6th April was to be followed by Civil Disobedience. For the purpose the committee of the Satyagraha Sabha had selected certain political laws for disobedience. And we commenced the distribution of prohibited literature of a perfectly healthy type, e.g., a pamphlet written by me on Home Rule, a translation of Ruskin's *Unto This Last, The Defence and Death of Socrates*, etc.

Disorder

But there is no doubt that the 6th of April found India vitalized as never before. The people who were fear-stricken ceased to fear authority. Moreover, hitherto the masses had lain inert. The leaders had not really acted upon them. They were undisciplined. They had found a new force but they did not know what it was and how to use it.

At Delhi the leaders found it difficult to restrain the very large number of people who had remained unmoved before. At Amritsar, Dr Satyapal was anxious that I should go there and show to the people the peaceful nature of Satyagraha. Swami Shraddhanandji from Delhi and Dr Satyapal from Amritsar wrote to me asking me to go to their respective places for pacifying the people and for explaining to them the nature of Satyagraha. I had never been to Amritsar and for that matter to the Punjab before. These two messages were sent by the authorities and they knew that I was invited to both the places for peaceful purposes.

I left Bombay for Delhi and the Punjab on the 8th April and had telegraphed to Dr Satyapal whom I had never met before to meet me at Delhi. But after passing Mathura I was served with an order prohibiting me from entering the Province of Delhi. I felt that I was bound to disregard this order and I proceeded on my journey. At Palwal I was served with an order prohibiting me from entering the Punjab and confining me to the Bombay Presidency. And I was arrested by a party of Police and taken off the train at that station. The Superintendent of the Police who arrested me acted with every courtesy. I was taken to Mathura by the first available train and thence by goods train early in the morning to Siwai Madhupur, where I joined the Bombay Mail from Peshawar and was taken charge of by Superintendent Bowring. I was discharged at Bombay on the 10th April.

But the people of Ahmedabad and Viramgam and in Gujarat generally had heard of my arrest. They became furious, shops were closed, crowds gathered and murder, arson, pillage, wire-cutting and attempts at derailment followed.

Young India, 14-1-'20

4

MEANS AND ENDS

Reader : Why should we not obtain our goal, which is good, by any means whatsoever, even by using violence ? Shall I think of the means when I have to deal with a thief in the house ? My duty is to drive him out anyhow. You seem to admit that we have received nothing, and that we shall receive nothing by petitioning. Why, then, may we not do so by using brute force ? And, to retain what we may receive we shall keep up the fear by using the same force to the extent that it may be necessary. You will not find fault with a continuance of force to prevent a child from thrusting its foot into fire ? Somehow or other we have to gain our end.

Editor : Your reasoning is plausible. It has deluded many. I have used similar arguments before now. But I think I know better now, and I shall endeavour to undeceive you. Let us first take the argument that we are justified in gaining our end by using brute force because the English gained theirs by using similar means. It is perfectly true that they used brute force and that it is possible for us to do likewise, but by using similar means we can get only the same thing that they got. You will admit that we do not want that. Your belief that there is no connection between the means and the end is a great mistake. Through that mistake even men who have been considered religious have committed grievous crimes. Your reasoning is the same as saying that we can get a rose through planting a noxious weed. If I want to cross the ocean, I can do so only by means of a vessel ; if I were to use a cart for that purpose, both the cart and I would soon find the bottom. " As is the God, so is the votary ", is a maxim worth considering. Its meaning has been distorted and men have gone astray. The means may be likened to a seed, the end to a tree ; and there is just the same inviolable connection between the means and the end as there is between the seed and the tree. I am not likely to obtain the result flowing from the worship of God by laying myself prostrate before Satan. If, therefore, any one were to say : " I want to worship God ; it does not matter that I do so by means of Satan," it would be set down as ignorant folly. We reap exactly as we sow. The English in 1833 obtained greater voting power by violence. Did they by using brute force better appreciate their duty ? They wanted the right of voting, which they obtained by using physical force. But real rights are a result of performance of duty ; these rights they have not obtained. We, therefore, have before us in England the force of everybody wanting and insisting on his rights, nobody thinking of his duty. And, where everybody wants rights, who shall give them to whom? I do not wish to imply that they do no duties. They don't perform the duties corresponding to those rights; and as they do not perform that particular duty, namely, acquire fitness, their rights have proved a burden to them. In other words, what they have obtained is an exact result of the means they adopted. They used the means corresponding to the end. If I want to deprive you of your watch, I shall certainly have to fight for it; if I want to buy your watch, I shall have to pay for it; and if I want a gift, I shall have to plead for it; and, according to the means I employ, the watch is stolen property, my own property, or a donation. Thus we see three different results from three different means. Will you still say that means do not matter?

Now we shall take the example given by you of the thief to be driven out. I do not agree with you that the thief may be driven out by any means. If it is my father who has come to steal I shall use one kind of means. If it is an acquaintance I shall use another; and in the case of a perfect stranger I shall use a third. If it is a white man, you will perhaps say you will use means different from those you will adopt with an Indian thief. If it is a weakling, the means will be different from those to be adopted for dealing with an equal in physical strength; and if the thief is armed from top to toe, I shall simply remain quiet. Thus we have a variety of means between the father and the armed man. Again, I fancy that I should pretend to be sleeping whether the thief was my father or that strong armed man. The reason for this is that my father would also be armed and I should succumb to the strength possessed by either and allow my things to be stolen. The strength of my father would make me weep with pity; the strength of the armed man would rouse in me anger and we should become enemies. Such is the curious situation. From these examples we may not be able to agree as to the means to be adopted in each case. I myself seem clearly to see what should be done in all these cases, but the remedy may frighten you. I therefore hesitate to place it before you. For the time being I will leave you to guess it, and if you cannot, it is clear you will have to adopt different means in each case. You will also have seen that any means will not avail to drive away the thief. You will have to adopt means to fit each case. Hence it follows that your duty is not to drive away the thief by any means you like.

Let us proceed a little further. That well-armed man has stolen your property ; you have harboured the thought of his act ; you are filled with anger ; you argue that you want to punish that rogue, not for your own sake, but for the good of your neighbours ; you have collected a number of armed men, you want to take his house by assault ; he is duly informed of it, he runs away ; he too is incensed. He collects his brother robbers, and sends you a defiant message that he will commit robbery in broad daylight. You are strong, you do not fear him, you are prepared to receive him. Meanwhile, the robber pesters your neighbours. They complain before you. You reply that you are doing all for their sake, you do not mind that your own goods have been stolen. Your neighbours reply that the robber never pestered them before, and that he commenced his depredations only after you declared hostilities against him. You are between Scylla and Charybdis. You are full of pity for the poor men. What they say is true. What are you to do ? You will be disgraced if you now leave the robber alone. You, therefore, tell the poor men : " Never mind. Come, my wealth is yours, I will give you arms, I will teach you how to use them ; you should belabour the rogue ; don't you leave him alone." And so the battle grows ; the robbers increase in numbers ; your neighbours have deliberately put themselves to inconvenience. Thus the result of wanting to take revenge upon the robber is that you have disturbed your own peace ; you are in perpetual fear of being robbed and assaulted ; your courage has given place to cowardice. If you will patiently examine the argument, you will see that I have not overdrawn the picture. This is one of the means. Now let us examine the other. You set this armed robber down as an ignorant brother; you intend to reason with him at a suitable opportunity; you argue that he is, after all, a fellow man; you do not know what prompted him to steal. You, therefore, decide that, when you can, you will destroy the man's motive for stealing. Whilst you are thus reasoning with yourself, the man comes again to steal. Instead of being angry with him you take pity on him. You think that this stealing habit must be a disease with him. Henceforth, you, therefore, keep your doors and windows open, you change your sleeping-place, and you keep your things in a manner most accessible to him. The robber comes again and is confused as all this is new to him; nevertheless, he takes away your things. But his mind is agitated. He inquires about you in the village, he comes to learn about your broad and loving heart, he repents, he begs your pardon, returns you your things, and leaves off the stealing habit. He becomes your servant, and you will find for him honourable employment. This is the second method. Thus, you see, different means have brought about totally different results. I do not wish to deduce from this that robbers will act in the above manner or that all will have the same pity and love like you, but I only wish to show that fair means alone can produce fair results, and that, at least in the majority of cases, if not indeed in all, the force of love and pity is infinitely greater than the force of arms. There is harm in the exercise of brute force, never in that of pity.

Now we will take the question of petitioning. It is a fact beyond dispute that a petition, without the backing of force, is useless. However, the late Justice Ranade used to say that petitions served a useful purpose because they were a means of educating people. They give the latter an idea of their condition and warn the rulers. From this point of view, they are not altogether useless. A petition of an equal is a sign of courtesy; a petition from a slave is a symbol of his slavery. A petition backed by force is a petition from an equal and, when he transmits his demand in the form of a petition, it testifies to his nobility. Two kinds of force can back petitions. "We

shall hurt you if you do not give this," is one kind of force ;
it is the force of arms, whose evil results we have already
examined. The second kind of force can thus be stated :
" If you do not concede our demand, we shall be no longer
your petitioners. You can govern us only so long as we
remain the governed ; we shall no longer have any dealings with you." The force implied in this may be
described as love-force, soul-force, or, more popularly but
less accurately, passive resistance.* This force is indes-
tructible. He who uses it perfectly understands his position. We have an ancient proverb which literally means :
" One negative cures thirty-six diseases." The force of
arms is powerless when matched against the force of love
or the soul.

Now we shall take your last illustration, that of the
child thrusting its foot into fire. It will not avail you.
What do you really do to the child ? Supposing that it
can exert so much physical force that it renders you
powerless and rushes into fire, then you cannot prevent it.
There are only two remedies open to you — either you
must kill it in order to prevent it from perishing in the
flames, or you must give your own life because you do
not wish to see it perish before your very eyes. You will
not kill it. If your heart is not quite full of pity, it is possible that you will not surrender yourself by preceding the
child and going into the fire yourself. You, therefore,
helplessly allow it to go to the flames. Thus, at any rate,
you are not using physical force. I hope you will not consider that it is still physical force, though of a low order,
when you would forcibly prevent the child from rushing
towards the fire if you could. That force is of a different
order and we have to understand what it is.

Remember that, in thus preventing the child, you are
minding entirely its own interest, you are exercising
authority for its sole benefit. Your example does not apply
to the English. In using brute force against the English

---

* Finding the word misleading Gandhiji later called the same force
Satyagraha or non-violent resistance.   — Ed.

you consult entirely your own, that is the national, interest. There is no question here either of pity or of love.
If you say that the actions of the English, being evil,
represent fire, and that they proceed to their actions
through ignorance, and that therefore they occupy the
position of a child and that you want to protect such a
child, then you will have to overtake every evil action of
that kind by whomsoever committed and, as in the case
of the evil child, you will have to sacrifice yourself. If
you are capable of such immeasurable pity, I wish you
well in its exercise.

Hind Swaraj or Indian Home Rule, chap. xvi

5

SATYAGRAHA OR PASSIVE RESISTANCE

Reader : Is there any historical evidence as to the
success of what you have called soul-force or truth-force ?
No instance seems to have happened of any nation having
risen through soul-force. I still think that the evil-doers
will not cease doing evil without physical punishment.

Editor : The poet Tulsidas has said : " Of religion,
pity, or love, is the root, as egotism of the body. Therefore, we should not abandon pity so long as we are alive."
This appears to me to be a scientific truth. I believe in it
as much as I believe in two and two being four. The force
of love is the same as the force of the soul or truth. We
have evidence of its working at every step. The universe
would disappear without the existence of that force. But
you ask for historical evidence. It is, therefore, necessary
to know what history means. The Gujarati equivalent
means : " It so happened ". If that is the meaning of
history, it is possible to give copious evidence. But, if it
means the doings of kings and emperors, there can be no
evidence of soul-force or passive resistance in such history.
You cannot expect silver ore in a tin mine. History, as
we know it, is a record of the wars of the world, and so

there is a proverb among Englishmen that a nation which
has no history, that is, no wars, is a happy nation. How
kings played, how they became enemies of one another,
how they murdered one another, is found accurately recorded in history, and if this were all that had happened
in the world, it would have been ended long ago. If the
story of the universe had commenced with wars, not a
man would have been found alive today. Those people
who have been warred against have disappeared as, for
instance, the natives of Australia of whom hardly a man
was left alive by the intruders. Mark, please, that these
natives did not use soul-force in self-defence, and it does
not require much foresight to know that the Australians
will share the same fate as their victims. "Those that
take the sword shall perish by the Sword." With us the
proverb is that professional swimmers will find a watery
grave.

The fact that there are so many men still alive in the
world shows that it is based not on the force of arms but
on the force of truth or love. Therefore, the greatest and
most unimpeachable evidence of the success of this force
is to be found in the fact that, in spite of the wars of the
world, it still lives on.

Thousands, indeed tens of thousands, depend for their
existence on a very active working of this force. Little
quarrels of millions of families in their daily lives disappear before the exercise of this force. Hundreds of
nations live in peace. History does not and cannot take
note of this fact. History is really a record of every
interruption of the even working of the force of love or
of the soul. Two brothers quarrel; one of them repents
and re-awakens the love that was lying dormant in him;
the two again begin to live in peace; nobody takes note
of this. But if the two brothers, through the intervention
of solicitors or some other reason, take up arms or go to
law — which is another form of the exhibition of brute
force — their doing would be immediately noticed in the
press, they would be the talk of their neighbours and
would probably go down to history. And what is true of

families and communities is true of nations. There is no reason to believe that there is one law for families and another for nations. History, then, is a record of an interruption of the course of nature. Soul-force, being natural, is not noted in history.

Reader: According to what you say, it is plain that instances of this kind of passive resistance are not to be found in history. It is necessary to understand this passive resistance more fully. It will be better, therefore, if you enlarge upon it.

Editor: Passive resistance is a method of securing rights by personal suffering ; it is the reverse of resistance by arms. When I refuse to do a thing that is repugnant to my conscience, I use soul-force. For instance, the Government of the day has passed a law which is applicable to me. I do not like it. If by using violence I force the Government to repeal the law, I am employing what may be termed body-force. If I do not obey the law and accept the penalty for its breach, I use soul-force. It involves sacrifice of self.

Everybody admits that sacrifice of self is infinitely superior to sacrifice of others. Moreover, if this kind of force is used in a cause that is unjust, only the person using it suffers. He does not make others suffer for his mistakes. Men have before now done many things which were subsequently found to have been wrong. No man can claim that he is absolutely in the right or that a particular thing is wrong because he thinks so, but it is wrong for him so long as that is his deliberate judgment. It is therefore meet that he should not do that which he knows to be wrong, and suffer the consequence whatever it may be. This is the key to the use of soul-force.

Reader: You would then disregard laws — this is rank disloyalty. We have always been considered a law-abiding nation. You seem to be going even beyond the extremists. They say that we must obey the laws that have been passed, but that if the laws be bad, we must drive out the law-givers even by force.

Editor : Whether I go beyond them or whether I do not is a matter of no consequence to either of us. We simply want to find out what is right and to act accordingly. The real meaning of the statement that we are a law-abiding nation is that we are passive resisters. When we do not like certain laws, we do not break the heads of law-givers but we suffer and do not submit to the laws. That we should obey laws whether good or bad is a new-fangled notion. There was no such thing in former days. The people disregarded those laws they did not like and suffered the penalties for their breach. It is contrary to our manhood if we obey laws repugnant to our conscience. Such teaching is opposed to religion and means slavery. If the Government were to ask us to go about without any clothing, should we do so? If I were a passive resister, I would say to them that I would have nothing to do with their law. But we have so forgotten ourselves and become so compliant that we do not mind any degrading law.

A man who has realized his manhood, who fears only God, will fear no one else. Man-made laws are not necessarily binding on him. Even the Government does not expect any such thing from us. They do not say : "You must do such and such a thing," but they say : "If you do not do it, we will punish you." We are sunk so low that we fancy that it is our duty and our religion to do what the law lays down. If man will only realize that it is unmanly to obey laws that are unjust, no man's tyranny will enslave him. This is the key to self-rule or home-rule.

It is a superstition and ungodly thing to believe that an act of a majority binds a minority. Many examples can be given in which acts of majorities will be found to have been wrong and those of minorities to have been right. All reforms owe their origin to the initiation of minorities in opposition to majorities. If among a band of robbers a knowledge of robbing is obligatory, is a pious man to accept the obligation? So long as the superstition that men should obey unjust laws exists, so long will their slavery exist. And a passive resister alone can remove such a superstition.

To use brute-force, to use gunpowder, is contrary to passive resistance, for it means that we want our opponent to do by force that which we desire but he does not. And, if such a use of force is justifiable, surely he is entitled to do likewise by us. And so we should never come to an agreement. We may simply fancy, like the blind horse moving in a circle round a mill, that we are making progress. Those who believe that they are not bound to obey laws which are repugnant to their conscience have only the remedy of passive resistance open to them. Any other must lead to disaster.

Hind Swaraj or Indian Home Rule, chap. XVII

6

EVIDENCE BEFORE THE HUNTER COMMITTEE

(Extracts)

1. Examination by Lord Hunter

Q. I take it, Mr Gandhi, that you are the author of the Satyagraha movement.

A. Yes, Sir.

Q. Will you explain it briefly ?

A. It is a movement intended to replace methods of violence and a movement based entirely upon truth. It is, as I have conceived it, an extension of the domestic law on the political field, and my experience has led me to the conclusion that that movement, and that alone, can rid India of the possibility of violence spreading throughout the length and breadth of the land, for the redress of grievances.

Q. It was adopted by you in connection with the opposition to the Rowlatt Act. And in that connection you asked the people to sign the Satyagraha pledge.

A. Yes, Sir.

Q. Was it your intention to enlist as many men as possible in the movement ?

A. Yes, consistently with the principle of truth and non-violence. If I got a million men ready to act according to those principles, I would not mind enlisting them all.

Q. Is it not a movement essentially antagonistic to Government because you substitute the determination of the Satyagraha Committee for the will of the Government?

A. That is not the spirit in which the movement has been understood by the people.

Q. I ask you to look at it from the point of view of the Government. If you were a Governor yourself, what would you say to a movement that was started with the object of breaking those laws which your Committee determined?

A. That would not be stating the whole case of the Satyagraha doctrine. If I were in charge of the Government and brought face to face with a body who, entirely in search of truth, were determined to seek redress from unjust laws without inflicting violence, I would welcome it and would consider that they were the best constitutionalists, and, as a Governor I would take them by my side as advisers who would keep me on the right path.

Q. People differ as to the justice or injustice of particular laws?

A. That is the main reason why violence is eliminated and a Satyagrahi gives his opponent the same right of independence and feelings of liberty that he reserves to himself, and he will fight by inflicting injuries on his own person.

Lord Hunter: I was looking at it from the point of view of the continuance of Government. Would it be possible to continue the Government if you had set up against the Government a body of men who would not accept the Government view but the view of an independent Committee?

A. I have found from my experience that it was possible to do so during the eight years of continuous struggle in South Africa. I found General Smuts, who went through the whole of that campaign, at the end of it saying that if all conducted themselves as the Satyagrahis had done, they should have nothing to fear.

Q. But there was no such pledge in that campaign as is prescribed here ?

A. Certainly there was. Every Satyagrahi was bound to resist all those laws which he considered to be unjust and which were not of a criminal character, in order to bend the Government to the will of the people.

Q. I understand your vow contemplates breaking of laws which a Committee may decide.

A. Yes, my Lord. I want to make it clear to the Committee that that part of the vow was meant to be a restraint on individual liberty. As I intended to make it a mass movement, I thought the constitution of some such Committee as we had appointed was necessary, so that no man should become a law unto himself, and, therefore, we conceived the plan that the Committee would be able to show what laws might be broken.

Q. We hear that doctors differ, and, even Satyagrahis might differ ?

A. Yes, I found it so to my cost.

Q. Supposing a Satyagrahi was satisfied that a particular law was a just law and that the Committee did not obey this law, what is a Satyagrahi to do ?

A. He is not bound to disobey that law. We had such Satyagrahis in abundance.

Q. Is it not rather a dangerous campaign ?

A. If you will conceive the campaign as designed in order to rid the country of violence, then you will share with me the same concern for it ; I think that at any cost a movement of this character should live in the country in a purified state.

Q. By your pledge are you not binding a man's conscience ?

A. Not according to my interpretation of it. If my interpretation of the pledge is found to be incorrect, I shall mend my error if I have to start the movement again. (*Lord Hunter* — No, no, Mr Gandhi, I do not pretend to advise you.)

I wish I could disabuse the Committee of the idea that it is a dangerous doctrine. It is conceived entirely with the object of ridding the country of the idea of violence.

Lord Hunter here briefly detailed the circumstances preceding the passage of the Rowlatt Act, the widespread general Indian opposition to the Act etc., and asked Mr Gandhi to describe the essence of his objection to the legislation.

A. I have read the Rowlatt Committee's report to the end and the legislation foreshadowed in it, and I came to the conclusion that the legislation was not warranted by the facts produced by the Committee. I thought it was very restrictive of human liberty and that no self-respecting person or nation could allow such legislation. When I saw the debates in the Legislative Council, I felt that the opposition to it was universal. When I found the agitation against it, I felt that for me as a self-respecting individual and a member of a vast Empire, there was no course left open, but to resist that law to the utmost.

Q. So far as the objects of that legislation are concerned, have you any doubt that they are to put down revolutionary and anarchical crimes ?

A. They are quite laudable objects.

Q. Your complaint, then, must be as regards the methods adopted ?

A. Entirely.

Q. The method is, I understand, that greater power has been given to the executive than they enjoyed before.

A. That is so.

Q. But is it not the same power that the executive enjoyed under the Defence of India Act ?

A. That is true, but that was essentially an emergency measure designed to secure the co-operation of everybody in order to put down any violence that may be offered by any section of the community in connection with the successful carrying on of the war. It was assented to with the greatest reluctance. The Rowlatt legislation is of a different character altogether, and now the

experience of the working of the former Act has strengthened my objections to the Rowlatt Act.

Q. Mr Gandhi, the Rowlatt legislation is only to
operate if the local Government is satisfied that there is
anarchy.

A. I would not, as a legislator, leave that power in
the hands of an executive whom I have known to run mad
in India at times.

Q. Then really, your objection comes to this, that
the Government of India, in the prosecution of a laudable
object, adopted a wrong method. Therefore, is not the
proper method of dealing with that, from a constitutional
point of view, to endeavour to get the legislation remedied
by satisfying Government of the inexpediency of it?

A. I approached on bended knees Lord Chelmsford.
and pleaded with him and with every English officer I
had the pleasure of meeting, and placed my views before
them, but they said they were helpless, and that the
Rowlatt Committee's recommendations had to be given
effect to. We had exhausted all the methods open to us.

Q. If an opponent differs from you, you cannot
satisfy him all of a sudden. You must do it by degrees.
Is it not rather a drastic way of attempting it by refusing
to obey the law?

A. I respectfully beg to differ from Your Lordship.
If I find that even my father has imposed upon me a law
which is repugnant to my conscience, I think it is the
least drastic course that I could adopt, to respectfully tell
him that I cannot obey it. By that course I do nothing
but justice to my father, and, if I may say so without any
disrespect to the Committee, I have myself followed that
course with the greatest advantage and I have preached
that ever since. If it is not disrespectful to say so to my
father, it is not so to a friend and for that matter to my
Government.

Lord Hunter: In the prosecution of your Satyagraha
movement against the Rowlatt legislation you resolved
upon a general *hartal* throughout India. That *hartal* was
to be a day when no business was to be done and people

were generally to indicate by their attitude that they disapproved of the Government's action. A *hartal* means a general cessation throughout the whole country. Would it not create a very difficult situation?

A. Cessation for a great length of time would create a difficult situation.

Mr Gandhi here explained how the observance of the *hartal* in some part of the country on the 30th March, and all over the country on the 6th April came about not on account of any miscalculation, but on account of the people in one part coming to know of the Viceregal assent to the Act earlier than the people in other parts.

Q. You agree that the abstention from work should be entirely voluntary?

A. Yes, entirely voluntary, in the sense that persuasion on the day of the *hartal* would not be allowed, whereas persuasion by means of leaflets and other propaganda work on the other days would be perfectly legitimate, so long as no physical force was employed.

Q. You disapprove of people interfering with *tongas* on the day of the *hartal*?

A. Certainly.

Q. You would not object to the police interfering in the case of such a disapprovable interference on the people's part?

A. I would not if they acted with proper restraint and forbearance.

Q. But you agree that on the day of the *hartal* it was highly improper to jostle with other people and stop *tongas*?

A. From a Satyagrahi standpoint I would hold it to be criminal.

Lord Hunter: Your leading lieutenant in Delhi, Swami Shraddhananda — *Mr Gandhi* interrupting: I would not call him my lieutenant, but an esteemed co-worker. — Did he write you a letter on the subject, and indicate to you that after what had occurred in Delhi and the Punjab, it was manifest that you could not prosecute a general *hartal* without violence inevitably ensuing?

A. I cannot recall the contents of that letter. I think he went much further and said that it was not possible that the law-breaking campaign could be carried on with impunity among the masses. He did not refer to *hartal* proceeding. There was a difference of opinion between me and Swami Shraddhananda when I suspended civil disobedience. I found it necessary to suspend it because I had not obtained sufficient control, to my satisfaction, over the people. What Swami Shraddhananda said was that Satyagraha could not be taken as a mass movement. But I did not agree with his view and I do not know that he is not converted to my view today. The suspension of civil disobedience was as much necessary as prosecution for offences against law. I would like the Committee to draw a sharp distinction between *hartal* and civil disobedience. *Hartal* was designed to strike the imagination of the people and the Government. Civil disobedience was a discipline for those who were to offer disobedience. I had no means of understanding the mind of India except by some such striking movement. *Hartal* was a proper indication to me how far I would be able to carry civil disobedience.

Q. If there is a *hartal* side by side with the preaching of Satyagraha would it not be calculated to promote violence ?

A. My experience is entirely to the contrary. It was an amazing scene for me to see people collected in their thousands — men, women and even little children and babies marching peacefully in procession. The peaceful *hartals* would not have been at all possible if Satyagraha was not preached in the right way.

But as I have said a *hartal* is a different thing from civil disobedience in practice.

*   *   *

Lord Hunter : Now, the only matters that we have got to deal with here are as regards Ahmedabad itself. In Ahmedabad, as we have been told, you enjoy great popularity among the mill workers ?

Mr Gandhi : Yes.

Lord Hunter : And your arrest seems to have caused great resentment on their part and led to the very unfortunate actions of the mob on April 10, 11 and 12 in Ahmedabad and Viramgam ?

Mr Gandhi : Yes.

Lord Hunter : So far as those incidents are concerned you have no personal knowledge of them ?

Mr Gandhi : No.

Lord Hunter : I don't know whether there is anything that you can communicate to us in connection with those events to help us to form an opinion.

Mr Gandhi : I venture to present the opinion that I considered that the action of the mob, whether at Ahmedabad or at Viramgam, was totally unjustified, and I think that it was a sad thing that they lost self-control. But, at the same time, I would like to say that the people among whom, rightly or wrongly, I was popular, were put to a severe test by Government. They should have known better. I do not say that the Government committed an unpardonable error of judgment and the mob committed no error. On the contrary, I hold that it was more unpardonable on the part of the mob than on the part of Government.

Proceeding, Mr Gandhi narrated how he endeavoured to do what he could to repair the error. He placed himself entirely at the disposal of the authorities. He had a long interview with Mr Pratt and other officials. He was to have held a meeting of the people on the 13th but he was told that it would not be possible to hold it that day, not on account of Colonel Fraser's order, because he was promised every assistance in connection with the meeting, but that the notice of the meeting would not reach all the people that day. The meeting took place on the 14th. There he adumbrated what had happened. There he had to use the terms *organized* and *educated* both of which terms had been so much quoted against him and against the people. The speech was in Gujarati. Mr Gandhi explained and hoped Sir Chimanlal Setalwad would bear him out on a reference to the Gujarati speech that the word only means those who can read and write, and that he used the word and expressed the opinion as he sensed the thing at that time.

He emphasized it was not a previous organization that he meant ; he only meant to say, and there could be no mistaking the actual words in his speech, that the acts were done in an *organized manner*. He further emphasized that he was speaking of Ahmedabad only, that he had then no knowledge of what had happened even at Viramgam, and that he would not retract a single statement from that speech. In his opinion, said Mr Gandhi, violence was done in an organized manner. It cannot be interpreted to mean a deep-laid conspiracy. He laid special emphasis on the fact that while he used these expressions he was addressing the people, and not the police authorities.

If Mr Guider stated that a single name of the offenders was not forthcoming from him, he was entirely mistaken about his mission and had put an improper valuation upon the term *organization*. The crimes committed by the mob were the result of their being deluded by the wicked rumour of the arrest of Miss Anasuya. There was a class of half-educated people who possessed false ideas obtained from sources such as cinematographs and from silly novels and from political leaders. He knew that school. He had mixed with them and endeavoured to wean them. He had so far succeeded in his endeavours that there were today hundreds of people who had ceased to belong to the school of revolution.

Proceeding, Mr Gandhi said he had now given the whole meaning of what he had said. He had never meant that there were University men behind the disturbances. He did not say they were incapable of those acts, but he was not aware of any highly educated man directing the mob.

Lord Hunter : Do you imply that there was a common purpose on the part of the rioters ?

Mr Gandhi : I don't say that. It would be exaggerating to say that, but I think the common purpose was restricted to two or three men or parties who instigated the crimes.

Q. Did the agitation take an anti-European character ?

A. It was certainly an anti-Government movement. I would fain believe it was not anti-European, but I have not yet made up my mind as to that.

Lord Hunter: I do not know whether you want to answer this or not. According to the Satyagraha doctrine, is it right that people who have committed crimes should be punished by the civil authorities ?

Mr Gandhi: It is a difficult question to answer, because (through punishment) you anticipate pressure from outside. I am not prepared to say that it is wrong, but there is a better method. But I think, on the whole, it would be proper to say that a Satyagrahi cannot possibly quarrel with any punishment that might be meted out to an offender, and therefore he cannot be anti-Government in that sense.

Lord Hunter: But apparently it is against the doctrine of Satyagraha to give assistance to Government by way of placing the information that a Satyagrahi has that would lead to the conviction of offenders ?

Mr Gandhi: According to the principle of Satyagraha it is inconsistent, for the simple reason that a Satyagrahi's business is not to assist the police in the method which is open to the police, but he helps the authorities and the police to make the people more law-abiding and more respectable to authority.

Lord Hunter: Supposing a Satyagrahi has seen one of the more serious crimes committed in these riots in his own presence. Would there be no obligation on him to inform the police ?

Mr Gandhi: Of course I answered that question to Mr Guider before and I think I must answer it to Your Lordship. I don't want to misguide the youth of the country, but even then he cannot go against his own brother. When I say brother, I do not, of course, make any distinction of country or nationality. A Satyagrahi is wholly independent of such a distinction. The Satyagrahi's position is somewhat similar to that of a counsel defending an accused. I have known criminals of the deadliest type and I may humbly claim to have been instrumental in weaning them from crimes. I should be forfeiting their confidence if I disclosed the name of a single man. But supposing I found myself wanting in weaning them I would surely not take the next step to go and inform the police about them ; I do not hesitate to say that for a Satyagrahi it is the straightest thing not to give evidence of a crime done even under his nose. But there can be only the rarest uses of this doctrine and even today I am not able to say whether I would not give evidence against a criminal whom I saw caught in the act.

Young India, 21-1-'20

2. Examination by Sir Chimanlal Setalwad

Sir Chimanlal : With regard to your Satyagraha doctrine, so far as I understand it, it involves the pursuit of truth and in that pursuit you invite suffering on yourself and do not cause violence to anybody else.

Mr Gandhi : Yes, Sir.

Q. However honestly a man may strive in his search for truth his notions of truth may be different from the notions of others. Who then is to determine the truth ?

A. The individual himself would determine that.

Q. Different individuals would have different views as to truth. Would that not lead to confusion ?

A. I do not think so.

Q. Honestly striving after truth is different in every case.

A. That is why the non-violence part was a necessary corollary. Without that there would be confusion and worse.

Q. Must not the person wanting to pursue truth be of high moral and intellectual equipment ?

A. No. It would be impossible to expect that from every one. If A has evolved a truth by his own efforts which B, C and others are to accept I should not require them to have the equipment of A.

Q. Then it comes to this that a man comes to a decision and others of lower intellectual and moral equipment would have to blindly follow him.

A. Not blindly. All I wish to urge is that each individual, unless he wants to carry on his pursuit of truth independently, needs to follow someone who has determined truth.

Q. Your scheme involves the determination of truth by people of high moral and intellectual equipment and a large number of people may follow them blindly being themselves unable to arrive at similar conclusions by reason of their lower intellectual equipment.

A. I would exact from them nothing more than I would expect from an ordinary being.

Q. I take it that the strength of the propaganda must depend on the number of its followers.

A. No. In Satyagraha success is possible even if there is only one Satyagrahi of the proper stamp.

Q. Mr Gandhi, you said you do not consider yourself a perfect Satyagrahi yet. The large mass of people are then even less so.

A. No. I do not consider myself an extraordinary man. There may be people more capable of determining truth than myself. Forty thousand Indians in South Africa, totally uncultured, came to the conclusion that they could be Satyagrahis and if I could take you through those thrilling scenes in the Transvaal you will be surprized to hear what restraint your countrymen in South Africa exhibited.

Q. But there you were all unanimous.

A. I have more solidity of opinion here than in South Africa.

Q. But there you had a clear-cut issue, not here.

A. Here too we have a clear-cut issue, viz. the Rowlatt Act.

Mr Gandhi then explained how he presented

Satyagraha as an instrument of infinitely greater power than violence.

Q. Does not suffering and going on suffering require extraordinary self-control ?

A. No ; no extraordinary self-control is required. Every mother suffers. Your countrymen, I submit, have got such control and they have exhibited that in a very large measure.

Q. Take Ahmedabad. Did they exhibit control here ?

A. All I say is, throughout India where you find these isolated instances of violence you will find a very large number of people who exercised self-restraint. Ahmedabad and other places show that we had not attained proper mastery over self. The Kaira people in the midst of grave provocation last year acted with the greatest self-restraint.

Q. Do you mean to say these acts of violence were mere accidents ?

A. Not accidents. But they were rare and would be rarer for a clear conception of Satyagraha. The country, I think, has sufficiently well realized the doctrine to warrant a second trial. I do feel sure that the country is all the purer and better for having gone through the fire of Satyagraha.

Q. Ordinarily your doctrine contemplates co-operation with the Government and elimination of race-hatred and inviting self-suffering. Does not suffering create ill-will ?

A. It is contrary to my thirty years' experience that people have by suffering been filled with any ill-will against the Government. In South Africa after a bitter struggle the Indians have lived on the best of terms with the Government, and Gen. Smuts was the recipient of an address which was voluntarily voted by the Indians.

Q. Is it possible to take part in the movement without taking the Satyagraha vow ?

A. I would ask them to take part in the non-civil-resistance part of the movement. The masses unless they took the pledge were not to do the civil-disobedience part of the pledge. For those who were not civil resisters, therefore, another vow was devised asking people to follow truth at all costs and to refrain from violence. I had suspended civil resistance then, and as it is open to a leader to emphasize one part of the vow, I eliminated the civil-resistance part which was not for that season suited to the people, and placed the truth part before them.

*   *   *

Q. Is not the underlying idea embarrassment of Government?

A. Certainly not. A Satyagrahi relies not upon embarrassment but upon self-suffering for securing relief.

Q. Would not ordered Government be impossible?

A. Ordered Government cannot be impossible if totally inoffensive people break the laws. But I would certainly make Government impossible if I found it had taken leave of its senses.

Q. In your message you ask people to refrain from violence and still violence occurred. Does it not show that the ordinary mind finds it very difficult to practise the theory of non-violence?

A. After having used methods of violence for years it is difficult for them to practise abstention.

Young India, 21-1-'20

3. Examination by Pandit Jagatnarain

Q. It is alleged that the Satyagraha movement would embarrass the Government. Are you not afraid of any such result of your movement?

A. The Satyagraha movement is not started with the intention of embarrassing the Government while ordinary political agitation is often started with that object. If a Satyagrahi finds his activities resulting in embarrassing the Government, he will not hesitate to face it.

Q. But you will agree with me that every political agitation depends for its success on the number of followers?

A. I do not regard the force of numbers as necessary in a just cause, and in such a cause every man, be he high or low, can have his remedy.

Q. But you would certainly try to have as many men in your movement as possible ?

A. Not exactly so. A Satyagrahi depends only on truth and his capacity to suffer for truth.

Q. But in politics, Mahatmaji, how can a single man's voice be heard ?

A. That is exactly what I have been attempting to disprove.

Q. Do you believe that an English officer will take any notice of isolated attempts ?

A. Why, that is my experience. Lord Bentinck became an ordinary Mr at the instance of Keshavachandra Sen.

Q. Oh, you cite an example of an extraordinary man.

A. Men of ordinary abilities also can develop morality. No doubt I regard illiteracy among my people as deplorable and I consider it necessary to educate them, but it is not at all impossible for an absolutely illiterate man to imbibe the Satyagraha principle. This is my long-standing experience.

Here Mr Gandhi briefly cleared the distinction between *hartal* and Satyagraha. *Hartal* was no integral part of Satyagraha. It should be resorted to only when necessary. He tried and tried it successfully in connection with the deportation of Mr Horniman and the Khilafat movement.

Q. You can resort to no other remedy to oppose the irresponsible, foreign officials and that is why you have started this movement. Is it not ?

A. I cannot say that with certainty. I can conceive the necessity of Satyagraha in opposition to the would-be full responsible self-government. Our ministers can never claim to defend themselves on the score of their ignorance, whereas such a defence is available today for the English officers.

Q. But with all the rights of self-government we shall be able to dismiss the ministers.

A. I cannot feel on that point so assured for ever. In England it often happens that ministers can continue in the executive even though they lose all the confidence of the public. The same thing may happen here too and therefore I can imagine a state of things in this country which would need Satyagraha even under Home Rule.

Q. Would you think that there should be no unrest coming after the Satyagraha movement ?

A. Not only I do not think so, I would be disappointed if there were no unrest in case Anasuyabehn and I were arrested. But that unrest will not take the shape of violence. It pains a Satyagrahi to see others suffering ; Satyagrahis will follow each other to jail. I do wish for such unrest.

Young India, 4-2-'20

7

THE THEORY AND PRACTICE OF SATYAGRAHA

[The following is taken from an article by Gandhiji contributed to the Golden Number of *Indian Opinion* which was issued in 1914 as a souvenir of the eight years' Satyagraha in South Africa :]

Carried out to its utmost limit, Satyagraha is independent of pecuniary or other material assistance ; certainly, even in its elementary form, of physical force or violence. Indeed, violence is the negation of this great spiritual force, which can only be cultivated or wielded by those who will entirely eschew violence. It is a force that may be used by individuals as well as by communities. It may be used as well in political as in domestic affairs. Its universal applicability is a demonstration of its permanence and invincibility. It can be used alike by men, women and children. It is totally untrue to say that it is a force to be used only by the weak so long as they are not capable of meeting violence by violence. This superstition arises from the incompleteness of the English expression, *passive resistance*. It is impossible for those who consider themselves to be weak to apply this force. Only those who realize that there is something in man which is superior to the brute nature in him and that the latter always yields to it, can effectively be Satyagrahis. This force is to violence, and, therefore, to all tyranny, all injustice, what light is to darkness. In politics, its use is based upon the immutable maxim, that government of the people is possible only so long as they consent either consciously or unconsciously to be governed. We did not want to be governed by the Asiatic Act of 1907 of the Transvaal, and it had to go before this mighty force. Two courses were open to us : to use violence when we were called upon to submit to the Act, or to suffer the penalties prescribed under the Act, and thus to draw out and exhibit the force of the soul within us for a period long enough to appeal to the sympathetic chord in the governors or the law-makers. We have taken long to achieve what we set about striving for. That was because our Satyagraha was not of the most complete type. All Satyagrahis do not understand the full value of the force, nor have we men who always from conviction refrain from violence. The use of this force requires the adoption of poverty, in the sense that we must be indifferent whether we have the wherewithal to feed or clothe ourselves. During the past struggle, all Satyagrahis, if any at all, were not prepared to go that length. Some again were only Satyagrahis so called. They came without any conviction, often with mixed motives, less often with impure motives. Some even, whilst engaged in the struggle, would gladly have resorted to violence but for most vigilant supervision. Thus it was that the struggle became prolonged ; for the exercise of the purest soul-force, in its perfect form, brings about instantaneous relief. For this exercise, prolonged training of the individual soul is an absolute necessity, so that a perfect Satyagrahi has to be almost, if not entirely, a perfect man. We cannot all suddenly become such men, but if my proposition is correct — as I know it to be correct — the greater the spirit of Satyagraha in us, the better men will we become. Its use, therefore, is, I think, indisputable, and it is a force, which, if it became universal, would revolutionize social ideals and do away with despotisms and the ever-growing militarism under which the nations of the West are groaning and are being almost crushed to death, and which fairly promises to overwhelm even the nations of the East. If the past struggle has produced even a few Indians who would dedicate themselves to the task of becoming Satyagrahis as nearly perfect as possible, they would not only have served themselves in the truest sense of the term, they would also have served humanity at large. Thus viewed, Satyagraha is the noblest and best education. It should come, not after the ordinary education in letters, of children, but it should precede it. It will not be denied, that a child, before it begins to write its alphabet and to gain worldly knowledge, should know what the soul is, what truth is, what love is, what powers are latent in the soul. It should be an essential of real education that a child should learn, that in the struggle of life, it can easily conquer hate by love, untruth by truth, violence by self-suffering.

Young India, 3-11-'27

SECTION SECOND: DISCIPLINE FOR SATYAGRAHA

8

SATYAGRAHA ASHRAM VOWS

[The vows were the principles which Gandhiji believed every Satyagrahi should follow in his daily life. The following were sent as a series of weekly discourses on the vows during 1930 from the Yeravda Jail to members of his Ashram at Sabarmati. We include discourses on only four of the vows here, viz. those of Truth, Non-violence, Chastity and Non-possession. The remaining seven are: Fearlessness, Control of the Palate, Non-stealing, Bread-Labour, Equality of Religions, Anti-untouchability and Swadeshi. The interested reader is referred for Gandhiji's discourses on them to his booklet *From Yeravda Mandir* (published by the Navajivan Publishing House, Ahmedabad). — Ed.]

Importance of Vows

Taking vows is not a sign of weakness, but of strength. To do at any cost something that one ought to do constitutes a vow. It becomes a bulwark of strength. A man who says that he will do something 'as far as possible', betrays either his pride or his weakness. I have noticed in my own case, as well as in the case of others, that the limitation 'as far as possible' provides a fatal loophole. To do something 'as far as possible' is to succumb to the very first temptation. There is no sense in saying that one would observe truth 'as far as possible'. Even as no businessman will look at a note in which a man promises to pay a certain amount on a certain date 'as far as possible', so will God refuse to accept a promissory note drawn by a man, who will observe truth as far as possible.

God is the very image of the vow. God would cease to be God if He swerved from His own laws even by a

37

hair's breadth. The sun is a greater keeper of observances ; hence the possibility of measuring time and publishing almanacs. All business depends upon men fulfilling their promises. Are such promises less necessary in character building or self-realization ? We should therefore never doubt the necessity of vows for the purpose of self-purification and self-realization.

I

Truth

I deal with Truth first of all, as the Satyagraha Ashram owes its very existence to the pursuit and the attempted practice of Truth.

The word *Satya* (Truth) is derived from *Sat*, which means 'being'. Nothing is or exists in reality except Truth. That is why *Sat* or Truth is perhaps the most important name of God. In fact it is more correct to say that Truth is God, than to say that God is Truth. But as we cannot do without a ruler or a general, names of God such as 'King of Kings' or 'the Almighty' are and will remain generally current. On deeper thinking, however, it will be realized, that *Sat* or *Satya* is the only correct and fully significant name for God.

And where there is Truth, there also is knowledge which is true. Where there is no Truth, there can be no true knowledge. That is why the word *Chit* or knowledge is associated with the name of God. And where there is true knowledge, there is always bliss (*Ananda*). Sorrow has no place there. And even as Truth is eternal, so is the bliss derived from it. Hence we know God as *Sat-chit-ananda*, One who combines in Himself Truth, Knowledge and Bliss.

Devotion to this Truth is the sole justification for our existence. All our activities should be centred in Truth. Truth should be the very breath of our life. When once this stage in the pilgrim's progress is reached, all other rules of correct living will come without effort, and obedience to them will be instinctive. But without Truth it would be impossible to observe any principles or rules in life.

Generally speaking, observation of the law of Truth is understood merely to mean that we must speak the truth. But we in the Ashram should understand the word *Satya* or Truth in a much wider sense. There should be Truth in thought, Truth in speech, and Truth in action. To the man who has realized this Truth in its fulness, nothing else remains to be known, because all knowledge is necessarily included in it. What is not included in it is not Truth, and so not true knowledge ; and there can be no inward peace without true knowledge. If we once learn how to apply this never-failing test of Truth, we will at once be able to find out what is worth doing, what is worth seeing, what is worth reading.

But how is one to realize this Truth, which may be likened to the philosopher's stone or the cow of plenty ? By single-minded devotion (*abhyasa*) and indifference to all other interests in life (*vairagya*) — replies the *Bhagavadgita*. In spite, however, of such devotion, what may appear as truth to one person will often appear as untruth to another person. But that need not worry the seeker. Where there is honest effort, it will be realized that what appear to be different truths are like the countless and apparently different leaves of the same tree. Does not God Himself appear to different individuals in different aspects ? Yet we know that He is one. But Truth is the right designation of God. Hence there is nothing wrong in every man following Truth according to his lights. Indeed it is his duty to do so. Then if there is a mistake on the part of any one so following Truth, it will be automatically set right. For the quest of Truth involves *tapas* — self-suffering, sometimes even unto death. There can be no place in it for even a trace of self-interest. In such selfless search for Truth nobody can lose his bearings for long. Directly he takes to the wrong path he stumbles, and is thus redirected to the right path. Therefore the pursuit of Truth is true *bhakti* (devotion). It is the path that leads to God. There is no place in it for cowardice, no place for defeat. It is the talisman by which death itself becomes the portal to life eternal.

In this connection it would be well to ponder over the lives and examples of Harishchandra, Prahlad, Ramachandra, Imam Hasan and Imam Husain, the Christian saints, etc.' How beautiful it would be, if all of us, young and old, men and women, devoted ourselves wholly to Truth in all that we might do in our waking hours, whether working, eating, drinking or playing, till dissolution of the body makes us one with Truth ? God as Truth has been for me a treasure beyond price ; may He be so to every one of us.

II

Ahimsa or Love

We saw last week how the path of Truth is as narrow as it is straight. Even so is that of *ahimsa*. It is like balancing oneself on the edge of a sword. By concentration an acrobat can walk on a rope. But the concentration required to tread the path of Truth and *ahimsa* is far greater. The slightest inattention brings one tumbling to the ground. One can realize Truth and *ahimsa* only by ceaseless striving.

But it is impossible for us to realize perfect Truth so long as we are imprisoned in this mortal frame. We can only visualize it in our imagination. We cannot, through the instrumentality of this ephemeral body, see face to face Truth which is eternal. That is why in the last resort one must depend on faith.

It appears that the impossibility of full realization of Truth in this mortal body led some ancient seeker after Truth to the appreciation of *ahimsa*. The question which confronted him was : " Shall I bear with those who create difficulties for me, or shall I destroy them ? " The seeker realized that he who went on destroying others did not make headway but simply stayed where he was, while the man who suffered those who created difficulties marched ahead, and at times even took the others with him.

The first act of destruction taught him that the Truth which was the object of his quest was not outside himself but within. Hence the more he took to violence, the more he receded from Truth. For in fighting the imagined enemy without, he neglected the enemy within.

We punish thieves, because we think they harass us. They may leave us alone ; but they will only transfer their attentions to another victim. This other victim however is also a human being, ourselves in a different form, and so we are caught in a vicious circle. The trouble from thieves continues to increase, as they think it is their business to steal. In the end we see that it is better to endure the thieves than to punish them. The forbearance may even bring them to their senses. By enduring them we realize that thieves are not different from ourselves, they are our brethren, our friends, and may not be punished. But whilst we may bear with the thieves, we may not endure the infliction. That would only induce cowardice. So we realize a further duty. Since we regard the thieves as our kith and kin, they must be made to realize the kinship. And so we must take pains to devise ways and means of winning them over. This is the path of *ahimsa*. It may entail continuous suffering and the cultivating of endless patience. Given these two conditions, the thief is bound in the end to turn away from his evil ways. Thus step by step we learn how to make friends with all the world ; we realize the greatness of God — of Truth. Our peace of mind increases in spite of suffering ; we become braver and more enterprising ; we understand more clearly the difference between what is everlasting and what is not ; we learn how to distinguish between what is our duty and what is not. Our pride melts away, and we become humble. Our worldly attachments diminish, and the evil within us diminishes from day to day.

Ahimsa is not the crude thing it has been made to appear. Not to hurt any living thing is no doubt a part of *ahimsa*. But it is its least expression. The principle of *ahimsa* is hurt by every evil thought, by undue haste, by lying, by hatred, by wishing ill to anybody. It is also violated by our holding on to what the world needs. But the world needs even what we eat day by day. In the place where we stand there are millions of micro-organisms to whom the place belongs, and who are hurt by our presence there. What should we do then? Should we commit suicide? Even that is no solution, if we believe, as we do, that so long as the spirit is attached to the flesh, on every destruction of the body it weaves for itself another. The body will cease to be only when we give up all attachment to it. This freedom from all attachment is the realization of God as Truth. Such realization cannot be attained in a hurry. The body does not belong to us. While it lasts, we must use it as a trust handed over to our charge. Treating in this way, the things of the flesh, we may one day expect to become free from the burden of the body. Realizing the limitations of the flesh, we must strive day by day towards the ideal with what strength we have in us.

It is perhaps clear from the foregoing, that without *ahimsa* it is not possible to seek and find Truth. *Ahimsa* and Truth are so intertwined that it is practically impossible to disentangle and separate them. They are like the two sides of a coin, or rather of a smooth unstamped metallic disc. Who can say, which is the obverse, and which is the reverse? Nevertheless *ahimsa* is the means; Truth is the end. Means to be means must always be within our reach, and so *ahimsa* is our supreme duty. If we take care of the means, we are bound to reach the end sooner or later. When once we have grasped this point, final victory is beyond question. Whatever difficulties we encounter, whatever apparent reverses we sustain, we may not give up the quest for Truth which alone is, being God Himself.

III

Brahmacharya or Chastity

The third among our observances is *brahmacharya*. As a matter of fact all observances are deducible from

Truth, and are meant to subserve it. The man, who is wedded to Truth and worships Truth alone, proves unfaithful to her, if he applies his talents to anything else. How then can he minister to the senses? A man, whose activities are wholly consecrated to the realization of Truth, which requires utter selflessness, can have no time for the selfish purpose of begetting children and running a household. Realization of Truth through self-gratification should, after what has been said before, appear a contradiction in terms.

If we look at it from the standpoint of *ahimsa* (nonviolence), we find that the fulfilment of *ahimsa* is impossible without utter selflessness. *Ahimsa* means Universal Love. If a man gives his love to one woman, or a woman to one man, what is there left for all the world besides? It simply means, " We two first, and the devil take all the rest of them." As a faithful wife must be prepared to sacrifice her all for the sake of her husband, and a faithful husband for the sake of his wife, it is clear that such persons cannot rise to the height of Universal Love, or look upon all mankind as kith and kin. For they have created a boundary wall round their love. The larger their family, the farther are they from Universal Love. Hence one who would obey the law of *ahimsa* cannot marry, not to speak of gratification outside the marital bond.

Then what about people who are already married? Will they never be able to realize Truth? Can they never offer up their all at the altar of humanity? There is a way out for them. They can behave as if they were not married. Those who have enjoyed this happy condition will be able to bear me out. Many have to my knowledge successfully tried the experiment. If the married couple can think of each other as brother and sister, they are freed for universal service. The very thought that all the women in the world are his sisters, mothers or daughters will at once ennoble a man and snap his chains. The husband and wife do not lose any thing here, but only add to their resources and even to their family. Their love becomes free from the impurity of lust and so grows stronger. With

the disappearance of this impurity, they can serve each
other better, and the occasions for quarrelling become
fewer. There are more occasions for quarrelling where
the love is selfish and bounded.

If the foregoing argument is appreciated, a consideration of the physical benefits of chastity becomes a matter
of secondary importance. How foolish it is intentionally
to dissipate vital energy in sensual enjoyment! It is a
grave misuse to fritter away for physical gratification that
which is given to man and woman for the full development of their bodily and mental powers. Such misuse is
the root cause of many a disease.

Brahmacharya, like all other observances, must be
observed in thought, word and deed. We are told in the
Gita, and experience will corroborate the statement, that
the foolish man, who appears to control his body, but is
nursing evil thoughts in his mind, makes a vain effort.
It may be harmful to suppress the body, if the mind is at
the same time allowed to go astray. Where the mind
wanders, the body must follow sooner or later.

It is necessary here to appreciate a distinction. It is
one thing to allow the mind to harbour impure thoughts ;
it is a different thing altogether if it strays among them in
spite of ourselves. Victory will be ours in the end, if we
non-co-operate with the mind in its evil wanderings.

We experience every moment of our lives, that often
while the body is subject to our control, the mind is not.
This physical control should never be relaxed, and in
addition we must put forth a constant endeavour to bring
the mind under control. We can do nothing more, nothing
less. If we give way to the mind, the body and the mind
will pull different ways, and we shall be false to ourselves.
Body and mind may be said to go together, so long as we
continue to resist the approach of every evil thought.

The observance of *brahmacharya* has been believed to
be very difficult, almost impossible. In trying to find a
reason for this belief, we see that the term *brahmacharya*
has been taken in a narrow sense. Mere control of animal
passion has been thought to be tantamount to observing

brahmacharya. I feel, that this conception is incomplete and wrong. *Brahmacharya* means control of all the organs of sense. He, who attempts to control only one organ, and allows all the others free play, is bound to find his effort futile. To hear suggestive stories with the ears, to see suggestive sights with the eyes, to taste stimulating food with the tongue, to touch exciting things with the hands, and then at the same time expect to control the only remaining organ is like putting one's hands in the fire, and expecting to escape being burnt. He therefore who is resolved to control the one must be likewise determined to control the rest. I have always felt, that much harm has been done by the narrow definition of *brahmacharya.* If we practise simultaneous self-control in all directions, the attempt will be scientific and possible of success. Perhaps the palate is the chief sinner. That is why in the Ashram we have assigned to control of the palate a separate place among our observances.

Let us remember the root meaning of *brahmacharya.* *Charya* means course of conduct ; *brahma-charya* conduct adapted to the search of *Brahma,* i.e., Truth. From this etymological meaning arises the special meaning, viz., control of all the senses. We must entirely forget the incomplete definition which restricts itself to the sexual aspect only.

IV

Non-possession

Possession implies provision for the future. A seeker after Truth, a follower of the law of Love cannot hold anything against tomorrow. God never stores for the morrow ; He never creates more than what is strictly needed for the moment. If therefore we repose faith in His providence, we should rest assured that He will give us every day our daily bread, meaning everything that we require. Saints and devotees, who have lived in such faith, have always derived a justification for it from their experience. Our ignorance or negligence of the Divine Law, which gives to man from day to day his daily bread and no more, has given rise to inequalities with all the miseries attendant upon them. The rich have a superfluous store of things which they do not need, and which are therefore neglected and wasted ; while millions are starved to death for want of sustenance. If each retained possession only of what he needed, no one would be in want, and all would live in contentment. As it is, the rich are discontented no less than the poor. The poor man would fain become a millionaire, and the millionaire a multi-millionaire. The rich should take the initiative in dispossession with a view to a universal diffusion of the spirit of contentment. If only they keep their own property within moderate limits, the starving will be easily fed, and will learn the lesson of contentment along with the rich.

Perfect fulfilment of the ideal of Non-possession requires, that man should, like the birds, have no roof over his head, no clothing and no stock of food for the morrow. He will indeed need his daily bread, but it will be God's business, and not his, to provide it. Only the fewest possible, if any at all, can reach this ideal. We ordinary seekers may not be repelled by the seeming impossibility. But we must keep the ideal constantly in view, and in the light thereof, critically examine our possessions, and try to reduce them. Civilization, in the real sense of the term, consists not in the multiplication, but in the deliberate and voluntary reduction of wants. This alone promotes real happiness and contentment, and increases the capacity for service. Judging by this criterion, we find that in the Ashram we possess many things, the necessity for which cannot be proved, and we thus tempt our neighbours to thieve.

From the standpoint of pure Truth, the body too is a possession. It has been truly said that desire for enjoyment creates bodies for the soul. When this desire vanishes, there remains no further need for the body, and man is free from the vicious cycle of births and deaths. The soul is omnipresent ; why should she care to be confined within the cagelike body, or do evil and even kill for the sake of that cage ? We thus arrive at the ideal of total renunciation, and learn to use the body for the purposes of service so long as it exists, so much so that service, and not bread, becomes with us the staff of life. We eat and drink, sleep and wake, for service alone. Such an attitude of mind brings us real happiness, and the beatific vision in the fulness of time. Let us all examine ourselves from this standpoint.

We should remember, that Non-possession is a principle applicable to thoughts, as well as to things. A man who fills his brain with useless knowledge violates that inestimable principle. Thoughts, which turn us away from God, or do not turn us towards Him, constitute impediments in our way.

From Yeravda Mandir, chapters I to III & VI

9

YAJNA OR SACRIFICE

Yajna means an act directed to the welfare of others, done without desiring any return for it, whether of a temporal or spiritual nature. 'Act' here must be taken in its widest sense, and includes thought and word, as well as deed. 'Others' embraces not only humanity, but all life. Therefore, and also from the standpoint of *ahimsa*, it is not a *yajna* to sacrifice lower animals even with a view to the service of humanity. It does not matter that animal sacrifice is alleged to find a place in the *Vedas*. It is enough for us, that such sacrifice cannot stand the fundamental tests of Truth and Non-violence. I readily admit my incompetence in *Vedic* scholarship. But the incompetence, so far as this subject is concerned, does not worry me, because even if the practice of animal sacrifice be proved to have been a feature of *Vedic* society, it can form no precedent for a votary of *ahimsa*.

Again a primary sacrifice must be an act, which conduces the most to the welfare of the greatest number in the widest area, and which can be performed by the largest number of men and women with the least trouble.

It will not therefore be a *yajna*, much less a *mahayajna*, to wish or to do ill to any one else, even in order to serve a so-called higher interest. And the *Gita* teaches, and experience testifies, that all action that cannot come under the category of *yajna* promotes bondage.

The world cannot subsist for a single moment without *yajna* in this sense, and therefore the *Gita*, after having dealt with true wisdom in the second chapter, takes up in the third the means of attaining it, and declares in so many words, that *yajna* came with the Creation itself. This body therefore has been given us, only in order that we may serve all Creation with it. And therefore, says the *Gita*, he who eats without offering *yajna* eats stolen food. Every single act of one who would lead a life of purity should be in the nature of *yajna*. *Yajna* having come to us with our birth, we are debtors all our lives, and thus for ever bound to serve the universe. And even as a bondslave receives food, clothing and so on from the master whom he serves, so should we gratefully accept such gifts as may be assigned to us by the Lord of the universe. What we receive must be called a gift; for as debtors we are entitled to no consideration for the discharge of our obligations. Therefore we may not blame the Master, if we fail to get it. Our body is His to be cherished or cast away according to His will. This is not a matter for complaint or even pity ; on the contrary, it is a natural and even a pleasant and desirable state, if only we realize our proper place in God's scheme. We do indeed need strong faith, if we would experience this supreme bliss. "Do not worry in the least about yourself, leave all worry to God," — this appears to be the commandment in all religions.

This need not frighten any one. He who devotes himself to service with a clear conscience will day by day grasp the necessity for it in greater measure, and will continually grow richer in faith. The path of service can hardly be trodden by one, who is not prepared to renounce self-interest, and to recognize the conditions of his birth. Consciously or unconsciously every one of us does render some service or other. If we cultivate the habit of doing this service deliberately, our desire for service will steadily grow stronger, and will make not only for our own happiness, but that of the world at large.

Again, not only the good, but all of us are bound to place our resources at the disposal of humanity. And if such is the law, as evidently it is, indulgence ceases to hold a place in life and gives way to renunciation. The duty of renunciation differentiates mankind from the beast.

Some object, that life thus understood becomes dull and devoid of art, and leaves no room for the householder. But renunciation here does not mean abandoning the world and retiring into the forest. The spirit of renunciation should rule all the activities of life. A householder does not cease to be one, if he regards life as a duty rather than as an indulgence. A merchant, who operates in the sacrificial spirit, will have crores passing through his hands, but he will, if he follows the law, use his abilities for service. He will therefore not cheat or speculate, will lead a simple life, will not injure a living soul and will lose millions rather than harm anybody. Let no one run away with the idea that this type of merchant exists only in my imagination. Fortunately for the world, it does exist in the West as well as in the East. It is true, such merchants may be counted on one's fingers' ends, but the type ceases to be imaginary, as soon as even one living specimen can be found to answer to it. No doubt such sacrificers obtain their livelihood by their work. But livelihood is not their objective, but only a by-product of their vocation. A life of sacrifice is the pinnacle of art, and is full of true joy. *Yajna* is not *yajna* if one feels it to be burdensome or annoying. Self-indulgence leads to destruction, and renunciation to immortality. Joy has no independent existence. It depends upon our attitude to life. One man will enjoy theatrical scenery, another the ever new scenes which unfold themselves in the sky. Joy, therefore, is a matter of individual and national education. We shall delight in things which we have been taught to delight in as children. And illustrations can be easily cited of different national tastes.

Again, many sacrificers imagine that they are free to receive from the people everything they need, and many things they do not need, because they are rendering disinterested service. Directly this idea sways a man, he ceases to be a servant, and becomes a tyrant over the people.

One who would serve will not waste a thought upon his own comforts, which he leaves to be attended to or neglected by his Master on high. He will not therefore encumber himself with everything that comes his way; he will take only what he strictly needs and leave the rest. He will be calm, free from anger and unruffled in mind even if he finds himself inconvenienced. His service, like virtue, is its own reward, and he will rest content with it.

Again, one dare not be negligent in service, or be behindhand with it. He, who thinks that he must be diligent only in his personal business, and unpaid public business may be done in any way and at any time he chooses, has still to learn the very rudiments of the science of sacrifice. Voluntary service of others demands the best of which one is capable, and must take precedence over service of self. In fact, the pure devotee consecrates himself to the service of humanity without any reservation whatever.

From Yeravda Mandir, chapters XIV-XV

10

PROTECTING HINDUISM

For self-defence, I would restore the spiritual culture. The best and most lasting self-defence is self-purification. I refuse to be lifted off my feet because of the scares that haunt us today. If Hindus would but believe in themselves and work in accordance with their traditions, they will have no reason to fear bullying. The moment they recommence the real spiritual training the Mussalman will respond. He cannot help it. If I can get together a band of young Hindus with faith in themselves and, therefore, faith in the Mussalmans, the band will become a shield for the weaker ones. They (the young Hindus) will teach how to die without killing. I know no other way. When our ancestors saw affliction surrounding them, they went in for *tapasya* — purification. They realized the helplessness of the flesh and in their helplessness they prayed till they compelled the Maker to obey their call. 'Oh yes,' says my Hindu friend, 'but then God sent some one to wield arms.' I am not concerned with denying the truth of the retort. All I say to the friend is that as a Hindu he may not ignore the cause and secure the result. It will be time to fight, when we have done enough *tapasya*. Are we purified enough I ask? Have we even done willing penance for the sin of untouchability, let alone the personal purity of individuals? Are our religious preceptors all that they should be? We are beating the air whilst we simply concentrate our attention upon picking holes in the Mussalman conduct.

Young India, 19-6-'24

11

MORAL REQUIREMENTS FOR SATYAGRAHA

Reader: I deduce that passive resistance * is a splendid weapon of the weak, but that when they are strong they may take up arms.

Editor: This is gross ignorance. Passive resistance, that is, soul-force, is matchless. It is superior to the force of arms. How, then, can it be considered only a weapon of the weak? Physical-force men are strangers to the courage that is requisite in a passive resister. Do you believe that a coward can ever disobey a law that he dislikes? Extremists are considered to be advocates of brute force. Why do they, then, talk about obeying laws? I do not blame them. They can say nothing else.

---

* Throughout this chapter the words *passive resistance* are generally used for Satyagraha.

When they succeed in driving out the English and they themselves become governors, they will want you and me to obey their laws. And that is a fitting thing for their constitution. But a passive resister will say he will not obey a law that is against his conscience, even though he may be blown to pieces at the mouth of a cannon.

What do you think ? Wherein is courage required — in blowing others to pieces from behind a cannon, or with a smiling face to approach a cannon and be blown to pieces ? Who is the true warrior — he who keeps death always as a bosom-friend, or he who controls the death of others ? Believe me that a man devoid of courage and manhood can never be a passive resister.

This, however, I will admit : that even a man weak in body is capable of offering this resistance. One man can offer it just as well as millions. Both men and women can indulge in it. It does not require the training of an army ; it needs no jiu-jitsu. Control over the mind is alone necessary, and when that is attained, man is free like the king of the forest and his very glance withers the enemy.

Passive resistance is an all-sided sword, it can be used anyhow ; it blesses him who uses it and him against whom it is used. Without drawing a drop of blood it produces far-reaching results. It never rusts and cannot be stolen. Competition between passive resisters does not exhaust. The sword of passive resistance does not require a scabbard. It is strange indeed that you should consider such a weapon to be a weapon merely of the weak.

Reader : You have said that passive resistance is a speciality of India. Have cannons never been used in India ?

Editor : Evidently, in your opinion, India means its few princes. To me it means its teeming millions on whom depends the existence of its princes and our own.

Kings will always use their kingly weapons. To use force is bred in them. They want to command, but those who have to obey commands do not want guns : and these are in a majority throughout the world. They have to learn either body-force or soul-force. Where they learn the former, both the rulers and the ruled become like so many mad men ; but where they learn soul-force, the commands of the rulers do not go beyond the point of their swords, for true men disregard unjust commands. Peasants have never been subdued by the sword, and never will be. They do not know the use of the sword, and they are not frightened by the use of it by others. That nation is great which rests its head upon death as its pillow. Those who defy death are free from all fear. For those who are labouring under the delusive charms of brute-force, this picture is not overdrawn. The fact is that, in India, the nation at large has generally used passive resistance in all departments of life. We cease to co-operate with our rulers when they displease us. This is passive resistance.

I remember an instance when, in a small principality, the villagers were offended by some command issued by the prince. The former immediately began vacating the village. The prince became nervous, apologized to his subjects and withdrew his command. Many such instances can be found in India. Real Home Rule is possible only where passive resistance is the guiding force of the people. Any other rule is foreign rule.

Reader : Then you will say that it is not at all necessary for us to train the body ?

Editor : I will certainly not say any such thing. It is difficult to become a passive resister unless the body is trained. As a rule, the mind, residing in a body that has become weakened by pampering, is also weak, and where there is no strength of mind there can be no strength of soul. We shall have to improve our physique by getting rid of infant marriages and luxurious living. If I were to ask a man with a shattered body to face a cannon's mouth I should make a laughing-stock of myself.

Reader : From what you say, then, it would appear that it is not a small thing to become a passive resister, and, if that is so, I should like you to explain how a man may become one.

Editor : To become a passive resister is easy enough but it is also equally difficult. I have known a lad of fourteen years become a passive resister ; I have known also sick people do likewise ; and I have also known physically strong and otherwise happy people unable to take up passive resistance. After a great deal of experience it seems to me that those who want to become passive resisters for the service of the country have to observe perfect chastity, adopt poverty, follow truth, and cultivate fearlessness.

Chastity is one of the greatest disciplines without which the mind cannot attain requisite firmness. A man who is unchaste loses stamina, becomes emasculated and cowardly. He whose mind is given over to animal passions is not capable of any great effort. This can be proved by innumerable instances. What, then, is a married person to do is the question that arises naturally ; and yet it need not. When a husband and wife gratify the passions, it is no less an animal indulgence on that account. Such an indulgence, except for perpetuating the race, is strictly prohibited. But a passive resister has to avoid even that very limited indulgence because he can have no desire for progeny. A married man, therefore, can observe perfect chastity. This subject is not capable of being treated at greater length. Several questions arise : How is one to carry one's wife with one, what are her rights, and other similar questions. Yet those who wish to take part in a great work are bound to solve these puzzles.

Just as there is necessity for chastity, so is there for poverty. Pecuniary ambition and passive resistance cannot well go together. Those who have money are not expected to throw it away, but they are expected to be indifferent about it. They must be prepared to lose every penny rather than give up passive resistance.

Passive resistance has been described in the course of our discussion as truth-force. Truth, therefore, has necessarily to be followed and that at any cost. In this connection, academic questions such as whether a man may not lie in order to save a life, etc., arise, but these questions occur only to those who wish to justify lying. Those who want to follow truth every time are not placed in such a quandary ; and if they are, they are still saved from a false position.

Passive resistance cannot proceed a step without fearlessness. Those alone can follow the path of passive resistance who are free from fear, whether as to their possessions, false honour, their relatives, the government, bodily injuries or death.

These observances are not to be abandoned in the belief that they are difficult. Nature has implanted in the human breast ability to cope with any difficulty or suffering that may come to man unprovoked. These qualities are worth having, even for those who do not wish to serve the country. Let there be no mistake, as those who want to train themselves in the use of arms are also obliged to have these qualities more or less. Everybody does not become a warrior for the wish. A would-be warrior will have to observe chastity and to be satisfied with poverty as his lot. A warrior without fearlessness cannot be conceived of. It may be thought that he would not need to be exactly truthful, but that quality follows real fearlessness. When a man abandons truth, he does so owing to fear in some shape or form. The above four attributes, then, need not frighten any one. It may be as well here to note that a physical-force man has to have many other useless qualities which a passive resister never needs. And you will find that whatever extra effort a swordsman needs is due to lack of fearlessness. If he is an embodiment of the latter, the sword will drop from his hand that very moment. He does not need its support. One who is free from hatred requires no sword. A man with a stick suddenly came face to face with a lion and instinctively raised his weapon in self-defence. The man saw that he had only prated about fearlessness when there was none in him. That moment he dropped the stick and found himself free from all fear.

Hind Swaraj or Indian Home Rule, chap. XVII

CONDITIONS FOR SUCCESSFUL SATYAGRAHA

There can be no Satyagraha in an unjust cause. Satyagraha in a just cause is vain, if the men espousing it are not determined and capable of fighting and suffering to the end ; and the slightest use of violence often defeats a just cause. Satyagraha excludes the use of violence in any shape or form, whether in thought, speech, or deed. Given a just cause, capacity for endless suffering and avoidance of violence, victory is a certainty.

Young India, 27-4-'21

13

NON-RETALIATION

Victory is impossible until we are able to keep our temper under the gravest provocation. Calmness under fire is a soldier's indispensable quality. A non-co-operator is nothing if he cannot remain calm and unperturbed under a fierce fire of provocation.

There should be no mistake. There is no civil disobedience possible, until the crowds behave like disciplined soldiers. And we cannot resort to civil disobedience, unless we can assure every Englishman that he is as safe in India as he is in his own home. It is not enough that we give the assurance. Every Englishman and Englishwoman must feel safe, not by reason of the bayonet at their disposal but by reason of our living creed of non-violence. That is the condition not only of success but our own ability to carry on the movement in its present form. There is no other way of conducting the campaign of non-co-operation.

Young India, 25-8-'21

14

COURAGE AND DISCIPLINE NECESSARY

The pledge of non-violence does not require us to co-operate in our humiliation. It, therefore, does not require us to crawl on our bellies or to draw lines with our noses or to walk to salute the Union Jack or to do anything degrading at the dictation of officials. On the contrary our creed requires us to refuse to do any of these things even though we should be shot. It was, therefore, for instance, no part of the duty of the Jalianwala Bagh people to run away or even to turn their backs when they were fired upon. If the message of non-violence had reached them, they would have been expected when fire was opened on them to march towards it with bare breasts and die rejoicing in the belief that it meant the freedom of their country. Non-violence laughs at the might of the tyrant and stultifies him by non-retaliation and non-retiral. We played into General Dyer's hands because we acted as he had expected. He wanted us to run away from his fire, he wanted us to crawl on our bellies and to draw lines with our noses. That was a part of the game of 'frightfulness'. When we face it with eyes front, it vanishes like an apparition. We may not all evolve that type of courage. But I am certain that Swaraj is unattainable this year if some of us have not the courage which enables us to stand firm like a rock without retaliating. The might of the tyrant recoils upon himself when it meets with no response, even as an arm violently waved in the air suffers dislocation.

And just as we need the cool courage described above, we need perfect discipline and training in voluntary obedience to be able to offer civil disobedience. Civil disobedience is the active expression of non-violence. Civil disobedience distinguishes the non-violence of the strong from the passive, i.e. negative non-violence of the weak. And as weakness cannot lead to Swaraj, negative non-violence must fail to achieve our purpose.

Have we then the requisite discipline? Have we, a friend asked me, evolved the spirit of obedience to our own rules and resolutions? Whilst we have made tremendous headway during the past twelve months, we have certainly not made enough to warrant us in embarking upon civil disobedience with easy confidence. Rules voluntarily passed by us and rules which carry no sanction save the disapproval of our own conscience must be like debts of honour held far more binding than rules superimposed upon us or rules whose breach we can purge by paying the penalty thereof. It follows that if we have not learnt the discipline of obeying our own rules, in other words carrying out our own promises, we are ill adapted for disobedience that can be at all described as civil. I do, therefore, suggest to every Congressman, every non-co-operator, and above all to every member of the All India Congress Committee to set himself or herself right with the Congress and his or her creed by carrying on the strictest self-examination and by correcting himself or herself wherever he or she might have failed.

Young India, 20-10-'21

15

THE NEED FOR HUMILITY

The spirit of non-violence necessarily leads to humility. Non-violence means reliance on God, the Rock of Ages. If we would seek His aid, we must approach Him with a humble and a contrite heart. Non-co-operationists may not trade upon their amazing success at the Congress. We must act, even as the mango tree which droops as it bears fruit. Its grandeur lies in its majestic lowliness. But one hears of non-co-operationists being insolent and intolerant in their behaviour towards those who differ from them. I know that they will lose all their majesty and glory, if they betray any inflation. Whilst we may not be dissatisfied with the progress made so far, we have little to our credit to make us feel proud. We have to sacrifice much more than we have done to justify pride, much less elation. Thousands, who flocked to the Congress *pandal*, have undoubtedly given their intellectual assent to the doctrine but few have followed it out in practice. Leaving aside the pleaders, how many parents have withdrawn their children from schools ? How many of those who registered their vote in favour of non-co-operation have taken to hand-spinning or discarded the use of all foreign cloth ?

Non-co-operation is not a movement of brag, bluster or bluff. It is a test of our sincerity. It requires solid and silent self-sacrifice. It challenges our honesty and our capacity for national work. It is a movement that aims at translating ideas into action. And the more we do, the more we find that much more must be done than we had expected. And this thought of our imperfection must make us humble.

A non-co-operationist strives to compel attention and to set an example not by his violence but by his unobtrusive humility. He allows his solid action to speak for his creed. His strength lies in his reliance upon the correctness of his position. And the conviction of it grows most in his opponent when he least interposes his speech between his action and his opponent. Speech, especially when it is haughty, betrays want of confidence and it makes one's opponent sceptical about the reality of the act itself. Humility therefore is the key to quick success. I hope that every non-co-operationist will recognize the necessity of being humble and self-restrained. It is because so little is really required to be done and because all of that little depends entirely upon ourselves that I have ventured the belief that Swaraj is attainable in less than one year.

Young India, 12-1-'21

WORK IN JAILS

An esteemed friend asks me whether now that the
Government have provided an opportunity for hundreds to
find themselves imprisoned and as thousands are respond-
ing, will it not be better for the prisoners to refuse to do any
work in the gaols at all? I am afraid that the suggestion
comes from a misapprehension of the moral position. We
are not out to abolish gaols as an institution. Even under
Swaraj we would have our gaols. Our civil disobedience,
therefore, must not be carried beyond the point of breaking the unmoral laws of the country. Breach of the laws
to be civil assumes the strictest and willing obedience to
gaol discipline because disobedience of a particular rule
assumes a willing acceptance of the sanction provided for
its breach. And immediately a person quarrels both with
the rule and the sanction for its breach, he ceases to be
civil and lends himself to the precipitation of chaos and
anarchy. A civil resister is, if one may be permitted such
a claim for him, a philanthropist and a friend of the State.
An anarchist is an enemy of the State and is, therefore,
a misanthrope. I have permitted myself to use the language
of war because the so-called constitutional method has
become so utterly ineffective. But I hold the opinion
firmly that civil disobedience is the purest type of constitutional agitation. Of course it becomes degrading and
despicable if its civil, i.e., non-violent character is a mere
camouflage. If the honesty of non-violence be admitted,
there is no warrant for condemnation even of the fiercest
disobedience because of the likelihood of its leading to
violence. No big or swift movement can be carried on
without bold risks and life will not be worth living if it
is not attended with large risks. Does not the history of
the world show that there would have been no romance
in life if there had been no risks? It is the clearest proof
of a degenerate atmosphere that one finds respectable

people, leaders of society, raising their hands in horror and indignation at the slightest approach of danger or upon an outbreak of any violent commotion. We do want to drive out the beast in man, but we do not want on that account to emasculate him. And in the process of finding his own status, the beast in him is bound now and again to put up his ugly appearance. As I have often stated in these pages what strikes me down is not the sight of blood under every conceivable circumstance. It is blood spilt by the non-co-operator or his supporters in breach of his declared pledge, which paralyses me as I know it ought to paralyse every honest non-co-operator.

Therefore, to revert to the original argument, as civil resisters we are bound to guard against universal indiscipline. Gaol discipline must be submitted to until gaol government itself becomes or is felt to be corrupt and immoral. But deprivation of comfort, imposition of restrictions and such other inconveniences do not make gaol government corrupt. It becomes that when prisoners are humiliated or treated with inhumanity as when they are kept in filthy dens or are given food unfit for human consumption. Indeed, I hope that the conduct of non-co-operators in the gaol will be strictly correct, dignified and yet submissive. We must not regard gaolers and warders as our enemies but as fellow human beings not utterly devoid of the human touch. Our gentlemanly behaviour is bound to disarm all suspicion or bitterness. I know that this path of discipline on the one hand and fierce defiance on the other is a very difficult path, but there is no royal road to Swaraj. The country has deliberately chosen the narrow and the straight path. Like a straight line it is the shortest distance. But even as you require a steady and experienced hand to draw a straight line, so are steadiness of discipline and firmness of purpose absolutely necessary if we are to walk along the chosen path with an unerring step.

Young India, 15-12-'21

17

A MODEL PRISONER

"Should non-co-operators shout *Bande Mataram* inside jails against jail discipline which may excite ordinary prisoners to violence, should non-co-operators go on hunger strike for the improvement of food or other conveniences, should they strike work inside jails on *hartal* days and other days? Are non-co-operators entitled to break rules of jail discipline unless they affect their conscience?" Such is the text of a telegram I received from a non-co-operator friend in Calcutta. From another part of India when a friend, again a non-co-operator, heard of the indiscipline of non-co-operator prisoners, he asked me to write on the necessity of observing jail discipline. As against this I know prisoners who are scrupulously observing in a becoming spirit all the discipline imposed upon them.

It is necessary, when thousands are going to jail to understand exactly the position a non-co-operator prisoner can take up consistently with his pledge of non-violence. Non-co-operation, when its limitations are not recognized, becomes a licence instead of being a duty and therefore becomes a crime. The dividing line between right and wrong is often so thin as to become indistinguishable. But it is a line that is breakable and unmistakable.

What is then the difference between those who find themselves in jails for being in the right and those who are there for being in the wrong? Both wear often the same dress, eat the same food and are subject outwardly to the same discipline. But while the latter submit to discipline most unwillingly and would commit a breach of it secretly, and even openly if they could, the former will willingly and to the best of their ability conform to jail discipline and prove worthier and more serviceable to their cause than when they are outside. We have observed that the most distinguished among the prisoners are of greater service inside jails than outside. The coefficient of service is raised to the extent of the strictness with which jail discipline is observed.

Let it be remembered that we are not seeking to destroy jails as such. I fear that we shall have to maintain jails even under Swaraj. It will go hard with us, if we let the real criminals understand that they will be set free or be very much better treated when Swaraj is established. Even in reformatories by which I would like to replace every jail under Swaraj, discipline will be exacted. Therefore, we really retard the advent of Swaraj if we encourage indiscipline. Indeed the swift programme of Swaraj has been conceived on the supposition that we being a cultured people are capable of evolving high discipline within a short time.

Indeed whilst on the one hand civil disobedience authorizes disobedience of unjust laws or unmoral laws of a State which one seeks to overthrow, it requires meek and willing submission to the penalty of disobedience and, therefore, cheerful acceptance of jail discipline and its attendant hardships.

It is now, therefore, clear that a civil resister's resistance ceases and his obedience is resumed as soon as he is under confinement. In confinement he claims no privileges because of the civility of his disobedience. Inside the jail by his exemplary conduct he reforms even the criminals surrounding him, he softens the hearts of jailors and others in authority. Such meek behaviour springing from strength and knowledge ultimately dissolves the tyranny of the tyrant. It is for this reason that I claim that voluntary suffering is the quickest and the best remedy for the removal of abuses and injustices.

It is now manifest that shouts of *Bande Mataram* or any other in breach of jail discipline are unlawful for a non-co-operator to indulge in. It is equally unlawful for him to commit a stealthy breach of jail regulations. A non-co-operator will do nothing to demoralize his fellow prisoners. The only occasion when he can openly disobey jail regulations or hunger-strike is when an attempt is made to humiliate him or when the warders themselves break, as they often do, the rules for the comfort of prisoners or when food that is unfit for human consumption is issued as it often is. A case for civil disobedience also arises when there is interference with any obligatory religious practice.

Young India, 29-12-'21

18

SATYAGRAHI PRISONER'S CONDUCT

Whether all of us realize or not the method of non-co-operation is a process of touching the heart and appealing to reason, not one of frightening by rowdyism. Rowdyism has no place in a non-violent movement.

I have often likened Satyagrahi prisoners to prisoners of war. Once caught by the enemy, prisoners of war act towards the enemy as friends. It will be considered dishonourable on the part of a soldier as a prisoner of war to deceive the enemy. It does not affect my argument that the Government does not regard Satyagrahi prisoners as prisoners of war. If we act as such, we shall soon command respect. We must make the prison a neutral institution in which we may, nay, must co-operate to a certain extent.

We would be highly inconsistent and hardly self-respecting if on the one hand we deliberately break prison rules and in the same breath complain of punishment and strictness. We may not, for instance, resist and complain of search and at the same time conceal prohibited things in our blankets or our clothes. There is nothing in Satyagraha that I know whereby we may under certain circumstances tell untruths or practise other deception.

When we say that if we make the lives of prison officials uncomfortable, the Government will be obliged to sue for peace, we either pay them a subtle compliment or regard them as simpletons. We pay a subtle compliment when we consider that even though we may make prison officials' lives uncomfortable, the Government will look on in silence and hesitate to award us condign punishment so as utterly to break our spirit. That is to say we regard the administrators to be so considerate and humane that they will not severely punish us even though we give them sufficient cause. As a matter of fact, they will not and do not hesitate to throw over-board all idea of decency and award not only authorized but even unauthorized punishments on given occasions.

But it is my deliberate conviction that had we but acted with uniform honesty and dignity, behoving Satyagrahis, we would have disarmed all opposition on the part of the Government and such strictly honourable behaviour on the part of so many prisoners would have at least shamed the Government into confessing their error in imprisoning so many honourable and innocent men. For is it not their case that our non-violence is but a cloak for our violence ? Do we not therefore play into their hands every time we are rowdy ?

In my opinion therefore as Satyagrahis we are bound, when we become prisoners,

1. to act with the most scrupulous honesty ;

2. to co-operate with the prison officials in their administration ;

3. to set by our obedience to all reasonable discipline an example to co-prisoners ;

4. to ask for no favours and claim no privileges which the meanest of prisoners do not get and which we do not need strictly for reasons of health ;

5. not to fail to ask what we do so need and not to get irritated if we do not obtain it ;

6. to do all the tasks allotted, to the utmost of our ability.

It is such conduct which will make the Government position uncomfortable and untenable. It is difficult for them to meet honesty with honesty for their want of faith and unpreparedness for such a rare eventuality. Rowdyism they expect and meet with a double dose of it. They were able to deal with anarchical crime but they have not yet found out any way of dealing with non-violence save by yielding to it.

The idea behind the imprisonment of Satyagrahis is that he expects relief through humble submission to suffering. He believes that meek suffering for a just cause has a virtue all its own and infinitely greater than the virtue of the sword. This does not mean that we may not resist when the treatment touches our self-respect. Thus for instance we must resist to the point of death the use of abusive language by officials or if they were to throw our food at us which is often done. Insult and abuse are no part of an official's duty. Therefore we must resist them. But we may not resist search because it is part of prison regulations.

Nor are my remarks about mute suffering to be construed to mean that there should be no agitation against putting innocent prisoners like Satyagrahis in the same class as confirmed criminals. Only as prisoners we may not ask for favours. We must be content to live with the confirmed criminals and even welcome the opportunity of working moral reform in them. It is however expected of a government that calls itself civilized to recognize the most natural divisions.

Young India, 5-6-'24

19

PRE-REQUISITES FOR SATYAGRAHA *

Public opposition is effective only where there is strength behind it. What does a son do when he objects to some action of his father ? He requests the father to desist from the objectionable course, i.e. presents respectful petitions. If the father does not agree in spite of repeated prayers, he non-co-operates with him to the extent even of leaving the paternal roof. This is pure

---

* From Gandhiji's Presidential Speech at the 3rd Kathiawad Political Conference, Bhavnagar.

justice. Where father and son are uncivilized, they quarrel, abuse each other and often even come to blows. An obedient son is ever modest, ever peaceful and ever loving. It is only his love which on due occasion compels him to non-co-operate. The father himself understands this loving non-co-operation. He cannot endure abandonment by or separation from the son, is distressed at heart and repents. Not that it always happens thus. But the son's duty of non-co-operation is clear.

Such non-co-operation is possible between a prince and his people. In particular circumstances it may be the people's duty. Such circumstances can exist only where the latter are by nature fearless and are lovers of liberty. They generally appreciate the laws of the State and obey them voluntarily without the fear of punishment. Reasoned and willing obedience to the laws of the State is the first lesson in non-co-operation.

The second is that of tolerance. We must tolerate many laws of the State, even when they are inconvenient. A son may not approve of some orders of the father and yet he obeys them. It is only when they are unworthy of tolerance and immoral that he disobeys them. The father will at once understand such respectful disobedience. In the same way it is only when a people have proved their active loyalty by obeying the many laws of the State that they acquire the right of Civil Disobedience.

The third lesson is that of suffering. He who has not the capacity of suffering cannot non-co-operate. He who has not learnt to sacrifice his property and even his family when necessary can never non-co-operate. It is possible that a prince enraged by non-co-operation will inflict all manner of punishments. There lies the test of love, patience, and strength. He who is not ready to undergo the fiery ordeal cannot non-co-operate. A whole people cannot be considered fit or ready for non-co-operation when only an individual or two have mastered these three lessons. A large number of the people must be thus prepared before they can non-co-operate. The result of hasty non-co-operation can only lead to harm. Some patriotic young men who do not understand the limitations noted by me grow impatient. Previous preparation is needed for non-co-operation as it is for all important things. A man cannot become a non-co-operator by merely wishing to be one. Discipline is obligatory. I do not know that many have undergone the needful discipline in any part of Kathiawad. And when the requisite discipline has been gone through probably non-co-operation will be found to be unnecessary.

As it is, I observe the necessity for individuals to prepare themselves in Kathiawad as well as in other parts of India. Individuals must cultivate the spirit of service, renunciation, truth, non-violence, self-restraint, patience, etc. They must engage in constructive work in order to develop these qualities. Many reforms would be effected automatically if we put in a good deal of silent work among the people.

Young India, 8-1-'25

20

MY POLITICAL PROGRAMME

[Some American friends sent Gandhiji a gift of 145 dollars to be spent on that part of his work which appealed to them most, viz. anti-untouchability and Hindu-Muslim unity, and said that they knew too little about his political programme to wish to help in that part of his work also. In reply, Gandhiji wrote as follows: — Ed.]

My political programme is extremely simple. If the donors had added the spinning wheel to untouchability and unity, they would have practically completed it. My opinion is becoming daily more and more confirmed that we shall achieve our real freedom only by effort from within, i.e., by self-purification and self-help, and therefore, by the strictest adherence to truth and non-violence. Civil Disobedience is no doubt there in the background. But Civil Disobedience asks for and needs not a single farthing for its support. It needs and asks for stout hearts with a faith that will not flinch from any danger and will shine the brightest in the face of severest trial. Civil Disobedience is a terrifying synonym for suffering. But it is better often to understand the terrible nature of a thing if people will truly appreciate its benignant counterpart. Disobedience is a right that belongs to every human being and it becomes a sacred duty when it springs from civility, or, which is the same thing, love. The anti-untouchability reformers are offering Civil Disobedience against entrenched orthodoxy. Protagonists of Hindu-Muslim unity are resisting with their whole soul those who will divide classes and sects. Just as there may be this resistance against those who will hinder the removal of untouchability or promotion of unity, so must there be resistance against a rule that is stunting India's manhood. It is daily grinding down the starving millions of this vast country. Heedless of future consequences the rulers are pursuing a course of conduct regarding intoxicating drinks and drugs that must, if it remains unchecked, corrupt the toilers of the land and make posterity ashamed of us who are making use of this immoral source of revenue for educating our children. But the condition of this terrible resistance — resistance against orthodoxy, resistance against enemies of unity, and resistance against Government — is possible of fulfilment only by a strong, and if need be, a long course of self-purification and suffering.

Young India, 1-4-'26

21

LIMITATIONS OF SATYAGRAHA

All Civil Disobedience is a part or branch of Satyagraha, but all Satyagraha is not Civil Disobedience. And seeing that the Nagpur friends have suspended what they were pleased to call Satyagraha or Civil Disobedience, let me suggest for their information and that of others how Satyagraha can be legitimately offered with reference to the Bengal detenus. If they will not be angry with me or laugh at me, let me commence by saying that they can offer Satyagraha by developing the power of the people through *khadi*, and through *khadi* achieving boycott of foreign cloth. They can offer Satyagraha by becoming precursors of Hindu-Muslim unity, by allowing their heads to be broken whenever there is a quarrel between the two, and whilst there is no active quarrel in their parts by performing silent acts of service to those of the opposite faith to theirs. If such constructive methods are too flat for them, and if they will be satisfied by nothing less than Civil Disobedience in spite of the violence of thought, word and deed raging round us, I suggest the following prescription of individual Civil Disobedience, which even one man can offer, not indeed in the hope of securing immediate release of detenus, but certainly in the hope of the individual sacrifice ultimately eventuating in such release. Let a batch, or only one person, say from Nagpur, march on foot to the Government House in Calcutta, and if a march is irksome or impossible then let him, her, or them beg enough money for trainfare from friends, and having reached Calcutta let only one Satyagrahi march to the Government House and walk on to the point where he or she is stopped. There let him or her stop and demand the release of detenus or his or her own arrest. To preserve intact the civil nature of this disobedience the Satyagrahi must be wholly unarmed, and in spite of insults, kicks or worse must meekly stand the ground, and be arrested without the slightest opposition. He may carry his own food in his pocket, a bottleful of water, take his *Gita*, the Koran, the Bible, the Zend Avesta or the Granth Sahib, as the case may be, and his *takli*. If there are many such real Satyagrahis, they will certainly transform the atmosphere in an immensely short time, even as one gentle shower transforms the plains of India into a beautiful green carpet in one single day.

The question will legitimately be asked, ' If you really mean what you say, why don't you take the lead, never mind whether any one follows you or not ? ' My answer is : I do not regard myself as pure enough to undertake such a heroic mission. I am trying every moment of my life to attain the requisite purity of thought, word and deed. As it is, I confess that I am swayed by many passions. Anger wells up in my breast when I see or hear about what I consider to be misdeeds. All I can humbly claim for myself is that I can keep these passions and moods under fair subjection, and prevent them from gaining mastery over me. But the standard of purity that I want, for any such heroic measure is not to have such passions at all and yet to hate the wrong. When I feel that I have become incapable even of thinking evil, and I hold it to be possible for every God-fearing man to attain that state, I shall wait for no man's advice, and even at the risk of being called the maddest of men, I shall not hesitate to knock at the Viceregal gate or go wherever God leads me, and demand what is due to this country which is being ground to dust today.

Meanwhile let no man mock at Satyagraha. Let no man parody it. If it is at all possible, leave Satyagraha alone, and the whole field is open for unchecked action. On a chartless sea in which there is no light-house a captain dares whither he wills. But a captain who knowing the existence of a light-house and its position, sails anyhow, or takes no precaution for knowing the light-house from deceiving stars, will be considered unfit for his post. If the reader can bear with me, let him understand that I claim to be the keeper of the light-house called Satyagraha in the otherwise chartless sea of Indian politics. And, therefore, it is that I have suggested, that those who make for Satyagraha will do well to go to its keeper. But I know that I have no patent rights in Satyagraha. I can, therefore, merely rely upon the indulgence of fellow-workers for recognition of my office.

Young India, 14-7-'27

A GREAT SATYAGRAHI

[In his speech at Chidambaram, Gandhiji paid this tribute to the great ' untouchable ' saint Nandanar :]

I know that Chidambaram must be a place of pilgrimage for me. I have never claimed to be the one original Satyagrahi. What I have claimed is to have made the application of that doctrine on an almost universal scale, and it yet remains to be seen and demonstrated that it is a doctrine which is capable of assimilation by thousands upon thousands of peoples in all ages and climes. I know, therefore, that mine is an experiment still in the making and it, therefore, always keeps me humble and rooted to the soil, and in that state of humility I always cling to every true example of Satyagraha that comes under my notice as a child clings to its mother's breast, and so when I heard and read the story of Nandanar and his lofty Satyagraha, and his great success, my head bowed before his spirit, and all day long I have felt elevated to be able to be in a place hallowed by the holy feet of Nanda, and it will not be without a wrench that I shall be leaving this place in a few minutes' time.

Nanda broke down every barrier and won his way to freedom not by brag, not by bluster, but by the purest form of self-suffering. He did not swear against his persecutors, he would not even condescend to ask his persecutors for what was his due. But he shamed them into doing justice by his lofty prayer, by the purity of his character, and if one may put it in human language he compelled God Himself to descend and made Him open the eyes of his persecutors. And what Nanda did in his time and in his own person, it is open to every one of us to do today in our own person.

Young India, 22-9-'27

NEILL STATUE SATYAGRAHA

In accordance with the promise made by the volunteers connected with this movement, they have sent me papers giving the particulars I had asked for. From them it appears that during the six weeks that the struggle had been on when the papers were sent to me thirty volunteers had courted imprisonment. Of these 29 are Hindus and one Mussalman, one lady aged 35 and one girl aged 9, her daughter. Of these thirty, two apologized, and got themselves released. The apology of a few, if it does not become infectious, does not matter. 'Blacklegs' will be found in every struggle. The men who have gone to gaol are not noted men. This is no loss, rather it is a gain in a Satyagraha struggle which requires no prestige save that of truth, and no strength save that of self-suffering which comes only from an immovable faith in one's cause and from a completely non-violent spirit.

The volunteers must not be impatient. Impatience is a phase of violence. A Satyagrahi has nothing to do with victory. He is sure of it, but he has also to know that it comes from God. His is but to suffer.

The papers give me an account of income and expenditure. Let the Satyagrahis understand that they have to use every pice they get as a miser uses his hoards. I suggest their getting a local man of note to take charge of their moneys and a philanthropic auditor to audit their accounts free of charge. Strictest honesty and care are necessary in the handling of public funds. This is an indispensable condition of growth of a healthy public life.

The third paper I have before me is their appeal to the public. A Satyagrahi's appeal must contain moderate language. The appeal before me though unexceptionable admits of improvement. 'Not only Neill but all of his nefarious breed must go,' is a sentence that mars the appeal. General Neill is no more. What we have to deal with is the statue and not even the statue as such. We seek to destroy the principle for which the statue stands. We wish to injure no man. And we wish to gain our object by enlisting public opinion not excluding English opinion in our favour by self-suffering. Here there is no room for the language of anger and hate.

So much for the volunteers.

The public owe a duty to them. They may not go to gaol but they can supervise, control and guide and help the movement in many ways. Agitation for the removal of the statue is agitation for the removal of but a symptom of a grave disease. And while the removal of the statue will not cure the disease it will alleviate the agony and point the way to reaching the disease itself. It is also often possible to reach a deep-seated disease by dealing with some of its symptoms. So long therefore as the Satya-grahi volunteers fight the battle in a clean manner and strictly in accordance with the conditions applicable to Satyagraha they deserve public support and sympathy.

Young India, 13-10-'27

24

A HIMALAYAN MISCALCULATION

Almost immediately after the Ahmedabad meeting I went to Nadiad. It was here that I first used the expression *Himalayan miscalculation* which obtained such a wide currency afterwards. Even at Ahmedabad I had begun to have a dim perception of my mistake. But when I reached Nadiad and saw the actual state of things there and heard reports about a large number of people from Kheda district having been arrested, it suddenly dawned upon me that I had committed a grave error in calling upon the people in the Kheda district and elsewhere to launch upon civil disobedience prematurely, as it now seemed to me. I was addressing a public meeting. My confession brought down upon me no small amount of ridicule. But

I have never regretted having made that confession. For I have always held that it is only when one sees one's own mistakes with a convex lens, and does just the reverse in the case of others, that one is able to arrive at a just relative estimate of the two. I further believe that a scrupulous and conscientious observance of this rule is necessary for one who wants to be a Satyagrahi.

Let us now see what that Himalayan miscalculation was. Before one can be fit for the practice of civil disobedience one must have rendered a willing and respectful obedience to the State laws. For the most part we obey such laws for fear of the penalty for their breach, and this holds good particularly in respect of such laws as do not involve a moral principle. For instance, an honest, respectable man will not suddenly take to stealing whether there is a law against stealing or not, but this very man will not feel any remorse for failure to observe the rule about carrying headlights on bicycles after dark. Indeed, it is doubtful whether he would even accept advice kindly about being more careful in this respect. But he would observe any obligatory rule of this kind, if only to escape the inconvenience of facing a prosecution for a breach of the rule. Such compliance is not, however, the willing and spontaneous obedience that is required of a Satyagrahi. A Satyagrahi obeys the laws of society intelligently and of his own free will, because he considers it to be his sacred duty to do so. It is only when a person has thus obeyed the laws of society scrupulously that he is in a position to judge as to which particular rules are good and just and which unjust and iniquitous. Only then does the right accrue to him of the civil disobedience of certain laws in well-defined circumstances. My error lay in my failure to observe this necessary limitation. I had called upon the people to launch upon civil disobedience before they had thus qualified themselves for it, and this mistake seemed to me of Himalayan magnitude. As soon as I entered the Kheda district, all the old recollections of the Kheda Satyagraha struggle came back to me, and I wondered how I could have failed to perceive what was so obvious. I realized that before a people could be fit for offering civil disobedience, they should thoroughly understand its deeper implications. That being so, before re-starting civil disobedience on a mass scale, it would be necessary to create a band of well-tried, pure-hearted volunteers who thoroughly understood the strict conditions of Satyagraha. They could explain these to the people, and by sleepless vigilance keep them on the right path.

With these thoughts filling my mind I reached Bombay, raised a corps of Satyagrahi volunteers through the Satyagraha Sabha there, and with their help commenced the work of educating the people with regard to the meaning and inner significance of Satyagraha. This was principally done by issuing leaflets of an educative character bearing on the subject.

But whilst this work was going on, I could see that it was a difficult task to interest the people in the peaceful side of Satyagraha. The volunteers too failed to enlist themselves in large numbers. Nor did all those who actually enlisted take anything like a regular systematic training, and as the days passed by, the number of fresh recruits began gradually to dwindle instead of to grow. I realized that the progress of the training in civil disobedience was not going to be as rapid as I had at first expected.

The Story of My Experiments with Truth, pt. V, chap. XXXIII

25

QUALIFICATIONS FOR SATYAGRAHA

Satyagraha presupposes self-discipline, self-control, self-purification, and a recognized social status in the person offering it. A Satyagrahi must never forget the distinction between evil and the evil-doer. He must not harbour ill-will or bitterness against the latter. He may not even employ needlessly offensive language against the evil person, however unrelieved his evil might be. For it should be an article of faith with every Satyagrahi that there is none so fallen in this world but can be converted by love. A Satyagrahi will always try to overcome evil by good, anger by love, untruth by truth, *himsa* by *ahimsa*. There is no other way of purging the world of evil. Therefore a person who claims to be a Satyagrahi always tries by close and prayerful self-introspection and self-analysis to find out whether he is himself completely free from the taint of anger, ill-will and such other human infirmities, whether he is not himself capable of those very evils against which he is out to lead a crusade. In self-purification and penance lies half the victory of a Satyagrahi. A Satyagrahi has faith that the silent and undemonstrative action of truth and love produces far more permanent and abiding results than speeches or such other showy performances.

But although Satyagraha can operate silently, it requires a certain amount of action on the part of a Satyagrahi. A Satyagrahi, for instance, must first mobilize public opinion against the evil which he is out to eradicate, by means of a wide and intensive agitation. When public opinion is sufficiently roused against a social abuse even the tallest will not dare to practise or openly to lend support to it. An awakened and intelligent public opinion is the most potent weapon of a Satyagrahi. When a person supports a social evil in total disregard of unanimous public opinion, it indicates a clear justification for

his social ostracism. But the object of social ostracism
should never be to do injury to the person against whom
it is directed. Social ostracism means complete non-co-
operation on the part of society with the offending
individual; nothing more, nothing less, the idea being
that a person who deliberately sets himself to flout society
has no right to be served by society. For all practical
purposes this should be enough. Of course, special action
may be indicated in special cases and the practice may
have to be varied to suit the peculiar features of each
individual case.

Young India, 8-8-'29

26

SOME RULES OF SATYAGRAHA

Satyagraha literally means insistence on truth. This
insistence arms the votary with matchless power. This
power or force is connoted by the word *Satyagraha*.
Satyagraha, to be genuine, may be offered against one's
wife or one's children, against rulers, against fellow
citizens, even against the whole world.

Such a universal force necessarily makes no distinction
between kinsmen and strangers, young and old, man and
woman, friend and foe. The force to be so applied can
never be physical. There is in it no room for violence.
The only force of universal application can, therefore, be
that of *ahimsa* or love. In other words it is soul-force.

Love does not burn others, it burns itself. Therefore,
a Satyagrahi, i.e. a civil resister, will joyfully suffer even
unto death.

It follows, therefore, that a civil resister, whilst he
will strain every nerve to compass the end of the existing
rule, will do no intentional injury in thought, word or
deed to the person of a single Englishman. This necessarily brief explanation of Satyagraha will perhaps enable the

reader to understand and appreciate the following rules:

As an Individual

1. A Satyagrahi, i.e., a civil resister will harbour no anger.

2. He will suffer the anger of the opponent.

3. In so doing he will put up with assaults from the opponent, never retaliate; but he will not submit, out of fear of punishment or the like, to any order given in anger.

4. When any person in authority seeks to arrest a civil resister, he will voluntarily submit to the arrest, and he will not resist the attachment or removal of his own property, if any, when it is sought to be confiscated by the authorities.

5. If a civil resister has any property in his possession as a trustee, he will refuse to surrender it, even though in defending it he might lose his life. He will however, never retaliate.

6. Non-retaliation excludes swearing and cursing.

7. Therefore a civil resister will never insult his opponent, and therefore also not take part in many of the newly coined cries which are contrary to the spirit of *ahimsa*.

8. A civil resister will not salute the Union Jack, nor will he insult it or officials, English or Indian.

9. In the course of the struggle if any one insults an official or commits an assault upon him, a civil resister will protect such official or officials from the insult or attack even at the risk of his life.

As a Prisoner

10. As a prisoner, a civil resister, will behave courteously towards prison officials, and will observe all such discipline of the prison as is not contrary to self-respect; as for instance, whilst he will *salaam* officials in the usual manner, he will not perform any humiliating gyrations and refuse to shout 'Victory to *Sarkar*' or the like. He will take cleanly cooked and cleanly served food, which is not contrary to his religion, and will refuse to take food insultingly served or served in unclean vessels.

11. A civil resister will make no distinction between an ordinary prisoner and himself, will in no way regard himself as superior to the rest, nor will he ask for any conveniences that may not be necessary for keeping his body in good health and condition. He is entitled to ask for such conveniences as may be required for his physical or spiritual well-being.

12. A civil resister may not fast for want of conveniences whose deprivation does not involve any injury to one's self-respect.

As a Unit

13. A civil resister will joyfully obey all the orders issued by the leader of the corps, whether they please him or not.

14. He will carry out orders in the first instance even though they appear to him insulting, inimical or foolish, and then appeal to higher authority. He is free before joining to determine the fitness of the corps to satisfy him, but after he has joined it, it becomes a duty to submit to its discipline irksome or otherwise. If the sum total of the energy of the corps appears to a member to be improper or immoral, he has a right to sever his connection, but being within it, he has no right to commit a breach of its discipline.

15. No civil resister is to expect maintenance for his dependents. It would be an accident if any such provision is made. A civil resister entrusts his dependents to the care of God. Even in ordinary warfare wherein hundreds of thousands give themselves up to it, they are able to make no previous provision. How much more, then, should such be the case in Satyagraha ? It is the universal experience that in such times hardly anybody is left to starve.

In Communal Fights

16. No civil resister will intentionally become a cause of communal quarrels.

17. In the event of any such outbreak, he will not take sides, but he will assist only that party which is demonstrably in the right. Being a Hindu he will be

generous towards Mussalmans and others, and will sacrifice himself in the attempt to save non-Hindus from a Hindu attack. And if the attack is from the other side, he will not participate in any retaliation but will give his life in protecting Hindus.

18. He will, to the best of his ability, avoid every occasion that may give rise to communal quarrels.

19. If there is a procession of Satyagrahis they will do nothing that would wound the religious susceptibilities of any community, and they will not take part in any other processions that are likely to wound such susceptibilities.

Young India, 27-2-'30

27

FULL SURRENDER

As a Satyagrahi I believe in the absolute efficacy of full surrender. Numerically Hindus happen to be the major community. Therefore, they may give to the minorities what they may want. But even if the Hindus were in a minority, as a Satyagrahi and Hindu I should say that the Hindus would lose nothing in the long run by full surrender.

To this argument a retort has thoughtlessly been made, "Why then do you not advise India to surrender to the English? Give them the domination they want and be happy." The hasty retort ignores the vital fact that I have not advised surrender to the bayonet. In the code of the Satyagrahi there is no such thing as surrender to brute force. Or the surrender then is the surrender of suffering and not to the will of the wielder of the bayonet. A Satyagrahi's surrender has to come out of his strength, not out of weakness. The surrender advised by me is not of honour but of earthly goods. There is no loss of honour in surrendering seats and positions of emoluments. There is loss of honour in haggling about them. Let the Englishmen give up the bayonet and live in our midst as simple friends and I should plead for them. The law of surrender and suffering is a universal law admitting of no exceptions.

Young India, 30-4-'31

28

TO WEAKEN COMMUNALISM

My implicit faith in non-violence does mean yielding to minorities when they are really weak. The best way to weaken communalists is to yield to them. Resistance will only rouse their suspicion and strengthen their opposition. A Satyagrahi resists when there is threat of force behind obstruction. I know that I do not carry the Congressmen in general with me in this what to me appears as very sensible and practical point of view. But if we are to come to Swaraj through non-violent means, I know that this point of view will be accepted.

Young India, 2-7-'31

29

POLITICAL POWER *v.* SATYAGRAHA

If I want political power it is for the sake of the reforms for which the Congress stands. Therefore when the energy to be spent in gaining that power means so much loss of energy required for the reforms, as threatens to be the case if the country is to engage in a duel with the Mussalmans or Sikhs, I would most decidedly advise the country to let the Mussalmans and Sikhs take all the power and I would go on with developing the reforms.

If we were to analyse the activities of the Congress during the past twelve years, we would discover that the capacity of the Congress to take political power has increased in exact proportion to its ability to achieve success in the constructive effort. That is to me the substance of political power. Actual taking over of the Government machinery is but a shadow, an emblem. And it could easily be a burden if it came as a gift from without, the people having made no effort to deserve it.

It is now perhaps easy to realize the truth of my statement that the needful can be 'gained more quickly and more certainly by Satyagraha than by political power'. Legislation in advance of public opinion has often been demonstrated to be futile. Legal prohibition of theft in a country in which the vast majority are thieves would be futile. Picketing and the other popular activities are therefore the real thing. If political power was a thing apart from these reforms, we would have to suspend the latter and concentrate on the former. But we have followed the contrary course. We have everywhere emphasized the necessity of carrying on the constructive activities as being the means of attaining Swaraj. I am convinced that whenever legal prohibition of drinks, drugs and foreign cloth comes, it will come because public opinion had demanded it. It may be said that public opinion demands it today but the foreign Government does not respond. This is only partly right. Public opinion in this country is only now becoming a vital force and developing the real sanction which is Satyagraha.

Young India, 2-7-'31

30

FOR 'FOLLOWERS'

A friend sends me the following :

"It will be very helpful if you will kindly guide your followers about their conduct when they have to engage in a political controversy. Your guidance on the following points is particularly needed :

(a) Vilification so as to lower the opponent in public estimation ;

(b) Kind of criticism of the opponent permissible ;

(c) Limit to which hostility should be carried ;

(d) Whether effort should be made to gain office and power."

I have said before in these pages that I claim no followers. It is enough for me to be my own follower. It is by itself a sufficiently taxing performance. But I know that many claim to be my followers. I must therefore answer the questions for their sakes. If they will follow what I endeavour to stand for rather than me they will see that the following answers are derived from truth and *ahimsa.*

(a)   Vilification of an opponent there can never be. But this does not exclude a truthful characterization of his acts. An opponent is not always a bad man because he opposes. He may be as honourable as we may claim to be and yet there may be vital differences between him and us.

(b)   Our criticism will therefore be if we *believe* him to be guilty of untruth to meet it with truth, of discourtesy with courtesy, of bullying with calm courage, of violence with suffering, of arrogance with humility, of evil with good. " My follower " would seek not to condemn but to convert.

(c)   There is no question of any limit to which hostility may be carried. For there should be no hostility to persons. Hostility there must be to acts when they are subversive of morals or the good of society.

(d)   Office and power must be avoided. Either may be accepted when it is clearly for greater service.

Young India, 7-5-'31

31

MAINTENANCE ALLOWANCE

[In the course of his speech at the Deshaseva Mandal, Sind, on the occasion of its second anniversary Gandhiji said :]

The question has been asked me whether the workers who join such institutions should receive some allowance for their livelihood or not. There are some who think it a humiliation to receive any allowance and would prefer to work without any. They do not seem to realize that if we act on that principle we shall have to search for millionaire workers. Millionaires are few and far between and it is very rarely that we get volunteer workers from that class. I must say that there is a subtle self-conceit in the insistence that we should work without drawing any allowance. There is not only no humiliation in receiving an allowance for one's livelihood but a clear duty. Gokhale began his life of service with an allowance of Rs 40 a month and never in his life drew more than Rs 75 monthly. He contented himself with that much all his life. He did not feel it below his dignity to draw an humble allowance for his livelihood, but considered it an act of duty and of merit. Why then should we pretend to have a higher sense of self-respect than he ? Even a millionaire's son, if he becomes a member should, instead of depending on his millions, make a gift of his millions to such a society and draw his monthly allowance as other members may be doing.

There is one thing more which I should like to bring home to you. Bodies like these ought to be governed by strict rules and regulations. A man without a pledge or a code of conduct is like a ship without a rudder.

I am told that a worker in Sind finds it difficult to live without less than a hundred rupees a month. I find it difficult to swallow this. It may be so in Sind because we have artificially increased our wants. But my experience tells me that it is possible to do with very much less. Lalaji's Servants of the People Society and Gokhale's Servants of India Society we know because of the great names of their founders, but there are many other societies of volunteer workers where the individual allowance is not more than Rs 25 to Rs 30. In Utkal Rs 25 to Rs 30 is an exception and Rs 15 is the rule. We have, therefore, to cut our coat according to our cloth, and limit our needs in accordance with the conditions of our people.

Young India, 30-4-'31

A NON-VIOLENT ARMY

The Congress should be able to put forth a non-violent army of volunteers numbering not a few thousands but lakhs who would be equal to every occasion where the police and the military are required. Thus, instead of one brave Pashupatinath Gupta who died in the attempt to secure peace, we should be able to produce hundreds. And a non-violent army acts unlike armed men, as well in times of peace as of disturbances. They would be constantly engaged in constructive activities that make riots impossible. Theirs will be the duty of seeking occasions for bringing warring communities together, carrying on peace propaganda, engaging in activities that would bring and keep them in touch with every single person, male and female, adult and child, in their parish or division. Such an army should be ready to cope with any emergency, and in order to still the frenzy of mobs should risk their lives in numbers sufficient for the purpose. A few hundred, maybe a few thousand, such spotless deaths will once for all put an end to the riots. Surely a few hundred young men and women giving themselves deliberately to mob fury will be any day a cheap and braver method of dealing with such madness than the display and use of the police and the military.

Harijan, 26-3-'38

TO VOLUNTEERS

I have received several letters offering the writers' names for enrolment as volunteers ready to immolate themselves at times of rioting and the like. To these writers I would suggest that they enlist co-workers themselves, form local corps, and begin training in accordance with the suggestion I have made. Let them not confine themselves merely to preparedness for emergencies, but for the daily walk of life in all its departments, personal, domestic, social, economic, political, religious. Only thus will they find themselves more than ready for dealing with emergencies in their own localities or beats. They may not aim, except indirectly, at influencing events happening hundreds of miles away from their scene of activity. That ability will come, if the right beginning is made in the first instance.

Harijan, 23-4-'38

34

REQUISITE QUALIFICATIONS

The four days' fast set me thinking of the qualifications required in a Satyagrahi. Though they were carefully considered and reduced to writing in 1921 they seem to have been forgotten.

In Satyagraha, it is never the numbers that count; it is always the quality, more so when the forces of violence are uppermost.

Then it is often forgotten that it is never the intention of a Satyagrahi to embarrass the wrong-doer. The appeal is never to his fear; it is, must be, always to his heart. The Satyagrahi's object is to convert, not to coerce, the wrong-doer. He should avoid artificiality in all his doings. He acts naturally and from inward conviction.

Keeping these observations before his mind's eye, the reader will perhaps appreciate the following qualifications which, I hold, are essential for every Satyagrahi in India :

1. He must have a living faith in God, for He is his only Rock.

2. He must believe in truth and non-violence as his creed and therefore have faith in the inherent goodness of human nature which he expects to evoke by his truth and love expressed through his suffering.

3. He must be leading a chaste life and be ready and willing for the sake of his cause to give up his life and his possessions.

4. He must be a habitual *khadi*-wearer and spinner. This is essential for India.

5. He must be a teetotaller and be free from the use of other intoxicants in order that his reason may be always unclouded and his mind constant.

6. He must carry out with a willing heart all the rules of discipline as may be laid down from time to time.

7. He should carry out the jail rules unless they are specially devised to hurt his self-respect.

The qualifications are not to be regarded as exhaustive. They are illustrative only.

Harijan, 25-3-'39

35

QUALIFICATIONS OF A PEACE BRIGADE

Some time ago I suggested the formation of a Peace Brigade whose members would risk their lives in dealing with riots, especially communal. The idea was that this Brigade should substitute the police and even the military. This reads ambitious. The achievement may prove impossible. Yet, if the Congress is to succeed in its non-violent struggle, it must develop the power to deal peacefully with such situations.

Let us therefore see what qualifications a member of the contemplated Peace Brigade should possess.

(1) He or she must have a living faith in non-violence. This is impossible without a living faith in God. A non-violent man can do nothing save by the power and grace of God. Without it he won't have the courage to die without anger, without fear and without retaliation. Such courage comes from the belief that God sits in the hearts of all and that there should be no fear in the presence of God. The knowledge of the omnipresence of God also means respect for the lives of even those who may be called opponents or *goondas*. This contemplated intervention is a process of stilling the fury of man when the brute in him gets mastery over him.

(2) This messenger of peace must have equal regard for all the principal religions of the earth. Thus, if he is a Hindu, he will respect the other faiths current in India. He must therefore possess a knowledge of the general principles of the different faiths professed in the country.

(3) Generally speaking this work of peace can only be done by local men in their own localities.

(4) The work can be done singly or in groups. Therefore no one need wait for companions. Nevertheless one would naturally seek companions in one's own locality and form a local brigade.

(5) This messenger of peace will cultivate through personal service contacts with the people in his locality or chosen circle, so that when he appears to deal with ugly situations, he does not descend upon the members of a riotous assembly as an utter stranger liable to be looked upon as a suspect or an unwelcome visitor.

(6) Needless to say, a peace-bringer must have a character beyond reproach and must be known for his strict impartiality.

(7) Generally, there are previous warnings of coming storms. If these are known, the peace brigade will not wait till the conflagration breaks out but will try to handle the situation in anticipation.

(8) Whilst, if the movement spreads, it might be well if there are some whole-time workers, it is not absolutely necessary that there should be. The idea is to have as many good and true men and women as possible. These can be had only if volunteers are drawn from those who are engaged in various walks of life but have leisure enough to cultivate friendly relations with the people living in their circle and otherwise possess the qualifications required of a member of the Peace Brigade.

(9) There should be a distinctive dress worn by the members of the contemplated brigade so that in course of time they will be recognized without the slightest difficulty.

These are but general suggestions. Each centre can work out its own constitution on the basis here suggested.

Lest false hopes may be raised, I must warn workers against entertaining the hope that I can play any active part in the formation of Peace Brigades. I have not the health, energy or time for it. I find it hard enough to cope with the tasks I dare not shirk. I can only guide and make suggestions through correspondence or these columns. Therefore let those who appreciate the idea and feel they have the ability, take the initiative themselves. I know that the proposed Brigade has great possibilities and that the idea behind it is quite capable of being worked out in practice.

Harijan, 18-6-'38

THE NECESSITY OF TRAINING

I am not likely, lightly and in the near future, to advise mass Satyagraha anywhere. There is neither adequate training nor discipline among the people. I have not the shadow of a doubt that the people at large should pass one or more positive tests. Mere abstention from physical violence will not answer our purpose. In the centre of this programme of positive tests I unhesitatingly put the spinning wheel and all it means. If there is quick response, this can be a short course. But it may well be a long course if the people do not make an enthusiastic response. I know no other programme than the fourfold constructive programme of 1920. If the people do not take it up whole-heartedly, it is proof enough for me that they have no *ahimsa* in them, or not the *ahimsa* of my conception, or say they have no confidence in the present leadership. For me there is no other test but what I have ever put before the nation since 1920. The new light tells me that I must not weaken as I have done before in exacting the discipline I have mentioned. I can quite clearly see my way to advise civil disobedience wherever the conditions mentioned are amply fulfilled. That civil disobedience will be individual, but in terms of *ahimsa* far more effective than any mass civil disobedience of the past. I must own that the past movements have been more or less tainted. I have no regret for them. For I knew no better then. I had the sense and humility to retrace my steps whenever I discovered blunders. Hence the nation has gone forward from step to step. But the time has come for a radical change in the direction indicated.

Harijan, 10-6-'39

PHYSICAL TRAINING FOR THE SATYAGRAHI

Ahimsa requires certain duties which can be done only by those with a trained physique. It is, therefore, most necessary to consider what kind of physical training a non-violent person should receive.

Very few of the rules applying to a violent army will apply to a non-violent body. A violent army will not have its arms for show but for definitely destructive purposes. A non-violent body will have no use for such weapons and will, therefore, beat its swords into plough-shares and spears into pruning hooks, and will shrink from the thought of using them as lethal weapons. The violent soldier will be trained in the use of violence by being taught to shoot. The non-violent soldier will have no time for this pastime. He will get all his training through nursing the sick, saving those in danger at the risk of his own life, patrolling places which may be in fear of thieves and dacoits, and in laying down his life, if necessary, in dissuading them from their purpose. Even the uniforms of the two will differ. The violent man will wear a coat of mail for his protection, and his uniform will be such as can dazzle people. The uniform of the non-violent man will be simple, in conformity with the dress of the poor, and betokening humility. Its purpose will be just to keep him from heat and cold and rain. A violent soldier's protection will be his arms, no matter how much he takes God's name. He will not shrink from spending millions on armaments. The first and last shield and buckler of the non-violent person will be his unwavering faith in God. And the minds of the two will be as poles asunder. The violent man will always be casting about for plans to work the destruction of his enemy and will pray to God to fulfil his purpose. The national anthem of the British people is worth considering in this connection. It prays to God to save the King, to frustrate the enemy's knavish tricks, and to destroy him. Millions of Englishmen sing this anthem aloud with one voice standing respectfully. If God is the Incarnation of Mercy, He is not likely to listen to such prayer, but it cannot but affect the minds of those who sing it, and in times of war it simply kindles their hatred and anger to white heat. The one condition of winning a violent war is to keep the indignation against the enemy burning fiercely.

In the dictionary of the non-violent there is no such word as an external enemy. But even for the supposed enemy he will have nothing but compassion in his heart. He will believe that no man is intentionally wicked, that there is no man but is gifted with the faculty to discriminate between right and wrong, and that if that faculty were to be fully developed, it would surely mature into non-violence. He will therefore pray to God that He may give the supposed enemy a sense of right and bless him. His prayer for himself will always be that the spring of compassion in him may ever be flowing, and that he may ever grow in moral strength so that he may face death fearlessly.

Thus since the minds of both will differ as the poles, their physical training will also differ in the same degree.

We all know more or less what military training is like. But we have hardly ever thought that non-violent training must be of a different kind. Nor have we ever cared to discover whether in the past such training was given anywhere in the world. I am of opinion that it used to be given in the past and is even now being given in a haphazard way. The various exercises of *Hatha Yoga* are in this direction. The physical training given by means of these imparts among other things physical health, strength, agility, and the capacity to bear heat and cold. Shri Kuvalayanandji is making scientific researches in the technique and benefits of these exercises. I have no knowledge of the progress he has made, nor do I know whether he is making his experiments with *ahimsa* as his goal. My reference to *Hatha Yoga* is meant only with a view to showing that this ancient type of non-violent training still exists, though I know that there is room in it for improvement. I do not know either that the author of this science had any idea of mass non-violence. The exercises had at their back the desire for individual salvation. The object of the various exercises was to strengthen and purify the body in order to secure control of the mind. The mass non-violence we are now thinking of applies to people of all religions and therefore the rules that may be framed must be such as can be accepted by all believers in *ahimsa*. And then as we are thinking of a non-violent army, that is to say, of bringing into being a Satyagraha *sangha*, we can but build anew accepting the old as our foundation. Let us then think of the physical training required by a Satyagrahi. If the Satyagrahi is not healthy in mind and body, he may perhaps fail in mustering complete fearlessness. He should have the capacity to stand guard at a single spot day and night; he must not fall ill even if he has to bear cold and heat and rain; he must have the strength to go to places of peril, to rush to scenes of fire, and the courage to wander about alone in desolate jungles and haunts of death; he will bear, without a grumble, severe beatings, starvation and worse, and will keep to his post of duty without flinching; he will have the resourcefulness and capacity to plunge into a seemingly impenetrable scene of rioting; he will have the longing and capacity to run with the name of God on his lips to the rescue of men living on the top storeys of buildings enveloped in flames; he will have the fearlessness to plunge into a flood in order to rescue people being carried off by it or to jump down a well to save a drowning person.

This list can be extended *ad libitum*. The substance of it all is that we should cultivate the capacity to run to the rescue of people in danger and distress and to suffer cheerfully any amount of hardship that may be inflicted upon us. He who accepts this fundamental principle will easily be able to frame rules of physical training for Satyagrahis. I have a firm conviction that the very foundation of this training is faith in God. If that is absent, all the training one may have received is likely to fail at the critical moment.

Let no one poohpooh my statement by saying that the Congress has many people who are ashamed to take the name of God. I am simply trying to state the view in terms of the science of Satyagraha as I have known and developed it. The only weapon of the Satyagrahi is God, by whatsoever name one knows Him. Without Him the Satyagrahi is devoid of strength before an opponent armed with monstrous weapons. Most people lie prostrate before physical might. But he who accepts God as his only Protector will remain unbent before the mightiest earthly power.

As faith in God is essential in a Satyagrahi, even so is *brahmacharya*. Without *brahmacharya* the Satyagrahi will have no lustre, no inner strength to stand unarmed against the whole world. *Brahmacharya* may have here the restricted meaning of conservation of the vital energy brought about by sexual restraint, and not the comprehensive definition I have given of it. He who intends to live on spare diet and without any external remedies, and still wants to have physical strength, has need to conserve his vital energy. It is the richest capital man can ever possess. He who can preserve it ever gains renewed strength out of it. He who uses it up, consciously or unconsciously, will ultimately be impotent. His strength will fail him at the right moment. I have often written about the ways and means of conserving this energy. Let the reader turn to my writings and carry out the instructions. He who lusts with the eye or the touch can never conserve his vital energy, nor the man who lusts after flesh-pots. Those who hope to conserve this energy without strict observance of the rules will no more succeed than those who hope to swim against the current without being exhausted. He who restrains himself physically and sins with his thoughts will fare worse than he who, without professing to observe *brahmacharya*, lives the life of a restrained householder. For he who lusts with the thought will ever remain unsated and will end his life a moral wreck and burden on the earth. Such a one can never be a full Satyagrahi. Nor can one who hankers after wealth and fame.

This is the foundation of the physical training for a Satyagrahi. The detailed structure of the course can easily be built in consonance with this foundation.

It should now be clear that in the physical training of a Satyagrahi there is no room for lethal weapons like the sword or the spear. For far more terrible weapons than we have seen are in existence today, and newer ones are being invented every day. Of what fear will a sword rid him who has to cultivate the capacity to overcome all fear — real or imaginary ? I have not yet heard of a man having shed all fear by learning sword-play. Mahavir and others who imbibed *ahimsa* did not do so because they knew the use of weapons, but because, in spite of the knowledge of their use, they shed all fear.

A slight introspection will show that he who has always depended on the sword will find it difficult to throw it away. But having deliberately discarded it he is likely to find his *ahimsa* more lasting than that of him who, not knowing its use, fancies he will not fear it. But that does not mean that in order to be truly non-violent one must beforehand possess and know the use of arms. By parity of reasoning, one might say that only a thief can be honest, only a diseased person can be healthy, and only a dissolute person can be a *brahmachari*. The fact is that we have formed the habit of thinking along traditional grooves and will not get out of them. And as we cannot take a detached view, we cannot draw the right conclusions and get caught in delusive snares.

If I have the time, I hope to present the reader with a model course of training.

Harijan, 13-10-'40

38

BRAHMACHARYA FOR SATYAGRAHA

There must be power in the word of a Satyagraha general — not the power that the possession of limitless arms gives, but the power that purity of life, strict vigilance, and ceaseless application produce. This is impossible without the observance of *brahmacharya*. It must be as full as it is humanly possible. *Brahmacharya* here does not mean mere physical self-control. It means much more. It means complete control over all the senses. Thus an impure thought is a breach of *brahmacharya* ; so is anger. All power comes from the preservation and sublimation of the vitality that is responsible for creation of life. If the vitality is husbanded instead of being dissipated, it is transmuted into creative energy of the highest order. This vitality is continuously and even unconsciously dissipated by evil, or even rambling, disorderly, unwanted, thoughts. And since thought is the root of all speech and action, the quality of the latter corresponds to that of the former. Hence perfectly controlled thought is itself power of the highest potency and can become self-acting. That seems to me to be the meaning of the silent prayer of the heart. If man is after the image of God, he has but to will a thing in the limited sphere allotted to him and it becomes. Such power is impossible in one who dissipates his energy in any way whatsoever, even as steam kept in a leaky pipe yields no power. The sexual act divorced from the deliberate purpose of generation is a typical and gross form of dissipation and has therefore been specially and rightly chosen for condemnation. But in one who has to organize vast masses of mankind for non-violent action the full control described by me has to be attempted and virtually achieved.

This control is unattainable save by the grace of God. There is a verse in the second chapter of the *Gita* which freely rendered means : " Sense-effects remain in abeyance whilst one is fasting or whilst the particular sense is starved, but the hankering does not cease except when one sees God face to face." This control is not mechanical or temporary. Once attained it is never lost.

Harijan, 23-7-'38

39

DISCIPLINE — SATYAGRAHI AND MILITARY

I have not yet known a general who has not altered time and again the plans of his campaign and made eleventh-hour alterations in his orders. The ordinary fighting soldier knows nothing of these plans. In fact they are a closely guarded secret unknown to all but the general himself. That is why Tennyson wrote those immortal lines — " Theirs not to reason why, theirs not to make reply, theirs but to do and die." But these words apply, if you please, to a Satyagrahi army more appropriately than to the ordinary army. For a military general may change his plans in view of the changing situations every day. Military strategy depends on the changing tactics of the enemy. The Satyagrahi general has to obey his inner voice, for over and above the situation outside, he examines himself constantly and listens to the dictates of the Inner Self. But both in Satyagraha and military warfare the position of the soldier is very nearly the same. He knows no rest, no certainty of movements, the only certainty for him is to face heavy odds and even death. His promise to be under discipline and to obey the general's command applies even during the period of suspension of hostilities. But I have not asked for this kind of discipline. I have always tried to carry conviction to my co-workers, to carry their hearts and their reason with me. I shall go on doing so always, but where you cannot follow you will have to have faith. In ordinary warfare a soldier cannot reason why. In our warfare there is enough scope for reasoning, but there is a limit to it. You will go on arguing until you are convinced, but when no conviction comes, you must fall back on faith.

Harijan, 10-6-'39

40

SCORCHED EARTH

There is no bravery in my poisoning my well or filling it in so that my brother who is at war with me may not use the water. Let us assume that I am fighting him in the orthodox manner. Nor is there sacrifice in it, for it does not purify me, and sacrifice, as its root meaning implies, presupposes purity. Such destruction may be likened to cutting one's nose to spite one's face. Warriors of old had wholesome laws of war. Among the excluded things were poisoning wells and destroying food crops. But I do claim that there are bravery and sacrifice in my leaving my wells, crops and homestead intact, bravery in that I deliberately run the risk of the enemy feeding himself at my expense and pursuing me, and sacrifice in that the sentiment of leaving something for the enemy purifies and ennobles me.

Harijan, 12-4-'42

41

TRAINING FOR A NON-VIOLENT ARMY

Q. What should be the training and discipline for a non-violent army ? Should not certain aspects of conventional military training form a part of the syllabus ?

A. A very small part of the preliminary training received by the military is common to the non-violent army. These are discipline, drill, singing in chorus, flag hoisting, signalling and the like. Even this is not absolutely necessary and the basis is different. The positively necessary training for a non-violent army is an immovable faith in God, willing and perfect obedience to the chief of the non-violent army and perfect inward and outward co-operation between the units of the army.

Harijan, 12-5-'46

42

CONSTRUCTIVE PREPARATION

Advising Rajkot workers on how to produce an atmosphere of non-violence of the brave, Gandhiji said :

" This depends on individual workers cultivating non-violence in thought, word and deed, by means of a concentrated effort in the fulfilment of the fourfold constructive programme. Maximum of work and minimum of speech must be your motto. In the centre of the programme is the spinning wheel — no haphazard programme of spinning, but scientific understanding of every detail, including the mechanics and the mathematics of it, study of cotton and its varieties, and so on. There is the programme of literacy. You must concentrate exclusively on it, and not talk of any other thing. The work should be systematic and according to time-table. Don't talk of politics — not even of non-violence — but talk to them of the advantages of literacy. There is prohibition of drink and intoxicating drugs and of gambling. There is medical relief by means of the propagation of simple rules of hygiene and sanitation and elementary preventive measures, and of cheap home remedies and training intelligent village folk in these.

" There should not be one house in Rajkot with which you have not established contact from the point of view of pure service. You have to cultivate the Mussalmans, serve them unselfishly. There are the Harijans. Establish living contact with them.

" All this constructive work should be for its own sake. And yet be sure that it will develop the quality required for non-violent responsible government. That is how I began my work in South Africa. I began with serving them. I did not know that I was training them for civil disobedience. I did not know myself that I was so training myself. But you all know what happened in the end.

" This constructive programme may go on endlessly. Why should you be tired of it? Do you know the Hundred Years' War in England? If they fought for a hundred years, we should be prepared to fight for a thousand years, inasmuch as we are a continent. That we will have given our contribution to the fight for freedom, will be our reward.

" That is the mass constructive programme I want you to do, and that is the basis of the training for the non-violence of the brave. It is whole and indivisible, and those who do not believe in it whole-heartedly must leave me and work according to their own lights."

Harijan, 10-6-'39

SECTION THIRD : NON-CO-OPERATION AND CIVIL DISOBEDIENCE

43

THE NATIONAL WEEK

[The Rowlatt Act was passed in the third week of March 1919. It was meant to deal with the situation arising from the expiry of the Defence of India Act soon after World War I. It gave arbitrary powers to the authorities to arrest, confine, imprison or otherwise punish persons who were suspected to be concerned in movements prejudicial to the security of the State. Gandhiji regarded the Act as subversive of the elementary principles of justice and destructive of civil liberties, and therefore by no means to be tolerated.

During World War I, Lloyd George, the then Premier of England made solemn promises to Indian Muslims that the suzerainty of their religious head, the Khalif, who was also the Sultan of Turkey, will be respected. Indian Muslims were thus induced to fight against their co-religionists of Turkey. But after the war, these pledges were broken and Turkey was deprived of her territories which were then distributed between England and France under the guise of mandates. This enraged not only the Muslims but also the other communities in India, who naturally looked upon this act as downright betrayal by Britain of her plighted word. This was the origin of the Khilafat movement, in which Hindus joined with the Muslims against the British.

These two issues led to intense agitation culminating on the 13th April, 1919, in the Jalianwala massacre, where peaceful people who had assembled in a political meeting in a small park were mercilessly killed by gun-fire ordered by a British commanding officer. Thereupon political passions rose to white heat, and Gandhiji organized his non-co-operation movement against the British Govt. in India. He also instituted the week, April 6th to 13th, of terrible happenings in 1919, as a National Week of prayer and fasting celebrated ever since, even to this day.   — Ed.]

The sixth of April again saw the inauguration of a definite plan of Hindu-Muslim unity and Swadeshi.

It was the 6th of April which broke the spirit underlying the Rowlatt Act and made it a dead letter. The 13th of April saw not merely the terrific tragedy but in that tragedy Hindu-Muslim blood flowed freely in a mingled stream and sealed the compact.

How to commemorate or celebrate these two great national events? I venture to suggest that those who will, should devote the 6th of April next to fast (twenty-four hours' abstention from food) and prayer.

The whole of the week beginning from the 6th should be devoted to some work connected with the tragedy of the 13th.

Then the 13th. That day of days should be devoted to fasting and prayer. It should be free from ill-will or anger. We want to cherish the memory of the innocent dead. We do not want to remember the wickedness of the deed. The nation will rise by readiness to sacrifice, not by preparing to revenge. On that day I would also have the nation to remember the mass excesses and feel penitent for them.

I would further urge that during the week each one does his or her best in his or her own person to realize more fully than ever the principles of Satyagraha, Hindu-Muslim unity and Swaraj. In order to emphasize Hindu-Muslim unity, I would advise joint meetings of Hindus and Mussalmans on Friday the 12th April at 7 p.m., urging that the Khilafat question be decided in accordance with the just Muslim sentiments.

Thus this national week should be a week of purification, self-examination, sacrifice, exact discipline and expression of cherished national sentiments. There should be no trace of bitterness, no violence of language, but absolute fearlessness and firmness.

I respectfully trust that all parties and all classes will see their way to take their full share in the observances of the National Week and make it an event for the true and definite progress in national awakening.

Young India, 10-3-'20 (reprinted in the issue of 30-3-'22)

44

THE SATYAGRAHA WEEK

First and foremost in the programme for the holy National Week I put fasting and prayer. I have said enough to emphasize the necessity of both these for the unfoldment of our national life. I speak of these from personal experience. But writing to a friend on this very matter of prayer, I came across a beautiful thing from Tennyson, which I present to the readers of *Young India*, if per chance I might convert them to a definite belief in the efficacy of prayer.

Here is the gem :

" ....More things are wrought by prayer
" Than this world dreams of. Wherefore, let thy voice
" Rise like a fountain for me night and day.
" For what are men better than sheep or goats
" That nourish a blind life within the brain,
" If, knowing God, they lift not hands of prayer
" Both for themselves and those who call them friend ?
" For so the whole round earth is every way
" Bound by gold chains about the feet of God."

Throughout my wanderings in India, I have had the privilege of mixing with men of all creeds, of mixing with thousands of women, hundreds upon hundreds of students. I have discussed with them national problems with a passion which I am unable to describe. I have found that we have not yet reached a conscious recognition of our national state. We have not had the discipline necessary for a realization of that state and I venture to say that there is nothing so powerful as fasting and prayer that would give us the requisite discipline, spirit of self-sacrifice, humility and resoluteness of will without which there can be no real progress. I hope, therefore, that millions throughout India will open the Satyagraha Week with sincere fasting and prayer.

I do not wish, during this week, to emphasize the civil-resistance part of Satyagraha. I would like us to contemplate Truth and Non-violence, and to appreciate their invincibility. Indeed, if all of us regulated our lives by this eternal law of *Satya* and *Ahimsa*, there will be no occasion for civil or other resistance. Civil resistance comes into play when only a small body of men endeavour to follow truth in the face of opposition. It is difficult to know what is truth, when to defend it to the point of civil resistance, and how to avoid error in the shape of violence in one's pursuit after truth. There may well be differences of opinion as to the advisability of preaching civil resistance as a creed during a week devoted to national uplift, in which one seeks the co-operation of all without distinction of party, class or creed.

Young India, 30-3-'22

45

JALIANWALA BAGH

There was an unfortunate hitch about the purchase of this Bagh for the nation. Thanks to the efforts of the Hon'ble Pandit Madan Mohan Malaviya, Sannyasi Swami Shri Shraddhananda and the local leaders, it has now become the property of the nation subject to full payment of the purchase price within three months from the 6th instant. The purchase price is Rs 5,36,000. And the amount must be raised within the prescribed period.

It is, therefore, necessary to examine the propriety of making this purchase on behalf of the nation, especially as it has been questioned even in enlightened quarters. With the Cawnpore Memorial before us the attitude is not to be wondered at. But with all respect to objectors, I cannot help saying that if the Bagh had not been acquired, it would have been a national disgrace. Can we afford to forget those five hundred or more men who were killed although they had done nothing wrong either morally or legally? If they had died knowingly and willingly, if realizing their innocence they had stood their ground and faced the shots from the fifty rifles, they would have gone down to history as saints, heroes and patriots. But even as it was, the tragedy became one of first class national importance. Nations are born out of travail and suffering. We should forfeit all title to be considered a nation, if we failed to treasure the memory of those, who in our battle for political freedom might, innocently or for the crimes of others, lose their lives or otherwise suffer. We were unable to protect our helpless countrymen when they were ruthlessly massacred. We may decline, if we will, to avenge the wrong. The nation will not lose if we did. But shall we — can we afford to — decline to perpetuate the memory and to show to the surviving members of the families of the dead that we are sharers in their sufferings, by erecting a national tombstone and by telling the world thereby that in the death of these men each one of us has lost dear relations ? If national instinct does not mean at least this much kinship, it has no meaning for me. I hold it to be our duty to tell the present generation and generations yet unborn that in our march towards true freedom, we must be prepared for repetitions of the wrongs such as the Jalianwala Bagh massacre. We must provide against them, we must not seek them, but we must be ready to face them if they came again. I would not have us flinch from the battle of national life. The supreme lesson of the Amritsar Congress was that the sufferings of the Punjab did not dishearten the nation but that the nation treated them as a matter of course. Some of us made stupid mistakes and the innocent suffered for them. We must in future try to avoid the mistakes but in spite of our best effort, we may fail to convert every one to sanity. We must, therefore, be ready for the repetition of the sufferings of the guiltless by telling the country now that they and theirs shall not be forgotten, but that the memory of the innocent dead shall be regarded as a sacred trust, and that the surviving relations shall have the right to look to the nation for maintenance in case of need. This is the primary meaning of the memorial. And has not the blood of the Mohammedan mixed with that of the

Hindu ? Has not the blood of the Sikh mixed with that of the Sanatanist and the Samajist ? The memorial should be a national emblem of an honest and sustained effort to achieve Hindu-Muslim unity.

But the objector's objection still remains unanswered. Will not the memorial also perpetuate bitterness and ill-will ? It will depend upon the trustees. And if I know them, I know that that is not their intention at all. I know that such was not the intention of the vast assembly. I do not wish to convey that bitterness was not there. It was there, and not in any way suppressed. But the idea of the memorial had nothing of bitterness in it. The people want to, they must be encouraged to, forget the doer and his madness. What General Dyer did we may all do if we had his irresponsibility and opportunity. To err is human, and it must be held to be equally human to forgive if we, though being fallible, would like rather to be forgiven than punished and reminded of our mis-deeds. Nor does this mean that we may not ask for General Dyer's dismissal. A lunatic cannot be kept in a position from which he can do harm to his neighbours. But just as we do not bear ill-will towards a lunatic, so too may we not bear ill-will even towards General Dyer. I would therefore eschew from the memorial all idea of bitterness and ill-will, but treat it as a sacred memory and regard the Bagh as a place of pilgrimage to be visited by all irrespective of class, creed or colour. I would invite Englishmen to appreciate our feeling in the matter, ask them by subscribing to the memorial in the spirit of the Royal Proclamation to make common cause with us in our endeavour to regain consciousness, to realize the same freedom that they enjoy under the same constitution and to realize Hindu-Muslim unity without which there can be no true progress for India.

Young India, 18-2-'20

46

NEITHER A SAINT NOR A POLITICIAN

A kind friend has sent me the following cutting from the April number of the *East and West* :

"Mr Gandhi has the reputation of a saint but it seems that the politician in him often dominates his decisions. He has been making great use of *hartals* and there can be no gainsaying that under his direction *hartal* is becoming a powerful political weapon for uniting the educated and the uneducated on a single question of the day. The *hartal* is not without its disadvantages. It is teaching direct action, and direct action however potent does not work for unity. Is Mr Gandhi quite sure that he is serving the highest behests of *ahimsa*, harmlessness ? His proposal to commemorate the shooting at Jalianwala Bagh is not likely to promote concord. It is a tragic incident into which our Government was betrayed, but is the memory of its bitterness worth retaining ? Can we not commemorate the event by raising a temple of peace, to help the widows and orphans, to bless the souls of those who died without knowing why ? The world is full of politicians and petti-foggers who, in the name of patriotism, poison the inner sweetness of man and, as a result, we have wars and feuds and such shameless slaughter as turned Jalianwala Bagh into a shambles. Shall we not now try for a larger symbiosis such as Buddha and Christ preached, and bring the world to breathe and prosper together ? Mr Gandhi seemed destined to be the apostle of such a movement, but circumstances are forcing him to seek the way of raising resistances and group unities. He may yet take up the larger mission of uniting the world."

I have given the whole of the quotation. As a rule I do not notice criticism of me or my methods except when thereby I acknowledge a mistake or enforce still further the principles criticized. I have a double reason for noticing the extract. For, not only do I hope further to elucidate the principles I hold dear, but I want to show my regard for the author of the criticism whom I know and whom I have admired for many years for the singular beauty of his character. The critic regrets to see in me a politician whereas he expected me to be a saint. Now I think that the word *saint* should be ruled out of present life. It is too sacred a word to be lightly applied to anybody, much less to one like myself who claims only to be a humble searcher after truth, knows his limitations, makes mistakes, never hesitates to admit them when he makes them, and frankly confesses that he, like a scientist, is making experiments about some 'of the eternal verities' of life, but cannot even claim to be a scientist because he can show no tangible proof of scientific accuracy in his methods or such tangible results of his experiments as modern science demands. But though by disclaiming sainthood I disappoint the critic's expectations, I would have him to give up his regrets by answering him that the politician in me has never dominated a single decision of mine, and if I seem to take part in politics, it is only because politics encircle us today like the coil of a snake from which one cannot get out, no matter how much one tries. I wish therefore to wrestle with the snake, as I have been doing with more or less success consciously since 1894, unconsciously, as I have now discovered, ever since reaching years of discretion. Quite selfishly, as I wish to live in peace in the midst of a bellowing storm howling round me, I have been experimenting with myself and my friends by introducing religion into politics. Let me explain what I mean by religion. It is not the Hindu religion, which I certainly prize above all other religions, but the religion which transcends Hinduism, which changes one's very nature, which binds one indissolubly to the truth within and which ever purifies. It is the permanent element in human nature which counts no cost too great in order to find full expression and which leaves the soul utterly restless until it has found itself, known its Maker and appreciated the true correspondence between the Maker and itself.

It was in that religious spirit that I came upon *hartal*. I wanted to show that it is not a knowledge of letters that would give India consciousness of herself, or that would bind the educated together. The *hartal* illuminated the whole of India as if by magic on the 6th of April, 1919. And had it not been for the interruption of the 10th of April, brought about by Satan whispering fear into the ears of a Government conscious of its own wrong and inciting to anger a people that were prepared for it by utter distrust of the Government, India would have risen to an unimaginable height. The *hartal* had not only been taken up by the great masses of people in a truly religious spirit but it was intended to be a prelude to a series of direct actions.

But my critic deplores direct action. For, he says, "it does not work for unity." I join issue with him. Never has anything been done on this earth without direct action. I rejected the word *passive resistance* because of its insufficiency and its being interpreted as a weapon of the weak. It was direct action in South Africa which told and told so effectively that it converted General Smuts to sanity. He was in 1906 the most relentless opponent of Indian aspirations. In 1914, he took pride in doing tardy justice by removing from the Statute Book of the Union a disgraceful measure which, in 1909 he had told Lord Morley, would be never removed, for he then said South Africa would never tolerate repeal of a measure which was twice passed by the Transvaal Legislature. But what is more, direct action sustained for eight years left behind it not only no bitterness but the very Indians who put up such a stubborn fight against General Smuts ranged themselves round his banner in 1915 and fought under him in East Africa. It was direct action in Champaran which removed an agelong grievance. A meek submission when one is chafing under a disability or a grievance which one would gladly see removed, not only does not make for unity, but makes the weak party acid, angry and prepares him for an opportunity to explode. By allying myself with the weak party, by teaching him direct, firm, but harmless action, I make him feel strong and capable of defying the physical might. He feels braced for the struggle, regains confidence in himself and knowing that the remedy lies with himself, ceases to harbour the spirit of revenge and learns to be satisfied with a redress of the wrong he is seeking to remedy.

It is working along the same line that I have ventured to suggest a memorial about Jalianwala Bagh. The writer in *East and West* has ascribed to me a proposal which has never once crossed my mind. He thinks that I want "to commemorate the shooting at Jalianwala Bagh". Nothing can be further from my thought than to perpetuate the memory of a black deed. I dare say that before we have come to our own we shall have a repetition of the tragedy and I will prepare the nation for it by treasuring the memory of the innocent dead. The widows and the orphans have been and are being helped, but we cannot "bless the souls of those who died without knowing why," if we will not acquire the ground which has been hallowed by innocent blood and there erect a suitable memorial for them. It is not to serve, if I can help it, as a reminder of a foul deed, but it shall serve as an encouragement to the nation that it is better to die helpless and unarmed and as victims rather than as tyrants. I would have the future generations remember that we who witnessed the innocent dying did not ungratefully refuse to cherish their memory. As Mrs Jinnah truly remarked when she gave her mite to the fund, the memorial would at least give us an excuse for living. After all it will be the spirit in which the memorial is erected that will decide its character.

What was the larger 'symbiosis' that Buddha and Christ preached? Buddha fearlessly carried the war into the enemy's camp and brought down on its knees an arrogant priesthood. Christ drove out the money-changers from the temple of Jerusalem and drew down curses from Heaven upon the hypocrites and the pharisees. Both were for intensely direct action. But even as Buddha and Christ chastized they showed unmistakable gentleness and love behind every act of theirs. They would not raise a finger against their enemies, but would gladly surrender themselves rather than the truth for which they lived. Buddha would have died resisting the priesthood, if the majesty of his love had not proved to be equal to the task of bending the priesthood. Christ died on the cross with a crown of thorns on his head defying the might of a whole empire. And if I raise resistances of a non-violent character I simply and humbly follow in the footsteps of the great teachers named by my critic.

Lastly, the writer of the paragraph quarrels with my ' grouping unities' and would have me to take up 'the larger mission of uniting the world'. I once told him under a common roof that I was probably more cosmopolitan than he. I abide by that expression. Unless I group unities I shall never be able to unite the whole world. Tolstoy once said that if we would but get off the backs of our neighbours the world would be quite all right without any further help from us. And if we can only serve our immediate neighbours by ceasing to prey upon them, the circle of unities thus grouped in the right fashion will ever grow in circumference till at last it is conterminous with that of the whole world. More than that it is not given to any man to try or achieve. यथा पिंडे तथा ब्रह्मांडे* is as true today as ages ago when it was first uttered by an unknown *rishi*.

Young India, 12-5-'20

47

THE LAW OF SUFFERING

No country has ever risen without being purified through the fire of suffering. Mother suffers so that her child may live. The condition of wheat growing is that the seed grain should perish. Life comes out of Death. Will India rise out of her slavery without fulfilling this eternal law of purification through suffering ?

If my advisers are right, evidently India will realize her destiny without travail. For their chief concern is that the events of April, 1919, should not be repeated. They fear non-co-operation because it would involve the sufferings of many. If Hampdon had argued thus he would not have withheld payment of ship-money, nor would Wat Tayler have raised the standard of revolt.

---

* As the atom, so the universe.

English and French histories are replete with instances of men continuing their pursuit of the right irrespective of the amount of suffering involved. The actors did not stop to think whether ignorant people would not have involuntarily to suffer. Why should we expect to write our history differently ? It is possible for us, if we would, to learn from the mistakes of our predecessors to do better, but it is impossible to do away with the law of suffering which is the one indispensable condition of our being. The way to do better is to avoid, if we can, violence from our side and thus quicken the rate of progress and to introduce greater purity in the methods of suffering. We can, if we will, refrain, in our impatience, from bending the wrong-doer to our will by physical force as Sinn Feiners are doing today, or from coercing our neighbours to follow our methods as was done last year by some of us in bringing about *hartal*. Progress is to be measured by the amount of suffering undergone by the sufferer. The purer the suffering, the greater is the progress. Hence did the sacrifice of Jesus suffice to free a sorrowing world. In his onward march he did not count the cost of suffering entailed upon his neighbours whether it was undergone by them voluntarily or otherwise. Thus did the sufferings of a Harishchandra suffice to re-establish the kingdom of truth. He must have known that his subjects would suffer involuntarily by his abdication. He did not mind because he could not do otherwise than follow truth.

I have already stated that I do not deplore the massacre of Jalianwala Bagh so much as I deplore the murders of Englishmen and destruction of property by ourselves. The frightfulness at Amritsar drew away public attention from the greater though slower frightfulness at Lahore where attempt was made to emasculate the inhabitants by slow processes. But before we rise higher we shall have to undergo such processes many more times till they teach us to take up suffering voluntarily and to find joy in it. I am convinced that the Lahorians never deserved the cruel insults that they were subjected to ;

they never hurt a single Englishman ; they never destroyed any property. But a wilful ruler was determined to crush the spirit of a people just trying to throw off his chafing yoke. And if I am told that all this was due to my preaching Satyagraha, my answer is that I would preach Satyagraha all the more forcibly for that so long as I have breath left in me, and tell the people that next time they would answer O'Dwyer's insolence not by opening shops by reason of threats of forcible sales but by allowing the tyrant to do his worst and let him sell their all but their unconquerable souls. Sages of old mortified the flesh so that the spirit within might be set free, so that their trained bodies might be proof against any injury that might be inflicted on them by tyrants seeking to impose their will on them. And if India wishes to revive her ancient wisdom and to avoid the errors of Europe, if India wishes to see the Kingdom of God established on earth instead of that of Satan which has enveloped Europe, then I would urge her sons and daughters not to be deceived by fine phrases, the terrible subtleties that hedge us in, the fears of suffering that India may have to undergo, but to see what is happening today in Europe and from it understand that we must go through suffering even as Europe has gone through, but not the process of making others suffer. Germany wanted to dominate Europe and the Allies wanted to do likewise by crushing Germany. Europe is no better for Germany's fall. The Allies have proved themselves to be just as deceitful, cruel, greedy and selfish as Germany was or would have been. Germany would have avoided the sanctimonious humbug that one sees associated with the many dealings of the Allies.

The miscalculation that I deplored last year was not in connection with the sufferings imposed upon the people, but about the mistakes made by them and violence done by them owing to their not having sufficiently understood the message of Satyagraha. What then is the meaning of non-co-operation in terms of the law of suffering ? We must voluntarily put up with the losses and inconveniences that arise from having to withdraw our support from a Government that is ruling against our will. Possession of power and riches is a crime under an unjust Government, poverty in that case is a virtue, says Thoreau. It may be that in the transition state we may make mistakes ; there may be avoidable suffering. These things are preferable to national emasculation.

We must refuse to wait for the wrong to be righted till the wrong-doer has been roused to a sense of his iniquity. We must not, for fear of ourselves or others having to suffer, remain participators in it. But we must combat the wrong by ceasing to assist the wrong-doer directly or indirectly.

If a father does an injustice it is the duty of his children to leave the parental roof. If the headmaster of a school conducts his institution on an immoral basis, the pupils must leave the school. If the chairman of a corporation is corrupt the members thereof must wash their hands clean of his corruption by withdrawing from it ; even so if a Government does a grave injustice the subjects must withdraw co-operation wholly or partially, sufficiently to wean the ruler from his wickedness. In each case conceived by me there is an element of suffering whether mental or physical. Without such suffering it is not possible to attain freedom.

Young India, 16-6-'20

48

HOW TO WORK NON-CO-OPERATION

Perhaps the best way of answering the fears and criticism as to non-co-operation is to elaborate more fully the scheme of non-co-operation. The critics seem to imagine that the organizers propose to give effect to the whole scheme at once. The fact however is that the organizers have fixed definite, progressive four stages. The first is the giving up of titles and resignation of honorary posts. If there is no response or if the response received is not effective, recourse will be had to the second stage. The second stage involves much previous arrangement. Certainly not a single servant will be called out unless he is either capable of supporting himself and his dependents or the Khilafat Committee is able to bear the burden. All the classes of servants will not be called out at once and never will any pressure be put upon a single servant to withdraw himself from Government service. Nor will a single private employee be touched, for the simple reason that the movement is not anti-English. It is not even anti-Government. Co-operation is to be withdrawn because the people must not be party to a wrong — a broken pledge — a violation of deep religious sentiment. Naturally, the movement will receive a check, if there is any undue influence brought to bear upon any Government servant, or if any violence is used or countenanced by any member of the Khilafat Committee. The second stage must be entirely successful, if the response is at all on an adequate scale. For no Government — much less the Indian Government — can subsist if the people cease to serve it. The withdrawal therefore of the police and the military — the third stage — is a distant goal. The organizers however wanted to be fair, open and above suspicion. They did not want to keep back from Government or the public a single step they had in contemplation even as a remote contingency. The fourth, i.e. suspension of taxes, is still more remote. The organizers recognize that suspension of general taxation is fraught with the greatest danger. It is likely to bring a sensitive class in conflict with the police. They are therefore not likely to embark upon it, unless they can do so with the assurance that there will be no violence offered by the people.

I admit, as I have already done, that non-co-operation is not unattended with risk, but the risk of supineness in the face of a grave issue is infinitely greater than the danger of violence ensuing from organizing non-co-operation. To do nothing is to invite violence for a certainty.

It is easy enough to pass resolutions or write articles

condemning non-co-operation. But it is no easy task to restrain the fury of a people incensed by a deep sense of wrong. I urge those who talk or work against non-co-operation to descend from their chairs and go down to the people, learn their feelings and write, if they have the heart, against non-co-operation. They will find, as I have found, that the only way to avoid violence is to enable them to give such expression to their feelings as to compel redress. I have found nothing save non-co-operation. It is logical and harmless. It is the inherent right of a subject to refuse to assist a government that will not listen to him.

Non-co-operation as a voluntary movement can only succeed, if the feeling is genuine and strong enough to make people suffer to the utmost. If the religious sentiment of the Mohammedans is deeply hurt and if the Hindus entertain neighbourly regard towards their Muslim brethren, they both will count no cost too great for achieving the end. Non-co-operation will not only be an effective remedy but will also be an effective test of the sincerity of the Muslim claim and the Hindu profession of friendship.

Young India, 5-5-'20

49

HOW AND WHEN TO ACT

The following is a statement issued by the Non-co-operation Committee for public information and guidance :

Many questions have been asked of the Non-co-operation Committee as to its expectation and the methods to be adopted for beginning non-co-operation.

The Committee wish it to be understood that whilst they expect every one to respond to their recommendation to the full, they are desirous of carrying the weakest members also with them. The Committee want to enlist the passive sympathy, if not the active co-operation, of the whole of the country in the method of non-co-operation.

Those, therefore, who cannot undergo physical

sacrifice will help by contributing funds or labour to the movement.

Should non-co-operation become necessary, the Committee has decided upon the following as part of the first stage :

(1) Surrender of all titles of honour and honorary offices.

(2) Non-participation in Government loans.

(3) Suspension by lawyers of practice and settlement of civil disputes by private arbitration.

(4) Boycott of Government schools by parents.

(5) Boycott of the Reformed Councils.

(6) Non-participation in Government parties, and such other functions.

(7) Refusal to accept any civil or military post, in Mesopotamia, or to offer as Units for the army especially for service in the Turkish territories now being administered in violation of pledges.

(8) Vigorous prosecution of Swadeshi, inducing the people, at the time of this national and religious awakening, to appreciate their primary duty to their country by being satisfied with its own productions and manufactures.

Swadeshi must be pushed forward without waiting for the 1st of August, for it is an eternal rule of conduct not to be interrupted even when the settlement arrives.

In order not to commit themselves, people will refrain now from taking service either civil or military. They will also suspend taking Government loans, new or old.

For the rest, it should be remembered that non-co-operation does not commence before 1st August next.

Every effort is being, and will still be, made to avoid resort to such a serious breach with the Government by urging His Majesty's Ministers to secure the revision of a Treaty which has been so universally condemned.

Those who realize their responsibility and gravity of the cause will not act independently, but in concert with the Committee. Success depends entirely upon disciplined and concerted non-co-operation and the later is dependent upon strict obedience to instructions, calmness and absolute freedom from violence.

Young India, 7-7-'20

50

AT THE CALL OF THE COUNTRY

Dr Sapru delivered before the Khilafat Conference at Allahabad an impassioned address sympathizing with the Mussalmans in their trouble but dissuaded them from embarking on non-co-operation. He was frankly unable to suggest a substitute but was emphatically of opinion that whether there was a substitute or not non-co-operation was a remedy worse than the disease. He said further that the Mussalmans will be taking upon their shoulders a serious responsibility if, whilst they appealed to the ignorant masses to join them, they could not appeal to the Indian judges to resign, and if they did they would not succeed.

I acknowledge the force of Dr Sapru's last argument. At the back of Dr Sapru's mind is the fear that non-co-operation by the ignorant people would lead to distress and chaos and would do no good. In my opinion any non-co-operation is bound to do some good. Even the Viceregal door-keeper saying, " Please Sir, I can serve the Government no longer because it has hurt my national honour," and resigning is a step mightier and more effective than the mightiest speech declaiming against the Government for its injustice.

Nevertheless, it would be wrong to appeal to the door-keeper until one has appealed to the highest in the land. And as I propose, if the necessity arose, to ask the door-keepers of the Government to dissociate themselves from an unjust Government, I propose now to address an appeal to the Judges and the Executive Councillors to join the protest that is rising from all over India against the double wrong done to India, on the Khilafat and the Punjab questions. In both national honour is involved.

I take it that these gentlemen have entered upon their high offices not for the sake of emolument, nor I hope for the sake of fame, but for the sake of serving their country. It was not for money, for, they were earning more than they do now. It must not be for fame, for, they cannot buy fame at the cost of national honour. The only consideration that can at the present moment keep them in office must be service of the country.

When the people have faith in the Government, when it represents the popular will, the judges and the executive officials possibly serve the country. But when that Government does not represent the will of the people, when it supports dishonesty and terrorism, the judges and the executive officials by retaining office become instruments of dishonesty and terrorism. And the least therefore that these holders of high offices can do is to cease to become agents of a dishonest and terrorizing Government.

For the judges the objection will be raised that they are above politics, and so they are and should be. But the doctrine is true only in so far as the Government is on the whole for the benefit of the people and at least represents the will of the majority. Not to take part in politics means not to take sides. But when a whole country has one mind, one will, when a whole country has been denied justice, it is no longer a question of party politics, it is a matter of life and death. It then becomes the duty of every citizen to refuse to serve a Government which misbehaves and flouts national wish. The judges are at that moment bound to follow the nation if they are ultimately its servants.

There remains another argument to be examined. It applies to both the judges and the members of the executive. It will be urged that my appeal could only be meant for the Indians and what good can it do by Indians renouncing offices which have been won for the nation by hard struggle. I wish that I could make an effective appeal to the English as well as the Indians. But I confess that I have written with the mental reservation that the appeal is addressed only to the Indians. I must therefore examine the argument just stated. Whilst it is true that these offices have been secured after a prolonged struggle, they are of use not because of the struggle but because they are intended to serve the nation. The moment they cease to possess that quality, they become useless and as in the present case harmful, no matter how hard-earned and therefore valuable they may have been at the outset.

I would submit too to our distinguished countrymen who occupy high offices that their giving up their offices will bring the struggle to a speedy end and would probably obviate the danger attendant upon the masses being called upon to signify their disapproval by withdrawing co-operation. If the title-holders gave up their titles, if the holders of honorary offices gave up their appointments and if the high officials gave up their posts, and the would-be councillors boycotted the councils, the Government would quickly come to its senses, and give effect to the people's will. For the alternative before the Government then would be nothing but despotic rule pure and simple. That would probably mean military dictatorship. The world's opinion has advanced so far that Britain dare not contemplate such dictatorship with equanimity. The taking of the steps suggested by me will constitute the peacefullest revolution the world has ever seen. Once the infallibility of non-co-operation is realized, there is an end to all bloodshed and violence in any shape or form.

Undoubtedly a cause must be grave to warrant the drastic method of national non-co-operation. I do say that the affront such as has been put upon Islam cannot be repeated for a century. Islam must rise now or 'be fallen' if not for ever, certainly for a century. And I cannot imagine a graver wrong than the massacre of Jalianwala and the barbarity that followed it, the white-wash by the Hunter Committee, the dispatch of the Government of India, Mr Montagu's letter upholding the Viceroy and the then Lieutenant-Governor of the Punjab, the refusal to remove officials who made of the lives of the Punjabis 'a hell' during the Martial Law period. These acts constitute a complete series of continuing wrongs against India which if India has any sense of honour, she must right at the sacrifice of all the material wealth she possesses. If she does not, she will have bartered her soul for a ' mess of pottage '.

Young India, 21-7-'20

51

THE FIRST OF AUGUST

It is hardly likely that before the 1st August there will be on the part of His Majesty's Ministers promise of a revision of the peace terms and the consequent suspension of the inauguration of non-co-operation. The first of August next will be as important an event in the history of India as was the 6th of April last year. The sixth of April marked the beginning of the end of the Rowlatt Act. No one can consider the Rowlatt Act can possibly live in the face of the agitation that has only been suspended — never given up. It must be clear to any one that the power that wrests justice from an unwilling Government in the matter of the Punjab and the Khilafat will be the power that will secure repeal of the Rowlatt Act. And that power is the power of Satyagraha whether it is known by the name of civil disobedience or non-co-operation.

Many people dread the advent of non-co-operation, because of the events of last year. They fear madness from the mob and consequent repetition of last year's reprisals almost unsurpassed in their ferocity in the history of modern times. Personally I do not mind Governmental fury as I mind mob fury. The latter is a sign of national distemper and therefore more difficult to deal with than the former which is confined to a small corporation. It is easier to oust a Government that has rendered itself unfit to govern than it is to cure unknown people in a mob of their madness. But great movements cannot be stopped altogether because a Government or a people or both go wrong. We learn and profit through our mistakes and failures. No general worth the name gives up a battle because he has suffered reverses, or which is the same thing, made mistakes. And so we must approach non-co-operation with confidence and hope. As in the past, the commencement is to be marked by fasting and prayer — a sign of the religious character of the demonstration. There should also be on that day suspension of business, and meetings to pass resolutions praying for revision of the peace terms and justice for the Punjab, and inculcating non-co-operation until justice has been done.

The giving up of titles and honorary posts should also commence from the first of August. Doubt has been expressed as to the sufficiency of notice regarding surrender of titles and honorary posts. It is however quickly dispelled by bearing in mind that the first of August marks the commencement of the surrender of titles. It is not the only day on which surrender has to take place. Indeed I do not expect a very large response on the first day. A vigorous propaganda will have to be carried on and the message delivered to every title- or post-holder and the argument presented to him proving the duty of such surrender.

But the greatest thing in this campaign of non-co-operation is to evolve order, discipline, co-operation among the people and co-ordination among the workers. Effective non-co-operation depends upon complete organization. Thousands of men who have filled meetings throughout the Punjab have convinced me that the people want to withdraw co-operation from the Government but they must know how. Most people do not understand the complicated machinery of the Government. They do not realize that every citizen silently but none-the-less certainly sustains the Government of the day in ways of which he has no knowledge. Every citizen therefore renders himself responsible for every act of his Government. And it is quite proper to support it so long as the actions of the Government are bearable. But when they hurt him and his nation, it becomes his duty to withdraw his support.

But as I have said, every citizen does not know how to do so in an orderly manner. Disorderliness comes from anger, orderliness out of intelligent resistance. The first condition therefore of real success is to ensure entire absence of violence. Violence done to persons representing the Government or to persons who don't join our ranks, i.e., the supporters of the Government, means in every case retrogression in our case, cessation of non-co-operation and useless waste of innocent lives. Those, therefore, who wish to make non-co-operation a success in the quickest possible time will consider it their first duty to see that in their neighbourhood complete order is kept.

Young India, 28-7-'20

52

WHO IS DISLOYAL ?

Mr Montagu has discovered a new definition of disloyalty. He considers my suggestion to boycott the visit of the Prince of Wales to be disloyal, and some newspapers taking the cue from him have called persons who have made the suggestion 'unmannerly'. They have even attributed to these 'unmannerly' persons the suggestion of 'boycotting the Prince'. I draw a sharp and fundamental distinction between boycotting the Prince and boycotting any welcome arranged for him. Personally I would extend the heartiest welcome to His Royal Highness if he came or could come without official patronage and the protecting wings of the Government of the day. Being the heir to a constitutional monarch, the Prince's movements are regulated and dictated by the ministers, no matter how much the dictation may be concealed beneath diplomatically polite language. In suggesting the boycott therefore the promoters have suggested boycott of an insolent bureaucracy and dishonest ministers of His Majesty.

You cannot have it both ways. It is true that under a constitutional monarchy, the royalty is above politics. But you cannot send the Prince on a political visit for the purpose of making political capital out of him, and then complain that those, who will not play your game and, in order to checkmate you, proclaim a boycott of the Royal visit, do not know constitutional usage. For the Prince's visit is not for pleasure. His Royal Highness is to come, in Mr Lloyd George's words, as the 'ambassador of the British nation', in other words, his own ambassador in order to issue a certificate of merit to him and possibly to give the ministers a new lease of life. The wish is designed to consolidate and strengthen a power that spells mischief for India. Even as it is, Mr Montagu has foreseen that the welcome will probably be excelled by any hitherto extended to Royalty, meaning that the people are not really and deeply affected and stirred by the official atrocities in the Punjab and the manifestly dishonest breach of official declarations on the Khilafat. With the knowledge that India was bleeding at heart, the Government of India should have told His Majesty's ministers that the moment was inopportune for sending the Prince. I venture to submit that it is adding insult to injury to bring the Prince and through his visit to steal honours and further prestige for a Government that deserves to be dismissed with disgrace. I claim that I prove my loyalty by saying that India is in no mood, is too deeply in mourning to take part in any welcome to His Royal Highness, and that the ministers and the Indian Government show their disloyalty by making the Prince a cat's paw of their deep political game. If they persist, it is the clear duty of India to have nothing to do with the visit.

Young India, 4-8-'20

53

NON-VIOLENCE AND SWADESHI

Before a crowded meeting of Mussalmans in the Muzaffarabad at Bombay held on the 29th July, speaking on the impending non-co-operation which commenced on the 1st of August, Mr Gandhi said the time for speeches on non-co-operation was past and the time for practice had arrived. But two things were needful for complete success : an environment free from any violence on the part of the people and a spirit of self-sacrifice. Non-co-operation, as the speaker had conceived it, was an impossibility in an atmosphere surcharged with the spirit of violence. Violence was an exhibition of anger and any such exhibition was dissipation of valuable energy. Subduing of one's anger was a storing up of national energy, which, when set free in an ordered manner, would produce astounding results. His conception of non-co-operation did not involve rapine, plunder, incendiarism and all the concomitants of mass madness. His scheme presupposed ability on their part to control all the forces of evil. If, therefore, any disorderliness was found on the part of the people which they could not control, he for one would certainly help the Government to control them. In the presence of disorder it would be for him a choice of evil, and evil though he considered the present Government to be, he would not hesitate for the time being to help the Government to control disorder. But he had faith in the people. He believed that they knew that the cause could only be won by non-violent methods. To put it at the lowest, the people had not the power, even if they had the will, to resist with brute strength the unjust Governments of Europe who had, in the intoxication of their success, disregarding every canon of justice, dealt so cruelly by the only Islamic Power in Europe.

Matchless Weapon

In non-co-operation they had a matchless and powerful weapon. It was a sign of religious atrophy to sustain an unjust Government that supported an injustice by resorting to untruth and camouflage. So long therefore as the Government did not purge itself of the canker of injustice and untruth, it was their duty to withdraw all help from it, consistently with their ability to preserve order in the social structure. The first stage of non-cooperation was, therefore, so arranged as to involve minimum of danger to public peace and minimum of sacrifice on the part of those who participated in the movement. And if they might not help an evil Government nor receive any favours from it, it followed that they must give up all titles of honour which were no longer a proud possession. Lawyers, who were in reality honorary officers of the Court, should cease to support Courts that upheld the prestige of an unjust Government and the people must be able to settle their disputes and quarrels by private arbitration. Similarly, parents should withdraw their children from the public schools and they must evolve a system of national education or private education totally independent of the Government. An insolent Government, conscious of its brute strength, might laugh at such withdrawals by the people especially as the Law Courts and schools were supposed to help the people, but he had not a shadow of doubt that the moral effect of such a step could not possibly be lost even upon a Government whose conscience had become stifled by the intoxication of power.

Swadeshi

He had hesitation in accepting Swadeshi as a plank in non-co-operation. To him Swadeshi was as dear as life itself. But he had no desire to smuggle in Swadeshi through the Khilafat movement, if it could not legitimately help that movement. But conceived as non-co-operation was in a spirit of self-sacrifice, Swadeshi had a legitimate place in the movement. Pure Swadeshi meant sacrifice of their liking for fineries. He asked the nation to sacrifice its liking for the fineries of Europe and Japan and be satisfied with the coarse but beautiful fabrics woven on their handlooms out of yarns spun by millions of their sisters. If the nation had become really awakened to a sense of the danger to its religions and its self-respect, it could not but perceive the absolute and immediate necessity of the adoption of Swadeshi in its intense form, and if the people of India adopted Swadeshi with religious zeal he begged to assure them that its adoption would arm them with a new power and would produce an unmistakable impression throughout the whole world. He, therefore, expected the Mussalmans to give the lead by giving up all the fineries they were so fond of and adopt the simple cloth that could be produced by the manual labour of their sisters and brethren in their own cottages. And he hoped that the Hindus would follow suit. It was a sacrifice in which the whole nation, every man, woman and child, could take part.

Young India, 4-8-'20

54

PROGRAMME FOR SATYAGRAHA

[From a letter written by Gandhiji to Hakim Ajmal Khan from Sabarmati Jail, dated 12th March, 1922.]

A staunch Mussalman, you have shown in your own life what Hindu-Muslim unity means.

We all now realize, as we have never before realized, that without that unity we cannot attain our freedom, and I make bold to say that without that unity the Mussalmans of India cannot render the Khilafat all the aid they wish. Divided, we must ever remain slaves. This unity, therefore, cannot be a mere policy to be discarded when it does not suit us. We can discard it only when we are tired of Swaraj. Hindu-Muslim unity must be our creed to last for all time and under all circumstances.

Nor must that unity be a menace to the minorities — the Parsees, the Christians, the Jews or the powerful Sikhs. If we seek to crush any of them, we shall some day want to fight each other.

I have been drawn so close to you chiefly because I know that you believe in Hindu-Muslim unity in the full sense of the term.

This unity, in my opinion, is unattainanble without our adopting non-violence as a firm policy. I call it a policy because it is limited to the preservation of that unity. But it follows that thirty crores of Hindus and Mussalmans, united not for a time but for all time, can defy all the powers of the world and should consider it a cowardly act to resort to violence in their dealings with the English administrators. We have hitherto feared them and their guns in our simplicity. The moment we realize our combined strength, we shall consider it unmanly to fear them and, therefore, ever to think of striking them. Hence am I anxious and impatient to persuade my countrymen to feel non-violent, not out of our weakness but out of our strength. But you and I know that we have not yet evolved the non-violence of the strong. And we have not done so, because the Hindu-Muslim union has not gone much beyond the stage of policy. There is still too much mutual distrust and consequent fear. I am not disappointed. The progress we have made in that direction is indeed phenomenal. We seem to have covered in eighteen months' time the work of a generation. But infinitely more is necessary. Neither the classes nor the masses feel instinctively that our union is necessary as the breath of our nostrils.

For this consummation we must, it seems to me, rely more upon quality than quantity. Given a sufficient number of Hindus and Mussalmans with almost a fanatical faith in everlasting friendship between the Hindus and the Mussalmans of India, we shall not be long before the unity permeates the masses. A few of us must first clearly understand that we can make no headway without accepting non-violence in thought, word and deed for the full realization of our political ambition. I would, therefore, beseech you and the members of the Working Committee and the All-India Congress Committee to see that our ranks contain no workers who do not fully realize the essential truth I have endeavoured to place before you. A living faith cannot be manufactured by the rule of majority.

To me the visible symbol of all-India unity and, therefore, of the acceptance of non-violence as an indispensable means for the realization of our political ambition is undoubtedly the *charkha*, i.e. khaddar. Only those who believe in *cultivating* a non-violent spirit and eternal friendship between Hindus and Mussalmans will daily and religiously spin. Universal hand-spinning and the universal manufacture and use of hand-spun and hand-woven khaddar will be a substantial, if not absolute, proof of real unity and non-violence. And it will be a recognition of a living kinship with the dumb masses. Nothing can possibly unify and revivify India as the acceptance by all India of the spinning wheel as a daily sacrament and khaddar wear as a privilege and a duty.

Whilst, therefore, I am anxious that more title-holders should give up their titles, lawyers law-courts, scholars Government schools or colleges, Councillors the Councils, and the soldiers and the civilians their posts, I would urge the nation to restrict its activity in this direction only to the consolidation of the results already achieved and to trust its strength to command further abstentions from association with a system we are seeking to mend or end.

Moreover, the workers are too few. I would not waste a single worker today on destructive work when we have such an enormous amount of constructive work. But perhaps the most conclusive argument against devoting further time to destructive propaganda is the fact that the spirit of intolerance which is a form of violence has never been so rampant as now. Co-operators are estranged from us ; they fear us. They say that we are establishing a worse bureaucracy than the existing one. We must remove every cause for such anxiety. We must go out of our way to win them to our side. We must make Englishmen safe from all harm from our side. I should not have to labour the point, if it was clear to every one as it is to you and to me that our pledge of non-violence implies utter humility and goodwill even towards our bitterest opponent. This necessary spirit will be automatically realized, if only India will devote her sole attention to the work of construction suggested by me.

I flatter myself with the belief that my imprisonment is quite enough for a long time to come. I believe in all humility that I have no ill-will against any one. Some of my friends would not have to be as non-violent as I am. But we contemplated the imprisonment of the most innocent. If I may be allowed that claim, it is clear that I should not be followed to prison by anybody at all. We do want to paralyze the Government considered as a system — not, however, by intimidation, but by the irresistible pressure of our innocence. In my opinion it would be intimidation to fill the jails anyhow. And why should more innocent men seek imprisonment till one considered to be the most innocent has been found inadequate for the purpose.

My caution against further courting of imprisonment does not mean that we are now to shirk imprisonment. If the Government will take away every *non-violent* non-co-operator, I should welcome it. Only it should not be because of our civil disobedience, defensive or aggressive. Nor, I hope, will the country fret over those who are in jail. It will do them and the country good to serve the full term of their imprisonment. They can be fitly discharged before their time only by an act of the Swaraj Parliament. And I entertain an absolute conviction that universal adoption of khaddar is Swaraj.

I have refrained from mentioning untouchability. I am sure every good Hindu believes that it has got to go. Its removal is as necessary as the realization of Hindu-Muslim unity.

I have placed before you a programme which is in my opinion the quickest and the best. No impatient Khilafatist can devise a better. May God give you health and wisdom to guide the country to her destined goal.

Young India, 16-3-'22

55

THE DOCTRINE OF THE SWORD

In this age of the rule of brute force, it is almost impossible for any one to believe that any one else could possibly reject the law of the final supremacy of brute force. And so I receive anonymous letters advising me that I must not interfere with the progress of non-co-operation even though popular violence may break out. Others come to me and, assuming that secretly I must be plotting violence, inquire when the happy moment for declaring open violence will arrive. They assure me that the English will never yield to anything but violence secret or open. Yet others, I am informed, believe that I am the most rascally person living in India because I never give out my real intention, and that they have not a shadow of doubt that I believe in violence just as much as most people do.

Such being the hold that the doctrine of the sword has on the majority of mankind, and as success of non-co-operation depends principally on absence of violence during its pendency, and as my views in this matter affect the conduct of a large number of people, I am anxious to state them as clearly as possible.

I do believe that where there is only a choice between cowardice and violence I would advise violence. Thus when my eldest son asked me what he should have done, had he been present when I was almost fatally assaulted in 1908, whether he should have run away and seen me killed or whether he should have used his physical force which he could and wanted to use, and defended me, I told him that it was his duty to defend me even by using violence. Hence it was that I took part in the Boer War, the so-called Zulu rebellion and the late War. Hence also do I advocate training in arms for those who believe in the method of violence. I would rather have India resort to arms in order to defend her honour than that she should in a cowardly manner become or remain a helpless witness to her own dishonour.

But I believe that non-violence is infinitely superior to violence, forgiveness is more manly than punishment. क्षमा वीरस्य भूषणम् । (Forgiveness adorns a soldier). But abstinence is forgiveness only when there is the power to punish; it is meaningless when it pretends to proceed from a helpless creature. A mouse hardly forgives a cat when it allows itself to be torn to pieces by her. I therefore appreciate the sentiment of those who cry out for the condign punishment of General Dyer and his ilk. They would tear him to pieces if they could. But I do not believe India to be helpless. I do not believe myself to be a helpless creature. Only I want to use India's and my strength for a better purpose.

Let me not be misunderstood. Strength does not come from physical capacity. It comes from an indomitable will. An average Zulu is any way more than a match for an average Englishman in bodily capacity. But he flees from an English boy, because he fears the boy's revolver or those who will use it for him. He fears death and is nerveless in spite of his burly figure. We in India may in a moment realize that one hundred thousand Englishmen need not frighten three hundred million human beings. A definite forgiveness would therefore mean a definite recognition of our strength. With enlightened forgiveness must come a mighty wave of strength in us, which would make it impossible for a Dyer and a Frank Johnson to heap affront upon India's devoted head. It matters little to me that for the moment I do not drive my point home. We feel too downtrodden not to be angry and revengeful. But I must not refrain from saying that India can gain more by waiving the right of punishment. We have better work to do, a better mission to deliver to the world.

I am not a visionary. I claim to be a practical idealist. The religion of non-violence is not meant merely for *rishis* and saints. It is meant for the common people as well. Non-violence is the law of our species as violence is the law of the brute. The spirit lies dormant in the brute and he knows no law but that of physical might. The dignity of man requires obedience to a higher law — to the strength of the spirit.

I have therefore ventured to place before India the ancient law of self-sacrifice. For Satyagraha and its off-shoots, non-co-operation and civil resistance, are nothing but new names for the law of suffering. The *rishis*, who discovered the law of non-violence in the midst of violence, were greater geniuses than Newton. They were themselves greater warriors than Wellington. Having themselves known the use of arms, they realized their uselessness and taught a weary world that its salvation lay not through violence but through non-violence.

Non-violence in its dynamic condition means con-scious suffering. It does not mean meek submission to the will of the evil-doer, but it means the pitting of one's whole soul against the will of the tyrant. Working under this law of our being, it is possible for a single individual to defy the whole might of an unjust empire, to save his honour, his religion, his soul and lay the foundation for that empire's fall or its regeneration.

And so I am not pleading for India to practise non-violence because she is weak. I want her to practise non-violence being conscious of her strength and power. No training in arms is required for realization of her strength. We seem to need it because we seem to think that we are but a lump of flesh. I want India to rcognize that she has a soul that cannot perish and that can rise triumphant above every physical weakness and defy the physical com-bination of a whole world. What is the meaning of Rama, a mere human being, with his host of monkeys, pitting himself against the insolent strength of ten-headed Ravana surrounded in supposed safety by the raging waters on all sides of Lanka ? Does it not mean the conquest of physical might by spiritual strength ? However, being a practical man, I do not wait till India recognizes the practicability of the spiritual life in the political world. India considers herself to be powerless and paralyzed before the machine-guns, the tanks and the aeroplanes of the English. And she takes up non-co-operation out of her weakness.

It must still serve the same purpose, namely, bring her delivery from the crushing weight of British injustice if a sufficient number of people practise it.

I isolate this non-co-operation from Sinn Feinism, for, it is so conceived as to be incapable of being offered side by side with violence. But I invite even the school of violence to give this peaceful non-co-operation a trial. It will not fail through its inherent weakness. It may fail because of poverty of response. Then will be the time for real danger. The high-souled men, who are unable to suffer national humiliation any longer, will want to vent their wrath. They will take to violence. So far as I know, they must perish without delivering themselves or their country from the wrong. If India takes up the doctrine of the sword, she may gain momentary victory. Then India will cease to be the pride of my heart. I am wedded to India because I owe my all to her. I believe absolutely that she has a mission for the world. She is not to copy Europe blindly. India's acceptance of the doctrine of the sword will be the hour of my trial. I hope I shall not be found wanting. My religion has no geographical limits. If I have a living faith in it, it will transcend my love for India herself. My life is dedicated to service of India through the religion of non-violence which I believe to be the root of Hinduism.

Meanwhile I urge those who distrust me not to disturb the even working of the struggle that has just commenced, by inciting to violence in the belief that I want violence. I detest secrecy as a sin. Let them give non-violent non-co-operation a trial and they will find that I had no mental reservation whatsoever.

Young India, 11-8-'20

56

RENUNCIATION OF MEDALS

[Mr Gandhi has addressed the following letter to the Viceroy :]

It is not without a pang that I return the Kaiser-i-Hind gold medal granted to me by your predecessor for my humanitarian work in South Africa, the Zulu War medal granted in South Africa for my services as officer in charge of the Indian volunteer ambulance corps in 1906 and the Boer War medal for my services as assistant superintendent of the Indian volunteer stretcher-bearer corps during the Boer War of 1899-1900. I venture to return these medals in pursuance of the scheme of non-co-operation inaugurated today in connection with the Khilafat movement. Valuable as these honours have been to me, I cannot wear them with an easy conscience so long as my Mussalman countrymen have to labour under a wrong done to their religious sentiment. Events that have happened during the past month have confirmed me in the opinion that the Imperial Government have acted in the Khilafat matter in an unscrupulous, immoral and unjust manner and have been moving from wrong to wrong in order to defend their immorality. I can retain neither respect nor affection for such a Government.

The attitude of the Imperial and Your Excellency's Governments on the Punjab question has given me additional cause for grave dissatisfaction. I had the honour, as Your Excellency is aware, as one of the Congress commissioners to investigate the causes of the disorders in the Punjab during the April of 1919. And it is my deliberate conviction that Sir Michael O'Dwyer was totally unfit to hold the office of Lieutenant Governor of the Punjab and that his policy was primarily responsible for infuriating the mob at Amritsar. No doubt the mob excesses were unpardonable ; incendiarism, murder of five innocent Englishmen and the cowardly assault on Miss Sherwood were most deplorable and uncalled for. But the punitive measures taken by General Dyer, Col. Frank

Johnson, Col. O'Brien, Mr Bosworth Smith, Rai Shriram Sud, Mr Malik Khan and other officers were out of all proportion to the crime of the people and amounted to wanton cruelty and inhumanity almost unparallelled in modern times. Your Excellency's light-hearted treatment of the official crime, your exoneration of Sir Michael O'Dwyer, Mr Montagu's dispatch and above all the shameful ignorance of the Punjab events and callous disregard of the feelings of Indians betrayed by the House of Lords, have filled me with the gravest misgivings regarding the future of the Empire, have estranged me completely from the present Government and have disabled me from tendering, as I have hitherto whole-heartedly tendered, my loyal co-operation.

In my humble opinion the ordinary method of agitating by way of petitions, deputations and the like is no remedy for moving to repentance a Government so hopelessly indifferent to the welfare of its charge as the Government of India has proved to be. In European countries, condonation of such grievous wrongs as the Khilafat and the Punjab would have resulted in a bloody revolution by the people. They would have resisted at all cost national emasculation such as the said wrongs imply. But half of India is too weak to offer violent resistance and the other half is unwilling to do so. I have therefore ventured to suggest the remedy of non-co-operation which enables those who wish, to dissociate themselves from the Government and which if it is unattended by violence and undertaken in an ordered manner, must compel it to retrace its steps and undo the wrongs committed. But whilst I shall pursue the policy of non-co-operation in so far as I can carry the people with me, I shall not lose hope that you will yet see your way to do justice. I, therefore, respectfully ask Your Excellency to summon a conference of the recognized leaders of the people and in consultation with them find a way that would placate the Mussalmans and do reparation to the unhappy Punjab.

Young India, 4-8-'20

57

NON-PAYMENT OF FINES

All the readers of *Young India* may not know that Ahmedabad came under a heavy fine for the misdeeds of the April of last year. The fine was collected from the residents of Ahmedabad but some were exempted at the discretion of the Collector. Among those who were called upon to pay fines were income-tax payers. They had to pay a third of the tax paid by them. Mr V. J. Patel, a noted barrister, and Dr Kanuga, a leading medical practitioner, were among those who were unable to pay. They had admittedly helped the authorities to quell the disturbance. No doubt they were Satyagrahis but they had endeavoured to still the mob fury even at some risk to their own persons. But the authorities would not exempt them. It was a difficult thing for them to use discretion in individual cases. It was equally difficult for these two gentlemen to pay any fine when they were not to blame at all. They did not wish to embarrass the authorities and yet they were anxious to preserve their self-respect. They carried on no agitation but simply notified their inability to pay the fines in the circumstances set forth above. Therefore, an attachment order was issued. Dr Kanuga is a very busy practitioner and his cash box is always full. The watchful attaching official attached his cash box and extracted enough money to discharge the writ of execution. A lawyer's business cannot be conducted on those lines. Mr Patel sported no cash box. A sofa of his sitting room was therefore attached and advertised for sale and duly sold. Both these Satyagrahis thus completely saved their consciences.

Wiseacres may laugh at the folly of allowing writs of attachment and paying for the collection of fines. Multiply such instances and imagine the consequence to the authorities of executing thousands of writs. Writs are possible when they are confined to a few recalcitrants.

They are troublesome when they have to be executed against many high-souled persons who have done no wrong and who refuse payment to vindicate a principle. They may not attract much notice when isolated individuals resort to this method of protest. But clean examples have a curious method of multiplying themselves. They bear publicity and the sufferers instead of incurring odium receive congratulations. Men like Thoreau brought about the abolition of slavery by their personal examples. Says Thoreau, " I know this well, that if one thousand, if one hundred, if ten men whom I could name, — if ten *honest* men only — aye, if *one honest* man, in this State of Massachusetts *ceasing to hold slaves* were actually to withdraw from this co-partnership and be locked up in the country gaol therefor, it would be the abolition of slavery in America. For it matters not how small the beginning may seem to be, what is once well done is done for ever." Again he says, " I have contemplated the imprisonment of the offender rather than seizure of his goods — though both will serve the same purpose, because they who assert the purest right and consequently are most dangerous to a corrupt State, commonly have not spent much time in accumulating property." We, therefore, congratulate Mr Patel and Dr Kanuga on the excellent example set by them in an excellent spirit and in an excellent cause.

Young India, 7-7-'20

58

NON-PAYMENT OF TAXES

I observe a desire in some places to precipitate mass civil disobedience by suspending payment of taxes. But I would urge the greatest caution before embarking upon the dangerous adventure. We must not be indifferent about violence. and we must make sure of masses exercising self-control whilst they are witnesses to the confiscation of their crops and cattle or forfeiture of their holdings. I know that withholding of payment of taxes is one of the quickest methods of overthrowing a government. I am equally sure that we have not yet evolved that degree of strength and discipline which are necessary for conducting a successful campaign of non-payment of taxes. Not a single *tahsil* in India is yet ready, except perhaps Bardoli and, to a lesser degree, Anand. More than fifty percent of the population of such *tahsil* has to rid itself of the curse of untouchability, must be dressed in *khadi* manufactured in the *tahsil*, must be non-violent in thought, word and deed, and must be living in perfect friendliness with all whether co-operators or non-co-operators. Non-payment of taxes without the necessary discipline will be an act of unpardonable madness. Instead of leading to Swaraj, it is likely to lead to no-*raj*.

Young India, 19-1-'22

59

NON-PAYMENT OF TAXES

The validity of the objection * (against non-payment of taxes) lies in the statement that the non-payment campaign will bring into the movement people, who are not as yet saturated with the principle of non-violence. This is very true, and because it is true, non-payment does 'hold out a material bait'. It follows, therefore, that we must not resort to non-payment because of the possibility of a ready response. The readiness is a fatal temptation. Such non-payment will not be civil or non-violent, but it will be criminal or fraught with the greatest possibility of violence. Let us remember the experience of Pandit Jawaharlal Nehru when the peasants, after they had taken the pledge of non-violence, told him that if he advised them to do violence, they would be certainly ready to do so. Not until the peasantry is trained to understand

---

* Reference is to apprehensions expressed by a friend " in deep sympathy with the national movement ".

the reason and the virtue of *civil* non-payment and is prepared to look with calm resignation upon the confiscation (which can only be temporary) of their holdings and the forced sale of their cattle and other belongings, may they be advised to withhold payment of taxes. They must be told what happened in holy Palestine. The Arabs who were fined were surrounded by soldiers. Aeroplanes were hovering overhead. And the sturdy men were dispossessed of their cattle. The latter were impounded and left without fodder and even water. When the Arabs, stupefied and rendered helpless, brought the fine and additional penalty, as if to mock them, they had their dead and dying cattle returned to them. Worse things can and certainly will happen in India. Are the Indian peasantry prepared to remain absolutely non-violent, and see their cattle taken away from them to die of hunger and thirst ? I know that such things have already happened in Andhra Desh. If the peasantry in general knowingly and deliberately remain peaceful even in such trying circumstances, they are nearly ready for non-payment.

I say ' nearly ready ', for non-payment is intended to transfer the power from the bureaucracy into our hands. It is, therefore, not enough that the peasantry remain non-violent. Non-violence is certainly nine-tenths of the battle, but it is not all. The peasantry may remain non-violent, but may not treat the untouchables as their brethren ; they may not regard Hindus, Mussalmans, Christians, Jews, Parsis, as the case may be, as their brethren ; they may not have learnt the economic and the moral value of the *charkha* and khaddar. If they have not, they cannot gain Swaraj. They will not do all these things after Swaraj, if they will not do them now. They must be taught to know that the practice of these national virtues means Swaraj.

Thus civil non-payment of taxes is a privilege capable of being exercised only after rigorous training. And even as *civil* disobedience is difficult in the case of a habitual offender against the laws of the State, so is *civil* non-payment difficult for those who have hitherto been in the habit of withholding payment of taxes on the slightest pretext. Civil non-payment of taxes is indeed the last stage in non-co-operation. We must not resort to it till we have tried the other forms of civil disobedience. And it will be the height of unwisdom to experiment with non-payment in large or many areas in the beginning stages.

Young India, 26-1-'22

60

BOYCOTT OF COURTS AND SCHOOLS

The Non-co-operation Committee has included, in the first stage, boycott of Law Courts by lawyers and of Government schools and colleges by parents or scholars as the case may be. I know that it is only my reputation as a worker and fighter, which has saved me from an open charge of lunacy for having given the advice about boycott of Courts and schools.

I venture, however, to claim some method about my madness. It does not require much reflection to see that it is through Courts that a Government establishes its authority and it is through schools that it manufactures clerks and other employees. They are both healthy institutions when the Government in charge of them is on the whole just. They are death-traps when the Government is unjust.

I submit that national non-co-operation requires suspension of their practice by lawyers. Perhaps no one co-operates with a Government more than lawyers through its Law Courts. Lawyers interpret laws to the people and thus support authority. It is for that reason that they are styled ' officers of the Court '. They may be called honorary office-holders. It is said that it is the lawyers who have put up the most stubborn fight against the Government. This is no doubt partly true. But that does not undo the mischief that is inherent in the profession.

So when the nation wishes to paralyze the Government, that profession, if it wishes to help the nation to bend the Government to its will, must suspend practice. But, say the critics, the Government will be too pleased, if the pleaders and barristers fell into the trap laid by me. I do not believe it. What is true in ordinary times is not true in extraordinary times. In normal times the Government resent fierce criticism of their manners and methods by lawyers, but in the face of fierce action they would be loath to part with a single lawyer's support through his practice in the Courts.

Moreover, in my scheme, suspension does not mean stagnation. The lawyers are not to suspend practice and enjoy rest. They will be expected to induce their clients to boycott Courts. They will improvise arbitration boards in order to settle disputes. A nation, that is bent on forcing justice from an unwilling Government, has little time for engaging in mutual quarrels. This truth the lawyers will be expected to bring home to their clients. The readers may not know that many of the most noted lawyers of England suspended their work during the late war. The lawyers, then, upon temporarily leaving their profession, became whole time workers instead of being workers only during their recreation hours. Real politics are not a game. The late Mr Gokhale used to deplore that we had not gone beyond treating politics as a pastime. We have no notion as to how much the country has lost by reason of amateurs having managed its battles with the serious-minded, trained and wholetime working bureaucracy.

Now for the Schools

I feel that if we do not have the courage to suspend the education of our children, we do not deserve to win the battle.

I contend that there is no sacrifice involved in emptying the schools. We must be specially unfit for non-co-operation if we are so helpless as to be unable to manage our own education in total independence of the Government. Every village should manage the education of its own children. I would not depend upon Government aid.

If there is a real awakening the schooling need not be
interrupted for a single day. The very schoolmasters who
are now conducting Government schools, if they are good
enough to resign their office, could take charge of national
schools and teach our children the things they need, and
not make of the majority of them indifferent clerks. I do
look to the Aligarh College to give the lead in this matter.
The moral effect created by the emptying of our *madrassas*
will be tremendous. I doubt not that the Hindu parents
and scholars would not fail to copy their Mussalman
brethren.

Indeed what could be grander education than that the
parents and scholars should put religious sentiment before
a knowledge of letters ? If therefore no arrangement
could be immediately made for the literary instruction of
youths who might be withdrawn, it would be most profitable training for them to be able to work as volunteers
for the cause which may necessitate their withdrawal
from Government schools. For as in the case of the lawyers, so in the case of boys, my notion of withdrawal does
not mean an indolent life. The withdrawing boys will,
each according to his worth, be expected to take their
share in the agitation.

Young India, 11-8-'20

61

EMPIRE GOODS BOYCOTT

It is curious how the question of the Empire goods boycott continues to challenge public attention from time to time. From the standpoint of non-violent non-co-operation it seems to me to be wholly indefensible. It is retaliation pure and simple and as such punitive. So long, therefore, as the Congress holds to *non-violent* non-co-operation, so long must boycott of British, as distinguished from other foreign goods, be ruled out. And if I am the only Congressman holding the view, I must move a resolution at the next Congress repealing the resolution in the matter carried at the last Special Session.

But for the moment, I propose to discuss not the ethics but the utility of the retaliatory boycott. The knowledge that even the Liberals joined the boycott campaign cannot make one shrink from the inquiry. On the contrary, if they come to believe with me that the retaliatory boycott that they and the Congress took up was not only ineffective but was one more demonstration of our impotent rage and waste of precious energy, I would appeal to them to take up with zeal and determination the boycott of all foreign cloth and replacing same not with Indian mill-cloth but with hand-spun khaddar.

If our rage did not blind us, we should be ashamed of the boycott resolution when we realized that we depended upon British goods for some of our national requirements. When we may not do without English books and English medicines, should we boycott English watches because we can procure Geneva watches? And if we will not do without English books because we need them, how shall we expect the importer of British watches or perfumes to sacrifice his trade? My very English efficient nurse whom I loved to call 'tyrant' because she insisted in all loving ways on my taking more food and more sleep than I did, with a smile curling round her lips and insidious twinkle in her eyes, gently remarked after I was safely removed to a private ward escorted by the house-surgeon and herself: "As I was shading you with my umbrella I could not help smiling that you, a fierce boy-cotter of everything British, probably owed your life to the skill of a British surgeon handling British surgical instruments, administering British drugs, and to the ministrations of a British nurse. Do you know that as we brought you here, the umbrella that shaded you was of British make?" The gentle nurse as she finished the last triumphant sentence evidently expected my complete collapse under her loving sermon. But happily I was able to confound her self-assurance by saying: "When will you people begin to know things as they are? Do you know that I do not boycott anything merely because it is British? I simply boycott all foreign cloth because the dumping down of foreign cloth in India has reduced millions of my people to pauperism." I was even able to interest her in the khaddar movement. Probably she became a convert to it. Anyway she understood the propriety, the necessity and the utility of khaddar, but she could only laugh (and rightly) against the wholly ineffective and meaningless boycott of British goods.

If the champions of this retaliatory boycott will look at their homes and their own belongings, they will, I have no doubt, discover the ludicrousness of their position even as my nurse friend did, under the supposition that I belonged to that boycott school.

Young India, 15-5-'24

62

SOCIAL BOYCOTT

It would be a dangerous thing if, for differences of opinion, we were to proclaim social boycott. It would be totally opposed to the doctrine of non-violence to stop the supply of water and food. This battle of non-co-operation is a programme of propaganda by reducing profession to practice, not one of compelling others to yield obedience by violence direct or indirect. We must try patiently to convert our opponents. If we wish to evolve the spirit of democracy out of slavery, we must be scrupulously exact in our dealings with opponents. We may not replace the slavery of the Government by that of the non-co-operationists. We must concede to our opponents the freedom we claim for ourselves and for which we are fighting. The stoutest co-operationist will bend to the stern realities of practice if there is real response from the people.

But there is a non-violent boycott which we shall be bound to practise if we are to make any impression. We must not compromise with what we believe to be an untruth, whether it resides in a white skin or a brown. Such boycott is political boycott. We may not receive favours from the new Councillors. The voters, if they are true to their pledge, will be bound to refrain from making use of the services of those whom they have declined to regard as their representatives. They must ratify their verdict by complete abstention from any encouragement of the so-called representatives.

The public will be bound, if they are non-co-operationists, to refrain from giving these representatives any prestige by attending their political functions or parties.

I can conceive the possibility of non-violent social ostracism under certain extreme conditions, when a defiant minority refuses to bend to the majority, not out of any regard for principle but from sheer defiance or worse. But that time has certainly not arrived. Ostracism of a violent character, such as the denial of the use of public wells is a species of barbarism, which I hope will never be practised by any body of men having any desire for national self-respect and national uplift. We will free neither Islam nor India by processes of coercion, whether among ourselves or against Englishmen.

Young India, 8-12-'20

63

SOCIAL BOYCOTT

Non-co-operation being a movement of purification is bringing to the surface all our weaknesses as also excesses of even our strong points. Social boycott is an age-old institution. It is coeval with caste. It is the one terrible sanction exercised with great effect. It is based upon the notion that a community is not bound to extend its hospitality or service to an excommunicate. It answered when every village was a self-contained unit, and the occasions of recalcitrancy were rare. But when opinion is divided, as it is today, on the merits of non-co-operation, when its new application is having a trial, a summary use of social boycott in order to bend a minority to the will of the majority is a species of unpardonable violence. If persisted in, such boycott is bound to destroy the movement. Social boycott is applicable and effective when it is not felt as a punishment and accepted by the object of boycott as a measure of discipline. Moreover, social boycott to be admissible in a campaign of non-violence must never savour of inhumanity. It must be civilized. It must cause pain to the party using it, if it causes inconvenience to its object. Thus, depriving a man of the services of a medical man, as is reported to have been done in Jhansi, is an act of inhumanity tantamount in the moral code to an attempt to murder. I see no difference in murdering a man and withdrawing medical aid from a man who is on the point of dying. Even the laws of war, I apprehend, require the giving of medical relief to the enemy in need of it. To deprive a man of the use of an only village well is notice to him to quit that village. Surely, non-co-operators have acquired no right to use that extreme pressure against those who do not see eye to eye with them. Impatience and intolerance will surely kill this great religious movement. We may not make people pure by compulsion. Much less may we compel them by violence to respect our opinion. It is utterly against the spirit of democracy we want to cultivate.

I hope, therefore, that non-co-operation workers will beware of the snares of social boycott. But the alternative to social boycott is certainly not social intercourse. A man who defies strong clear public opinion on vital matters is not entitled to social amenities and privileges. We may not take part in his social functions such as marriage feasts, we may not receive gifts from him. But we dare not deny social service. The latter is a duty. Attendance at dinner parties and the like is a privilege, which it is optional to withhold or extend. But it would be wisdom to err on the right side and to exercise the weapon even in the limited sense described by me on rare and well-defined occasions. And in every case the user of the weapon will use it at his own risk. The use of it is not as yet in any form a duty. No one is entitled to its use if there is any danger of hurting the movement.

Young India, 16-2-'21

64

SYMPATHETIC STRIKES

Any premature precipitation of sympathetic strikes will result in infinite harm to our cause. In the programme of non-violence, we must rigidly exclude the idea of gaining anything by embarrassing the Government. If our activity is pure and that of the Government impure, the latter is embarrassed by our purity, if it does not itself become pure. Thus, a movement of purification benefits both parties. Whereas a movement of mere destruction leaves the destroyer unpurified, and brings him down to the level of those whom he seeks to destroy.

Even our sympathetic strikes, therefore, have to be strikes of self-purification, i.e., non-co-operation. And so, when we declare a strike to redress a wrong, we really cease to take part in the wrong, and thus leave the wrong-doer to his own resources, in other words, enable him to see the folly of continuing the wrong. Such a strike can only succeed, when behind it is the fixed determination not to revert to service.

Speaking, therefore, as one having handled large successful strikes, I repeat the following maxims, already stated in these pages, for the guidance of all strike leaders :

1. There should be no strike without a real grievance.

2. There should be no strike, if the persons concerned are not able to support themselves out of their own savings or by engaging in some temporary occupation, such as carding, spinning and weaving. Strikers should never depend upon public subscriptions or other charity.

3. Strikers must fix an unalterable minimum demand, and declare it before embarking upon their strike.

A strike may fail in spite of a just grievance and the ability of strikers to hold out indefinitely, if there are workers to replace them. A wise man, therefore, will not strike for increase of wages or other comforts, if he feels that he can be easily replaced. But a philanthropic or patriotic man will strike in spite of supply being greater than the demand, when he feels for and wishes to associate himself with his neighbour's distress. Needless to say, there is no room in a civil strike of the nature described by me for violence in the shape of intimidation, incendiarism or otherwise. I should, therefore, be extremely sorry to find, that the recent derailment near Chittagong was due to mischief done by any of the strikers. Judged by the tests suggested by me, it is clear that the friends of the strikers should never have advised them to apply for or receive Congress or any other public funds for their support. The value of the strikers' sympathy was diminished to the extent, that they received or accepted financial aid. The merit of a sympathetic strike lies in the inconvenience and the loss suffered by the sympathizers.

Young India, 22-9-'21

65

MORE OBJECTIONS ANSWERED

I do not know from where the information has been derived that I have given up the last two stages of non-co-operation. What I have said is that they are a distant goal. I abide by it. I admit that all the stages are fraught with some danger but the last two are fraught with the greatest — the last most of all. The stages have been fixed with a view to running the least possible risk. The last two stages will not be taken up unless the Committee has attained sufficient control over the people to warrant the belief that the laying down of arms or suspension of taxes will, humanly speaking be free from an outbreak of violence on the part of the people. I do entertain the belief that it is possible for the people to attain the discipline necessary for taking the two steps. When once they realize that violence is totally unnecessary to bend an unwilling Government to their will and that the result can be obtained with certainty by dignified non-co-operation, they will cease to think of violence even by way of retaliation. The fact is that hitherto we have not attempted to take concerted and disciplined action from the masses. Some day, if we are to become truly a self-governing nation, that has to be made. The present, in my opinion, is a propitious movement. Every Indian feels the insult to the Punjab as a personal wrong, every Mussalman resents the wrong done to the Khilafat. There is, therefore, a favourable atmosphere for expecting cohesive and restrained movement on the part of the masses.

So far as response is concerned, I agree with the Editor that the quickest and the largest response is to be expected in the matter of suspension of payment of taxes, but as I have said, so long as the masses are not educated to appreciate the value of non-violence even whilst their holdings are being sold, so long must it be difficult to take up the last stage into any appreciable extent.

I agree too that a sudden withdrawal of the military and the police will be a disaster if we have not acquired the ability to protect ourselves against robbers and thieves. But I suggest that when we are ready to call out the military and the police on an extensive scale, we would find ourselves in a position to defend ourselves. If the police and the military resign from patriotic motives, I would certainly expect them to perform the same duty as national volunteers, not as hirelings but as willing protectors of the life and liberty of their countrymen. The movement of non-co-operation is one of automatic adjustment. If the Government schools are emptied, I would certainly expect national schools to come into being. If the lawyers as a whole suspended practice, they would devise arbitration courts and the nation will have expeditious and cheaper method of settling private disputes and awarding punishment to the wrong-doer. I may add that the Khilafat Committee is fully alive to the difficulty of the task and is taking all the necessary steps to meet the contingencies as they arise.

Regarding the leaving of civil employment, no danger is feared, because no one will leave his employment, unless he is in a position to find support for himself and family either through friends or otherwise.

Disapproval of the proposed withdrawal of students betrays, in my humble opinion, lack of appreciation of the true nature of non-co-operation. It is true enough that we pay the money wherewith our children are educated. But when the agency imparting the education has become corrupt, we may not employ it without partaking of the agent's corruption. When students leave schools or colleges I hardly imagine that the teachers will fail to perceive the advisability of themselves resigning. But even if they do not, money can hardly be allowed to count where honour or religion are the stake.

As to the boycott of the councils, it is not the entry of the Moderates or any other persons that matters so much as the entry of those who believe in non-co-operation. You may not co-operate at the top and non-co-operate at the bottom. A councillor cannot remain in the council and ask the *gumasta* who cleans the council table to resign.

Young India, 18-8-'20

66

ANSWERS TO QUESTIONS

My experience of last year shows me that in spite of aberrations in some parts of India, the country was entirely under control, that the influence of Satyagraha was profoundly for its good and that where violence did break out, there were local causes that directly contributed to it. At the same time I admit that even the violence that did take place on the part of the people and the spirit of lawlessness that was undoubtedly shown in some parts should have remained under check. I have made ample acknowledgment of the miscalculation I then made. But all the painful experience that I then gained did not in any way shake my belief in Satyagraha or in the possibility of that matchless force being utilized in India. Ample provision is being made this time to avoid the mistakes of the past. But I must refuse to be deterred from a clear course because it may be attended by violence totally unintended and in spite of extraordinary efforts that are being made to prevent it. At the same time I must make my position clear. Nothing can possibly prevent a Satyagrahi from doing his duty because of the frown of the authorities. I would risk, if necessary, a million lives so long as they are voluntary sufferers and are innocent, spotless victims. It is the mistakes of the people that matter in a Satyagraha campaign. Mistakes, even insanity must be expected from the strong and the powerful, and the moment of victory has come when there is no resort to the mad fury of the powerful but a voluntary, dignified and quiet submission, but not submission to the will of the authority that has put itself in the wrong. The secret of success lies, therefore, in holding every English life and the life of every officer serving the Government as sacred as those of our own dear ones. All the wonderful experience I have gained now during nearly 40 years of conscious existence, has convinced me that there is no gift so precious as that of life. I make bold to say that the moment Englishmen feel that although they are in India in a hopeless minority, their lives are protected against harm not because of the matchless weapons of destruction which are at their disposal, but because Indians refuse to take the lives even of those whom they may consider to be utterly in the wrong, that moment will see a transformation in the English nature in its relation to India, and that moment will also be the moment when all the destructive cutlery that is to be had in India will begin to rust. I know that this is a far-off vision. That cannot matter to me. It is enough for me to see the light and to act up to it, and it is more than enough when I gain companions in the onward march. I have claimed in private conversations with English friends that it is because of my incessant preaching of the gospel of non-violence and my having successfully demonstrated its practical utility that so far the forces of violence, which are undoubtedly in existence in connection with the Khilafat movement, have remained under complete control.

I consider non-co-operation to be such a powerful and pure instrument, that if it is enforced in an earnest spirit, it will be like seeking first the Kingdom of God and everything else following as a matter of course. People will have then realized their true power. They would have learnt the value of discipline, self-control, joint action, non-violence, organization and everything else that goes to make a nation great and good, and not merely great.

I do not know that I have a right to arrogate greater purity for myself than for our Mussalman brethren. But I do admit that they do not believe in my doctrine of non-violence to the full extent. For them it is a weapon of the weak, an expedient. They consider non-co-operation without violence to be the only thing open to them in the way of direct action. I know that if some of them could offer successful violence, they would today. But they are convinced that humanly speaking it is an impossibility. For them, therefore, non-co-operation is a matter not merely of duty but also of revenge. Whereas I take up non-co-operation against the Government as I have actually taken it up in practice against members of my own family. I entertain very high regard for the British Constitution. I have not only no enmity against Englishmen but I regard much in English character as worthy of my emulation. I count many as my friends. It is against my religion to regard any one as an enemy. I entertain similar sentiments with respect to Mohammedans. I find their cause to be just and pure. Although therefore their view-point is different from mine I do not hesitate to associate with them and invite them to give my method a trial, for, I believe that the use of a pure weapon even from a mistaken motive does not fail to produce some good, even as the telling of truth, if only because for the time being it is the best policy, is at least so much to the good.

Young India, 2-6-'20

67

NON-CO-OPERATION EXPLAINED

A representative of this journal * called on Mr M. K. Gandhi yesterday at his temporary residence in the Pursewalkum High Road for an interview on the subject of non-co-operation. Mr Gandhi, who has come to Madras on a tour to some of the principal Muslim centres in Southern India, was busy with a number of workers discussing his programme ; but he expressed his readiness to answer questions on the chief topic which is agitating Muslims and Hindus.

" After your experience of the Satyagraha agitation last year, Mr Gandhi, are you still hopeful and convinced of the wisdom of advising non-co-operation ? "

" Certainly."

" How do you consider conditions have altered since the Satyagraha movement of last year ? "

" I consider that people are better disciplined now than they were before. In this I include even the masses whom I have had opportunities of seeing in large numbers in various parts of the country."

" And you are satisfied that the masses understand the spirit of Satyagraha ? "

" Yes."

" And that is why you are pressing on with the programme of non-co-operation ? "

" Yes. Moreover, the danger that attended the civil-disobedience part of Satyagraha does not apply to non-co-operation, because in non-co-operation we are not taking up civil disobedience of laws as a mass movement. The result hitherto has been most encouraging. For instance, people in Sindh and Delhi, in spite of the irritating restrictions upon their liberty by the authorities, have

---

* The present article is the report of a talk the representative of *The Madras Mail* had with Gandhiji. It was reproduced in the *Young India* from that paper.

carried out the Committee's instructions in regard to the Seditious Meetings Proclamation and to the prohibition of posting placards on the walls which we hold to be inoffensive but which the authorities consider to be offensive."

" What is the pressure which you expect to bring to bear on the authorities if co-operation is withdrawn ? "

"I believe, and everybody must grant, that no Government can exist for a single moment without the co-operation of the people, willing or forced, and if people suddenly withdraw their co-operation in every detail, the Government will come to a stand-still."

" But is there not a big ' If ' in it ? "

" Certainly, there is."

" And how do you propose to succeed against the big ' If ' ? "

" In my plan of campaign expediency has no room. If the Khilafat movement has really permeated the masses and the classes, there must be adequate response from the people."

" But are you not begging the question ? "

" I am not begging the question, because so far as the data before me go, I believe that the Muslims keenly feel the Khilafat grievance. It remains to be seen whether their feeling is intense enough to evoke in them the measure of sacrifice adequate for successful non-co-operation."

" That is, your survey of the conditions, you think, justifies your advising non-co-operation in the full conviction that you have behind you the support of the vast masses of the Mussalman population ? "

" Yes."

" This non-co-operation, you are satisfied, will extend to complete severance of co-operation with the Government ? "

" No ; nor is it at the present moment my desire that it should. I am simply practising non-co-operation to the extent that is necessary to make the Government realize the depth of popular feeling in the matter and the dissatisfaction with the Government that all that could be done has not been done either by the Government of India or by the Imperial Government, whether on the Khilafat question or on the Punjab question."

"Do you, Mr Gandhi, realize that even amongst Mohammedans there are sections of people who are not enthusiastic over non-co-operation however much they may feel the wrong that has been done to their community?"

"Yes, but their number is smaller than those who are prepared to adopt non-co-operation."

"And yet does not the fact that there has not been an adequate response to your appeal for resignation of titles and offices and for boycott of elections of the Councils indicate that you may be placing more faith in their strength of conviction than is warranted?"

"I think not; for the reason that the stage has only just come into operation and our people are always most cautious and slow to move. Moreover, the first stage largely affects the uppermost strata of society, who represent a microscopic minority though they are undoubtedly an influential body of people."

"This upper class, you think, has sufficiently responded to your appeal?"

"I am unable to say either one way or the other at present. I shall be able to give a definite answer at the end of this month."

"Do you think that without one's loyalty to the King and the Royal Family being questioned, one can advocate non-co-operation in connection with the Royal visit?"

"Most decidedly; for the simple reason that if there is any disloyalty about the proposed boycott of the Prince's visit, it is disloyalty to the Government of the day and not to the person of His Royal Highness."

"What do you think is to be gained by promoting this boycott in connection with the Royal visit?"

"I want to show that the people of India are not in sympathy with the Government of the day and that they strongly disapprove of the policy of the Government in regard to the Punjab and Khilafat, and even in respect of other important administrative measures. I consider that the visit of the Prince of Wales is a singularly good opportunity to the people to show their disapproval of the present Government. After all, the visit is calculated to have tremendous political results. It is not to be a non-political event, and seeing that the Government of India and the Imperial Government want to make the visit a political event of first-class importance, namely, for the purpose of strengthening their hold upon India, I for one consider that it is the bounden duty of the people to boy-cott the visit which is being engineered by the two Govern-ments in their own interest which at the present moment is totally antagonistic to the people."

" Do you mean that you want this boycott promoted because you feel that the strengthening of the hold upon India is not desirable in the best interests of the country ? "

" Yes. The strengthening of the hold of a Government so wicked as the present one is not desirable for the best interests of the people. Not that I want the bond between England and India to become loosened for the sake of loosening it, but I want that bond to become strengthened only in so far as it adds to the welfare of India."

" Do you think that non-co-operation and the non-boycott of the Legislative Councils are consistent ? "

" No ; because a person who takes up the programme of non-co-operation cannot consistently stand for Coun-cils."

" Is non-co-operation, in your opinion, an end in itself or a means to an end, and if so, what is the end ? "

" It is a means to an end, the end being to make the present Government just, whereas it has become mostly unjust. Co-operation with a just Government is a duty ; non-co-operation with an unjust Government is equally a duty."

" Will you look with favour upon the proposal to enter the Councils and to carry on either obstructive tactics or to decline to take the oath of allegiance as consistent with your non-co-operation ? "

"No; as an accurate student of non-co-operation, I consider that such a proposal is inconsistent with the true spirit of non-co-operation. I have often said that a Government really thrives on obstruction, and so far as the proposal not to take the oath of allegiance is concerned, I can really see no meaning in it; it amounts to a useless waste of valuable time and money."

"In other words, obstruction is no stage in non-co-operation?"

"No."

"Are you satisfied that all efforts at constitutional agitation have been exhausted and that, non-co-operation is the only course left us?"

"I do not consider non-co-operation to be unconstitutional, but I do believe that of all the constitutional remedies now left open to us, non-co-operation is the only one left for us."

"Do you consider it constitutional to adopt it with a view merely to paralyze Government?"

"Certainly, it is not unconstitutional, but a prudent man will not take all the steps that are constitutional if they are otherwise undesirable, nor do I advise that course. I am resorting to non-co-operation in progressive stages because I want to evolve true order out of untrue order. I am not going to take a single step in non-co-operation unless I am satisfied that the country is ready for that step, namely, non-co-operation will not be followed by anarchy or disorder."

"How will you satisfy yourself that anarchy will not follow?"

"For instance, if I advise the police to lay down their arms, I shall have satisfied myself that we are able by voluntary assistance to protect ourselves against thieves and robbers. That was precisely what was done in Lahore and Amritsar last year by the citizens by means of volunteers when the military and the police had withdrawn. Even where Government had not taken such measures in a place, for want of adequate force, I know people have successfully protected themselves."

"You have advised lawyers to non-co-operate by suspending their practice. What is your experience? Has the lawyers' response to your appeal encouraged you to hope that you will be able to carry through all stages of non-co-operation with the help of such people?"

"I cannot say that a large number has yet responded to my appeal. It is too early to say how many will respond. But I may say that I do not rely merely upon the lawyer class or highly educated men to enable the Committee to carry out all the stages of non-co-operation. My hope lies more with the masses so far as the later stages of non-co-operation are concerned."

Young India, 18-8-'20

68

LOVE

I accept the interpretation of *ahimsa,* namely, that it is not merely a negative state of harmlessness but it is a positive state of love, of doing good even to the evil-doer. But it does not mean helping the evil-doer to continue the wrong or tolerating it by passive acquiescence. On the contrary, love, the active state of *ahimsa,* requires you to resist the wrong-doer by dissociating yourself from him even though it may offend him or injure him physically. Thus if my son lives a life of shame, I may not help him to do so by continuing to support him; on the contrary, my love for him requires me to withdraw all support from him although it may mean even his death. And the same love imposes on me the obligation of welcoming him to my bosom when he repents. But I may not by physical force compel my son to become good. That in my opinion is the moral of the story of the Prodigal Son.

Non-co-operation is not a passive state, it is an intensely active state — more active than physical resistance or violence. Passive resistance is a misnomer. Non-co-operation in the sense used by me must be non-violent and, therefore, neither punitive nor vindictive nor based on malice, ill-will or hatred. It follows therefore that it would be sin for me to serve General Dyer and co-operate with him to shoot innocent men. But it will be an exercise of forgiveness or love for me to nurse him back to life, if he was suffering from a physical malady. I would co-operate a thousand times with this Government to wean it from its career of crime, but I will not for a single moment co-operate with it to continue that career. And I would be guilty of wrong-doing if I retained a title from it or "a service under it or supported its Law Courts or schools." Better for me a beggar's bowl than the richest possession from hands stained with the blood of the innocents of Jalianwala. Better by far a warrant of imprisonment than honeyed words from those who have wantonly wounded the religious sentiment of my seventy million brothers.

Young India, 25-8-'20

69

THE POET'S ANXIETY

The Poet of Asia, as Lord Hardinge called Dr Tagore, is fast becoming, if he has not already become, the Poet of the world. Increasing prestige has brought to him increasing responsibility. His greatest service to India must be his poetic interpretation of India's message to the world. The Poet is, therefore, sincerely anxious that India should deliver no false or feeble message in her name. He is naturally jealous of his country's reputation. He says he has striven hard to find himself in tune with the present movement. He confesses that he is baffled. He can find nothing for his lyre in the din and the bustle of non-co-operation. In three forceful letters he has endeavoured to give expression to his misgivings, and he has come to the conclusion that non-co-operation is not dignified enough for the India of his vision, that it is a doctrine of negation and despair. He fears that it is a doctrine of separation, exclusiveness, narrowness and negation.

No Indian can feel anything but pride in the Poet's exquisite jealousy of India's honour. It is good that he should have sent to us his misgivings in language at once beautiful and clear.

In all humility I shall endeavour to answer the Poet's doubts. I may fail to convince him or the reader who may have been touched by his eloquence, but I would like to assure him and India that non-co-operation in conception is not any of the things he fears, and he need have no cause to be ashamed of his country for having adopted non-co-operation. If in actual application it appears in the end to have failed, it will be no more the fault of the doctrine, than it would be of Truth if those who claim to apply it in practice do not appear to succeed. Non-co-operation may have come in advance of its time. India and the world must then wait, but there is no choice for India save between violence and non-co-operation.

Nor need the Poet fear that non-co-operation is intended to erect a Chinese wall between India and the West. On the contrary, non-co-operation is intended to pave the way to real, honourable and voluntary co-operation based on mutual respect and trust. The present struggle is being waged against compulsory co-operation, against one-sided combination, against the armed imposition of modern methods of exploitation masquerading under the name of civilization.

Non-co-operation is a protest against an unwitting and unwilling participation in evil.

The Poet's concern is largely about the students. He is of opinion that they should not have been called upon to give up Government schools before they had other schools to go to. Here I must differ from him. I have never been able to make a fetish of literary training. My experience has proved to my satisfaction that literary training by itself adds not an inch to one's moral height and that character-building is independent of literary training. I am firmly of opinion that the Government schools have unmanned us, rendered us helpless and Godless. They have filled us with discontent, and providing no remedy for the discontent, have made us despondent. They have made us what we were intended to become — clerks and interpreters. A Government builds its prestige upon the apparently voluntary association of the governed. And if it was wrong to co-operate with the Government in keeping us slaves, we were bound to begin with those institutions in which our association appeared to be most voluntary. The youth of a nation are its hope. I hold that as soon as we discovered that the system of Government was wholly, or mainly evil, it became sinful for us to associate our children with it.

It is no argument against the soundness of the proposition laid down by me, that the vast majority of the students went back after the first flush of enthusiasm. Their recantation is proof rather of the extent of our degradation than of the wrongness of the step. Experience has shown that the establishment of national schools has not resulted in drawing many more students. The strongest and the truest of them came out without any national schools to fall back upon, and I am convinced that these first withdrawals are rendering service of the highest order.

But the Poet's protest against the calling out of the boys is really a corollary to his objection to the very doctrine of non-co-operation. He has a horror of everything negative. His whole soul seems to rebel against the negative commandments of religion. I must give his objection in his own inimitable language. " R. in support of the present movement has often said to me that passion for rejection is a stronger power in the beginning than the acceptance of an ideal. Though I know it to be a fact, I cannot take it as a truth.... *Brahmavidya* in India has for its object *mukti* (emancipation), while Buddhism has *nirvana* (extinction). *Mukti* draws our attention to the positive and *nirvana* to the negative side of truth. Therefore, he emphasized the fact of *duhkha* (misery) which had to be avoided and the *Brahmavidya* emphasized the fact of *ananda* (joy) which had to be attained." In these and kindred passages the reader will find the key to the Poet's mentality. In my humble opinion, rejection is as much an ideal as the acceptance of a thing. It is as necessary to reject untruth as it is to accept truth. All religions teach that two opposite forces act upon us and that the human endeavour consists in a series of eternal rejections and acceptances. Non-co-operation with evil is as much a duty as co-operation with good. I venture to suggest that the Poet has done an unconscious injustice to Buddhism in describing *nirvana* as merely a negative state. I make bold to say that *mukti* (emancipation) is as much a negative state as *nirvana*. Emancipation from or extinction of the bondage of the flesh leads to *ananda* (eternal bliss). Let me close this part of my argument by drawing attention to the fact that the final word of the *Upanishads* (*Brahmavidya*) is *Not*. *Neti* was the best description the authors of the *Upanishads* were able to find for *Brahman*.

I, therefore, think that the Poet has been unnecessarily alarmed at the negative aspect of non-co-operation. We had lost the power of saying 'no'. It had become disloyal, almost sacrilegious to say 'no' to the Government. This deliberate refusal to co-operate is like the necessary weeding process that a cultivator has to resort to before he sows. Weeding is as necessary to agriculture as sowing. Indeed, even whilst the crops are growing, the weeding fork, as every husbandman knows, is an instrument almost of daily use. The nation's non-co-operation is an invitation to the Government to co-operate with it on its own terms as is every nation's right and every good Government's duty. Non-co-operation is the nation's notice that it is no longer satisfied to be in tutelage. The nation has taken to the harmless (for it), natural and religious doctrine of non-co-operation in the place of the unnatural and irreligious doctrine of violence. And if India is ever to attain the Swaraj of the Poet's dream, she will do so only by non-violent non-co-operation. Let him deliver his message of peace to the world, and feel confident that India through her non-co-operation, if she remains true to her pledge, will have exemplified his message. Non-co-operation is intended to give the very meaning to patriotism that the Poet is yearning after. An India prostrate at the feet of Europe can give no hope to humanity. An India awakened and free has a message of peace and goodwill to a groaning world. Non-co-operation is designed to supply her with a platform from which she will preach the message.

Young India, 1-6-'21

70

WHAT IT IS NOT

"The situation in India illustrates another curious basis of difference between us. I hold to the 'non-resistance' idea. Gandhi, as I understand him, proclaims the Way of Love. And yet he does not see that 'Non-co-operation is a way of violence.' Suppose the milk drivers of New York had a real and just and even terrible grievance. Suppose that they should strike and cut off the milk supply from the babies of New York. They might never raise a hand in violent attack on any one and yet their way would be the way of violence. Over the dead bodies of little children they would by 'non-co-operation' win their victory. As Bertrand Russell said of the Bolsheviki, 'such suffering makes us question the means used to arrive at a desired end.' Non-co-operation means suffering in Lancashire and is an appeal in the end to violence rather than reason.

"This is not quite to the point and yet it does illustrate in a way what I have in mind. The advocates of Home Rule in India are now in the legislative bodies and there they propose to block progress by non-co-operative methods. In England, the country in which by historical accident civil institutions got a chance to develop, as John Fiske pointed out, through absence of war, the process of growth has been by the method of co-operation."

The above is an extract from an article in *Unity* (Feb. 14, '24) sent by an unknown American friend.

The article is a letter addressed to Mr Holmes by Mr Arthur I. Weatherly. The letter is an endeavour to show that an idealist, if he will be practical, has to water his ideal down to suit given circumstances. The writer has packed his letter with illustrations in support of his argument. As I am not for the moment concerned with his main argument, I hope I am doing no violence to him by merely giving an extract from his letter. My purpose is to show that Mr Weatherly's view of Indian non-co-operation cannot fail to be of general interest to the reader.

Mr Weatherly has laid down a universal proposition that ' non-co-operation is a way of violence.' A moment's thought would have shown the falsity of the proposition. I non-co-operate when I refuse to sell liquor in a liquor-shop, or help a murderer in his plans. My non-co-operation, I hold, is not only not a way of violence, but may be an act of love, if love is the motive that has prompted my refusal. The fact is that all non-co-operation is not violent, and non-violent non-co-operation can never be an act of violence. It may not be always an act of love. For love is an active quality which cannot always be inferred from the act itself. A surgeon may perform a most successful operation and yet he may have no love for his patient.

Mr Weatherly's illustration is most unhappy and incomplete for the purpose of examination. If the milk drivers of New York have a grievance against its Municipality for criminal mismanagement of its trust and if, in order to bend it, they decided to cut off the milk supply of the babies of New York, they would be guilty of a crime against humanity. But suppose that the milk drivers were underpaid by their employers, that they were consequently starving, they would be justified, if they have tried every other available and proper method of securing better wages, in refusing to drive the milk carts even though their action resulted in the death of the babies of New York. Their refusal will certainly not be an act of violence though it will not be an act of love. They were not philanthropists. They were driving milk carts for the sake of their maintenance. It was no part of their duty as employees under every circumstance to supply milk to babies. There is no violence when there is no infraction of duty. Suppose further that the milk drivers in question knew that their employers supplied cheap but adulterated milk and another dairy company supplied better but dearer milk and they felt for the welfare of the babies of New York, their refusal to drive the milk carts will be an act of love even though some short-sighted mother of New York might be deprived of the adulterated milk and may not have bought better but dearer milk from the more honest dairy company whose existence has been assumed for the purpose of our argument.

From the imaginary heartless milk drivers and the heaps of dead bodies of New York babies, the writer in *Unity* takes us to Lancashire and pictures its ruin when Indian non-co-operation has succeeded. In his haste to prove his main argument, the writer has hardly taken the trouble to study even simple facts. Indian non-co-operation is not designed to injure Lancashire or any other part of the British Isles. It has been undertaken to vindicate India's right to administer her own affairs. Lancashire's trade with India was established at the point of the bayonet and it is sustained by similar means. It has ruined the one vital cottage-industry which supplemented the resources of millions of India's peasants and kept starvation from their doors. If India now strives to revive her cottage industry and hand-spinning and refuses to buy any foreign cloth or even cloth manufactured by Indian mills and Lancashire or Indian mills suffer thereby, non-co-operation cannot by any law of morals be held to be an act of violence. India never bound herself to maintain Lancashire. Visitors to taverns or houses of ill fame would be congratulated on their self-restraint, and will be held even as benefactors of keepers of taverns or questionable houses, if they ceased to visit those places even without notice and even if their abstention resulted in the starvation of the keepers of those houses. Similarly, if customers of money-lenders ceased to borrow and the latter starved, the former cannot be regarded as violent by reason of their withdrawal. But they might be so considered if they transferred their custom from one money-lender to another through ill-will or spite and without just cause.

Thus it is clear that non-co-operation is not violence when the refusal of the restraint is a right and a duty even though by reason of its performance some people may have to suffer. It will be an act of love when non-co-operation is resorted to solely for the good of the wrong-doer. Indian non-co-operation is a right and a duty, but cannot be regarded as an act of love because it has been undertaken by a weak people in self-defence.

Young India, 10-4-'24

71

THE NON-CO-OPERATION OF A SATYAGRAHI

Q. It has been suggested in Bombay that you went to the Governor uninvited, in fact you forced yourself upon his attention. If so, was it not co-operation even without response ? What could you have to do with the Governor, I wonder ?

A. My answer is that I am quite capable even of forcing myself upon the attention of my opponent when I have strength. I did so in South Africa. I sought interviews after interviews with General Smuts when I knew that I was ready for battle. I pleaded with him to avoid the untold hardships that the Indian settlers must suffer, if the great historic march had to be undertaken. It is true that he in his haughtiness turned a deaf ear ; but I lost nothing. I gained added strength by my humility. So would I do in India when we are strong enough to put a real fight for freedom. Remember that ours is a non-violent struggle. It pre-supposes humility. It is a truthful struggle and consciousness of truth should give us firmness. We are not out to destroy men. We own no enemy. We have no ill-will against a single soul on earth. We mean to convert by our suffering. I do not despair of converting the hardest-hearted or the most selfish Englishman. Every opportunity of meeting him is, therefore, welcome to me.

Let me distinguish. Non-violent non-co-operation means renunciation of the benefits of a system with which we non-co-operate. We, therefore, renounce the benefits of schools, courts, titles, legislatures and offices set up under the system. The most extensive and permanent part of our non-co-operation consists in the renunciation of foreign cloth which is the foundation for the vicious system that is crushing us to dust. It is possible to think of other items of non-co-operation. But owing to our weakness or want of ability, we have restricted ourselves to these items only. If then I go to any official for the purpose of seeking the benefits above-named, I co-operate. Whereas if I go to the meanest official for the purpose of converting him, say to khaddar, or weaning him from his service or persuading him to withdraw his children from Government schools, I fulfil my duty as a non-co-operator. I should fail, if I did not go to him with that definite and direct purpose.

Young India, 27-5-'26

72

CIVIL DISOBEDIENCE

Civil disobedience was on the lips of every one of the members of the All India Congress Committee. Not having really ever tried it, every one appeared to be ena-moured of it from a mistaken belief in it as a sovereign remedy for our present-day ills. I feel sure that it can be made such if we can produce the necessary atmosphere for it. For individuals there always is that atmosphere except when their civil disobedience is certain to lead to bloodshed. I discovered this exception during the Satya-graha days. But even so a call may come which one dare not neglect, cost it what it may. I can clearly see the time coming to me when I *must* refuse obedience to every single State-made law, even though there may be a certainty of bloodshed. When neglect of the call means a denial of God, civil disobedience becomes a peremptory duty.

Mass civil disobedience stands on a different footing. It can only be tried in a calm atmosphere. It must be the calmness of strength not weakness, of knowledge not ignorance. Individual civil disobedience may be and often is vicarious. Mass civil disobedience may be and often is selfish in the sense that individuals expect personal gain from their disobedience. Thus in South Africa, Kallenbach and Polak offered vicarious civil disobedience. They had nothing to gain. Thousands offered it because they expected personal gain also in the shape, say, of the removal of the annual poll-tax levied upon ex-indentured men and their wives and grown-up children. It is sufficient in mass civil disobedience if the resisters understand the working of the doctrine.

It was in a practically uninhabited tract of country that I was arrested in South Africa when I was marching into prohibited area with over two to three thousand men and some women. The company included several Pathans and others who were able-bodied men. It was the greatest testimony of merit the Government of South Africa gave to the movement. They knew that we were as harmless as we were determined. It was easy enough for that body of men to cut to pieces those who arrested me. It would have not only been a most cowardly thing to do, but it would have been a treacherous breach of their own pledge, and it would have meant ruin to the struggle for freedom and the forcible deportation of every Indian from South Africa. But the men were no rabble. They were disciplined soldiers and all the better for being unarmed. Though I was torn from them, they did not disperse, nor did they turn back. They marched on to their destination till they were, every one of them, arrested and imprisoned. So far as I am aware, this was an instance of discipline and non-violence for which there is no parallel in history. Without such restraint I see no hope of successful mass civil disobedience here.

We must dismiss the idea of overawing the Government by huge demonstrations every time some one is arrested. On the contrary, we must treat arrest as the normal condition of the life of a non-co-operator. For we must seek arrest and imprisonment, as a soldier who goes to battle seeks death. We expect to bear down the opposition of the Government by courting and not by avoiding imprisonment, even though it be by showing our supposed readiness to be arrested and imprisoned *en masse*. Civil disobedience then emphatically means our desire to surrender to a single unarmed policeman. Our triumph consists in thousands being led to the prisons like lambs to the slaughter house. If the lambs of the world had been willingly led, they would have long ago saved themselves from the butcher's knife. Our triumph consists again in being imprisoned for no wrong whatsoever. The greater our innocence, the greater our strength and the swifter our victory.

As it is, this Government is cowardly, we are afraid of imprisonment. The Government takes advantage of our fear of gaols. If only our men and women welcome gaols as health-resorts, we will cease to worry about the dear ones put in gaols which our countrymen in South Africa used to nickname His Majesty's Hotels.

We have too long been mentally disobedient to the laws of the State and have too often surreptitiously evaded them, to be fit all of a sudden for civil disobedience. Disobedience to be civil has to be open and non-violent.

Complete civil disobedience is a state of peaceful rebellion — a refusal to obey every single State-made law. It is certainly more dangerous than an armed rebellion. For it can never be put down if the civil resisters are prepared to face extreme hardships. It is based upon an implicit belief in the absolute efficiency of innocent suffering. By noiselessly going to prison a civil resister ensures a calm atmosphere. The wrong-doer wearies of wrongdoing in the absence of resistance. All pleasure is lost when the victim betrays no resistance. A full grasp of the conditions of successful civil resistance is necessary at least on the part of the representatives of the people before we can launch out on an enterprise of such magnitude. The quickest remedies are always fraught with the greatest danger and require the utmost skill in handling them. It is my firm conviction that if we bring about a successful boycott of foreign cloth, we shall have produced an atmosphere that would enable us to inaugurate civil disobedience on a scale that no Government can resist. I would, therefore, urge patience and determined concentration on Swadeshi upon those who are impatient to embark on mass civil disobedience.

Young India, 4-8-'21

73

CIVIL DISOBEDIENCE

We dare not pin our faith solely on civil disobedience. It is like the use of a knife to be used most sparingly if at all. A man who cuts away without ceasing cuts at the very root, and finds himself without the substance he was trying to reach by cutting off the superficial hard crust. The use of civil disobedience will be healthy, necessary, and effective only if we otherwise conform to the laws of all growth. We must therefore give its full and therefore greater value to the adjective ' civil ' than to ' disobedience '. Disobedience without civility, discipline, discrimination, non-violence is certain destruction. Disobedience combined with love is the living water of life. Civil disobedience is a beautiful variant to signify growth, it is not discordance which spells death.

Young India, 5-1-'22

74

THE RIGHT OF CIVIL DISOBEDIENCE

I wish I could persuade everybody that civil disobedience is the inherent right of a citizen. He dare not give it up without ceasing to be a man. Civil disobedience is never followed by anarchy. Criminal disobedience can lead to it. Every State puts down criminal disobedience by force. It perishes, if it does not. But to put down civil disobedience is to attempt to imprison conscience. Civil disobedience can only lead to strength and purity. A civil resister never uses arms and hence he is harmless to a State that is at all willing to listen to the voice of public opinion. He is dangerous for an autocratic State, for he brings about its fall by engaging public opinion upon the matter for which he resists the State. Civil disobedience therefore becomes a sacred duty when the State has become lawless, or which is the same thing, corrupt. And a citizen that barters with such a State shares its corruption or lawlessness.

It is therefore possible to question the wisdom of applying civil disobedience in respect of a particular act or law ; it is possible to advise delay and caution. But the right itself cannot be allowed to be questioned. It is a birthright that cannot be surrendered without surrender of one's self-respect.

At the same time that the right of civil disobedience is insisted upon, its use must be guarded by all conceivable restrictions. Every possible provision should be made against an outbreak of violence or general lawlessness. Its area as well as its scope should also be limited to the barest necessity of the case.

Young India, 5-1-'22

AGGRESSIVE *v.* DEFENSIVE

It is now necessary to understand the exact distinction between aggressive civil disobedience and defensive. Aggressive, assertive or offensive civil disobedience is non-violent, wilful disobedience of laws of the State whose breach does not involve moral turpitude and which is undertaken as a symbol of revolt against the State. Thus disregard of laws relating to revenue or regulation of personal conduct for the convenience of the State, although such laws in themselves inflict no hardship and do not require to be altered, would be assertive, aggressive or offensive civil disobedience.

Defensive civil disobedience, on the other hand, is involuntary or reluctant non-violent disobedience of such laws as are in themselves bad and obedience to which would be inconsistent with one's self-respect or human dignity. Thus formation of volunteer corps for peaceful purposes, holding of public meetings for like purposes, publication of articles not contemplating or inciting to violence in spite of prohibitory orders, is defensive civil disobedience. And so is conducting of peaceful picketing undertaken with a view to wean people from things or institutions picketed in spite of orders to the contrary. The fulfilment of the conditions mentioned above is as necessary for defensive civil disobedience as for offensive civil disobedience.

Young India, 9-2-'22

MY FAITH

[Extract from Gandhiji's Presidential Address at the 39th Session of the Indian National Congress, Belgaum, Dec. 1924.]

Non-co-operation and civil disobedience are but different branches of the same tree called Satyagraha. It is my *Kalpadruma* — my *Jam-i-Jam* — the Universal Provider. Satyagraha is search for Truth ; and God is Truth. *Ahimsa* or non-violence is the light that reveals that Truth to me. Swaraj for me is part of that Truth. This Satyagraha did not fail me in South Africa, Kheda, or Champaran and in a host of other cases I could mention. It excludes all violence or hate. Therefore, I cannot and will not hate Englishmen. Nor will I bear their yoke. I must fight unto death the unholy attempt to impose British methods and British institutions on India. But I combat the attempt with non-violence. I believe in the capacity of India to offer non-violent battle to the English rulers. The experiment has not failed. It has succeeded, but not to the extent we had hoped and desired. I do not despair. On the contrary, I believe that India will come to her own in the near future, and that only through Satyagraha. The proposed suspension is part of the experiment. Non-co-operation need never be resumed if the programme sketched by me can be fulfilled. Non-violent non-co-operation in some form or other, whether through the Congress or without it, will be resumed if the programme fails. I have repeatedly stated that Satyagraha never fails and that one perfect Satyagrahi is enough to vindicate Truth. Let us all strive to be perfect Satyagrahis. The striving does not require any quality unattainable by the lowliest among us. For Satyagraha is an attribute of the spirit within. It is latent in every one of us. Like Swaraj it is our birthright. Let us know it.

Young India, 26-12-'24

SECTION FOURTH : VYKOM SATYAGRAHA

[The Vykom Satyagraha was undertaken in 1924 and 1925 to obtain permission for " untouchables " and " unapproachables " to use certain roads round about the temple in Vykom in Travancore, South India. — Ed.]

77

VYKOM

The anti-untouchability campaign at Vykom is providing an interesting study in Satyagraha, and as it is being conducted in a calm spirit, it must prove of great use for future workers along similar lines. The Travancore authorities, whilst they still remain unbending regarding the prohibition order, are carrying out their purpose in a courteous manner. The public already know how quickly the authorities tried to check violence against Satyagrahis. The treatment in the gaols too is in keeping with their conduct in the open.

Why Petition ?

Surprise has been expressed over the advice I have tendered to the Satyagrahis that whilst Satyagraha continues, the organizers should leave no stone unturned by way of petitions, public meetings, deputations, etc., in order to engage the support of the State and public opinion on their side. The critics argue that I am partial to the State authorities because they represent Indian rule, whereas I am hostile to the British authorities because they represent an alien rule. For me every ruler is alien that defies public opinion. In South Africa Indians continued to negotiate with the authorities up to the last moment even though Satyagraha was going on. In British India we are non-co-operating and we are doing so because we are bent on mending or ending the whole system of Government, and therefore the method of petition is a hopeless effort.

In Travancore the Satyagrahis are not attacking a whole system. They are not attacking it at any point at all. They are fighting sacerdotal prejudice. The Travancore State comes in by a side door as it were. Satyagrahis would therefore be deviating from their path if they did not try to court junction with the authorities and cultivate public support by means of deputations, meetings, etc. Direct action does not always preclude other consistent methods. Nor is petitioning etc. in every case a sign of weakness on the part of a Satyagrahi. Indeed he is no Satyagrahi who is not humble.

Some Implications

I have been also asked to develop the argument against sending aid apart from public sympathy from outside Travancore. I have already stated the utilitarian argument in an interview. But there is a root objection too to getting, indeed even accepting, such support. Satyagraha is either offered by a few self-sacrificing persons in the name of the many weak, or by very few in the face of enormous odds. In the former case, which is the case in Vykom, many are willing but weak, and a few are willing and capable of sacrificing their all for the cause of the " untouchables ". In such a case it is obvious they need no aid whatsoever. But suppose that they took outside aid, how would it serve the " untouchable " countrymen ? The weak Hindus in the absence of strong ones rising in their midst will not prevail against the strong opponents. The sacrifice of helpers from other parts of India will not convert the opponents and it is highly likely that the last state of the " untouchables " will be worse than the first. Let it be remembered that Satyagraha is a most powerful process of conversion. It is an appeal to the heart. Such an appeal cannot be successfully made by people from other parts of India flocking to Vykom.

Nor should a campaign conducted from within need outside monetary support. All the weak but sympathetic Hindus of Travancore may not court arrest and other suffering, but they can and should render such pecuniary assistance as may be needed. I could not understand their sympathy without such support.

In the case too of a very few offering Satyagraha against heavy odds, outside support is not permissible. Public Satyagraha is an extension of private or domestic Satyagraha. Every instance of public Satyagraha should be tested by imagining a parallel domestic case. Thus suppose in my family I wish to remove the curse of untouchability. Suppose further that my parents oppose the view, that I have the fire of the conviction of Prahlad, that my father threatens penalties, calls in even the assistance of the State to punish me. What should I do? May I invite my friends to suffer with me the penalties my father has devised for me? Or is it not up to me, meekly to bear all the penalties my father inflicts on me and absolutely rely on the law of suffering and love to melt his heart and open his eyes to the evil of untouchability? It is open to me to bring in the assistance of learned men, the friends of the family, to explain to my father what he may not understand from me his child. But I may allow no one to share with me the privilege and the duty of suffering. What is true of this supposed case of domestic Satyagraha is equally true and no less of the case we have imagined of public Satyagraha. Whether therefore the Vykom Satyagrahis represent a hopeless minority or as I have been informed a majority of the Hindus concerned, it is clear that they should avoid aid from outside save that of public sympathy. That in every such case we may not be able to conform to the law, that in the present case too, we may not be able to do so may be true. Let us not however forget the law and let us conform to it as far as ever we can.

Young India, 24-4-'24

78

VYKOM SATYAGRAHA

Vykom Satyagraha has attracted such wide public attention, and though restricted to a small area, presents so many problems for solution that I offer no apology to the reader for constantly engaging his attention for it.

I have received several important and well thought-out letters protesting against my countenancing it in any way whatsoever. One such letter even urges me to use whatever influence I may have, for stopping it altogether. I am sorry that I am unable to publish all these letters. But I hope to cover all the points raised in these letters or otherwise brought to my notice.

The first may be cleared at once. Exception has been taken to Mr George Joseph — a Christian — having been allowed to replace Mr Menon as leader and organizer. In my humble opinion the exception is perfectly valid. As soon as I heard that Mr Joseph was 'invited to take the lead' and he contemplated taking it, I wrote to him as follows on 6th April:

"As to Vykom, I think that you shall let the Hindus do the work. It is they who have to purify themselves. You can help by your sympathy and by your pen, but not by organizing the movement and certainly not by offering Satyagraha. If you refer to the Congress resolution of Nagpur, it calls upon the Hindu members to remove the curse of untouchability. I was surprised to learn from Mr Andrews that the disease had infected even the Syrian Christians."

Unfortunately before the letter could reach him, Mr Menon was arrested and Mr George Joseph had taken his place. But he had nothing to expiate, as every Hindu has, in the matter of untouchability as countenanced by the Hindus. His sacrifice cannot be appropriated by the Hindus in general as expiation made, say, by Malaviyaji would be. Untouchability is the sin of the Hindus. They must suffer for it, they must purify themselves, they must pay the debt they owe to their suppressed brothers and sisters. Theirs is the shame and theirs must be the glory when they have purged themselves of the black sin. The silent loving suffering of one single pure Hindu as such will be enough to melt the hearts of millions of Hindus; but the sufferings of thousands of non-Hindus on behalf of the "untouchables" will leave the Hindus unmoved. Their blind eyes will not be opened by outside inter- ference, however well-intentioned and generous it may be ; for it will not bring home to them the sense of guilt. On the contrary, they would probably hug the sin all the more for such interference. All reform to be sincere and lasting must come from within.

But why may the Vykom Satyagrahis not receive monetary aid from outside, especially if it be from Hindus ? So far as non-Hindu assistance is concerned, I am as clear about such pecuniary help as I am about such personal help. I may not build my Hindu temple with non-Hindu money. If I desire a place of worship I must pay for it. This removal of untouchability is much more than building a temple of brick and mortar. Hindus must bleed for it, must pay for it. *They* must be prepared to forsake wife, children and all for the sake of removing the curse. As for accepting assistance from Hindus from outside, such acceptance would betray unreadiness on the part of the local Hindus for the reform. If the Satyagrahis have the sympathy of the local Hindus, they must get locally all the money they may need. If they have not, the very few who may offer Satyagraha must be content to starve. If they are not, it is clear that they will evoke no sympathy among the local Hindus whom they want to convert. Satyagraha is a process of conversion. The reformers, I am sure, do not seek to force their views upon the community ; they strive to touch its heart. Outside pecuniary help must interfere with the love process if I may so describe the method of Satyagraha. Thus viewed the proposed Sikh free kitchen, I can only regard, as a menace to the frightened Hindus of Vykom.

There is no doubt in my mind about it that the orthodox Hindus who still think that worship of God is inconsistent with touching a portion of their own co-religionists, and that a religious life is summed up in ablutions and avoidance of physical pollutions merely, are alarmed at the developments of the movement at Vykom. They believe that their religion is in danger. It behoves the organizers, therefore, to set even the most orthodox and the most bigoted at ease and to assure them that they do not seek to bring about the reform by compulsion. The Vykom Satyagrahis must stoop to conquer. They must submit to insults and worse at the hands of the bigoted and yet love them, if they will change their hearts.

But a telegram says in effect, ' the authorities are barricading the roads ; may we not break or scale the fences ? May we not fast ? For we find that fasting is effective.'

My answer is : If we are Satyagrahis, we dare not scale or break fences. Breaking or scaling fences will certainly bring about imprisonment but the breaking will not be civil disobedience. It will be essentially incivil and criminal. Nor may we fast. I observe that my letter to Mr Joseph with reference to fasting has been misunderstood. For the sake of ready reference I reproduce below the relevant part :

" ' Omit fasting but stand or squat in relays with quiet submission till arrested.'

" The above is the wire sent to you in reply to yours. Fasting in Satyagraha has well-defined limits. You cannot fast against a tyrant, for it will be a species of violence done to him. You invite penalty from him for disobedience of his orders but you cannot inflict on yourselves penalties when he refuses to punish and renders it impossible for you to disobey his orders so as to compel infliction of penalty. Fasting can only be resorted to against a lover, not to extort rights but to reform him, as when a son fasts for a father who drinks. My fast at Bombay and then at Bardoli was of that character. I fasted to reform those who loved me. But I will not fast to reform, say, General Dyer, who not only does not love me but who regards himself as my enemy. Am I quite clear ? "

It need not be pointed out that the above remarks are of a general character. The words *tyrant* and *lover* have also a general application. The one who does an injustice is styled ' tyrant '. The one who is in sympathy with you is the ' lover '. In my opinion, in the Vykom movement opponents of the reform are the ' tyrant '. The State may or may not be that. In this connection I have considered the State as merely the police striving to keep the peace. In no case is the State or the opponents in the position of ' lover '. The supporters of Vykom Satyagrahis enjoy that status. There are two conditions attached to a Satyagrahi fast. It should be against the lover and for his reform, not for extorting rights from him. The only possible case in the Vykom movement when a fast will be justified, would be when the local supporters go back upon their promise to suffer. I can fast against my father to cure him of a vice, but I may not in order to get from him an inheritance. The beggars of India who sometimes fast against those who do not satisfy them are no more Satyagrahis than children who fast against a parent for a fine dress. The former are impudent, the latter are childish. My Bardoli fast was against fellow-workers who ignited the Chauri-chaura spark and for the sake of reforming them. If the Vykom Satyagrahis fast because the authorities will not arrest them, it will be, I must say in all humility, the beggar's fast described above. If it proves effective, it shows the goodness of the authorities, not that of the cause or of the actors. A Satyagrahi's first concern is not the effect of his action. It must always be its propriety. He must have faith enough in his cause and his means, and know that success will be achieved in the end.

Some of my correspondents object altogether to Satyagraha in an Indian State. In this matter too, let me quote the remaining portion of my foregoing letter to Mr Joseph :

"You must be patient. You are in an Indian State. Therefore, you may wait in deputation on the Dewan and the Maharaja. Get up a monster petition by the orthodox Hindus who may be well-disposed towards the movement. See also those who are opposing. You can support the gentle direct action in a variety of ways. You have already drawn public attention to the matter by preliminary Satyagraha. Above all see to it that it neither dies nor by impatience becomes violent."

Satyagraha in an Indian State by the Congress for the attainment of its object is, I think, clearly forbidden. But Satyagraha in an Indian State in connection with local abuses may be legitimately taken up at any time provided the other necessary conditions are fulfilled. As in an Indian State there can be no question of non-co-operation, the way of petitions and deputations is not only always open, but it is obligatory. But, say some of my correspondents, the conditions for lawful Satyagraha do not exist in Vykom. They ask :

1. Is unapproachability exclusively observed at Vykom or is it general throughout Kerala ?

2. If it is general, then what is the special reason for selecting Vykom in preference to places within the British territory in Kerala ?

3. Did the Satyagrahis petition the Maharaja, the local Assembly etc. ?

4. Did they consult the orthodox sections ?

5. Is not the use of the road the thin end of the wedge, is it not a step towards the abolition of caste altogether ?

6. Is not the road a private road ?

The first two questions are irrelevant. Unapproachability and untouchability have to be tackled wherever they exist. Wherever the workers consider a place or time suitable, it is their duty to start work whether by Satyagraha or other legitimate means.

My information goes to show that the method of petition etc. was tried not once but often.

They did consult the orthodox people and thought that they had the latter's support.

I am assured that the use of the road is the final goal of the Satyagrahis. It is however not to be denied that the present movement throughout India is to throw open to the suppressed classes all the *public* roads, *public* schools, *public* wells and *public* temples which are accessible to non-Brahmins.

It is in fact a movement to purify caste by ridding it of its most pernicious result. I personally believe in Varnashrama, though it is true that I have my own meaning for it. Any way, anti-untouchability movement does not aim at inter-dining or inter-marrying. Those who mix up the touch and the last two things together are doing harm to the cause of the suppressed classes as also to that of inter-dining and inter-marriage.

I have letters which protest that the road in question is a public road. In fact my informants tell me it was some years ago even accessible to the " unapproachables " as to other non-Brahmins.

In my opinion, therefore, there is a just cause for the Vykom Satyagraha and so far as it is kept within proper limits and conducted with the strictest regard to non-violence and truth, it deserves full public sympathy.

Young India, 1-5-'24

79

VYKOM SATYAGRAHA

His Holiness Shri Narayan Guru, spiritual leader of the Tiyas, is reported to have disapproved of the present methods of Satyagraha at Vykom. He suggests that volunteers should advance along barricaded roads and scale the barricades. They should enter temples and sit with others to dine. Though I have compressed the interview I have reproduced almost the exact words. Now the action proposed is not Satyagraha. For scaling barricades is open violence. If you may scale barricades, why not break open temple doors and even pierce through temple walls ? How are volunteers to pierce through a row of policemen except by using physical force ? I do not for one moment suggest that by the methods proposed the Tiyas if they are strong and are willing to die in sufficient numbers cannot gain their point. All I submit is that they will have gained it by something the reverse of Satyagraha ; and then too they would not have converted the orthodox to their view but would have imposed it on them by force. A friend who has sent me the press cutting recording the interview suggests that by reason of the violent advice of the *Guru* I should ask the local Congress committee to call off Satyagraha. I feel that would mean want of faith in one's means and surrender to violence. So long as the organizers strictly keep within the limits which they have prescribed for themselves there is no cause for calling off Satyagraha. The friend cites Chaurichaura as an illustration. In doing so, he has betrayed confusion of thought or ignorance of facts. The Bardoli Satyagraha was suspended because Congress and Khilafat men were implicated in the Chaurichaura outrage. If Congressmen connected with the Vykom movement entertain the suggestions said to be favoured by the Tiya spiritual leader, there would be a case for penance and therefore suspension but not otherwise. I would therefore urge the organizers at Vykom to make redoubled efforts and at the same time keep stricter watch on the conduct of those who take part in the movement. Whether it takes long or short to reach the goal, the way is the way of peaceful conversion of the orthodox by self-suffering and self-purification and no other.

Young India, 19-6-'24

80

VYKOM

The Vykom Satyagraha has entered upon probably the last stage. The newspapers report — and the report is confirmed by private advice — that the Travancore authorities have now practically abandoned the Satyagrahis to the tender mercies of *goondas*. This is euphemistically called the organized opposition of the orthodox section. Every one knows that orthodoxy is often unscrupulous. It has as a rule prestige and public opinion behind it in comparison with the reformer. It, therefore, does things with impunity which the poor reformer dare not. But what baffles one is the attitude of the Travancore authorities. Are they conniving at this open violence against the innocent Satyagrahis? Has such an advanced State like Travancore abdicated its elementary function of protection of life and property? The violence of the *goondas* is said to be of a particularly barbarous type. They blind the eyes of volunteers by throwing lime into them.

The challenge of the *goondas* must be taken up. But the Satyagrahis must not lose their heads. The khaddar dress of the volunteers is said to have been torn from them and burnt. This is all most provoking. They must remain cool under every provocation and courageous under the hottest fire. Loss even of a few hundred lives will not be too great a price to pay for the freedom of the "unapproachables". Only the martyrs must die clean. Satyagrahis like Caesar's wife must be above suspicion.

Young India, 3-7-'24

81

VYKOM SATYAGRAHA

The Vykom Satyagraha has perhaps a meaning deeper than is generally realized. The young men who have organized it are stern in discipline and gentle in their dealings with the orthodox section. But this is the least part of their trials. Some of them are suffering too the persecution of social boycott. We of the western presidency have no idea of what this persecution can mean. These young men who are taking part in the movement are not only being denied social amenities but are threatened even with the deprivation of their share in the family property. If they would go to law, probably they would get their due. But a Satyagrahi cannot go to law for a personal wrong. He sets out with the idea of suffering persecution. In a reform that the Vykom struggle seeks to achieve, the Satyagrahi seeks to convert his opponent by sheer force of character and suffering. The purer he is and the more he suffers, the quicker the progress. He must therefore resign himself to being excommunicated, debarred from the family privileges and deprived of his share in the family property. He must not only bear such hardships cheerfully but he must actively love his persecutors. The latter honestly believe that the reformer is doing something sinful and, therefore, resort to the only means they know to be effective to wean him from his supposed error. The Satyagrahi on the other hand does not seek to carry out his reform by a system of punishments but by penance, self-purification and suffering. Any resentment of the persecution, therefore, would be an interruption of the course of discipline he has imposed upon himself. It may be a prolonged course, it may even seem to be never-ending. A little bullying or even moral suasion or coercion may appear more expeditious. What, however, I am showing here is not the greater efficacy of Satyagraha but the implications of the method the Satyagrahi has deliberately chosen for himself. Indeed I have often shown in these pages that Satyagraha is, as a matter of fact and in the long run, the most expeditious course. But my purpose here is merely to show what the young Satyagrahis of Vykom are doing. The public know much of what they are doing in the shape of picketing, but they know nothing of the silent suffering some of them are undergoing at the hands of their families and caste-men. But I know that it is this silent and loving suffering which will finally break the wall of prejudice. I am anxious therefore that the reformers should realize their responsibility to the full and not swerve by a hair's breadth from their self-imposed discipline.

Young India, 18-9-'24

82

VYKOM SATYAGRAHA

[Extract from Gandhiji's reply to a letter from a Vykom Satyagrahi.]

Satyagrahis must not be dejected. They dare not give way to despair. Of all my Tamil lessons one proverb at least abides with me as an evergreen. Its literal meaning is, " God is the only Help for the helpless." The grand theory of Satyagraha is built upon a belief in that truth. Hindu religious literature, indeed all religious literature, is full of illustrations to prove the truth. The Travancore Durbar may have failed them. I may fail them. But God will never fail them, if they have faith in Him. Let them know that they are leaning on a broken reed if they are relying on me. I am living at a safe distance from them. I may wipe their tears, but suffering is their sole privilege. And victory will surely come out of their sufferings provided they are pure. God tries His votaries through and through, but never beyond endurance. He gives them strength enough to go through the ordeal He prescribes for them. For the Satyagrahis of Vykom their Satyagraha is not a mere experiment to be given up if it does not succeed within a prescribed time or after a prescribed force of suffering. There is no time limit for a Satyagrahi nor is there a limit to his capacity for suffering. Hence there is no such thing as defeat in Satyagraha. Their so-called defeat may be the dawn of victory. It may be the agony of birth.

The Vykom Satyagrahis are fighting a battle of no less consequence than that of Swaraj. They are fighting against an age-long wrong and prejudice. It is supported by orthodoxy, superstition, custom and authority. Theirs is only one among the many battles that must be fought in the holy war against irreligion masquerading as religion, ignorance appearing in the guise of learning. If their battle is to be bloodless, they must be patient under the severest trials. They must not quail before a raging fire.

The Congress Committee may give them no help. They may get no pecuniary help, they may have to starve. Their faith must shine through all these dark trials.

Theirs is 'direct action'. They dare not be irritated against their opponents. They know no better. They are not all dishonest men as Satyagrahis are not all honest men. They are resisting what they honestly believe to be an encroachment upon their religion. The Vykom Satyagraha is the argument of suffering. The hardest heart and the grossest ignorance must disappear before the rising sun of suffering without anger and without malice.

Young India, 19-2-'25

VYKOM SATYAGRAHA

I cannot help endorsing the remark of Dewan Bahadur T. Raghaviah that "there is a world of difference between Satyagraha meant to be an educative force and Satyagraha intended as an instrument for the coercion of the Government and through them of the orthodox Hindu. What the Satyagrahis should aim at is the conversion of the orthodox to whom untouchability is part of their faith." I make bold to state that from the very outset Satyagraha at Vykom was intended to be an educative force and never an instrument of coercion of the orthodox. It was for that reason that the fast against the orthodox was abandoned. It was to avoid coercion of the Government by embarrassment that the barricades have been scrupulously respected. It was for that reason that no attempt was made to dodge the Police. It has been recognized that what appears to the reformers as a gross and sinful superstition is to the orthodox a part of their faith. The Satyagrahi's appeal has therefore been to the reason of the orthodox. But experience has shown that mere appeal to the reason produces no effect upon those who have settled convictions. The eyes of their understanding are opened not by argument but by the suffering of the Satyagrahi. The Satyagrahi strives to reach the reason through the heart. The method of reaching the heart is to awaken public opinion. Public opinion for which one cares is a mightier force than that of gunpowder. The Vykom Satyagraha has vindicated itself in that it has drawn the attention of the whole of India to the cause and it has been instrumental in the Travancore Assembly considering in a remarkable debate a resolution favouring the reform sought for and lastly in eliciting a considered reply from the Dewan of Travancore. I am sure that victory is a certainty if only the Satyagrahis will retain their patience and their spirit of suffering.

Young India, 19-3-'25

SATYAGRAHI'S DUTY

[The following is almost a verbatim report of the quiet talk I gave to the inmates of the Satyagraha Ashram at Vykom. The Ashram has at the present moment over fifty volunteers who stand or squat in front of the four barricades which are put up to guard the four entrances to the Vykom temple. They spin whilst they are stationed there and remain there at a stretch for six hours. They are sent in two relays. I reproduce the talk as being of general interest and applicable to all Satyagrahis.   —M. K. G.]

I want to tell you as briefly as I can what I expect of you. I would ask you to forget the political aspect of the programme. Political consequences of this struggle there are, but you are not to concern yourself with them. If you do, you will miss the true result and also miss the political consequences, and when the real heat of the struggle is touched you will be found wanting. I am therefore anxious, even if it frightens you, to explain to you the true nature of the struggle. It is a struggle deeply religious for the Hindus. We are endeavouring to rid Hinduism of its greatest blot. The prejudice we have to fight against is an age-long prejudice. The struggle for the opening of the roads round the temple which we hold to be public to the "unapproachables" is but a small skirmish in the big battle. If our struggle was to end with the opening of the roads in Vykom you may be sure I would not have bothered my head about it. If, therefore, you think that the struggle is to end with opening of the roads in Vykom to the "unapproachables" you are mistaken. The road must be opened. It has got to be opened. But that will be the beginning of the end. The end is to get all such roads throughout Travancore to be opened to the "unapproachables"; and not only that, but we expect that our efforts may result in amelioration of the general condition of the "untouchables" and "unapproachables". That will require tremendous sacrifice. For our aim is not to do things by violence to

192

opponents. That will be conversion by violence or compulsion; and if we import compulsion in matters of religion, there is no doubt that we shall be committing suicide. We should carry on this struggle on the lines of strict non-violence, i.e. by suffering in our own persons. That is the meaning of Satyagraha. The question is whether you are capable of every suffering that may be imposed upon you or may be your lot in the journey towards the goal. Even whilst you are suffering you may have no bitterness — no trace of it — against your opponents. And I tell you it is not a mechanical act at all. On the contrary I want you to feel like loving your opponents, and the way to do it is to give them the same credit for honesty of purpose which you would claim for yourself. I know that it is a difficult task. I confess that it was a difficult task for me yesterday whilst I was talking to those friends who insisted on their right to exclude the "unapproachables" from the temple roads. I confess there was selfishness behind their talk. How then was I to credit them with honesty of purpose? I was thinking of this thing yesterday and also this morning, and this is what I did. I asked myself: 'Wherein was their selfishness or self-interest? It is true that they have their ends to serve. But so have we our ends to serve. Only we consider our ends to be pure and, therefore, selfless. But who is to determine where selflessness ends and selfishness begins? Selflessness may be the purest form of selfishness.' I do not say this for the sake of argument. But that is what I really feel. I am considering their condition of mind from their point of view and not my own. Had they not been Hindu they would not have talked as they did yesterday. And immediately we begin to think of things as our opponents think of them, we shall be able to do them full justice. I know that this requires a detached state of mind, and it is a state very difficult to reach. Nevertheless for a Satyagrahi it is absolutely essential. Three-fourths of the miseries and misunderstandings in the world will disappear, if we step into the shoes of our adversaries and understand their

standpoint. We will then agree with our adversaries
quickly or think of them charitably. In our case there is
no question of our agreeing with them quickly as our
ideals are radically different. But we may be charitable
to them and believe that they actually mean what they
say. They do not want to open the roads to the " unapproachables ". Now whether it is their self-interest or
ignorance that tells them to say so, we really believe that
it is wrong of them to say so. Our business, therefore,
is to show them that they are in the wrong and we should
do so by *our* suffering. I have found that mere appeal
to reason does not answer where prejudices are age-long
and based on supposed religious authority. Reason has
to be strengthened by suffering and suffering opens the
eyes of understanding. Therefore, there must be no trace
of compulsion in our acts. We must not be impatient,
and we must have an undying faith in the means we are
adopting. The means we are adopting just now are that
we approach the four barricades, and as we are stopped,
there we sit down and spin away from day to day, and we
must believe that through it the roads must be opened. I
know that it is a difficult and slow process. But if you
believe in the efficacy of Satyagraha, you will rejoice in this
slow torture and suffering, and you will not feel the discomfort of your position as you go and sit in the boiling
sun from day to day. If you have faith in the cause and
the means and in God the hot sun will be cool for you. You
must not be tired and say, ' how long ', and never get
irritated. That is only a small portion of your penance for
the sin for which Hinduism is responsible.

I regard you as soldiers in this campaign. It is not
possible for you to reason out things for yourselves. You
have come to the Ashram because you have faith in the
management. That does not mean faith in me. For I am
not manager. I am directing the movement, so far as
ideals and general direction are concerned. Your faith
therefore must be in those who are managers for the time
being. The choice before coming to the Ashram was
yours. But having made your choice and come to the

Ashram it is not for you to reason why. If we are to become a powerful nation you must obey all directions that may be given to you from time to time. That is the only way in which either political or religious life can be built up. You must have determined for yourselves certain principles and you must have joined the struggle in obedience to these principles. Those who remain in the Ashram are taking as much part in the struggle as those who go and offer Satyagraha at the barricades. Every piece of work in connection with the struggle is just as important as any other piece, and, therefore, the work of sanitation in the Ashram is just as important as spinning away at the barricades. And if in this place the work of cleaning the closets and compound is more distasteful than spinning it should be considered far more important and profitable. Not a single minute should be wasted in idle conversation, but we must be absorbed in the work before us, and if every one of us works in that spirit you will see that there is pleasure in the work itself. Every bit of property, any thing in the Ashram should be regarded by you as your own property and not property that can be wasted at pleasure. You may not waste a grain of rice or a scrap of paper, and similarly a minute of your time. It is not ours. It belongs to the nation and we are trustees for the use of it.

I know that all this will sound hard and difficult for you. My presentation may be hard, but it has not been possible for me to present the thing in any other way. For it will be wrong on my part if I deceive you or myself in believing that this is an easy thing.

Much corruption has crept into our religion. We have become lazy as a nation, we have lost the time sense. Selfishness dominates our action. There is mutual jealousy amongst the tallest of us. We are uncharitable to one another. And if I did not draw your attention to the things I have, it will not be possible for us to rid ourselves of all these evils. Satyagraha is a relentless search for truth and a determination to reach truth. I can only hope you will realize the import of what you are doing. And if you do, your path will be easy — easy because you will take delight in difficulties and you will laugh in hope when everybody is in despair. I believe in the illustrations the *rishis* or poets have given in religious books. For example, I literally believe in the possibility of a Sudhanva smiling away whilst he was being drowned in the boiling oil. For to him it was greater torture to forget his Maker than to be in boiling oil. And so it can be in a lesser measure here, if we have a spark of Sudhanva's faith in this struggle.

Young India, 19-3-'25

85

VYKOM

And now for the "unapproachables" miscalled. I understand that they are getting restive. They have a right to do so. I am further told that they are losing faith in Satyagraha. If so, their want of faith betrays ignorance of the working of Satyagraha. It is a force that works silently and apparently slowly. In reality, there is no force in the world that is so direct or so swift in working. But sometimes apparent success is more quickly attained by brute force. To earn one's living by body-labour is a method of earning it by Satyagraha. A gamble on the stock-exchange or house-breaking, either of which is the reverse of Satyagraha, may apparently lead to an instantaneous acquisition of wealth. But the world has by now, I presume, realized that gambling and house-breaking are no methods of earning one's livelihood, and that they do harm rather than good to the gambler or the thief. The "unapproachables" may force their way by engaging in a free fight with the superstitious *savarnas* but they will not have reformed Hinduism. Theirs will be a method of forcible conversion. But I am further told that some of them even threaten to seek shelter in Christianity, Islam or Buddhism if relief is not coming soon. Those who use the threat do not, in my humble opinion, know the meaning of religion. Religion is a matter of life and death. A man does not change religion as he changes his garments. He takes it with him beyond the grave. Nor does a man profess his religion to oblige others. He professes a religion because he cannot do otherwise. A faithful husband loves his wife as he would love no other woman. Even her faithlessness would not wean him from his faith. The bond is more than blood-relationship. So is the religious bond if it is worth anything. It is a matter of the heart. An "untouchable" who loves his Hinduism in the face of persecution at the hands of those Hindus who arrogate to themselves a superior status is a better Hindu than the self-styled superior Hindu, who by the very act of claiming superiority denies his Hinduism. Therefore, those who threaten to renounce Hinduism are in my opinion betraying their faith.

But the Satyagrahi's course is plain. He must stand unmoved in the midst of all these cross-currents. He may not be impatient with blind orthodoxy, nor be irritated over the unbelief of the suppressed people. He must know that his suffering will melt the stoniest heart of the stoniest fanatic and that it will also be a wall of protection for the wavering *panchama* brother who has been held under suppression for ages. He must know that relief will come when there is the least hope for it. For such is the way of that cruelly kind Deity who insists upon testing His devotees through a fiery furnace and delights in humbling him to the dust. In his hour of distress let the Satyagrahi recall to his mind the prayer of the fabled godly Elephant King who was saved only when he thought he was at his last gasp.

86

TRUE SATYAGRAHA

For a long time I have purposely refrained from writing anything in these columns about Vykom and its struggle against unapproachability. Nor do I want as yet to say anything directly bearing on it. But I do want to tell the reader how the Satyagrahis at Vykom are passing their time.

A letter was received at Calcutta from Vykom dated the 1st of August. It has remained unpublished through oversight. But the substance of it is as fresh today as it was when it was received. I reproduce it below :

" Now there are only ten volunteers including myself. One of us daily does the kitchen-work while others except one offer Satyagraha for three hours each. Including the time taken to go and return the time for Satyagraha comes to four hours. We regularly get up at 4-30 a.m. and prayer takes half an hour. From 5 to 6 we have sweeping, drawing water and cleaning vessels. By seven all of us except two (who go for Satyagraha at 5-45 after bath) return after bath and spin or card till it is time for going to the barricade. Most of us regularly give 1,000 yards each per day and some of us even more. The average output is over 10,000 yards per day. I do not insist on our doing any work on Sundays when each does according to his will. Some of us card and spin for two or three more hours on Sundays too. Anyhow no yarn is returned on Sundays. Those who are Congress members spin for the Congress franchise on Sundays. Some of us are now spinning on Sundays and other spare hours for our humble gift towards All India Deshabandhu Memorial Fund which you have instituted. We wish to pack a small bundle of yarn to you on the 4th September (G. O. M. Centenary Day). I hope you will be glad to receive it. This we shall spin apart from our routine work. We mean either to beg or to spin the whole of that auspicious day and to send whatever is obtained. We have not yet settled what we should do."

This shows that the Satyagrahis of Vykom have understood the spirit of their work. There is no bluster, there is no fireworks display ; but there is here a simple determination to conquer by exact conduct. A Satyagrahi should be able to give a good account of every minute at his disposal. This the Vykom Satyagrahis are doing. The reader cannot fail to notice the honesty in spinning Congress yarn, and the yarn for the G. O. M. Centenary during their off day. The idea too of spinning for the All India Deshabandhu Memorial is in keeping with the rest of their doings. The letter before me gives me details of each member's spinning during the preceding week omitting Sunday. The largest quantity spun by a single inmate is 6,895 yards of 17 counts. The lowest is 2,936 yards of 18 counts. The remark against his name is that he was absent on leave for three days. The average per man per day during that week was 866.6 yards. I have also before me the figures for the week ending 26th August. The highest during that week was 7,700 for a single individual, and the lowest was 2,000, the spinner having spun only two days during the week. The reader may ask what connection is there between the removal of untouchability and spinning. Apparently nothing. In reality much. It is not any single isolated act which can be called Satyagraha apart from the spirit behind. Here, there is the spirit behind the spinning which is bound to tell in the long run ; for, spinning to these young men is a sacrificial national act calculated unconsciously to exhibit true humility, patience and pertinacity — qualities indispensable for clean success.

Young India, 24-9-'25

87

VYKOM SATYAGRAHA

Hindu reformers who are intent on removal of untouchability should understand the implications of Vykom Satyagraha and its results. The immediate goal of the Satyagrahis was the opening of the roads surrounding the temple, not their entry into the latter. Their contention was that the roads should be opened to the so-called untouchables as they were to all other Hindus and even non-Hindus. That point has been completely gained. But whilst Satyagraha was directed to the opening of roads, the ultimate aim of reformers is undoubtedly removal of every disability that " the untouchables " are labouring under and which the other Hindus are not. It, therefore, includes access to temples, wells, schools etc. to which other non-Brahmins are freely admitted. But for achieving these reforms much remains to be done before the method of direct action can be adopted. Satyagraha is never adopted abruptly and never till all other and milder methods have been tried. The reformers of the South have to cultivate public opinion in the matter of temple-entry etc. This is, moreover, a disability not peculiar to the South but unfortunately and, to our shame, it must be admitted, common, to more or less extent, to Hinduism throughout India. I, thereore, welcome the decision of Sjt. Kellappen Nayar who was in charge of the camp at Vykom to concentrate his effort on working among the unhappiest and the most suppressed among " the untouchables ", i.e., Puliyas whose very shadow defiles. It is a golden rule to follow out every direct action with constructive work, i.e., work of conservation. Reform has to be undertaken at both ends to make *savarnas* do their duty by the " untouchables " whom they have so cruelly suppressed and to help the latter to become more presentable and to shed habits for which they can in no way be held accountable but which nevertheless have to be given up if they are to occupy their proper place in the social scale.

88

SATYAGRAHA *v.* COMPULSION

An earnest but impatient worker has been trying to have temples and public places thrown open to Harijans. He had some success but nothing to be proud of. In his impatience, therefore, he writes :

> "It is no use waiting for these orthodox men to make a beginning. They will never move unless compelled to do so. Drastic steps are required to wipe off untouchability. I therefore beg you to kindly favour me with your opinion if Satyagraha at the entrance of the temples, by workers and Harijans preventing orthodox persons from entering the temples, will be an effective method. Appeals and entreaties have produced no effect, and to lose more time on these will, in my humble opinion, be sheer waste of valuable time."

Such blocking the way will be sheer compulsion. And there should be no compulsion in religion or in matters of any reform. The movement for the removal of untouchability is one of self-purification. No man can be purified against his will. Therefore, there can be no force directly or indirectly used against the orthodox. It should be remembered that many of us were like the orthodox people before our recognition of the necessity of the removal of untouchability. We would not then have liked anybody to block our way to the temples, because we in those days believed, no doubt wrongly as we now think, that Harijans should not be allowed to enter temples. Even so may we not block the way of the orthodox to the temples.

I should also remind correspondents that the word Satyagraha is often most loosely used and is made to cover veiled violence. But as the author of the word I may be allowed to say that it excludes every form of violence, direct or indirect, veiled or unveiled, and whether in thought, word or deed. It is breach of Satyagraha to wish ill to an opponent or to say a harsh word to him or of him with the intention of harming him. And often the evil thought or the evil word may, in terms of Satyagraha, be more dangerous than actual violence used in the heat of the moment and perhaps repented and forgotten the next moment. Satyagraha is gentle, it never wounds. It must not be the result of anger or malice. It is never fussy, never impatient, never vociferous. It is the direct opposite of compulsion. It was conceived as a complete substitute for violence.

Nevertheless, I fully agree with the correspondent that 'most drastic steps are required to wipe off untouchability'. But these steps have to be taken against ourselves. The orthodox people sincerely believe that untouchability, as they practise it, is enjoined by the *Shastras* and that great evil will befall them and Hinduism if it was removed. How is one to cope with this belief? It is clear that they will never change their belief by being compelled to admit Harijans to their temples. What is required is not so much the entry of Harijans to the temples as the conversion of the orthodox to the belief that it is wrong to prevent Harijans from entering the temples. This conversion can only be brought about by an appeal to their hearts, i.e. by evoking the best that is in them. Such an appeal can be made by the appellants' prayers, fasting and other suffering in their own persons, in other words, by their ever increasing purity. It has never yet been known to fail. For it is its own end. The reformer must have consciousness of the truth of his cause. He will not then be impatient with the opponent, he will be impatient with himself. He must be prepared even to fast unto death. Not every one has the right or the capacity to do so. God is most exacting. He exacts humility from His votaries. Even fasts may take the form of coercion. But there is nothing in the world that in human hands does not lend itself to abuse. The human being is a mixture of good and evil, Jekyll and Hyde. But there is the least likelihood of abuse when it is a matter of self-suffering.

Harijan, 15-4-'33

89

RELIGIOUS SATYAGRAHA

Mixing up of motives is damaging in any species of Satyagraha; but in religious Satyagraha it is altogether inadmissible. It is fatal to use or allow religious Satyagraha to be used as a cloak or a device for advancing an ulterior political or mundane objective.

As with regard to the goal so with the means, unadulterated purity is of the very essence in this species of Satyagraha. The leader in such a movement must be a man of deeply spiritual life, preferably a *brahmachari* — whether married or unmarried. He must be a believer in — as in fact everybody participating in such a movement must be — and practiser of the particular religious observance for which the movement is launched. The leader must be versed in the science of Satyagraha. Truth and *ahimsa* should shine through his speech. All his actions must be transparent through and through. Diplomacy and intrigue can have no place in his armoury.

Absolute belief in *ahimsa* and in God is an indispensable condition in such Satyagraha.

In religious Satyagraha there can be no room for aggressiveness, demonstrativeness, show. Those who take part in it must have equal respect and regard for the religious convictions and susceptibilities of those who profess a different faith from theirs. The slightest narrowness in their outlook is likely to be reflected magnified multifold in the opponent.

Religious Satyagraha is, above all, a process of self-purification. It disdains mere numbers and external aids since these cannot add to the Satyagrahi's self-purification. Instead, it relies utterly on God who is the fountainhead of all strength. Religious Satyagraha, therefore, best succeeds under the leadership of a true man of God who will compel reverence and love even of the opponent by the purity of his life, the utter selflessness of his mission and the breadth of his outlook.

Harijan, 27-5-'39

SECTION FIFTH: KHEDA AND BARDOLI

SATYAGRAHAS

[Owing to failure of crops, conditions approaching famine prevailed in the Kheda District in Gujarat in 1918. The Gujarat Sabha, of which Gandhiji was President, sent petitions and telegrams to Government, but these had no effect. Thereupon Gandhiji after consulting co-workers advised the Patidars of the area to resort to Satyagraha and withhold payment of land revenue. This campaign soon came to a successful termination, Government granting remission to the poorer peasants.

Bardoli, an area in Gujarat, was where Gandhiji wanted to experiment with mass civil disobedience, as the people there were well disciplined. The idea, however, was given up in February 1922 owing to outbreaks of violence in other parts of the country. But Bardoli had its opportunity in 1928, when it was to have its periodical settlement of land revenue, and the Government wished to raise the revenue by about 25 per cent. The people insisted that there should be a public enquiry into conditions before the revenue was enhanced. On the Government refusing, a No-tax campaign was organized and successfully carried through by the people till the Government yielded to their wishes. — Ed.]

90

THE KHEDA SATYAGRAHA

A condition approaching famine had arisen in the Kheda District owing to a widespread failure of crops, and the Patidars of Kheda were considering the question of getting the revenue assessment for the year suspended.

Sjt. Amritlal Thakkar had already inquired into and reported on the situation, and personally discussed the question with the Commissioner, before I gave any definite advice to the cultivators. Sjt. Mohanlal Pandya and Shankarlal Parikh had also thrown themselves into the fight, and had set up an agitation in the Bombay Legislative Council through Sjt. Viththalbhai Patel and the late Sir Gokuldas Kahandas Parekh. More than one deputation had waited upon the Governor in that connection.

I was at this time President of the Gujarat Sabha. The Sabha sent petitions and telegrams to the Government and even patiently swallowed the insults and threats of the Commissioner. The conduct of the officials on this occasion was so ridiculous and undignified as to be almost incredible now.

The cultivators' demand was as clear as daylight, and so moderate as to make out a strong case for its acceptance. Under the Land Revenue Rules, if the crop was four annas * or under, the cultivators could claim full suspension of the revenue assessment for the year. According to the official figures the crop was said to be over four annas. The contention of the cultivator, on the other hand, was that it was less than four annas. But the Government was in no mood to listen, and regarded the popular demand for arbitration as *lese majeste*. At last all petitioning and prayer having failed, after taking counsel with co-workers, I advised the Patidars to resort to Satyagraha.

Besides the volunteers of Kheda, my principal comrades in this struggle were Sjt. Vallabhbhai Patel, Shankarlal Banker, Shrimati Anasuyabehn, Sjts. Indulal Yajnik, Mahadev Desai and others. Sjt. Vallabhbhai, in joining the struggle, had to suspend a splendid and growing practice at the bar, which for all practical purposes he was never able to resume.

We fixed up our headquarters at the Nadiad Anathashram, no other place being available which would have been large enough to accommodate all of us.

The following pledge was signed by the Satyagrahis:

" Knowing that the crops of our villages are less than four annas, we requested the Government to suspend the collection of revenue assessment till the ensuing year, but the Government has not acceded to our prayer. Therefore, we, the undersigned, hereby solemnly declare that we shall not, of our own accord, pay to the Government the full or the remaining revenue for the year. We shall let the Government take whatever legal steps it may think fit and gladly suffer the consequences of our non-payment. We shall rather let our lands be forfeited than

---

* i.e. 4 annas in the rupee meaning 25 per cent of the normal crop.

that by voluntary payment we should allow our case to be considered false or should compromise our self-respect. Should the
Government, however, agree to suspend collection of the second
instalment of the assessment throughout the district, such among
us as are in a position to pay will pay up the whole or the
balance of the revenue that may be due. The reason why those
who are able to pay still withold payment is that, if they pay
up, the poorer ryots may in a panic sell their chattels or incur
debts to pay their dues, and thereby bring suffering upon themselves. In these circumstances we feel that, for the sake of the
poor, it is the duty even of those who can afford to pay to withhold
payment of their assessment."

I cannot devote many chapters to this struggle. So a
number of sweet recollections in this connection will have
to be crowded out. Those who want to make a fuller and
deeper study of this important fight would do well to read
the full and authentic history of the Kheda Satyagraha by
Sjt. Shankarlal Parikh of Kathlal, Kheda.

'The Onion Thief'

The Gujaratis were deeply interested in the fight,
which was for them a novel experiment. They were ready
to pour forth their riches for the success of the cause. It
was not easy for them to see that Satyagraha could not
be conducted simply by means of money. Money is a thing
that it least needs. In spite of my remonstrance, the
Bombay merchants sent us more money than necessary, so
that we had some balance left at the end of the campaign.

At the same time the Satyagrahi volunteers had to
learn the new lesson of simplicity. I cannot say that they
imbibed it fully, but they considerably changed their ways
of life.

For the Patidar farmers, too, the fight was quite a
new thing. We had, therefore, to go about from village to
village explaining the principles of Satyagraha.

The main thing was to rid the agriculturists of their
fear by making them realize that the officials were not the
masters but the servants of the people, inasmuch as they
received their salaries from the taxpayer. And then it
seemed well nigh impossible to make them realize the
duty of combining civility with fearlessness. Once they had
shed the fear of the officials, how could they be stopped

from returning their insults ? And yet if they resorted to incivility it would spoil their Satyagraha, like a drop of arsenic in milk. I realized later that they had less fully learnt the lesson of civility than I had expected. Experience has taught me that civility is the most difficult part of Satyagraha. Civility does not here mean the mere outward gentleness of speech cultivated for the occasion, but an inborn gentleness and desire to do the opponent good. These should show themselves in every act of a Satyagrahi.

In the initial stages, though the people exhibited much courage, the Government did not seem inclined to take strong action. But as the people's firmness showed no signs of wavering, the Government began coercion. The attachment officers sold people's cattle and seized whatever movables they could lay hands on. Penalty notices were served, and in some cases standing crops were attached. This unnerved the peasants, some of whom paid up their dues, while others desired to place safe movables in the way of the officials so that they might attach them to realize the dues. On the other hand some were prepared to fight to the bitter end.

While these things were going on, one of Sjt. Shankarlal Parikh's tenants paid up the assessment in respect of his land. This created a sensation. Sjt. Shankarlal Parikh immediately made amends for his tenant's mistake by giving away for charitable purposes the land for which the assessment had been paid. He thus saved his honour and set a good example to others.

With a view to steeling the hearts of those who were frightened, I advised the people, under the leadership of Sjt. Mohanlal Pandya, to remove the crop of onion, from a field which had been, in my opinion, wrongly attached. I did not regard this as civil disobedience, but even if it was, I suggested that this attachment of standing crops, though it might be in accordance with law, was morally wrong, and was nothing short of looting, and that therefore it was the people's duty to remove the onion in spite of the order of attachment. This was a good opportunity for the people to learn a lesson in courting fines or imprisonment, which was the necessary consequence of such disobedience. For Sjt. Mohanlal Pandya it was a thing after his heart. He did not like the campaign to end without some one undergoing suffering in the shape of imprisonment for something done consistently with the principles of Satyagraha. So he volunteered to remove the onion crop from the field, and in this seven or eight friends joined him.

It was impossible for the Government to leave them free. The arrest of Sjt. Mohanlal and his companions added to the people's enthusiasm. When the fear of jail disappears, repression puts heart into the people. Crowds of them besieged the court-house on the day of the hearing. Pandya and his companions were convicted and sentenced to a brief term of imprisonment. I was of opinion that the conviction was wrong, because the act of removing the onion could not come under the definition of 'theft' in the Penal Code. But no appeal was filed as the policy was to avoid the law courts.

A procession escorted the 'convicts' to jail, and on that day Sjt. Mohanlal Pandya earned from the people the honoured title of *dungli chor* (onion thief) which he enjoys to this day.

Autobiography, pt. v, ch. xxiii, xxiv.

(*Young India*, 20-9-'28 and 27-9-'28)

91

BARDOLI'S DECISION

30th January, 1922

Bardoli has come to a momentous decision. It has made its final and irrevocable choice. Viththalbhai Patel, the President, addressed a conference of the representatives of the Taluka in a speech impressive for its warning. He certainly did not mince matters. There was an audience of khaddar-clad representatives numbering 4,000. There were five hundred women, a large majority of whom were also in khaddar. They were interested and interesting listeners. It was an audience of sober, responsible men and women with a stake.

I followed Viththalbhai and went through every one of the conditions of mass civil disobedience laid down by the Congress. I took the sense of the meeting on every one of the conditions separately. They understood the implications of Hindu-Muslim-Parsi-Christian unity. They realized the significance and the truth of non-violence. They saw what the removal of untouchability meant; they were prepared, not merely to take into national schools, but to induce 'untouchable' children to join them; they have had no objection to the 'untouchable' drawing water from the village wells. They knew that they were to nurse the 'untouchable' sick as they would nurse their ailing neighbours. They knew that they could not exercise the privilege of non-payment of revenue and other forms of civil disobedience until they had purified themselves in the manner described by me. They knew too that they had to become industrious and spin their own yarn and weave their own khaddar. And lastly, they were ready to face forfeiture of their movables, their cattle and their land. They were ready to face imprisonment and even death, if necessary, and they would do all this without resentment.

There was an old dissentient voice on the question of untouchability. He said that what I said was right in theory, but it was difficult in practice to break down the custom all of a sudden. I drove the point home but the audience had made up its mind.

Before the larger meeting, I had met the real workers about fifty in number. Before that meeting, Viththalbhai Patel, some workers and I conferred together and felt that we would pass a resolution postponing the decision for about a fortnight, to make the Swadeshi preparation more complete and removal of untouchability more certain, by actually having 'untouchable' children in all the sixty national schools. The brave and earnest workers of Bardoli would not listen to the postponement. They were certain that more than 50 per cent of the Hindu population were quite ready about untouchability and they were sure of being able to manufacture enough khaddar for their future wants. They were bent on trying conclusions with the Government. They bore down every objection raised by Viththalbhai Patel ; and Abbas Tyabji, with his hoary beard and ever smiling face, was there to utter the warning. But they would not budge an inch from their position and so the resolution which I give below was unanimously passed.

"After having fully understood and considered the conditions essential for the starting of mass civil disobedience, this Conference of the inhabitants of the Bardoli Taluka resolves that this Taluka is fit for mass civil disobedience.

"This Conference is of opinion —

(a) That for the redress of India's grievances, unity among Hindus, Mohammedans, Parsis, Christians and other communities of India is absolutely necessary.

(b) That non-violence, patience and endurance are the only remedy for the redress of the said grievances.

(c) That the use of the spinning wheel in every home, and the adoption of hand-spun and hand-woven garments to the exclusion of all other cloth by every individual are indispensable for India's freedom.

(d) That Swaraj is impossible without complete removal of untouchability by the Hindus.

(e) That for the people's progress and for the attainment of freedom, readiness to sacrifice movable and immovable property, to suffer imprisonment and, if necessary, to lay down one's life, is indispensable.

"This Conference hopes that the Bardoli Taluka will have the privilege to be the first for the aforesaid sacrifices, and this Conference hereby respectfully informs the Working Committee that unless the Working Committee otherwise decides or unless the proposed Round Table Conference is held, this Taluka will immediately commence mass civil disobedience under the advice and guidance of Mr Gandhi and the President of the Conference.

"This Conference recommends that those tax-payers of the Taluka who are ready and willing to abide by the conditions laid down by the Congress for mass civil disobedience, will refrain, till further instruction, from paying land revenue and other taxes due to the Government."

Who knows the issue ? Who knows whether the men and women of Bardoli will stand the repression that the Government may resort to ? God only knows. In His name has the battle been undertaken. He must finish it.

The Government have acted hitherto in a most exemplary manner. They might have prohibited the Conference. They did not. They know the workers. They would have removed them long ago. They have not done so. They have not interfered with any of the activities of the people. They have permitted them to make all preparations. I have watched their conduct with wonder and admiration. Both sides have up to the time of writing behaved in a manner worthy of chivalrous warriors of old. In this battle of peace it ought not to be otherwise. If the battle continues in this fashion, it will end only in one way. Whoever has the ear of 85,000 men and women of Bardoli will gain the day.

The Working Committee has to sit and pass its judgment upon Bardoli's decision. The Viceroy has still choice and will have yet another choice given to him. No charge of hurry, want of preparation or thought, no charge of discourtesy will it be possible to bring against the people of Bardoli.

Therefore,

> Lead, kindly Light, amid the encircling gloom,
> Lead Thou me on :
> The night is dark and I am far from home,
> Lead Thou me on.

92

BARDOLI ON TRIAL

One may hastily think that the Government is on its trial in Bardoli. But that would be a wrong opinion. The Government has been tried and found wanting scores of times. "Frightfulness" is its code of conduct when its vital parts are affected. If its prestige or its revenue is in danger, it seeks to sustain it by means either fair or foul. It does not hesitate to resort to terrorism and cover it with unblushing untruths. The latest information that Pathans are now being posted in villages with instructions to surround the houses of the villagers day and night need not cause either surprise or anger. The surprise is that they have not yet let loose in Bardoli a punitive police and declared martial law. We ought by this time to know what a punitive police or martial law means. It is evident that by the latest form of "frightfulness" the Government is seeking to goad people into some act of violence, be it ever so slight, to justify their enactment of the last act in the tragedy.

Will the people of Bardoli stand this last trial? They have already staggered Indian humanity. They have shown heroic patience in the midst of great provocation. Will they stand the greatest provocation that can be offered? If they will, they will have gained everything. Imprisonments, forfeitures, deportations, death must all be taken in the ordinary course by those who count honour before everything else. When the terror becomes unbearable, let the people leave the land they have hitherto believed to be theirs. It is wisdom to vacate houses or places that are plague-infected. Tyranny is a kind of plague and when it is likely to make us angry or weak it is wisdom to leave the scene of such temptation. History is full of instances of brave people having sought exile in preference to surrender to *zoolum*.

Let me hope however that such a step will not be

necessary. One hears rumours of intercessions by well-meaning friends. They have the right, it may be even their duty, to intercede. But let these friends realize the significance of the movement. They are not to represent a weak cause or a weak people. The people of Bardoli stand for an absolutely just cause. They ask no favour, they seek only justice. They do not ask any one to consider their case to be true. Their cause is to seek an independent, open, judicial inquiry, and they undertake to abide by the verdict of such a tribunal. To deny the tribunal is to deny justice which the Government have hitherto done. The means at the disposal of the people are self-suffering. In such a cause then minimum and maximum are almost convertible terms. Those who rely upon self-suffering for redress of a grievance cannot afford to rate it higher than it actually is. Those therefore who will intervene will harm the people and their cause, if they do not appreciate the implications of the struggle which cannot be lightly given up or compromised.

The public have a duty to perform by the Satyagrahis. The response is already being made to Vallabhbhai's appeal for funds. It will be remembered that he refused to make the appeal as long as it was possible to refrain. The imprisonments have made the appeal imperative. I have no doubt that the response will be quick and generous. Equally necessary is the expression of enlightened public opinion. Let the public study the facts carefully and then cover the whole of the land with public meetings. I like the suggestion made by Sjt. Jairamdas that June 12th or any other suitable date should be proclaimed as Bardoli Day when meetings representing all parties may be held to pass resolutions and make collections in aid of the sufferers of Bardoli.

Young India, 31-5-'28

93

NON-CO-OPERATION OR CIVIL RESISTANCE?

Fear has been entertained in Government circles that the movement going on in Bardoli is one of non-co-operation. It is necessary, therefore, to distinguish between non-co-operation and civil resistance. Both are included in the wider term Satyagraha which covers any and every effort based on truth and non-violence. The term non-co-operation was designed to include among other things the items named in the programme of 1920 at the special session of the Congress at Calcutta and reaffirmed the same year at Nagpur with the object of attaining Swaraj. Under it no negotiation with or petition to the Government of the day was possible except for the purpose of attaining Swaraj. Whatever the Bardoli struggle may be, it clearly is not a struggle for the direct attainment of Swaraj. That every such awakening, every such effort as that of Bardoli brings Swaraj nearer and may bring it nearer even than any direct effort is undoubtedly true. But the struggle of Bardoli is to seek redress of a specific grievance. It ceases the moment the grievance is redressed. The method adopted in the first instance was through conventional prayer and petition. And when the conventional method failed utterly, the people of Bardoli invited Sjt. Vallabhbhai Patel to lead them in civil resistance. The civil resistance does not mean even civil disobedience of the laws and rules promulgated by constituted authority. It simply means non-payment of a portion of a tax which former, the aggrieved ryots contend, has been improperly and unjustly imposed on them. This is tantamount to the repudiation by a private debtor of a part of the debt claimed by his creditor as due to him. If it is the right of a private person to refuse payment of a debt he does not admit, it is equally the right of the ryot to refuse to pay an imposition which he believes to be unjust. But it is not the purpose here to prove the correctness of the action of the people of Bardoli. My purpose is to distinguish between non-co-operation with attainment of Swaraj as its object and civil resistance as that of Bardoli with the redress of a specific grievance as its object. This I hope is now made clear beyond doubt. That Sjt. Vallabhbhai and the majority of the workers under his command are confirmed non-co-operators is beside the point. The majority of those whom they represent are not. National non-co-operation is suspended. The personal creed of a non-co-operator does not preclude him from representing the cause of those who are helplessly co-operators.

Young India, 19-7-'28

94

LIMITATIONS OF SATYAGRAHA

Sardar Sardul Singh is an esteemed worker. His open letter advising me to invite sympathetic civil disobedience for Bardoli demands a reply especially because it enables me to clear my own position. If Bardoli Satyagraha were a campaign of lawlessness as the Government paint it, nothing would be more tempting or more natural than sympathetic Satyagraha and that too without the limits prescribed in the Sardar's letter. But the Sardar rightly says : ' I find in prominent Gujarat workers a tendency to allow Bardoli peasants to be kept isolated. This impression has been created in my mind by the reports of Sjt. Vallabhbhai's speeches and your writings. Friends think that any more scruples on this point go beyond the limits of practical politics.'

The Sardar's impression is correct. In order strictly to limit the scope of the struggle to the purely local and economic issue and to keep it non-political Sjt. Vallabhbhai would not let Sjt. Rajagopalachari and other leaders to go to Bardoli. It was only when the Government gave it a political character and made it an all-India issue by their coercive measures that the reins were loosened and

Vallabhbhai could no longer prevent public men from going to Bardoli, though where his advice or permission was sought, he said, ' Not yet.'

I do not know what Sjt. Vallabhbhai Patel would say to the Sardar's suggestion , but I can say, ' Not yet.' Time has not come even for limited sympathetic Satyagraha. Bardoli has still to prove its mettle. If it can stand the last heat and if the Government go to the farthest limit, nothing that I or Sjt. Vallabhbhai can do will stop the spread of Satyagraha or limit the issue to a bona fide re-inquiry and its logical consequences. The limit will then be prescribed by the capacity of India as a whole for self-sacrifice and self-suffering. If that manifestation is to come it will be natural and incapable of being stayed by any agency no matter how powerful. But so far as I understand the spirit of Satyagraha and its working, it is the duty of Sjt. Vallabhbhai and myself to keep to the original limits in spite of the Government provocations which are strong enough even as they are to warrant the crossing of the original boundary.

The fact is that Satyagraha presupposes the living presence and guidance of God. The leader depends not on his own strength but on that of God. He acts as the Voice within guides him. Very often, therefore, what are practical politics so called are unrealities to him, though in the end his prove to be the most practical politics. All this may sound foolish and visionary on the eve of what bids fair to become the toughest battle that India has hitherto had to face. But I would be untrue to the nation and myself if I failed to say what I feel to be the deepest truth. If the people of Bardoli are what Vallabhbhai believes them to be, all will be well, in spite of the use of all the weapons that the Government may have at its command. Let us wait and see. Only let the M. L. C.'s and others who are interested in compromises not take a single weak step in the hope of saving the people of Bardoli. They are safe in the hands of God.

Young India, 2-8-'28

95

ALL'S WELL

It is a matter for sincere joy that the settlement has at last been reached over the Bardoli Satyagraha. All's well that ends well. I tender my congratulations both to the Government of Bombay and the people of Bardoli and Valod and Sjt. Vallabhbhai without whose firmness as well as gentleness the settlement would have been impossible. The reader will note that the Satyagrahis have achieved practically all that they had asked for. The terms of reference to the Committee of Enquiry are all that could be desired. True, there is to be no inquiry into the allegations about the coercive measures adopted by the Government to enforce payment. But it was generous on the part of Sjt. Vallabhbhai to waive the condition, seeing that the lands forfeited including lands sold are to be restored, the *talatis* are to be reinstated, and other minor matters are to be attended to. It is well not to rake up old wrongs for which beyond the reparation made there can be no other remedy. The inquiry into the assessment question will be carried in a calmer atmosphere for the waiver of the clause about the coercive processes.

Let not the Satyagrahis sleep over their well-deserved victory. They have to collect and collate material to prove their allegations about the assessment.

And above all, if they are to consolidate their position, they must proceed with constructive work with redoubled vigour. Their strength lies in their ability and willingness to handle this difficult, slow and unpretentious work of construction. They have to rid themselves of many social abuses. They must better their economic condition by attention to the *charkha*. It was the *charkha* that led to the awakening among them. They must remove the reproach of drink from their midst. They must attend to village sanitation and have a properly managed school in every village. The so-called higher classes must befriend

217

the depressed and the suppressed classes. The greater the attention given to these matters, the greater will be their ability to face crises like the one they have just gone through.

Young India, 9-8-'28

96

A SIGN OF THE TIMES

Bardoli is a sign of the times. It has a lesson both for the Government and the people — for the Government if they will recognize the power of the people when they have truth on their side and when they can form a non-violent combination to vindicate it. By such recognition a wise Government consolidates its power which is then built upon people's goodwill and co-operation not merely in act enforced by brute power but in speech and thought as well. Non-violent energy properly stored up sets free a force that becomes irresistible.

Let us then turn to the people of Bardoli. The lesson that they have to learn is that so long as they remain united in non-violence they have nothing to fear, not even unwilling officials. But have they learnt that lesson, have they recognized the unseen power of non-violence, have they realized that if they had committed one single act of violence, they would have lost their cause? If they have, then they will know from day to day that they will not become a non-violent organization unless they undergo a process of what may be called continuous corporate cleansing. This they can only do by engaging in carrying out a well thought out constructive programme requiring combined effort and promoting common good. In other words before they can claim to have become a non-violent organization, they must receive education in non-violence not through speeches or writings, necessary as both may be, but through an unbroken series of corporate acts, each evoking the spirit of non-violence. Sjt. Vallabhbhai

Patel knows what he is about. He has set for himself this more difficult task of constructive effort or internal reform. May God grant him therein the same measure of success that has attended the struggle against the Government.

Young India, 16-8-'28

SECTION SIXTH : SALT SATYAGRAHA

[Gandhiji launched civil disobedience in 1930 to rectify some of the evils of British rule, and symbolically singled out the Salt Laws for violation. He regarded these laws as iniquitous as they taxed salt which was the only flavouring to a bowlful of rice or other grain which the poorest in the land could afford.   — Ed.]

97

" NEVER FAILETH "

अहिंसाप्रतिष्ठायां तत्सन्निधौ वैरत्याग: ।

' Hate dissolves in the presence of Love.'

"In the opinion of the Working Committee civil disobedience should be initiated and controlled by those who believe in non-violence for the purpose of achieving *Purna Swaraj* as an article of faith, and as the Congress contains in its organization not merely such men and women, but also those who accept non-violence as a policy essential in the existing circumstances in the country, the Working Committee welcomes the proposal of Mahatma Gandhi and authorizes him and those working with him who believe in non-violence as an article of faith to the extent above indicated to start civil disobedience as and when they desire and in the manner and to the extent they decide. The Working Committee trusts that when the campaign is actually in action all Congressmen and others will extend to the civil resisters their full co-operation in every way possible, and that they will observe and preserve complete non-violence notwithstanding any provocation that may be offered. The Working Committee further hopes that in the event of a mass movement taking place, all those who are rendering voluntary co-operation to the Government, such as lawyers, and those who are receiving so-called benefits from it, such as students, will withdraw their co-operation or renounce benefits as the case may be, and throw themselves into the final struggle for freedom. The Working Committee trusts, that in the event of the leaders being arrested and imprisoned, those, who are left behind and have the spirit of sacrifice and service in them, will carry on the Congress organization, and guide the movement to the best of their ability."

This resolution of the Working Committee gives me my charter of freedom if it also binds me in the tightest chains. It is the formula of which I have been in search these long and weary months. For me the resolution is not so much a political as a religious effort. My difficulty was fundamental. I saw that I could not work out *ahimsa* through an organization holding a variety of mentalities. It could not be subject to the decision of majorities. To be consistent with itself, it might have to be inconsistent with the whole world.

A person who has a choice before him is ever exposed to temptation. The instinct of those, therefore, with whom non-violence is a policy, when tempted by violence, may fail them. That of those who have no remedy but non-violence open to them can never fail them if they have non-violence in them in reality. Hence the necessity for freedom from Congress control. And I was thankful that the members of the Working Committee saw the utter correctness of my position.

It is to be hoped that no one will misunderstand the position. Here there is no question of superiority. Those, who hold non-violence for the attainment of freedom as an article of faith, are in no way superior to those with whom it is a mere policy, even as there is no such inequality between brown men and yellow men. Each acts according to his lights.

The responsibility devolving on me is the greatest I have ever undertaken. It was irresistible. But all will be well, if it is *ahimsa* that is guiding me. For the seer who knew what he gave to the world said, 'Hate dissolves in the presence of *ahimsa*.' The true rendering of the word in English is love or charity. And does not the Bible say :

" Love worketh no ill to his neighbour,
" Believeth all things,
" Hopeth all things,
" Never faileth."

Civil disobedience is sometimes a peremptory demand of love. Dangerous it undoubtedly is, but no more than the encircling violence. Civil disobedience is the only non-violent escape from its soul-destroying heat. The danger lies only in one direction, in the outbreak of violence side by side with civil disobedience. If it does I know now the way; not the retracing as at the time of Bardoli. The struggle, in freedom's battle, of non-violence against violence, no matter from what quarter the latter comes, must continue till a single representative is left alive. More no man can do, to do less would be tantamount to want of faith.

Young India, 20-2-'30

98

TO ENGLISH FRIENDS

[On the eve of starting Civil Disobedience. An extract.]

Hatred and ill-will there undoubtedly are in the air. They are bound sooner or later to burst into acts of fury if they are not anticipated in time. The conviction has deepened in me that civil disobedience alone can stop the bursting of that fury. The nation wants to feel its power more even than to have independence. Possession of such power *is* independence.

That civil disobedience may resolve itself into violent disobedience is, I am sorry to have to confess, not an unlikely event. But I know that it will not be the cause of it. Violence is there already corroding the whole body politic. Civil Disobedience will be but a purifying process and may bring to the surface what is burrowing under and into the whole body. And British officials, if they choose, may regulate civil disobedience so as to sterilize the forces of violence. But whether they do so, or whether, as many of us fear, they will, directly or indirectly, consciously or unconsciously, provoke violence, my course is clear. With the evidence I have of the condition of the country and with the unquenchable faith I have in the method of civil resistance, I must not be deterred from the course the Inward Voice seems to be leading me to.

But whatever I do and whatever happens, my English friends will accept my word, that whilst I am impatient to break the British bondage, I am no enemy of Britain.

Young India, 23-1-'30

99

WHEN I AM ARRESTED

It must be taken for granted, that when civil disobedience is started, my arrest is a certainty. It is, therefore, necessary to consider what should be done when the event takes place.

On the eve of my arrest in 1922 I had warned co-workers against any demonstration of any kind save that of mute, complete non-violence, and had insisted that constructive work, which alone could organize the country for civil disobedience, should be prosecuted with the utmost zeal. The first part of the instructions was, thanks be to God, literally and completely carried out — so completely that it has enabled an English noble contemptuously to say, ' Not a dog barked.' For me when I learnt in the jail that the country had remained absolutely non-violent, it was a demonstration that the preaching of non-violence had had its effect and that the Bardoli decision was the wisest thing to do. It would be foolish to speculate what might have happened if ' dogs ' had barked and violence had been let loose on my arrest. One thing, however, I can say, that in that event there would have been no Independence Resolution at Lahore, and no Gandhi with his confidence in the power of non-violence left to contemplate taking the boldest risks imaginable.

Let us, however, think of the immediate future. This time on my arrest there is to be no mute, passive non-violence, but non-violence of the activest type should be set in motion, so that not a single believer in non-violence as an article of faith for the purpose of achieving India's goal should find himself free or alive at the end of the effort to submit any longer to the existing slavery. It would be, therefore, the duty of every one to take up such civil disobedience or civil resistance as may be advised and conducted by my successor, or as might be taken up by the Congress. I must confess, that at the present moment, I have no all-India successor in view. But I have sufficient faith in the co-workers and in the mission itself to know that circumstances will give the successor. This peremptory condition must be patent to all that he must be an out-and-out believer in the efficacy of non-violence for the purpose intended. For without that living faith in it he will not be able at the crucial moment to discover a non-violent method.

It must be parenthetically understood that what is being said here in no way fetters the discretion and full authority of the Congress. The Congress will adopt only such things said here that may commend themselves to Congressmen in general. If the nature of these instructions is to be properly understood, the organic value of the charter of full liberty given to me by the Working Committee should be adequately appreciated. Non-violence, if it does not submit to any restrictions upon its liberty, subjects no one and no institution to any restriction whatsoever, save what may be self-imposed or voluntarily adopted. So long as the vast body of Congressmen continue to believe in non-violence as the only policy in the existing circumstances and have confidence not only in the bona fides of my successor and those who claim to believe in non-violence as an article of faith to the extent indicated but also in the ability of the successor wisely to guide the movement, the Congress will give him and them its blessings and even give effect to these instructions and his.

So far as I am concerned, my intention is to start the movement only through the inmates of the Ashram and those who have submitted to its discipline and assimilated the spirit of its methods. Those, therefore, who will offer battle at the very commencement will be unknown to fame. Hitherto the Ashram has been deliberately kept in reserve in order that by a fairly long course of discipline it might acquire stability. I feel, that if the Satyagraha Ashram is to deserve the great confidence that has been reposed in it and the affection lavished upon it by friends, the time has arrived for it to demonstrate the qualities implied in the word *satyagraha*. I feel that our self-imposed restraints have become subtle indulgences, and the prestige acquired has provided us with privileges and conveniences of which we may be utterly unworthy. These have been thankfully accepted in the hope that some day we would be able to give a good account of ourselves in terms of Satyagraha. And if at the end of nearly 15 years of its existence, the Ashram cannot give such a demonstration, it and I should disappear, and it would be well for the nation, the Ashram and me.

When the beginning is well and truly made I expect the response from all over the country. It will be the duty then of every one who wants to make the movement a success to keep it non-violent and under discipline. Every one will be expected to stand at his post except when called by his chief. If there is a spontaneous mass response, as I hope there will be, and if previous experience is any guide, it will largely be self-regulated. But every one who accepts non-violence whether as an article of faith or policy would assist the mass movement. Mass movements have, all over the world, thrown up unexpected leaders. This should be no exception to the rule. Whilst, therefore, every effort imaginable and possible should be made to restrain the forces of violence, civil disobedience once begun this time cannot be stopped and must not be stopped so long as there is a single civil resister left free or alive. A votary of Satyagraha should find himself in one of the following states :

1. In prison or in an analogous state ; or
2. Engaged in civil disobedience ; or
3. Under orders at the spinning wheel, or at some constructive work advancing Swaraj.

Young India, 27-2-'30

100

LETTER TO THE VICEROY

[On the eve of launching on Civil Disobedience Gandhiji wrote a letter on 2-3-'30 to the Viceroy stating the evils which required to be removed immediately from the British Government of India. He ended it by pointing out the method of Satyagraha he would adopt in case there was no adequate response. We reproduce below the concluding part of his letter. —Ed.]

Sinful to Wait Any Longer

It is common cause that, however disorganized, and, for the time being, insignificant, it may be, the party of violence is gaining ground and making itself felt. Its end is the same as mine. But I am convinced that it cannot bring the desired relief to the dumb millions. And the conviction is growing deeper and deeper in me that nothing but unadulterated non-violence can check the organized violence of the British Government. Many think that non-violence is not an active force. My experience, limited though it undoubtedly is, shows that non-violence can be an intensely active force. It is my purpose to set in motion that force as well against the organized violent force of the British rule as the unorganized violent force of the growing party of violence. To sit still would be to give rein to both the forces above mentioned. Having an unquestioning and immovable faith in the efficacy of non-violence, as I know it, it would be sinful on my part to wait any longer.

This non-violence will be expressed through civil disobedience, for the moment confined to the inmates of the Satyagraha Ashram, but ultimately designed to cover all those who choose to join the movement with its obvious limitations.

My Ambition — Conversion of British People

I know that in embarking on non-violence I shall be running what might fairly be termed a mad risk. But the victories of truth have never been won without risks, often of the gravest character. Conversion of a nation that has consciously or unconsciously preyed upon another, far more numerous, far more ancient and no less cultured than itself, is worth any amount of risk.

I have deliberately used the word *conversion*. For my ambition is no less than to convert the British people through non-violence, and thus make them see the wrong they have done to India. I do not seek to harm your people. I want to serve them even as I want to serve my own. I believe that I have always served them. I served them up to 1919 blindly. But when my eyes were opened and I conceived non-co-operation, the object still was to serve them. I employed the same weapon that I have in all humility successfully used against the dearest members of my family. If I have equal love for your people with mine it will not long remain hidden. It will be acknowledged by them even as the members of my family acknowledged it after they had tried me for several years. If the people join me, as I expect they will, the sufferings they will undergo, unless the British nation sooner retraces its steps, will be enough to melt the stoniest hearts.

If You Cannot See Your Way

The plan through Civil Disobedience will be to combat such evils as I have sampled out. If we want to sever the British connection it is because of such evils. When they are removed the path becomes easy. Then the way to friendly negotiation will be open. If the British commerce with India is purified of greed, you will have no difficulty in recognizing our independence. I respectfully invite you then to pave the way for immediate removal of those evils, and thus open a way for a real conference between equals, interested only in promoting the common good of mankind through voluntary fellowship and in arranging terms of mutual help and commerce equally suited to both. You have unnecessarily laid stress upon the communal problems that unhappily affect this land. Important though they undoubtedly are for the consideration of any scheme of Government, they have little bearing on the greater problems which are above communities and which affect them all equally. But if you cannot see your way to deal with these evils and my letter makes no appeal to your heart, on the 11th day of this month, I shall proceed with such co-workers of the Ashram as I can take, to disregard the provisions of the Salt laws. I regard this tax to be the most iniquitous of all from the poor man's standpoint. As the Independence movement is essentially for the poorest in the land the beginning will be made with this evil. The wonder is that we have submitted to the cruel monopoly for so long. It is, I know, open to you to frustrate my design by arresting me. I hope that there will be tens of thousands ready, in a disciplined manner, to take up the work after me, and, in the act of disobeying the Salt Act, to lay themselves open to the penalties of a law that should never have disfigured the Statute Book.

No Threat but a Sacred Duty

I have no desire to cause you unnecessary embarrassment, or any at all, so far as I can help. If you think that there is any substance in my letter, and if you will care to discuss matters with me, and if to that end you would like me to postpone publication of this letter, I shall gladly refrain on receipt of a telegram to that effect soon after this reaches you. You will, however, do me the favour not to deflect me from my course unless you can see your way to conform to the substance of this letter.

This letter is not in any way intended as a threat but is a simple and sacred duty peremptory on a civil resister. Therefore, I am having it specially delivered by a young English friend who believes in the Indian cause and is a full believer in non-violence and whom Providence seems to have sent to me, as it were, for the very purpose.

Young India, 12-3-'30

101

SOME QUESTIONS & ANSWERS

The Risk of Violence

Q. Will not your movement lead to violence ?

A. It may, though I am trying my best to prevent any outbreak of violence. Today there is a greater risk of violence, in the absence of any safety-valve in the shape of a movement of non-violence like the one I am contemplating.

Q. Yes, I have heard you say that you are launching this campaign for the very purpose of stopping violence.

A. It is one argument, but that is not the most conclusive argument. The other and most conclusive argument for me is that if non-violence has to prove its worth, it must prove its worth today. It must cease to be the passive or even impotent instrument that it has come to be looked upon in certain quarters. And when it is exercised in the most effective way, it must act in spite of the most fatal *outward* obstructions. In fact non-violence by its very nature must neutralize all *outward* obstruction. On the contrary, inward obstacles in the shape of fraud, hatred, and ill-will would be fatal to the movement. Up to now I used to say, ' Let me get control over the forces of violence.' It is growing upon me now that it is only by setting the force of non-violence in motion that I can get those elements under control.

But I hear people say, ' History will have to repeat itself in India.' Let it repeat itself, if it must. I for one must not postpone the movement unless I am to be guilty of the charge of cowardice. I must fight unto death the system based on violence and thus bring under control the force of political violence. When real organic non-violence is set to work, the masses also will react manfully.

A Miracle

Q. But after you are removed the movement will no longer be in your control ?

A. In South Africa the movement was not in my control during the latter part of it, when it gained considerable momentum without any action on my part. Thousands joined the movement instinctively. I had not even seen the faces of them, much less known them. They joined because they felt that they must. They had possibly only heard my name, but they saw in the twinkling of an eye that it was a movement for their liberation ; they knew that there was a man prepared to fight the £ 3 tax and they took the plunge. And against what odds ? Their mines were converted into jails ; the men who oppressed them day and night were appointed warders over them. They knew that there would be hell let loose on them. And yet they did not waver or falter. It was a perfect miracle.

The Opportunity of a Lifetime

Q. But would not the movement add to the already numerous divisions existing in the country ?

A. I have no such fear. The forces of disunion can be kept under control, even as the forces of violence. You may say that there is fear elsewhere. The party of violence may not respond to my advances and the masses might behave unthinkingly. I am an optimist and have an abiding faith in human nature. The party of violence will give me fair play and the masses will act rightly by instinct. It is possible that I may be living in a fool's paradise. But no general can possibly provide for all contingencies. For me it is the opportunity of a lifetime. The movement is none of my seeking. Almost in spite of myself I was irresistibly drawn to Calcutta. I entered into a compromise to which I was driven. The period of two years I changed to one, simply because it did not involve any moral principle. In Lahore I had to conceive and frame practically every resolution. There I saw the forces of violence and non-violence in full play, acting side by side ; and I found that non-violence ultimately triumphed over violence.

How is the Time Ripe Now ?

Q. You said some time ago that the time was not ripe for civil disobedience. What has happened between that time and today that has helped you to alter your view ?

A. I am quite positive that it is fully ripe. The reason I will tell you. Nothing has happened externally, but the internal conflict in me, which was the only barrier, has ceased ; and I am absolutely certain now that the campaign had been long overdue. I might have started it long before this.

Q. And what was that internal conflict ?

A. You know I have always been guided solely by my attitude towards non-violence, but I did not know then how to translate that attitude into action in the face of growing violence. But now I see as clearly as daylight that, pursuing the course that I have adopted, I minimize the risk I am taking.

Q. Are you sure that the salt campaign will lead you to jail ?

A. I have not a shadow of doubt that it will. How long exactly it will take is more than I can say, but I feel that it will be much sooner than most people would be inclined to think. I expect a crisis to be soon reached which would lead to a proper Conference — not a Round Table Conference, but a Square Table one where everybody attending it would know his bearings. The exact lineaments of that Conference I cannot at present depict, but it will be a Conference between equals met to lay their heads together to devise ways and means for the establishment of an Independent Constitution in India.

About the Interview

Q. Were you not responsible for allowing the Viceregal negotiations to come to an abrupt end ?

A. I know that is the impression in certain quarters ; the public blamed me for a time, but now it has come to understand the true position.

Q. Are you quite sure that in the position you took, the influence of the younger generation did not weigh with you ?

A. No. Not a bit. I had never been sanguine about the Round Table Conference. I went of course as far as I could. But the central thing I always insisted on was that the Conference should apply itself to a scheme of Dominion Status suited to the needs of India. If the Viceroy had said ' Yes,' I should gladly have asked him to proceed to the other points.

Q. Then you had no objection to the scheme coming into operation some years hence ?

A. If the scheme was such as to come into operation at a future time, I should rule it out. But I may not talk about our interview with the Viceroy. The public might know more about it some day. I can assure you, however, that there was no question of a real Dominion Status scheme being framed.

The Eleven Points

Q. Just a question about your now famous eleven points. If some of them are conceded, would there be room for a compromise ?

A. If they were to concede a few main points and couple the concession with a promise that the rest would be conceded as soon as possible, I would be prepared to consider a proposition for a Conference. But the justice of all those demands must be admitted. You will agree that there is nothing new about them. Most have been handed down to us from Dadabhai Naoroji's time.

Q. Supposing they conceded your demand about the reduction of civil and military expenditure, would you not regard it as a sufficient proof of their bona fides ?

A. I should seriously reconsider my position, but it would all depend on the spirit in which the concession was made.

102

ON THE EVE OF THE MARCH

[Gandhiji addressed these words to the vast audience assembled on the sands of the Sabarmati near the Sabarmati Ashram after prayer on the eve of his Salt Satyagraha March to Dandi:]

In all probability this will be my last speech to you. Even if the Government allow me to march tomorrow morning, this will be my last speech on the sacred banks of the Sabarmati. Possibly these may be the last words of my life here.

I have already told you yesterday what I had to say. Today I shall confine myself to what you should do after my companions and I are arrested. The programme of the march to Jalalpur must be fulfilled as originally settled. The enlistment of volunteers for this purpose should be confined to Gujarat. From what I have seen and heard during the last fortnight, I am inclined to believe that the stream of civil resisters will flow unbroken.

But let there be not a semblance of breach of peace even after all of us have been arrested. We have resolved to utilize all our resources in the pursuit of an exclusively non-violent struggle. Let no one commit a wrong in anger. This is my hope and prayer. I wish these words of mine reached every nook and corner of the land. My task shall be done if I perish and so do my comrades. It will then be for the Working Committee of the Congress to show you the way and it will be up to you to follow its lead. That is the only meaning of the Working Committee's resolution. The reins of the movement will still remain in the hands of those of my associates who believe in non-violence as an article of faith. Of course, the Congress will be free to chalk out what course of action commends itself to it. So long as I have not reached Jalalpur, let nothing be done in contravention to the authority vested in me by the Congress. But once I am arrested, the whole general responsibility shifts to the Congress. No one who believes in non-violence, as a creed, need therefore sit still. My compact with the Congress ends as soon as I am arrested. In that case there should be no slackness in the enrolment of volunteers. Wherever possible, civil disobedience of Salt laws should be started. These laws can be violated in three ways. It is an offence to manufacture salt wherever there are facilities for doing so. The possession and sale of contraband salt (which includes natural salt or salt earth) is also an offence. The purchasers of such salt will be equally guilty. To carry away the natural salt deposits on the sea-shore is likewise a violation of law. So is the hawking of such salt. In short, you may choose any one or all of these devices to break the salt monopoly.

We are, however, not to be content with this alone. Wherever there are Congress Committees, wherever there is no ban by the Congress and wherever the local workers have self-confidence, other suitable measures may be adopted. I prescribe only one condition, viz., let our pledge of truth and non-violence as the only means for the attainment of Swaraj be faithfully kept. For the rest, every one has a free hand. But that does not give a licence to all and sundry to carry on on their individual responsibility. Wherever there are local leaders, their orders should be obeyed by the people. Where there are no leaders and only a handful of men have faith in the programme, they may do what they can, if they have enough self-confidence. They have a right, nay it is their duty, to do so. The history of the world is full of instances of men who rose to leadership by sheer force of self-confidence, bravery and tenacity. We too, if we sincerely aspire to Swaraj and are impatient to attain it, should have similar self-confidence. Our ranks will swell and our hearts strengthen as the number of our arrests by Government increases.

Let nobody assume that after I am arrested there will be no one left to guide you. It is not I but Pandit Jawaharlal who is your guide. He has the capacity to lead. Though the fact is that those who have learnt the lesson of fearlessness and self-effacement need no leader. If we lack these virtues, not even Jawaharlal will be able to produce them in us.

Much can be done in other ways besides these. Liquor and foreign cloth shops can be picketed. We can refuse to pay taxes if we have the requisite strength. The lawyers can give up practice. The public can boycott the Courts by refraining from litigation. Government servants can resign their posts. In the midst of the despair reigning all round people quake with fear of losing employment. Such men are unfit for Swaraj. But why this despair? The number of Government servants in the country does not exceed a few hundred thousand. What about the rest? Where are they to go? Even free India will not be able to accommodate a greater number of public servants. A Collector then will not need the number of servants he has got today. He will be his own servant. How can a poor country like India afford to provide a Collector with separate servants for performing the duties of carrying his papers, sweeping, cooking, latrine cleaning and letter carrying? Our starving millions can by no means afford this enormous expenditure. If, therefore, we are sensible enough, let us bid good-bye to Government employment, no matter if it is the post of a judge or a peon. It may be difficult for a judge to leave his job, but where is the difficulty in the case of a peon? He can earn his bread everywhere by honest manual labour. This is the easiest solution of the problem of freedom: Let all who are co-operating with the Government in one way or another, be it by paying taxes, keeping titles, or sending children to official schools etc., withdraw their co-operation in all or as many ways as possible. One can devise other methods too of non-co-operating with the Government. And then there are women who can stand shoulder to shoulder with men in this struggle.

You may take it as my will. It was the only message that I desired to impart to you before starting on the march or for the jail. I wish that there should be no suspension or abandonment of the war that commences tomorrow morning, or earlier if I am arrested before that time. I shall eagerly await the news that ten batches are ready as soon as my batch is arrested. I believe there are men in India to complete the work begun by me today. I have faith in the righteousness of our cause and the purity of our weapons. And where the means are clean, there God is undoubtedly present with His blessings. And where these three combine, there defeat is an impossibility. A Satyagrahi, whether free or incarcerated, is ever victorious. He is vanquished only when he forsakes truth and non-violence and turns a deaf ear to the Inner Voice. If, therefore, there is such a thing as defeat for even a Satyagrahi, he alone is the cause of it. God bless you all and keep off all obstacles from the path in the struggle that begins tomorrow. Let this be our prayer.

Young India, 20-3-'30

103

ASHRAM DISCIPLINE DURING THE MARCH

It may be mentioned in passing that in spite of the weary marches Gandhiji has insisted on the Ashram routine being followed by every one of the pilgrims, especially in the three essentials, viz., prayer, spinning and writing up the daily diary. It is easy enough to attend the prayers, inasmuch as the hours of march depend on the due observance of the hours of prayer, but the other two items are often difficult of achievement. One often feels dead tired and falls off to sleep before writing up the diary ; in some places it is difficult to get the spinning wheel, or, at any rate, a sufficient number of spinning wheels, and for a slow spinner it is difficult to do the quota of 212 yards on the *takli* in anything less than three hours. But Gandhiji would listen to no such excuse. " Ours is a sacred pilgrimage," he said, " and we should be able to account for every minute of our time. Let those who cannot finish their quota or do not find time to spin or to write up their diaries see me. I shall discuss the thing with them. There must be something wrong about their time-table and I should help them to readjust it. We should be resourceful enough to do all our daily duties without the march coming in our way. I dare say we are not hardy enough for a strenuous trek, and I am therefore providing for a weekly day of rest. But I should listen to no proposal for the relaxation of the regular discipline of the Ashram. I repeat that ours is a sacred pilgrimage, and self-examination and self-purification are essentials without which we cannot do. The diary is a great help in this matter. This regular spinning, counting the yards spun each day, the daily diary — all these things were thought out by me in the Yeravda Jail, and for us whose ambition it is to lay the foundation of the edifice of Swaraj, inasmuch as ours will be the first sacrificial offering, it should be as unsullied as possible. Those who follow us may dispense with the rigid discipline we are going through, but for us there is no escape. That rigorous self-discipline will generate in us a force which will enable us to retain what we have won. It is the natural result of active non-violence and should stand us in good stead after Swaraj. It is hardly likely that when we are imprisoned, we shall all be kept together. Therefore if our life is well regulated from now, we should not have the slightest difficulty in going regularly through our daily task."

Young India, 20-3-'30

104

DUTY OF DISLOYALTY

The spectacle of three hundred million people being cowed down by living in the dread of three hundred men is demoralizing alike for the despots as for the victims. It is the duty of those who have realized the evil nature of the system, however attractive some of its features, torn from their context, may appear to be, to destroy it without delay. It is their clear duty to run any risk to achieve the end.

But it must be equally clear that it would be cowardly for three hundred million people to seek to destroy the three hundred authors or administrators of the system. It is a sign of gross ignorance to devise means of destroying these administrators or their hirelings. Moreover, they are but creatures of circumstances. The purest man entering the system will be affected by it and will be instrumental in propagating the evil. The remedy therefore naturally is, not being enraged against the administrators and therefore hurting them, but to non-co-operate with the system by withdrawing all the voluntary assistance possible and refusing all its so-called benefits. A little reflection will show that civil disobedience is a necessary part of non-co-operation. You assist an administration most effectively by obeying its orders and decrees. An evil administration never deserves such allegiance. Allegiance to it means partaking of the evil. A good man will therefore resist an evil system or administration with his whole soul. Disobedience of the laws of an evil State is therefore a duty. Violent disobedience deals with men who can be replaced. It leaves the evil itself untouched and often accentuates it. Non-violent, i.e. civil, disobedience is the only and the most successful remedy and is obligatory upon him who would dissociate himself from evil.

There is danger in civil disobedience only because it is still only a partially tried remedy and has always to be tried in an atmosphere surcharged with violence. For when tyranny is rampant much rage is generated among the victims. It remains latent because of their weakness and bursts in all its fury on the slightest pretext. Civil disobedience is a sovereign method of transmitting this undisciplined life-destroying latent energy into disciplined life-saving energy whose use ensures absolute success. The attendant risk is nothing compared to the result promised. When the world has become familiar with its use and when it has had a series of demonstrations of its successful working, there will be less risk in civil disobedience than there is in aviation, in spite of that science having reached a high stage of development.

Young India, 27-3-'30

105

SOME SUGGESTIONS

The resolution passed by the A. I. C. C. at its Ahmedabad meeting throws the burden on me of giving the signal for starting civil disobedience all over the country, assuming that I am kept free till I reach Dandi. The reason is obvious. The A. I. C. C. wishes to take every reasonable precaution against mishaps. In the event of my arrest, it would be dangerous to stop the movement. Before my arrest, the A. I. C. C. will not anticipate me. So far as I can judge now, the workers may assume that the date for making an all-India start will be the 6th of April. It is the day of commencement of the national week. It is the day of Satyagraha that in 1919 witnessed a mass awakening unknown before. The seven days that followed witnessed some dark deeds on our part and culminated in the inhuman Jalianwala massacre. If all goes well I should reach Dandi on April 5th. April 6th therefore appears to me to be the most natural day for commencing Satyagraha. But the workers, while they may make preparations, must await the final word.

The release of the embargo however does not mean that every province or every district is bound at once to commence civil disobedience although it may not be ready and although its First Servant does not feel the inner urge. He will refuse to be hustled into action if he has no confidence in himself or in his immediate surroundings. No one will be blamed for inaction, but blame will most decidedly descend upon the shoulders of him who instead of controlling the surroundings is carried away by them.

What we all are after is mass civil disobedience. It cannot be made. It must be spontaneous, if it is to deserve the name and if it is to be successful. And there certainly will be no mass response where the ground has not been previously tilled, manured and watered. The greatest precaution has to be taken everywhere against an outbreak of violence. Whilst it is true, as I have said, that civil resistance this time will continue even though violence may break out, it is equally true that violence on our part will harm the struggle and retard its progress. Two opposite forces can never work concurrently so as to help each other. The plan of civil disobedience has been conceived to neutralize and ultimately entirely to displace violence and enthrone non-violence in its stead, to replace hatred by love, to replace strife by concord.

The meaning then of not suspending the fight in spite of any outbreak of violence simply is that votaries of non-violence will allow themselves, will even seek, to be consumed in the flames if any should rise. They will not care to remain helpless witnesses either of the organized violence of the Government or of the sporadic violence of an enraged group or nation. The workers will therefore take, in each province, all precautions humanly possible and then plunge into the fight even though in so doing they run the greatest risks imaginable. It follows that everywhere there will be willing submission to the judgment of those who may be in their own provinces known for their belief in non-violence as an article of faith for the purpose of gaining *Purna Swaraj*.

There has been talk of disobeying other laws. The proposal has not attracted me. I believe in concentrating attention upon the Salt laws. Salt mines are to be found almost everywhere. The idea is not to manufacture salt in saleable quantities but through manufacture and otherwise to commit a deliberate and open breach of Salt laws.

The *chaukidari* tax laws have been suggested for possible disobedience. This tax does not in my opinion comply with the conditions that the Salt tax fulfils. The idea is to disobey such laws as are bad for all time as far as can be seen today. We do not want the Salt tax even under Swaraj. *Chaukidari* tax is perhaps not such a tax. We may need *chaukidars* even under Swaraj. If such is the case, it may be wise not to touch that tax so long as we have other taxes or other laws to combat.

Then there are the forest laws. I have not studied them. I must therefore write with reserve. There can be no doubt that we do not want our forests to be destroyed altogether or wood to be cut uneconomically. There is a need, I have little doubt, for mending these laws. There is greater need perhaps for humaner administration of these laws. The reform may well await the establishment of Swaraj. Nor so far as I am aware has there been any popular education about the grievances arising out of these laws or their administration.

Closely allied to the forests are grazing areas. I do not know that regulations governing their use are so irksome as to be a just grievance.

Much better from my standpoint is the picketing of liquor shops, opium dens and foreign cloth shops. Though picketing is not by itself illegal, past experience shows that the Government will want to suppress all effective picketing. That does not much matter. We are out to resist it wherever we can, consistently with our creed. But I fear the unscrupulous behaviour of liquor dealers and the ignorant wrath of foreign cloth dealers. I should like public opinion to consolidate itself more fully around these two evils and would like workers to undertake more systematic education of the dealers as also of their customers.

We have to eradicate both the evils some day or other. Wherever, therefore, workers have confidence in their ability to carry on picketing without taking undue risks of the type I have mentioned, they should start the campaign, but in no case because they must be doing something when the word is given for action and because they do not see their way to take up the Salt laws. It seems to me to be the safest thing to take up the latter for the time being ; what I have said above is merely by way of caution. Wherever workers feel that they have the real inner call for action and are themselves free from violence, they are at liberty, as soon as the word is given, to take up such civil disobedience as they may consider necessary and desirable, subject of course to the A. I. C. C. control.

Meanwhile between now and the 6th of April the provinces should lose no time in making their preparation for mobilization.

Young India, 27-3-'30

106

TURNING THE SEARCHLIGHT INWARD

[Condensed translation by Gandhiji himself of an introspective speech he delivered at Bhatgam (Dist. Surat) on 29-3-'30 during the Dandi March. — Ed.]

Only this morning at the prayer time I was telling my companions that as we had entered the district in which we were to offer civil disobedience, we should insist on greater purification and intenser dedication. I warned them that as the district was more organized and contained many intimate co-workers, there was every likelihood of our being pampered. I warned them against succumbing to their pampering. We are not angels. We are very weak, easily tempted. There are many lapses to our debit. God is great. Even today some were discovered. One defaulter confessed his lapse himself whilst I was brooding over the lapses of the pilgrims. I discovered that my warning was given none too soon. The local workers had ordered milk from Surat to be brought in a motor lorry and they had incurred other expenses which I could not justify. I therefore spoke strongly about them. But that did not allay my grief. On the contrary it increased with the contemplation of the wrongs done.

The Right to Criticize

In the light of these discoveries, what right had I to write to the Viceroy the letter in which I have severely criticized his salary which is more than 5,000 times our average income? How could he possibly do justice to that salary? And how can we tolerate his getting a salary out of all proportion to our income? But he is individually not to be blamed for it. He has no need for it. God has made him a wealthy man. I have suggested in my letter that probably the whole of his salary is spent in charity. I have since learnt that my guess is largely likely to be true. Even so, of course, I should resist the giving of such a large salary. I could not vote Rs 21,000 per month, not perhaps even Rs 2,100 per month. But when could I offer such resistance? Certainly not if I was myself taking from the people an unconscionable toll. I could resist it only if my living bore some correspondence with the average income of the people. We are marching in the name of God. We profess to act on behalf of the hungry, the naked and the unemployed. I have no right to criticize the Viceregal salary, if we are costing the country say fifty times seven pice, the average daily income of our people. I have asked the workers to furnish me with an account of the expenses. And the way things are going, I should not be surprised if each of us is costing something near fifty times seven pice. What else can be the result if they will fetch for me from whatever source possible, the choicest oranges and grapes, if they will bring 120 when I should want 12 oranges, if when I need one pound of milk, they will produce three? What else can be the result if we would take all the dainties you may place before us under the excuse that we would hurt your feeling, if we did not take them. You give us guavas and grapes and we eat them because they are a free gift from a princely farmer. And then imagine me with an easy conscience writing the Viceregal letter on costly glazed paper with a fountain pen, a free gift from some accommodating friend ! ! ! Will this behove you and me ? Can a letter so written produce the slightest effect ?

Trustees of the Dumb Millions

To live thus would be to illustrate the immortal verse of Akho Bhagat who says, " stolen food is like eating unprocessed mercury." And to live above the means befitting a poor country is to live on stolen food. This battle can never be won by living on stolen food. Nor did I bargain to set out on this march for living above our means. We expect thousands of volunteers to respond to the call. It will be impossible to keep them on extravagant terms. My life has become so busy that I get little time to come in close touch even with the eighty companions so as to be able to identify them individually. There was therefore no course open to me but to unburden my soul in public. I expect you to understand the central point of my message. If you have not, there is no hope of Swaraj through the present effort. We must become real trustees of the dumb millions.

I have exposed our weaknesses to the public gaze. I have not yet given you all the details, but I have told you enough to enable you to realize our unworthiness to write the letter to the Viceroy.

Now the local co-workers will understand my agony. Weak, ever exposed to temptations, ever failing, why will you tempt us and pamper us ? We may not introduce these incandescent burners in our villages. It is enough that one hundred thousand men prey upon three hundred million. But how will it be when we begin to prey upon one another ? In that event dogs will lick our corpses.

Account for Every Pice

These lights are merely a sample of the extravagance I have in mind. My purpose is to wake you up from torpor. Let the volunteers account for every pice spent.

I am more capable of offering Satyagraha against ourselves than against the Government. I have taken many years before embarking upon civil resistance against the Government. But I should not take as many days for offering it against ourselves. The risk to be incurred is nothing compared to what has to be incurred in the present Satyagraha.

Therefore in your hospitality towards servants like us, I would have you to be miserly rather than lavish. I shall not complain of unavoidable absence of things. In order to procure goat's milk for me you may not deprive poor women of milk for their children. It would be like poison if you did. Nor may milk and vegetables be brought from Surat. We can do without them if necessary. Do not resort to motor cars on the slightest pretext. The rule is, do not ride, if you can walk. This is not a battle to be conducted with money. It will be impossible to sustain a mass movement with money. Any way it is beyond me to conduct the campaign with a lavish display of money.

Extravagance has no room in this campagin. If we cannot gather crowds unless we carry on a hurricane expensive propaganda, I would be satisfied to address half a dozen men and women. Success depends not upon our high skill. It depends solely upon God. And He only helps the vigilant and the humble.

A Humiliating Sight

We may not consider anybody as low. I observed that you had provided for the night journey a heavy kitson burner mounted on a stool which a poor labourer carried on his head. This was a humiliating sight. This man was being goaded to walk fast. I could not bear the sight. I therefore put on speed and outraced the whole company. But it was no use. The man was made to run after me. The humiliation was complete. If the weight had to be carried, I should have loved to see some one among ourselves carrying it. We would then soon dispense both with the stool and the burner. No labourer would carry such a load on his head. We rightly object to

begar (forced labour). But what was this if it was not
begar ? Remember that in Swaraj we would expect one
drawn from the so-called lower class to preside over India's
destiny. If then we do not quickly mend our ways, there
is no Swaraj such as you and I have put before the people.

From my outpouring you may not infer that I shall
weaken in my resolve to carry on the struggle. It will
continue no matter how co-workers or others act. For
me there is no turning back whether I am alone or joined
by thousands. I would rather die a dog's death and have
my bones licked by dogs than that I should return to the
Ashram a broken man.

(Turning to the women I concluded and nearly broke
down as I finished the last sentences.)

I admit that I have not well used the money you have
given out of the abundance of your love. You are entitled
to regard me as one of those wretches described in the
verses sung in the beginning. Shun me.

Young India, 3-4-'30

107

NOTES ON THE WAY TO DANDI

Dog in the Manger

The volume of information being gained daily shows
how wickedly the Salt tax has been designed. In order
to prevent the use of salt that has not paid the tax which
is at times even fourteen times its value, the Government
destroys the salt it cannot sell profitably. Thus it taxes
the nation's vital necessity, it prevents the public from
manufacturing it and destroys what nature manufactures
without effort. No adjective is strong enough for charac-
terizing this wicked dog-in-the-manger policy. From
various sources I hear tales of such wanton destruction
of nation's property in all parts of India. Maunds if not
tons of salt are said to be destroyed on the Konkan coast.
The same tale comes from Dandi. Wherever there is

likelihood of natural salt being taken away by the people living in the neighbourhood of such areas for their personal use, salt officers are posted for the sole purpose of carrying on destruction. Thus valuable national property is destroyed at national expense and salt taken out of the mouths of the people.

Nor is this all. I was told on entering the Olpad Taluka that through the poor people being prevented from collecting the salt that was prepared by nature or from manufacturing it they were deprived of the supplementary village industry they had in addition to the spinning wheel.

The salt monopoly is thus a fourfold curse. It deprives the people of a valuable easy village industry, involves wanton destruction of property that nature produces in abundance, the destruction itself means more national expenditure, and fourthly, to crown this folly, an unheard of tax of more than 1,000 per cent is exacted from a starving people.

I cannot help recalling in this connection the hue and cry that was raised when I first proposed the burning of foreign cloth. It was considered to be an inhuman, wasteful proposal. It is generally admitted that foreign cloth is harmful to the people. Salt on the other hand is a vital necessity. Yet it has been and is daily being wantonly destroyed in the interest of wicked exaction.

This tax has remained so long because of the apathy of the general public. Now that it is sufficiently roused, the tax has to go. How soon it will be abolished depends upon the strength the people are able to put forth. Happily the test will not be long delayed.

Exaggerated Statements

Paragraphs have appeared in the press to the effect that 18 of my companions have become ill and incapacitated. This is a gross exaggeration. It is quite true that that number had to take a two days' rest at the Broach Sevashram. But that was because they were fatigued and footsore. With the exception of the case of smallpox which proved to be quite mild, there was no illness worth the name. One of the companions certainly had high fever. But that fever too proved to be due to overzeal in marching. He had a wiry constitution and was over-confident about his ability to pull through without resting. He would not therefore rest till nature absolutely compelled him. But both are quite well now though being weak they are still being made to rest a few days. They expect to join the company at Surat. A third, though still a little footsore, insisted on walking, but had to rest at Ankleshvar. All the others are fit and marching daily. It has become necessary to make this statement in order to prevent anxiety on the part of guardians and friends. It would be ungrateful not to mention here the great attention the villagers are paying to the Satyagrahis and the exceptional care that was bestowed upon the smallpox patient by the Charotar Education Society at Anand and on the footsore men by Dr Chandulal's staff at Sevashram.

A moral may also be drawn from these accidents. The modern generation is delicate, weak and much pampered. If they will take part in national work, they must take ample exercise and become hardy. And exercise is as good and as effective as long vigorous marches. Gymnastics and the like are good and may be added to walking. They are no substitute for walking, justly called the prince of exercises. Our march is in reality child's play. Less than twelve miles per day in two stages with not much luggage should cause no strain. Those who have not been footsore have gained in weight. I may add too that the hot Condy's fluid, baths and wet-sheet packs are proving a most efficient remedy for smallpox.

The True Spirit

Shrimati Khorshedbai Naoroji came the other day to Sandhiar, a halting station during the march. She was accompanied by Mridulabehn, the daughter of Sjt. Ambalal Sarabhai, Madalasa the little daughter of Jamnalalji, Shrimati Vasumatibehn and Radhabehn from the Ashram. They had to await a lift for Sandhiar. They wanted to turn to national account the time at their disposal. They saw that the surroundings of the place were not over clean.

They therefore decided to clean up the rubbish and so asked for brooms from the surprised villagers. As soon as the villagers realized what had happened, they also joined these national scavengers some of whom were drawn from aristocratic families and the village of Sayan perhaps never looked as clean as when these sisters utilized their spare time for scavenging. I commend this true service, this mute speech of the sisters to the army of young men who are pining to serve and free the country. Freedom will come only when we deliver a simultaneous attack on all the weak points. Let it be known that all these sisters have enlisted as civil resisters and are eagerly, even impatiently, awaiting marching orders. In this campaign of Swaraj by self-purification, it will be nothing surprising if the women outdo the men.

Young India, 3-4-'30

108

REMEMBER 6TH APRIL

This will be in the readers' hands on Thursday 3rd instant. If there is no previous cancelling, they all may regard this as the word from me that all are free, and those who are ready are expected to start mass civil disobedience regarding the Salt laws, as from 6th April.

Let me gather up what has been said in these pages at various times.

The only stipulation for civil disobedience is perfect observance of non-violence in the fullest sense of the term.

Mass civil disobedience means spontaneous action. The workers will merely guide the masses in the beginning stages. Later the masses will regulate the movement themselves.

Congress volunteers will watch developments and render aid wherever needed. They will be expected to be in the forefront.

Volnteers may not take sides in any communal quarrels.

Wherever there is a violent eruption, volunteers are expected to die in the attempt to quell violence.

Perfect discipline and perfect co-operation among the different units are indispensable for success.

If there is true mass awakening, those who are not engaged in civil disobedience are expected to occupy themselves and induce others to be engaged in some national service such as *khadi* work, liquor and opium picketing, foreign cloth exclusion, village sanitation, assisting the families of civil resistance prisoners in a variety of ways.

Indeed if there is a real response about civil resistance regarding the Salt tax, we should by proper organization secure boycott of foreign cloth through *khadi* and secure total prohibition. This should mean a saving of 91 crores per year, and supplementary work for the millions of unemployed. If we secure these things, we cannot be far from independence. And not one of these things is beyond our capacity.

Young India, 3-4-'30

109

HINDU-MUSLIM QUESTION

[Summary of a speech delivered at Broach on 26th March, 1930, on the communal question.]

A Muslim youth has sent me questions on the Hindu-Muslim problem. One of them is : ' Do you expect to win Swaraj through your own single effort or assisted merely by the Hindus ? ' I have never dreamt that I could win Swaraj merely through my effort or assisted only by the Hindus. I stand in need of the assistance of Mussalmans, Parsis, Christians, Sikhs, Jews and all other Indians. I need the assistance even of Englishmen. But I know too that all this combined assistance is worthless if I have not one other assistance, that is from God. All is vain without

His help. And if He is with this struggle no other help is necessary.

But to realize His help and guidance in this struggle, I need your blessings, the blessings of all communities. The blessings of thousands of men and women belonging to all communities that have attended this march are to me a visible sign of the hand of God in this struggle.

Now is the Time

I know that there are occasions when the hand of God has to be traced in the curses of men. But this is not such an occasion. Today I am doing what the nation has been yearning for during the past ten years. Have I not been rebuked for delaying civil resistance? Have not friends angrily said, "You are stopping the progress of the nation towards its goal. You have only to say, 'Let there be civil resistance, behold! there is Swaraj.'"? There is some truth in the taunt. Full civil resistance does mean Swaraj. But I was staying my hand. I had no confidence in myself. I was straining my ear to listen to the still small voice within, but only up to yesterday there was no response. It was in Lahore I had told a journalist that I saw nothing on the horizon to warrant civil resistance. But suddenly, as in a flash, I saw the light in the Ashram. Self-confidence returned. Englishmen and some Indian critics have been warning me against the hazard. But the voice within is clear. I must put forth all my effort or retire altogether and for all time from public life. I feel that now is the time or it will be never.

And so I am out for battle and am seeking help on bended knee from this white beard (pointing to Sjt. Abbas Tyabji) as also the little girls. For in this battle even they can help; and thank God, they are eager to do so. I have insistent letters from them demanding enlistment.

The Satyagrahi's Strength

Thus the answer to the Muslim youth's question is complete. I need the help of all races and from all climes.

A Satyagrahi has no power he can call his own. All the power he may seem to possess is from and of God. He therefore moves towards his goal carrying the world's opinion with him. Without the help of God he is lame, blind, groping.

Ever since 1921 I have been reiterating two words, *self-purification* and *self-sacrifice*. God will not assist him without these two. The world is touched by sacrifice. It does not then discriminate about the merits of a cause. Not so God. He is all seeing. He insists on the purity of the cause and on adequate sacrifice therefor.

The question was put by a Mussalman representing a powerful interest. But had a little Parsi girl representing but a hundred thousand Parsis asked the question, I should have given the same answer and said, 'Without the help of Parsis there is no Swaraj.' I am thankful to be able to say that I have had during the march abundant proof of the blessings of these communities. I have read friendliness in the eyes and in the speech of the Mussalmans who along with the rest have lined our route or attended the meetings. They have even given material aid.

Yet I know that I have not the Ali Brothers with me. Maulana Shaukat Ali will no longer have me in his pocket. Do not think, I do not miss him. I hold no distinction between him and a blood brother. His resistance therefore can only be short-lived. If truth is in me, the brothers must capitulate. They cannot long keep out of the battle. I crave too the assistance of Englishmen. It was neither empty formula nor a touch of vanity that prompted me to send an English friend with my letter to the Viceroy. By choosing Reginald Reynolds as my messenger, I sealed the bond between them and me. For my enmity is not against them, it is against their rule. I seem to be born to be an instrument to compass the end of that rule. But if a hair of an English head was touched I should feel the same grief as I should over such a mishap to my brother. I say to them as a friend, 'Why will you not understand that your rule is ruining this country? It has got to be destroyed even though you may pound us to powder or drown us. We must declare what we feel.'

The Congress Pledge

The second question is 'Under Swaraj how many

seats will Mussalmans have in the legislatures ? ' What answer can I return to such a question ? If I were Viceroy of India I should say to the Mussalmans, Sikhs, Christians, Parsis &c., ' Take what you like, the balance will go to the Hindus.' It is true that the *Sanatani* Hindu will never let me become Viceroy. The fact is that I am unfit to do such accounting. But it should be sufficient to know that the Congress has pledged itself not to accept any communal solution that does not satisfy the parties concerned. I am bound by that pledge. For the Congress all are one. They are all Indians and therefore their freedom is guaranteed. No more can be expected by any community.

Civil resistance will merely give the power to the nation to assert her will. But when the time comes for its assertion, the document embodying the will will have to be sealed by all the communities. Thus without the co-operation of all communities, there is no independence.

But what should we do meanwhile ? We must at least be true to the salt we eat. Her starving millions are the salt of India's earth. To be true to them we must free the salt from a tax which they have to pay equally with the rich and in the same proportion as the rich. In our ignorance we have been paying this inhuman imposition. Having realized our folly we will be traitors to the starving millions, if we submit to the exaction any longer.

Who can help liking this poor man's battle ? The cruel tax is no respecter of persons. It is therefore as much the interest of the Mussalman as of the Hindu to secure its abolition. This is a fight undertaken in the name of God and for the sake of the millions of paupers of this country.

Young India, 3-4-'30

110

BARBAROUS

The threatened has after all happened. I congratulate the Government on having commenced arrests in right earnest of Salt tax resisters at least in Gujarat. They have arrested Sjt. Manilal Kothari and all his companions, so also Sjt. Amritlal Sheth and his companions, Dr Chandulal Desai of Broach Sevashram and his companions. They have arrested Darbar Gopaldas, Sjt. Fulchand, Sjt. Ravishankar the intrepid reformer who has weaned the brave but ignorant Rajputs of Kheda from many an error. They have arrested Ramdas Gandhi, Keshavbhai Ganeshji, Chimanlal Pranshankar and others. All this the Government had the right to do. But they had no right to do what they did today at the village Aat four miles from Dandi. The police tried by force to snatch salt from the civil resisters. This they had no right to do, if they were representing a civilized Government. There was no provocation offered. The resisters were not running away. Their names could have been taken. But they insulted these brave men and through them the nation by touching their sacred persons without warrant and without just cause. One of the resisters by name Ukabhai Rama of Bardoli was slightly injured on the wrist. I admit that the police went unarmed to the scene of action. They will probably admit that there never was the slightest occasion for carrying arms, for the people were obviously and absolutely peaceful. Nevertheless this laying hands on the people for the purpose of seizing the salt they were carrying was morally wrong, and even wrong I fancy according to English common law. But I do not know what powers are given by a statute that makes a crime of undefined cowardice.

This first drawing of blood, however little, brought down practically the whole of the village to the scene. Women were just yet to take no part in the act of civil disobedience, nor were the men of the village expected as yet to do so. But they, men and women (some with babies in arms), immediately they heard that salt was being forcibly seized and that one of the volunteers was injured, rushed out, and men on one side and women on the other descended to the channel and began to dig out the salt. As soon as I heard of the attempt at forcible seizure from the persons of the resisters, Monday being my day of silence, I wrote on a piece of paper that Shrimati Sarojini Devi and Sjt. Abbas Tyabji should go, and if the police did not desist they should also dig out salt and challenge them to seize it from their hands. But I charitably assume that the police had seen their mistake before these friends reached the scene and had not the heart to touch a whole villageful of people including women. The Satyagrahis, however, would not be satisfied without my presence although I might not speak. They wanted me evidently to see with my own eyes how they had behaved and with what zest the whole village was participating in the struggle. Ukabhai Rama was brought to me with the salt rescued. I went. For me it was a soul-stirring sight. The forcible seizure served a good purpose. It brought life to the whole village. Nevertheless, for the sake of the Government and for the sake of keeping the salt war on the gentlemanly plane, I wish this ugly incident had not happened.

Legal procedure may be a cumbersome business for the Government. But since they have begun well let them not end ill. Let it be a pure trial of strength between them and the people. If they will resort to terrorism and if I am not mistaken, they will find the people, men as well as women, ready for any ordeal they may prepare for them. Salt in the hands of Satyagrahis represents the honour of the nation. It cannot be yielded up except to force that will break the hand to pieces. Ukabhai as he was describing the action of the police said, 'God gives strength to a Satyagrahi to defend what is entrusted to him.' Let the people defend the salt in their possession till they break in the attempt, but they should do so without malice, without anger, without an angry word. The police have the easiest way open to them of taking possession of the salt. Let them arrest the civil resisters, and they can take possession of the salt for they have possession of their persons. But it can become forfeit only after conviction, not before.

Young India, 10-4-'30

111

THE INHUMAN TAX

Every new experience gained of the incidence of the Salt tax shows it to be more inhuman than it appeared at first. Living and moving as I am in the midst of the salt area in Gujarat, I find that villages have been ruined because of the prohibition of salt manufacture by the villagers. The only use the people can make of the land is to extract salt from it which nature deposits in abundance from month to month. This was the poor man's staple industry in these parts. Now all this land lies fallow. Dandi itself has a tragic history. It is a beautiful seaside place. It takes its name from the fact that it was a place for a *diva dandi,* i.e. a lighthouse. Now it is a deserted village. A European and then Indians tried against nature to reclaim the soil for cultivation. As I walk about the otherwise beautiful peace-giving shore and listen for the heavenly music of the gentle waves, I see about me wasted human effort in the shape of dilapidated embanked fields without a patch of vegetation. These very fields immediately the hateful salt monopoly is gone, will be valuable salt pans from which villagers will extract fresh, white sparkling salt without much labour, and it will give them a living as it did their ancestors.

Mahadev Desai has already shown that the Government communique that this salt is injurious to health is a wicked falsehood. In spite of the inhuman regulations, the people round about this area have used none but the salt that nature provides here in abundance. They do not seem to have felt any the worse for it. Thousands all over this area have been during the past week eating this salt with impunity. I hear that in Konkan people have all these years used what they regard as Swadeshi salt in contradistinction to the taxed salt which they regard as *sarkari* or 'foreign', although in the first instance it was yielded by India's earth and seas. The recipe which I publish in this issue has been prepared by two careful men who have graduated in science. According to it every household can prepare its own salt without any expense whatsoever. One boy has merely to fetch a *lotaful* of salt water and it has merely to be strained or filtered and put near the fire in a shallow pan and treated in accordance with the recipe, and the householders have every day's supply of salt much cleaner and healthier than the *sarkari* or 'foreign' dirty salt to be had in the bazars. Let the salt Satyagrahis (and they are to be counted in their tens of thousands now) not waste a single grain of Swadeshi salt. Law or no law there is now no excuse for any one to eat the bazar salt. Swadeshi salt must be introduced even where there are no salt beds. It can be easily transported in small quantities from place to place. Let the Government prosecute tens of thousands of men and women or if they dare, send their officials to search their persons and brutally force it from them. Let them say : 'The Salt law allows it.' I have already shown that the Salt regulations are as inhuman as the tax itself. If the history of the administration in the early stages of these regulations were known, it would be found that these inhuman regulations were as inhumanly administered in order to deprive the people of their natural calling and compel them to take the blood-stained *sarkari* salt. Let the reader know that even palanquins bearing *pardanashin* women were searched in order to prevent the transport of illicit salt. If today we have to bear hardships in the attempt to have this iniquitous tax removed, we are but doing a modicum of penance for our past neglect and shameful submission to the impost. The reader will thus see that it is not merely the tax, heavy as it is, that is offensive. It has not one redeeming feature about it. The revenue it brings is not the only cost to the nation. The cost to the nation is probably twenty crores per year besides the loss of an equal amount of salt which is wantonly destroyed or prevented from being gathered.

Young India, 17-4-'30

112

A SURVEY

The mass manifestation in Gujarat has exceeded all expectations. Bombay and its suburbs have done no less. And the reports slowly coming to me at this out of the way place from all over India are fully encouraging. It is the matter of the keenest joy to me to see Maharashtra united once more and Sjt. N. C. Kelkar and his friends joining the struggle. Sjt. Kelkar's and Sjt. Aney's resignations are events of great importance in the struggle. Bengal is the most tempestuous province in all India. It is pulsating with life. Its very factions are symptomatic of its great awakening. If Bengal responds in the right style it is likely to overshadow every other province. I do not know that any province, even Maharashtra, can claim the credit that Bengal can for voluntary sacrifice. If its emotional side is its weakness, it is also its greatest strength. It has the capacity for reckless abandon to non-violence, if such use of language is permissible. Sjt. Sen Gupta's action in response to the wanton assault on the students' meeting has evoked the sentiment above expressed. The sentence of Dr Suresh Bannerji and others pales into insignificance before the possibilities of the move on the part of the Bengal students and the savage counter move on the part of the police. I know what the Calcutta Commissioner of Police will say, if he sees these lines. I hear him saying ' But you do not know my Bengal.' Well, I know his Bengal more than he ever will. His Bengal is the creation of the Government. If the Government will cease to molest Bengal and not keep India from her cherished goal, Bengal will be as gentle as the greatest province of India. If Bengal is seething with the violent spirit, it is because of her sufferings.

But I expect Bengal's imagination to come to her assistance and to realize that non-violence is the trump-card. All the suffering must be dedicated to the Goddess of *Ahimsa*.

Soon after the Jalianwala massacre, I used to express and reiterate the hope that next time in no part of India must people run away on bullets being discharged against them, and that they must receive them in their chests with arms folded and with courageous resignation. That testing time seems to be coming faster than I had expected. And if we are to train ourselves to receive the bullet wounds or bayonet charges in our bare chests, we must accustom ourselves to standing unmoved in the face of cavalry or baton charges. I know that it is easier said than done. Nevertheless, I must say it if we are ever to complete our training in mass non-violence. That mass non-violence is a perfect possibility has been sufficiently demonstrated during the past eight days. Mahadev Desai has given a realistic account of the brutal treatment of volunteers in the Dholera salt bed and the volunteers suffering the brutality with meek heroism. What thousands in Bombay did when the police acted with rashness and harshness if also with comparative considerateness can be studied from a condensed translation published in this issue of a graphic description sent to me by Pt. Mukund Malaviya. His report is in the main corroborated by Dahyabhai, Sardar Vallabhbhai's son, who was also an eyewitness.

Perinbai and her companions as also Kamaladevi acted with rare courage and calmness. But they would allow me to say that they would have done better to remain outside the venue of the men's fight. For women to be in the midst of such danger as they put themselves in was against the rule of chivalry. Any way that time is not yet. Let them by all means manufacture salt in their thousands. But they may not remain deliberately in crowds which they know are likely to be charged. I have in all humility suggested to them an exclusive field in which they are at liberty and are expected to show their best qualities. There is in that field enough scope for adventure and heroism.

To revert, if then we are to stand the final heat of the battle, we must learn to stand our ground in the face of cavalry or baton charges and allow ourselves to be trampled under horses' hoofs or bruised with baton charges. An armed crowd could stand firm and retaliate if there were such charges. We, if we would learn the lesson of non-violence, should show greater courage by standing our ground without anger, without retaliation. Then a reincarnation of Dyer will find us ready for receiving bullets in the bare breast.

People have already begun to defend their salt pans. If we have evolved that sufficient amount of courage, it must be done methodically and regularly. As soon as the police come to charge us and break through the living wall, women should, if the police give the opportunity, stand aside and let their men be wounded. They do so all the world over in armed conflict; let them do so in a conflict in which one party deliberately chooses to remain unarmed.

When there are no men left to fight the battle of free salt, if they have courage let them take up the work deserted by men. But I have no doubt that men will give a good account of themselves in this struggle.

I have already examined elsewhere the argument that the police must use force if people will not surrender the contraband salt in their possession. Here I would only remind these critics that even from confirmed thieves they do not take stolen property by force except after they are brought under arrest and then too never if they are not to be brought to trial. The property still remains the thief's until he is convicted and the court adjudges the property not to be his. That the salt regulations make the policeman the arresting officer, prosecutor and judge all rolled

into one is no answer to my charge of barbarity in respect
of the procedure adopted by the authorities.

Young India, 17-4-'30

113

THE BLACK REGIME

The past week has not been one of unmixed joy. It has
seen the disturbances in Calcutta and Karachi. And now
comes the sad news from Chittagong. It shows that in
spite of the striking demonstration of non-violence all over
the country, there is still violence in the air and cities
are the storehouses of it. Calcutta and Karachi can be
distinguished from Chittagong. The first two appear to
have been mad outbursts of the moment. Chittagong
seems to be a deliberate planning. Whatever they were,
they are most regrettable and interfere with the growth
of the movement which is otherwise shaping itself marve-
llously well and gaining fresh momentum from day to day.
I can only appeal to those who believe in violence not to
disturb the free flow of the non-violent demonstration.
Whether they listen or not, this movement will go on.
Violence is bound to impede the progress towards
independence. I am unable to demonstrate how it will
impede. Those who survive the struggle will know how.

Meanwhile Satyagrahis must continue their activity
with redoubled vigour. We must deal with the double-
edged violence ranged against us. For me popular violence
is as much an obstruction in our path as the Government
violence. Indeed I can combat the Government violence
more successfully than the popular. For one thing, in
combating the latter, I should not have the same support
as in the former. Then again one motive in the latter being
as honourable as that of the Satyagrahis, the method to be
employed has to be somewhat different from that employed
in regard to Government violence.

I hope that as in Karachi, so in Calcutta and Chittagong,

there were Satyagrahis attempting to check mob violence. Brave young Dattatreya Mane who is said to have known nothing of Satyagraha and being an athlete had merely gone to assist in keeping order, received a fatal bullet wound, Meghraj Revachand, 18 years old, has also succumbed to a bullet wound. Thus did seven men, including Jairamdas, receive bullet wounds. Jairamdas's injury gave me unmixed joy. It is the injury to leaders that would bring relief. The law of sacrifice is uniform throughout the world. To be effective it demands the sacrifice of the bravest and the most spotless. And Jairamdas is of the bravest and the cleanest. I therefore could not help wiring when I heard of Jairamdas's wound that a wound in the thigh was better than prison and wound in the heart better still.

Whilst therefore I tender my sympathy to the parents of the two brave lads who lost their lives, my inmost desire is to congratulate them for the finished sacrifices of their sons, if they would accept my congratulations. A warrior's death is never a matter for sorrow, still less that of a Satyagrahi warrior. One of the lessons that a nation yearning for freedom needs to learn is to shed several fears of losing title, wealth, position, fear of imprisonment, of bodily injury and lastly death.

Accounts from all over India tell the same tale of growing fearlessness. The Bihar letter published elsewhere in this issue makes soul-stirring reading.

One thing we must get rid of quickly. Lawless physical violence must be stopped even if it is to be through forcing the Government to use its guns. And this can be done non-violently.

I give only one out of several samples of indecent assaults by the police at Viramgam :

Statement of Aniruddha Vyas, a student of Dakshinamurti Vidyarthi Bhavan, Volunteer No. 35/3.

"I with a number of my companions got down from the 6-30 evening mail with bags of salt at the Viramgam Railway Station, when from 8 to 10 policemen surrounded us. To save the salt from being seized, I sat down with the bag of salt on the ground, clinging to it with all my might.

"All efforts of the police to make me get up having failed, one of them thrust apart my legs and squeezed my private parts with his hands so as to compel me to get up. But the weight of my body and the push and the pull of the surrounding police disengaged the parts and I fell down. I was then pulled up again. But I bent double and held the salt bag tight under my crossed arms. A policeman thereupon straightened my back by poking it with his foot which caused me intense pain. Then two policemen gave a violent jerk, twisted my fingers as they liked and loosened my arms and wrested the bag from me. I was then let go, one officer taking my name and number."

Mahadev Desai tells me that those assaults have stopped for the time being. But there is no knowing that they have stopped for ever and there certainly is not the slightest ground for supposing that they will not occur in other parts of Gujarat or of other provinces. In Broach things are growing from bad to worse. A bullet wound is any day better than these barbarous, unnecessary, unprovoked assaults. The person of a citizen must be held inviolate. It can only be touched to arrest or to prevent violence, never in the manner being done now. It is a prostitution even of the Salt laws to use them against civil resisters. The provisions were designed to deal (even then unjustly as I hold) with surreptitious breaches of its new provisions, never to deal with masses of men openly defying them. If the Government do not stop this brutal violation of the body, they will find the Satyagrahis presently compelling them to use the guns against them. I do not want this to happen. But if the Government will have it, I should have no hesitation whatsoever in giving them the opportunity. They must not physically interfere with the bands of civil resisters manufacturing or vending salt, they may arrest every man, woman and child if they wish. If they will neither arrest nor declare salt free, they will find people marching to be shot rather than be tortured.

It is true that the barbarous interference with the body and the indecent assaults are a heritage of the past. This Government by its tacit approval has given it a currency which it never had before.

As I am writing these notes two volunteers have brought me salt said to have been poisoned. Not only do the authorities wantonly destroy salt and salt pans now, they are said to poison the sources of salt manufacture. If the report is true the blackness of the regime becomes blacker still. And all this against a people who without hurting anybody are seeking to gain freedom through self-suffering !

Young India, 24-4-'30

114

PURITY IN ACCOUNT KEEPING

Simple people are in pure faith pouring in their copper, silver and paper coins into the bowls of volunteers who sell salt or otherwise collect money. No unauthorized volunteers should make collections or sell salt at fancy prices. Accounts should be accurately kept and frequently published. Books should be weekly examined by auditors. It will be well if moneyed men of proved honesty were to constitute themselves treasurers to take charge of and collect funds and work in full co-operation with Congress volunteers. Active workers are being quickly picked up and it may be difficult before long for local organizations to hold funds and keep proper accounts. As it is, the public have everywhere taken over the financing of the movement. Let it be done responsibly and methodically.

Young India, 24-4-'30

115

CALM HEROISM

Sjt. Shriprakash writes from Banaras :

" I felt I must convey to you the story of volunteer Hiralal who seems to me to have got nearest to your instructions regarding our conduct when the police seize our salt. We started our salt campaign here on the 8th, and every day batches of 10 manufacture salt for 24 hours when they are relieved by the next batch.

" On the third day in the afternoon about 60 constables with their officers suddenly invaded the site and demanded the delivery of the salt and pan. The volunteers clung to the burning pan desperately and it could only be forcibly snatched from them after fully 20 minutes of resistance. Volunteer Hiralal caught hold of the ring of the burning pan and clung to it desperately. The result was that his right hand was completely burnt and it will be many weeks before he is able to recover the use of his fingers. Almost all other volunteers were injured, but this volunteers' conduct deserves mention and convey to you his name with pride."

Young men like Hiralal will be the makers of Swaraj.

Young India, 24-4-'30

116

MAHADEV DESAI AND HIS SUCCESSOR

In the midst of chaos going under the false name of Government, Mahadev's arrest was a courteous and reluctant business on the part of the authorities. Though he set ablaze the whole of Gujarat from Viramgam and Dholera to Ahmedabad, the authorities recognized that it was a life-giving fire, that they were safer under Mahadev's rule than their own and that he was well able to control the forces he had brought into being.

But Mahadev made it impossible for the authorities to keep him free. He had managed to ' smuggle in ' a lorry load of salt from Dholera. The authorities were wide awake. They intercepted the lorry. They had hoped not to find Mahadev in it. But when he saw that the lorry was to be arrested together with its precious load, he got out of the car in which he was following and jumped into the lorry. And so if they were to arrest the lorry they could not help arresting him. Nor could Mahadev help jumping into the lorry in the circumstances. With him was a youth who was to have appeared for his final LL.B. the following day, two were young men from the Gujarat College and two were sons of wealthy men. The lorry was given by Sjt. Ranchhodlal, a mill-owner who when warned what might befall the lorry said, ' What fear about the loss of the lorry, when I am prepared to lose all for Swaraj ? '

Mahadev has got his well-deserved rest. For hundreds of strenuous workers the jail has become a resting house. Mahadev yearned as he says after ' a better fate but evidently had not yet deserved it.'

He had appointed as his successor Imamsaheb Abdul Kadir Bavazeer, a comrade from South Africa and Vice Chairman of the Ashram committee and one of its trustees. Imamsaheb is an elderly man hardly capable of strenuous labour. He may be said to be illiterate. But he is a seasoned soldier and son of a devoted Muslim who was till the time of his death muezzin of the Juma Musjid of Bombay. He is himself styled Imam because he officiated as priest in several mosques in South Africa. He is an orthodox Mussalman in the sense that he never misses his prayers or his fasts. But he is also most liberal-minded or he could not have lived with me in the closest contact in the midst of all sorts of people for an unbroken period of nearly twenty years.

But the Swaraj of my — our — dream recognizes no race or religious distinctions. Nor is it to be the monopoly of lettered persons nor yet of moneyed men. Swaraj is to be for all, including the former, but emphatically including the maimed, the blind, the starving toiling millions. A stout-hearted, honest, sane, illiterate man may well be the first servant of the nation as Imamsaheb has become in

Gujarat, and another still less known friend, by name Abdullabhai, has become one in Vile Parle. He is the successor of Swami Anand who by his inexhaustible energy and amazing self-denial made Navajivan Karyalaya, though a purely philanthropic institution, also a sound business proposition which has been bringing to the doors of the Gujaratis the truest gems of Gujarati literature understandable by the masses. But these are not rare instances. These are typical of what the struggle has thrown up all over India.

Young India, 1-5-'30

117

GOONDA RAJ

If what is going on in Gujarat is any indication of what is going on in other parts of India, even Dyerism pales into insignificance. This may appear to be an exaggerated statement. But it is meant to be literally true. The massacre of Jalianwala was a clean sweep. It created an impression both in the intended and the unintended sense.

The death by inches that is being dealt out in Gujarat is unimpressive either way, and may, if care is not taken, prove utterly demoralizing. It may weaken the victims and decidedly debases the tyrants.

If I have the time I shall summarize the events of the past week for these columns. In any case the reader will find the whole of the evidence in the daily press.

Mahadev Desai had hugged the belief that after the efforts he made by going there himself and sending lawyer friends, the barbarous torture had ceased at Viramgam. But it was not to be. A volunteer was for a few minutes isolated from his company, and this gave the representatives of law and order an opportunity of falling upon their victim and treating him as his predecessors had been treated at Viramgam.

That is what Dr Narsinbhai Mehta, a retired Chief

Medical Officer of Junagadh, who at the age of 66, was enthused with the spirit of Satyagraha, saw with his own eyes :

"I brought a party of about 120 Satyagrahis, each with a bag of ten lb. of contraband salt from Wadhwan Camp this evening.

"As I led the party, I was the first to meet the inspecting party consisting of one European officer, two Indian officers and about 4 or 5 police constables. Over and above this there were about fifty spare constables watching the entrance of the staircase.

"I was asked what I had got in the bag under my armpit. I replied, 'Ten lb. of contraband salt.' 'All right, old doctor, you can go,' they said. I said, 'I am leading a party of about 120 Satyagrahis, each with a bag of such salt. So I want to see personally how you deal with them, or whether you allow them to go freely just like other passengers.' He said, 'All right, you stand apart on one side, and watch.' One by one the Satyagrahis were made to pass through the said inspecting party and immediately all the seven or eight of them, including the European officer, caught hold of each resister and snatched the bag from the hands of the Satyagrahi, handling the resister most roughly. Almost every Satyagrahi was treated likewise. It was a disgraceful proceeding. I had a very high opinion of Englishmen throughout my life. This was my first experience of the kind during sixty-six years.

"When I could bear the treatment no longer and expostulated, the officer said: 'Speak to the public outside about this and write to the papers!' And the whole performance went on as before."

Mark the callousness with which Dr Mehta's entreaty was met. It was a jolly performance for the British officer and his fellow loyalists to indulge in the sport of dispossessing young men of their precious possession. It was no use telling them that the victims were not running away nor hiding anything. The law had to be respected without any waiting for the law's delay on the part of its administrators.

But even this was nothing compared to the scenes enacted in the Kheda district. I own that the brave sons and daughters of Kheda have carried out fairly successfully the legitimate boycott of officials who are no longer able to impose their will upon the people. They have brutally struck a graduate and professor of the Gujarat Vidyapith who had committed no offence, but who had gone simply to see what was happening when he heard the beating. In the same district near Borsad a few police supported by a local Thakore and his minions armed with long-armed sickles without notice put out the lights at a meeting and mercilessly fell upon their victims. The audience consisted of Patidars and Rajputs who were fully able to defend themselves. But not a stone was thrown, not a word was uttered. For the sake of discipline they suffered. One man narrowly escaped death. Seven are still lying in a hospital. Altogether thirty-five have been traced as having been injured. This was a cowardly edition of Jalianwala.

Then take Ahmedabad. A liquor dealer finding his till empty from day to day got so exasperated that he savagely attacked the pickets one of whom lay senseless. The picketing was of the most peaceful as acknowledged by everybody. There was not even any demonstration. Only the names of those who visited this were taken down by the pickets who knew them. The success of the picketing lies in this case in moving the caste machinery which still works fairly among the labouring classes.

Have the administrators of law and order done anything to prevent this savagery? No. They have secretly enjoyed it. They are welcome to the joy of it. Only let this be not called 'law and order'. Let it be called *Goonda Raj*.

The duty before the people is clear. They must answer this organized hooliganism with great suffering. If they have the will and the power, freedom is assured. Freedom is a fruit of suffering, licence is born of violence. What we are all pining for is freedom that imposes restraints upon itself for the sake of society. Licence imposes suffering upon society so that it may enjoy exclusive privileges. This is a Government of unbridled licence because it is a Government whose chief, if not sole, aim is to exploit Indian society.

118

MESSAGE TO THE NATION

[The following is an English translation of a message dictated by Gandhiji at Dandi on April 9th, when there was a strong rumour of his impending arrest.]

At last the long expected hour seems to have come.

In the dead of night my colleagues and companions have roused me from deep slumber and requested me to give them a message. I am therefore dictating this message, although I have not the slightest inclination to give any.

Messages I have given enough already. Of what avail would this message be if none of the previous messages evoked a proper response? But information received until this midnight leads me to the belief that my message did not fall flat, but was taken up by the people in right earnest.

The people of Gujarat seem to have risen in a body as it were. I have seen with my own eyes thousands of men and women at Aat and Bhimrad, fearlessly breaking the Salt Act. Not a sign of mischief, not a sign of violence have I seen, despite the presence of people in such large numbers. They have remained perfectly peaceful and non-violent, although Government officers have transgressed all bounds.

Here in Gujarat well-tried and popular public servants have been arrested one after another, and yet the people have been perfectly non-violent. They have refused to give way to panic, and have celebrated the arrests, by offering civil disobedience in ever increasing numbers. This is just as it should be.

If the struggle auspiciously begun is continued in the same spirit of non-violence to the end, not only shall we see *Purna Swaraj* established in our country before long, but we shall have given to the world an object lesson worthy of India and her glorious past.

Swaraj won without sacrifice cannot last long. I would therefore like our people to get ready to make the highest sacrifice that they are capable of. In true sacrifice all the suffering is on one side — one is required to master the art of getting killed without killing, of gaining life by losing it. May India live up to this *mantra*.

At present India's self-respect, in fact her all, is symbolized as it were in a handful of salt in the Satyagrahi's hand. Let the fist holding it, therefore, be broken, but let there be no voluntary surrender of the salt.

Let the Government, if it claims to be a civilized Government, jail those who help themselves to contraband salt. After their arrest the civil resisters will gladly surrender the salt, as they will their bodies into the custody of their jailors.

But by main force to snatch the salt from the poor, harmless Satyagrahis' hands is barbarism pure and simple and an insult to India. Such insult can be answered only by allowing our hand to be fractured without loosening the grasp. Even then the actual sufferer or his comrades may not harbour in their hearts anger against the wrong-doer. Incivility should be answered not by incivility but by a dignified and calm endurance of all suffering in the name of God.

Let not my companions or the people at large be perturbed over my arrest, for it is not I, but God who is guiding this movement. He ever dwells in the hearts of all and He will vouchsafe to us the right guidance if only we have faith in Him. Our path has already been chalked out for us. Let every village fetch or manufacture contraband salt. Sisters should picket liquor shops, opium dens and foreign-cloth dealers' shops. Young and old in every home should ply the *takli* and spin and get woven heaps of yarn every day. Foreign cloth should be burnt. Hindus should eschew untouchability. Hindus, Mussalmans, Sikhs, Parsis, and Christians should all achieve heart unity. Let the majority rest content with what remains after the minorities have been satisfied. Let students leave Government schools and colleges, and Government servants resign their service and devote themselves to service of the people, and we shall find that *Purna Swaraj* will come knocking at our doors.

Young India, 8-5-'30

119

THE SECOND LETTER

[The following is the text of Gandhiji's letter to the Viceroy drafted on the eve of his arrest.]

Dear Friend,

God willing, it is my intention on....to set out for Dharasana and reach there with my companions on.... and demand possession of the Salt Works. The public have been told that Dharasana is private property. This is mere camouflage. It is as effectively under Government control as the Viceroy's House. Not a pinch of salt can be removed without the previous sanction of the authorities.

It is possible for you to prevent this raid, as it has been playfully and mischievously called, in three ways :

1. by removing the Salt tax ;

2. by arresting me and my party unless the country can, as I hope it will, replace every one taken away ;

3. by sheer *goondaism* unless every head broken is replaced, as I hope it will.

It is not without hesitation that the step has been decided upon. I had hoped that the Government would fight the civil resister in a civilized manner. I could have had nothing to say if in dealing with the civil resisters the Government had satisfied itself with applying the ordinary processes of law. Instead, whilst the known leaders have been dealt with more or less according to the legal formality, the rank and file has been often savagely and in some cases even indecently assaulted. Had these been isolated cases, they might have been overlooked. But accounts have come to me from Bengal, Bihar, Utkal, U.P., Delhi and Bombay, confirming the experiences of Gujarat of which I have ample evidence at my disposal. In Karachi,

Peshawar and Madras, the firing would appear to have been unprovoked and unnecessary. Bones have been broken, private parts have been squeezed, for the purpose of making volunteers give up, to the Government value-less, to the volunteers precious, salt. At Mathura an Assistant Magistrate is said to have snatched the national flag from a ten-year old boy. The crowd that demanded restoration of the flag thus illegally seized, is said to have been mercilessly beaten back. That the flag was subsequently restored betrayed a guilty conscience. In Bengal there seem to have been only a few prosecutions and assaults about salt, but unthinkable cruelties are said to have been practised in the act of snatching flags from volunteers. Paddy fields are reported to have been burnt, eatables forcibly taken. A vegetable market in Gujarat has been raided because the dealers would not sell vegetables to officials. These acts have taken place in front of crowds who, for the sake of Congress mandate, have submitted without retaliation. I ask you to believe the accounts given by men pledged to truth. Repudiation even by high officials has, as in the Bardoli case, often proved false. The officials, I regret to have to say, have not hesitated to publish falsehoods to the people even during the past five weeks. I take the following samples from Government notices issued from Collectors' offices in Gujarat :

"1. Adults use five pounds of salt per year, therefore, pay three annas per year as tax.........If Government removed the monopoly people will have to pay higher prices and in addition make good to the Government the loss sustained by the removal of the monopoly......The salt you take from the seashore is not eatable therefore, the Government destroys it."

" 2. Mr Gandhi says that Government has destroyed hand-spinning in this country, whereas everybody knows that this is not true, because throughout the country, there is not a village where hand-spinning of cotton is not going on. Moreover, in every province cotton spinners are shown superior methods and are provided with better instruments at less price and are thus helped by Government."

" 3. Out of every five rupees of the debt that the Government has incurred rupees four have been beneficially spent."

I have taken these three sets of statements from three different leaflets. I venture to suggest that every one of these statements is demonstrably false. The daily consumption of salt by an adult is three times the amount stated and therefore the poll tax, that the Salt tax undoubtedly is, is at least 9 as. per head per year. And this tax is levied from man, woman, child and domestic cattle irrespective of age and health.

It is a wicked falsehood to say that every village has a spinning wheel, and that the spinning movement is in any shape or form encouraged or supported by the Government. Financiers can better dispose of the falsehood, that four out of every five rupees of the public debt is used for the benefit of the public. But those falsehoods are mere samples of what people know is going on in everyday contact with the Government. Only the other day a Gujarati poet, a brave man, was convicted on perjured official evidence, in spite of his emphatic statement that at the time mentioned he was sleeping soundly in another place.

Now for instances of official inactivities. Liquor dealers have assaulted pickets admitted by officials to have been peaceful and sold liquor in contravention of regulations. The officials have taken no notice either of the assaults or the illegal sales of liquor. As to the assaults, though they are known to everybody, they may take shelter under the plea that they have received no complaints.

And now you have sprung upon the country a Press Ordinance surpassing any hitherto known in India. You have found a short cut through the law's delay in the matter of the trial of Bhagatsingh and others by doing away with the ordinary procedure. Is it any wonder if I call all these official activities and inactivities a veiled form of Martial Law ? Yet this is only the fifth week of the struggle !

Before then the reign of terrorism that has just begun overwhelms India, I feel that I must take a bolder step, and if possible divert your wrath in a cleaner if more drastic channel. You may not know the things that I have described. You may not even now believe in these. I can but invite your serious attention to them.

Any way I feel that it would be cowardly on my part not to invite you to disclose to the full the leonine paws of authority so that the people who are suffering tortures and destruction of their property may not feel that I, who had perhaps been the chief party inspiring them to action that has brought to right light the Government in its true colours, had left any stone unturned to work out the Satyagraha programme as fully as it was possible under given circumstances.

For, according to the science of Satyagraha, the greater the repression and lawlessness on the part of authority, the greater should be the suffering courted by the victims. Success is the certain result of suffering of the extremest character, voluntarily undergone.

I know the dangers attendant upon the methods adopted by me. But the country is not likely to mistake my meaning. I say what I mean and think. And I have been saying for the last fifteen years in India and outside for twenty years more and repeat now that the only way to conquer violence is through non-violence pure and undefiled. I have said also that every violent act, word and thought interferes with the progress of non-violent action. If in spite of such repeated warnings people will resort to violence, I must disown responsibility save such as inevitably attaches to every human being for the acts of every other human being. But the question of responsibility apart, I dare not postpone action on any cause whatsoever, if non-violence is the force the seers of the world have claimed it to be and if I am not to belie my own extensive experience of its working.

But I would fain avoid the further step. I would therefore ask you to remove the tax which many of your illustrious countrymen have condemned in unmeasured terms and which, as you could not have failed to observe, has evoked universal protest and resentment expressed in civil disobedience. You may condemn civil disobedience as much as you like. Will you prefer violent revolt to civil disobedience ? If you say, as you have said, that the civil disobedience must end in violence, history will pronounce the verdict that the British Government, not bearing because not understanding non-violence, goaded human nature to violence, which it could understand, and deal with. But in spite of the goading I shall hope that God will give the people of India wisdom and strength to withstand every temptation and provocation to violence.

If, therefore, you cannot see your way to remove the Salt tax, and remove the prohibition on private salt-making, I must reluctantly commence the march adumbrated in the opening paragraph of my letter.

I am,

Your sincere friend,

M. K. Gandhi

Young India, 8-5-'30

120

THE GREAT ARREST

[The following is the account of Gandhiji's arrest at Karadi Camp (Dist. Surat) on the morning of 12th May, 1930, as given by Mirabehn.]

At dead of night, like thieves they came, to steal him away. For, " when they sought to lay hold on him, they feared the multitudes, because they took him for a prophet."

At twelve forty-five at night the District Magistrate of Surat, two Indian police officers, armed with pistols, and some thirty policemen, armed with rifles, silently and suddenly came into the peaceful little compound where Gandhiji and his Satyagrahis were sleeping. They immediately surrounded the party, and the English officer going up to the bed and turning a torch-light on to Gandhiji's face, said :

" Are you Mohandas Karamchand Gandhi ? "

" You want me ? " enquired Gandhiji gently, and added, " Please give me time for my ablutions."

He commenced to clean his teeth and the officers, time-piece in hand, stood watching him. Gandhiji here asked if there was a warrant and the Magistrate forthwith read out the following order :

"Whereas the Governor-in-Council views with alarm the activities of Mohandas Karamchand Gandhi, he directs that the said Mohandas Karamchand Gandhi should be placed under restraint under Regulation xxv of 1827, and suffer imprisonment during the pleasure of the Government; and that he be immediately removed to the Yeravda Central Jail."

The ablutions finished, his few little necessities packed up, and his papers handed over to one of his party, Gandhiji again turned to the officers and said, "Please give me a few minutes more for prayer." This was granted, and he forthwith stood and prayed with his companions, surrounded by the ring of police.

As soon as the prayer was over, they hurried him away, put him into a motor-lorry and drove him off accompanied by the three officers and some eight policemen.

All telephonic and telegraphic communications were cut off, and the police guarded the roads.

Swift, silent secrecy.

No trial, no justice.

The Government is making its own statements and the accused lies buried in the silence of the prison cell.

They may take his frail body and cast it into jail. They may stifle his pure voice with the heavy prison walls. But they cannot stifle the Great Soul. Its radiance will penetrate all earthly barriers. The more they strive to smother it, the brighter and brighter will it shine, filling not only India, but the whole world.

Ah India, India, now is thy hour of greatest trial. May God lead thee on the path to Victory and Peace.

He who loves and knows thee with a love and knowledge surpassing all mortal words, has told thee that Freedom is now within thy reach if thou hast the strength and courage to stick to the Pure Path — the Path which he has shown thee of Truth and Non-violence. May God give thee that strength and fill thee with that courage.

Young India, 8-5-'30

121

MORE ABOUT THE SETTLEMENT

[The Civil Disobedience Movement continued unabated till early in 1931, when Gandhiji was released to negotiate a settlement with the Viceroy. After the settlement had been made Gandhiji addressed a mammoth meeting on the 17th March, 1931 in Bombay. Extracts from that speech relating to Satyagraha are given below: — Ed.]

For full twelve months we have developed a war mentality : we thought of war, we talked of war and nothing but war. Now we have to sing a completely different tune. We are in the midst of truce. With some of us, I know the very mention of the word *truce* sends a shiver through their bodies. That is because we had thought of nothing but war and had believed that there could be no compromise. But that was not a position becoming a true Satyagrahi. The Satyagrahi whilst he is ever ready for fight must be equally eager for peace. He must welcome any honourable opportunity for peace. The Working Committee of the Congress saw such an opportunity and availed itself of it. The essential condition of a compromise is that there should be nothing humiliating, nothing panicky about it. You may be sure that whilst I was being inundated with telegrams to make peace at any price, I was absolutely unmoved by them. I am inured to such things and I was absolutely firm that I must not allow any of these telegrams to make me flinch from whatever decision my inner voice gave me. Whilst however a Satyagrahi never yields to panic or hesitancy, neither does he think of humiliating the other party, of reducing it to an abject surrender. He may not swerve from the path of justice and may not dictate impossible terms. He may not pitch his demands too high, neither may he pitch them too low. The present settlement, I submit, satisfies all these conditions. One of the terms of the settlement seems to have caused some disappointment in certain quarters and some have rushed in to condemn the settlement on that account. They complain that we ought not to have entered into the settlement until we had secured the release of *all* political prisoners. I may tell you that we could not in justice make this demand. Not that there was any lack of will on our part, but the power to make the demand irresistible was lacking. That power will come as soon as we fulfil in letter and in spirit all the terms of the settlement that apply to us.

I may inform you that local Governments have been remiss in fulfilling their part of the contract. Some prisoners who ought to have been released are still in jail, some prosecutions — like the Chirner firing case — that ought to have been withdrawn are still going on. It is a matter for sorrow. If the remissness or failure is deliberate it would be culpable. But it would add to *our* power and make our case for Swaraj more irresistible than ever. One would like to think however that such remissness would not be deliberate in view of the stupendous machinery of Government. There is likely to be unintentional delay and inadvertance. But if there is deliberate breach of faith, we have our sovereign remedy. If you look at the settlement the last clause empowers Government to set its machinery of law and order in motion in the event of failure on the part of the Congress to fulfil its part of the settlement. Need I tell you that the clause necessarily includes its converse? Even as it would be open to Government to set its machinery in motion, it is open to us also to resort to our infallible weapon as soon as we find that there is a deliberate breach.

But the present delays need not agitate or irritate you. For there is no occasion for it. A Satyagrahi has infinite patience, abundant faith in others, ample hope.

And now a word of warning. The settlement is obviously provisional. But it necessitates a change in our method of work. Whilst civil disobedience and jail going, or direct action was the method to be followed before the settlement, the way of argument and negotiation takes its place. But let no one forget that the settlement is provisional and the negotiations may break down at any stage. Let us therefore keep our powder ever dry and our armour ever bright. Failure should not find us napping, but ready to mobilize at the first command. In the meanwhile let us carry on the process of self-purification with greater vigour and greater faith, so that we may grow in strength day by day.

Young India, 19-3-'31

122

THE CONGRESS

The Congress will be upon us in a few days from now. The broken-up organizations will hardly have been put together by that time. The delegates, half of whom will be ex-prisoners, will hardly have had time to collect themselves. And yet, it will meet with a greater prestige than ever before, and with a consciousness of its new strength born of a knowledge of suffering undergone by tens of thousands of men, women and children, and perhaps unparallelled in history in the sense that the sufferers suffered without retaliation.

But it would be wrong to brood over the sufferings, to exaggerate them, or to be puffed up with pride. True suffering does not know itself and never calculates. It brings its own joy which surpasses all other joys. We shall, therefore, be guilty of suicide if we live upon the capital amassed during the past twelve months. Whilst we must try always to avoid occasions for needless suffering, we must ever be ready for them. Somehow or other, those who will walk along the right path cannot avoid suffering notwithstanding the attempt to avoid it. It is the privilege of the patriot, the reformer and, still greater, of the Satyagrahi.

The settlement, provisional though it is, has come through God's grace. During the negotiations there were times when breakdown seemed a certainty. Beyond doubt, the suffering would have been ten times multiplied if a breakdown had taken place. And yet, I would have been obliged to ask the nation to go through it, had an honourable peace proved impossible. But I am not sure that it will be possible to reach the goal without further, wider and deeper suffering. The measure of our purification seems hardly equal to the prize to be won. We have not yet consciously, and on a national scale, got rid of the curse of untouchability, we have not shed distrust of one another. Great though the awakening has been among the rich, they have not yet made common cause with the poor ; their life bears no resemblance to that of the poor. Though much progress has been made in the case of drink and drugs, much more yet remains to be done ; the progress made is still uncertain. The drunkard has yielded to pressure of public opinion. He has not yet definitely given up the habit. He knows the evil but has not been taught to shun it as poison. The word *taught* has been used advisedly. The workers have confined their attention to the drink and drug shops, they have not made a serious attempt to touch the heart of the addict. We have not shed the desire for foreign cloth and fineries, nor have the cloth merchants fully realized the magnitude of the wrong they have done to the nation by their trade. Many of them still parade the doctrine of individual freedom. These and several other evils that can be easily recalled show how much still remains to be done in the matter of self-purification. And so, it is little wonder if we do not find the atmosphere of *Purna Swaraj* pervading us. How far, therefore, the method of consultation and conference will succeed, it is difficult to forecast. This much is certain that argument is not what will carry conviction. The British conviction will be in exact proportion to the strength we have developed. And since the nation has decided that we will acquire strength only through self-purification, if we have not attained the wisdom during these good months of grace to rid ourselves of the evils I have enumerated, then we must go through a fiercer fire of suffering than ever before. Let us, therefore, approach the Congress with a humbled spirit and with a will bent on removing every form of weakness from our midst. We

must not give undue weight to conferences and the like.
The past twelve months have made it clear for us that
Swaraj will come when it does, from within, by internal
effort, not as a free gift from above or by simple argument.

Young India, 19-3-'31

123

LET US REPENT

"But the hatred which was created and which has been
shown in words and actions has been so intolerable that it must
set one to think whether release of such mighty forces of
hatred all round the country is advisable. From morning till
late night one heard through talks, songs, through slogans and
felt such mighty torrents of hatred that it was sickening to
find such a degradation in large masses of people. I use the word
degradation with full responsibility. It appeared that speaking
lies was a matter of full licence and liberty. To attack Government officers, police officers, men who disagreed, for something
which was entirely untrue, for something which never happened,
was a daily common event seen on the roads and everywhere.
More than words can express the cruelties and the injustice
inflicted on the traders of British goods especially, and some
other foreign goods, were wide, intolerable, and unbearable. To
request a man not to deal in one article and to request another
not to purchase an article is one thing, but to *force* a man by
all possible means, by abusing him, by obstructing him, by
making his life miserable in every way is another thing, and
there, I must admit, non-violence has miserably failed. I am
certain in my mind that the hatred created and the cruelties
inflicted were far from non-violence and against all principles
and teachings of Mahatmaji. It was a common practice to
obstruct and inflict with all kinds of tactics to make persons'
lives miserable whenever one disagreed with the general movement. In every province there were different types of activities
and it appears that either one had to accept such dictation of
somebody or one had to go through whatever was inflicted upon
him by any small or large band of children, ladies or full grown
up men. According to them, to differ in any way was pro-British,
pro-Government or unfaithfulness to the country, and today one
can see clearly mental victims of these forces of hatred in several
houses.

"But the danger is still greater. The taste of blood viz.

breaking laws, has been so attractive that one finds today this blessed Satyagraha on the lips of every one. As soon as you differ anywhere, be it in a school, in a house, in a group, in a circle of friends, in business, in an office, you find immediately threat of Satyagraha pointed out to you at every time. Between employer and employee, landlord and tenant, parents and children, teachers and pupils, brothers and friends, everywhere this pointed bayonet of Satyagraha seems to be ready for use. To break laws and rules of society or of the State seems to be so easy and handy. If a college professor suggests discipline, if a municipal officer recommends extra tax, if children are requested not to make noise, if hawkers are told to remove obstructions on roads, if changes or transfers are being arranged, if anything is done which does not suit anybody else, there is this dagger of Satyagraha pointed at you. Discrimination where to use and how to use seems to have been entirely lost in the whole nation, and this is a danger-signal for any nation or country. It is exactly like an aeroplane, which is being used generally to fly from one country to another speedily and is also used for throwing bombs. It is exactly like matches, which give light, and are also used for burning a house. One can clearly see this danger-signal in the Satyagraha weapon also. Satyagraha can be used to advantage but it can also be misused to entire destruction. I feel that unless those who proclaim Satyagraha as the best weapon to the wide world, did feel their responsibility in this matter, they would soon find the tables turned not only against themselves but on the whole country. If I can humbly suggest, I feel that some of the rigidly trained leaders, free from hatred, should now do nothing else, but pass some years of their lives in each province and each city and village to make people understand what real Satyagraha or true non-violence means, how it can be brought into operation and when it ought to be brought into operation. I would humbly suggest a regular school of non-violence in every province, where high-minded souls who thoroughly understand this subject scientifically and religiously ought to be teachers to the students of politics who in return should be kept as all-time workers to go round the country, give this message and teach what it is in reality. This can be the only safeguard for saving the country in my opinion."

Jamshed Mehta, the Lord Mayor of Karachi, is a patriot of the purest type. But for his identification with the Congress to the extent he was capable of and but for his having placed at the disposal of the Reception Committee all the resources of his Municipality, the wonderful Congress city would not have been brought into being in the incredibly short space of twenty-five days. His sympahy for the Satyagrahis when the campaign was going on is well known. Any criticism from one like him must, therefore, arrest attention. The quotation given above is an extract from Sjt. Jamshed Mehta's article in a Karachi Anglo-Gujarati weekly called *Parsi Sansar and Lokasevak*. The criticism I have copied follows a glowing tribute paid by him to the Satyagrahis who bore sufferings without retaliation. But we have no reason to be puffed up with pride over certificates of merit. In so far as we observed non-violence we only did our duty.

It is then the warning of this true friend of humanity and his country that we must treasure and profit by. What he has said of Karachi is likely to be true more or less of other places.

Non-violence to be a potent force must begin with the mind. Non-violence of the mere body without the co-operation of the mind is non-violence of the weak or the cowardly and has therefore no potency. It is, as Jamshedji says truly, a degrading performance. If we bear malice and hatred in our bosoms and pretend not to retaliate, it must recoil upon us and lead to our destruction. For abstention from mere bodily non-violence, i.e., not to be injurious, it is at least necessary not to entertain hatred if we cannot generate active love. All the songs and speeches betokening hatred must be taboo.

It is equally true to say that indiscriminate resistance to authority must lead to lawlessness, unbridled licence and consequent self-destruction.

If Jamshedji's criticism was not more than balanced by his appreciation, that is to say, if the sum total of real non-violence had not overbalanced the unreal, India would not have gone forward as it has done. But better even than the Karachi Lord Mayor's appreciation is the undoubted fact that the villagers have instinctively observed non-violence in a manner never before thought of. It is their non-violence that has conduced to the growth of national consciousness.

The mysterious effect of non-violence is not to be

measured by its visible effect. But we dare not rest content so long as the poison of hatred is allowed to permeate society. This struggle is a stupendous effort at conversion. We aim at nothing less than the conversion of the English. It can never be done by harbouring ill-will and still pretending to follow non-violence. Let those therefore who want to follow the path of non-violence and yet harbour ill-will retrace their steps and repent of the wrong they have done to themselves and the country.

Young India, 2-4-'31

124

POWER OF AHIMSA

A correspondent writes a Gujarati letter of which the following is a translation :

" For all that one can see, the support that world opinion has given to India in her present struggle has been most halting and feeble. Is it not surprising, in the face of this, to find Gandhiji claiming that we have received the fullest support from world-opinion ? An unarmed race struggling to win back its own from a most ruthless imperialistic power on earth armed to the teeth can only be compared to a poor, helpless woman defending herself against a ruffian in the face of heavy odds. Imagine this woman being brutally struck with *lathis* again and again by the heartless ruffian. Would it not make the blood of any human being boil with indignation ? Yet do we find signs of such moral indignation in the world today with regard to what was done to India ? And does not the absence of this moral indignation bespeak an indifferently developed sense of humanity in the world ? And if we admit that the question arises, can the weapon of *ahimsa* be at all effective in a world that is so devoid of humanity ? Why cannot Gandhiji see that the world has failed to rise at the sight of unarmed India's blood to that pitch of moral indignation which is essential to the success of truth and *ahimsa* ? "

If I have anywhere referred to India having received the fullest support from world opinion, it should be set down as an unconscious exaggeration. I should like to be shown such a statement of mine if I have made one. For myself I have absolutely no idea of having made any such statement.

The correspondent, by comparing the condition of unarmed India pitted against the British military power to that of a defenceless woman thrown at the tender mercy of a ruffian, has done an injustice to the strength as well of non-violence as of woman. Had not man in his blind selfishness crushed woman's soul as he has done or had she not succumbed to the 'enjoyments' she would have given the world an exhibition of the infinite strength that is latent in her. What she showed in the last fight was but a broken and imperfect glimpse of it. The world shall see it in all its wonder and glory when woman has secured an equal opportunity for herself with man and fully developed her powers of mutual aid and combination.

And it is wrong to say that a person is unarmed in the sense of being weak who has *ahimsa* as his weapon. The correspondent is evidently a stranger to the real use or the immeasurable power of *ahimsa*. He has used it, if at all, only mechanically and as an expedience for want of a better. Had he been saturated with the spirit of *ahimsa*, he would have known that it can tame the wildest beast, certainly the wildest man.

If, therefore, the world's blood did not boil over the brutalities of the past year, it was not because the world was brutal or heartless but because our non-violence, widespread though it was, good enough though it was for the purpose intended, was not the non-violence of the strong and the knowing. It did not spring from a living faith. It was but a policy, a temporary expedient. Though we did not retaliate, we had harboured anger, our speech was not free from violence, our thoughts still less so. We generally refrained from violent action, because we were under discipline. The world marvelled even at this limited exhibition of non-violence and gave us, without any propaganda, the support and sympathy that we deserved and needed. The rest is a matter of the rule of three. If we had the support that we received for the limited and mechanical non-violence we were able to practise during the recent struggle, how much more support should we command when we have risen to the full height of *ahimsa*? Then the world's blood will certainly boil. I know we are still far away from that divine event. We realized our weakness at Kanpur, Banaras, Mirzapur. When we are saturated with *ahimsa* we shall not be non-violent in our fight with the bureaucracy and violent among ourselves. When we have a living faith in non-violence, it will grow from day to day till it fills the whole world. It will be the mightiest propaganda that the world will have witnessed. I live in the belief that we will realize the vital *ahimsa*.

Young India, 7-5-'31

125

GOONDAISM WITHIN THE CONGRESS

The Congress has become a vast democratic body. It reached a high water-mark during the past twelve months. Without being technically on the register millions took possession of it and added lustre to it. But *goondaism* also entered the Congress to a much larger extent than hitherto. It was inevitable. The ordinary rules prescribed for the selection of volunteers were practically set aside during the last stages of the struggle. The result has been that in some places *goondaism* has made itself felt. Some Congressmen have even been threatened with disaster if they will not give the money demanded of them. Of course, professional *goondas* may also take advantage of the atmosphere and ply their trade.

The wonder is that the cases I have in mind are so very few compared to what they might have been, regard being had to the great mass awakening. My conviction is that this happy state is due to the Congress creed of non-violence, even though we have but crudely followed it. But there has been sufficient expression of *goondaism* to warn us to take time by the forelock and adopt preventive and precautionary measures.

The measures that suggest themselves to me are naturally and certainly a scientific and more intelligent and disciplined application of non-violence. In the first place, if we had a firmer faith in non-violence than we have shown, not one man or woman who did not strictly conform to the rules regarding the admission of volunteers would have been taken. It would be no answer to say that in that case there would have been no volunteers during the final stage and therefore there would have been a perfect failure. My experience teaches me to the contrary. It is possible to fight a non-violent battle even with one Satyagrahi. But it, i.e. a non-violent battle, cannot be fought with a million non-Satyagrahis. And I would welcome even an utter failure with non-violence unimpaired rather than depart from it by a hair's breadth to achieve a doubtful success. Without adopting a non-compromising attitude so far as non-violence is concerned, I can see nothing but disaster in the end. For, at the critical moment we may be found wanting, weighed in the scales of non-violence, and may be found hopelessly unprepared to meet the forces of disorder that might suddenly be arrayed against us.

But having made the mistake of indiscriminate recruiting how are we to repair the mischief in a non-violent way ? Non-violence means courage of the highest order and, therefore, readiness to suffer. There should, therefore, be no yielding to bullying, bluff or worse, even though it may mean the loss of a few precious lives. Writers of threatening letters should be made to realize that their threats will not be listened to. But at the same time their disease must be diagnosed and properly treated. Even the *goondas* are part of us and therefore they must be handled gently and sympathetically. People generally do not take to *goondaism* for the love of it. It is a symptom of a deeper-seated disease in the body politic. The same law should govern our relations with internal *goondaism* that we apply in our relations with the *goondaism* in the system of Government. And if we have felt that we have the ability to deal with that highly organized *goondaism* in a non-violent manner how much more should we feel the ability to deal with the internal *goondaism* by the same method ?

It follows that we may not seek police assistance to deal with the disease although it is open during the truce, to any Congressman to seek it precisely in the same manner as any other citizen. The way I have suggested is the way of reform, conversion, love. Seeking police assistance is the way of punishment, fear, want of affection if not actual disaffection. The two methods therefore cannot run together. The way of reform appears at some stage or other to be difficult but it is in reality the easiest.

Young India, 7-5-'31

126

CONQUEST OVER BODY

It is a fundamental principle of Satyagraha that the tyrant whom the Satyagrahi seeks to resist has power over his body and material possessions but he can have no power over the soul. The soul can remain unconquered and unnconquerable even when the body is imprisoned. The whole science of Satyagraha was born from a knowledge of this fundamental truth. In the purest form of Satyagraha there should be no need for conveyances, carriage fare or even of doing *Hijrat*. And in case *Hijrat* has to be performed it will be done by journeying on foot. The *Hijratis* would have to be satisfied with whatever hard fare falls to their lot and keep smiling when even that fails. When we have developed this ' be careful for nothing ' attitude, we shall be saved from many a botheration and trouble and freedom will dance attendance upon us. Nor should one suppose that a ' careful for nothing ' person shall have always to be starving. God that provides the little ant its speck of food and to the elephant his daily one maund bolus will not neglect to provide man with his daily meal. Nature's creatures do not worry or fret about tomorrow but simply wait on tomorrow for the daily sustenance. Only man in his overweening pride and egotism imagines himself to be the lord and master of the earth, and goes on piling up for himself goods that perish. Nature tries every day by its rude shocks to wean him from his pride but he refuses to shed it. Satyagraha is a specific for bringing home to one the lesson of humility. We have travelled so much distance during the last year, we have gone through so much suffering and had so many rich experiences that we ought to have sufficient faith in us to be able to feel that if we throw ourselves upon God's mercy untroubled by doubt or fear, it would be well with us.

Young India, 21-5-'31

SECTION SEVENTH : INDIAN STATES SATYAGRAHA

[Rajkot was one of the States of Kathiawad, ruled by a Prince. Its people had, like those in other States of India, demanded Constitutional Reform, but their efforts met with repression buttressed by British authority. Gandhiji, whose childhood was spent in that State, had many personal links with the Ruler. He therefore went to Rajkot to bring about a peaceful settlement, especially to see that the agreement concluded by the Ruler with the people's leaders was kept. Towards this end, Gandhiji undertook a fast in Rajkot in 1939, and then appealed to the Viceroy, who intervened and brought about arbitration. The award was in Gandhiji's favour, but the latter felt that his fast was tainted by an element of coercion, and therefore denied himself the benefits of the award. — Ed.]

127

SUSPEND CIVIL DISOBEDIENCE

In Satyagraha there is no such thing as disappointment or heartburning. The struggle always goes on in some shape or other till the goal is reached. A Satyagrahi is indifferent whether it is civil disobedience or some other phase of the struggle to which he is called. Nor does he mind if, in the middle of the civil disobedience march, he is called upon to halt and do something else. He must have faith that it is all for the best. My own experience hitherto has been that each suspension has found the people better equipped for the fight and for control over forces of violence. Therefore, in advising suspension, I dismiss from my mind the fear that it may lead to desertion and disbelief. If it does, I should not feel sorry, for it would be to me a sign that the deserters did not know what Satyagraha was and the movement was better without those who did not know what they were doing.

Harijan, 1-4-'39

RAJKOT SATYAGRAHA

In the course of conversation Gandhiji again put Rajkot Satyagraha under the lens : " I think the initial mistake was made when all Kathiawadis were permitted to join Rajkot Satyagraha. That step introduced an element of weakness in the fight. Thereby we put our reliance on numbers, whereas a Satyagrahi relies solely upon God who is the help of the helpless. A Satyagrahi always says to himself, ' He in whose name Satyagraha was launched, will also see it through.' If the people of Rajkot had thought in these terms, there would have been no temptation to organize big processions or mass demonstrations and probably there would have been no atrocities such as Rajkot has had to experience. A genuine Satyagrahi proceeds by setting the opponent at his ease. His action never creates panic in the breast of the ' enemy '. Supposing as a result of rigid enforcement of the rules of Satyagrahis Rajkot Satyagraha had been confined to a few hundred or even a few score true Satyagrahis and they had carried on their Satyagraha in the right spirit till their last breath, theirs would have served as a heroic example."

Harijan, 20-5-'39

ABOUT THE RAJKOT AWARD

[In the Rajkot dispute over which Gandhiji fasted, the Viceroy had to intervene and give his award, on Gandhiji appealing to him. Gandhiji, however, regarded this move of his as unworthy of a true Satyagrahi and repented in the following words :]

The very possession of this Award has made me a coward, and I am afraid if I were to retain it, it would make cowards of you too. A Satyagrahi does not depend for his strength on external means. His strength comes from within, from his reliance on God. God becomes his shield when he throws down all his earthly weapons. But if he were to hide a firearm in his pocket, his inner strength would go and he would cease to feel invulnerable. The Award was very like a firearm in the pocket of a votary of *ahimsa* like me. It stood between me and my God. It shamed me and made a coward of me. I have thrown it away as Christian did his load of sin, and I am feeling again free and invulnerable and one with my Maker.

Harijan, 3-6-'39

130

SUSPENSION OF CIVIL DISOBEDIENCE

In the afternoon the talks with the Travancore friends were resumed. They were afraid that indefinite suspension of civil disobedience would bring in depression from which it would be difficult for the people to recover. Gandhiji regarded this as a very disquieting symptom. It showed that what people had so far been practising was not genuine Satyagraha. The inwardness was lacking. They must start again from the very beginning. "Suspension should never bring despondency and weakness in a

Satyagraha struggle. Even though people may be ready and non-violence ensured, and suspension is ordered through a miscalculation of the general, it cannot jeopardize the future of the movement. Satyagraha means readiness to suffer and a faith that the more innocent and pure the suffering the more potent will it be in its effect. Helplessness is thus ruled out in Satyagraha. Suspension of civil disobedience, if it resulted in an accentuation of repression would itself become Satyagraha in its ideal form.

"Today the opponent is afraid of your numbers. You cannot expect him to show a change of heart while he is filled with panic. He senses in your action a spirit of retaliation which irritates him the more. It thus becomes a species of violence.

"Your struggle hereafter may have to be restricted to a few men only, but their Satyagraha will tell. While we are playing with non-violence we are only giving a chance to the powers that be in Travancore to organize the brute in man. This must not be."

He developed the theme further in his discussion with the Jaipur workers who came next : "Provoking *lathi* charges or receiving *lathi* blows on your body in a spirit of bravado is not Satyagraha. True Satyagraha consists in the readiness to face blows if they come in the course of performing one's duty.

"Today the whole atmosphere in the country is reeking of violence as was evidenced at Tripuri. Under violence I include corruption, falsehood, hypocrisy, deceit and the like. If our Satyagraha is to survive this atmosphere, we *ahimsaites* shall have to be more strict with ourselves. Let only the purest and the most innocent go to jail. It does not matter if they have to remain immured behind the prison bars for a whole lifetime. Their sacrifice will fill the prison with a sweet fragrance and its influence will even travel outside and subtly transform the entire atmosphere. They will never long for their release nor doubt that their sacrifice is being 'wasted'. They will realize that a consecrated resolve is more potent in its action than mere physical action can ever be. The discipline that they will be acquiring in prison will help the non-violent organization of the people outside and instil fearlessness among them.

"So much for those who are in prison, what about those outside? They must engage in constructive work as the embodiment of the active principle of *ahimsa*. If it does not appeal to them, it will only betray their lack of faith in *ahimsa*.

"The other thing is internal. They must cultivate a living faith in God — an attitude of utter reliance on Him to the exclusion of all external aids. A single Satyagrahi imbued with such faith will inspire the whole people by his example and may induce a heart change even in the opponent who, freed from fear, will the more readily appreciate his simple faith and respect it."

Harijan, 3-6-'39

131

ITS IMPLICATIONS

The positive implication of the Rajkot chapter in my life is the discovery that the non-violence claimed for the movement since 1920, marvellous though it was, was not unadulterated. The results though brilliant would have been far richer if our non-violence had been complete. A non-violent action accompanied by non-violence in thought and word should never produce enduring violent reaction upon the opponent. But I have observed that the movement in the States has produced violent reaction on the Princes and their advisers. They are filled with distrust of the Congress. They do not want what they call interference from it. In some cases the very name *Congress* is anathema. This should not have been the case.

The value of the discovery lies in its reaction upon me. I have definitely stiffened in my demands upon would-be Satyagrahis. If my stiffness reduces the number to an insignificant figure, I should not mind. If Satyagraha is a universal principle of universal application, I must find an effective method of action even through a handful. And when I say I see the new light only dimly, I mean that I have not yet found with certainty how a handful can act effectively. It may be, as has happened throughout my life, that I shall know the next step only after the first has been taken. I have faith that when the time for action has arrived, the plan will be found ready.

But the impatient critic will say, ' The time has always been there for action ; only you have been found unready ! ' I cannot plead guilty. I know to the contrary. I have been for some years saying that there is no warrant for resumption of Satyagraha.

The reasons are plain.

The Congress has ceased to be an effective vehicle for launching nation-wide Satyagraha. It has become unwieldy, it has corruption in it, there is indiscipline among Congressmen, and rival groups have come into being which would radically change the Congress programme, if they could secure a majority. That they have failed hitherto to secure it is no comfort to me. The majority has no living faith in its own programme. In any case Satyagraha through a majority is not a feasible proposition. The whole weight of the Congress should be behind any nation-wide Satyagraha.

Then there is the ever-growing communal tension. Final Satyagraha is inconceivable without an honourable peace between the several communities composing the Indian nation.

Lastly, there is the provincial autonomy. I adhere to my belief that we have not done any thing like justice to the task undertaken by the Congress in connection with it. It must be confessed that the Governors have on the whole played the game. There has been very little interference on their part with the ministerial actions. But the interference, sometimes irritating, has come from Congressmen and Congress organizations. Popular violence there should not have been whilst the Congressmen were in office. Much of the ministerial energy has been devoted to dealing with the demands and opposition of Congressmen. If the ministers are unpopular, they can and should be dismissed. Instead they have been allowed to function without the active co-operation of many Congressmen.

It will be contrary to every canon of Satyagraha to launch upon the extreme step till every other is exhausted. Such haste will itself constitute violence.

It may be said in reply with some justification that if all the conditions I have mentioned are insisted upon civil disobedience may be well-nigh impossible. Is that a valid objection? Every measure carries with it conditions for its adoption. Satyagraha is no exception. But I feel within me that some active form of Satyagraha, not necessarily civil disobedience, must be available in order to end an impossible situation. India is facing an impossible situation. There must be either effective non-violent action or violence and anarchy within a measurable distance of time. I must examine this position on a future occasion.

Harijan, 24-6-'39

132

NON-VIOLENCE *v.* VIOLENCE

I must resume the argument about the implications of the Rajkot step, where I left it the week before.

In theory, if there is sufficient non-violence developed in any single person, he should be able to discover the means of combating violence, no matter how widespread or severe, within his jurisdiction. I have repeatedly admitted my imperfections. I am no example of perfect *ahimsa.* I am evolving. Such *ahimsa* as has been developed in me has been found enough to cope with situations that have hitherto arisen. But today I feel helpless in the face of the surrounding violence. There was a penetrating article in the *Statesman* on my Rajkot statement. The editor had therein contended that the English had never taken our movement to be true Satyagraha, but being practical people they had allowed the myth to continue though they had known it to be a violent revolt. It was none the less so because the rebels had no arms. I have quoted the substance from memory. When I read the article, I felt the force of the argument. Though I had intended the movement to be pure non-violent resistance, as I look back upon the happenings of those days, there was undoubtedly violence among the resisters. I must own that had I been perfectly tuned to the music of *ahimsa*, I would have sensed the slightest departure from it and my sensitiveness would have rebelled against any discord in it.

It seems to me that the united action of the Hindus and the Muslims blinded me to the violence that was lurking in the breasts of many. The English who are trained diplomats and administrators are accustomed to the line of least resistance, and when they found that it was more profitable to conciliate a big organization than to crush it by extensive frightfulness, they yielded to the extent that they thought was necessary. It is, however, my conviction that our resistance was predominantly non-violent in action and will be accepted as such by the future historian. As a seeker of truth and non-violence, however, I must not be satisfied with mere action if it is not from the heart. I must declare from the house-tops that the non-violence of those days fell far short of the non-violence as I have so often defined.

Non-violent action without the co-operation of the heart and the head cannot produce the intended result. The failure of our imperfect *ahimsa* is visible to the naked eye. Look at the feud that is going on between Hindus and Muslims. Each is arming for the fight with the other. The violence that we had harboured in our breasts during the non-co-operation days is now recoiling upon ourselves. The violent energy that was generated among the masses, but was kept under check in the pursuit of a common objective, has now been let loose and is being used among and against ourselves.

The same phenomenon is discernible, though in a less

crude manner, in the dissension among Congressmen themselves and the use of forcible methods that the Congress
ministers are obliged to adopt in running the administra-
tions under their charge.

This narrative clearly shows that the atmosphere is
surcharged with violence. I hope it also shows that non-
violent mass movement is an impossibility unless the
atmosphere is radically changed. To blind one's eyes to
the events happening around us is to court disaster. It
has been suggested to me that I should declare mass civil
disobedience and all internal strife will cease, Hindus and
Muslims will compose their differences, Congressmen will
forget mutual jealousies and fights for power. My reading
of the situation is wholly different. If any mass movement
is undertaken at the present moment in the name of non-
violence, it will resolve itself into violence largely
unorganized and organized in some cases. It will bring
discredit on the Congress, spell disaster for the Congress
struggle for independence and bring ruin to many a home.
This may be a wholly untrue picture born of my weakness.
If so, unless I shed that weakness, I cannot lead a movement which requires great strength and resolution.

Harijan, 8-7-'39

SECTION EIGHTH : INDIVIDUAL SATYAGRAHA AGAINST WAR

[When Britain involved India in World War II in 1939 without so much as consulting her, public opinion in the country was enraged, especially as Britain was unwilling to promise independence to India, and it was therefore felt that the War was being fought only to maintain the British Empire and not for the freedom of suppressed nations. Accordingly, the people were anxious to proclaim civil disobedience against the Government. Gandhiji did his best to restrain them, as he did not think it proper to embarrass the British when they were facing a crisis, and also because he did not feel that our people were sufficiently non-violent. But when after a whole year of such restraint, the people appeared to feel stifled, he permitted what was called individual Satyagraha to assert freedom of speech, and gave the right to individuals chosen by himself for their character, public work and belief in non-violence to offer civil disobedience by preaching against war and courting imprisonment. This limited kind of Satyagraha went on during 1940 and 1941. When the Cripps Mission sent out by the British in 1942 failed to bring about a settlement, Gandhiji started his Quit India slogan. This was followed by his imprisonment and that of his followers. As the *Harijan* was under a Government ban from November 1940, his instructions to his followers regarding Satyagraha came to an end. Gandhiji was permitted to publish the *Harijan* again only in February, 1946. — Ed.]

133

NO SUPPRESSION

A Bengal friend came to me during the week and said that though Bengal was ready for battle the Working Committee and especially I were suppressing it and thus damaging the nation's cause. This is a serious charge. The Working Committee can take care of itself. So far as I know, it has suppressed no province and no person. But I can say as the sole authority on Satyagraha that I have never suppressed any body or organization. Satyagraha does not admit of such suppression. Thus though I have been ignorantly accused of suppressing the people of Rajkot, I never suppressed them. They were at liberty, as they are now, to civilly resist authority. Even one person could do so if he had the conviction. If he is wrong, he can only harm himself, not his opponent. Hence it is that I have called Satyagraha the most harmless, if also the most potent, remedy against wrongs.

What, however, I did in the case of Rajkot was to use the authority the Satyagrahis of Rajkot had given me, to suspend civil resistance. It was open to them to reject my advice — it could hardly be dignified by the name of command. If they had, and if they had got responsible government, they would have received my congratulations.

Some readers may remember that the Working Committee had refused to sanction civil resistance in Chirala Perala but had left the Chirala people to declare it at their own risk. Likewise it is open to Bengal, as also to any other province, on its own initiative and at its own risk, to offer civil resistance. What it cannot have is my approval or support. And if the Bengal Provincial Congress Committee wholly repudiates the authority of the Working Committee, it can, with all the greater force and propriety, do as it likes. If it succeeds, it will cover itself with glory, overthrow the present leadership, and rule the Congress organization as it will deserve to. I have prescribed the conditions of successful civil resistance. But if the Bengal Provincial Congress Committee thinks that the Muslim masses are with the Congress, if it thinks that both Hindus and Muslims are ready for the fight, if it thinks that neither non-violence nor the *charkha* is necessary or that non-violence has no connection with the *charkha*, and if it fails to declare war, it will then be untrue to itself and to the country. What I have said applies to every province and part of India. But as the most experienced Satyagrahi I must be allowed to utter a note of warning to all concerned that whoever declares civil resistance without the proper training and a full appreciation of the conditions of Satyagraha is likely to bring disaster to the cause he espouses.

Harijan, 20-1-'40

134

EVERY CONGRESS COMMITTEE
A SATYAGRAHA COMMITTEE

In the coming struggle, if it must come, no half-hearted loyalty will answer the purpose. Imagine a general marching to battle with doubting, ill-prepared soldiers. He will surely march to defeat. I will not consciously make any such fatal experiment. This is not meant to frighten Congressmen. If they have the will, they will not find my instructions difficult to follow. Correspondents tell me that, though they have no faith in me or the *charkha*, they ply the latter for the sake of discipline. I do not understand this language. Can a general fight on the strength of soldiers who, he knows, have no faith in him ? The plain meaning of this language is that the correspondents believe in mass action but do not believe in the connection I see between it and the *charkha*, etc., if the action is to be non-violent. They believe in my hold on the masses, but they do not believe in the things which I believe have given me that hold. They merely want to exploit me and will grudgingly pay the price which my ignorance or obstinacy (according to them) demands. I do not call this discipline. True discipline gives enthusiastic obedience to instructions even though they do not satisfy reason. A volunteer exercises his reason when he chooses his general, but after having made the choice, he does not waste his time and energy in scanning every instruction and testing it on the anvil of his reason before following it. His is " not to reason why ".

Now for my instructions :

Every Congress Committee should become a Satyagraha Committee and register such Congressmen who believe in the cultivation of the spirit of goodwill towards all, who have no untouchability in them in any shape or form, who would spin regularly, and who habitually use *khadi* to the exclusion of all other cloth. I would expect those who thus register their names with their Committees to devote the whole of their spare time to the constructive programme. If the response is sincere, these Satyagraha Committees would become busy spinning depots. They will work in conjunction with and under the guidance of the A. I. S. A. branches in a businesslike manner so that there remain, in the jurisdiction of the Committees, no Congressmen who have not adopted *khadi* for exclusive use. I shall expect businesslike reports to be sent from provincial headquarters to the A. I. C. C. as to the progress of the work of the Satyagraha Committees. Seeing that this registration is to be purely voluntary, the reports would mention the numbers both of those who give their names for registration and those who do not.

The registered Satyagrahis will keep a diary of the work that they do from day to day. Their work, besides their own spinning, will consist in visiting the primary members and inducing them to use *khadi*, spin and register themselves. Whether they do so or not, contact should be maintained with them.

There should be visits paid to Harijan homes and their difficulties removed so far as possible.

Needless to say that names should be registered only of those who are willing and able to suffer imprisonment.

No financial assistance is to be expected by Satyagrahi prisoners whether for themselves or their dependants.

So much for the active Satyagrahis. But there is a much larger class of men and women who, though they will not spin or court or suffer imprisonment, believe in the two cardinal principles of Satyagraha and welcome and wish well to the struggle. These I will call passive Satyagrahis. They will help equally with the active ones, if they will not interfere with the course of the struggle by themselves courting imprisonment or aiding or precipitating strikes of labourers or students. Those who out of overzeal or for any other cause will act contrary to these instructions will harm the struggle and may even compel me to suspend it. When the forces of violence are let loose all over the world and when nations reputed to be most civilized cannot think of any force other than that of arms for the settlement of their disputes, I hope that it will be possible to say of India that she fought and won the battle of freedom by purely peaceful means.

I am quite clear in my mind that, given the co-operation of politically-minded India, the attainment of India's freedom is perfectly possible through unmixed nonviolence. The world does not believe our pretension of non-violence. Let alone the world, I, the self-styled general, have repeatedly admitted that we have violence in our hearts, that we are often violent to one another in our mutual dealings. I must confess that I will not be able to fight so long as we have violence in our midst. But I will fight if the proposed register is honest and if those who courageously keep out will not disturb the even course of the struggle.

Harijan, 30-3-'40

135

THE CHARKHA AND SATYAGRAHA

One of the speakers (at the open Congress Session) said that he had no quarrel with the *charkha*, but he wanted the *charkha* to be divorced from Satyagraha. Well I tell you, as I have been telling you these 20 years, that there is a vital connection between Satyagraha and the *charkha*, and the more I find that belief challenged the more I am confirmed in it. Otherwise I am no fool to persist in turning the *charkha*, day in and day out, at home and even on trains, in the teeth of medical advice. I want you too to be turning the *charkha* with the same faith. And unless you do it and unless you habitually use *khadi* you will deceive me and deceive the world.

I know that you will not fight unless you have me with you, but then you must know that I am here and I would fight only as a representative of those dumb millions for whom I live and for whom I want to die. My loyalty to them is greater than any other loyalty, and it is for them that I would not give up the *charkha* even if you were to forsake me or kill me. For I know that, if I were to relax the conditions of the *charkha*, I should bring ruin upon those dumb millions for whom I have to answer before God. If, therefore, you do not believe in the *charkha* in the sense I believe in it, I implore you to leave me. The *charkha* is an outward symbol of truth and non-violence, and unless you have them in your hearts you will not take to the *charkha* either. Remember, therefore, that you have to fulfil both the internal and external conditions. If you fulfil the internal condition, you will cease to hate your opponent, you will not seek or work for his destruction, but pray to God to have mercy on him. Do not, therefore, concentrate on showing the misdeeds of the Government, for we have to convert and befriend those who run it. And after all no one is wicked by nature. And if others are wicked, are we the less so? That attitude is inherent in Satyagraha, and if you do not subscribe to it, even then I would ask you to leave me. For without a belief in my programme and without an acceptance of my condition you will ruin me, ruin yourself and ruin the cause.

Harijan, 30-3-'40

136

CIVIL DISOBEDIENCE

Civil disobedience, if it is really civil, must appear so even to the opponent. He must feel that the resistance is not intended to do him any harm. At the present moment the average Englishman thinks that non-violence is merely a cloak. The Muslim Leaguers think that civil disobedience is aimed at them more than at the British. I protest with all the strength at my command that, so far as I am concerned, I have no desire whatsoever to embarrass the British, especially at a time when it is a question of life and death with them. All I want the Congress to do through civil disobedience is to deny the British Government the moral influence which Congress co-operation would give. The material resources of India and her man power are already being exploited by the British Government by reason of their control of the whole of this sub-continent.

If by civil disobedience the Congress has no desire to embarrass the British people, it has still less to embarrass the Muslim League. And I can say this on behalf of the Congress with far greater assurance than I can with regard to the British. Working in the midst of suspicion and terrible misrepresentation on the one hand and the prevailing lawlessness outside and inside the Congress on the other, I have to think a thousand times before embarking on civil disobedience.

So far as I can see, at present mass civil disobedience is most unlikely. The choice lies between individual civil disobedience on a large scale, very restricted, or confined only to me. In every case there must be the backing of the whole of the official Congress organization and the millions who, though not on the Congress register, have always supported the organization with their mute but most effective co-operation.

I have repeatedly shown in these columns that the

most effective and visible co-operation which all Congressmen and the mute millions can show is by not interfering with the course civil disobedience may take and by themselves spinning and using *khadi* to the exclusion of all other cloth. If it is allowed that there is a meaning in people wearing primroses on Primrose Day, surely there is much more in a people using a particular kind of cloth and giving a particular kind of labour to the cause they hold dear. From their compliance with the *khadi* test I shall infer that they have shed untouchability, and that they have nothing but brotherly feeling towards all without distinction of race, colour or creed. Those who will do this are as much Satyagrahis as those who will be singled out for civil disobedience.

Harijan, 27-4-'40

137

NOT YET

Many Congressmen are playing at non-violence. They think in terms of civil disobedience anyhow, meaning the filling of jails. This is a childish interpretation of the great force that civil disobedience is. I must continue to repeat, even though it may cause nausea, that prison-going without the backing of honest constructive effort and goodwill in the heart for the wrong-doer is violence and therefore forbidden in Satyagraha. Force generated by non-violence is infinitely greater than the force of all the arms invented by man's ingenuity. Non-violence, therefore, is the decisive factor in civil disobedience. I have been told that people cannot be non-violent overnight. I have never contended they can. But I have held that by proper training they can be, if they have the will. Active non-violence is necessary for those who will offer civil disobedience, but the will and proper training are enough for the people to co-operate with those who are chosen for civil disobedience. The constructive work prescribed by the

Congress is the proper training. Those, therefore, who wish to see India realize her destiny through non-violence should devote every ounce of their energy towards the fulfilment of the constructive programme in right earnest without any thought of civil disobedience.

Harijan, 1-6-'40

138

TO THE READER

You must have seen through my Press notice that the publication of *Harijan* and the other two weeklies * has been suspended. In it, I had expressed the hope that the suspension might be only for a week. But I see that the hope had no real foundation. I shall miss my weekly talks with you, as I expect you too will miss them. The value of those talks consisted in their being a faithful record of my deepest thoughts. Such expression is impossible in a cramped atmosphere. As I have no desire to offer civil disobedience, I cannot write freely. As the author of Satyagraha I cannot, consistently with my professions, suppress the vital part of myself for the sake of being able to write on permissible subjects such as the constructive programme. It would be like dealing with the trunk without the head. The whole of the constructive programme is to me an expression of non-violence. I would be denying myself if I could not preach non-violence. For that would be the meaning of submission to the latest Ordinance. The suspension must, therefore, continue while the gagging lasts. It constitutes a Satyagrahi's respectful protest against the gag. Is not Satyagraha giving an ell when an inch is asked for by the wrong-doer, is it not giving the cloak also when only the coat is demanded? It may be asked why this reversal of the ordinary process? The ordinary process is based on violence. If my life were

---

* *Harijansevak* and *Harijanbandhu* — Hindi and Gujarati editions of the English *Harijan.*

regulated by violence in the last resort, I would refuse to give an inch lest an ell might be asked for. I would be a fool if I did otherwise. But if my life is regulated by non-violence, I should be prepared to and actually give an ell when an inch is asked for. By so doing I produce on the usurper a strange and even pleasurable sensation. He would also be confounded and would not know what to do with me. So much for the ' enemy '. I, having made up my mind to surrender every non-essential, gain greater strength than ever before to die for the defence and preservation of what I hold to be essential. I was therefore wrongly accused by my critics of having advised cowardly surrender to Nazism by Englishmen when I suggested that they should lay down external arms, let the Nazis overrun Britain if they dare, but develop internal strength to refuse to sell themselves to the Nazis. Full surrender of non-essentials is a condition precedent to accession of internal strength to defend the essential by dying.

But I am not writing this to convert the English to my view. I am writing this to suggest to you that my surrender to the framers of the gaging Ordinance is an object-lesson to you, the Reader, in Satyagraha. If you will quietly work out in your own life the implications of the lesson, you will then not need the weekly aid from the written word in *Harijan*. Even without your weekly *Harijan* you will know how I shall myself work out the full implications of giving an ell when an inch is wanted. A correspondent pleads with me that on no account should I suspend *Harijan*, for he says his non-violence is sustained by the weekly food he gets therefrom. If he has really done so, then this self-imposed restraint should teach him more than a vapid continuation of the weekly *Harijan*.

Harijan. 10-11-'40

139

FASTING AS PENANCE

Once when I was in Johannesburg I received tidings
of the moral fall of two of the inmates of the Ashram. News
of an apparent failure or reverse in the Satyagraha struggle would not have shocked me, but this news came upon
me like a thunderbolt. The same day I took the train for
Phoenix. Mr Kallenbach insisted on accompanying me.
He had noticed the state I was in. He would not brook the
thought of my going alone, for he happened to be the bearer
of the tidings which had so upset me.

During the journey my duty seemed clear to me. I
felt that the guardian or teacher was responsible, to some
extent at least, for the lapse of his ward or pupil. So my
responsibility regarding the incident in question became
clear to me as daylight. My wife had already warned me
in the matter, but being of a trusting nature, I had ignored
her caution. I felt that the only way the guilty parties
could be made to realize my distress, and the depth of their
own fall would be for me to do some penance. So I imposed
upon myself a fast for seven days and a vow to have only
one meal a day for a period of four months and a half.
Mr Kallenbach tried to dissuade me, but in vain. He finally
conceded the propriety of the penance, and insisted on
joining me. I could not resist his transparent affection.

I felt greatly relieved, for the decision meant a heavy
load off my mind. The anger against the guilty parties
subsided and gave place to the purest pity for them. Thus
considerably eased, I reached Phoenix. I made further

investigation and acquainted myself with some more details I needed to know.

My penance pained everybody, but it cleared the atmosphere. Everyone came to realize what a terrible thing it was to be sinful, and the bond that bound me to the boys and girls became stronger and truer.

A circumstance arising out of this incident compelled me, a little while after, to go into a fast for fourteen days, the results of which exceeded even my expectations.

It is not my purpose to make out from these incidents that it is the duty of a teacher to resort to fasting whenever there is a delinquency on the part of his pupils. I hold, however, that some occasions do call for this drastic remedy. But it presupposes clearness of vision and spiritual fitness. Where there is no true love between the teacher and the pupil, where the pupil's delinquency has not touched the very being of the teacher and where the pupil has no respect for the teacher, fasting is out of place and may even be harmful. Though there is thus room for doubting the propriety of fasts in such cases, there is no question about the teacher's responsibility for the errors of his pupil.

Autobiography, pt. IV, chap. XXXVI

140

THE SATYAGRAHA WAY WITH CHILDREN

[Gandhiji went on a seven-day fast owing to some error in the conduct of his Ashram children. In this connection he wrote :]

I discovered errors among the boys and somewhat among the girls. I know that hardly a school or any other institution is free from the errors I am referring to. I am anxious to see the Ashram free from errors which are sapping the manhood of the nation and undermining the character of the youth. It was not permissible to punish the boys. Experience gained in two schools under my control has taught me that punishment does not purify, if anything it hardens children. In such cases in South Africa I have resorted to fasts with, in my opinion, the best of results. I have resorted to the same process here and let me say of a milder type. The basis of the action is mutual love. I know that I possess the love of the boys and the girls. I know too that if the giving up of my life can make them spotless, it would be my supreme joy to give it. Therefore, I could do no less to bring the youngsters to a sense of their error. So far the results seem to be promising.

What, however, if I cannot perceive the fruit? I can but do the will of God as I feel it. The result is in His disposing. This suffering for things great and small is the keynote of Satyagraha.

But why should not the teachers perform the penance? They cannot, so long as I remain the chief. If they had fasted with me all work would have come to a standstill. As with big institutions so with small ones. As the king must share the sins of his subjects even as he arrogates to himself all their virtues, so must I, a tiny chosen king in the little Ashram, atone for the sins of the least among the children of the Ashram, if I may proudly claim the presence in it of many noble characters. If I am to identify myself with the grief of the least in India, aye, if I have the power, the least in the world, let me identify myself with the sins of the little ones who are under my care. And so doing in all humility I hope some day to see God — Truth — face to face.

Young India, 3-12-'25

SATYAGRAHA — TRUE AND FALSE

There are many forms of Satyagraha, of which fasting may or may not be one, according to the circumstances of the case. A friend has put the following poser :

> " A man wants to recover money another owes him. He cannot do so by going to law as he is a non-co-operator, and the debtor in the intoxication of the power of his wealth pays him no heed, and refuses even to accept arbitration. If in these circumstances, the creditor sits *dhurna* at the debtor's door, would it not be Satyagraha ? The fasting creditor seeks to injure no one by his fasting. Ever since the golden age of Rama we have been following this method. But I am told you regard this as intimidation. If you do, will you kindly explain ? "

I know the correspondent. He has written from the purest motive. But I have no doubt that he is mistaken in his interpretation of Satyagraha. Satyagraha can never be resorted to for personal gain. If fasting with a view to recovering money is to be encouraged, there would be no end of scoundrels blackmailing people by resorting to the means. I know that many such people are to be met with in the country. It is not right to argue that those who rightly resort to fasting need not be condemned because it is abused in a few cases. Any and every one may not draw his own distinction between fasting — Satyagraha — true and false. What one regards as true Satyagraha may very likely be otherwise. Satyagraha, therefore, cannot be resorted to for personal gain, but only for the good of others. A Satyagrahi should always be ready to undergo suffering and pecuniary loss. That there would not be wanting dishonest people to reap an undue advantage from the boycott of Law Courts practised by good people was a contingency not unexpected at the inception of non-co-operation. It was then thought that the beauty of non-co-operation lay just in taking those risks.

But Satyagraha in the form of fasting cannot be undertaken as against an opponent. Fasting can be resorted to only against one's nearest and dearest, and that solely for his or her good.

In a country like India, where the spirit of charity or pity is not lacking, it would be nothing short of an outrage to resort to fasting for recovering money. I know people who have given away money, quite against their will, but out of a false sense of pity. The Satyagrahi has, therefore, to proceed warily in a land like ours. It is likely that some men may succeed in recovering money due to them, by resorting to fasting; but instead of calling it a triumph of Satyagraha, I would call it a triumph of *duragraha* or violence. The triumph of Satyagraha consists in meeting death in the insistence on truth. A Satyagrahi is always unattached to the attainment of the object of Satyagraha ; one seeking to recover money cannot be so unattached. I am, therefore, clear that fasting for the sake of personal gain is nothing short of intimidation and the result of ignorance.

Young India, 30-9-'26

142

FAST AS AN ELEMENT IN SATYAGRAHA

Suffering even unto death and, therefore, even through a perpetual fast is the last weapon of a Satyagrahi. That is the last duty which it is open to him to perform. Therefore, fast is a part of my being as, I hold, it has been, to a large or small extent, of every seeker of Truth. I am making an experiment in *ahimsa* on a scale perhaps unknown in history. That I may be wholly wrong is quite possible, but quite irrelevant to the present purpose. So long as I am not conscious of the error, but, on the contrary, am sure, as far as it is humanly possible to be, of being in the right, I must go on with my pursuit to the farthest end. And in this manner, but in no other, a fast or a series of fasts are always a possibility in my life. I have undergone many before now since childhood. There should be no alarm felt if they are undertaken for public causes. Nor must any one exploit them in anticipation. When they come, they will produce their own effect and result, whether anybody wills or no. But it is wrong to speculate over the contingency.

I, therefore, implore the public to dismiss from their minds, and be unaffected by the remote possibility of another fast by me in this campaign against untouchability and to accept my assurance that, if such a fast does come, it will have come in obedience to the call of Truth which is God. I will not be a traitor to God to please the whole world.

Harijan, 18-2-'33

143

FAST AS PRAYER

[After his fast for the Harijan cause in May, 1933, Gandhiji wrote :]

The fast was an uninterrupted twenty-one days' prayer whose effect I can feel even now. I know now more fully than ever that there is no prayer without fasting, be the latter ever so little. And this fasting relates not merely to the palate, but all the senses and organs. Complete absorption in prayer must mean complete exclusion of physical activities till prayer possesses the whole of our being and we rise superior to, and are completely detached from, all physical functions. That state can only be reached after continual and voluntary crucifixion of the flesh. Thus all fasting, if it is a spiritual act, is an intense prayer or a preparation for it. It is a yearning of the soul to merge in the divine essence. My last fast was intended to be such a preparation. How far I have succeeded, how far I am in tune with the Infinite, I do not know. But I do know that the fast has made the passion for such a state intenser than ever.

Harijan, 8-7-'33

144

IS FAST COERCION ?

[In reply to Rev. Stanley Jones, Gandhiji said :]

If it is agreed that my fast sprang from love, then it was coercion, only if love of parents for their children or of the latter for the former, or love of husband for wife and wife for husband, or, to take a sweeping illustration, love of Jesus for those who own Him as their all, is coercion. It is the implicit and sacred belief of millions of Christians that love of Jesus keeps them from falling and that it does so against themselves. His love bends the reason and the emotion of thousands of His votaries to His love. I know that, in my childhood, love of my parents kept me from sinning, and, even after fifty years of age, love of my children and friends kept me positively from going to perdition, which I would have done most assuredly but for the definite and overwhelming influence of that love. And, if all this love could be regarded as coercion, then the love that prompted my fast and, therefore, my fast, was coercion, but it was that in no other sense. Fasting is a great institution in Hinduism, as perhaps in no other religion, and, though it has been abused by people not entitled to fast, it has, on the whole, done the greatest good to Hinduism. I believe that there is no prayer without fasting and there is no real fast without prayer. My fast was the prayer of a soul in agony.

Harijan, 11-2-'33

145

FAST AS THE LAST RESORT

Sacrifice of self even unto death is the final weapon in the hands of a non-violent person. It is not given to man to do more. I, therefore, suggest to this co-worker and all the others that in this religious battle against untouchability they must be prepared joyously even to "fast unto death", if such an urgent call comes to them. If they feel that they are party to the September pledge given unsolicited to the Harijans and if they cannot make good the pledge in spite of ordinary effort, how else, being non-violent, will they propose to deliver the goods except by laying down their lives?

The *shastras* tell us that, when people in distress prayed to God for relief and He seemed to have hardened His heart, they declared a 'fast unto death' till God listened to their prayer. Religious history tells us of those who survived their fast, because God listened to them, but it tells us nothing of those who silently and heroically perished in the attempt to win the answer from a deaf God. I am certain that many have died in that heroic manner, but without their faith in God and non-violence being in the slightest degree diminished. God does not always answer prayers in the manner we want Him to. For Him life and death are one, and who is able to deny that all that is pure and good in the world persists because of the silent death of thousands of unknown heroes and heroines!

Harijan, 4-3-'33

FAST AS SELF-SURRENDER

Although the Sanatanists swear at me for the fast, and Hindu co-workers may deplore it, they know that fasting is an integral part of even the present-day Hinduism. They cannot long affect to be horrified at it. Hindu religious literature is replete with instances of fasting, and thousands of Hindus fast even today on the slightest pretext. It is the one thing that does the least harm. There is no doubt that, like everything that is good, fasts are abused. That is inevitable. One cannot forbear to do good, because sometimes evil is done under its cover.

My real difficulty is with my Christian Protestant friends, of whom I have so many and whose friendship I value beyond measure. Let me confess to them that, though from my very first contact with them I have known their dislike for fasts, I have never been able to understand it.

Mortification of the flesh has been held all the world over as a condition of spiritual progress. There is no prayer without fasting, taking fasting in its widest sense. A complete fast is a complete and literal denial of self. It is the truest prayer. "Take my life, and let it be consecrated, Lord, to Thee," is not, should not be, a mere lip or figurative expression. It has to be a wreckless and joyous giving without the least reservation. Abstention from food and even water is but the mere beginning, the least part of the surrender.

It is only proper that friends should know my fundamental position. I have a profound belief in the method of the fast, both private and public. It may come again any day without any warning even to me. If it comes, I shall welcome it as a great privilege and a joy.

Harijan, 15-4-'33

REQUIREMENTS FOR SATYAGRAHA FAST

But the mere fast of the body is nothing without the will behind it. It must be a genuine confession of the inner fast, an irrepressible longing to express truth and nothing but truth. Therefore, those only are privileged to fast for the cause of truth, who have worked for it and who have love in them even for opponents, who are free from animal passion and who have abjured earthly possessions and ambitions. No one, therefore, may undertake, without previous preparation and discipline the fast I have foreshadowed.

Harijan, 6-5-'33

148

COERCIVE FASTS

If the expression 'coercive effect' can be lawfully used for my fasts, then in that sense, all fasts can be proved to have that effect to a greater or less extent. The fact is that all spiritual fasts always influence those who come within the zone of their influence. That is why spiritual fasting is described as *tapas*. And all *tapas* invariably exerts purifying influence on those in whose behalf it is undertaken.

Of course, it is not to be denied that fasts can be really coercive. Such are fasts to attain a selfish object. A fast undertaken to wring money from a person or for fulfilling some such personal end would amount to the exercise of coercion or undue influence. I would unhesitatingly advocate resistance of such undue influence. I have myself successfully resisted it in the fasts that have been undertaken or threatened against me. And if it is argued that the dividing line between a selfish and an unselfish end is often very thin, I would urge that a person who regards the end of a fast to be selfish or otherwise base should resolutely refuse to yield to it, even though the refusal may result in the death of the fasting person. If people will cultivate the habit of disregarding fasts which in their opinion are taken for unworthy ends, such fasts will be robbed of the taint of coercion and undue influence. Like all human institutions, fasting can be both legitimately and illegitimately used. But as a great weapon in the armoury of Satyagraha, it cannot be given up because of its possible abuse. Satyagraha has been designed as an effective substitute for violence. This use is in its infancy and, therefore, not yet perfected. But as the author of modern Satyagraha I cannot give up any of its manifold uses without forfeiting my claim to handle it in the spirit of a humble seeker.

Harijan, 6-5-'33

149

FASTING

Fasting is a potent weapon in the Satyagraha armoury. It cannot be taken by every one. Mere physical capacity to take it is no qualification for it. It is of no use without a living faith in God. It should never be a mechanical effort nor a mere imitation. It must come from the depth of one's soul. It is therefore always rare. I seem to be made for it. It is noteworthy that not one of my colleagues on the political field has felt the call to fast. And I am thankful to be able to say that they have never resented my fasts. Nor have fellow-members of the Ashram felt the call except on rare occasions. They have even accepted the restriction that they may not take penitential fasts without my permission, no matter how urgent the inner call may seem to be.

Thus fasting, though a very potent weapon, has necessarily very strict limitations and is to be taken only by those who have undergone previous training. And, judged by my standard, the majority of fasts do not at all come under the category of Satyagraha fasts and are, as they are popularly called, hunger-strikes undertaken without previous preparation and adequate thought. If the process is repeated too often, these hunger-strikes will lose what little efficacy they may possess and will become objects of ridicule.

Harijan, 18-3-'39

150

FASTING IN SATYAGRAHA

Nowadays quite a number of fasts are undertaken in the name of Satyagraha. Many of the known fasts have been meaningless, many may be said to have been impure. Fasting is a fiery weapon. It has its own science. No one, as far as I am aware, has a perfect knowledge of it. Unscientific experimentation with it is bound to be harmful to the one who fasts, and it may even harm the cause espoused. No one who has not earned the right to do so should, therefore, use this weapon. A fast may only be undertaken by him who is associated with the person against whom he fasts. The latter must be directly connected with the purpose for which the fast is being undertaken. Bhagat Fulsinghji's recent fast was such a one. He was closely connected with the people of Moth village; he had served the Harijans of the place too. The wrong that was being enacted was done by the villagers to the Harijans. When every means of obtaining justice had failed there was no option left for a man like Fulsinghji except to resort to fasting. He did and succeeded. Success or failure depends entirely on the will of God and is not relevant to the issue under discussion.

All my public fasts have been of this category. Out of all of them perhaps there is most to be learnt from the Rajkot one. It has been roundly condemned by many people. Originally it was pure and necessary. The blemish crept in when I asked the Viceroy to intervene. Had I not done so, I am convinced that its result would have been brilliant. Even as it was, the result was a victory for the cause. Because God wanted to open my eyes, he took the bread out of my mouth, so to speak. The Rajkot fast is thus a useful study for the Satyagrahi. In regard to its necessity there is no doubt, assuming that the principles for fasting which I have laid down are accepted. The important thing to note about it is how a pure undertaking can become tainted owing to lack of watchfulness on the part of the doer. There can be no room for selfishness, anger, lack of faith, or impatience in a pure fast. It is no exaggeration to admit that all these defects crept into my Rajkot fast. My selfishness lay in the fact that inasmuch as its being given up depended on certain conditions being fulfilled by the late Thakoresaheb, I had in me the selfish desire for the realization of the fruit of my labour. If there had been no anger in me, I would not have looked to the Viceroy for assistance. My love should have deterred me from doing so. For if he was really as a son to me, why should I have complained about him to his overlord? I betrayed want of faith in that I thought the Thakoresaheb would not be melted by my love and I was impatient to break the fast. All these shortcomings were bound to make my fast impure. It would be irrelevant here to ponder over the many results of the Rajkot fast, and I therefore refrain from doing so. But we have learnt how infinitely watchful and prayerful he who fasts has to be and how even a little carelessness can damage a good cause. It is now apparent that in addition to truth and non-violence a Satyagrahi should have the confidence that, God will grant him the necessary strength and that, if there is the slightest impurity in the fast, he will not hesitate to renounce it at once. Infinite patience, firm resolve, single-mindedness of purpose, perfect calm, and no anger must of necessity be there. But since it is impossible for a person to develop all these qualities all at once, no one who has not devoted himself to following the laws of *ahimsa* should undertake a Satyagrahi fast.

I should like readers to note that I have not here dealt with fasts undertaken for bodily or spiritual purification. Nature-cure doctors should be consulted for the former. The greatest of sinners can undertake the latter. And for this type of fast we possess a veritable mine of literature. Fasts for spiritual purification have really been forgotten in our day. If they are ever undertaken, they are either purely imitative or merely for the sake of tradition, and we cannot therefore derive the benefit from them that we should. Those who want to go in for a Satyagrahi fast should certainly possess some personal experience of fasts for spiritual purification. Fasts for ridding the body of impurities are also beneficial. In the end, of course, there is only one basis for the whole ideal of fasting, and that is purification.

Harijan, 13-10-'40

151

FASTING IN THE AIR

I have had the temerity to claim that fasting is an infallible weapon in the armoury of Satyagraha. I have used it myself, being the author of Satyagraha. Any one whose fast is related to Satyagraha should seek my permission and obtain it in writing before embarking on it. If this advice is followed, there is no need for framing rules, at any rate, in my lifetime.

One general principle, however, I would like to enunciate. A Satyagrahi should fast only as a last resort when all other avenues of redress have been explored and have failed. There is no room for imitation in fasts. He who has no inner strength should not dream of it, and never with attachment to success. But if a Satyagrahi once undertakes a fast from conviction, he must stick to his resolve whether there is a chance of his action bearing fruit or not. This does not mean that fasting cannot or does not bear fruit. He who fasts in the exectation of fruit generally fails. And even if he does not seemingly fail, loses all the inner joy which a true fast holds.

Whether one should take fruit juices or not depends on one's physical powers of endurance. But no more fruit juice than is absolutely necessary for the body should be taken. He probably has the greatest inner strength who takes only water.

It is wrong to fast for selfish ends, e.g., for increase in one's own salary. Under certain circumstances it is permissible to fast for an increase in wages on behalf of one's group.

Ridiculous fasts spread like plague and are harmful. But when fasting becomes a duty it cannot be given up. Therefore, I do fast when I consider it to be necessary and cannot abstain from it on any score. What I do myself I cannot prevent others from doing under similar circumstances. It is common knowledge that the best of good things are often abused. We see this happening every day.

Harijan, 21-4-'46

152

TO THE WOMEN OF INDIA

The impatience of some sisters to join the good fight
is to me a healthy sign. It has led to the discovery that
however attractive the campaign against the Salt tax may
be, for them to confine themselves to it would be to
change a pound for a penny. They will be lost in the crowd,
there will be in it no suffering for which they are thirsting.

In this non-violent warfare, their contribution should
be much greater than men's. To call woman the weaker
sex is a libel ; it is man's injustice to woman. If by
strength is meant brute strength, then indeed is woman
less brute than man. If by strength, is meant moral power,
then woman is immeasurably man's superior. Has she
not greater intuition, is she not more self-sacrificing, has
she not greater powers of endurance, has she not greater
courage ? Without her man could not be. If non-violence
is the law of our being, the future is with woman.

I have nursed this thought now for years. When the
women of the Ashram insisted on being taken along with
men something within me told me that they were destined
to do greater work in this struggle than merely breaking
salt laws.

I feel that I have now found that work. The picketing of liquor shops and foreign cloth shops by men, though
it succeeded beyond expectations up to a point for a time
in 1921, failed because violence crept in. If a real
impression is to be created, picketing must be resumed.
If it remains peaceful to the end, it will be the quickest
way of educating the people concerned. It must never be
a matter of coercion but conversion, moral suasion. Who
can make a more effective appeal to the heart than
woman ?

Prohibition of intoxicating liquors and drugs and boycott of foreign cloth have ultimately to be by law. But the law will not come till pressure from below is felt in no uncertain manner.

That both are vitally necessary for the nation, nobody will dispute. Drink and drugs sap the moral well-being of those who are given to the habit. Foreign cloth undermines the economic foundations of the nation and throws millions out of employment. The distress in each case is felt in the home and therefore by the women. Only those who have drunkards as their husbands know what havoc the drink devil works in homes that once were orderly and peace-giving. Millions of women in our hamlets know what unemployment means. Today the Charkha Sangha covers over one hundred thousand women against less than 10,000 men.

Let the women of India take up these two activities, specialize in them, they would contribute more than men to national freedom. They would have access of power and self-confidence to which they have hitherto been strangers.

Their appeal to the merchants and buyers of foreign cloth and to the liquor dealers and addicts to the habit cannot but melt their hearts. At any rate the women can never be suspected of doing or intending violence to these four classes. Nor can Government long remain supine to an agitation so peaceful and so resistless.

The charm will lie in the agitation being initiated and controlled exclusively by women. They may take and should get as much assistance as they need from men, but the men should be in strict subordination to them.

In this agitation thousands of women literate and illiterate can take part.

Highly educated women have in this appeal of mine an opportunity of actively identifying themselves with the massess and helping them both morally and materially.

They will find when they study the subject of foreign cloth boycott that it is impossible save through *khadi*. Mill-owners will themselves admit that mills cannot manufacture in the near future enough cloth for Indian requirements. Given a proper atmosphere, *khadi* can be manufactured in our villages, in our countless homes. Let it be the privilege of the women of India to produce this atmosphere by devoting every available minute to the spinning of yarn. The question of production of *khadi* is surely a question of spinning enough yarn. During the past ten days of the march under pressure of circumstances I have discovered the potency of the *takli* which I had not realized before. It is truly a wonder worker. In mere playfulness my companions have without interrupting any other activity spun enough yarn to weave 4 square yards per day of *khadi* of 12 counts. *Khadi* as a war measure is not to be beaten. The moral results of the two reforms are obviously great. The political result will be no less great. Prohibition of intoxicating drinks and drugs means the loss of twenty-five crores of revenue. Boycott of foreign cloth means the saving by India's millions of at least sixty crores. Both these achievements would monetarily be superior to the repeal of the Salt tax. It is impossible to evaluate the moral results of the two reforms.

" But there is no excitement and no adventure in liquor and foreign cloth picketing," some sisters may retort. Well, if they will put their whole heart into this agitation they will find more than enough excitement and adventure. Before they have done with the agitation, they might even find themselves in prison. It is not improbable that they may be insulted and even injured bodily. To suffer such insult and injury would be their pride. Such suffering if it comes to them will hasten the end.

If the women of India will listen and respond to my appeal, they must act quickly. If the all-India work cannot be undertaken at once, let those provinces which can organize themselves do so. Their example will be quickly followed by the other provinces.

Young India, 10-4-'30

153

WOMEN IN CONFERENCE

The conference of women on Sunday last at Dandi became a Congress as I had wanted it to be. Thanks to the Government prohibition against the Baroda territory cars plying between Navasari and Dandi, many had walked the full 12 miles to Dandi. The following resolutions were unanimously adopted :

1. This conference of the women of Gujarat assembled at Dandi on 13th April 1930 having heard Gandhiji, resolves that the women assembled will picket liquor and toddy shops of Gujarat and appeal to the shop-keepers and the shop-goers to desist from plying their trade or drinking intoxicating liquors as the case may be, and will similarly picket foreign cloth shops and appeal to the dealers and the buyers to desist from the practice of dealing in or buying foreign cloth as the case may be.

2. This conference is of opinion that boycott of foreign cloth is possible only through *khadi* and therefore the women assembled resolve henceforth to use *khadi* only and will so far as possible spin regularly and will learn all the previous processes and preach the message of *khadi* among their neighbours, teach them the processes up to spinning and encourage them to spin regularly.

3. This conference appoints the following Executive Committee * with power to draw up a constitution and to amend it from time to time and add to their number.

4. This conference hopes that women all over Gujarat and the other provinces will take up the movement initiated at this conference.

I regard this extension of the Swaraj movement as of the highest importance. I need not reiterate the argument already advanced in these pages. Mithubehn has already commenced operations. She is not the woman to let the grass grow under her feet. The idea is for twenty to twenty-five women to go in one batch and plant themselves near each liquor shop and come in personal contact with every visitor to the liquor or toddy shops, and wean them from the habit. They will also appeal to the shop-keepers

---

* The names were to be published later.

to give up the immoral traffic and earn their livelihood through better means.

Foreign cloth shops are to be treated in the same way as liquor shops as soon as there are enough trained women volunteers. Though the same committee will carry on the two boycotts it will necessarily have two branches. It will be open to any woman to offer her services for only one branch of work, nor is it necessary that every worker should belong to the Congress. Only this must be clearly understood, that the work is part of the Congress programme and has tremendous political results if it has also equally great moral and economic consequences.

Those who will belong to the foreign cloth boycott branch should realize that without the constructive work of *khadi* production the mere boycott will be a mischievous activity. Its very success without the production of *khadi* will prove the ruin of the national movement for independence. For the millions will take it up in simple faith. But they will curse us if they discover that they have no cloth to wear or the cloth they can get is too dear for their purse. The formula therefore is : Discard foreign cloth and make your own *khadi* and wear it. Already there is a dearth of *khadi*. Most of the *khadi* workers are in the salt campaign. Therefore the production has suffered a temporary check.

But there need never be any dearth of cloth the moment the country gets disabused of the superstition that it must buy cloth to cover its nakedness. It would be on a par with some one saying that we must starve if we cannot get Manchester or Delhi biscuits. Even as we cook our food and eat it so can we, if we but will it, make our own cloth and wear it. We did it only a hundred years ago and we can relearn the trick now. All the vital processes are almost too simple to learn. At this supreme crisis, this turning point in the nation's history, we must not hesitate and nurse idleness. I do not need to restate the argument about our mills. Even if every mill were genuinely Swadeshi and even if all became patriotic, they could not supply all our wants. Whichever way we look at it, whether we like it or not, we cannot escape *khadi* if we are to achieve independence through non-violent means and if we are to achieve the boycott of foreign cloth on which we began concentration in 1920.

Young India, 17-4-'30

154

MEN'S PART

[The following is a free rendering of extracts from my speech delivered before men just after the women's conference at Dandi on 13th instant. — M. K. G.]

I have just finished the women's conference. You will like to know what part we men may take in the women's movement. In the first place, we men may not meddle with the women's picketing of liquor and foreign cloth shops. If we do, we are likely to make a hash of it as we did in 1921. We can assist them in a variety of ways. The two classes of picketing have been designed to provide them with a special and exclusive field of activity. We can help by making the acquaintance of liquor and toddy dealers and interviewing them personally and asking them to give up the traffic now that the nation is going through the throes of a new birth. One can help also by showing greater and more delicate respect towards our women. Such general levelling up of the atmosphere will act upon the liquor dealer and also the foreign cloth dealer and buyer and the drinker, as neither will then be able to resist the appeal made to the heart by the gentle sex. In my opinion, these are virtues in which *women* excel men. *Ahimsa* is pre-eminently such a virtue. Woman exercises it naturally and intuitively when man reaches it through a laborious analytical process. Women left to themselves are likely quicker to reach the goal than if we men were to meddle with their picketing though we may help them with advice and guidance whenever they need them. Dr Sumant Mehta and Sjt. Kanjibhai have already undertaken that task.

But there is the constructive activity of the women, i.e. manufacture of *khadi*. This is an activity which requires the assistance of every man, woman and child. We must all learn how to pick cotton, gin it, card it and spin it. These are all easy processes easily learnt if we have the will. It is no more difficult to learn than it is to cook or swim. Believe me there will be no boycott of foreign cloth, if we do not learn to manufacture *khadi* in our homes. The problem of *khadi* manufacture is the problem of every one becoming his or her own spinner. This natural and universal distribution of one simple process solves the whole of the problem of cloth supply. We have enough weavers in the land, we have not enough spinners. And when we have yarn spun from day to day by millions of hands, we men must approach the weavers and get them to weave it. This requires some organizing in the beginning. But it will be done as soon as we have made up our minds, as we have about the Salt tax.

So much for what we may and ought to do. Now for what we may never do. I have complaints from correspondents in Bombay that the forcible seizing of foreign caps from other people's heads has begun as happened in 1921. I do not know to what extent this is true. But whatever the extent, it must not be repeated. We may not use compulsion even in the matter of doing a good thing. Any compulsion will ruin the cause. I feel that we are within reach of the goal. But all the marvellous work done during this week of self-purification will be undone if the movement is vitiated by the introduction of compulsion. This is a movement of conversion, not of compulsion, even of the tyrant. We can offer Satyagraha against those whom we know as our friends or associates when they will not do a good thing or when they break promises. If you have the strength and the purity, you can offer Satyagraha, say by fasting, against your associates when they do not listen to a good thing. If I had the strength and the purity I should do so today against the nation. I confess I have not developed it to the extent required. It is not a mechanical art. Something within you impels you to it and then no one on earth can prevent you. I have no such impelling force as yet. If *you* have it, you can do it. I did it in 1921 when Bombay went mad. I did it in 1917 when the mill hands who had made a promise in the name of God were about to break it in a moment of weakness. In each case the act was spontaneous and its effect was electrical.

But this was a process of conversion. The exercise of compulsion by our men simply unnerves me and unfits me for service. This time whatever happens, the struggle has to go on. There is no turning back. But that is one thing and my capacity for service is another. I can promise not to suspend the movement but I have no capacity for promising not to die or collapse through sickness or weakness during the struggle. I admit that I am utterly weak in the face of any violence on our part and when I hear of any such thing, a doctor examining my pulse would at once detect a ruffle in the heart beat. It really takes a few moments, a waiting on God for help before I regain the normal beat of the heart. I cannot help this weakness of mine. Rather do I nurse it. This sensitiveness keeps me fit for service and true guidance, and keeps me humble and ever reliant on God. He only knows when I may become so upset and disconcerted by some violent act of ours as to declare a perpetual or temporary fast. It is the last weapon of a Satyagrahi against loved ones. If India continually takes resolutions in the name of God about non-violence, *khadi*, untouchability, communal unity and what not and as often denies God by breaking them, — India that has in her infatuation for me made me a *Mahatma*, — I do not know when God within may provoke me to offer the final Satyagraha against her who has loved me not wisely but too well. May the occasion never arise ; but if it does, may God give me the strength and the purity to undertake that final sacrifice.

Young India, 17-4-'30

155

NOTES

The Frontier Provinces

When I marched to Dandi, friends in the Frontier Provinces had offered to send some volunteers to help me. I sent them thanks in appreciation of their offer but did not avail myself of it. How nice perhaps it would have been if they had not actively participated in the movement. Those who not being sure of perfect non-violence being observed, do not take an active part in the struggle, are most assuredly helping it. Those who wanting to serve take part in it and violence results, as happened at Peshawar, are as assuredly harming the movement. That the people in Peshawar meant well I have no doubt. They are perhaps more impatient (if such a thing were possible) than I am to win freedom. But nobody can get freedom today in this land except through non-violence. We cannot get India's freedom through the way of violence ; we are within reach of it, if we would but keep up non-violence to the end. The way lies not through the burning of armoured cars and taking the lives of administrators of the Government machinery ; it lies through disciplined organized self-suffering. I deeply regret the occurrences in Peshawar. Brave lives have been thrown away without the cause itself being served.

Boycott and Picketing

There is a great deal of bartering among us. The position taken up by foreign cloth merchants is but a symptom of that spirit. They want to give up foreign cloth trade only if they can do so without suffering any loss. But patriotism does not admit of barter. People are expected like Dattatreya to face death, like Kachhalia in South Africa to face compulsory insolvency, like the late Gopabandhu Das and others, not known to fame, to face poverty, and like the widow of Viththalbhai of Ambheti to suffer the death of nearest and dearest ones. Therefore the reluctance of foreign cloth merchants to suffer losses, in my opinion, betrays want of real patriotism.

But the Delhi merchants contend that the local Congress Committee has bound itself to stop picketing under certain conditions. If that be so, the promise has to be fulfilled at any cost. If the word of a Congressman or a Congress organization cannot be relied upon, we shall ultimately lose the battle. Satyagraha means insistence on truth. Breach of promise is a base surrender of truth. I have therefore advised the parties that if they cannot agree as to the text of the promise, if any, to refer the matter to arbitration.

I understand, too, that in Delhi, they have resorted to mixed picketing. I have suggested that it should be confined only to women. It does not matter if picketing is suspended for want of sufficient women pickets. Every occasion for violence must be avoided. Men can produce, by careful propaganda and production of *khadi,* an irresistible atmosphere for the boycott. But picketing whereever it is done must be confined to women.

Young India, 1-5-'30

156

HOW TO DO THE PICKETING

1. At least ten women are required for picketing a liquor or foreign cloth shop. They must choose a leader from among themselves.

2. They should all first go in a deputation to the dealer and appeal to him to desist from carrying on the traffic and present him with leaflets setting forth facts and figures regarding drink or foreign cloth as the case may be. Needless to say the leaflets should be in the language understood by the dealer.

3. If the dealer refuses to suspend traffic, the volunteers should guard the shop leaving the passage free and make a personal appeal to the would-be purchasers.

4. The volunteers should carry banners or light boards bearing warnings in bold letters against buying foreign cloth or indulging in intoxicating drinks, as the case may be.

5. Volunteers should be as far as possible in uniforms.

6. Volunteers should at frequent intervals sing suitable *bhajans* bearing on the subject.

7. Volunteers should prevent compulsion or interference by men.

8. On no account should vulgarity, abuse, threat or unbecoming language be used.

9. The appeal must always be to the head and the heart, never to fear of force.

10. Men should on no account congregate near the place of picketing nor block the traffic. But they should carry on propaganda generally through the area against foreign cloth and drink. They should help and organize processions of women to parade through the area carrying the message of temperance and *khadi* and the necessity of boycott of drink and foreign cloth.

11. There should be at the back of these picketing units a network of organizations for spreading the message of the *takli* and the *charkha* and thinking out new leaflets and new lines of propaganda.

12. There should be an absolutely accurate and systematic account of all receipts and expenditure. This should be periodically audited. This again should be done by men under the supervision of women. The whole scheme pre-supposes on the part of men a genuine respect for women and sincere desire for their rise.

Young India, 24-4-'30

157

SOME PICKETING RULES

In picketing foreign cloth or intoxicating drinks and drugs, let it be remembered, that the aim is to convert the addict or the buyer. Our object is moral and economic reform. The political consequence is but a bye-product. If Lancashire ceased to send us its cloth and the Government ceased to use the *abkari* revenue for any purpose save that of weaning the drunkard or opium-eater from his vice, we should still be engaged in picketing work and allied propaganda. The following rules, therefore, must be read in that light:

1. In picketing shops your attention must be rivetted on the buyer.

2. You should never be rude to the buyer or the seller.

3. You may not attract crowds or form cordons.

4. Yours must be a silent effort.

5. You must seek to win over the buyer or the seller by your gentleness, not by the awe of numbers.

6. You may not obstruct traffic.

7. You may not cry *hai hai* or use other expressions of shame.

8. You should know every buyer and his address and occupation and penetrate his or her home and heart. This presupposes continuity of same picketers.

9. You should try to understand the difficulties of buyers and sellers, and where you cannot remove them you should report them to your superiors.

10. If you are picketing foreign cloth, you should have some *khadi* or at least a sample book with prices and should know the nearest *khadi* shop to which you could take the buyer. If the buyer does not wish to buy *khadi* and insists on mill cloth, you should direct the buyer to an indigenous mill-cloth seller.

11. You should have relevant literature upon your person for distribution among the buyers.

12. You should join or organize processions, lectures with or without magic lantern, *bhajan* parties etc.

13. You should keep an accurate diary of your day's work.

14. If you find your effort failing do not be disheartened but rely upon the universal law of cause and effect and be assured that no good thought, word or deed goes fruitless. To think well, to speak well is ours, reward is in the hands of God.

Young India, 19-3-'31

158

A STERN REPROOF

[To certain foreign-cloth dealers who presented Gandhiji with a purse and an address in Navasari Gandhiji administered the following reproof :]

This function appears to me to be to a great extent out of place and uncalled for. The association of merchants, dealers as they are in foreign cloth, ought not to have thought of presenting the address to me or the Sardar. The presentation, if it must be made, ought to be accompanied by a pledge that they would never in future have anything to do with foreign cloth and also the intimation that they have either burnt their present stock or sealed it. How can we, whose daily prayer is for the entire extinction of this trade, accept an address and a purse from dealers in it? I would, therefore, plead with the friends to take back their purse and their address. The address affords no information about the association and reads as though it was a citizens' address. That smacks somewhat of a bogus translation, as I said to the Sardar. Satyagraha eschews all make-believe. I have no relish for the title of the *Mahatma* given me by the people, if only because I am unworthy of it but I have given myself a title of which I am proud. I call myself a Satyagrahi, and so I must live up to it. I cannot but utter the bitter truth, whenever there is an occasion for it. The acceptance of the purse and the address would be a bitter dose for me, as its presentation should be for you too. But, if I cannot convince you, I must ask you to take both of them back. I have had occasions in my life when I have practised Satyagraha against my brother and my wife, and today's occasion can be no exception. I would have to return the address and the purse, as I would return a title from a government with which I non-co-operate or a gift from a liquor seller. I want you to understand that I would compromise myself to the cause if I agreed to accept your address. I would, however, spare you a sudden shock, hold the address and the purse in trust for you. You can ponder over what I have said and decide whether you will present them on my terms or take them back because you will not give up foreign-cloth trade.

Young India, 19-3-'31

159

PICKETING

My critics are shocked over my recent remarks on picketing. They think that in describing as a species of violence the formation of a living wall of pickets in order to prevent the entry of persons into picketed places, I have contradicted my sayings and doings during the civil disobedience campaign. If such is really the case, my recent writing must be held as cancelling my comparatively remote sayings and doings. Though my body is deteriorating through age, no such law of deterioration, I hope, operates against wisdom which I trust is not only not deteriorating but even growing. Whether it is or not, my mind is clear on the opinion I have given on picketing. If it does not appeal to Congressmen, they may reject it, and if they do, they will violate the laws of peaceful picketing. But there is no discrepancy between my past practice and the present statement. When civil disobedience was first organized by me in South Africa, my companions discussed with me the question of picketing. The registration office had to be picketed in Johannesburg, and the suggestion made was that we should form there a living wall of pickets. I at once rejected the idea as violent. And pickets were posted in marked positions in a big public square so that no one could elude the eagle eyes of the pickets and yet every one could go to the registration office, if he liked, without touching any one. Reliance was put upon the force of public opprobrium which would be evoked by the publication of the names of the ' blacklegs '. This method was copied by me here when liquor shops were to be picketed. The work was specially entrusted to the women as better representatives of non-violence than men. Thus there was no question of the formation of a living wall. Many unauthorized things were no doubt done during those days as they are now. But I cannot recall a single instance in which I countenanced the kind of picketing condemned by the article that has come in for sharp criticism. And is there really any difficulty about regarding a living wall of pickets as naked violence ? What is the difference between force used against a man wanting to do a particular thing, and force exercised by interposing yourself between him and the deed ? When, during the non-co-operation days, the students in Banaras blocked the passage to the University gates I had to send a peremptory message and, if my recollection serves me right, I strongly condemned their action in the columns of *Young India*. Of course, I have no argument against those who hold different views from mine regarding violence and non-violence.

Harijan, 27-8-'38

WHEN IS PICKETING PEACEFUL ?

A correspondent writes :

"I find that here in Bombay this weapon of 'peaceful picketing' is being misused on the ground that peaceful picketing, with whatsoever just or unjust object it may be resorted to, is no offence. The aggrieved party against whom such picketing is aimed at. fails to get any protection either from the police or law. For instance, A happens to be a shop-keeper. B an employee of A, having no legal claim against A, threatens A with picketing his shop in case A does not accede to B's demands and actually, with the help of C and D posing as 'leaders', starts picketing A's shop and misleads A's customers, with a view to dissuading them from patronizing A's shop. Would such picketing, even though there be no actual physical force used, be termed 'peaceful' ? "

I cannot speak about the legality of such picketing, but I can say that such picketing cannot be called peaceful, i.e. non-violent. All picketing without indubitably just cause is violent even though no physical force is used. Picketing without such cause becomes a nuisance and interferes with the exercise of private right. Generally no picketing should be resorted to by individuals unless it is promoted by a responsible organization. Picketing like civil disobedience has its well-defined limits without a strict observance of which it becomes illegitimate and reprehensible.

Harijan, 2-12-'39

PICKETING AND LOVE

A writer in the public Press indignantly asks : " How can I reconcile picketing with my doctrine of love ? Is not picketing a form of violence or undue pressure ? " It can be that certainly. It has been that in several cases, I am sorry to say. But it has been also an act of love, I know. Several sisters and young lads have gone on picketing purely out of love. Nobody has accused me of hatred against Marwadis. Nobody can possibly accuse Sheth Jamnalalji of hatred against his own caste-men and fellow merchants. And yet both he and I are countenancing picketing of Marwadi foreign-cloth shops. When a daughter stands guard over her erring father, she does it purely out of love. The fact is, that there are certain acts that are common to all classes of men. And when they are not in themselves objectionable, the motive alone decides their quality.

Young India, 22-9-'21

162

STUDENTS' NOBLE SATYAGRAHA

In referring to the universality of Satyagraha I have time and again observed in these columns that it is capable of application in the social no less than in the political field. It may equally be employed against Government, society, or one's own family, father, mother, husband or wife, as the case may be. For it is the beauty of this spiritual weapon that when it is completely free from the taint of *himsa* and its use is actuated purely and solely by love it may be used with absolute impunity, in any connection and in any circumstance whatever. A concrete instance of its use against a social evil was furnished by the brave and spirited students of Dharmaj (in Kheda District) a few days back. The facts as gleaned from the various communications about the incident received by me were as follows :

A gentleman of Dharmaj, some days back, gave a caste dinner in connection with the twelfth-day ceremony of the death of his mother. It was preceded by a keen controversy about the subject among the young men of the place who shared with a number of other local inhabitants their strong dislike of this custom. They felt that on this occasion something must be done. Accordingly, most of them took all or some of the following three vows :

1.   Not to join their elders at the dinner or otherwise partake of the food served on that occasion.

2.   To fast on the day of the dinner as an emphatic protest against this practice.

3.   To bear patiently and cheerfully any harsh treatment that might be accorded to them by their elders for taking this step.

In pursuance of this decision quite a large number of students, including some children of tender age, fasted on the day on which the dinner was given and took upon themselves the wrath of their so-called elders. Nor was the step free from the dangers of serious pecuniary consequences to the students. The 'elders' threatened to stop the allowances of their boys and even to withdraw any financial aid that they were giving to local institutions, but the boys stood firm. As many as two hundred and eighty-five students thus refused to take part in the caste dinner and most of them fasted.

I tender my congratulations to these boys and hope that everywhere students will take a prominent part in effecting social reform. They hold in their pocket, as it were, the key to social reform and the protection of their religion just as they have in their possession the key to Swaraj — though they may not be aware of it owing to their negligence or carelessness. But I hope that the example set by the students of Dharmaj will awaken them to a sense of their power. In my opinion, the true *shraddha* of the deceased lady was performed by these young men fasting on that day, while those who gave the dinner wasted good money and set a bad example to the poor. The rich, moneyed class ought to use their God-given wealth for philanthropic purposes. They should understand that the poor cannot afford to give caste dinners on wedding or on funeral ceremonies. These bad practices have proved to be the ruin of many a poor man. If the money that was spent in Dharmaj on the caste dinner had been used for helping poor students, or poor widows, or for *khadi*, or cow-protection, or the amelioration of the 'untouchables', it would have borne fruit and brought peace to the departed soul. But as it is, the dinner has already been forgotten. It has profited nobody and it has caused pain to the students and the sensible section of the Dharmaj public.

Let no one imagine that the Satyagraha has gone in vain because it did not succeed in preventing the dinner in question from taking place. The students themselves knew that there was little possibility of their Satyagraha producing any immediate tangible result. But we may safely take it that if they do not let their vigilance go to sleep no *shethia* will again dare to give a post-mortem dinner. A chronic and long-standing social evil cannot be swept away at a stroke ; it always requires patience and perseverence.

When will the ' elders ' of our society learn to recognize the signs of the times ? How long will they be slaves to custom instead of using it as a means for the amelioration of society and the country ? How long will they keep their children divorced from a practical application of the knowledge which they are helping them to acquire ? When will they rescue their sense of right and wrong from its present state of trance and wake up and be *mahajans* in the true sense of the word ?

Young India, 1-3-'28

163
LIMITS OF SATYAGRAHA

A correspondent impatient to stop the marriages of aged men with young girls writes :

" This evil requires drastic remedies. Twenty-five young men of character should form themselves into a band of Satyagrahis proceed to the place of the marriage eight or ten days before the event and plead with both the parties, with the heads of the caste organization, and with all concerned. They should parade the streets with suitable placards condemning such marriages and produce an atmosphere of opposition to the proposed marriage. They should persuade the people of the town or village to declare a peaceful boycott against the parties to the marriage, and court arrest or whatever other punishment that comes to them.

" Thus the Satyagrahi band would soon become a power in the locality, and these marriages would be a thing of the past."

The suggestion looks attractive, but I am afraid it cannot be of use on more than one occasion. Where lust and cupidity join hands the slaughter of the innocents becomes almost impossible to avoid. As soon as lustful old candidates for brides and the greedy parents get scent of the invasion of the Satyagrahi band, they will evade the band by performing the wedding secretly, and they will find enough priests and wedding guests to help them in the ceremony. The readers of *Navajivan* may be aware of an incident that happened some time ago. The old man in that case feigned contrition, and successfully threw dust into the eyes of all by a hollow public apology. The reformers were delighted, but before they had finished congratulating themselves the old man managed to get secretly married. What happened in one case may happen in many cases. We should, therefore, devise other means to grapple with the evil. I have an idea that it may be easier to reach the greedy father of the bride than the slave of his lust. There is a great necessity for cultivating public opinion in the matter. The parents who readily sell away their girls, out of cupidity, should be sought out and pleaded with, and caste organizations should be persuaded to pass resolutions condemning such marriages. Evidently such reforms cannot be carried out all at once by the same band in large areas. Their field must needs be circumscribed. A Satyagrahi band in Cape Comorin will not be able to prevent a monstrous marriage in Kashmir. The reformers will have, therefore, to recognize their limitations. We may not attempt the impossible.

Love and *ahimsa* are matchless in their effect. But in their play there is no fuss, show, noise or placards. They presuppose self-confidence which in its turn presupposes self-purification. Men of stainless character and self-purification will easily inspire confidence and automatically purify the atmosphere around them. I have long believed that social reform is a tougher business than political reform. The atmosphere is ready for the latter, people are interested in it, and there is an impression abroad that it is possible without self-purification. On the other hand, people have little interest in social reform, the result of agitation does not appear to be striking and there is little room for congratulations and addresses. The social reformers will have therefore to plod on for some time, hold themselves in peace, and be satisfied with apparently small results.

I may here throw out a practical suggestion. The most effective means of creating an atmosphere against the marriages of aged persons with young girls is to create public opinion against the actual marriage and to set in motion a peaceful social boycott against the aged bridegroom and the greedy father of the bride.

If a successful boycott can be carried out even in one single instance, parents will hesitate to sell their daughters and old men will hesitate to run after young brides.

It will not be easy to wean lustful old men from their lust. They may be, therefore, induced to marry old widows, if they must marry. In Europe old men easily seek out old widows.

In conclusion, we must be clear about our objective in opposing these marriages. It cannot be our object to wean old men from their lust; if it is we will have first to deal with lustful young men. But that is a tall order. Our objective can be only to save young girls from the clutches of lustful old men and the cupidity of their parents. The reformer must, therefore, address himself to carrying on a crusade against the sale of brides. It is the bride's parents who have to be reached. Let the Satyagrahi, therefore, chalk out the field of his activities, have a census of all girls of a marriageable age living in that area, let him get into touch with their parents, and awaken them to a sense of their duty towards their daughters.

Let not the reformer go outside these limits if he wants to achieve success. The scheme proposed in the correspondent's letter easily transgresses these limits.

Young India, 6-9-'28

SATYAGRAHA AGAINST THE COLOUR BAR BILL

[With reference to the Colour Bar Bill which was due to be passed in South Africa, Gandhiji wrote:]

What are then our countrymen in South Africa to do? There is nothing in the world like self-help. The world helps those who help themselves. Self-help in this case, as perhaps in every other, means self-suffering; self-suffering means Satyagraha. When their honour is at stake, when their rights are being taken away, when their livelihood is threatened, they have the right and it becomes their duty to offer Satyagraha. They offered it during 1907 and 1914 and won the support even of the Government of India, indeed the recognition of the Europeans and the Government of South Africa. They can do likewise again if they have the will and the courage to suffer for the common good.

That time is not yet. They must, as they are doing, exhaust every diplomatic remedy. They must await the result of the negotiations the Government of India are carrying on with the Union Government. And when they have explored and tried every other available channel and failed to find a way out, the case for Satyagraha is complete. Then it would be cowardice to flinch. And victory is a certainty. No power on earth can make a person do a thing against his will. Satyagraha is a direct result of the recognition of this great Law and is independent of numbers participating in it.

Young India, 18-2-'26

THE JEWS

The German persecution of the Jews seems to have no parallel in history. Can the Jews resist this organized and shameless persecution? Is there a way to preserve their self-respect, and not to feel helpless, neglected and forlorn? I submit there is. No person who has faith in a living God need feel helpless or forlorn. Jehovah of the Jews is a God more personal than the God of the Christians, the Mussalmans or the Hindus, though, as a matter of fact, in essence, He is common to all and one without a second and beyond description. But as the Jews attribute personality to God and believe that He rules every action of theirs, they ought not to feel helpless. If I were a Jew and were born in Germany and earned my livelihood there, I would claim Germany as my home even as the tallest gentile German may, and challenge him to shoot me or cast me in the dungeon ; I would refuse to be expelled or to submit to discriminating treatment. And for doing this, I should not wait for the fellow Jews to join me in civil resistance but would have confidence that in the end the rest are bound to follow my example. If one Jew or all the Jews were to accept the prescription here offered, he or they cannot be worse off than now. And suffering voluntarily undergone will bring them an inner strength and joy which no number of resolutions of sympathy passed in the world outside Germany can. Indeed even if Britain, France and America were to declare hostilities against Germany, they can bring no inner joy, no inner strength. The calculated violence of Hitler may even result in a general massacre of the Jews by way of his first answer to the declaration of such hostilities. But if the Jewish mind could be prepared for voluntary suffering, even the massacre I have imagined could be turned into a day of thanksgiving and joy that Jehovah had wrought deliverance of the race even at the hands of the tyrant. For to the God-fearing, death has no terror. It is a joyful sleep to be followed by a waking that would be all the more refreshing for the long sleep.

It is hardly necessary for me to point out that it is easier for the Jews than for the Czechs to follow my prescription. And they have in the Indian Satyagraha campaign in South Africa an exact parallel. There the Indians occupied precisely the same place that the Jews occupy in Germany. The persecution had also a religious tinge. President Kruger used to say that the white Christians were the chosen of God and Indians were inferior beings created to serve the whites. A fundamental clause in the Transvaal Constitution was that there should be no equality between the whites and coloured races including Asiatics. There too the Indians were consigned to ghettoes described as locations. The other disabilities were almost of the same type as those of the Jews in Germany. The Indians, a mere handful, resorted to Satyagraha without any backing from the world outside or the Indian Government. Indeed the British officials tried to dissuade the Satyagrahis from their contemplated step. World opinion and the Indian Government came to their aid after eight years of fighting. And that too was by way of diplomatic pressure not of a threat of war.

But the Jews of Germany can offer Satyagraha under infinitely better auspices than the Indians of South Africa. The Jews are a compact, homogeneous community in Germany. They are far more gifted than the Indians of South Africa. And they have organized world opinion behind them. I am convinced that if someone with courage and vision can arise among them to lead them in nonviolent action, the winter of their despair can in the twinkling of an eye be turned into the summer of hope. And what has today become a degrading man-hunt can be turned into a calm and determined stand offered by unarmed men and women possessing the strength of suffering given to them by Jehovah. It will be then a truly religious resistance offered against the godless fury of dehumanized man. The German Jews will score a lasting victory over the German gentiles in the sense that they will have converted the latter to an appreciation of human dignity. They will have rendered service to fellow-Germans and proved their title to be the real Germans as against those who are today dragging, however unknowingly, the German name into the mire.

Harijan, 26-11-'38

166

THE SATYAGRAHA WAY WITH CRIME

A villager was brought to him with injuries on his body, received at the hands of thieves who had taken away ornaments etc. from his house. There were three ways, Gandhiji told the villagers of Uruli, of dealing with the case. The first was the stereotyped orthodox way of reporting to the police. Very often, it only provided the police a further opportunity for corruption and brought no relief to the victim. The second way, which was followed by the general run of the village people, was to passively acquiesce in it. This was reprehensible as it was rooted in cowardice. Crime would flourish, while cowardice remained. What was more, by such acquiescence we ourselves became party to the crime. The third way, which Gandhiji commended, was that of pure Satyagraha. It required that we should regard even thieves and criminals as our brothers and sisters, and crime as a disease of which the latter were the victims and needed to be cured. Instead of bearing ill-will towards a thief or a criminal and trying to get him punished they should try to get under his skin, understand the cause that had led him into crime and try to remedy it. They should, for instance, teach him a vocation and provide him with the means to make an honest living and thereby transform his life. They should realize that a thief or a criminal was not a different being from themselves. Indeed, if they turned the searchlight inward and closely looked into their own souls, they would find that the difference between them was only one of degree. The rich, moneyed man who made his riches by exploitation or other questionable means, was no less guilty of robbery than the thief who picked a pocket or broke into a house and committed theft. Only the former took refuge behind the facade of respectability and escaped the penalty of law. Strictly speaking, remarked Gandhiji, all amassing or hoarding of wealth, above and beyond one's legitimate requirements was theft. There would be no occasion for thefts and, therefore, no thieves, if there was a wise regulation of riches and absolute social justice prevailed. In the Swaraj of his conception, there would be no thieves and no criminals, or else it would be Swaraj only in name. The criminal was only an indication of the social malady and since nature cure, as he envisaged it, included the triple cure for body, mind and soul, they must not be satisfied with merely banishing physical illness from Uruli, their work must include the healing of the mind and soul, too, so that there would be perfect social peace in their midst.

The Way of Satyagraha

If they followed the nature-cure way of dealing with the criminal, which, as he had already explained, was the way of Satyagraha, they could not sit still in the face of crime. Only a perfect being could afford to lose himself within himself and withdraw completely from the cares and responsibilities of the world. But who could claim that perfection? "On the high sea a sudden calm is always regarded by experienced pilots and mariners with concern. Absolute calm is not the law of the ocean. It is the same with the ocean of life. More often than not, it portends rough weather. A Satyagrahi would, therefore, neither retaliate nor would he submit to the criminal, but seek to cure him by curing himself. He will not try to ride two horses at a time, viz. to pretend to follow the law of Satyagraha, while at the same time, seek police aid. He must forswear the latter, in order to follow the former. If the criminal himself chooses to hand himself over to the police, it would be a different matter. You cannot expect to touch his heart and win his confidence, if at the same time you are prepared to go to the police and inform against him. That would be gross betrayal of trust. A reformer cannot afford to be an informer." And by way of illustration, he mentioned several instances of how he had refused to give information to the police, about persons who had been guilty of violence and came and confessed to him. No police officer could compel a Satyagrahi to give evidence against a person who had confessed to him. A Satyagrahi would never be guilty of a betrayal of trust. He wanted the people of Uruli to adopt the method of Satyagraha for dealing with crime and criminals. They should contact the criminals in their homes, win their confidence and trust by loving and selfless service, wean them from evil and unclean habits and help to rehabilitate them by teaching them honest ways of living.

Harijan, 11-8-'46

167

SOCIALISM AND SATYAGRAHA

Truth and *ahimsa* must incarnate in socialism. In order that they can, the votary must have a living faith in God. Mere mechanical adherence to truth and *ahimsa*, is likely to break down at the critical moment. Hence have I said that truth is God. This God is a living Force. Our life is of that Force. That Force resides in, but is not the body. He who denies the existence of that great Force, denies to himself the use of that inexhaustible Power and thus remains impotent. He is like a rudderless ship which, tossed about here and there, perishes without making any headway. The socialism of such takes them nowhere, what to say of the society in which they live.

The fact is that it has always been a matter of strenuous research to know this great Force and its hidden possibilities.

My claim is that in the pursuit of that search lies the discovery of Satyagraha. It is not, however, claimed that all the laws of Satyagraha have been laid down or found. This I do say, fearlessly and firmly, that every worthy object can be achieved by the use of Satyagraha. It is the highest and infallible means, the greatest force. Socialism will not be reached by any other means. Satyagraha can rid society of all evils, political, economic and moral.

Harijan, 20-7-'47

168

SOME QUESTIONS

With reference to the imminent civil disobedience some pertinent questions have been put by friends as well as critics. These need answering.

Q. Surely you are not so impatient as to start your campaign without letting the authorities know your plans and giving them an opportunity of meeting you and arresting you?

A. Those who know my past should know that I hold it to be contrary to Satyagraha to do anything secretly or impatiently. My plans will be certainly sent to the Viceroy before I take any definite step. A Satyagrahi has no secrets to keep from his opponent or so-called enemy.

Q. Did you not say even at Lahore that the country was not prepared for civil disobedience, especially, no-tax campaign on a mass scale?

A. I am not even now sure that it is. But it has become clear to me as never before that the unpreparedness in the sense that a non-violent atmosphere is wanting will as time goes by, very likely increase as it has been increasing all these years. Young men are impatient. I know definitely many stayed their violent designs because in 1921 the Congress had decided to offer civil disobedience. That school has been more active than before because of my repeated declarations that the country was not prepared for civil disobedience. I feel then that if non-violence is an active force, as I know it is, it should work even in the face of the most violent atmosphere. One difficulty in the way was that the Congress claiming to represent the whole nation could not very well offer civil disobedience and disown

354

responsibility for violence especially by Congressmen. I have procured discharge from that limitation by taking over the responsibility for launching on civil disobedience. I represent no one but myself and at the most those whom I may enrol for the campaign. And I propose at present to confine myself only to those who are amenable to the Ashram discipline and have actually undergone it for some time. It is true that I may not shirk responsibility indirectly for any violence that may break out on the part of the nation and in the course of the campaign. But such responsibility will always be there and can be only a degree more than the responsibility I share with the British rulers in their sins against the nation in so far as I give my co-operation however reluctantly and ever so slightly. For instance I give my co-operation by paying taxes direct or indirect. The very salt I eat compels my voluntary co-operation. Moreover it has dawned on me never so plainly as now that if my non-violence has suffered the greatest incarnation of violence which the British Imperialistic rule is, it must suffer the crude and ineffective violence of the impatient patriots who know not that by their ineffectiveness they are but helping that imperialistic rule and enabling it to consolidate the very thing they seek to destroy. I see now as clearly as daylight that my non-violence working as it has done against the British misrule has shaken it somewhat. Even so will it shake the counter-violence of the patriot if taking courage in both my hands I set my non-violence actively in motion, i.e., civil disobedience. I reduce the risk of the outbreak of counter-violence to a minimum by taking sole charge of the campaign. After all is said and done, however, I feel the truth of the description given to my proposal by the *Times of India*. It is indeed 'the last throw of a gambler'. I have been a 'gambler' all my life. In my passion for finding the truth and in relentlessly following out my faith in non-violence, I have counted no stake too great. In doing so I have erred, if at all, in the company of the most distinguished scientist of any age and any clime.

Q. But what about your much vaunted faith in Hindu-Muslim unity? Of what value will even independence be without that unity?

A. My faith in that unity is as bright as ever. I do not want independence at the cost even of the weakest minority, let alone the powerful Mussalman and the no less powerful Sikh. The Lahore Congress resolution on unity finally sums up all its previous effort in that behalf. The Congress rules out all solutions proposed on a communal basis. But if it is ever compelled to consider such a solution it will consider only that, which will give (not merely justice) but satisfaction to all the parties concerned. To be true to its word, therefore, the Congress cannot accept any scheme of independence that does not give satisfaction, so far as communal rights are concerned, to the parties concerned. The campaign that is about to be launched is calculated to generate power for the whole nation to be independent. But it will not be in fact till all the parties have combined. To postpone civil disobedience which has nothing to do with communalism till the latter is set at rest will be to move in a vicious circle and defeat the very end that all must have in view. What I am hoping is that the Congress being free from the communal incubus will tend it, if it remains true to the nation as a whole, to become the strongest centre party jealously guarding the rights of the weakest members. Such a Congress will have only servants of the nation, not office-seekers. Till independence is achieved or till unity is reached it will have nothing to do with any office or favours from the Government of the day in competition with the minorities. Happily the Congress has now nothing to do with the legislatures which have perhaps more than anything else increased communal bitterness. It is no doubt unfortunate that at the present moment the Congress contains largely only the Hindu element. But if the Congress Hindus cease to think communally and will take no advantage that cannot be shared to the full with all the other communities, it will presently disarm all suspicion and will attract to itself the noblest among

Mussalmans, Sikhs, Parsis, Christians, Jews and all those who are of India. But whether the Congress ever approaches this ideal or not, my course is, as it always has been, perfectly clear. This unity among all is no new love with me. I have treasured it, acted up to it from my youth upward. When I went to London as a mere lad in 1889 I believed in it as passionately as I do now. When I went to South Africa in 1893 I worked it out in every detail of my life. Love so deep seated as it is in me will not be sacrificed even for the realm of the whole world. Indeed this campaign should take the attention of the nation off the communal problem and rivet it on the things that are common to all Indians, no matter to what religion or sect they may belong.

Q. Then you will raise, if you can, a force ultimately hostile to the British ?

A. Never. My love for non-violence is superior to every other thing mundane or supramundane. It is equalled only by my love for Truth which is to me synonymous with non-violence through which and which alone I can see and reach Truth. My scheme of life, if it draws no distinction between different religionists in India, it also draws none between different races. For me " man is a man for a' that." I embark upon the campaign as much out of my love for the Englishman as for the Indian. By self-suffering I seek to convert him, never to destroy him.

Q. But may not all this be your hallucination that can never come to pass in this matter-of-fact world of ours ?

A. It may well be that. It is not a charge wholly unfamiliar to me. My hallucinations in the past have served me well. This last is not expected to fail me. If it does, it will but harm me and those who may come or put themselves under its influence. If my hallucination is potent to the authorities, my body is always at their disposal. If owing to my threatened action any Englishman's life is put in greater danger than it is now, the arm of English authority is long enough and strong enough to overtake any outbreak that may occur between Kashmir and Cape Comorin or Karachi and Dibrugarh. Lastly, no campaign need take place, if all the politicians and editors instead of addressing themselves to me will address themselves to the authorities and ask them to undo the continuing wrongs some of which I have inadequately described in these pages.

Young India, 20-2-'30

169

ON NON-VIOLENCE

Questions in Paris and Geneva

"In the method we are adopting in India, fraud, lying, deceit and all the ugly brood of violence and untruth have absolutely no room. Everything is done openly and above board, for truth hates secrecy. The more open you are the more truthful you are likely to be. There is no such thing as defeat or despair in the dictionary of a man who bases his life on truth and non-violence. And yet the method of non-violence is not in any shape or form a passive or inactive method. It is essentially an active movement, much more active than the one involving the use of sanguinary weapons. Truth and non-violence are perhaps the activest forces you have in the world. A man who wields sanguinary weapons and is intent upon destroying those whom he considers his enemies, does at least require some rest and has to lay down his arms for a while in every twenty-four hours. He is, therefore, essentially inactive, for a certain part of the day. Not so the votary of truth and non-violence, for the simple reason that they are not external weapons. They reside in the human breast and they are actively working their way whether you are awake or whether you are asleep, whether you are walking leisurely or playing an active game. The panoplied warrior of truth and non-violence is ever and incessantly active."

"How then can one be effectively non-violent? By simply refusing to take up arms?"

" I would say that merely to refuse military service is not enough. To refuse to render military service when the particular time arrives is to do the thing after all the time for combating the evil is practically gone. Military service is only a symptom of the disease which is deeper. I suggest to you that those who are not on the register of military service are equally participating in the crime if they support the State otherwise. He or she who supports a State organized in the military way — whether directly or indirectly — participates in the sin. Each man old or young takes part in the sin by contributing to the maintenance of the State by paying taxes. That is why I said to myself during the war that so long as I ate wheat supported by the army whilst I was doing everything short of being a soldier, it was best for me to enlist in the army and be shot; otherwise I should retire to the mountains and eat food grown by nature. Therefore, all those who want to stop military service can do so by withdrawing all co-operation. Refusal of military service is much more superficial than non-co-operation with the whole system which supports the State. But then one's opposition becomes so swift and so effective that you run the risk of not only being marched to jail, but of being thrown into the streets."

" Then may not one accept the non-military services of the State ? "

" Now," said Gandhiji, " you have touched the tenderest spot in human nature. I was faced with the very question as author of the non-co-operation movement. I said to myself, there is no State either run by Nero or Mussolini which has not good points about it, but we have to reject the whole, once we decide to non-co-operate with the system. There are in our country grand public roads, and palatial educational institutions, said I to myself, but they are part of a system which crushes the nation. I should not have anything to do with them. They are like the fabled snake with a brilliant jewel on its head, but which has fangs full of poison. So I came to the conclusion that the British rule in India had crushed the spirit of the nation and stunted its growth, and so I decided to deny myself all the privileges — services, courts, titles. The policy would vary with different countries but sacrifice and self-denial are essential."

"But is there not a big difference between an independent nation and a subject nation? India may have a fundamental quarrel with an alien Government, but how can the Swiss quarrel with their State?"

"Difference there undoubtedly is," said Gandhiji. "As a member of a subject nation I could best help by shaking myself rid of my subjection. But here I am asked as to how best to get out of a military mentality. You are enjoying your amenities on condition that you render military service to the State. There you have to get the State rid of its military mentality."

In answer to a similar question at another meeting Gandhiji said : "Non-co-operation in military service and service in non-military matters are not compatible. 'Definitely' military service is an ill-chosen word. You are all the while giving military service by deputy because you are supporting a State which is based on military service. In Transvaal and other countries some are debarred from military service, but they have to pay money to the State. You will have to extend the scope of non-co-operation to your taxes."

"How could a disarmed neutral country allow other nations to be destroyed? But for our army which was waiting ready at our frontier during the last war we should have been ruined."

"At the risk of being considered a visionary or a fool I must answer this question in the only manner I know. It would be cowardly of a neutral country to allow an army to devastate a neighbouring country. But there are two ways in common between soldiers of war and soldiers of non-violence, and if I had been a citizen of Switzerland and a President of the Federal State what I would have done would be to refuse passage to the invading army by refusing all supplies. Secondly, by re-enacting a Thermopylae in Switzerland, you would have presented a living wall of men and women and children and invited the invaders to walk over your corpses. You may say that such a thing is beyond human experience and endurance. I say that it is not so. It was quite possible. Last year in Gujarat women stood *lathi* charges unflinchingly and in Peshawar thousands stood hails of bullets without resorting to violence. Imagine these men and women staying in front of an army requiring a safe passage to another country. The army would be brutal enough to walk over them, you might say. I would then say you will still have done your duty by allowing yourself to be annihilated. An army that dares to pass over the corpses of innocent men and women would not be able to repeat that experiment. You may, if you wish, refuse to believe in such courage on the part of the masses of men and women, but then you would have to admit that non-violence is made of sterner stuff. It was never conceived as a weapon of the weak, but of the stoutest hearts."

"Is it open to a soldier to fire in the air and avoid violence?"

"A soldier who having enlisted himself flattered himself that he was avoiding violence by shooting in the air did no credit to his courage or to his creed of non-violence. In my scheme of things such a man would be held to be guilty of untruth and cowardice both — cowardice in that in order to escape punishment he enlisted, and untruth in that he enlisted to serve as soldier and did not fire as expected. Such a thing discredits the cause of waging war against war. The War Resisters have to be like Caesar's wife — above suspicion. Their strength lies in absolute adherence to the morality of the question."

Young India, 31-12-'31

170

WHAT ARE BASIC ASSUMPTIONS

An esteemed correspondent, who has for years been following, as a student, the non-violent action of the Congress and who ultimately joined the Congress, expresses certain doubts with lucid argument. Whilst the argument is helpful to me it is unnecessary to reproduce it here. He lays down three basic assumptions and argues that India is hardly able to satisfy these assumptions under all circumstances.

The suggested basic assumptions are :

"1. Complete unity of the people in their desire and demand for freedom ;

"2. Complete appreciation and assimilation of the doctrine in all its implications by the people as a whole with consequent control over one's natural instincts for resort to violence either in revenge or as a measure of self-defence ; and (this is the most important of all).

"3. Implicit belief that the sight of suffering on the part of multitudes of people will melt the heart of the aggressor and induce him to desist from his course of violence."

For the application of the remedy of non-violence complete unity is not an indispensable condition. If it was, the remedy would possess no special virtue. For complete unity will bring freedom for the asking. Have I not said repeatedly in the columns of *Young India* and these columns that even a few true Satyagrahis would suffice to bring us freedom ? I have maintained that we would require a smaller army of Satyagrahis than that of soldiers trained in modern warfare, and the cost will be insignificant compared to the fabulous sums devoted by nations to armaments.

Nor is the second assumption necessary. Satyagraha by the vast mass of mankind will be impossible if they had all to assimilate the doctrine in all its implications. I cannot claim to have assimilated all its implications nor do I claim even to know them all. A soldier of an army does not know the whole of the military science ; so also does a Satyagrahi not know the whole science of Satyagraha. It is enough if he trusts his commander and honestly follows his instructions and is ready to suffer unto death without bearing malice against the so-called enemy.

The third assumption has to be satisfied. I should word it differently, but the result would be about the same.

My friend says there is no historical warrant for the third assumption. He cites Ashoka as a possible exception. For my purpose, however, Ashoka's instance is unnecessary. I admit that there is no historical instance to my knowledge. Hence it is that I have been obliged to claim uniqueness for the experiment. I have argued from the analogy of what we do in families or even clans. The humankind is one big family. And if the love expressed is intense enough it must apply to all mankind. If individuals have succeeded even with savages, why should not a group of individuals succeed with a group, say, of savages ? If we can succeed with the English, surely it is merely an extension of faith to believe that we are likely to succeed with less cultured or less liberally-minded nations. I hold that if we succeed with the English, with unadulterated non-violent effort, we must succeed with the others, or which is the same thing as saying that if we achieve freedom with non-violence, we shall defend it also with the same weapon. If we have not achieved that faith our non-violence is a mere expedient, it is alloy, not pure gold.

Harijan, 22-10-'38

171

BELIEF IN GOD

In his inaugural address before the annual conference of the Gandhi Seva Sangh at Brindavan (Bihar), Gandhiji had said that belief in God was one of the indispensable qualifications of a Satyagrahi. One of the members asked if some of the Socialists and Communists who did not believe in God could not be Satyagrahis.

"I am afraid not. For a Satyagrahi has no other stay but God, and he who has any other stay or depends on any other help cannot offer Satyagraha. He may be a passive resister, non-co-operator and so on, but not a true Satyagrahi. It is open to you to argue that this excludes brave comrades, whereas it may include men who profess a belief in God but who in their daily lives are untrue to their profession. I am not talking of those who are untrue to their profession, I am talking of those who are prepared in the name of God to stake their all for the sake of their principle. Don't ask me again why I am enunciating this principle today and did not do so 20 years ago. I can only say that I am no prophet, I am but an erring mortal, progressing from blunder towards truth. 'What about the Buddhists and Jains, then?' someone has asked. Well, I will say that if the Buddhists and Jains raise this objection themselves, and say that they would be disqualified if such a strict rule were observed, I should say to them that I agree with them.

"But far be it from me to suggest that you should believe in the God that I believe in. Maybe your definition is different from mine, but your belief in that God must be your ultimate mainstay. It may be some Supreme Power or some Being even indefinable, but belief in it is indispensable. To bear all kinds of tortures without a murmur of resentment is impossible for a human being without the strength that comes from God. Only in His strength we are strong. And only those who can cast their cares and their fears on that immeasurable Power have faith in God."

Other Conditions of Satyagraha

But someone may not be a *khadi*-wearer and yet his heart may be fired with patriotism. He may even have given up his legal practice and yet may not be a *khadi*-wearer. What about him ?

"Such a one may be an estimable man. But why should he do civil disobedience? There are various ways of service. Millions need not be civil resisters. The field of constructive work is open to them. Some special rigid discipline is necessary for civil resisters. The privilege of resisting or disobeying a particular law or order accrues only to him who gives willing and unswerving obedience to the laws laid down for him. This may exclude men who may be otherwise far worthier than the common men who observe the Satyagrahi's code. Those others may perform worthier tasks, but not civil disobedience."

On another occasion speaking on the same topic and in the same strain he said : "You know that word *Himalayan blunder* which has now passed into the English language and is flung at me on all occasions. It was coined by me to translate a Gujarati word. I had to condemn my own blunder in placing civil disobedience before the people in Kheda and Ahmedabad in 1919. In Kheda the proportion of crime is greater than in any other district. These people with cries of *Mahatma Gandhiji ki jai* on their lips pulled out rails and derailed trains and, but for a lucky accident, would have killed hundreds of soldiers. The mill workmen in Ahmedabad did likewise. A false rumour was spread that Anasuyabehn was arrested or assaulted. They attacked police stations, seized an English sergeant, killed him and burnt him on the streets ; they burnt telegraph offices and did much other damage. I realized that I had committed a Himalayan blunder in placing civil disobedience before those who had never learnt the art of civil disobedience. The art comes instinctively to those who are by nature law-abiding. I was by nature law-abiding. In South Africa I was neither desirous of registering the births of my children nor of getting them vaccinated. But I obeyed the laws. Then I became a confirmed anti-vaccinationist. In jail it was no easy thing to defy the rule regarding vaccination. But they respected my conscientious objection, because they knew that I had systematically respected all the civil and moral laws of the State. It is from this obedience that the capacity for civil defiance springs, and therefore my civil disobedience sits well upon me."

There were still more questions. " There is one who believes in *ahimsa* and truth, satisfies other conditions, but is compelled by circumstances, say, to sell foreign cloth. Would he come under the ban ? "

" Of course. We cannot be too strict in this matter."

" And what is the scope of freedom from bad habits ? Is tobacco-smoking a bad habit ? Or *pan**-chewing ? "

" I may not fix the limit. It must be understood that all intoxicants warp or cloud a man's intellect, and he who allows his intellect to be warped or clouded cannot offer Satyagraha. But I will not be judge in this matter. *Ganja, bhang,* opium, etc. are recognized intoxicants and come under prohibition. Not so tobacco, though I cannot quite understand how men can bear to foul their mouths with smoking and tobacco-chewing."

" Is it permissible to offer Satyagraha in jail against inhuman treatment ? "

" It is, but inhuman treatment is a very difficult term to define and anything and everything may not come under it. A Satyagrahi goes prepared to put up with tortures, brutal treatments, even humiliations, but he may do nothing that outrage his sense of self-respect or honour. However, Satyagraha is not a weapon to be used lightly or easily and at the slightest provocation. It is better that he who is easily provoked does not go to jail."

Harijan, 3-6-'39

---

* A kind of leaf chewed by people with slacked lime and betel nut.

NOT GUILTY

Dr Lohia has sent me a long well-reasoned letter on the current controversy on the Congress resolution on Satyagraha. There is a portion in it which demands public discussion. Here it is :

" You will not permit the slightest separation of the principle of Satyagraha from your own specific programme. Is it not possible to universalize the principle of Satyagraha, to make it the bed-rock of programmes other than your own? Perhaps, it is not; but I have this argument against you that you have not permitted and encouraged any such experiment. The people today do not regard your own programme of ministerial action and constructive activities as wholly adequate; they are experimenting with such programmes as those of peasant action. These newer programmes entail an amount of local and isolated action even during such times when there is no general Satyagraha. Will you stop these little Satyagrahas till you have found the formula for a general Satyagraha? In such a course of action there is the danger of anarchy that arises out of suppression. Non-violent collective action is among the rarest and most precious gifts received by mankind in all history; we may not, however, know how to treasure it and continue it."

Not only have I not prohibited separation of the principle of Satyagraha from my own specific programme, I have often invited new programmes. But hitherto I have not known a single case of any new programme. I have never suggested that there can never be any departure from or addition to my programme. What, however, I have said and would like to repeat here is that I cannot bless or encourage a new programme that makes no appeal to me. My programme I claim is a deduction from the Satyagraha of my conception. It is therefore likely that if there was any such vital activity favouring the growth of Satyagraha, it would not escape me.

I am painfully conscious of the fact that my programme has not made a general appeal to the Congress intelligentsia. I have already pointed out that the reason for the apathy of Congressmen is not to be sought in any

inherent defect in the programme, but that it is due to
the want of a living faith in *ahimsa*. What can be more
patent than that we should have complete communal
harmony, eradication of untouchability, sacrifice of the
drink revenue by the closing of liquor shops, and the
replacement of mill cloth by *khadi*? I suggest that non-
violent Swaraj is impossible if Hindus, Muslims and others
do not shed their mutual distrust and do not live as
blood-brothers, if Hindus do not purify themselves by
removing the curse of untouchability and thus establish
intimate contact with those whom they have for ages put
beyond the pale of society, if the wealthy men and women
of India will not tax themselves so that the poor who are
helpless victims of the drink and drug habit may have the
temptation removed from them by the closing of drink
and drug shops, and, lastly, if we all will not identify
ourselves with the semi-starved millions by giving up the
taste for mill cloth and revert to *khadi* produced by the
many million hands in the cottages of India. In all that
has been written against the constructive programme, I
have not come across a single convincing argument against
either its intrinsic merit or its merit in terms of non-
violent Swaraj. I make bold to say that if all Congressmen
concentrate themselves on this constructive programme,
we shall soon have the requisite non-violent atmosphere
throughout the length and breadth of the land for cent
per cent Satyagraha.

Take the peasant action suggested by Dr Lohia as a
possible new programme. I regret to have to say that in
most cases the peasants are not being educated for non-
violent action. They are being kept in a state of perpetual
excitement and made to entertain hopes which can never
be fulfilled without a violent conflict. The same may
safely be said about labour. My own experience tells me
that both the peasantry and labour can be organized for
effective non-violent action, if Congressmen honestly work
for it. But they cannot, if they have no faith in the ultimate success of non-violent action. All that is required
is the proper education of the peasantry and labour. They

need to be informed that if they are properly organized they have more wealth and resources through their labour than the capitalists through their money. Only capitalists have control over the money market, labour has not over its labour market, although if labour had been well served by its chosen leaders, it would have become conscious of the irresistible power that comes from proper instruction in non-violence. Instead, labour in many cases is being taught to rely on coercive methods to compel compliance with its demands. The kind of training that labour generally receives today leaves it in ignorance, and relies upon violence as the ultimate sanction. Thus it is not possible for me to regard the present peasant or labour activity as a new programme for the preparation of Satyagraha.

Indeed what I see around me is not preparation for a non-violent campaign but for an outbreak of violence, however unconscious or unintended it may be. If I was invited to hold myself responsible for this ending to the past twenty years' effort, I should have no hesitation in pleading guilty. Have I not said as much already in these columns? But my admission will not take us anywhere, unless it results in the retracing of our steps, the undoing of the wrong already done. This means having a reasoned faith in the non-violent method as the only means of gaining complete independence. When we have that faith, all bickerings within the Congress will cease, there will be no longer an ungainly scramble for power, and there will be mutual help instead of mutual mud-flinging. But it may be that Congressmen have come to believe that non-violence of my definition is played out or is not possible of attainment. In that case there should be a conference, formal or informal, between all Congress groups or a special meeting of the A. I. C. C. to consider the question whether time has not come to revise the policy of non-violence and the consequent constructive programme and to find out and frame a programme in consonance with and answering the present temper of Congressmen.

Harijan, 29-7-'39

173

QUESTION BOX

A Domestic Difficulty

Q. You have rightly said that no one who has not renounced untouchability in every shape and form can take part in Satyagraha. Supposing a Congressman's wife does not share his conviction in this regard and won't let him bring Harijans into his house, what should he do — coerce his wife into conformity with his views, renounce her, or renounce the Satyagraha struggle ?

A. No occasion for coercing your wife. You should let her go her way and you should go yours. This would mean her having a separate kitchen for herself and, if she likes, also a separate room. Thus there is no question of renouncing the struggle.

The More Essential

Q. Which is the more essential requirement in your mind for starting civil disobedience — your inner urge which may make you fight even single-handed, or the fulfilment of your conditions by Congressmen ? What will be the position if they are prepared and you have not felt the call ?

A. There can be no inner urge if my conditions are not fulfilled. It is possible that there may be apparent fulfilment of conditions but there may be no inner response in me. In such a case I cannot declare civil disobedience ; but it will be open to the Congress to repudiate me and declare civil disobedience independently of me.

Secrecy

Q. You should give your opinion clearly about secrecy. During the last struggle there was a great deal of secrecy to outwit the authorities.

A. I am quite clear that secrecy does no good to our cause. It certainly gave joy to those who were able successfully to outwit the police. Their cleverness was undoubted. But Satyagraha is more than cleverness. Secrecy takes away from its dignity. Satyagrahis have no reason to have secret books or secret funds. I am aware that my opinion has not found favour among many co-workers. But I have seen no reason to change it. I admit I was lukewarm before. Experience has taught me that I should have been firm.

Damage to Property

Q. You know that many Congressmen openly preached that there was no violence in damaging property, i.e. destroying rails, burning *thanas* when they are not occupied, cutting telegraph poles, burning post boxes, etc.

A. I have never been able to understand this reasoning. It is pure violence. Satyagraha is self-suffering and not inflicting suffering on others. There is surely often more violence in burning a man's property than doing him physical injury. Have not so-called Satyagrahis preferred imprisonment to fines or confiscation of their property? Well has one of my critics said that I have succeeded in teaching disruptive disobedience till at last it has come home to roost, but that I have signally failed in teaching people the very difficult art of non-violence. He has also said that in my haste I have put the cart before the horse and therefore all my talk of civil disobedience is folly if not worse. I am not able to give a satisfactory reply to this criticism. I am but a poor mortal. I believe in my experiment and in my uttermost sincerity. But it may be that the only fitting epitaph after my death will be "He tried but signally failed."

Harijan, 13-4-'40

174

QUESTION BOX

Spinning Regularly

Q. What do you mean by 'spinning regularly'? If one spins for a couple of hours during a month or for half an hour once or twice a week, would he be deemed to have satisfied the condition about spinning regularly?

A. 'Regularly' was put in the place of 'daily'. This was meant to provide for accidental or unavoidable omissions. Therefore, spinning every week or at stated intervals will not meet the case. A Satyagrahi will be expected to spin daily except for valid reasons such as sickness, travelling or the like.

Satyagraha Camps and Untouchability

Q. Satyagraha camps are being organized for the training of volunteers all over the country. But the principle with regard to the renunciation of untouchability in every shape and form is not being rigorously enforced. Don't you agree that it ought to be made an absolute rule in the camps that no one who regards the touch of Harijans as polluting and does not freely mix with them should be permitted to attend them?

A. I have no hesitation whatsoever in saying that he who has the slightest untouchability in him is wholly unfit for enrolment in the Satyagraha *sena*. I regard untouchability as the root cause of our downfall and of Hindu-Muslim discord. Untouchability is the curse of Hinduism and therefore of India. The taint is so pervasive that it haunts a man even after he has changed over to another faith.

Legal Practice and Satyagraha

Q. Knowing as you do how lying and deceit have become the stock-in-trade of the legal profession in this country, would you permit practising lawyers to enlist as active Satyagrahis?

A. I am unable to subscribe to your sweeping proposition. The fact that a lawyer wants to become a Satyagrahi presupposes on his part a certain standard of purification. No doubt there may be, to my knowledge there are, black sheep in the Congress. This is inevitable in any big organization. But it would be unbecoming of a Satyagrahi to condemn a man because he belongs to a certain profession.

Satyagraha and Obstructionism

Q. Is the policy of obstructionism compatible with Satyagraha? Can a Satyagrahi, who is supposed to stand for principles rather than party, adopt one attitude with regard to a measure when it is sponsored by his party, and another when the same measure is sponsored by the opposite party? Would you approve of this policy in Municipalities and District Boards as is being done by some Congressmen at present?

A. I have always opposed obstruction as being anti-Satyagraha. Congressmen, to be correct in their behaviour, should always give co-operation to their opponents when the latter are in a majority and adopt any wise measure. The object of Congressmen should never be attainment of power for power's sake. Indeed such discriminatory co-operation will enhance the prestige of the Congress and may even give it majority.

Harijan, 25-5-'40

FIVE QUESTIONS

1. Can Satyagrahis (i.e. those who have signed the Satyagraha pledge) offer defence when they are arrested ?
2. May a Satyagrahi make an effort to get better class treatment, i.e. 'A' or 'B' ?
3. Ought a Satyagrahi in jail to acquiesce in the conditions imposed upon him, or should he endeavour to secure what he regards more humane and satisfactory treatment ?
4. What is the minimum time for which a Satyagrahi ought to spin or what is the minimum quantity of yarn he should produce ?
5. Can a man sign the Satyagraha pledge immediately you declare civil disobedience and court arrest, or is there any definite period for which he should have remained a Satyagrahi to be eligible to take part in the civil disobedience campaign ?

Answers

1. There is no objection to offering defence, and in certain cases it would be a duty to do so as, say, in the Ajmer case.

2. In my opinion he should not make any attempt to alter the class. Personally I am against any classification.

3. He is entitled to make every legitimate effort for change to human conditions.

4. I think one hour per day should be the minimum and 300 rounds per hour is a reasonable speed. Men engaged in public work may spin less.

5. A man who intentionally refrains from signing a pledge in order to avoid fulfilment of conditions is a cheat and unworthy of being a Satyagrahi. But I can conceive an honest man just signing the pledge and straightaway going to jail. Even at the risk of losing prospective pledge-takers and those who have taken the pledge, I would say that there is no immediate prospect of my giving the call.

Harijan, 25-5-'40

THE SERMON ON THE MOUNT

Q. You often refer to the Sermon on the Mount. Do you believe in the verse, " If any man will take away thy coat, let him have thy cloak also " ? Does it not follow from the principle of non-violence ? If so, then do you advise the weak and poor tenant of a village to submit gladly to the violent encroachment of the zamindar on his ' *abadi* land ' or tenancy rights, which so often occurs in a village these days ?

A. Yes, I would unhesitatingly advise tenants to evacuate the land belonging to a tyrant. That would be like giving your cloak also when only the coat is demanded. To take what is required may be profitable ; to have more given to you is highly likely to be a burden. To overload a stomach is to court slow death. A zamindar wants his rent, he does not want his land. It would be a burden on him when he does not want it. When you give more to a robber than he needs, you spring a surprise on him, you give him a shock although agreeable. He has not been used to it. Historical instances are on record to show that such non-violent conduct has produced a wholesome effect upon evil-doers. These acts cannot be done mechanically ; they must come out of conviction and love or pity for the other man. Nor need you work out all the apparent implications of my answer. If you do, you will come across blind alleys. Suffice it to say that in the verse quoted by you Jesus put in a picturesque and telling manner the great doctrine of non-violent non-co-operation. Your non-co-operation with your opponent is violent when you give a blow for a blow, and is ineffective in the long run. Your non-co-operation is non-violent when you give your opponent all in the place of just what he needs. You have disarmed him once for all by your apparent co-operation, which in effect is complete non-co-operation.

Harijan, 13-7-'40

WHAT CAN A SOLITARY SATYAGRAHI DO ?

Q. There is one solitary Satyagrahi in one of our villages. The rest do not worry about violence or non-violence. What discipline is that single Satyagrahi to undergo ?

A. Yours is a good question. The solitary Satyagrahi has to examine himself. If he has universal love and if he fulfils the conditions implied in such a state, it must find its expression in his daily conduct. He would be bound with the poorest in the village by ties of service. He would constitute himself the scavenger, the nurse, the arbitrator of disputes, and the teacher of the children of the village. Every one, young and old, would know him ; though a householder he would be leading a life of restraint ; he would make no distinction between his and his neighbour's children ; he would own nothing but would hold what wealth he has in trust for others, and would, therefore, spend out of it just sufficient for his barest needs. His needs would, as far as possible, approximate those of the poor, he would harbour no untouchability, and would, therefore, inspire people of all castes and creeds to approach him with confidence.

Such is the ideal Satyagrahi. Our friend will always endeavour to come up to, wherever he falls short of, the ideal, fill in the gaps in his education, will not waste a single moment. His house will be a busy hive of useful activities centring round spinning. His will be a well-ordered household.

Such a Satyagrahi will not find himself single-handed for long. The village will unconsciously follow him. But whether they do or not, at a time of emergency he will, single-handed, effectively deal with it or die in the attempt. But I firmly hold that he will have converted a number of others. I may add in this connection that I had come to Sevagram as a solitary Satyagrahi. Luckily or unluckily, I could not remain alone, several from outside came and settled with me. I do not know whether any inhabitant of the village proper can be counted as a Satyagrahi, but I do hope that some of them are unconsciously shaping themselves as such. Let me say that I do not fulfil all the tests I have laid down. But I should not have mentioned them, had I not been striving to put into practice all of them. My present ambition is certainly to make of Sevagram an ideal village. I know that the work is as difficult as to make of India an ideal country. But while it is possible for one man to fulfil his ambition with respect to a single village some day, one man's lifetime is too short to overtake the whole of India. But if one man can produce one ideal village, he will have provided a pattern not only for the whole country, but perhaps for the whole world. More than this a seeker may not aspire after.

Harijan, 4-8-'40

178

NON-VIOLENT NON-CO-OPERATION

Q. There is a report about some new scheme that you want to propound in one of your *Harijan* articles about non-violent non-co-operation if any invader came to India. Could you give us an idea ?

A. It is wrong. I have no plan in mind. If I had, I should give it to you. But I think nothing more need be added when I have said that there should be unadulterated non-violent non-co-operation, and if the whole of India responded and unanimously offered it, I should show that without shedding a single drop of blood Japanese arms — or any combination of arms — can be sterilized. That involves the determination of India not to give quarter on any point whatsoever and to be ready to risk loss of several milllion lives. But I would consider that cost very cheap and victory won at that cost glorious.

That India may not be ready to pay that price may be true. I hope it is not true, but some such price must be paid by any country that wants to retain its independence. After all, the sacrifice made by the Russians and the Chinese is enormous, and they are ready to risk all. The same could be said of the other countries also, whether aggressors or defenders. The cost is enormous. Therefore, in the non-violent technique I am asking India to risk no more than other countries are risking and which India would have to risk even if she offered armed resistance.

Harijan, 24-5-'42

179

SABOTAGE AND SECRECY

A friend put before Gandhiji some of his doubts. Was destruction of Government property violence ? " You say that nobody has a right to destroy any property not his own. If so, is not Government property mine ? I hold it is mine and I may destroy it."

" There is a double fallacy involved in your argument," replied Gandhiji. " In the first place, conceding that Government property is national property — which today it is not — I may not destroy it because I am dissatisfied with the Government. But even a national Government will be unable to carry on for a day if everybody claimed the right to destroy bridges, communications, roads, etc., because he disapproved of some of its activities. Moreover, the evil resides not in bridges, roads, etc., which are inanimate objects but in men. It is the latter who need to be tackled. The destruction of bridges, etc. by means of explosives does not touch this evil but only provokes a worse evil in the place of the one it seeks to end."

" I agree," rejoined the friend, " that the evil is within ourselves, not in the bridge which can be used for a good purpose as well as an evil one. I also agree that its blowing up provokes counter-violence of a worse type. But it may be necessary from a strategic point of view for the success of the movement and in order to prevent demoralization."

"It is an old argument," replied Gandhiji. "One used to hear it in the old days in defence of terrorism. Sabotage is a form of violence. People have realized the futility of physical violence but some people apparently think that it may be successfully practised in its modified form as sabotage. It is my conviction that the whole mass of people would not have risen to the height of courage and fearlessness that they have but for the working of full non-violence. How it works we do not yet fully know. But the fact remains that under non-violence we have progressed from strength to strength even through our apparent failures and setbacks. On the other hand terrorism resulted in demoralization. Haste leads to waste."

"We have found," rejoined the friend, "that a person who has had a schooling in violent activity comes nearer to true non-violence than one who has had no such experience."

"That can be true only in the sense that having tried violence again and again he has realized its futility. That is all. Would you maintain also that a person who has had a taste of vice is nearer to virtue than the one who has had none? For, that is what your argument amounts to."

The discussion then turned upon secrecy. The friend in question argued that whilst individual secrecy created a fear complex and was therefore an evil, organized secrecy might be useful. "It is no secrecy if the person concerned is boldly prepared to face the consequences of his action. He resorts to secrecy in order to achieve his object. He can refuse to take any part in subsequent interrogations during his trial. He need not make a false statement."

But Gandhiji was adamant. "No secret organization, however big, could do any good. Secrecy aims at building a wall of protection round you. *Ahimsa* disdains all such protection. It functions in the open and in the face of odds, the heaviest conceivable. We have to organize for action a vast people that have been crushed under the heel of unspeakable tyranny for centuries. They cannot be organized by any other than open truthful means. I have grown up from youth to 76 years in abhorrence of secrecy. There must be no watering down of the ideal. Unless we cling to the formula in its fulness, we shall not make any headway."

Harijan, 10-2-'46

180

SATYAGRAHA IN FACE OF HOOLIGANISM

A friend has gently posed the question as to what a Satyagrahi should do to prevent looting by *goondas*. If he had understood the secret of Satyagraha he would not have put it.

To lay down one's life, even alone, for what one considers to be right, is the very core of Satyagraha. More, no man can do. If a man is armed with a sword he might lop off a few hands but ultimately he must surrender to superior force or else die fighting. The sword of the Satyagrahi is love and the unshakable firmness that comes from it. He will regard as brothers the hundreds of *goondas* that confront him and instead of trying to kill them he will choose to die at their hands and thereby live.

This is straight and simple. But how can a solitary Satyagrahi succeed in the midst of a huge population? Hundreds of hooligans were let loose on the city of Bombay for arson and loot. A solitary Satyagrahi will be like a drop in the ocean. Thus argues the correspondent.

My reply is that a Satyagrahi may never run away from danger, irrespective of whether he is alone or in the company of many. He will have fully performed his duty if he dies fighting. The same holds good in armed warfare. It applies with greater force in Satyagraha. Moreover, the sacrifice of one will evoke the sacrifice of many and may possibly produce big results. There is always this possibility. But one must scrupulously avoid the temptation of a desire for results.

I believe that every man and woman should learn the art of self-defence in this age. This is done through arms in the West. Every adult man is conscripted for army training for a definite period. The training for Satyagraha is meant for all, irrespective of age or sex. The more important part of the training here is mental, not physical. There can be no compulsion in mental training. The surrounding atmosphere no doubt acts on the mind but that cannot justify compulsion.

It follows that shopkeepers, traders, mill-hands, labourers, farmers, clerks, in short, every one ought to consider it his or her duty to get the necessary training in Satyagraha.

Satyagraha is always superior to armed resistance. This can only be effectively proved by demonstration, not by argument. It is the weapon that adorns the strong. It can never adorn the weak. By weak is meant the weak in mind and spirit, not in body. That limitation is a quality to be prized and not a defect to be deplored.

One ought also to understand one of its other limitations. It can never be used to defend a wrong cause.

Satyagraha brigades can be organized in every village and in every block of buildings in the cities. Each brigade should be composed of those persons who are well-known to the organizers. In this respect Satyagraha differs from armed defence. For the latter the State impresses the service of everybody. For a Satyagraha brigade only those are eligible who believe in *ahimsa* and *satya*. Therefore, an intimate knowledge of the persons enlisted is necessary for the organizers.

Harijan, 17-3-'46

181

THE NON-VIOLENT SANCTION

Q. What is the place of Satyagraha in making the rich realize their duty towards the poor ?

A. The same as against the foreign power. Satyagraha is a law of universal application. Beginning with the family its use can be extended to every other circle. Supposing a land-owner exploits his tenants and mulcts them of the fruit of their toil by appropriating it to his own use. When they expostulate with him he does not listen and raises objections that he requires so much for his wife, so much for his children and so on. The tenants or those who have espoused their cause and have influence will make an appeal to his wife to expostulate with her husband. She would probably say that for herself she does not need his exploited money. The children will say likewise that they would earn for themselves what they need.

Supposing further that he listens to nobody or that his wife and children combine against the tenants, they will not submit. They will quit if asked to do so but they will make it clear that the land belongs to him who tills it. The owner cannot till all the land himself and he will have to give in to their just demands. It may, however, be that the tenants are replaced by others. Agitation short of violence will then continue till the replacing tenants see their error and make common cause with the evicted tenants. Thus Satyagraha is a process of educating public opinion, such that it covers all the elements of society and in the end makes itself irresistible. Violence interrupts the process and prolongs the real revolution of the whole social structure.

The conditions necessary for the success of Satyagraha are : (1) The Satyagrahi should not have any hatred in his heart against the opponent. (2) The issue must be true and substantial. (3) The Satyagrahi must be prepared to suffer till the end for his cause.

Harijan, 31-3-'46

SECTION ELEVENTH: CONCLUSION

182

MY FAITH IN NON-VIOLENCE

[From a talk after the evening prayer on board the ship at Suez on the way to London for the Round Table Conference.]

I have found that life persists in the midst of destruction and, therefore, there must be a higher law than that of destruction. Only under that law would a well-ordered society be intelligible and life worth living. And if that is the law of life, we have to work it out in daily life. Wherever there are jars, wherever you are confronted with an opponent, conquer him with love. In a crude manner I have worked it out in my life. That does not mean that all my difficulties are solved. I have found, however, that this law of love has answered as the law of destruction has never done. In India we have had an ocular demonstration of the operation of this law on the widest scale possible. I do not claim therefore that non-violence has necessarily penetrated the three hundred millions, but I do claim that it has penetrated deeper than any other message, and in an incredibly short time. We have not been all uniformly non-violent; and with the vast majority, non-violence has been a matter of policy. Even so, I want you to find out if the country has not made phenomenal progress under the protecting power of non-violence.

It takes a fairly strenuous course of training to attain to a mental state of non-violence. In daily life it has to be a course of discipline though one may not like it, like for instance, the life of a soldier. But I agree that, unless there is a hearty co-operation of the mind, the mere outward observance will be simply a mask, harmful both to the man himself and to others. The perfect state is reached only when mind and body and speech are in proper co-ordination. But it is always a case of intense mental struggle. It is not that I am incapable of anger, for instance, but I succeed on almost all occasions to keep my feelings under control. Whatever may be the result, there is always in me a conscious struggle for following the law of non-violence deliberately and ceaselessly. Such a struggle leaves one stronger for it. Non-violence is a weapon of the strong. With the weak it might easily be hypocrisy. Fear and love are contradictory terms. Love is reckless in giving away, oblivious as to what it gets in return. Love wrestles with the world as with the self and ultimately gains a mastery over all other feelings. My daily experience, as of those who are working with me, is that every problem lends itself to solution if we are determined to make the law of truth and non-violence the law of life. For truth and non-violence are, to me, faces of the same coin.

The law of love will work, just as the law of gravitation will work, whether we accept it or not. Just as a scientist will work wonders out of various applications of the law of nature, even so a man who applies the law of love with scientific precision can work greater wonders. For the force of non-violence is infinitely more wonderful and subtle than the material forces of nature, like, for instance, electricity. The men who discovered for us the law of love were greater scientists than any of our modern scientists. Only our explorations have not gone far enough and so it is not possible for every one to see all its working. Such, at any rate, is the hallucination, if it is one, under which I am labouring. The more I work at this law the more I feel the delight in life, the delight in the scheme of this universe. It gives me a peace and a meaning of the mysteries of nature that I have no power to describe.

The Nation's Voice, part II, pp. 109-10

183

THE FUTURE

A friend writing from America propounds the following two questions :

"1. Granted that Saytagraha is capable of winning India's independence, what are the chances of its being accepted as a principle of State policy in a free India ? In other words, would a strong and independent India rely on Satyagraha as a method of self-preservation, or would it lapse back to seeking refuge in the age-old institution of war, however defensive its character ? To restate the question on the basis of a purely theoretic problem : Is Satyagraha likely to be accepted only in an up-hill battle, when the phenomenon of martyrdom is fully effective, or is it also to be the instrument of a sovereign authority which has neither the need nor the scope of behaving on the principle of martyrdom ?

"2. Suppose a free India adopts Saytagraha as an instrument of State policy how would she defend herself against probable aggression by another sovereign State ? To restate the question on the basis of a purely theoretic problem : What would be the Satyagrahic action-patterns to meet the invading army at the frontier ? What kind of resistance can be offered the opponent before a common area of action, such as the one now existing in India between the Indian nationalists and the British Government, is established ? Or should the Satyagrahis withhold their action until after the opponent has taken over the country ? "

The questions are admittedly theoretical. They are also premature for the reason that I have not mastered the whole technique of non-violence. The experiment is still in the making. It is not even in its advanced stage. The nature of the experiment requires one to be satisfied with one step at a time. The distant scene is not for him to see. Therefore, my answers can only be speculative.

In truth, as I have said before, now we are not having unadulterated non-violence even in our struggle to win independence.

As to the first question, I fear that the chances of non-violence being accepted as a principle of State policy are very slight, so far as I can see at present. If India does not accept non-violence as her policy after winning independence, the second question becomes superfluous.

But I may state my own individual view of the potency of non-violence. I believe that a State can be administered on a non-violent basis if the vast majority of the people are non-violent. So far as I know, India is the only country which has a possibility of being such a State. I am conducting my experiment in that faith. Supposing, therefore, that India attained independence through pure non-violence, India could retain it too by the same means. A non-violent man or society does not anticipate or provide for attacks from without. On the contrary, such a person or society firmly believes that nobody is going to disturb them. If the worst happens, there are two ways open to non-violence. To yield possession but non-co-operate with the aggressor. Thus, supposing that a modern edition of Nero descended upon India, the representatives of the State will let him in but tell him that he will get no assistance from the people. They will prefer death to submission. The second way would be non-violent resistance by the people who have been trained in the non-violent way. They would offer themselves unarmed as fodder for the aggressor's cannon. The underlying belief in either case is that even a Nero is not devoid of a heart. The unexpected spectacle of endless rows upon rows of men and women simply dying rather than surrender to the will of an aggressor must ultimately melt him and his soldiery. Practically speaking there will be probably no greater loss in men than if forcible resistance was offered ; there will be no expenditure in armaments and fortifications. The non-violent training received by the people will add inconceivably to their moral height. Such men and women will have shown personal bravery of a type far superior to that shown in armed warfare. In each case the bravery consists in dying, not in killing. Lastly, there is no such thing as defeat in non-violent resistance. That such a thing has not happened before is no answer to my speculation. I have drawn no impossible picture. History is replete with instances of individual non-violence of the type I have mentioned. There is no warrant for saying or thinking that a group of men and women cannot by sufficient training act non-violently as a group or nation. Indeed the sum total of the experience of mankind is that men somehow or other live on. From which fact I infer that it is the law of love that rules mankind. Had violence, i.e. hate, ruled us, we should have become extinct long ago. And yet the tragedy of it is that the so-called civilized men and nations conduct themselves as if the basis of society was violence. It gives me ineffable joy to make experiments proving that love is the supreme and only law of life. Much evidence to the contrary cannot shake my faith. Even the mixed non-violence of India has supported it. But if it is not enough to convince an unbeliever, it is enough to incline a friendly critic to view it with favour.

Harijan, 13-4-'40

INDEX

ACCOUNT KEEPING, its purification, 264, 335

Action, if not *yajna*, promotes bondage, 48

Ahimsa, 40-42, 91-92; and Truth are two sides of a coin, 42; cannot be subject to decision of majority, 221; hurt by evil thought, 78; its power, 285-87; never faileth, 220-22; only force of universal application, 78; positive active state of love, 161; who obeys, cannot marry, 43; with, guiding all would be well, 221; see Non-violence

A. I. C. C., at Ahmedabad passes Satyagraha resolution (1930) under Gandhiji's leadership, 239

Allegiance, oath of, to British Government is meaningless, 160

Anand, Swami, made Navajivan sound business proposition, 267

Anarchist, enemy of State and misanthrope, 60

Anasuyabehn, Gandhiji's comrade in Kheda, 205; her arrest inflamed labour, 27

Aney, his resignation, 258

Anti-untouchability movement, does not aim at inter-dining or inter-marrying, 185; meant to throw open all public wells, roads, schools, temples etc. to suppressed classes, 185

Arms, laying down of, risky step in non-co-operation, 151

Army, daring to pass over corpses of non-violent men once would not repeat the experiment, 361

Arrest, normal condition of a non-co-operator, 172

Asiatic Act of 1907 of Transvaal, 35

Attachment, freedom from, is God-realization, 42

Auditing, 264, 335

BANDE MATARAM, 62, 63

Banker, Shankarlal, Gandhiji's comrade in Kheda, 205

Bardoli Satyagraha (1922) its resolution of no-tax campaign, 209-10; its suspension, 186; its suspension is the wisest, 223

Bardoli Satyagraha (1928), is sign of the times, 218; is to be kept isolated, 215; its refusal to pay unjust assessment, 214; its spread can be limited by how much government wants to go, 216; its success should be consolidated by constructive work, 217; means only non-payment of a portion of tax unjustly imposed, 214; not directed for attaining Swaraj, 214; people should recognize that non-violent combination to vindicate Truth can be formed, 218; Sardar Vallabhbhai invited to take lead, 214; seeks an independent, judicial and open enquiry, 213; settlement, 217-18

Bavazeer, Imamsaheb, 266

Belief, in God is Satyagrahi's mainstay, 364; that suffering would melt heart is necessary for Satyagraha, 363

Bengal, seethes with violence because of government oppression, 259

Bengal Provincial Congress Committee, may start Satyagraha on its initiative, 301

Blacklegs, would be found in every struggle, 73

Blocking, of ways to temples etc. is compulsion, 201

Blood, spilt by non-co-operators paralyses Gandhiji, 61

Body, is a possession, 46; must be trained for passive resistance, 53

Borsad, cowardly edition of Jalianwala Bagh, 269

Boycott, answers well when village was unit, 148; depriving in, medical service is murder, 148; must never savour of inhumanity, 148; of courts, 235; of Empire goods is indefensible, 145-46; of foreign cloth would be mischievous without *khadi* production, 329, 331; of liquor, 329; political, explained, 147

Boycott, of royal visit is disloyalty to British government, 158-59; social, 147-49

Brahmacharya, 97-98; essential for Satyagrahi, 95; means control of all senses, 45, 97; must be observed in thought, word and deed, 44; unattainable save by grace of God, 97

Brahmavidya, its final word is *Not*, 165

British commerce, with India should be purified of greed, 227

British imperialism, is the greatest incarnation of violence, 355

British national anthem, prays to God to destroy enemy, 92

Buddha, brought down arrogant priesthood by non-violence, 111

Bullying, there should be no yielding to, and bluffing, 288

CHAMPARAN SATYAGRAHA, 110

Character-building, is independent of literary training, 163

Charkha, and Satyagraha, 304-05; led to awakening in Bardoli, 27; Sangha helps one *lakh* women, 326; outward symbol of truth and non-violence, 305

Chidambaram, place of Nandanar, 72

Chirala Perala, may declare Satyagraha at their risk, 301

Christ, defied might of a whole empire, 111

Christian Protestants, dislike Gandhiji's fasts, 318

Cities, store-houses of *himsa*, 261

Citizen, his person is inviolate, 263

Civil Disobedience, 4, 170-76, 306-07; aggressive *v.* defensive, 175; branch of Satyagraha, 4, 69; complete, is peaceful rebellion, 172; conceived to neutralize & displace violence, 240; defined 3; individual, 70, is vicarious, 171; *v.* mass, 91, 170-71; inherent right of a citizen, 67, 174; is active non-violence, 57; is a discipline, 25; is never followed by anarchy, 174; is sacred duty when State is lawless, 174; its danger is not present in non-co-operation, 156; its implicit belief in absolute efficacy of innocent suffering, 172; its real guidance comes from God, 251; its suspension must never worry a Satyagrahi, 291; leads to strength & purity, 174; more dangerous than armed rebellion, 172; must be guarded from outbreak of lawlessness, 174; must not be stopped with violence cropping up, 225, 240; necessary part of non-co-operation, 238; needs stout hearts with faith, 68; on a mass scale must be spontaneous, 240; only non-violent escape from soul-destroying violence, 221-22; permitted in jail only against humiliation, 64; purely constitutional, 60; signifies growth, 173; sovereign method of transmuting fury into energy, 239; sovereign remedy for all our ills, 170; synonym for suffering, 69; to postpone, till communal solution is vicious, 356; would be confined in 1930 to Ashram inmates, but designed to cover all Satyagrahis in future, 226; see Civil Resistance & Satyagraha

Civility, difficult part of Satyagraha, 207

Civilization, consists in reduction of wants, 46

Civil Resistance, 105

Civil Resister, depends only on God, 80; harmless to a State listening to public opinion, 174; is dangerous to an autocratic State, 174; will not salute Union Jack, 79; would protect officials from attack & insult, 79; see Satyagrahi

Committee, is a restraint on individual liberty, 21

Communal tension, 82, 227, 296, 299

Communists, not believing in God cannot be Satyagrahis, 364

Compulsion, 331; by Congressmen unnerves Gandhiji, 332; in religion is suicide, 193; should not be used in mental training for Satyagraha, 381

Congress, corruption & indiscipline have set in, 296; interference is resented by princes, 295; is free to start Satyagraha if settlement fails, 279; its political power increased in proportion to its success in constructive programme, 82; Khilafat volunteers were implicated in Chaurichaura violence, 186; must have non-violent army of lakhs, 86; rules out all solutions proposed on communal basis, 356; should not think communally, 356

Congressmen, have interfered in ministerial actions, 296; have not living faith in ahimsa, 368; their qualifications for individual Satyagraha, 302

Constructive Programme, is basis for training in non-violence, 100; is embodiment of active ahimsa, 295, 308; is internal reform, 219; is means for attaining Swaraj, 83; would develop Satyagrahi qualities, 68; would make riots impossible, 86

Control, over mind is alone necessary for Satyagraha, 52

Conversion, of modern Britain by ancient India is worth any risk, 227

Cotton, would solve cloth problem if its processes are distributed universally, 331

Courage, 52, 57; and discipline, 57-58; must be used methodically, 260

Criminal, indicates social malady, 351

DADABHAI NAOROJI, 232

Dandi March, is a sacred pilgrimage, 236, 237

Dandi Marchers, act on behalf of the hungry and naked, 243; are trustees of dumb millions, 244

Death, by inches by means of oppressions may weaken victims, 267; has no terror for God-fearing, 349; is joyful sleep, 349; of few spotless would end riots, 86

Defeat, is impossible where God, clean cause and means are, 236

Defence of India Act, 102

Democracy, spirit of conversion necessary for its evolution, 147

Desai, Mahadev, arrested for Salt Satyagraha, 266; Gandhiji's comrade in Kheda, 205; shows natural salt is not injurious, 256

Diet, of a man of restraint differs from that of one of pleasure, 5; saltless, better for health, 4

Direct Action, does not preclude other consistent methods, 178

Discipline, its necessity in building political and religious life, 195;

requires enthusiastic obedience, 302; Satyagrahi and military, 98-99; specially rigid, is necessary for Satyagrahi, 365; uninsisted in jail would retard Swaraj, 63

Disloyalty, to British Government is a duty, 238-39

Disobedience, a symbol of revolt against State, 175; of laws not involving moral turpitude, 175; without civility is certain death, 173

Divine Law, its ignorance or negligence gives rise to inequalities, 45-46

Dominion Status, 232

Drinks and drugs, sap moral being, 326

Duty, of combining civility with fearlessness, 206

Dyer, General, his dismissal was demanded, 107

EATING, without *yajna* is stealing, 48

Education, in non-violence through non-violent corporate acts, 218

Elders, in society are slaves of customs, 344

Eleven Points, their justice must be admitted by Britain, 232

English Law, forbids laying hands on any person, 254

Englishmen, as trained diplomats are accustomed to line of least resistance, 298; have not taken the movement to be true Satyagraha, 298; must feel safe in India, 56, 154

Enjoyment, its desire creates bodies for soul, 46

Evil, and evil-doer are different, 71

FAITH in God, is foundation of Satyagrahi's training, 95; must never permit feeling helpless, 348

Faith in non-violence, gives power to discover non-violent methods at crucial moment, 224

Fast, and prayer, 103, 104, 316; as prayer, 315; as self-surrender, 318; can be undertaken against a lover, 182, 314, 331; can be undertaken after previous training, 320; coercive, 319-20; element of Satyagraha, 314-15; for selfish end is wrong, 324; great institution of Hinduism, 316; is last resort of Satyagrahi, 317; is of no use without faith in God, 320; is wreckless and joyous giving, 318; its uses are not still perfected, 320; must be a process of conversion, 332; not a coercion, 316; of all the senses and organs, 315; Satyagrahi, 310-24; its well-defined limits, 182; its requirements, 319; series of, is always a possibility in Gandhiji's life, 314; spiritual, is *tapas*, 319; spiritual *v.* nature-cure, 323; *v.* hunger-strike, 321; unto death, 317; weapon in Satyagrahi's armoury, 314, 320, 321, 323

Fearlessness, 55, 94

Firing, for Salt Satyagraha in Karachi, Peshawar and Madras, 273

Foreign cloth, 59; its boycott by *Khadi*, 70, 250, 326; reduced India to pauperism, 146; shops should be picketed, 235; undermines economic foundation, 326

Forest Laws, 241

Freedom, can be won by few Satyagrahis, 362; only by self-purification and self-help, 68

GANDHIJI, admits he is utterly weak in face of our violence, 332; admits his constructive programme has not appealed to Congress intelligentsia, 367; admonishes workers for over-expenses, 243; advocates resistance to selfish fasts, 319; arrested in South Africa while leading march, 171;

arrives at settlement (1931) with British Government, 278-80; believes Ali Brothers may join Civil Disobedience, 252; believes if non-violence succeeds with the English it would succeed with all, 363; believes if non-violence would help achieve freedom it would help retain it, 363; believes in full surrender in Satyagraha, 81-82; believes in India's capacity to fight Britain non-violently, 176; claims his search into force of God lies in discovery of Satyagraha, 353; claims no followers, 84; claims to be keeper of light-house of Satyagraha, 71; claims to have applied Satyagraha on a universal scale, 72; confines Satyagraha (1930) to himself and to his Ashram volunteers to begin with, 355; congratulates Sardar Vallabhbhai and others on Bardoli settlement, 217; congratulates students of Dharmaj on Satyagraha, 342-44; defines Satyagrahi fast, 322; delivers message to nation on his arrest (1930), 270-72; disapproves of mixed picketing, 334; disapproves of non-Hindus taking part in Vykom Satyagraha, 180; does not make a fetish of literary training, 163; entertains high regard for British Consti-tution, 155; explains non-co-ope-ration, 156-61; explains Satya-graha, 19; explains self-purifi-cation, 281; explains to Bardoli Conference all conditions of Satya-graha (1922), 209; fasts in Phoenix for one week, 310; fasts in Sabarmati Ashram for one week, 311-12; fasts for two weeks in Phoenix, 311; fasts for 3 weeks in Yeravda Jail, 315; gains added strength by interviewing oppo-nents, 169; gets light for C. D.

(Civil Disobedience) in Sabarmati Ashram, 251; gives maxims for strike leaders, 150-51; gives ultimatum to Viceroy to leave Ashram on 11-3-1930 for Salt Satyagraha, 228; glad to give up life if it would make children spotless, 312; has not mastered all technique of non-violence, 385; helps authorities to bring order in Ahmedabad, 26; his address on eve of Dandi March, 233-36; his ambition to convert British people, 226; his confidence to lead in 1930 is result of non-violence observed by people after his arrest in 1922, 223; his expec-tations from a Satyagrahi, 94; his experience that both peasants and labour can be organized for effective Satyagraha, 368; his faith in Satyagraha, 176; his fasts at Bombay and Bardoli, 183; his internal conflict which was only barrier regarding Satya-graha, ceased in 1930, 231; his letter to English friends, 222; his letter to Viceroy (1930), 226-28; his political programme, 68-69; his reply to Poet Tagore, 162-66; his scheme of life draws no distinc-tion between different religionists, 357; his sensitiveness to violence keeps him fit for service, 332; his suggestions to prospective Satyagrahis (1930), 239-42; his surrender to gagging order (1940) is object-lesson in Satyagraha, 309; his Swaraj would not be a monopoly of lettered or moneyed men, 266; hopes C. D. would shake counter-violence of British Government and violence-school, 226, 355; hopes to see God face to face by identifying with the least in the world, 312; insists on Dandi pilgrims Ashram discipline regarding prayer, spinning and diary, 236; intends to serve Britain even by non-co-operation, 227; invites prospective Satyagrahis to consult him, 71; is against classification in jails, 374; is arrested for Salt Satyagraha, 276-77; is authorized by Working Committee to start Salt Satyagraha, 220; is inundated with telegrams not to continue Satyagraha (1931), 278; is paralysed by blood spilt by non-co-operators, 61; issues instructions to individual Satyagrahis, 302; lays down rules for picketing, 334-37; on boycott and picketing of liquor and foreign cloth shops, 333-34; on boycott of British goods, 145-46; on *brahmacharya*, 95; on constructive programme, 100-01; on Dandi Women's Conference, 328-30; on Frontier Provinces violence, 333; on *hatha-yoga*, 93; on Hindu Muslim question, 250-51; on his picketing campaign in S. Africa, 339; on how to deal with a thief, 350; on how to resist foreign invasion by non-violence, 377-78; on Jews' persecution by Germans, 348-50; on Nandanar, 72; on Rajkot Award, 293; on Rajkot fast, 321-23; on relations between constructive programme and Satyagraha, 368; on Satyagraha against Colour Bar Bill, 347; on women's role in Satyagraha, 325-41; opines Indians are cautious and slow to move, 158; organizes Satyagraha in Kheda, 204-08; prescribes individual C.D. regarding Bengal detenus, 70; prohibited from going to Punjab, 9; protests he does not intend to embarrass either British or Muslim League, 306; proud of

Ashram having many noble characters, 312; raises Satyagrahi Corps in Bombay, 76; realizes his error in calling upon people to launch C. D. in 1920, 74; realizes progress of training in Satyagraha would not be rapid, 76; refuses to give information to police about persons confessing their guilt to him, 352; refuses (1930) to return to Ashram without Swaraj, 246; says all Satyagraha laws are not still found, 353; says chances of non-violence being accepted as a State policy are very slight, 385-87; says he counted no stake too great in following non-violence, 355; says he is by nature law-abiding, 365-66; says he is evolving, 297; says he is neither a saint nor a politician, 108-12; says he is not incapable of anger, 384; says he might offer Satyagraha by fast if violence is repeated, 332; says he would begin Dharasana raid to divert government wrath in a clean manner, 275; says his non-violence has somewhat shaken British misrule, 355; says his task will be done if he and his Dandi comrades perish in Satyagraha (1930), 233; serves Britain blindly till 1919, 227; stiffens in his demands upon would-be Satyagrahis, 295; still to demonstrate Satyagraha to be assimilable *en masse*, 72; suggests *hijrat* to Bardoli people, 212; suggests Satyagraha in 1930 must continue in spite of violence, 222; suspends C. D. (1919), 25; suspends Rajkot Satyagraha, 301; takes survey of Salt Satyagraha, 258-64; urges concentration on Swadeshi as a step to C. D., 173; utters warning to those intending to launch

Satyagraha without preparation, 301; visualizes great possibilities for Peace Brigade, 90; wants Congress through individual C. D. to deny to British Government moral influence, 306; writes to Viceroy intimating Dharasana raid, 272

Gaol discipline, 61, 62

God, and Satyagrahi, 95; belief in, indispensable for Satyagrahi, 364; is guiding Satyagraha, 271; never fails Satyagrahi, 189, 252, 289

Gokhale, 85

Goondaism, in Congress, 287-89; internal and external, 288; its challenge at Vykom must be taken up, 187; of British Government, 268-69; should be met by non-violence, 89, 289, 380-81

Government (British), cannot exist without co-operation of people, 157; destroys salt in various parts of India, 246; has no right to snatch salt from Satyagrahis, 254; has stunted India's manhood, 69; its embarrassment is not our aim, 149; its police is arresting officer, prosecutor and judge rolled into one, 260; its property is national, 378; its repression in Gujarat is worse than Dyerism, 267; not understanding non-violence goaded people to violence, 276; poisons salt, 264

Gujarat, disorder after C. D. in, in April 1920, 9; sends petitions to government in respect of Kheda, 205

Gupta, Pashupatinath, died to secure peace, 86

HAND-SPINNING, 59

Harijan, faithful record of Gandhiji's deepest thought, 308; Weeklies suspended, 308

Hartal, 23-24; designed to strike imagination, 25; illuminated the whole of India in 1919, 109; intended as a prelude to direct action, 110

Hathayoga, can be said to be training in non-violence, 93

Hijrat, has no place in true Satyagraha, 289; should be done on foot, 289; to Bardoli people is suggested by Gandhiji, 212

Himalayan blunder, 365

Hindu, his silent suffering is enough to melt million Hindus, 181

Hindus, being in majority should give all what minorities want 81; orthodox, are alarmed by Vykom movement, 182

Hindu Literature, is replete with instances of fasting, 318; on religion being full of illustrations of God's help, 189

Hiralal, his calm heroism in Salt Satyagraha, 265

Hitler, 348

Horniman, Satyagraha against his deportation, 33

Humiliation, no, in drawing allowance for service, 85

Humility, 58-59

Hunter, Lord, 19-29

ILLITERATE man, is able to imbibe Satyagraha, 33

Impatience, and intolerance will kill religious movement, 193; is a phase of violence, 73

Independence, is not possible without co-operation of all communities, 253; resolution at Lahore is result of non-violence observed by people after Gandhiji's arrest in 1922

India, alone has possibility of being a non-violent State, 386; at large has used passive resistance in life, 53; found herself vitalized on 6th April 1919, 8; free, has a message of peace, 166; her choice between violence and non-violence, 163; her mills cannot produce enough cloth for India, 326; her non-violence (1930) is not of the strong, 286; is never bound to maintain Lancashire, 168; means its teeming millions, 52; might win freedom through peace, 304

Indians, have lost power of saying no, 165; must accept bullets on chests, 259; should renounce benefits of schools, courts etc., 170; were mentally disobedient to State laws, 172

Indulgence, ceases to hold place in life of a man of service, 49; sexual, is prohibited except for perpetuating race, 54

JAGATNARAIN, PANDIT, examines Gandhiji in the Hunter Committee, 32

Jail Discipline, 62

Jairamdas Daulatram, receives bullets in Salt Satyagraha, 262; suggests 12th June as Bardoli Day, 213

Jalianwala Bagh, 162; its memorial is emblem of Hindu-Muslim unity, 107; massacre, 102; purchase, 105-07

Japanese invasion, can be sterilized by non-violent non-co-operation, 377

Jawaharlal, Pandit, is nation's guide, 234

Jesus, puts in a telling manner Satyagraha in Sermon on the Mount, 375

Jews, are better placed than Indians in S. Africa, 349; domiciled in Germany must refuse to be expelled, 348; their hunt must be turned into a calm and determined tand, 349; their massacre must be turned into joy by Satyagraha, 348; their Satyagraha has an exact parallel in S. Africa Satya-

graha, 349; would not be worse than now if they take to Satyagraha, 348

Joseph, George, leads Vykom Satyagraha, 180

KALLENBACH, joins Gandhiji in fast, 310; offers vicarious C. D., 171

Kasturba, gives up salt and pulses, 4-5

Kelkar, N. C. joins Salt Satyagraha, 258

Khadi, and *charkha* propaganda is indispensable part of foreign cloth boycott, 335; as a war measure cannot be beaten, 327; cannot be escaped for attainment of non-violent Swaraj, 330; develops people's power, 70; wear is meaningful, 307

Kheda, agriculturists are to be rid of fear, 206; cultivators demand arbitration, 205; famine, 204; Patidars consider getting annual revenue suspended, 204; Satyagraha, 204-08; Satyagraha by Shankarlal Parikh, 206; Satyagraha policy is to avoid law courts, 208

Khilafat, 157-58; Satyagraha, 33

Kruger, President, used to say Whites and not Indians are the Chosen of God, 349

Kuvalayanandji, is making experiments in Hathayoga, 93

LABOUR, would be, if properly served, conscious of the irresistable power of non-violence, 369

Lahore, Congress resolves finally its position regarding communal unity, 356

Lalaji, his Servants of People Society, 85

Lancashire, its trade ruined India, 168

Lawyers, should devise arbitration courts, 152

Leadership, by sheer force of self-confidence, bravery and tenacity, 234; not needed when fearlessness and self-effacement are there, 235

Legislatures, have increased communal bitterness, 356

Life, would have no romance without risks, 60

Liquor, shops should be picketed, 235

Lohia, Dr., 367

Love, and fear are contradictory terms, 384; gives indescribable peace and meaning to Gandhiji's life, 384; is law of life, 383, 387; its active state, 161-62; none so fallen but can be converted by, 77; of children and friends keep Gandhiji from going to perdition, 316; see *Ahimsa* and Non-violence

MAHAVIR, imbibed *ahimsa*, 96

Maintenance allowance, 84-85

Man, applying non-violence with scientific precision would work greater wonders than a material scientist, 384; having *yajna* come to him from birth, is a debtor all his life, 48; should follow his own truth, 39

Mane, Dattatreya, victim in Salt Satyagraha, 262

Married people, can behave as if not married, 43

Masses, begin understanding the spirit of Satyagraha, 156; would regulate movement (1930) at a later stage, 249

Mass movement, 151; in 1930 would be self-regulated, 225; in 1939, if undertaken, would resolve into violence both organized and unorganized, 299; throws up unexpected leaders, 225

Means and ends, 9-15

Meghraj Revachand, victim of Salt Satyagraha, 262

Mehta, Dr Sumant, 331

Mehta, Jamshed, on indiscipline in Congress ranks, 282-83

Mehta, Narsibhai, his account o Wadhwan Salt Satyagraha, 267-68

Men, are bound to place their resources at disposal of humanity 49; must not meddle with women's picketing of liquor and foreign cloth shops in 1930, 330

Menon, leads Vykom Satyagraha, 180

Military and Police, as national volunteers, 152; their withdrawal, 152

Military service, is a symptom of a deeper disease, 359; refusal of, is much more superficial than non-co-operation, 359

Millions, have always supported Congress, 306

Ministers, devote much time in dealing with demands of Congressmen, 297

Miscalculation, Himalayan, 74-76

Modern generation, is weak and delicate, 248

Mortification, of flesh is a condition of spiritual progress, 318

Mussalmans, do not believe in non-violence to full extent, 155

NADIAD, becomes Kheda Satyagraha headquarters, 205

Naidu, Sarojini, starts for Salt Satyagraha at Aat in Gujarat, 255

Nandanar, compelled God to open the eyes of his persecutors, 72; won his way by pure suffering, 72

Narayan Guru, disapproved of Vykom Satyagraha, 185

Nation, is born out of travail and suffering, 106; its notice of rejection of tutelage is non-co-operation, 165

National Week, 102-03

Nayar, Kellappen, decides to work among Puliyas of Vykom, 200

Neill Statue Satyagraha, 73-74

Non-co-operation, and C. D. distinguished, 214, 238; and hunger-strike, 62; and work strike, 62; and *Vande Mataram*, 62; between a father and a son, 67; between a prince and his people, 67; defined, 4; included co-operation to convert, 170; in military service in non-military matters is incompatible, 360; intensely active, 161; is an act of love, 167; is constitutional, 160; (of 1920) is designed for Swaraj, 214; is nation's notice of rejection of tutelage, 165; is neither punitive nor vindictive, 162; is not designed to injure Lancashire, 168; its method touches heart and appeals to reason, 64; may become a licence and a crime, 62; movement for purification, 148; national, is suspended, 215; need not be resumed if constructive programme is worked, 176; test of our sincerity, 59; with mind in evil wanderings, 44; would evolve order and not disorder, 160

Non-Hindus, their suffering for untouchables may leave Hindus unmoved, 181

Non-possession, 45-47; is applicable to thoughts and things, 47; its perfect ideal, 46

Non-retaliation, 56, 79

Non-violence, 176; alone is able to prepare India in a short time for freedom battle, 383; alone would enable us to meet forces of disorder, 288; as a creed, 221; as a policy, 221; as a State policy, 385-87; believes Nero is not devoid of heart, 386; complete unity of Indians is not its indispensable condition, 362; inward obstacles are fatal to, 229; is more wonderful than material forces of nature, 384; is of sterner stuff, 361; its basic assumptions, 362-63; its incessant preaching responsible for checking violence, 154; its more scientific and disciplined application to check *goondaism*, 288; its movement is a safety-valve against violence, 229; its votaries would even seek consuming in flames of violence, 240; means reliance on God, 58; mixed, of India supports Gandhiji's faith, 387; must act in spite of most fatal outward obstructions, 229; necessary corollary of Satyagraha, 29; non-compromising attitude regarding, alone would prevent disaster, 288; of activest type, 223, 226, 358; of Congress fell short of the ideal, 298; of the weak can be hypocrisy, 384; stultifies tyrant by non-retaliation, 57; taboos acceptance of non-military services of the State, 359; training in, requires co-ordination of mind, body and speech, 384; unadulterated, alone would check (British) government's violence, 226; *v.* violence, 297-99; would develop only by continuous cleansing, 218; see *Ahimsa*

Non-violent Army, its duties, 86; its training, 100; its volunteers must face emergencies in daily life, 87; would be constantly engaged in constructive activities, 86; would beat swords into plough-shares, 92; see Peace Brigade

Non-violent Resistance, can be fought even by one Satyagrahi, 288; has no defeat, 386; its loss in men would not be greater than what armed resistance would involve, 386

Nursing, real training for Satya-grahi, 92

OBEDIENCE, to State laws is necessary before C. D., 75

Obstructionism, is contrary to Satya-graha, 373

Office, and power can be accepted for only service, 84

Officials, are servants and not masters of people, 206

Old men, should be induced to marry old widows, 346

Opponent, must feel that C. D. is not intended to harm him, 306; non-violent dealing with, 147; not always bad, 84; vilification of, is not permitted in Satyagraha, 84

Ostracism, non-violent and social, 78, 147-48; see Boycott

PANDYA, MOHANLAL, 204; is convicted for 'theft', 208; nick-named 'Onion-thief', 206; removes onion crops from attached fields, 207

Parekh, Gokuldas, 204

Parikh, Shankarlal, 204; makes amends for his tenants' mistake, 207

Passive Resistance, explained, 3, 17, 51-55; is an all-sided sword, 52; is truth-force, 54

Passive Resister, 54-55

Patel, Vallabhbhai, Gandhiji's comrade in Kheda, 205; his appeal for Bardoli fund, 213; in-vited by Bardoli people to lead Satyagraha, 214; sets about con-structive work in Bardoli, 219; suspends growing practice, 205; would not let other leaders go to Bardoli, 215

Patel, Viththalbhai, 204, 209

Pathans, posted in Bardoli to coerce people, 212

Patrolling, places of danger is a training for Satyagraha, 92

Peace Brigade, its qualifications, 88-90; must have a distinctive dress, 90; should substitute police and military, 88; see Non-violent Army

Peace Brigade member, must have equal regard for all religions, 89; need not wait for companions, 89; should seek contact through service, 89

Peasants, are not being educated for non-violent action, 368; have never been subdued by swords, 53

People, must have positive tests before they go for Satyagraha, 76; must prove their loyalty by obeying laws, 67; must understand deeper implications of Satyagraha before launching it, 76; non-violent, would not co-operate with invader, 386; non-violent, would offer themselves as fodder for aggressor's cannon, 386; should march to be shot rather than be tortured for salt, 263; their representatives must have full grasp of conditions of successful C. D. 172

Petition, and deputation are obli-gatory in Indian States and not non-co-operation, 184; and prayer method is tried in Bardoli, 214; not always a sign of weakness of Satyagrahi, 178

Physical training, for a non-violent person, 92

Picketing, 175; and love can be reconciled, 341; formation of a living wall for, is violence, 338; its aim is conversion to moral and economic reform, 336; peaceful, 340; rules for, 334-37; of liquor and foreign cloth shops is special work of women, 241, 325

Poisoning of wells, and destruction of crops are excluded in Satyagraha, 99

Polak, offers vicarious C. D. in S. Africa, 171

Police and Military, 86

Political power, to work out Congress reforms, 82

Power, ungainly scramble for, in Congress, 369

Prayer, possesses the whole of our being, 315

Prejudices, are not removed by appeal to reason, 194

Prison, is a neutral institution, 64

Property, damages to, contrary to Satyagraha, 371

Public opinion, is developing real sanction of Satyagraha, 83; is most potent weapon, 77; must be consolidated against liquor and foreign cloth, 241; succeeds when there is strength behind it, 66

Punishment, does not purify but hardens a criminal, 312

Punjab suffering, did not dishearten India, 106

Purification, movement of, benefits both the parties, 151

RAJKOT AWARD, is thrown by Gandhiji, 293

Rajkot Fast, most important of public fasts, 321; viceregal interference made, impure, 322

Rajkot Satyagraha, 292, 301; its implications for Gandhiji's life, 295

Ranade, Justice, 13

Recruiting, in C. D. camps indiscriminately is a mistake, 288

Reform, to be sincere must come from within, 181

Reliance, on numbers is weakness of Satyagraha, 292

Religion, is a matter of life and death, 197

Renolds, Reginald, becomes Gandhiji's messenger, 252; is a believer in Indian cause and non-violence, 228

Renunciation, 49; of medals, 136-37

Research, to know God's great force and its hidden possibilities is Satyagraha, 352-53

Resistance, against orthodoxy, 69; its condition is long self-purification and self-suffering, 69

Resolve, consecrated, is more potent than mere physical action, 295

Restraint, whatsoever, is wholesome, 5

Rich people, must take initiative in dispossession, 46

Rowdyism, has no place in non-violence, 64

Rowlatt Act, 7, 22, 102-03; is not warranted by facts of the Committee, 22

Rules, for Satyagrahi prisoners, 65

SABOTAGE, is against Satyagraha, 379

Sacrifice, 47-50; in true, all suffering is on one side, 271; life of, is pinnacle of art, 49; of lower animals for higher ones is against non-violence, 47

Salt, is supplementary village industry on coast, 247; natural, is not injurious to health, 256; *swadeshi* and *sarkari*, 257; its annual cost to India is 20 crores, 258; its monopoly is fourfold curse, 247; its recipe for preparation, 257; its snatching from Satyagrahi's hands is insult to India, 271; laws cannot be used against Satyagrahis, 263; laws should be broken in three ways, 234; resolution of Congress Working Committee, 220

Salt Satyagraha, 220-90; disturbances at Calcutta, Karachi and Chittagong, 261-64; is trial of strength between people and government, 255

Salt Tax, is fourteen times its value, 246, 247; is iniquitous from poor man's standpoint, 228

Sardulsingh, Sardar, suggests Bardoli Satyagraha (1928) should be expanded, 215

Satya and Ahimsa, 105; see Truth and Non-violence

Satyagraha, against aged men marrying young girls, 344-46; against Colour Bar Bill, 347; against Neill Statue, 73-74; against war (individual Satyagraha) 1939, 300-09; and socialism, 352-53; can achieve every worthy object, 353; can adorn the weak in body and not weak in mind, 381; can never be physical, 78; can never be resorted to for personal gain, 313, 314; can never be used to defend a wrong cause, 381; constitutes evolution, 6; defined, 3; domestic, 4-5; educative v. coercive, 191; effective substitute for violence, 202, 320; excludes every form of violence, 201; forbids prison-going without constructive work and non-violence, 307; for social reform, 342-53; has no defeat, 190; includes both non-co-operation and C. D., 176, 214; in face of hooliganism, 380-81; in, quality counts and not numbers, 30, 87; in, reasoning has enough, though limited, scope, 99; is based upon belief in God's help, 189; is different from Passive Resistance, 35; is earning living by body labour, 196; is independent of pecuniary or material assistance, 34; is law of universal application, 382; is mightiest propaganda in the world, 287; is most expeditious course, 189; is most practical politics, 216;

is noblest and best education, 36; is non-violent sanction, 382; is process of conversion, 178, 181; is process of public education, 382; is prolonged course, 188; is real sanction, 83; is superior to armed resistance, 381; is used in political and domestic affairs, 34; its conditions for success, 56, 66-68, 365-66, 382; its difficult part is civility, 207; its education must precede ordinary education, 36; its limitations, 69-71, 215-16, 344-46; its moral requirements, 51-55; its one condition is truth and non-violence, 234; its rules, 78-81; its success depends on God, 245; its way to deal with crime, 350-52; means vindication of truth by self-suffering, 6, 294; must continue in spite of violence, 222; must not provoke lathi charge in a spirit of bravado, 294; must teach humility, 290; naturally comes to those who are law-abiding, 365; never fails, 176; not a dangerous doctrine, 22; of Gujarat and Peshawar, 361; on a vast scale is impossible if masses are expected to assimilate the doctrine in all its implications, 362; operates silently, 77; physical training for, 91-96; public, is extension of private Satyagraha, 179; qualifications for, 77-78; regarding Bengal Detenus, 69; requires adoption of poverty, 35; rules out helplessness, 294; taboos doing secretly or impatiently, 354; true and false, 313-14; v. passive resistance, 6; v. political power, 82-83; vitally connected with charkha, 304; works slowly and silently, 196; would do away with despotism and militarism, 36; would give the world an object lesson worthy of India, 270; would revolutionize social ideals, 36

Satyagraha in Indian States, 291-99; by Congress is forbidden, 184; has produced violent reaction in princes and their advisers, 295; in connection with local abuses can be undertaken, 184

Satyagraha (religious), 203; its leader's qualifications, 203; its specialities, 203; forbids mixing of motives, 203

Satyagraha leader, depends on God's strength and not on his, 216; obeys inner voice, 98; would be one who believes in non-violence as an article of faith, 240

Satyagrahashram, Sabarmati, its volunteers' discipline during Dandi march, 236-37; its vows, 37-47; should demonstrate qualities of Satyagraha, 224

Satyagraha Sabha, Bombay, 8, 76

Satyagraha Sangha, 94; see Peace Brigade and Non-violent Army

Satyagraha Week, 104-05; see National Week

Satyagrahi, as a prisoner, 64-66, 79-80; cannot go to law for personal wrong, 188; cannot quarrel with punishment meted out to offenders, 28; committees, 303; does not intend to embarrass wrong-doer, 87; expects relief through humble submission to suffering, 66; fast, 183; has to spend as a miser, 73; his death is a matter for congratulation, 262; his duties, 303; his faith in God is his shield, 92, 292; his first concern is propriety, not effect of his action, 183; his prayer would be that the spring of compassion may ever be flowing, 93; his qualifications, 87-88; his real training is in saving people

in danger, 92; his soul is unconquerable, 289; his triumph consists in thousands being led to prisons, 172; his victory is in purification and penance, 77; makes people more law-abiding, 28; must appeal by prayer, fasting and other suffering, 202; must be healthy in mind and body, 94; must be ready for pecuniary loss, 79, 313; must believe in inherent goodness in human nature, 88, 295; must cultivate capacity to run to rescue people in danger, 94; must defend salt till he breaks, 255; must distinguish between evil and evil-doer, 77; must keep diary, 303; must learn simplicity, 206; must love actively persecutors, 188; must mobilize public opinion against an evil, 77; must not care for tomorrow, 290; must not do anything which outrages his self-respect, 366; must not give evidence against a person who has confessed to him, 352; must stake his all in name of God, 364; must surrender fully, 81; must take drastic step against himself to wipe off untouchability, 202; must take imprisonments, forfeitures, deportations and death in the ordinary course, 212; must think also with standpoint of opponent, 193; perfect, is a perfect man, 35; reaches opponent's heart by awakening public opinion, 191; requires action for being effective, 77; seeks to carry out reform by penance, purification and suffering, 188; sets out for suffering persecution, 188; should bear no anger against snatcher of salt, 271; should better not give evidence of a crime he has seen, 28; should devote spare time to constructive work, 303;

should not be classed as confirmed criminal, 66; should not scale or break fences, 182; should walk to Calcutta Government House to have Bengal detenus released, 70; solitary, what he can do ? 376; suffers unto death joyfully, 78; would never surrender his trust, 79, 81; would obey before he would appeal, 80; would voluntarily court arrest, 79

Satyagraha of Vykom, 177-201; is fighting sacerdotal prejudices, 178; its barricades are respected by Satyagrahis, 191; deeply religious for Hindus, 192; is as important as Swaraj, 190; is educative and never coercive, 191; its implications, 200-01; its objective is supported by Travancore Assembly, 191; its suspension should never bring weakness to Satyagrahis, 293

Satyagrahis of Vykom, are abandoned to the mercies of goondas, 187; are gentle in their dealings with the orthodox section, 188; are threatened with deprivation of inheritance, 188; must remain cool under the hottest fire, 187; must submit to insults and yet must love, 182; seek to convert opponent by suffering, 188, 191, 192; should forget political part, 192; suffer social boycott, 188; their final goal is use of the road, 185

Schools, made Indians clerks and interpreters, 164

Scorched earth, 99

Secrecy, does no good to Satyagraha, 370; is against ahimsa, 380

Self-defence, its art must be learnt by everybody through non-violence, 381

Self-discipline, rigorous, is result of active non-violence, 237

Self-protection, against robbers and thieves, 152

Self-purification, and self-examination necessary for Satyagrahi, 237; is best self-defence, 50; would give strength to the nation, 280

Service, devotion to, 48; its co-efficient is raised in proportion to jail discipline, 63; its path, 48; silent acts of, to those of opposite faith, 70

Setalwad, Sir Chimanlal, examines Gandhiji, 29-32

Shastras, tell of fasts unto death till God hears prayers, 317

Shraddhanandji, Swami, 24

Shraddha, true, 343

Smuts, General, converted to sanity because of South African Satyagraha, 110; on South African Satyagraha, 20-21

Socialism, its votary must have a living faith in God, 352; truth and ahimsa must incarnate in, 352

Socialist, not beliving in God cannot be a Satyagrahi, 364

Social Reform, is tougher than political reform, 345; must begin against sale of brides, 346

Social Status, in a Satyagrahi, 77

Soldier, cannot fire in the air to avoid violence, 361; his position in Satyagraha and military warfare is the same, 98

Soul force, key to its use, 17; not noted in history, 17; purest, brings instantaneous relief, 35

South Africa, in, thousands joined Satyagraha instinctively, 230

Spinning, 88, 91; as the centre of Satyagrahi's programme, 91, 100; daily, is necessary for Satyagraha, 372, 374

Spiritual culture, for self-defence, 50

State, offers amenities on condition of rendering military service, 360

Strike, should be for self-purification, 150; should never depend upon charity, 150; sympathetic, 149-51

Students, of Dharmaj launch Satyagraha against caste dinner, 342-44, their withdrawal .from schools, 152

Suffering, and surrender, 82; does not create ill-will, 31; is the only answer to hooliganism 269; is the test of love, patience and strength, 67; its law,112-13; meek, is more powerful than sword, 66; mute, is impossible without strength coming from God, 66, 364; of extreme character would bring certain results, 275; of Satyagrahis would break wall of prejudices, 189

Swadeshi, 102-03, 126-28

Swaraj, in, a collector will not need many servants, 235; government in England unable to dismiss ministers losing public confidence, 34; in less than a year, 59; when, would come knocking at our doors, 272; won without sacrifice cannot last long, 271

Switzerland, would have re-enacted Thermopylae, 360; would have refused passage to the invading army by refusing all supplies, 360

Symbiosis, preached by Buddha and Christ, 111

Syrian Christians, are infected by untouchability, 180

TAKLI, is a wonder-worker, 327

Tapasya, 51

Taxes, their suspension, 138-42; is the last step in non-co-operation, 151

Teacher, his responsibilities for errors of his pupils, 311

Temple entry, 200

Terrorism, results in demoralization, 379

Thakkar, Amritlal, inquired into the famine conditions of Kheda district, 204

Theft, would not happen if there is wise regulation of riches, 351

Thief, is no more guilty than exploiting rich man, 351; is our brother, 41; or a criminal is not a different being from ourselves, 350

Thoreau, his masterly treatise on C. D., 3

Thought, or word which is evil is more dangerous than violence, 202; perfectly controlled, is highest power and self-acting, 97

Transvaal, its Constitution lays down inequality between whites and coloured races, 349

Truth, 38-39, 176; defined, 3; devotion to, sole justification of existence, 38; is God, 38; is in oneself and not outside, 41; its follower cannot hold anything against tomorrow, 45; its quest involves *tapas* 39; its realization is impossible in mortal body, 40; its realization is through *abhyasa* and *vairagya*, 39

Truth and non-violence, are facets of the same coin, 384; mechanical adherence to, is likely to break down at critical moment, 352; realizable only by ceaseless striving, 40; their actions are more abiding than speeches, 77

Tyabji, Abbas, 210, 255

Tyranny, generates fury, 239

"UNAPPROACHABLES", of Vykom threaten to leave Hinduism, 196

Union, Jack, 79

Untouchability, and unapproachability must be tackled wherever they exist 184; battle against, is religious, 317; is supported by orthodoxy, superstition, custom and authority, 190; its curse has infected even Syrian Christians, 180; its removal is vital to Satyagrahi, 372; sin of the Hindus, 180

Uruli-Kanchan, its work must include healing of mind and soul along with that of body, 351

VEGETARIANISM, 4

Villages, ideal, created by Satyagrahis would be a pattern for the world, 377

Violence, believers in, must not take part in Satyagraha, 333; eliminated from Satyagraha, 20; harboured during Satyagraha movements is recoiling upon ourselves, 298; has filled India as evidenced at Tripuri Congress, 294; includes corruption, falsehood, hypocrisy, deceit etc., 294; its school enables British rule to consolidate the very thing it seeks to destroy, 355; its school is more active in 1930 than in 1921, 354; one single act of, would have frustrated Bardoli Satyagraha, (1928), 218; party of, is gaining ground in India, 226; popular, is as much obstruction as government violence, 261; with, in 1922 after Gandhiji's arrest, he would have no confidence to resume leadership in 1930, 223

Volunteers, are expected to die in quenching violence, 250; must account for every pie spent, 244; should exercise reason only while choosing the general, not afterwards, 302

Votary, of truth and non-violence is active for 24 hours, 358

Vow, its importance, 37-38; taking of, is a bulwark of strength, 37

WALKING, is prince of exercises, 248

War, 16; nation without, is happy, 16; see Violence

Water and Food, stopping supply of, is against non-violence, 147

Weapons, lethal, have no place in Satyagrahi's training, 96

Women, are better representatives of non-violence than men, 325, 330, 339; hold conference at Dandi, 328-30; must not be in venue of Salt Satyagraha, 259; should organize *Khadi* production, 327, 331; should picket liquor, opium and foreign cloth shops, 271; should work shoulder to shoulder with men, 235; their appeal to liquor addicts and dealers would melt their hearts, 326; their taking part in Swaraj movement is an important extension of the movement, 328; would exhibit infinite strength if they do not succumb to 'enjoyments', 286

Working Committee, (Indian National Congress), authorizes Gandhiji (1930) to start Satyagraha, 220; trusts that Satyagraha would be taken up by the masses (1930) soon after the arrest of the leaders, 220

World, is based on force of truth and love, 16

Wrong-doer, is wearied in the absence of resistance, 172

YAJNA, explained, 47; see Sacrifice

Yajnik, Indulal, Gandhiji's comrade in Kheda Satyagraha, 205

A CATALOG OF SELECTED
DOVER BOOKS
IN ALL FIELDS OF INTEREST

A CATALOG OF SELECTED DOVER BOOKS IN ALL FIELDS OF INTEREST

100 BEST-LOVED POEMS, Edited by Philip Smith. "The Passionate Shepherd to His Love," "Shall I compare thee to a summer's day?" "Death, be not proud," "The Raven," "The Road Not Taken," plus works by Blake, Wordsworth, Byron, Shelley, Keats, many others. 96pp. 5³⁄₁₆ x 8¼. 0-486-28553-7

100 SMALL HOUSES OF THE THIRTIES, Brown-Blodgett Company. Exterior photographs and floor plans for 100 charming structures. Illustrations of models accompanied by descriptions of interiors, color schemes, closet space, and other amenities. 200 illustrations. 112pp. 8⅜ x 11. 0-486-44131-8

1000 TURN-OF-THE-CENTURY HOUSES: With Illustrations and Floor Plans, Herbert C. Chivers. Reproduced from a rare edition, this showcase of homes ranges from cottages and bungalows to sprawling mansions. Each house is meticulously illustrated and accompanied by complete floor plans. 256pp. 9⅜ x 12¼. 0-486-45596-3

101 GREAT AMERICAN POEMS, Edited by The American Poetry & Literacy Project. Rich treasury of verse from the 19th and 20th centuries includes works by Edgar Allan Poe, Robert Frost, Walt Whitman, Langston Hughes, Emily Dickinson, T. S. Eliot, other notables. 96pp. 5³⁄₁₆ x 8¼. 0-486-40158-8

101 GREAT SAMURAI PRINTS, Utagawa Kuniyoshi. Kuniyoshi was a master of the warrior woodblock print — and these 18th-century illustrations represent the pinnacle of his craft. Full-color portraits of renowned Japanese samurais pulse with movement, passion, and remarkably fine detail. 112pp. 8⅜ x 11. 0-486-46523-3

ABC OF BALLET, Janet Grosser. Clearly worded, abundantly illustrated little guide defines basic ballet-related terms: arabesque, battement, pas de chat, relevé, sissonne, many others. Pronunciation guide included. Excellent primer. 48pp. 4³⁄₁₆ x 5¾. 0-486-40871-X

ACCESSORIES OF DRESS: An Illustrated Encyclopedia, Katherine Lester and Bess Viola Oerke. Illustrations of hats, veils, wigs, cravats, shawls, shoes, gloves, and other accessories enhance an engaging commentary that reveals the humor and charm of the many-sided story of accessorized apparel. 644 figures and 59 plates. 608pp. 6 ⅛ x 9¼. 0-486-43378-1

ADVENTURES OF HUCKLEBERRY FINN, Mark Twain. Join Huck and Jim as their boyhood adventures along the Mississippi River lead them into a world of excitement, danger, and self-discovery. Humorous narrative, lyrical descriptions of the Mississippi valley, and memorable characters. 224pp. 5³⁄₁₆ x 8¼. 0-486-28061-6

ALICE STARMORE'S BOOK OF FAIR ISLE KNITTING, Alice Starmore. A noted designer from the region of Scotland's Fair Isle explores the history and techniques of this distinctive, stranded-color knitting style and provides copious illustrated instructions for 14 original knitwear designs. 208pp. 8⅜ x 10⅞. 0-486-47218-3

Browse over 9,000 books at www.doverpublications.com

ALICE'S ADVENTURES IN WONDERLAND, Lewis Carroll. Beloved classic about a little girl lost in a topsy-turvy land and her encounters with the White Rabbit, March Hare, Mad Hatter, Cheshire Cat, and other delightfully improbable characters. 42 illustrations by Sir John Tenniel. 96pp. 5³/₁₆ x 8¼.　　　　0-486-27543-4

AMERICA'S LIGHTHOUSES: An Illustrated History, Francis Ross Holland. Profusely illustrated fact-filled survey of American lighthouses since 1716. Over 200 stations — East, Gulf, and West coasts, Great Lakes, Hawaii, Alaska, Puerto Rico, the Virgin Islands, and the Mississippi and St. Lawrence Rivers. 240pp. 8 x 10¾.

0-486-25576-X

AN ENCYCLOPEDIA OF THE VIOLIN, Alberto Bachmann. Translated by Frederick H. Martens. Introduction by Eugene Ysaye. First published in 1925, this renowned reference remains unsurpassed as a source of essential information, from construction and evolution to repertoire and technique. Includes a glossary and 73 illustrations. 496pp. 6½ x 9¼.　　　　0-486-46618-3

ANIMALS: 1,419 Copyright-Free Illustrations of Mammals, Birds, Fish, Insects, etc., Selected by Jim Harter. Selected for its visual impact and ease of use, this outstanding collection of wood engravings presents over 1,000 species of animals in extremely lifelike poses. Includes mammals, birds, reptiles, amphibians, fish, insects, and other invertebrates. 284pp. 9 x 12.　　　　0-486-23766-4

THE ANNALS, Tacitus. Translated by Alfred John Church and William Jackson Brodribb. This vital chronicle of Imperial Rome, written by the era's great historian, spans A.D. 14-68 and paints incisive psychological portraits of major figures, from Tiberius to Nero. 416pp. 5³/₁₆ x 8¼.　　　　0-486-45236-0

ANTIGONE, Sophocles. Filled with passionate speeches and sensitive probing of moral and philosophical issues, this powerful and often-performed Greek drama reveals the grim fate that befalls the children of Oedipus. Footnotes. 64pp. 5³/₁₆ x 8 ¼.　　　　0-486-27804-2

ART DECO DECORATIVE PATTERNS IN FULL COLOR, Christian Stoll. Reprinted from a rare 1910 portfolio, 160 sensuous and exotic images depict a breathtaking array of florals, geometrics, and abstracts — all elegant in their stark simplicity. 64pp. 8⅜ x 11.　　　　0-486-44862-2

THE ARTHUR RACKHAM TREASURY: 86 Full-Color Illustrations, Arthur Rackham. Selected and Edited by Jeff A. Menges. A stunning treasury of 86 full-page plates span the famed English artist's career, from *Rip Van Winkle* (1905) to masterworks such as *Undine, A Midsummer Night's Dream*, and *Wind in the Willows* (1939). 96pp. 8⅜ x 11.

0-486-44685-9

THE AUTHENTIC GILBERT & SULLIVAN SONGBOOK, W. S. Gilbert and A. S. Sullivan. The most comprehensive collection available, this songbook includes selections from every one of Gilbert and Sullivan's light operas. Ninety-two numbers are presented uncut and unedited, and in their original keys. 410pp. 9 x 12.

0-486-23482-7

THE AWAKENING, Kate Chopin. First published in 1899, this controversial novel of a New Orleans wife's search for love outside a stifling marriage shocked readers. Today, it remains a first-rate narrative with superb characterization. New introductory Note. 128pp. 5³/₁₆ x 8¼.　　　　0-486-27786-0

BASIC DRAWING, Louis Priscilla. Beginning with perspective, this commonsense manual progresses to the figure in movement, light and shade, anatomy, drapery, composition, trees and landscape, and outdoor sketching. Black-and-white illustrations throughout. 128pp. 8⅜ x 11.　　　　0-486-45815-6

Browse over 9,000 books at www.doverpublications.com

THE BATTLES THAT CHANGED HISTORY, Fletcher Pratt. Historian profiles 16 crucial conflicts, ancient to modern, that changed the course of Western civilization. Gripping accounts of battles led by Alexander the Great, Joan of Arc, Ulysses S. Grant, other commanders. 27 maps. 352pp. 5⅜ x 8½. 0-486-41129-X

BEETHOVEN'S LETTERS, Ludwig van Beethoven. Edited by Dr. A. C. Kalischer. Features 457 letters to fellow musicians, friends, greats, patrons, and literary men. Reveals musical thoughts, quirks of personality, insights, and daily events. Includes 15 plates. 410pp. 5⅜ x 8½. 0-486-22769-3

BERNICE BOBS HER HAIR AND OTHER STORIES, F. Scott Fitzgerald. This brilliant anthology includes 6 of Fitzgerald's most popular stories: "The Diamond as Big as the Ritz," the title tale, "The Offshore Pirate," "The Ice Palace," "The Jelly Bean," and "May Day." 176pp. 5⅜ x 8½. 0-486-47049-0

BESLER'S BOOK OF FLOWERS AND PLANTS: 73 Full-Color Plates from Hortus Eystettensis, 1613, Basilius Besler. Here is a selection of magnificent plates from the *Hortus Eystettensis,* which vividly illustrated and identified the plants, flowers, and trees that thrived in the legendary German garden at Eichstätt. 80pp. 8⅜ x 11. 0-486-46005-3

THE BOOK OF KELLS, Edited by Blanche Cirker. Painstakingly reproduced from a rare facsimile edition, this volume contains full-page decorations, portraits, illustrations, plus a sampling of textual leaves with exquisite calligraphy and ornamentation. 32 full-color illustrations. 32pp. 9⅜ x 12¼. 0-486-24345-1

THE BOOK OF THE CROSSBOW: With an Additional Section on Catapults and Other Siege Engines, Ralph Payne-Gallwey. Fascinating study traces history and use of crossbow as military and sporting weapon, from Middle Ages to modern times. Also covers related weapons: balistas, catapults, Turkish bows, more. Over 240 illustrations. 400pp. 7¼ x 10⅛. 0-486-28720-3

THE BUNGALOW BOOK: Floor Plans and Photos of 112 Houses, 1910, Henry L. Wilson. Here are 112 of the most popular and economic blueprints of the early 20th century — plus an illustration or photograph of each completed house. A wonderful time capsule that still offers a wealth of valuable insights. 160pp. 8⅜ x 11. 0-486-45104-6

THE CALL OF THE WILD, Jack London. A classic novel of adventure, drawn from London's own experiences as a Klondike adventurer, relating the story of a heroic dog caught in the brutal life of the Alaska Gold Rush. Note. 64pp. 5³⁄₁₆ x 8¼. 0-486-26472-6

CANDIDE, Voltaire. Edited by Francois-Marie Arouet. One of the world's great satires since its first publication in 1759. Witty, caustic skewering of romance, science, philosophy, religion, government — nearly all human ideals and institutions. 112pp. 5³⁄₁₆ x 8¼. 0-486-26689-3

CELEBRATED IN THEIR TIME: Photographic Portraits from the George Grantham Bain Collection, Edited by Amy Pastan. With an Introduction by Michael Carlebach. Remarkable portrait gallery features 112 rare images of Albert Einstein, Charlie Chaplin, the Wright Brothers, Henry Ford, and other luminaries from the worlds of politics, art, entertainment, and industry. 128pp. 8⅜ x 11. 0-486-46754-6

CHARIOTS FOR APOLLO: The NASA History of Manned Lunar Spacecraft to 1969, Courtney G. Brooks, James M. Grimwood, and Loyd S. Swenson, Jr. This illustrated history by a trio of experts is the definitive reference on the Apollo spacecraft and lunar modules. It traces the vehicles' design, development, and operation in space. More than 100 photographs and illustrations. 576pp. 6¾ x 9¼. 0-486-46756-2

A CHRISTMAS CAROL, Charles Dickens. This engrossing tale relates Ebenezer Scrooge's ghostly journeys through Christmases past, present, and future and his ultimate transformation from a harsh and grasping old miser to a charitable and compassionate human being. 80pp. 5⁵⁄₁₆ x 8¼.   0-486-26865-9

COMMON SENSE, Thomas Paine. First published in January of 1776, this highly influential landmark document clearly and persuasively argued for American separation from Great Britain and paved the way for the Declaration of Independence. 64pp. 5⁵⁄₁₆ x 8¼.   0-486-29602-4

THE COMPLETE SHORT STORIES OF OSCAR WILDE, Oscar Wilde. Complete texts of "The Happy Prince and Other Tales," "A House of Pomegranates," "Lord Arthur Savile's Crime and Other Stories," "Poems in Prose," and "The Portrait of Mr. W. H." 208pp. 5⁵⁄₁₆ x 8¼.   0-486-45216-6

COMPLETE SONNETS, William Shakespeare. Over 150 exquisite poems deal with love, friendship, the tyranny of time, beauty's evanescence, death, and other themes in language of remarkable power, precision, and beauty. Glossary of archaic terms. 80pp. 5⁵⁄₁₆ x 8¼.   0-486-26686-9

THE COUNT OF MONTE CRISTO: Abridged Edition, Alexandre Dumas. Falsely accused of treason, Edmond Dantès is imprisoned in the bleak Chateau d'If. After a hair-raising escape, he launches an elaborate plot to extract a bitter revenge against those who betrayed him. 448pp. 5⁵⁄₁₆ x 8¼.   0-486-45643-9

CRAFTSMAN BUNGALOWS: Designs from the Pacific Northwest, Yoho & Merritt. This reprint of a rare catalog, showcasing the charming simplicity and cozy style of Craftsman bungalows, is filled with photos of completed homes, plus floor plans and estimated costs. An indispensable resource for architects, historians, and illustrators. 112pp. 10 x 7.   0-486-46875-5

CRAFTSMAN BUNGALOWS: 59 Homes from "The Craftsman," Edited by Gustav Stickley. Best and most attractive designs from Arts and Crafts Movement publication — 1903–1916 — includes sketches, photographs of homes, floor plans, descriptive text. 128pp. 8¼ x 11.   0-486-25829-7

CRIME AND PUNISHMENT, Fyodor Dostoyevsky. Translated by Constance Garnett. Supreme masterpiece tells the story of Raskolnikov, a student tormented by his own thoughts after he murders an old woman. Overwhelmed by guilt and terror, he confesses and goes to prison. 480pp. 5⁵⁄₁₆ x 8¼.   0-486-41587-2

THE DECLARATION OF INDEPENDENCE AND OTHER GREAT DOCUMENTS OF AMERICAN HISTORY: 1775-1865, Edited by John Grafton. Thirteen compelling and influential documents: Henry's "Give Me Liberty or Give Me Death," Declaration of Independence, The Constitution, Washington's First Inaugural Address, The Monroe Doctrine, The Emancipation Proclamation, Gettysburg Address, more. 64pp. 5⁵⁄₁₆ x 8¼.   0-486-41124-9

THE DESERT AND THE SOWN: Travels in Palestine and Syria, Gertrude Bell. "The female Lawrence of Arabia," Gertrude Bell wrote captivating, perceptive accounts of her travels in the Middle East. This intriguing narrative, accompanied by 160 photos, traces her 1905 sojourn in Lebanon, Syria, and Palestine. 368pp. 5⅜ x 8½.
0-486-46876-3

A DOLL'S HOUSE, Henrik Ibsen. Ibsen's best-known play displays his genius for realistic prose drama. An expression of women's rights, the play climaxes when the central character, Nora, rejects a smothering marriage and life in "a doll's house." 80pp. 5⅝⁄₁₆ x 8¼.   0-486-27062-9

DOOMED SHIPS: Great Ocean Liner Disasters, William H. Miller, Jr. Nearly 200 photographs, many from private collections, highlight tales of some of the vessels whose pleasure cruises ended in catastrophe: the *Morro Castle, Normandie, Andrea Doria, Europa,* and many others. 128pp. 8⅞ x 11¾. 0-486-45366-9

THE DORÉ BIBLE ILLUSTRATIONS, Gustave Doré. Detailed plates from the Bible: the Creation scenes, Adam and Eve, horrifying visions of the Flood, the battle sequences with their monumental crowds, depictions of the life of Jesus, 241 plates in all. 241pp. 9 x 12. 0-486-23004-X

DRAWING DRAPERY FROM HEAD TO TOE, Cliff Young. Expert guidance on how to draw shirts, pants, skirts, gloves, hats, and coats on the human figure, including folds in relation to the body, pull and crush, action folds, creases, more. Over 200 drawings. 48pp. 8¼ x 11. 0-486-45591-2

DUBLINERS, James Joyce. A fine and accessible introduction to the work of one of the 20th century's most influential writers, this collection features 15 tales, including a masterpiece of the short-story genre, "The Dead." 160pp. 5⁵⁄₁₆ x 8¼. 0-486-26870-5

EASY-TO-MAKE POP-UPS, Joan Irvine. Illustrated by Barbara Reid. Dozens of wonderful ideas for three-dimensional paper fun — from holiday greeting cards with moving parts to a pop-up menagerie. Easy-to-follow, illustrated instructions for more than 30 projects. 299 black-and-white illustrations. 96pp. 8⅜ x 11. 0-486-44622-0

EASY-TO-MAKE STORYBOOK DOLLS: A "Novel" Approach to Cloth Dollmaking, Sherralyn St. Clair. Favorite fictional characters come alive in this unique beginner's dollmaking guide. Includes patterns for Pollyanna, Dorothy from *The Wonderful Wizard of Oz,* Mary of *The Secret Garden,* plus easy-to-follow instructions, 263 black-and-white illustrations, and an 8-page color insert. 112pp. 8¼ x 11. 0-486-47360-0

EINSTEIN'S ESSAYS IN SCIENCE, Albert Einstein. Speeches and essays in accessible, everyday language profile influential physicists such as Niels Bohr and Isaac Newton. They also explore areas of physics to which the author made major contributions. 128pp. 5 x 8. 0-486-47011-3

EL DORADO: Further Adventures of the Scarlet Pimpernel, Baroness Orczy. A popular sequel to *The Scarlet Pimpernel,* this suspenseful story recounts the Pimpernel's attempts to rescue the Dauphin from imprisonment during the French Revolution. An irresistible blend of intrigue, period detail, and vibrant characterizations. 352pp. 5⁵⁄₁₆ x 8¼. 0-486-44026-5

ELEGANT SMALL HOMES OF THE TWENTIES: 99 Designs from a Competition, Chicago Tribune. Nearly 100 designs for five- and six-room houses feature New England and Southern colonials, Normandy cottages, stately Italianate dwellings, and other fascinating snapshots of American domestic architecture of the 1920s. 112pp. 9 x 12. 0-486-46910-7

THE ELEMENTS OF STYLE: The Original Edition, William Strunk, Jr. This is the book that generations of writers have relied upon for timeless advice on grammar, diction, syntax, and other essentials. In concise terms, it identifies the principal requirements of proper style and common errors. 64pp. 5⅜ x 8½. 0-486-44798-7

THE ELUSIVE PIMPERNEL, Baroness Orczy. Robespierre's revolutionaries find their wicked schemes thwarted by the heroic Pimpernel — Sir Percival Blakeney. In this thrilling sequel, Chauvelin devises a plot to eliminate the Pimpernel and his wife. 272pp. 5⁵⁄₁₆ x 8¼. 0-486-45464-9

AN ENCYCLOPEDIA OF BATTLES: Accounts of Over 1,560 Battles from 1479 B.C. to the Present, David Eggenberger. Essential details of every major battle in recorded history from the first battle of Megiddo in 1479 B.C. to Grenada in 1984. List of battle maps. 99 illustrations. 544pp. 6½ x 9¼. 0-486-24913-1

ENCYCLOPEDIA OF EMBROIDERY STITCHES, INCLUDING CREWEL, Marion Nichols. Precise explanations and instructions, clearly illustrated, on how to work chain, back, cross, knotted, woven stitches, and many more — 178 in all, including Cable Outline, Whipped Satin, and Eyelet Buttonhole. Over 1400 illustrations. 219pp. 8⅜ x 11¼. 0-486-22929-7

ENTER JEEVES: 15 Early Stories, P. G. Wodehouse. Splendid collection contains first 8 stories featuring Bertie Wooster, the deliciously dim aristocrat and Jeeves, his brainy, imperturbable manservant. Also, the complete Reggie Pepper (Bertie's prototype) series. 288pp. 5⅜ x 8½. 0-486-29717-9

ERIC SLOANE'S AMERICA: Paintings in Oil, Michael Wigley. With a Foreword by Mimi Sloane. Eric Sloane's evocative oils of America's landscape and material culture shimmer with immense historical and nostalgic appeal. This original hardcover collection gathers nearly a hundred of his finest paintings, with subjects ranging from New England to the American Southwest. 128pp. 10⅝ x 9. 0-486-46525-X

ETHAN FROME, Edith Wharton. Classic story of wasted lives, set against a bleak New England background. Superbly delineated characters in a hauntingly grim tale of thwarted love. Considered by many to be Wharton's masterpiece. 96pp. 5³⁄₁₆ x 8 ¼. 0-486-26690-7

THE EVERLASTING MAN, G. K. Chesterton. Chesterton's view of Christianity — as a blend of philosophy and mythology, satisfying intellect and spirit — applies to his brilliant book, which appeals to readers' heads as well as their hearts. 288pp. 5⅜ x 8½. 0-486-46036-3

THE FIELD AND FOREST HANDY BOOK, Daniel Beard. Written by a co-founder of the Boy Scouts, this appealing guide offers illustrated instructions for building kites, birdhouses, boats, igloos, and other fun projects, plus numerous helpful tips for campers. 448pp. 5³⁄₁₆ x 8¼. 0-486-46191-2

FINDING YOUR WAY WITHOUT MAP OR COMPASS, Harold Gatty. Useful, instructive manual shows would-be explorers, hikers, bikers, scouts, sailors, and survivalists how to find their way outdoors by observing animals, weather patterns, shifting sands, and other elements of nature. 288pp. 5⅜ x 8½. 0-486-40613-X

FIRST FRENCH READER: A Beginner's Dual-Language Book, Edited and Translated by Stanley Appelbaum. This anthology introduces 50 legendary writers — Voltaire, Balzac, Baudelaire, Proust, more — through passages from *The Red and the Black, Les Misérables, Madame Bovary,* and other classics. Original French text plus English translation on facing pages. 240pp. 5⅜ x 8½. 0-486-46178-5

FIRST GERMAN READER: A Beginner's Dual-Language Book, Edited by Harry Steinhauer. Specially chosen for their power to evoke German life and culture, these short, simple readings include poems, stories, essays, and anecdotes by Goethe, Hesse, Heine, Schiller, and others. 224pp. 5⅜ x 8½. 0-486-46179-3

FIRST SPANISH READER: A Beginner's Dual-Language Book, Angel Flores. Delightful stories, other material based on works of Don Juan Manuel, Luis Taboada, Ricardo Palma, other noted writers. Complete faithful English translations on facing pages. Exercises. 176pp. 5⅜ x 8½. 0-486-25810-6

Browse over 9,000 books at www.doverpublications.com

CATALOG OF DOVER BOOKS

FIVE ACRES AND INDEPENDENCE, Maurice G. Kains. Great back-to-the-land classic explains basics of self-sufficient farming. The one book to get. 95 illustrations. 397pp. 5⅜ x 8½. 0-486-20974-1

FLAGG'S SMALL HOUSES: Their Economic Design and Construction, 1922, Ernest Flagg. Although most famous for his skyscrapers, Flagg was also a proponent of the well-designed single-family dwelling. His classic treatise features innovations that save space, materials, and cost. 526 illustrations. 160pp. 9⅜ x 12¼.
0-486-45197-6

FLATLAND: A Romance of Many Dimensions, Edwin A. Abbott. Classic of science (and mathematical) fiction — charmingly illustrated by the author — describes the adventures of A. Square, a resident of Flatland, in Spaceland (three dimensions), Lineland (one dimension), and Pointland (no dimensions). 96pp. 5³⁄₁₆ x 8¼.
0-486-27263-X

FRANKENSTEIN, Mary Shelley. The story of Victor Frankenstein's monstrous creation and the havoc it caused has enthralled generations of readers and inspired countless writers of horror and suspense. With the author's own 1831 introduction. 176pp. 5³⁄₁₆ x 8¼. 0-486-28211-2

THE GARGOYLE BOOK: 572 Examples from Gothic Architecture, Lester Burbank Bridaham. Dispelling the conventional wisdom that French Gothic architectural flourishes were born of despair or gloom, Bridaham reveals the whimsical nature of these creations and the ingenious artisans who made them. 572 illustrations. 224pp. 8⅜ x 11. 0-486-44754-5

THE GIFT OF THE MAGI AND OTHER SHORT STORIES, O. Henry. Sixteen captivating stories by one of America's most popular storytellers. Included are such classics as "The Gift of the Magi," "The Last Leaf," and "The Ransom of Red Chief." Publisher's Note. 96pp. 5³⁄₁₆ x 8¼. 0-486-27061-0

THE GOETHE TREASURY: Selected Prose and Poetry, Johann Wolfgang von Goethe. Edited, Selected, and with an Introduction by Thomas Mann. In addition to his lyric poetry, Goethe wrote travel sketches, autobiographical studies, essays, letters, and proverbs in rhyme and prose. This collection presents outstanding examples from each genre. 368pp. 5⅜ x 8½. 0-486-44780-4

GREAT EXPECTATIONS, Charles Dickens. Orphaned Pip is apprenticed to the dirty work of the forge but dreams of becoming a gentleman — and one day finds himself in possession of "great expectations." Dickens' finest novel. 400pp. 5³⁄₁₆ x 8¼.
0-486-41586-4

GREAT WRITERS ON THE ART OF FICTION: From Mark Twain to Joyce Carol Oates, Edited by James Daley. An indispensable source of advice and inspiration, this anthology features essays by Henry James, Kate Chopin, Willa Cather, Sinclair Lewis, Jack London, Raymond Chandler, Raymond Carver, Eudora Welty, and Kurt Vonnegut, Jr. 192pp. 5⅜ x 8½. 0-486-45128-3

HAMLET, William Shakespeare. The quintessential Shakespearean tragedy, whose highly charged confrontations and anguished soliloquies probe depths of human feeling rarely sounded in any art. Reprinted from an authoritative British edition complete with illuminating footnotes. 128pp. 5³⁄₁₆ x 8¼. 0-486-27278-8

THE HAUNTED HOUSE, Charles Dickens. A Yuletide gathering in an eerie country retreat provides the backdrop for Dickens and his friends — including Elizabeth Gaskell and Wilkie Collins — who take turns spinning supernatural yarns. 144pp. 5⅜ x 8½. 0-486-46309-5

Browse over 9,000 books at www.doverpublications.com

HEART OF DARKNESS, Joseph Conrad. Dark allegory of a journey up the Congo River and the narrator's encounter with the mysterious Mr. Kurtz. Masterly blend of adventure, character study, psychological penetration. For many, Conrad's finest, most enigmatic story. 80pp. 5³⁄₁₆ x 8¼. 0-486-26464-5

HENSON AT THE NORTH POLE, Matthew A. Henson. This thrilling memoir by the heroic African-American who was Peary's companion through two decades of Arctic exploration recounts a tale of danger, courage, and determination. "Fascinating and exciting." — *Commonweal.* 128pp. 5⅜ x 8½. 0-486-45472-X

HISTORIC COSTUMES AND HOW TO MAKE THEM, Mary Fernald and E. Shenton. Practical, informative guidebook shows how to create everything from short tunics worn by Saxon men in the fifth century to a lady's bustle dress of the late 1800s. 81 illustrations. 176pp. 5⅜ x 8½. 0-486-44906-8

THE HOUND OF THE BASKERVILLES, Arthur Conan Doyle. A deadly curse in the form of a legendary ferocious beast continues to claim its victims from the Baskerville family until Holmes and Watson intervene. Often called the best detective story ever written. 128pp. 5³⁄₁₆ x 8¼. 0-486-28214-7

THE HOUSE BEHIND THE CEDARS, Charles W. Chesnutt. Originally published in 1900, this groundbreaking novel by a distinguished African-American author recounts the drama of a brother and sister who "pass for white" during the dangerous days of Reconstruction. 208pp. 5⅜ x 8½. 0-486-46144-0

THE HUMAN FIGURE IN MOTION, Eadweard Muybridge. The 4,789 photographs in this definitive selection show the human figure — models almost all undraped — engaged in over 160 different types of action: running, climbing stairs, etc. 390pp. 7⅞ x 10⅝. 0-486-20204-6

THE IMPORTANCE OF BEING EARNEST, Oscar Wilde. Wilde's witty and buoyant comedy of manners, filled with some of literature's most famous epigrams, reprinted from an authoritative British edition. Considered Wilde's most perfect work. 64pp. 5³⁄₁₆ x 8¼. 0-486-26478-5

THE INFERNO, Dante Alighieri. Translated and with notes by Henry Wadsworth Longfellow. The first stop on Dante's famous journey from Hell to Purgatory to Paradise, this 14th-century allegorical poem blends vivid and shocking imagery with graceful lyricism. Translated by the beloved 19th-century poet, Henry Wadsworth Longfellow. 256pp. 5³⁄₁₆ x 8¼. 0-486-44288-8

JANE EYRE, Charlotte Brontë. Written in 1847, *Jane Eyre* tells the tale of an orphan girl's progress from the custody of cruel relatives to an oppressive boarding school and its culmination in a troubled career as a governess. 448pp. 5³⁄₁₆ x 8¼.
0-486-42449-9

JAPANESE WOODBLOCK FLOWER PRINTS, Tanigami Kônan. Extraordinary collection of Japanese woodblock prints by a well-known artist features 120 plates in brilliant color. Realistic images from a rare edition include daffodils, tulips, and other familiar and unusual flowers. 128pp. 11 x 8¼. 0-486-46442-3

JEWELRY MAKING AND DESIGN, Augustus F. Rose and Antonio Cirino. Professional secrets of jewelry making are revealed in a thorough, practical guide. Over 200 illustrations. 306pp. 5⅜ x 8½. 0-486-21750-7

JULIUS CAESAR, William Shakespeare. Great tragedy based on Plutarch's account of the lives of Brutus, Julius Caesar and Mark Antony. Evil plotting, ringing oratory, high tragedy with Shakespeare's incomparable insight, dramatic power. Explanatory footnotes. 96pp. 5³⁄₁₆ x 8¼. 0-486-26876-4

Browse over 9,000 books at www.doverpublications.com

THE JUNGLE, Upton Sinclair. 1906 bestseller shockingly reveals intolerable labor practices and working conditions in the Chicago stockyards as it tells the grim story of a Slavic family that emigrates to America full of optimism but soon faces despair. 320pp. 5³⁄₁₆ x 8¼. 0-486-41923-1

THE KINGDOM OF GOD IS WITHIN YOU, Leo Tolstoy. The soul-searching book that inspired Gandhi to embrace the concept of passive resistance, Tolstoy's 1894 polemic clearly outlines a radical, well-reasoned revision of traditional Christian thinking. 352pp. 5³⁄₁₆ x 8¼. 0-486-45138-0

THE LADY OR THE TIGER?: and Other Logic Puzzles, Raymond M. Smullyan. Created by a renowned puzzle master, these whimsically themed challenges involve paradoxes about probability, time, and change; metapuzzles; and self-referentiality. Nineteen chapters advance in difficulty from relatively simple to highly complex. 1982 edition. 240pp. 5⅜ x 8½. 0-486-47027-X

LEAVES OF GRASS: The Original 1855 Edition, Walt Whitman. Whitman's immortal collection includes some of the greatest poems of modern times, including his masterpiece, "Song of Myself." Shattering standard conventions, it stands as an unabashed celebration of body and nature. 128pp. 5³⁄₁₆ x 8¼. 0-486-45676-5

LES MISÉRABLES, Victor Hugo. Translated by Charles E. Wilbour. Abridged by James K. Robinson. A convict's heroic struggle for justice and redemption plays out against a fiery backdrop of the Napoleonic wars. This edition features the excellent original translation and a sensitive abridgment. 304pp. 6⅛ x 9¼. 0-486-45789-3

LILITH: A Romance, George MacDonald. In this novel by the father of fantasy literature, a man travels through time to meet Adam and Eve and to explore humanity's fall from grace and ultimate redemption. 240pp. 5⅜ x 8½. 0-486-46818-6

THE LOST LANGUAGE OF SYMBOLISM, Harold Bayley. This remarkable book reveals the hidden meaning behind familiar images and words, from the origins of Santa Claus to the fleur-de-lys, drawing from mythology, folklore, religious texts, and fairy tales. 1,418 illustrations. 784pp. 5⅜ x 8½. 0-486-44787-1

MACBETH, William Shakespeare. A Scottish nobleman murders the king in order to succeed to the throne. Tortured by his conscience and fearful of discovery, he becomes tangled in a web of treachery and deceit that ultimately spells his doom. 96pp. 5³⁄₁₆ x 8¼. 0-486-27802-6

MAKING AUTHENTIC CRAFTSMAN FURNITURE: Instructions and Plans for 62 Projects, Gustav Stickley. Make authentic reproductions of handsome, functional, durable furniture: tables, chairs, wall cabinets, desks, a hall tree, and more. Construction plans with drawings, schematics, dimensions, and lumber specs reprinted from 1900s *The Craftsman* magazine. 128pp. 8⅛ x 11. 0-486-25000-8

MATHEMATICS FOR THE NONMATHEMATICIAN, Morris Kline. Erudite and entertaining overview follows development of mathematics from ancient Greeks to present. Topics include logic and mathematics, the fundamental concept, differential calculus, probability theory, much more. Exercises and problems. 641pp. 5⅜ x 8½. 0-486-24823-2

MEMOIRS OF AN ARABIAN PRINCESS FROM ZANZIBAR, Emily Ruete. This 19th-century autobiography offers a rare inside look at the society surrounding a sultan's palace. A real-life princess in exile recalls her vanished world of harems, slave trading, and court intrigues. 288pp. 5⅜ x 8½. 0-486-47121-7

Browse over 9,000 books at www.doverpublications.com

THE METAMORPHOSIS AND OTHER STORIES, Franz Kafka. Excellent new English translations of title story (considered by many critics Kafka's most perfect work), plus "The Judgment," "In the Penal Colony," "A Country Doctor," and "A Report to an Academy." Note. 96pp. 5³⁄₁₆ x 8¼. 0-486-29030-1

MICROSCOPIC ART FORMS FROM THE PLANT WORLD, R. Anheisser. From undulating curves to complex geometrics, a world of fascinating images abound in this classic, illustrated survey of microscopic plants. Features 400 detailed illustrations of nature's minute but magnificent handiwork. The accompanying CD-ROM includes all of the images in the book. 128pp. 9 x 9. 0-486-46013-4

A MIDSUMMER NIGHT'S DREAM, William Shakespeare. Among the most popular of Shakespeare's comedies, this enchanting play humorously celebrates the vagaries of love as it focuses upon the intertwined romances of several pairs of lovers. Explanatory footnotes. 80pp. 5³⁄₁₆ x 8¼. 0-486-27067-X

THE MONEY CHANGERS, Upton Sinclair. Originally published in 1908, this cautionary novel from the author of *The Jungle* explores corruption within the American system as a group of power brokers joins forces for personal gain, triggering a crash on Wall Street. 192pp. 5⅜ x 8½. 0-486-46917-4

THE MOST POPULAR HOMES OF THE TWENTIES, William A. Radford. With a New Introduction by Daniel D. Reiff. Based on a rare 1925 catalog, this architectural showcase features floor plans, construction details, and photos of 26 homes, plus articles on entrances, porches, garages, and more. 250 illustrations, 21 color plates. 176pp. 8⅜ x 11. 0-486-47028-8

MY 66 YEARS IN THE BIG LEAGUES, Connie Mack. With a New Introduction by Rich Westcott. A Founding Father of modern baseball, Mack holds the record for most wins — and losses — by a major league manager. Enhanced by 70 photographs, his warmhearted autobiography is populated by many legends of the game. 288pp. 5⅜ x 8½. 0-486-47184-5

NARRATIVE OF THE LIFE OF FREDERICK DOUGLASS, Frederick Douglass. Douglass's graphic depictions of slavery, harrowing escape to freedom, and life as a newspaper editor, eloquent orator, and impassioned abolitionist. 96pp. 5³⁄₁₆ x 8¼. 0-486-28499-9

THE NIGHTLESS CITY: Geisha and Courtesan Life in Old Tokyo, J. E. de Becker. This unsurpassed study from 100 years ago ventured into Tokyo's red-light district to survey geisha and courtesan life and offer meticulous descriptions of training, dress, social hierarchy, and erotic practices. 49 black-and-white illustrations; 2 maps. 496pp. 5⅜ x 8½. 0-486-45563-7

THE ODYSSEY, Homer. Excellent prose translation of ancient epic recounts adventures of the homeward-bound Odysseus. Fantastic cast of gods, giants, cannibals, sirens, other supernatural creatures — true classic of Western literature. 256pp. 5³⁄₁₆ x 8¼. 0-486-40654-7

OEDIPUS REX, Sophocles. Landmark of Western drama concerns the catastrophe that ensues when King Oedipus discovers he has inadvertently killed his father and married his mother. Masterly construction, dramatic irony. Explanatory footnotes. 64pp. 5³⁄₁₆ x 8¼. 0-486-26877-2

ONCE UPON A TIME: The Way America Was, Eric Sloane. Nostalgic text and drawings brim with gentle philosophies and descriptions of how we used to live — self-sufficiently — on the land, in homes, and among the things built by hand. 44 line illustrations. 64pp. 8⅜ x 11. 0-486-44411-2

Browse over 9,000 books at www.doverpublications.com

ONE OF OURS, Willa Cather. The Pulitzer Prize–winning novel about a young Nebraskan looking for something to believe in. Alienated from his parents, rejected by his wife, he finds his destiny on the bloody battlefields of World War I. 352pp. 5³⁄₁₆ x 8¼. 0-486-45599-8

ORIGAMI YOU CAN USE: 27 Practical Projects, Rick Beech. Origami models can be more than decorative, and this unique volume shows how! The 27 practical projects include a CD case, frame, napkin ring, and dish. Easy instructions feature 400 two-color illustrations. 96pp. 8¼ x 11. 0-486-47057-1

OTHELLO, William Shakespeare. Towering tragedy tells the story of a Moorish general who earns the enmity of his ensign Iago when he passes him over for a promotion. Masterly portrait of an archvillain. Explanatory footnotes. 112pp. 5³⁄₁₆ x 8¼. 0-486-29097-2

PARADISE LOST, John Milton. Notes by John A. Himes. First published in 1667, *Paradise Lost* ranks among the greatest of English literature's epic poems. It's a sublime retelling of Adam and Eve's fall from grace and expulsion from Eden. Notes by John A. Himes. 480pp. 5³⁄₁₆ x 8¼. 0-486-44287-X

PASSING, Nella Larsen. Married to a successful physician and prominently ensconced in society, Irene Redfield leads a charmed existence — until a chance encounter with a childhood friend who has been "passing for white." 112pp. 5⅜ x 8½. 0-486-43713-2

PERSPECTIVE DRAWING FOR BEGINNERS, Len A. Doust. Doust carefully explains the roles of lines, boxes, and circles, and shows how visualizing shapes and forms can be used in accurate depictions of perspective. One of the most concise introductions available. 33 illustrations. 64pp. 5⅜ x 8½. 0-486-45149-6

PERSPECTIVE MADE EASY, Ernest R. Norling. Perspective is easy; yet, surprisingly few artists know the simple rules that make it so. Remedy that situation with this simple, step-by-step book, the first devoted entirely to the topic. 256 illustrations. 224pp. 5⅜ x 8½. 0-486-40473-0

THE PICTURE OF DORIAN GRAY, Oscar Wilde. Celebrated novel involves a handsome young Londoner who sinks into a life of depravity. His body retains perfect youth and vigor while his recent portrait reflects the ravages of his crime and sensuality. 176pp. 5³⁄₁₆ x 8¼. 0-486-27807-7

PRIDE AND PREJUDICE, Jane Austen. One of the most universally loved and admired English novels, an effervescent tale of rural romance transformed by Jane Austen's art into a witty, shrewdly observed satire of English country life. 272pp. 5³⁄₁₆ x 8¼. 0-486-28473-5

THE PRINCE, Niccolò Machiavelli. Classic, Renaissance-era guide to acquiring and maintaining political power. Today, nearly 500 years after it was written, this calculating prescription for autocratic rule continues to be much read and studied. 80pp. 5³⁄₁₆ x 8¼. 0-486-27274-5

QUICK SKETCHING, Carl Cheek. A perfect introduction to the technique of "quick sketching." Drawing upon an artist's immediate emotional responses, this is an extremely effective means of capturing the essential form and features of a subject. More than 100 black-and-white illustrations throughout. 48pp. 11 x 8¼. 0-486-46608-6

RANCH LIFE AND THE HUNTING TRAIL, Theodore Roosevelt. Illustrated by Frederic Remington. Beautifully illustrated by Remington, Roosevelt's celebration of the Old West recounts his adventures in the Dakota Badlands of the 1880s, from round-ups to Indian encounters to hunting bighorn sheep. 208pp. 6¼ x 9¼. 0-486-47340-6

THE RED BADGE OF COURAGE, Stephen Crane. Amid the nightmarish chaos of a Civil War battle, a young soldier discovers courage, humility, and, perhaps, wisdom. Uncanny re-creation of actual combat. Enduring landmark of American fiction. 112pp. 5³⁄₁₆ x 8¼. 0-486-26465-3

RELATIVITY SIMPLY EXPLAINED, Martin Gardner. One of the subject's clearest, most entertaining introductions offers lucid explanations of special and general theories of relativity, gravity, and spacetime, models of the universe, and more. 100 illustrations. 224pp. 5⅜ x 8½. 0-486-29315-7

REMBRANDT DRAWINGS: 116 Masterpieces in Original Color, Rembrandt van Rijn. This deluxe hardcover edition features drawings from throughout the Dutch master's prolific career. Informative captions accompany these beautifully reproduced landscapes, biblical vignettes, figure studies, animal sketches, and portraits. 128pp. 8⅜ x 11. 0-486-46149-1

THE ROAD NOT TAKEN AND OTHER POEMS, Robert Frost. A treasury of Frost's most expressive verse. In addition to the title poem: "An Old Man's Winter Night," "In the Home Stretch," "Meeting and Passing," "Putting in the Seed," many more. All complete and unabridged. 64pp. 5³⁄₁₆ x 8¼. 0-486-27550-7

ROMEO AND JULIET, William Shakespeare. Tragic tale of star-crossed lovers, feuding families and timeless passion contains some of Shakespeare's most beautiful and lyrical love poetry. Complete, unabridged text with explanatory footnotes. 96pp. 5³⁄₁₆ x 8¼. 0-486-27557-4

SANDITON AND THE WATSONS: Austen's Unfinished Novels, Jane Austen. Two tantalizing incomplete stories revisit Austen's customary milieu of courtship and venture into new territory, amid guests at a seaside resort. Both are worth reading for pleasure and study. 112pp. 5⅜ x 8½. 0-486-45793-1

THE SCARLET LETTER, Nathaniel Hawthorne. With stark power and emotional depth, Hawthorne's masterpiece explores sin, guilt, and redemption in a story of adultery in the early days of the Massachusetts Colony. 192pp. 5³⁄₁₆ x 8¼.
0-486-28048-9

THE SEASONS OF AMERICA PAST, Eric Sloane. Seventy-five illustrations depict cider mills and presses, sleds, pumps, stump-pulling equipment, plows, and other elements of America's rural heritage. A section of old recipes and household hints adds additional color. 160pp. 8⅜ x 11. 0-486-44220-9

SELECTED CANTERBURY TALES, Geoffrey Chaucer. Delightful collection includes the General Prologue plus three of the most popular tales: "The Knight's Tale," "The Miller's Prologue and Tale," and "The Wife of Bath's Prologue and Tale." In modern English. 144pp. 5³⁄₁₆ x 8¼. 0-486-28241-4

SELECTED POEMS, Emily Dickinson. Over 100 best-known, best-loved poems by one of America's foremost poets, reprinted from authoritative early editions. No comparable edition at this price. Index of first lines. 64pp. 5³⁄₁₆ x 8¼. 0-486-26466-1

SIDDHARTHA, Hermann Hesse. Classic novel that has inspired generations of seekers. Blending Eastern mysticism and psychoanalysis, Hesse presents a strikingly original view of man and culture and the arduous process of self-discovery, reconciliation, harmony, and peace. 112pp. 5³⁄₁₆ x 8¼. 0-486-40653-9

SKETCHING OUTDOORS, Leonard Richmond. This guide offers beginners step-by-step demonstrations of how to depict clouds, trees, buildings, and other outdoor sights. Explanations of a variety of techniques include shading and constructional drawing. 48pp. 11 x 8¼. 0-486-46922-0

Browse over 9,000 books at www.doverpublications.com

SMALL HOUSES OF THE FORTIES: With Illustrations and Floor Plans, Harold E. Group. 56 floor plans and elevations of houses that originally cost less than $15,000 to build. Recommended by financial institutions of the era, they range from Colonials to Cape Cods. 144pp. 8⅜ x 11.   0-486-45598-X

SOME CHINESE GHOSTS, Lafcadio Hearn. Rooted in ancient Chinese legends, these richly atmospheric supernatural tales are recounted by an expert in Oriental lore. Their originality, power, and literary charm will captivate readers of all ages. 96pp. 5⅜ x 8½.   0-486-46306-0

SONGS FOR THE OPEN ROAD: Poems of Travel and Adventure, Edited by The American Poetry & Literacy Project. More than 80 poems by 50 American and British masters celebrate real and metaphorical journeys. Poems by Whitman, Byron, Millay, Sandburg, Langston Hughes, Emily Dickinson, Robert Frost, Shelley, Tennyson, Yeats, many others. Note. 80pp. 5³⁄₁₆ x 8¼.   0-486-40646-6

SPOON RIVER ANTHOLOGY, Edgar Lee Masters. An American poetry classic, in which former citizens of a mythical midwestern town speak touchingly from the grave of the thwarted hopes and dreams of their lives. 144pp. 5³⁄₁₆ x 8¼.

0-486-27275-3

STAR LORE: Myths, Legends, and Facts, William Tyler Olcott. Captivating retellings of the origins and histories of ancient star groups include Pegasus, Ursa Major, Pleiades, signs of the zodiac, and other constellations. "Classic." — *Sky & Telescope.* 58 illustrations. 544pp. 5⅜ x 8½.   0-486-43581-4

THE STRANGE CASE OF DR. JEKYLL AND MR. HYDE, Robert Louis Stevenson. This intriguing novel, both fantasy thriller and moral allegory, depicts the struggle of two opposing personalities — one essentially good, the other evil — for the soul of one man. 64pp. 5³⁄₁₆ x 8¼.   0-486-26688-5

SURVIVAL HANDBOOK: The Official U.S. Army Guide, Department of the Army. This special edition of the Army field manual is geared toward civilians. An essential companion for campers and all lovers of the outdoors, it constitutes the most authoritative wilderness guide. 288pp. 5³⁄₁₆ x 8¼.   0-486-46184-X

A TALE OF TWO CITIES, Charles Dickens. Against the backdrop of the French Revolution, Dickens unfolds his masterpiece of drama, adventure, and romance about a man falsely accused of treason. Excitement and derring-do in the shadow of the guillotine. 304pp. 5³⁄₁₆ x 8¼.   0-486-40651-2

TEN PLAYS, Anton Chekhov. *The Sea Gull, Uncle Vanya, The Three Sisters, The Cherry Orchard,* and *Ivanov,* plus 5 one-act comedies: *The Anniversary, An Unwilling Martyr, The Wedding, The Bear,* and *The Proposal.* 336pp. 5³⁄₁₆ x 8¼.   0-486-46560-8

THE FLYING INN, G. K. Chesterton. Hilarious romp in which pub owner Humphrey Hump and friend take to the road in a donkey cart filled with rum and cheese, inveighing against Prohibition and other "oppressive forms of modernity." 320pp. 5⅜ x 8½.   0-486-41910-X

THIRTY YEARS THAT SHOOK PHYSICS: The Story of Quantum Theory, George Gamow. Lucid, accessible introduction to the influential theory of energy and matter features careful explanations of Dirac's anti-particles, Bohr's model of the atom, and much more. Numerous drawings. 1966 edition. 240pp. 5⅜ x 8½. 0-486-24895-X

TREASURE ISLAND, Robert Louis Stevenson. Classic adventure story of a perilous sea journey, a mutiny led by the infamous Long John Silver, and a lethal scramble for buried treasure — seen through the eyes of cabin boy Jim Hawkins. 160pp. 5³⁄₁₆ x 8¼.

0-486-27559-0

Browse over 9,000 books at www.doverpublications.com

THE TRIAL, Franz Kafka. Translated by David Wyllie. From its gripping first sentence onward, this novel exemplifies the term "Kafkaesque." Its darkly humorous narrative recounts a bank clerk's entrapment in a bureaucratic maze, based on an undisclosed charge. 176pp. 5³⁄₁₆ x 8¼. 0-486-47061-X

THE TURN OF THE SCREW, Henry James. Gripping ghost story by great novelist depicts the sinister transformation of 2 innocent children into flagrant liars and hypocrites. An elegantly told tale of unspoken horror and psychological terror. 96pp. 5³⁄₁₆ x 8¼. 0-486-26684-2

UP FROM SLAVERY, Booker T. Washington. Washington (1856-1915) rose to become the most influential spokesman for African-Americans of his day. In this eloquently written book, he describes events in a remarkable life that began in bondage and culminated in worldwide recognition. 160pp. 5³⁄₁₆ x 8¼. 0-486-28738-6

VICTORIAN HOUSE DESIGNS IN AUTHENTIC FULL COLOR: 75 Plates from the "Scientific American – Architects and Builders Edition," 1885-1894, Edited by Blanche Cirker. Exquisitely detailed, exceptionally handsome designs for an enormous variety of attractive city dwellings, spacious suburban and country homes, charming "cottages" and other structures — all accompanied by perspective views and floor plans. 80pp. 9¼ x 12¼. 0-486-29438-2

VILLETTE, Charlotte Brontë. Acclaimed by Virginia Woolf as "Brontë's finest novel," this moving psychological study features a remarkably modern heroine who abandons her native England for a new life as a schoolteacher in Belgium. 480pp. 5³⁄₁₆ x 8¼. 0-486-45557-2

THE VOYAGE OUT, Virginia Woolf. A moving depiction of the thrills and confusion of youth, Woolf's acclaimed first novel traces a shipboard journey to South America for a captivating exploration of a woman's growing self-awareness. 288pp. 5³⁄₁₆ x 8¼. 0-486-45005-8

WALDEN; OR, LIFE IN THE WOODS, Henry David Thoreau. Accounts of Thoreau's daily life on the shores of Walden Pond outside Concord, Massachusetts, are interwoven with musings on the virtues of self-reliance and individual freedom, on society, government, and other topics. 224pp. 5³⁄₁₆ x 8¼. 0-486-28495-6

WILD PILGRIMAGE: A Novel in Woodcuts, Lynd Ward. Through startling engravings shaded in black and red, Ward wordlessly tells the story of a man trapped in an industrial world, struggling between the grim reality around him and the fantasies his imagination creates. 112pp. 6⅛ x 9¼. 0-486-46583-7

WILLY POGÁNY REDISCOVERED, Willy Pogány. Selected and Edited by Jeff A. Menges. More than 100 color and black-and-white Art Nouveau–style illustrations from fairy tales and adventure stories include scenes from Wagner's "Ring" cycle, *The Rime of the Ancient Mariner, Gulliver's Travels,* and *Faust.* 144pp. 8⅜ x 11. 0-486-47046-6

WOOLLY THOUGHTS: Unlock Your Creative Genius with Modular Knitting, Pat Ashforth and Steve Plummer. Here's the revolutionary way to knit — easy, fun, and foolproof! Beginners and experienced knitters need only master a single stitch to create their own designs with patchwork squares. More than 100 illustrations. 128pp. 6½ x 9¼. 0-486-46084-3

WUTHERING HEIGHTS, Emily Brontë. Somber tale of consuming passions and vengeance — played out amid the lonely English moors — recounts the turbulent and tempestuous love story of Cathy and Heathcliff. Poignant and compelling. 256pp. 5³⁄₁₆ x 8¼. 0-486-29256-8

Browse over 9,000 books at www.doverpublications.com

MORRIS AUTOMATED INFORMATION NETWORK

0 1029 0612472 6

WITHDRAWN

Parsippany-Troy Hill
Main Librar
449 Halsey RD
Parsippany NJ 07054
973-887-5150

Call Me Dad!

JUN 2 6 2012

First published in 2009 by New Holland Publishers (NZ) Ltd
Auckland • Sydney • London • Cape Town

www.newhollandpublishers.co.nz

218 Lake Road, Northcote, Auckland 0627, New Zealand
Unit 1, 66 Gibbes Street, Chatswood, NSW 2067, Australia
86–88 Edgware Road, London W2 2EA, United Kingdom
80 McKenzie Street, Cape Town 8001, South Africa

Copyright © 2009 in text DIYFather Ltd
Copyright © 2009 in photography DIYFather Ltd with the exception of pg 19 (Niamh
Baldock\Shutterstock); pg 26 (Gabrielle Martell-Turner); pg 37 (John van Eekelen\
Shutterstock); pg 59 (James Steidl\Shutterstock); pg 73 (Elena Schweitzer\
Shutterstock); pg 74 (Konstantins Visnevskis\Shutterstock); pg 79 (NASA); pg 95
(Phyllis Buchanan).

Commissioned by Louise Armstrong
Publishing manager: Christine Thomson
Editor: John Mackinven
Design: Seven
Photography: Karina Smith except as otherwise noted above

National Library of New Zealand Cataloguing-in-Publication Data

Korn, Stefan.
Call me Dad : a manual for new fathers / Stefan Korn,
Scott Lancaster and Eric Mooij.
Includes index.
ISBN 978-1-86966-237-0
1. Fatherhood. 2. Fathers. 3. Newborn infants—Care. 4. Infants
—Care. I. Lancaster, Scott. II. Mooij, Eric. III. Title.
306.8742—dc 22

10 9 8 7 6 5 4 3

Colour reproduction by Pica Digital Pte Ltd, Singapore
Printed in China by Toppan Leefung on paper sourced from sustainable forests.

All rights reserved. No part of this publication may be reproduced, stored in a
retrieval system, or transmitted in any form or by any means, electronic, mechanical,
photocopying, recording or otherwise, without the prior permission of the publishers
and copyright holders.

While every care has been taken to ensure the information contained in this book is
as accurate as possible, the authors and publishers can accept no responsibility for
any loss, injury or inconvenience sustained by any person using the advice contained
herein.

Readers are strongly advised to seek professional advice if they have any concerns
about their baby's health or well-being. The information in this book is intended to
provide general advice about caring for babies only and should not be regarded as an
alternative to seeking specific advice from a trained medical professional.

Call Me Dad!

A MANUAL FOR NEW FATHERS

From **pre-birth** to **12 months**

Scott Lancaster
Eric Mooij
Stefan Korn

ERIC MOOIJ

Eric Mooij is married to Andrea who welcomed baby Ava into the world in April 2008.

Eric is also father to Nastassja (14), Christian (13) and Amber (12). Although he is not living with his three older children, he has regular contact with them and supports them in every way possible.

Eric is keen to make a stand for separated families. Coming from a broken family himself and having relived this experience with his first three children, he works hard to be a positive role-model.

Outside of DIYFather, Eric works full-time in IT management.

SCOTT LANCASTER

Scott is the founder of DIYFather Ltd. He is the father of one daughter named Pyper and is married to Renee, who gave birth to Pyper in July 2007.

After discovering what little parenting information was available for fathers, Scott approached the other two directors, who helped him build DIYFather.

When not involved with DIYFather, Scott looks after Pyper full-time and also helps Renee with her business. Scott has an Applied Science degree majoring in Agriculture and comes from a farming background.

STEFAN KORN

Stefan describes himself as one of New Zealand's 'e-vangelists'. He is passionate about e-commerce and the Internet, and in general loves getting involved in new businesses. His wife Raquel gave birth to their son Noah in May 2007 and the experience of becoming a father, as well as the challenges of looking after Noah, prompted him to join DIYFather.

In addition to DIYFather, Stefan runs a web-investment company, WebFund, and helps his wife with her Spanish language school. Stefan is also actively engaged in community projects and enjoys tutoring for Wellington Community Education.

CONTENTS

1 WELCOME TO YOUR NEW LIFE — 9

Finding out you're going to be a dad — 14
So now what? — 16
We never said we didn't want kids — 16
Reality check — 17
From man to dad – the road ahead — 18
A word for sceptics –
    if you're not a natural-born dad — 20

2 PREGNANCY — 23

Pregnancy in five minutes — 24
Living with a pregnant woman — 27
The pregnant father — 31
Where do I fit in as a dad? — 32
The medical stuff –
    screenings and procedures — 33
A word on Braxton Hicks — 34
A word on midwives and obstetricians — 35
Problems and risks during pregnancy — 36
Let's talk about sex, baby — 37

3 PREPARING FOR THE BABY — 39

Decisions, decisions . . . — 40
Top (baby) gear – what to buy — 47
What not to buy — 60
Preparations — 62
The baby shower — 72
The dad shower — 74
Your role during labour — 75

4 SURVIVING BIRTH — 77

Last-minute preparations — 78
The final countdown — 79
It's not called 'labour' for nothing . . . — 80
The big moment: Baby is here! — 86

5 LIFE AFTER BIRTH: THE DAYS AFTER — 91

Handling a newborn — 93
Feeding — 94
Silent night? — 97
Newborn hygiene — 101
Looking after your partner — 101
The baby blues — 102
The trip home — 103
The first week — 104
Visitors — 109

6 THE FIRST THREE MONTHS — 111

The new routine — 112
Basic necessities of life: food, warmth,
clothing (and a whole lot more . . .) — 113
Out and about — 120
Toys, toys (and more toys) — 121
Making time for your child — 122
General health — 123
Getting support — 123
Don't forget your partner — 124
The end of the probationary period — 124
A word about SIDS — 125
Active movement –
    zero to three months — 126

7 THREE TO SIX MONTHS   131

Reviewing key decisions   132
The routines they are a-changin'   133
The food revolution –
   introducing solids   134
Don't forget the paperwork   138
Finances and insurances   139
Cool things you can do now with your
   baby that you couldn't do before   141
On the road again – baby travels   144
Baby on board   145
Nannies and babysitters   145
The wider family   146
Ceremonies   146
Active movement –
   three to six months   148

8 SIX TO TWELVE MONTHS   151

Routines for babies aged six to
   twelve months   152
Some new challenges   153
Child-proofing the house   159
The joy of everyday objects   163
Leaving them with others   164
Rejoining the workforce   165
Cool things to do with babies aged
   six to twelve months   166
Getting pregnant again   168
The first birthday   170
Finding your feet as a dad   171
The DIYFather Murphy's Law
   for babies   171
End of year-one test –
   what kind of parent are you?   172
Active movement –
   six to twelve months   174

9 THE FIRST YEAR:
LOOKING BACK   177

The experience of being a father   179
Dads look back   179
More advice for expectant fathers   180
More babies and what to expect
   from toddlers   182
Some final words of wisdom   183

GLOSSARY   186

INDEX   187

CHAPTER 1

WELCOME TO YOUR NEW LIFE

Why write a book for new dads? Surely there are enough parenting books already? Well, yes, it's true there are gazillions of parenting books available, and as new parents we've read many of them. But we felt, as dads, there was something missing – a book written especially for a new generation of dads.

Try as we might, we couldn't find a practical book for dads about the early fatherhood experience – one that was easy to read, instructional without being overly academic, and provided a male perspective on all the stuff first-time dads need to know. And one that reminds new dads not to forget the humorous side of parenting. Kids bring a lot of laughs into your life, so why should a book on fatherhood read like a dry report?

We believe there's quite a difference between how men and women approach parenting and how they choose to prepare for their new roles. There are different expectations, too, from society in general and, closer to home, from friends and family.

So, 'Dad', this book will help get you through pregnancy and the first 12 months of fatherhood. You'll find it tells you everything you need to know about babies, parenting and life with neonates (newborns) in general. If we don't tell you specifically, then we tell you where to find out. Since newborns don't come with an instruction manual, we hope you'll find *Call Me Dad!* to be the next best thing.

Call Me Dad! was written for a new generation of dads. There is a quiet revolution happening in parenting: fathers are now much more deeply involved. More and more dads are no longer content with traditional, stereotypical roles and are questioning their contribution to the upbringing of their children.

Occasionally, this 'dawn of the new dad' has been taken a bit too far and outspoken men's activist groups have made it into a

1. Dads are expected to be a bit more involved now than they were in our dads' day.

Call Me Dad!

OLD DAD	NEW DAD
+ Bring home the bacon	+ Cooking the bacon
+ Don't disturb your father	+ Go hang out with your father
+ Mum does the housework	+ We all do the housework
+ 'I want my son to be a successful lawyer'	+ I want to help my son be whatever he wants to be
+ Smacking as discipline	+ Time out on the naughty spot

campaign against the perceived stronghold of women in the parenting space. That is definitely not what this book is about. *Call Me Dad!* is simply about equipping you as a male with what you need to know to be a great father, written from a man's perspective, in language that works for men.

We – the authors – are all ordinary blokes who one day became dads. But in speaking to our parents about what it means to be a dad, we realised that things had changed, had moved on. The 'involved-father' movement is gaining momentum and its signs are showing everywhere in the form of mushrooming stay-at-home-dad groups, dad coffee groups and dad conventions.

The philosophy of this book can be summarised simply as 'dads can do'. 'Mums know best' remains an enduring myth, but in our personal experience, they don't always. They know a lot, but whether it's best or always right remains debatable. Mums can be just as clueless about babies as dads, but society has better support systems for preparing women for the big event, and they can always turn to their own mothers for advice (whereas our dads are not always a good source of information).

This book is meant as a guidebook and companion to take you on the fatherhood journey and transform you from zero to hero. It covers the mechanics of fathering (yep, that's where the nappies come in), but also the mentality of fathering (as in, 'You're having children? You must be mental . . . '). Most importantly though, it's about the joy of becoming and being a dad – a journey that lasts for the rest of your life. You don't suddenly graduate as a dad the day your first child is born – you earn the title over time. We think being a dad is actually not so much a role as a mindset, and we fundamentally believe that each and every guy can be a fantastic father.

Along with climate change, religion, politics and, of course, football, 'How best to look after a baby' is probably amongst the most controversial subjects on the planet. There are a myriad different approaches to parenting with countless support organisations advocating their own philosophies. We don't want to join the often passionate (and sometimes ridiculous) debates in parenting forums, playgroups, antenatal classes or midwifery seminars about who's right or wrong; we just want to help you be comfortable with your new role, and do well in it from the start.

That said, there is value in following and participating in such discussions, and we'd encourage all dads to do so. Whether it's home birthing vs. hospital, breast vs. bottle-feeding, or cloth vs. disposable nappies, the views are usually quite polarised and so you end up in a situation where all parties accuse each other of being out of touch with reality. Great fun! But in the end, you and your partner have to make your own informed decisions, and we trust this book will help you do that.

While we appreciate that many child-rearing approaches are backed by scientific research and/or generations of experience, there can still be a somewhat disturbing element of 'preaching' involved.

The problem with strong opinions on given parenting subjects is that they tend to alienate parents who've decided they would like to try a different approach. In some cases, couples are simply unable to adopt a certain approach however much they might want to (breastfeeding is a good example). So rather than telling parents how they're doing things wrong, we feel it's important to provide an overview of alternatives, and let you decide for yourselves.

That's how our approach differs – the purpose of the book is to inform, not to judge. We want to make sure that you as a new father know just about everything there is to know about fatherhood, and to encourage you to use your own judgement to make decisions.

Although there is no single right way to do things around babies, there are some inalienable truths you might as well accept from the start:

+ Each baby is different.
+ Babies develop rapidly and change their behaviour all the time – what worked really well last week may not work this week.
+ Official 'best practice' changes every now and then (depending on the latest research results).
+ Parenting styles come and go (whatever happened to laissez-faire?).
+ Parenting advice varies drastically by country, culture and religion – so depending on where you live and what beliefs you follow, you will be told different things.
+ Randomness . . . there is a certain random element to everything you do with babies which is beyond rational thought or prediction (so it's best to go with it rather than fight it!).

This book will help you develop and learn to trust your natural fatherly instincts. By all means do the research, listen to what others have to say, read all the books and talk to every man and his dog. But ultimately, talk it through with your partner and make your own decision.

Although we've just said that there's no single right way to do things around babies, there are some non-negotiable rules which we adhere to as fathers, and which we insist you do, too. These include not smoking around children, no violence towards and around children, and attending to the safety of children at all times – especially in vehicles.

As concerned fathers we feel obliged to take a stand on these issues. No matter what your parenting style is, there are no good reasons why your child should ever be exposed to smoke, violence or danger.

We've written *Call Me Dad!* in chronological order starting with that wonderful, indescribable moment when you discover you're going to be a dad. We then cover pregnancy and all the weird and wonderful things that happen to you as a dad during that period.

Since you're not the one who's pregnant, much of the pregnancy chapter is about preparation, but we felt there's a special need to gear up for the experience of birth and to help you through the birth itself (covered in Chapter 4).

Then suddenly people are calling you 'Dad', and you've got your little bundle of joy with you. From there on it's all about surviving the first few days and weeks, which is why we've dedicated an extra chapter to this critical period. Once you've coped with that, it's about honing your core skills and building on them to reach the first milestone, when your baby reaches the age of three months.

Some things get easier after that, others don't. A lot is happening with your baby between four and six months (covered in Chapter 7).

And finally we round things off with a look at what's happening as your baby goes through the second half of her first year to finish up at that major milestone, her first birthday. From there, your life as a dad continues with new challenges and more joy.

This book is based largely on our personal experiences as dads and the distilled wisdom of fatherly advice from a vast community of other dads we've had contact with in our personal networks and online travels. Many of the topics in this book are also actively discussed on our website www.DIYFather.com.

Throughout the book, when we refer to children, we alternate between both male and female genders, calling them him or her, he or she. It seems a shame to label a child 'it' or 'their' when children are real human beings oozing personality.

2. Now is a good time to find out what fatherhood's all about.

To add to our collective experiences we've also drawn on quality information from organisations such as Sport and Recreation New Zealand (SPARC), and we're thankful for their contributions.

Think you know it all already? Well, take our Dad Test. You can check your score online at: www.DIYFather.com/fathertest.

The DIYFather readiness assessment test:

+ How much does a disposable nappy cost?
+ What's an APGAR score?
+ What's considered a normal weight for a three-month-old baby?
+ On average, how long do you think labour lasts?
+ Who is Braxton Hicks?
+ What should you do when you can't get your baby to settle at night?
+ When is a good time to introduce 'solids'?
+ How many nappies does a newborn go through on average a day?
+ When do you think you'll have sex again after your partner has given birth?
+ What can you feed your newborn?
+ What is a capsule?
+ What preference do you have – boy or girl?

READY?

If your partner's already expecting, then the clock's ticking. You can't put off finding out what you need to know and getting ready to be a dad, because your baby is coming, ready or not!

But we don't want to scare you. This book is really a celebration of the 'coming out' of dads. Today, perhaps more than ever, our children need great fathers. Every father makes a unique contribution to the upbringing of his child, a contribution for which mothers cannot provide a total substitute.

There are so many aspects of parenting where male contributions are pivotal for baby and mum that if we listed them all here the book would be twice as long. Not only that, many of the influences you are going to have as a dad will be so subtle they might not even have a category yet. You will influence the development of your child in a thousand different ways every day, so you owe it to her to get fully involved, and to front up to the challenge of becoming the world's greatest dad.

FINDING OUT YOU'RE GOING TO BE A DAD

Finding out you're going to be a dad makes sense of that old saying, 'today is the first day of the rest of your life'. Your life with a kid. No matter what you thought when you found out ('Fantastic!' 'Shit!' 'But that's impossible!' Or, 'Finally – thank God'), it is always a very special moment. Savour it.

However you look at it, it's big news. So for the next few days you might enter some sort of parallel reality where you wake up convinced it was all a dream, or you might suddenly remember in the middle of a meeting that 'I'm going to be a DAD!'

Usually (though not always) there's a considerable period of time between finding out about the pregnancy and your partner giving birth, so relax for a while and let reality catch up with you.

> **SCOTT:**
> Renee and I had had an argument, and she was feeling very unwell. But then she did a pregnancy test and we found out we were expecting!

Many couples, sometimes on the advice of their health professionals, elect not to announce the pregnancy until about three months into it, i.e., once they're sure it's all going according to plan.

While keeping the news to yourselves the parallel reality might continue. It's a great time for lots of in-jokes with your partner and hidden smiles when friends or family talk about babies.

It's also an excellent time to listen to your thoughts and feelings and reflect on them. So, despite the fact you might be bursting to tell everyone, bear in mind that once you've told people you may not have the same space and quiet time to get your head around this new situation.

So spend some quality time with your partner and have fun sharing all the weird, wonderful and scary thoughts that are going through your head.

3. It's hard to predict how you or your partner are going to react to the big news. Expect the full emotional spectrum.

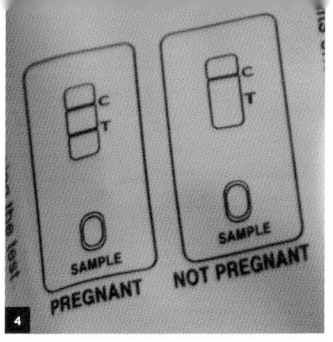
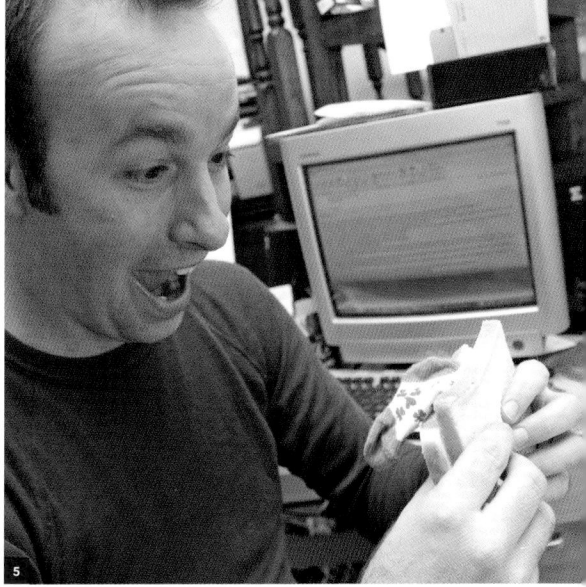

4. A home pregnancy test.

5. You might find out you're going to be a dad in a rather unusual way.

SCOTT:
The first thoughts that went through my head: what if our baby is ugly, what if she's weird, what if I pass out during the birth . . .

CHRIS:
I found out early in the morning. My wife was on 'period watch', and was acutely aware that the beginning of a new cycle had come and gone. Unbeknown to me (it was about 4.30 am), she had gone to the loo where she had a handy supply of home pregnancy tests. I was woken by the covers being flung off the bed and my wife jumping on me with the positive result clutched in her hand. 'WE'VE GOT TWO LINES!' she shouted.

RICHARD:
Clara and I were having a posh romantic dinner to celebrate my birthday. Towards the end of the meal she gave me a gift. When I opened it, I thought at first it was a pair of All Blacks boxers (maybe a hint about what was in store later!). Two seconds later, I realised it was a Babygro! I've kept the bill from that night – it was one of the last times we went to a flash restaurant for quite a while!

MATT:
I learnt I was going to be a father shortly after returning from my second trip to Iraq as a reporter. I had recently been on a medical transport plane alongside dozens of wounded service people in various states of injury and dismemberment – needless to say my own mortality was on my mind. I could have been any one of those guys. When my wife told me she was pregnant – 'there will be three of us for dinner tonight' is how she put it – I was extremely excited. But I also couldn't help thinking of my impending parenthood in light of the experiences I'd had while covering the war. Life is so very fragile. So I started thinking in terms of 'what can I give my daughter, right at this moment, which would benefit her if I weren't here tomorrow?' Perhaps it sounds a bit morbid, but it helps me determine what is important to me and what is important for her.

We've heard from a large number of guys who, once they reveal that they're going to be a dad to their mates, find themselves on the receiving end of a lot of comments that all carry a similar underlying message: the best days of your 'manhood' are over. You're going to be a family guy now. No more wild nights on the town. You'll have to sell that nice two-seater convertible and buy a station wagon. At least a 10-pack of condoms will last you a whole year now, and so on.

You'll almost certainly have to endure comments of that sort also, especially from your male mates who don't have kids. The thing is, though, these comments reflect the choices people have made, and have nothing to do with the inevitable path your approach to fatherhood has to take.

> **DANA:**
> We were trying to get pregnant, and my wife shared the news with me that we had scored a goal!

You can make your fatherhood experience whatever you like. There are some pretty cool dads out there who've successfully combined fatherhood with whatever else it is they want to do. You can be one of them.

From this point forward, you're going to be responsible for someone else's life and chances are you're going to find it pretty rewarding. You may as well put some effort in and do a reasonable job of it.

> **CHRIS:**
> Becoming a dad is the closest we can come in life to experiencing our own first breath of air or first mouthful of food. No one, nothing, can tell us what it's like, and from the moment we become a father we can't imagine life any other way.

> **CHRIS:**
> My biggest worry about becoming a dad was keeping the child alive. The most fastidious, responsible King of the Boy Scouts would still find himself scratching his head and wondering how it all worked. And I am no boy scout.

SO NOW WHAT?

Whichever way you look at it, over the next year or so your life is going to change pretty significantly. So take the time to acknowledge and celebrate the beginning of your journey as a father (and the beginning of your child's journey of life).

Top-10 things to do when you have just found out you're going to be a dad:

+ Cook a meal for your partner.
+ Sleep in; those nights of undisturbed sleep are about to end!
+ Think about what you do and don't want to pass on to your kid(s).
+ Give your partner lots of back rubs.
+ Write a letter to your unborn child.
+ Find a restaurant where you can have a meal with 17 courses and try them all.
+ Play naked twister and have lots of sex (she can't get pregnant twice!).
+ Whenever you watch a movie, check the titles for possible names for your child (or just buy a baby-name book).
+ Hire and watch a family/kids' movie.
+ Start a personal diary.

WE NEVER SAID WE DIDN'T WANT KIDS

At some stage you're going to have to let the cat out of the bag. This can be daunting if you're worried about what others might say. Alternatively, you might have the time of your life because you can't wait to share the news.

Whichever is the case – it's essential to have a think before you spill the beans. At the very least you'll want to synchronise with your partner. There'll be a certain pecking order for telling people, which only you can decide (usually parents first, then siblings and closest friends). Or you might want to stagger the announcement to coincide with a certain point in the pregnancy.

There's no rule that fits all – it's entirely up to you. The important thing is to discuss it as a couple and reach agreement first. She won't necessarily appreciate it if your first

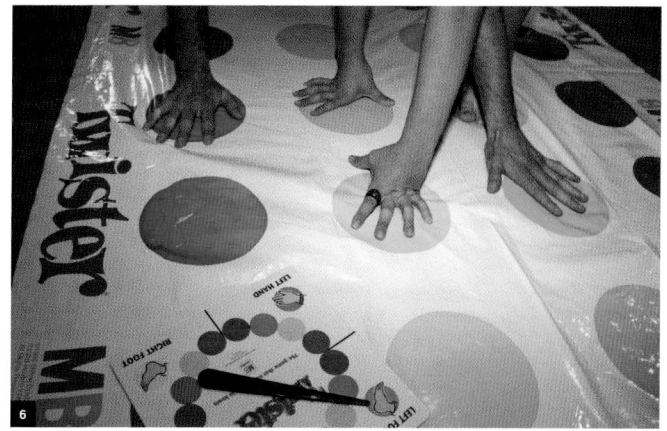

6. Enjoy a bit of playtime with your partner while you can.

7. Dinner for two . . . but not for long!

inclination is to head for the pub and shout your mates a celebratory round before anyone else knows!

> **DANA:**
> My biggest worry about becoming a dad was that I would be giving up all of my free time and wouldn't be able to have fun any more. I think everyone on the outside of parenting looks at parents and their kids and asks themselves: why would anyone subject themselves to that? But the truth is, regardless of the hardship and sacrifice, life is much more meaningful than ever before. That's the part most people can't see before they become parents.

REALITY CHECK

Once the dust has settled, take a moment to evaluate how a baby is going to affect your life now, and in the future:

+ What is your situation at the moment and how will a baby fit?
+ What adjustments do you need to make to your house, lifestyle and goals?
+ Who will look after the baby?
+ How are you going to support him?
+ What support is available where you live?
+ Who can help? (It takes a village to raise a child.) What about your family?
+ How involved do you want to be? Are you planning to be a stay-at-home dad?

Of course you don't need to answer all these questions immediately, but they make a good starting point for reflection on what's coming your way. The lead-up period to birth is a good time to discuss these details with your partner and reach some understanding of mutual expectations. One thing's for sure: don't leave it until after the baby's born – there won't be time.

Remember the old story about the bacon-and-egg pie: the chicken was involved, but the pig was committed!

STEF:

When I was about to become a father, I felt like Neo in *The Matrix* when he woke up in that spaceship – 'welcome to the real world'. However, unlike in *The Matrix*, where it was all about taking the blue or red pill, it was *not* taking a certain pill that got us into this position in the first place.

FROM MAN TO DAD – THE ROAD AHEAD

There are certain practical aspects involved with being a dad and in many cases nature has a gentle way of introducing you to the role. For example, baby poo doesn't smell much at the beginning (you'll be pleased to know).

Your partner's pregnancy is a gently evolving thing; slowly but surely her shape changes and you have all those weeks and months to adapt to and accommodate the changes.

MATT:

I like skydiving as a metaphor for fatherhood. When you skydive, no one takes you up in an aeroplane against your will and pushes you out the door. Instead, people who have done it – again and again and again - tell you what to expect, what to do once you're in the plane, once you've begun freefall, and as you approach the ground. The experience itself simply can't be explained, but you're a complete fool if you don't listen to those who have gone before you.

In other areas nature has decided that shock therapy is really the best way to get you to look after the baby. For example, a crying newborn is always louder than the telly and she's virtually impossible to ignore.

But be assured that over time you'll develop fantastic baby-handling skills and superhuman abilities to care for your baby. Naturally, just as you're getting more confident it gets more difficult. This usually happens just when you think you've got it sorted.

Mostly, becoming a dad involves a mindset change, and you'll notice a few things when this happens.

Your first thought in most situations is for the baby – including remembering to take a spare nappy or bottle before you leave the house with your baby. It doesn't take many mistakes to make this lesson stick (or sticky)!

You take charge. Your child looks to you for guidance and imitates everything you do. You get clarity about what values and which parts of your own knowledge of life you would like to pass on to your child. Having your own child puts a very clear focus on your own world and values.

You might see your own father (and mother) with different eyes as you realise what they must have gone through when they raised you.

MATT:

Becoming a dad is like looking in a mirror – a really clear mirror. All the things you like about yourself, and all of the things you don't, you will see reflected in your child's life. The things that are most important to you will be the things you choose to pass down to your child, consciously or subconsciously.

For some reason there seems to be a tendency among prenatal parents to underestimate everything – starting with the pain involved in bringing the baby into the world (on the mother's part), what it takes to look after a baby, the difficulties of fitting the baby's needs in neatly with your needs, but also the immense joy and hilarity of having a baby around.

8. A journey of a thousand miles starts with a single step.

So whatever you imagine the extent will be of the impact of baby's arrival on your life – double it and you might be close, or not!

Becoming a dad is like parachuting – nobody can tell you what it's really like, because it can only be experienced. There's only one way to truly find out and that's to step out of an aeroplane and let gravity do the rest. You'll soon realise the gravity of the situation when your new baby arrives, and all you can do is hope you've packed your 'chute properly.

RICHARD:
My biggest worry about becoming a dad was that I didn't think I was 'ready' or grown-up or responsible enough, even though I was 29. The reality is that I was, or at least I had to grow up quickly!

DANA:
Becoming a dad is like being born again. You give up so much of what you once were and, like it or not, you are reformed (for the better) by the challenges of being a parent.

Here are the five secrets of success for new dads:

+ Patience: whatever it is, it will pass, and over time things will settle by themselves, or change.
+ Ignorance: of the positive kind – i.e., don't pay too much attention to naughty behaviour in your child and you may well find they stop doing it all by themselves.
+ Distractions: reasoning with a crying baby doesn't work – distracting her just might do the trick.
+ Persistence: some things you just have to keep trying and trying.
+ Sense of humour: never lose it!

These will help you in almost every situation and sometimes you'll need to call on all five at once. One general rule to bear in mind is that you really need to 'lead by example'. Children tend to pick up your mood very quickly – so if you're grumpy they're likely to get grumpy as well. If you greet every setback with a laugh, they'll be much more easygoing.

A WORD FOR SCEPTICS –
IF YOU'RE NOT A NATURAL-BORN DAD

Me? A dad? No way! Fatherhood is something that happens to other people. Not me!

If that's what you're thinking right now and you can't get used to the idea of becoming a dad – relax. Although there is generally pressure from friends and family to charge into your new role immediately and become a natural-born dad, to instantly bond with your baby and transform into Superdad, give yourself some credit and allow the change to happen naturally.

Nature is cunning in the way she prepares us for this new role – mostly on an emotional level. Bonding with a neonate can take a while but it happens eventually, one way or another.

It is a bit weird suddenly to have to deal with a baby when you've never done it before, especially if you've never had younger siblings.

But then, as each day goes by, it gets easier and your interest in and love for the baby grows. You'll find that spending time with your baby is not something you have to do but something you want to do. The rest of life just gets in the way.

Also, the natural male protective instinct generally kicks in and you will want to make sure that your baby is OK. You can find yourself getting very protective, and emotional, on behalf of other kids and their circumstances. Those news stories about kids getting lost or going missing will suddenly take on a whole new significance. That could be your child.

For some dads the bonding process happens very quickly. For others it can take months, but either way it's a quiet transition that can easily happen virtually unnoticed – by you anyway. Others will certainly be aware! Before you know it, you suddenly realise: Hey! I love being a dad!

THE BABIES MADE THEM SUPERDADS!

NATURAL BORN FATHERS

9. Some guys are natural-born fathers and adapt to their new role easily, while others take a little more time to adjust.

CHAPTER 2

PREGNANCY

Now that you're on the path to fatherhood, suddenly the whole world seems to be coming along with you, and you'll notice pregnant women everywhere. You may even find yourself staring at them and trying to work out how far along they are, and whether their boobs were always that big. Don't worry, this is normal. Naturally, you'll notice changes in your partner as her pregnancy progresses. There are fundamental changes going on in both her body and mind and some will affect you more than others. Be prepared. Be very prepared.

There's a lot of detailed information available describing exactly – and to an almost infinite degree of detail – what happens during pregnancy.

We have found that a lot of the information goes far beyond the essentials, or what you really need to know. Unless, of course, the fatherhood experience is having such a profound impact on you that you're thinking about changing career and becoming an obstetrician.

Or maybe you'd like to take up the challenge and see whether you can pronounce all those medical terms correctly. Start with chorionic gonadotropin – if that doesn't put you off, you're on to a winner.

So here is our five-minute version of what happens during pregnancy, and if you want to explore it in greater depth, go to: www.DIYFather.com/pregnancy.

THE THREE TERMS

Pregnancy usually lasts for around 40 weeks and like all good things is split into three parts (like *The Lord of the Rings*, but hopefully with fewer battle scenes). They're called trimesters.

THE FIRST TRIMESTER
(NOUGHT TO THREE MONTHS)

You'll no doubt remember the first five minutes of this very well. But what happens immediately after that satisfying procreative process is that one of your little sperm buddies manages to beat all the competition in the freestyle to fertilise an egg in your partner's womb. This fusion of egg and sperm sets off a whole host of hormonal changes in a woman's body.

The majority of the significant hormonal changes during pregnancy take place during this first trimester, which is why many women experience various symptoms of discomfort, e.g., morning sickness, personality changes, mood swings, tiredness, and so on. These changes can sometimes be minor – the luckiest mums-to-be are the ones who hardly notice that they are pregnant – but sometimes the side-effects will be major. Either way your partner will need significant support and understanding from you. Remember, this period will pass.

In the first few weeks of this process your child is usually referred to as an 'embryo' by health professionals, while towards the end of the first trimester they start calling it a 'foetus'.

Although you might not see any changes in your partner's body, things are happening quickly on the inside. At the end of the first trimester the womb is about the size of a pear with your offspring floating around inside suspended in the amniotic fluid. At week 12 an average foetus measures around 5.5 centimetres (head to bum) and weighs around 15 grams.

Towards the end of the first trimester you can usually get your first baby photo, via an ultrasound scan. (A note of caution: this is a good time to remove all *Alien* DVDs from the house; do not

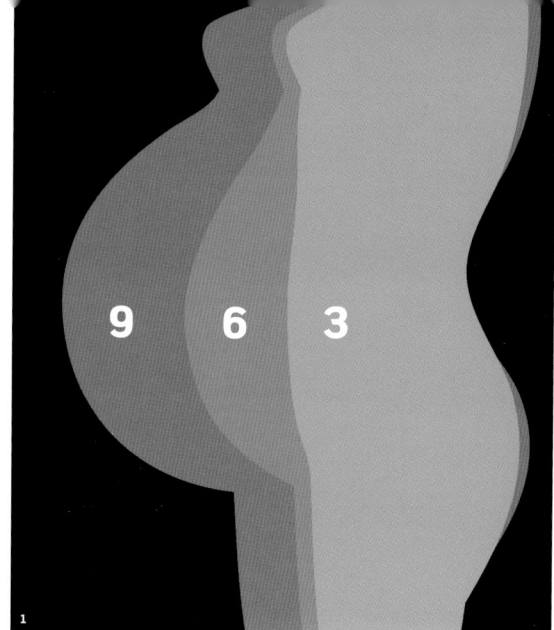

1. The three stages (or 'trimesters') of pregnancy. Remember, it's a baby in there, not an alien.

watch them over the next few months!) It's important that you as the dad-to-be go along to the first scan – this is an extremely exciting and amazing (if slightly surreal) experience. You can say hi to your baby as it appears on the screen, sometimes in surprising detail. Typically you can also ask for a 'nuchal-fold' test to be done, which gives you an indication of the statistical probability of your child being born with Down's syndrome.

THE SECOND TRIMESTER (FOUR TO SIX MONTHS)

The second trimester is often called the golden trimester because it's generally regarded as the period when most women experience the least amount of trouble and the most hormonal bliss. Some women get really horny during the second trimester, so watch out!

Your partner's body has now well and truly switched on to pregnancy mode and, provided there are no complications, everything should go swimmingly. After the initial scans your partner might now be having routine check-ups. There is often a 'big' check-up around about week 20. At this point health professionals check the

development of the baby and make sure all internal organs are OK.

In some cases, an amniocentesis or amniotic-fluid test (where they stick a needle in your partner's belly to extract some amniotic fluid from around the baby) might be suggested. This can provide a further indication about the genetic make-up of your baby, but it's not without its risks; there's a one- to two-per cent risk of losing the baby through amniocentesis testing. Be guided by your GP or other health professionals as to whether this is necessary for you, and don't be afraid to ask questions.

At about month four you might notice the little bump appear and your partner might feel the baby move for the first time. Putting your hand on her belly to share this experience is something really special. It's the first physical 'contact' you'll have with the baby, and brings home the truth in the best possible way: you're going to be a dad!

By week 26 most of your baby's external and internal organs are fully formed and the rest of the pregnancy is now mostly about the baby growing. An average baby measures around 35 centimetres (head to heel) and weighs around 750 grams at the end of the second trimester.

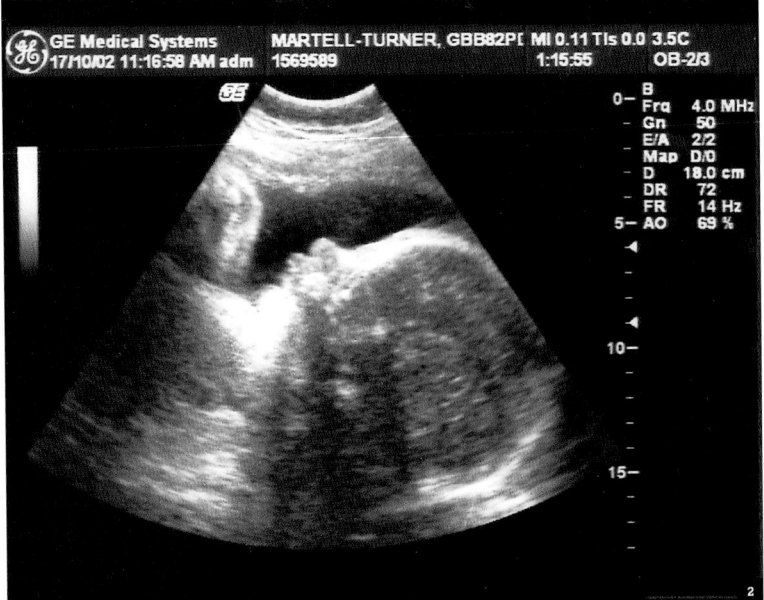

THE THIRD TRIMESTER
(SEVEN TO NINE MONTHS)

In this, the home-straight trimester, it's normally very obvious that your partner is pregnant. The pregnancy will definitely be 'showing' which means the two of you will need to invest in maternity clothes for your partner to wear (if you haven't already). Your partner's belly button might pop out like a turkey timer and you might notice a vertical dark line appearing on her belly (which is all perfectly normal). And she might well start nagging you to paint the baby's room, build a cot, redecorate . . .

This actually isn't nagging so much as an inbuilt nesting instinct. Don't forget, thousands of years ago you were Man the Provider and it would have been your job to do the hunting and gathering. So, naturally, today it's your job to paint the baby's bedroom. Be thankful you don't have to go out and kill wild boar with a club.

Your partner's bump will be getting bigger by the day and she'll feel the presence of the baby in many ways. The sheer size of the baby and resulting physical changes to her body means that things can start to get a bit uncomfortable. At the upper end of the womb there is now significant pressure on the stomach, which can cause digestive problems, such as heartburn. The lower end of the womb puts pressure on the bladder, which explains why you keep having to stop whatever you are doing so she can go to the toilet.

Sleeping beside her might become a little tricky as well, as the bump is always in the way. Your partner's body really has to do double the work now, so tiredness and exhaustion are common during these last few weeks. Your baby will put on quite a lot of weight during the third trimester (up to 300 or 400 grams a week towards the end) and the baby's movement can also be seen from the outside. You can 'touch' your baby's limbs through the skin. (Remember what we said about not watching *Alien* – it's more important now than ever!)

Finally, from about week 35 onwards you are entering the 'drop zone' . . . the baby can come at any time now, although most babies are born between weeks 38 and 42. That's about it in a nutshell – enjoy your pregnancy time!

Call Me Dad!

3

2. A typical second-trimester ultrasound.

3. Your pregnant partner needs full support from you – put your back into it!.

LIVING WITH A PREGNANT WOMAN

As your partner is going through these changes it's important that you offer and provide extra support. Although you're not physically carrying the baby, you are still pregnant as a couple, so you as one half of that equation (soon to be one third) have a major role to play. But before you get to be a Superdad, you can be a Super 'Looker-Afterer' of your partner.

There are all sorts of physical and emotional changes your partner will experience during pregnancy, not all of them obvious to you from the outside. Apart from the bulge, she might look the same as always, but she'll certainly feel different inside.

So you need to man-up and deal with it. You, as the person who 'did this with her' (or later, during the birth, more likely 'to her' . . .), now take on the role of caregiver, looking after the mother of your child. Yes, that's right: caring for and looking after the mother of your child. As the Greek goddess says, 'Just do it'.

Here are the DIYFather top 10 things you can do for your pregnant partner:

+ Offer to give her back rubs or rub her belly, as it grows, with coconut butter or baby oil (which helps prevent stretch marks). Most importantly, though, be interested in the changes in her body.
+ Cook her a nice meal.
+ Remind her often that you think she's beautiful. It's important that she knows you still think she's gorgeous, because she's probably feeling about as attractive as a beached whale.
+ Take photos of her belly, and of her looking radiant as a mum-to-be. Get a professional photographer to take a photo of the two of you together in the last days of the pregnancy.
+ Draw some funny stuff on her belly. Find the Travis music video *Flowers in the Window* on YouTube.
+ Go shopping with her (even if it's just window shopping) and show an interest in baby stuff.
+ Talk about the baby, and come up with a shortlist of names together.
+ Encourage her to do safe exercises by doing them with her and monitoring her technique.
+ Go along to scan appointments with her, and take her somewhere nice for lunch afterwards.
+ Buy her a new maternity dress or bra. This is not a joke – maternity wear in general has come a long way in recent years. Many maternity clothes look really flash or sexy . . . so treat her to something nice! If you want to surprise her, make sure you check the size of her other bras or dresses first.

Call Me Dad!

4. 'I'll save the horse for later.' Be prepared for some funny but powerful food cravings.

5. 'Don't push me!' Mood swings are all part of the deal during pregnancy.

DAD TIP #1:
During the third trimester, if your partner is worried because she hasn't felt the baby move for several hours, give her a glass of very cold water to drink. The baby should move after a few minutes.

DAD TIP #2:
Help your partner to refrain from drinking alcohol by not drinking yourself when you're together. In other words, don't rub it in that she can't drink for a while!

DADS IN THE KNOW
During pregnancy you need to display a bit of extra tolerance for your pregnant partner.

Expectant mums commonly experience:

+ Morning sickness;
+ Mood swings;
+ Food cravings;
+ Tiredness;
+ Leg cramps;
+ Heartburn – acid reflux;
+ Forgetfulness or mental fog;
+ Needing the toilet every five minutes;
+ Uncontrolled shopping for baby things;
+ Constipation and haemorrhoids.

Check out our landing page for tips on how to help your partner through all these and more at www.DIYFather.com/pregnancy.

It's important that you and your partner maintain a healthy lifestyle during pregnancy. The following might be stating the obvious, but it can't be said often enough. You might not be carrying the baby, but it will be so much easier for your partner to give up unhealthy indulgences if you're saying 'no' to them as well.

> **CAROLINE:**
> Try not to take our mood swings personally, and react with compassion even if you don't understand where it is all coming from. Just sit down, listen, make a cup of tea or something. Pretend you're working with nine months of PMT!

Some things should be avoided:

Smoking:
Smoking is not only bad for you, but bad for your baby as well. Smoking during pregnancy reduces the amount of oxygen that the baby receives and increases the risk of miscarriage and bleeding.

Alcohol:
Drinking may cause foetal alcohol syndrome, which can result in your child having a low birth weight, serious ongoing medical problems and behaviour abnormalities.

Recreational drugs:
Taking recreational drugs during pregnancy is linked to many additional health risks for mum and baby.

And these things should be reduced:

Caffeine:
Although the evidence is not conclusive on caffeine and its effects on the baby, you may want to reduce the amount of coffee and tea you drink anyway, just in case.

Drugs and herbal remedies:
Be extra careful about non-prescription drugs or herbal remedies as they may affect the development of your unborn child. If in doubt – don't take them. In general it is advisable to reduce the intake of non-prescription drugs like painkillers, also. ALWAYS read the labels on pharmaceuticals and check for any mention of adverse implications for pregnant women and their babies.

Exposure to chemicals:
Unfortunately, these days it is virtually impossible to altogether avoid exposure to potentially harmful chemicals. But you can alter your eating habits to reduce your exposure to herbicides and pesticides. Be extra careful when handling products that are known to contain dangerous chemicals (paints, wood stains, weedkillers, etc.).

DAD TIP #3:
The good news: during pregnancy your partner's breasts will probably increase in size. You might regard this as really good news (unless they're already huge – in which case this is bad news, but the one below is the 'really bad news'. . .).

DAD TIP #4:
The bad news: sorry, but there's a good chance you won't get to fully enjoy the feel of your partner's new big boobs, as she may find her breasts are pretty sore. Nipples, and the underlying tissue, go through a major transformation to prepare for breastfeeding, so you might not be welcome when you want to touch them.

> **STEF:**
> OK, I know that most people find it really amazing that you can feel the baby move inside your partner's belly, but it just FREAKED ME OUT. It's a really weird feeling to lie in bed all snuggled up with your partner and suddenly you feel the baby move. Especially towards the end when the baby runs out of space and you've got elbows and feet sticking out – how can you not think of all those films featuring creatures inside bodies . . .

In general it's important for you as the virtually pregnant parent to be proactive in keeping it together, to remain calm and in control (remember there are already plenty of emotions and hormones involved in the pregnancy without you losing the plot). To maintain a yin-yang balance, it's important for you to play the rational part.

Don't forget about some of the basics of life at this stage. These can include such things as talking to your partner about renegotiating her workload if she's not coping, planning a holiday, diet and nutrition, and all the other everyday stuff. Take care of the bill payments, and add things to the shopping list as they run out. It's all simple stuff, but the less she has to worry about the better, and she'll appreciate it, as will the new baby.

Remember that although you can't see the baby, it's very much there with you all the time. The physical and emotional states of your partner affect the baby in the womb, so the more comfortable you both are the better for all concerned. Question your partner regularly as to whether she's feeling OK, and help her to get a bit of 'me time' (or 'me and the baby time') whenever possible. You won't have much to spare once the baby has arrived!

> **ERIC:**
> Andrea had a good pregnancy, and carried well, experienced very little morning sickness, put on the recommended weight and tested well during every prenatal check-up. We put it down to a great nutritional intake of high-quality supplements, high in folic acid, vitamin B, bio omega oils, calcium and more of what is needed for optimal health during pregnancy.
>
> However, our unborn child had ideas of her own and turned breech at 37 weeks, and no amount of ancient or modern remedies were going to turn this child around the right way. Ideas of a vaginal birth were becoming a distant dream like my fantasy of catching our baby and cutting the umbilical cord. It was time to prepare for birth by caesarean section.

THE PREGNANT FATHER

Naturally, the attention at this stage is mostly on the woman as the bearer of the unborn child. But as we've mentioned, you are also pregnant, figuratively speaking, and are also affected by this major event.

So you also need to deal with what's happening inside you. Talk to male friends, your dad and other people you trust. Don't be afraid to approach dads you don't know if an opportunity presents itself. We found that some of the best advice we got came from other dads, and as we know from experience, new dads love to share what they've learnt!

PREGNANT-DAD EXERCISE

When you're not looking after your partner, or working, or doing the thousand other things you need to do each day, make sure you take a little bit of time out for yourself for some quiet reflection. This can be difficult and can feel weird to begin with, partly because we males are often action-oriented. But it's important to enjoy some quiet time and wait for thoughts and emotions to come. This won't happen unless you're calm, so open yourself up and go wherever your mind takes you.

AN INSPIRATION FOR DADS WHO SMOKE

If you smoke, right now might be a great time to enrol in a stop-smoking programme. There is a lot of research to support a smoke-free environment for kids and even unborn babies. So if you wonder what you can do for your child while your partner is pregnant – stopping smoking is probably one of the greatest gifts you can give. What better motivation could there be to kick the habit? Think about it.

> **DARIAN:**
> During the pregnancy I used to get random phone calls from my wife to say she'd just seen someone eating something on TV (one time it was cucumber club sandwiches), and that she really needed me to stop at the supermarket to get the necessary ingredients to replicate it.

6

WHERE DO I FIT IN AS A DAD?

Good question, and an important one to mull over. What does your partner want you to do? What's your role at this stage: to be a provider; to look after her; to look after everyone else? Remember that you're part of this pregnancy, too, and you fit in where your partner needs you to fit in. But your strengths are different from hers. So be the 'rock' that keeps everyone firmly on the ground, and don't let yourself be fooled into thinking: 'I'll just wait until the birth and then I'll look after both of them.'

It's a big responsibility to look after a little human life, so get used to taking an interest and start getting in touch with your fatherly side. Best way to do it? Get involved early and at every

6. Small shoes to fill: Take time to reflect on your role as a dad-to-be.

stage – not just when the baby arrives. You may also find it gets a bit lonely as a dad since everything is typically focused on the mum. So convey to your partner (and others perhaps) what is also happening to you. No dad is an island – so don't let yourself become one.

Let everyone who matters know that this is also a big deal for you, and that you, too, are going through some emotional changes. You need an adjustment period to get used to the idea that you are going to be a dad. Yes, you might take a ribbing from your mates, but hey, who's in charge here?

However, not all of your mates will be as fascinated by the details of pregnancy as you are, especially if they're not fathers themselves. For many in this position, listening to a dad-to-be warble on about morning sickness or how cute it was to see his baby on the ultrasound scan just doesn't do it for them. So know your audience if you feel like sharing. It's going to be hard enough to keep relations with your childless friends on the same level after the baby arrives, so go easy on them with baby-related stuff.

THE MEDICAL STUFF – SCREENINGS AND PROCEDURES

How to bring babies into the world in the best possible way is a controversial subject with opinions ranging from 'natural is best' to 'caesarean section is the way to go', and everything in between. Even before the birth there are lots of options as to how your partner can be looked after during pregnancy. You may choose to stick with your GP, find a dedicated midwife or engage an obstetrician. Regardless of which choice you make, there are common checks that you go through to make sure mum and baby are OK. The most common ones are:

ULTRASOUND SCANS
These are like radar for the unborn, where sound waves transmitted through the pregnant woman's tummy bounce off the developing baby to produce images on a screen, which are then printed for you to take away with you. You might have already come across these when other proud

dads-to-be you know have broken the news they were going to have a baby.

And yes, we also think that the initial scans are nearly always strange, if not disturbing, as the baby can look like a king prawn. The practitioner usually tells you how they can see all the baby's organs, but you'll most likely only see weird grey shapes on a grey background.

But it gets better as the baby gets older and more developed. Some of the more modern ultrasound machines are in colour, or even 3D – make sure you ask about that as it is even more fun to play around with these images on screen. Be sure to think about and tell your practitioner beforehand whether or not you want to know your baby's sex. It's not always obvious from the ultrasound, but if you'd definitely rather not know, say so!

DAD TIP #5:
Try and get along to all the screenings, and ask lots of questions. Get your money's worth out of the specialists and don't be afraid to ask for plain-English explanations if they drift off into medical lingo. Also, take a blank CD – you may be able to get a copy of the images.

The initial scan can be a very emotional occasion as this is the first time you and your partner get to see your offspring. Make sure you've got some tissues handy (mostly for yourself, but also for your partner).

Unfortunately, in some cases you may discover that everything is not as it should be. Most practitioners are well aware of this and prepare you for all possibilities. But just in case they don't, take the time to talk about this with your partner in advance of your appointment.

NUCHAL-FOLD TEST
Typically this test is done at 11–14 weeks by a specialist using an ultrasound scan to measure the space in the tissue at the back of the baby's neck (called the nuchal fold). The likelihood of Down's syndrome is assessed based on the baby's overall size, the measurement of the nuchal fold, and the mother's age.

DAD TIP #6:

If your partner doesn't mention the nuchal-fold test herself, ask her about it. Also talk through what you would do if the test came back with your baby having a higher than average risk of Down's syndrome. Again, it's important to have had this conversation before you do the test.

**20-WEEK SCREENING
(DETAILED ANATOMICAL SCAN)**

Usually undertaken at 18–22 weeks, this is a full check-up of baby's health and development at the 'halfway mark' and involves a number of tests. Assuming you decide to go ahead, it is likely to be the first time you get a really good look at your baby (which now looks less like a prawn and more like a human being, albeit with a huge head). If there are any serious problems with the baby's health or development, they will probably show up with this test, so take some extra time out for it. It usually takes 45–90 minutes. Also make sure you fully understand everything the specialists tell you. Never be afraid to ask questions, no matter how dumb this might make you feel.

DAD TIP #7:

Typically, about the time of the 20-week scan is when healthcare professionals can make a reasonable guess at the baby's sex. Usually the practitioner will ask you whether you want to know, but it's a good idea to agree on this first.

BLOOD TESTS

Depending on your healthcare provider or health-monitoring programme during pregnancy, your partner may have to undergo several blood tests. Generally between weeks 24 and 28 there is a glucose test you can request to check for 'gestational diabetes', which is a high blood-sugar condition that some women experience during pregnancy.

DAD TIP #8:

Try to go along to all the blood tests, especially if your partner has a tendency to feel a bit queasy afterwards. Perhaps go out for a quick snack when it's over.

AMNIOCENTESIS

Amniocentesis is the removal of a small quantity of fluid from the amniotic cavity, in other words, the womb. This fluid contains cells shed from the baby's skin. The fluid is sent to a laboratory where these cells are extracted and cultured. It takes two to three weeks for a sufficient number of cells to grow to allow an analysis of the chromosomes. The genetic code revealed can then be tested for abnormalities.

The test is done by inserting a fine needle through your partner's abdomen into the womb with ultrasound guidance. About 10 millilitres of fluid is required for the analysis of the chromosomes. Amniocentesis is a relatively safe procedure, although there is a small risk of miscarriage: figures we have come across range from one in 200 to one in 1600.

Your GP or healthcare professional may suggest an amniocentesis to get clarity on possible risk factors for genetic abnormalities as a result of ultrasound scans. If this procedure is suggested to you, make sure you ask for a counselling session with the practitioner beforehand to ensure you understand what is being done to your partner and how this could affect the baby. Make sure you also discuss the various outcomes of the amniocentesis with your partner.

A WORD ON BRAXTON HICKS

Braxton Hicks refers to the 'false' contractions women experience during the third (and sometimes second) trimester. They are typically thought of as 'training contractions' the body goes through to make sure it's all set for the big event. When your partner is experiencing Braxton Hicks, you need to hang on to the most important rule to remember around women who may or may not be in labour – don't panic . . . or panic later. It's likely the cramping sensation will stop altogether after a few minutes. However, if the contractions persist for a prolonged period (more than an hour) give your midwife or GP a call to double check.

Just in case you were curious, the original Braxton Hicks was not a legendary

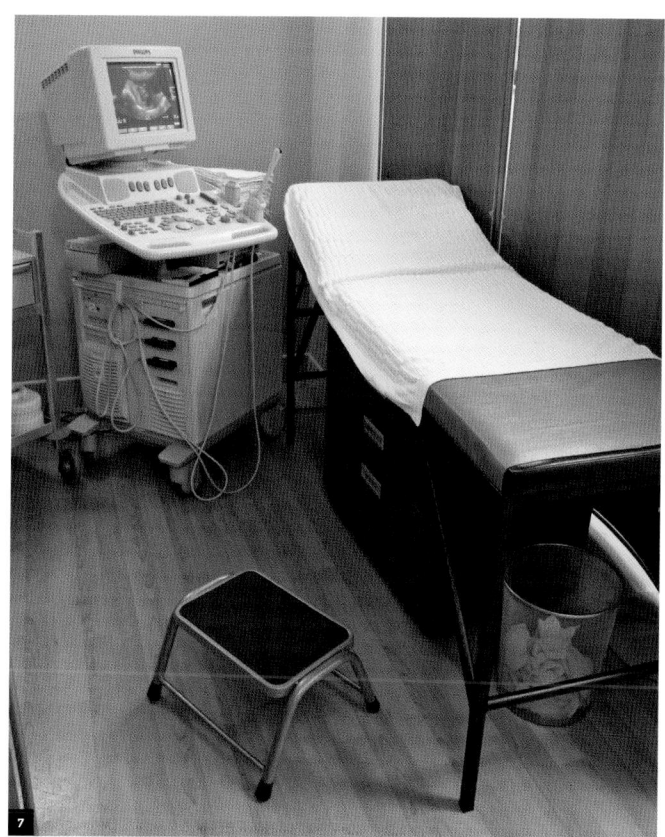

7. You are bound to feel nervous going for a scan, especially if it's the first, but don't let your anxieties deter you from asking questions.

soul singer from the 1950's. Rather, John Braxton Hicks was an English doctor who first described these 'false contractions' during a study of the latter stages of pregnancy in 1872.

A WORD ON MIDWIVES AND OBSTETRICIANS

If you decide to go with a midwife or obstetrician (or some other specialist), make sure you're satisfied they're right for you. Check them out by talking to others who have used them, and also check their professional backgrounds. You might also want to find out their personal opinions about some of the key decisions that need to be made during pregnancy. For example, some health professionals will have a

tendency to push you in a certain direction (putting pressure on you to breastfeed, for example). So ensure your values are in sync from the outset.

Finally – don't be intimidated by all their experience and years of study. Ultimately a lot of what is involved with having a baby is common sense, and you should always challenge the experts if any of their advice seems odd. After all, you and your partner are the parents. Your instincts and personal preferences are just as important as the specialist's professional opinion.

In some cases you may need to fight to get what you want – but also make sure you do your homework. The Internet is great for reading up on medical stuff – just make sure you use trustworthy, reputable sources. In the end, ask yourself what's best for baby.

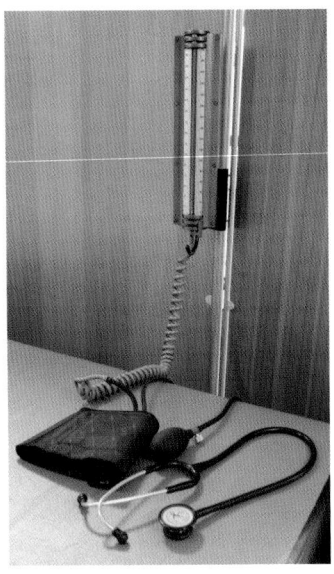
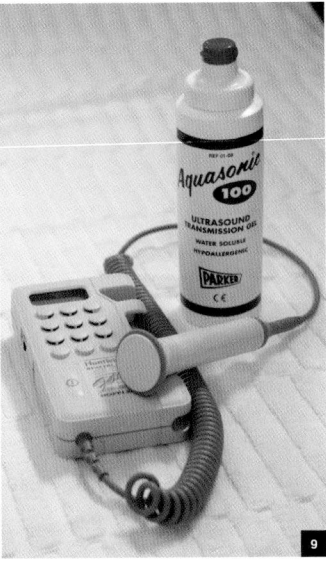

8. Blood pressure readings, taken during the latter two trimesters, are useful indicators of health conditions that may require management.

9. For an ultrasound scan a special gel is smeared over your partner's belly. A probe then traces through the gel, transmitting images to a monitor.

10. Don't forget the importance of you and your partner's relationship as a couple during pregnancy.

PROBLEMS AND RISKS DURING PREGNANCY

For some of us, nature throws in an extra challenge during pregnancy or labour. Sometimes things don't go according to plan and your health professional will tell you that mum or baby have a higher risk of developing . . . (insert unpronounceable medical term here). Unfortunately, many things during pregnancy are down to probability, often including the chances of certain problems showing up. Some risks you can positively influence include your partner stopping smoking, not drinking alcohol, eating well and getting some extra rest. Others you can't do much about, and in some cases you may have to wait until the baby is born to find out whether that unwelcome condition is present or not.

During pregnancy there are several indicators to watch out for – your healthcare professional or obstetrician will point them out to you. Examples include: unexplained vaginal bleeding or discharge, fevers or strong pain. If you or your partner are worried because of any unusual symptom, don't wait around – seek professional help right away.

If you are told about a particular medical condition that your baby or your partner are at an increased risk of, ask your healthcare professional about it. On top of that you can also do some research on it yourself and find out about support organisations in your area. If you have access to the Internet, Google the condition and add your location for contact details of local support organisations, e.g. 'spina bifida' + [the name of your town or city].

STEF:
After we found out Raquel was pregnant, we decided to go with an obstetrician and had our first appointment at week 10. Our obstetrician spent the first 50 minutes of the 90-minute appointment preparing us for what we were about to see. He told us that about one in six babies he checks at this stage has some kind of problem. I was quite shocked at first that the number was so high, but then it was a fantastic relief when we found out everything was OK with our little one. I'm glad he told us about all the potential problems first, though – it sort of means you are going in with low expectations.

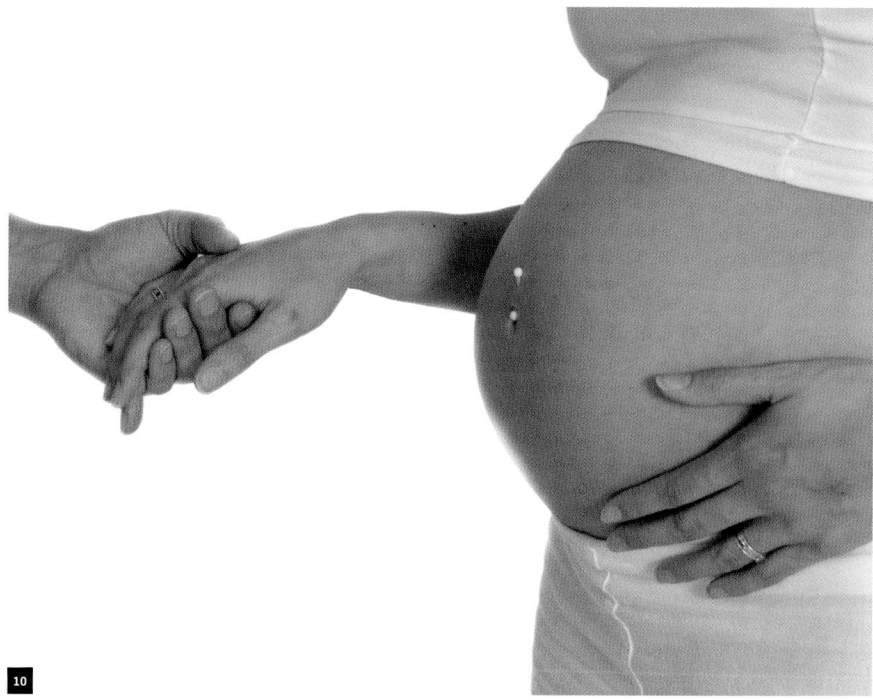

`10`

LET'S TALK ABOUT SEX, BABY

Sex during pregnancy? Of course! Why not? Any time, all the time!

Seriously though, this is important, because guys think about it a lot (according to Freud, every six seconds). But it's also important that your relationship doesn't take a back seat just because the focus is now on the arrival of the newest member of the family.

So sex during pregnancy is fine as long as you are both willing and able, unless of course your doctor says not to for some (good) reason. Don't expect too much though – it depends very much on your partner. Some women have a decreased libido, while others experience an increase.

If you're wondering how you're actually going to manage it, or whether you'll be disturbing the baby, relax. Sex during pregnancy is not usually as difficult as it seems, though it might take a wee while to get used to. And, of course, it might call for a bit of positional creativity on both sides, but that can be fun.

Towards the end of the pregnancy it can get a bit tricky on a practical level to actually have sex, but then again, sex is often cited as one of the ways to bring on labour. So there you go – you might get (doubly) lucky!

SCOTT:
My wife had a terrible pregnancy. When she wasn't just being sick, she was either working and being sick, or she was sleeping and being sick. So basically there wasn't a lot of sex, if any. A good friend of mine (female) who had a three-year-old at the time, suggested waiting until the third trimester. 'Your wife will be horny all the time,' she said. 'Best sex you will ever have.' Hmmm, famous last words. Renee was still 'sick and worse than ever, overweight, sore and pregnant' (her words not mine), and so far from horny.

CHAPTER 3

PREPARING FOR THE BABY

If you haven't already done so in the excitement of it all, then towards the end of the pregnancy is high time to prepare for the baby's arrival. This is a great time for fathers, as you can play to all your strengths in getting things organised – and there's a lot to do. So take the reins and get moving . . . especially if you're in week 38 and haven't yet ticked off any of the topics covered in this chapter!

DECISIONS, DECISIONS . . .

First off, there are a few key matters you should talk through with your partner.

We'll start with the mother of all controversial subjects, and probably the most passionately debated issue in recent (parenting) history: bottle-feeding vs breastfeeding.

BREAST OR FORMULA?

The feeding debate has taken on almost epic proportions, and the arguments on either side are deeply rooted in different parenting philosophies. The intention of this book is not to get involved in the discussion of which is best. You can make that choice yourselves based on your own feelings, circumstances and advice from health professionals and other sources.

However, we do want to encourage you to get support, no matter what your decision might be. Unfortunately, there are many examples of parents – particularly mothers – not receiving full support from friends, family or healthcare professionals because they have decided one way or the other.

Where this debate is concerned, it's important to remember that there is a difference between what science/research suggests, and how this relates to your individual situation.

Most healthcare professionals – GPs, obstetricians, midwives, and so on – tend to go with what the most recent evidence suggests is best. And care organisations often adopt an official line. As it stands, the World Health Organisation (WHO) and many other support and care organisations go with 'breast is best'.

On the other hand, supporters of bottle-feeding will point to the large number of babies who've been reared on formula and have grown up to be healthy individuals just like their breastfed peers.

At a practical level this means that staff and members of care organisations almost certainly have to support the official line of their organisations, regardless of what their personal opinions might be. And we're not saying this is wrong! We would simply like to make a case for supporting all parents – no matter what they decide. This means respecting the values, integrity and individual judgement of mothers and fathers making this decision.

Many people get so caught up in the debate that they forget that it's possible to both breast- and bottle-feed, a course which has a number of benefits, including greater overall flexibility along with the ability for dads to take responsibility for some of the feeding. One thing to bear in mind though is that if you don't breastfeed from the beginning, the mother's milk supply will cease after a few days, and that's pretty much it; no going back.

A note for dads

The formula vs. breast-milk conflict will be evident in many interactions you will have with your doctor, midwife, friends and family. As a father, you are in a perfect position to remain calm and ensure your partner is supported, no matter what. Don't put up with people not fully supporting you or your baby because you have chosen a different option. It's your baby, remember.

But, if it helps your conscience, make an informed decision together after gathering as much information as possible on formula and breastfeeding. Talk to the professionals, and talk to the other professionals – those parents who've already been through the different options and have come out (intact) on the other side.

WHAT'S IN A NAME?

This is another surprisingly controversial decision: choosing the baby's name(s). Let's face it, junior is likely to have to live with whatever names you give him for the rest of his life, so you owe it to him to give this whole thing serious thought.

Having said that, it can be quite tricky to agree on a first name for the baby, because the world is your oyster and the choices are almost infinite (especially now when babies are named after websites, city districts, or fruit and veg).

To pick an example: while a name like 'Apple' sounds really cute for a little baby girl, it will sound somewhat daft if she

1. Bottle-feeding vs. breastfeeding remains a hotly contested debate.

2. I'm not sure we'll get away with 'Skype'
as a name!

Call Me Dad!

ends up as the CEO of a major IT company. Anyway, bear the sanity of your child in mind and decide in her interest rather than on how many 'coolness' points you might score with your friends for having the most outrageous baby name.

> **SCOTT:**
> I think our little girl has to have one of the longest last names in history. My wife kept her family name of Heatherwick when we got married, and my last name is Lancaster, and we are both stubborn control freaks – so guess what we called our little girl? Pyper Jade Lancaster-Heatherwick.

Names go in and out of fashion. Read the most popular names of any given year and check what celebrities called their offspring that year – you might just find a connection.

> **MIKE:**
> I know of a trendy couple who, after having a baby boy back in the late 1970s, couldn't decide what to call him. So they nicknamed him 'Alias' because he would eventually be known as something else. In true hippy fashion they elected to leave the decision to him when he was old enough. So, at the age of 10 he finally decided to call himself . . . Alias.

When it comes to the last name, once again swallow your pride and act in the name (literally) of your baby. These days just about any combination of parents' last names in any order is possible. But think of the practicalities of the name the baby will end up with, both in terms of how it sounds, and how it looks on paper. Also consider what the initials spell!

If it all seems too hard, start a list of favourites (as identified between the two of you) and put it on the fridge. Live with it, and refer back to it regularly, gradually eliminating those names you both decide are unsuitable. This way at least you should end up with a shortlist, and maybe if you're lucky one name will continue to stand out from the rest.

Whatever you do – sleep on your final decision for your baby's name. Write it down a few times and read it back to yourself. If it still sounds good you might be on to a winner. You may want to delay a final decision until you've actually seen your baby. In many cultures it's not uncommon for the baby to go without a name for some weeks.

Finally, think about how your favourite first AND last name combination goes together. There are some unfortunate combinations, such as:

+ Tex Milaeda;
+ Harry Lipp;
+ Neil Down;
+ Rusti Nail;
+ Dick Butkus (Chicago Bears player).

THE NAPPY DRAMA
A slightly less dramatic, but still important, subject is that of dealing with the thousands (yes, this is not a joke) of nappies that your little offspring will fill. There are a number of ways you can go about this and they all have different implications for your finances, the environment and your sanity – or is that sanitation? Remember that a newborn will typically go through six to ten nappies a day, so choose well.

The main choices are:

Disposable nappies
Perhaps the most common and convenient choice on offer. Readily available in every supermarket, disposable nappies are used once and then binned. Depending on your choice of brand, this can either be pretty cheap or quite expensive. Environmentally, however, disposable nappies are the worst option, unless you're willing to pay extra for the eco-friendly disposable variety which are appearing in shops more and more.

Cloth nappies
You can buy these from most baby stores. Typically they are a plain, square piece of cloth, usually white. When they are full, you wash and reuse them. Many areas have a nappy-washing service, supplying

3. Expect to go through at least seven nappies a day.

4. 'Right, now this is precisely how the birth's going to go, honey.' (Yeah, right!)

you with fresh nappies as you hand them the used ones. You will need at least 10 a day and 20–30 in total if you want to wash them yourself. You might need to stock up on some emergency disposables, just in case. Cloth nappies are considered more environmentally friendly and slightly cheaper than disposables. However, there is the inconvenience factor of having to wash them, or get them washed.

Reusable pants with disposable pads
These are a sort of hybrid of the first two. Usually there is a reusable part (like pants) and a disposable part (a towel), and together they make a pretty good nappy. There are many different systems on the market but by and large they follow the same principle. Like a true hybrid, they combine many of the advantages, and unfortunately some of the disadvantages, of both disposables and reusable cloth nappies.

It's a good idea to speak to other new parents about what they use. Ask them about the pros and cons, and spend some time with them when they are changing their baby to find out what it's like.

The other thing to remember about nappies is that, while they do a reasonably good job of containing your baby's pee and

poo, you will frequently experience leaks. That's why you always need more baby clothes than you think.

BIRTH PLAN ANYONE?
This is an interesting concept often talked about in baby books and preparation courses, so we thought it was worth including here, too. The idea is to explore the various options with a view to deciding how, in an ideal world, both of you (but mostly your partner, of course) want to bring your baby into the world.

Birth plans typically include:

+ Who you want to have around during labour. Amazingly, people you'd really rather not have there sometimes try to muscle their way in at the last moment. It's your job, Dad, to be a good gatekeeper and ensure Great Aunt Bertha is barred from entering the delivery suite – if that's what your partner wants.
+ Where you want to give birth, e.g., at home, at the bottom of the garden, or in a hospital.
+ What position or technique you want to use, e.g., water birth.
+ Pain-relief options: epidural, gas,

Call Me Dad!

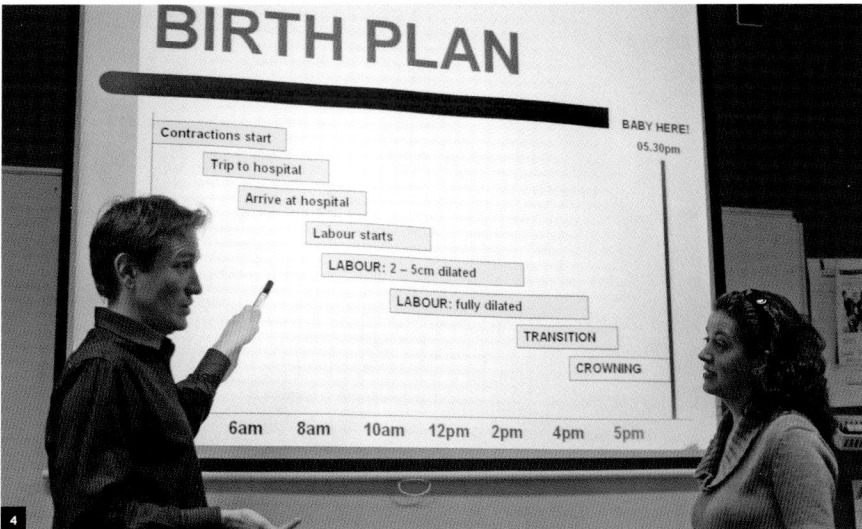

acupuncture, hypnosis, breathing techniques, etc.

+ What to do with the placenta.
+ The level of involvement you want from medical staff or other support people.

Your birth plan may also involve opting for an elective caesarean section, in which case you may be subject to comments like, 'Too posh to push, eh?' Just smile and wave, like the celebrities.

Any birth plan is going to be somewhat theoretical because in reality it absolutely depends on the condition of mum and baby at the time. But it's still good to find out about the various options and discuss them with your partner.

Be prepared to deviate from or even disregard your birth plan if need be. If there are any complications whatsoever, your obstetrician or midwife will take over and make the best decisions based on ensuring the birth proceeds smoothly.

A note for dads

Make sure you are involved in finding out about options for giving birth. Educate yourselves about the advantages and disadvantages of each. This is important because sometimes you may have to make

a quick decision about how to proceed when there is more than one option available.

In such circumstances medical staff will explain the consequences of each course of action to you, and give you some advice, but it's easier if you already know what the main options are and their implications.

> **DOMINIC:**
> The birth plan – perhaps it can be best described as the medical system's attempt to give parents, and especially mothers, the illusion of choice. When things don't go to plan during labour your birth plan is the first thing that goes out the window, which is probably just as well as the safety of the mother and baby needs to come first at that point.

STAY-AT-HOME DADS AND FULL-TIME MUMS

Here's another big issue to consider: who will look after the baby? The best time to sort this out is well before the baby arrives.

Looking after a baby is pretty much a round-the-clock job at the beginning, and you need to have a plan for who's going to do what and when. Usually there's a range of options and some even come with government support! Paternal leave is

becoming more common in some countries now, so check out all the support that your employer, government and healthcare system is able to offer.

The first thing to consider is whether one or both of you will look after the baby during the daytime, or whether you'll get someone else to do it. If you want to call on others to look after your child, you will need to check the availability and suitability of the various options (hiring a nanny, calling on family members, care centres, and so on).

Typically, your baby needs to be at least six weeks or, in some cases, three months old before you can use care centres, but if you are considering this, you will most likely need to book well in advance. And

for popular neighbourhoods, this means straight after conception!

If you've decided to look after the baby yourselves, make sure you understand what's involved and how you will organise your lives. Looking after a baby takes up a surprising amount of time and energy and can be difficult to combine with other activities. Spend some time with couples who have recently had a baby and you will learn a lot in a short time.

If you decide to be a SAHD (stay-at-home dad), great, but make sure you skill up on everything that needs to be done for the baby and around the house. Prepare as much as you can, as time will be precious (i.e., non-existent) once the baby arrives.

SCOTT (THOUGHTS FROM A REAL SAHD):

OK, so you have either decided (or been told) that you are going to be a SAHD. I thought this stood for sad or sudden, or something, and that the person who made up the acronym was dyslexic.

But this is going to be one of the best times of your life, believe me! Now you get to be moody, go off at your partner when they come home to a messy house with no dinner prepared, you get to have coffees with the mothers' groups, and you also get to share the best years of your child's life (until they get to the attitude stage – and then it's over to you, Supermum).

It's the best thing I have ever done. I now know my little girl inside out, and she knows me, too. And we also do lots together, and as such it's a challenge every day what to do next. The thing is, you know how to look after your baby and that brings 'street cred' with other dads who unfortunately have to work, and don't know as much.

Make sure you get into the routine as quickly as possible; do short stints by yourself and then full days. Have your days planned out well, and if you have to go into town think about your child's eating and sleeping regimes and how they'll work for both of you.

Every day I plan my work, etc., around Pyper; sometimes it's frustrating but usually it's a lot of fun when it comes down to it. Make sure you have an array of songs, and also books. What do you mean you can't sing?

5. All in a day's work for a stay-at-home-dad.

TOP (BABY) GEAR – WHAT TO BUY

We've heard many a sob story from expectant dads who have had to sell the sports car or the motorbike. The old toys had to go in favour of the baby-friendly variety. Simple.

Not as simple as you might think. Believe it or not, buying sensible stuff for babies is challenging. It's important to get organised before the baby arrives, as you won't have much time to make well-considered purchases later when you discover you're short of something you really need. Chances are you'll rush out and buy the first thing you see – which may be over-priced or impractical (and possibly both).

Buying for baby will introduce you to a whole new dimension of shopping. The baby-oriented retailers and products are out there, waiting to exploit your innocence and your highly emotional state. The result? You end up buying lots of crap that's either totally impractical, unsuitable, detrimental to the environment (and your wallet), or just utterly irrelevant. Fear not though, because we've compiled a list of must-haves in this chapter, and we'll tell you what not to buy in the next one.

SCOTT:

We already had a sensible car before getting pregnant so that was lucky for us, especially seeing as my wife traditionally over-packs whenever we go on holiday. She now packs Pyper's bag, too, so when we went away for a weekend, when Pyper was around three months old, holy shit! We had everything, and I mean everything: the exersaucer (a round play gym that babies sit in), the stroller plus accessories, the capsule, the travel cot, her bag, the milk machine . . . and this didn't include any of our clothes. It's lucky we had a station wagon, but I have to admit that was more a case of good luck than good management.

So you might want to take a critical look at your current vehicle and decide whether it needs replacing with something more practical.

6. Don't be fooled by
cute but impractical
clothes.

Check out the following list before you go on a shopping spree:

CLOTHES

Buying clothing for a new baby was traditionally the sole domain of mothers, expectant mothers or any female with a sniff of an impending arrival. Fortunately for the baby, in our opinion, the reality is quite different these days.

When it comes to buying baby clothes you might as well take the practical male approach because you will end up with a lot of the other type of clothes anyway: the ones that are impractical, expensive and possibly toxic, but make the baby look 'so cute'. (You'll hear that phrase a lot, by the way.) So don't leave the buying of baby clothes completely up to your partner or the other females in the family – get stuck in there!

It isn't actually necessary to buy new clothes either, you know. Babies outgrow clothing so quickly – you're sure to find that your friends and relatives with kids will have plenty of barely worn items that they will be only too happy to pass on to you. Don't be afraid to ask.

On that note, chances are your income will be taking a big drop with only one of you working, so if you can't afford new clothes, don't worry – there are plenty of second-hand baby clothes available from online auction sites. Let's face it, your baby is unlikely to know what he's wearing, and he certainly won't know how to use a mirror yet. Obviously, you'll want to give pre-loved clothes a really good wash before baby wears them for the first time, but no one but the most fashion-conscious will pick they aren't new.

Fashion aside, clothing for the baby is really important. The right kind of clothes can make all the difference between sailing through nocturnal dramas with ease, or wanting to rip your own head off at 4 am.

DAD TIP #9:

Cut off the labels of your baby clothes. Even with soft fabric especially designed for newborns, labels can be itchy or hard and may irritate your baby's skin.

The first thing to look for when shopping for baby clothes is the size. Typically you'll find most clothes are marked according to the following table:

00000	premature
0000	newborn
000	0–3 months
00	3–6 months
0	9–12 months
1	1 year
2	2 years

Babies' clothes vary a lot though (as do babies), as the sizes are approximate and can differ from garment to garment. Some manufacturers include measurements and equivalent age ratios for extra guidance, which is really helpful. But not all of them do, so have some fun getting to know your baby's body measurements – most importantly, the length from head to heel, and head circumference. ·

Now that you've got an idea about sizes you need to find your way through the maze of different baby-garment styles, including all the different opening and closing mechanisms out there (buttons, tied-downs, Velcro, laces, zips, etc.).

Before you buy, take a moment to do the mental dressing test Think of a baby vigorously waving her arms and legs and try to imagine you are dressing her in the item of clothing you're holding in your hands. Tricky? Then, don't buy it!

Even better, if you have convenient access to a baby, try the clothes on them (if it's allowed) before you commit to buying.

Basically, you need clothes that are practical and allow easy access to key body parts (mainly the head and the bum).

Talking softly to your baby while putting on her clothes and describing to her what you're doing can help reduce her wriggling. She might not know what you're saying, but she'll know something interesting is going on: 'Let's put this arm through this sleeve. Yes! Good girl! Can you put the other arm through? Oops! Let's have another go.' It might seem an embarrassing thing to do . . . or you might just find yourself doing it naturally.

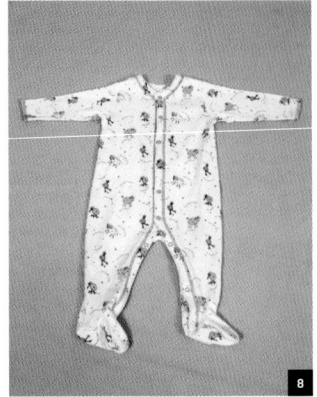

In a nutshell:

+ Buy clothes that are easy to put on and take off.
+ Look for simple fasteners, such as domes or Velcro. Avoid buttons.
+ White clothes are great – yeah right! Only if you like washing 24 hours a day!
+ Choose clothes that you can put on and take off without having to get them over your baby's head, i.e., they open at the back or side.
+ Go for clothes that stretch easily and have wide openings for arms and legs.

What you'll need – the minimum – immediately after the birth:

+ Lots of singlets/onesies (basically an undergarment that you put on as the first layer). You can never have enough of these, but you need at least five, and preferably more. Choose a variety; some long-sleeved, some short-sleeved.
+ Stretch-and-grows – make sure you have at least two.
+ T-shirts.
+ Trousers – some come with 'socks' attached.
+ Swaddling clothes – i.e., wraps. These are always good to have in the nappy bag, as they can be used to cover floors for little people to play on.
+ Lots of singlets, cardigans, all-in-ones (with long arms and legs) and booties, all

of which are readily available.
+ Nighties/pjs – ideally with inbuilt mittens and socks.
+ A sleep sack – babies tend to uncover themselves so if it's a bit cold in the room, a sleep sack is your best option to ensure they are covered for the whole night.
+ Easy-fit hats and socks.

Note: Wash new clothes before use to get rid of any starch or chemicals that might cause skin irritation. This will also help soften the clothes prior to use and give you an idea of the actual size, which will mean that in some cases they are now too small.

> **MATT:**
> We've been given some clothes that we thought were pretty ugly, that's for sure. But then something funny happens – you run out of all the cute clothes and you have to put your kid in the ugly clothes. And when you do, you step back and go, 'Well, hell, that's actually pretty cute.'

DAD TIP #10:
Take extra care when using clothes with lots of Velcro straps as they can sometimes irritate babies' skin. They shouldn't be anywhere where they can rub against your child's skin.

Call Me Dad!

7. Sleeves with fold-over mittens are great for keeping your baby from scratching herself.

8. Buy at least two handy stretch-and-grows.

9. Sleep sacks stop your child from kicking off the blankets and getting cold.

10. Onesies/singlets are perfect as the first layer of clothing.

11. Kimono suits are ultra easy to put on and take off.

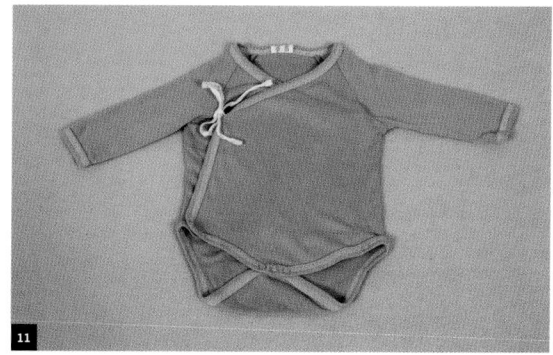

12. Preparing the nursery: time to put your DIY hat on.

THE NURSERY

The most exciting time to decorate the nursery is before the baby arrives. Before you decide on which of the rooms previously known as 'my room' will become the nursery, familiarise yourself with what the room will need.

Here's a brief overview of the most likely things you'll need:

+ A cot – they tend to be bigger than you think.
+ A changing table, ideally with some storage space underneath or a chest of drawers/changing table combination.
+ A feeding chair.
+ A large bucket/nappy disposal device for those nappy emergencies.
+ Some newborn-friendly toys.
+ Separate bassinette or Moses basket for the first few weeks.

For the first six weeks or so you may want to use a Moses basket or bassinette for the baby to sleep in. Newborns tend to be tiny and yours may not like to be put to sleep in a comparatively huge cot. If you want to use swaddling for the night, it may be easier to use a basket or bassinette. You can also put the Moses basket inside the cot – this means the baby is higher up (easier to take out and put in). They both come in really handy for transporting the baby as well – especially the Moses basket, as you can carry your baby everywhere. Great for visiting friends and family. You can switch to the cot when your baby is too big for the basket/bassinette.

DAD TIP #11:
If you are using a Moses basket or bassinette, use a pillowcase as an undersheet, with the opening at the foot end. No need to buy separate sheets for the basket/bassinette, particularly as babies can only sleep in them for a couple of months before they need to move to a cot.

If you have a cot and wish to use it from day one, you may want to adjust it so that the bottom of the cot is in the upper position (there are usually two positions).

Call Me Dad!

This means the baby is higher up and it is easier to put her down in the cot (your back will be grateful). Since babies don't move much at the beginning, there is no danger in their being higher up. When they start crawling and pulling themselves up on the sides, you need to readjust the cot to the lower position.

DAD TIP #12:
Get two mattress protectors. These are typically watertight or very absorbent and go under the sheet. You will almost certainly experience a leak at some point. If you have a spare, you simply change the protector and the sheet and you're good to go. It's much messier when you have to deal with a wet mattress . . .

A quick word on toys you can use from the start. This is a personal thing, of course, but babies don't really need 25 cuddly toys and 10 battery-operated devices that make all sorts of noises or operate elaborate mobiles. Chances are they will have one or two favourites and the rest won't get a look in! Definitely stay away from cuddly toys that have long-haired fur or are overly fluffy. There is some evidence that inhaling small fibres from these toys can cause breathing difficulties for newborns.

A few desirable characteristics of toys for newborns:

+ Durable.
+ No small removable parts.
+ Colourful or interesting geometric shapes.
+ Non-toxic, including non-toxic paints. Check if toys have been treated with chemicals, e.g., to make them water resistant.
+ Easy to clean.

Go especially easy on putting toys inside the cot. In the first few months babies won't be able to do anything with the toys, and in extreme cases some of them may represent a choking hazard. There's definitely a case for less is more when it comes to toys in the cot.

SCOTT:
It was a killer on my back, but I just used a spare bed instead of a changing table. I thought: 'Where the heck are we going to put such a large piece of furniture?'

Be realistic about places to change your baby, but at the end of the day be careful to ensure whatever you use is safe.

BABY HYGIENE
Baby hygiene generally consists of a number of routine tasks you have to take care of until your baby can do them for herself. These include:

+ Cleaning after a nappy change;
+ Quick washes (face/hands/feet);
+ Bathing.

At this stage, the last of these is the most relevant. Have a think about where you are going to bathe your baby. For the first few months you won't need to be too worried about making a mess as he'll keep relatively still, and you will have a firm grip on him at all times. Remember: babies can drown in only a few centimetres of water. The obvious place is the bathroom, but as you'll probably want to use a baby bath you can also make use of anywhere in the house. Baby baths are a great investment – they are small, easy-to-use and give you extra flexibility for bathing your baby. You can use them until your baby is at least a year old.

As well as a baby bath you will need the following hygiene accessories:

+ A change mat (goes on top of a changing table or any other surface you want to use for changing the baby). This is highly recommended as there is nothing less inspiring than baby poo on your bed or sofa.
+ A good body lotion suitable for newborns – olive oil is excellent, too.
+ Nappy-rash cream or powder.
+ Baby-friendly soap and shampoo.
+ Lots of baby wipes and cloths.
+ A soft hairbrush.
+ Hand sanitiser (for you).

CAR SEATS

Car seats generally come in three basic versions: capsules, fixed seats and booster seats. There are now many legislative requirements in place for car seats for children. Given our unregulated global economy, make sure you check that imported models are legal and safe. Remember too that booster seats are generally not suitable for newborns and babies younger than 18 months.

Capsules

You can use these for about the first six months (or up to a certain weight – e.g., nine kilograms). Capsules are strapped in, using seatbelts. Typically for the first few months your baby will be in a rear-facing position in the car. The most practical thing about a capsule is that you can carry your baby around in it when you leave the car. She can even sleep in it for a while, though longer than a couple of hours is not recommended.

Fixed car seats

These are usually mounted with a special hook (Tether Anchor) that clips into a safety bolt at the back of the car. Once properly installed, it takes a little while to get them out of the car.

Fixed car seats are not really suitable for carrying your baby. However, they offer superior safety to capsules – and as such are essential if you are planning to do lots of car travel with baby on board. Some fixed seats can be used from day one up until 24 or even 36 months (depending on the model). They typically have specific functions to accommodate both the front-facing and rear-facing positions, but you might need a degree in engineering to install one of these contraptions in your car. On a serious note – you may want to have the installation checked at your local car dealer before you start using it. Some will do this as a complimentary service.

Booster seats

These can only be used from when your baby is at least 18 months old and can sit up properly for long periods. Booster seats are usually front facing and strapped in using seatbelts, but offer good safety features for longer journeys.

13. A good car-seat is essential – if buying an import, make sure it meets local safety regulations.

14. Now I've got an idea how mummy felt with you in her tummy.

DAD TIP #13:

Before you go and buy a car seat, check with your local baby store or care organisation. Many of them have car-seat/capsule hire schemes. This is very useful for the first year; as you can use a hired capsule until your baby grows out of it, and then buy a fixed car seat which will keep you sorted for a while.

OTHER PRACTICAL ACCESSORIES

Nappy disposal

An industrial-sized waste container is an absolute must for your used disposable nappies. You will need to arrange with the local council to have a special replacement bin left at your place each day. OK, all joking aside, you will probably find a large nappy bucket useful. A baby initially goes through six to ten nappies a day (which are heavy and smelly), so your ordinary rubbish bins may not cope.

Front packs

Front packs are great during the early months when you just want to go for a short walk. You will probably need two people to do it up safely, but once it's on your baby is generally tucked in nicely. Most babies love the feeling of being close to you, hearing your heartbeat and feeling your body heat. Until your baby can support his own head, put him in facing the person carrying him. There is usually a support pad that goes behind his neck. After a few months, and when he is ready, you can put him in the other way and he can watch where you are going (and if he's a genius he'll give you directions).

Note: Backpacks for babies are also available, but these are generally not recommended for use until your baby is at least 9–12 months old.

Bottles and food containers

You will need lots of these – even if your partner is breastfeeding. There are lots of models available but in the end there are only minor differences. Almost all bottles and food containers these days are made of plastic and both come in all shapes, sizes and colours.

DAD TIP #14:

Try different teats or even bottles, as the teat shape and flow can make a big difference to how well your baby feeds depending on the shape and size of your baby's mouth. Fortunately most bottles are not that expensive, so you can try different types and brands. Some brands even offer different teat shapes or different materials, such as silicon or latex. If you are worried about chemicals leaching from plastic bottles into the milk or formula, use glass bottles.

Airtight containers are typically used when your baby starts eating solids, but they can also be handy earlier to store formula or teething rusks. Make sure they are easy to clean and are microwave and dishwasher safe.

Breast pumps

Though not absolutely essential, breast pumps are another great invention to make breastfeeding easier. Breast pumps are used to express milk for later use. You can keep breast milk in the fridge for up to 24 hours or freeze it for up to a month. Most breast pumps fit with a particular model or system of bottles, and some of them are even automated. Some shops or healthcare organisations have them for hire – so, once again, it will pay to check before you buy.

Other situations when your partner might decide to try a breast pump:

+ For sore nipples. Expressing milk can be easier on the nipples than your baby sucking them.
+ To find out exactly how much your baby is drinking. Your midwife may ask your partner to express into a bottle with measurements marked.
+ Feeding in public. If your partner is not comfortable with this but you want to stick with breastfeeding, expressing can offer the solution.
+ You want a piece of the feeding action, meaning you want to feed the baby and perhaps, more importantly, your partner needs a rest from it.

DAD TIP #15:

When heating expressed breast milk, don't use the microwave. Although microwaves are very convenient and good to have around when you have a baby, they have been known to kill the nutritional value of breast milk. Instead, place the bottle of breast milk in a pot of hot water to warm gently. Make sure the temperature is right before you give it to the baby.

Bags

A large-volume baby bag is a wise investment because it can hold a change of clothes, formula, wipes, spoons, sunscreen, nappies, change mat, toys, cold bottle, hot bottle in thermo bag, a hammer . . . the list goes on! There's no such thing as a baby bag that's too big. You'll see.

DAD TIP #16:

'Sunlight is the best disinfectant' may be something you heard your grandmother say, and it's still true today. Hang cloth nappies to dry in the sun whenever possible. Apart from the disinfecting qualities of the sunlight, the breeze will help keep them smelling clean and fresh.

> **SCOTT:**
> We have a 'Sangenic' for the dirty nappies and it's great. It takes all the smell out of the room. Basically, a Sangenic is a rectangular bucket with a double lid. Inside is a scented plastic bag into which the soiled nappy goes. You push this down, it falls into the bottom of the bucket, and you turn a lever which seals off the nappy in the bucket.

15.The baby bag complete with essentials: Never leave home without it.

16. If you're going out for longer than a couple of hours, you will want to fill the baby bag with spare clothing and various other necessities.

17. I'm all set, Dad. Let's get out of here!

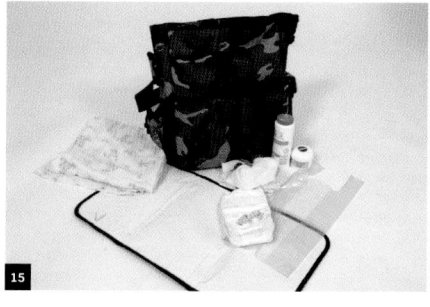

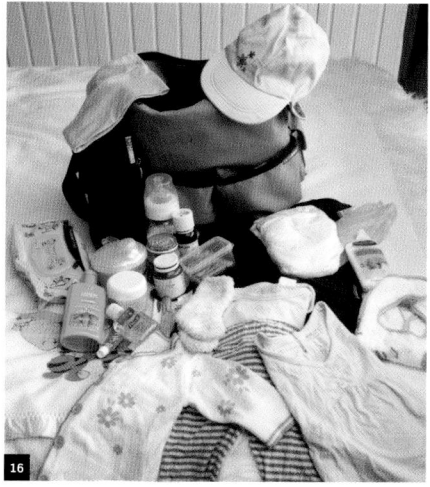

STROLLERS, PRAMS AND BUGGIES

The mode of transport you choose for your child when you're all ready to face the big wide world comes down to two things: practicality and cost. There's a huge range of strollers and buggies on the market, so doing some research in advance can save you both money and disappointment. If you are confused about strollers, prams and buggies, check the DIYFather website: www.DIYFather.com

So, where to start? Well, you need baby transport that's fit for a newborn. For the first three months you'll need a stroller or buggy that has a 'lie-flat' option, where the main compartment can be lowered into a fully horizontal position enabling baby to lie down. Newborns need to lie flat most of the time to make sure their spines can stretch and assume their normal shape.

Important: Most manufacturers suggest that you shouldn't leave a baby in a stroller or buggy for more than two hours at a time. So if you are going for a long walk, make sure you take her out now and then. Top-end buggies can be expensive but hey, you might want to compensate for that sports car you had to sell and buy a stylish stroller instead! As far as we know, they don't sell strollers with spoilers or alloy mags yet, but you could always install under-body neon lighting . . .

OK, let's get real about strollers and buggies. Consider how often you're going to use it. Do you travel a lot? Are you planning on running with it, or taking the baby for cross-country walks? There's lots to consider and it can be a bit like buying a car (and nearly as expensive) – you know which one you'd really like, but is it practical?

18

Call Me Dad!

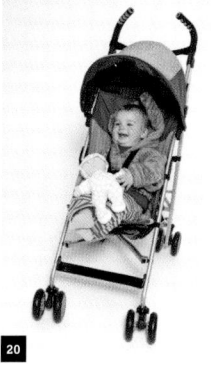

18. Buggy.
19. Buggy with rain cover.
20. Stroller.
21. Pram.

Important things to check when buying a stroller:

+ Are the brakes easy to operate?
+ Does it comply with the appropriate safety ratings and standards?
+ What are the different positions for the baby to sit or lie in, and is it easy to switch between them?
+ How heavy is it?
+ What is it primarily designed for – inner city, jogging, cross-country, etc.?
+ How easy will it be to pack down with an upset baby in one arm and a huge queue of people behind you waiting to get on the bus . . . ?
+ How big is it when collapsed and will it fit into the boot of your car or wagon?
+ How much storage space has it got?
+ How adaptable is it to different situations or people pushing it?

As ridiculous as it sounds, you may find you will need both a stroller and a buggy. Buggies are usually a lot cheaper and pack down more easily. They're quite light and you can easily take them on a plane, so are ideal for travelling. With a stroller, on the other hand, you have the option of lying your baby down or sitting him up in it. For most stroller and buggy models your baby needs to be at least three months old. Until then you'll most likely carry the baby around in the car-seat capsule.

One thing's for sure, you are firmly on man territory when it comes to buying a stroller. So choose a good one and don't let yourself get bullied into one that simply looks flash.

When in doubt, the lighter and less complex, the better. One of early parenthood's biggest time and effort wasters is getting the damn things in and out of the car.

By the way, if you've just bought a stroller or buggy and you think you're done – think again. The whole process really is like buying a car – because now you'll need accessories. There are a range of things you'll need such as a sun cover, rain cover, tow bar (just kidding). Unless of course the model you bought came 'fully loaded'. Make sure all accessories are right for your model and actually fit. Surprisingly, not all manufacturers provide accessories – so you may have to buy generic ones.

DAD TIP #17:
See if you can collapse the stroller/buggy using only one hand. When you're on your own and you've got baby in one arm, you have only one free hand. There are models which can be manipulated quite easily while still holding the baby.

ABOUT THAT SPORTS CAR . . .

Unfortunately the stereotype is true: with a baby, you do need a sedan or station wagon.

Although babies are comparatively small, you are just not going to be able to fit one into your sports car. He – and especially all his paraphernalia – will take up some serious room, not just for his own comfort but also for safety.

To start with, the baby must have a car seat, and no, that's not optional: you cannot travel safely or legally with a baby in a car unless they are appropriately secured.

Beyond his personal transport issues, you'll also have to take his buggy or stroller. Carrying him all the time is not an option, pleasant though it is to begin with, because sooner or later you'll get tired or the baby will get fed up and just wants to lie down. So you will also need room for his buggy, pram or stroller in the car.

Finally there's the all-important baby bag, bulging with nappies, changing mat, bottles and the multiple tools needed to change, feed and entertain your baby.

Now that you have either placed a 'For Sale' sign in the window of your sports car or covered it with a tarp after promising it you won't abandon it for too long, you need to consider what sort of car will suit your newly expanded family of two plus one (or more).

Things to consider:

+ Rear seats: bench seats are more practical than formed seats for two people in the back.
+ Car-seat anchor points: most sedans have anchor points near where the rear speakers are. Vans will usually have them on the ceiling, and some other vehicles might have them on the floor behind the seat where the car seat is to be installed.

Anchor points, like the approved baby seat itself, are not optional. They are really important to prevent your baby from becoming a projectile in a crash.

+ Boot space is very important, which is why many people choose a station wagon, SUV, people mover, van or 4×4. Apart from needing to fit the stroller, if you're thinking of going grocery shopping you'll need space for the groceries. Also, nappies don't come in small bags! Then there are the long trips, when you'll need to include you and your partner's luggage plus a portable cot. It's enough to warrant a small trailer, so you might want to look at whether the vehicle can take a roof rack or roof storage unit (comes in handy, especially for sports gear).
+ Good-sized rear doors: you need to be able to get the baby in and out of the car as easily as possible, another reason why people may go with SUVs because you don't need to bend down quite as much.
+ Seats: how many do you need? If you think you're going to need a seven-seater car, but won't use all seven seats too often, choose a vehicle where the two rear extra seats can fold down.

WHAT NOT TO BUY

Like those programmes on TV that tell you what not to wear, we think it's important to provide some advice on what not to buy.

This is the stuff nobody writes about, so we've taken it upon ourselves to be the educators. The reason for not buying generally falls into two categories: either you simply don't need it, or it's only marginally useful and there are much better options available.

Once you realise your friends are going to give you baby gifts that they like but which are completely impractical for your baby (like battery-operated pythons that trap blowflies), you will understand why we strongly advise that you refrain from buying anything that falls into the categories on p. 62.

22. The kid may be small but she sure comes with a lot of baggage!

DO NOT under any circumstances buy any of the following:

+ Dresses for newborns – they don't get used, are impossible to put on and your little girl will grow out of them in 10 minutes.
+ Jackets for newborns – especially suede or denim as they are too rigid and difficult to get on.
+ Shoes for newborns, especially designer brands which, apart from costing a fortune, are useless considering babies can't walk until they are at least seven months old! Some infant shoes can even impair the growth of your baby's feet.
+ Mittens for newborns – unless you buy them three sizes too big and you can tape them to your baby. Babies generally dislike them – you just watch!
  Note: you do need to find a solution for cold weather though – try proper gloves (long ones that go up over the wrist); they might last a few minutes.
+ Any battery-operated toy designed for newborns – they don't understand them and they spend most of their time sleeping or feeding anyway.

You probably won't need about 90 per cent of what's given to you by friends and colleagues, though that percentage should decrease slightly if you have friends who already have kids.

This isn't as bad as it seems and has to be considered in context. Those who are parents themselves are just doing some thoughtful and sensible recycling. The fact is they might be giving you useless things they were given themselves and have been waiting for an opportunity to offload.

DAD TIP #18:
Keep unwanted items intact in case you can return and swap them for something that you actually need. Point out to your friends that exchange vouchers are a really good idea. If a relative from overseas sends you something useless or impractical, pop it on baby, take a photo, and email them the photo as proof of use. Then discard the item.

DANA:
Top things to give to a mate who tells you they are going to be a dad:
1. A light sabre (yes, I'm a *Star Wars* geek).
2. A promise to be available to support them on this new journey.

What you will be given (whether you asked for it or not):

+ Every possible and impossible cuddly toy known to mankind.
+ Old knitted garments, usually made by friends or relatives and possibly for some other baby (or for you when you were a newborn). You will be expected to regard these as treasures for your own baby. Obviously, if they're handed down as precious heirlooms, but are downright ugly or musty, you'll need a lot of tact.
+ Tonnes of 0000-sized clothes, socks, mittens and shoes. Remember, your baby is growing like a watered and fertilised flower every day, therefore 0000 might last you for, oh, a week.

PREPARATIONS

Until now, you and your partner have been able to enjoy life and your home with nothing more demanding on your mind than mortgage payments and grocery shopping. You've had the luxury of having only yourselves to think about.

But soon – very soon – you'll be introducing a new person to your lives, a little person who will be absolutely and totally dependent on you for her health, welfare and happiness. This will not only be the biggest responsibility you've ever had to face, but also the event that transforms you from a couple into a family and turns your house into a home. So it's time to do some serious thinking about what needs to be done ahead of time.

DAD TIP #19:
A very useful thing to do in the weeks before your due date is to prepare some food and freeze it. Prepare some healthy dishes – don't just stock up on frozen pizzas or microwave meals.

Call Me Dad!

DAD TIP #20:

Organise help for the first few days after the birth (ask family or close friends if they'd mind staying with you for a while). It really helps to have an extra pair of hands to help with cooking, cleaning and looking after the baby, particularly in the first few days. That way taking care of the baby feels less like you're always on duty (which can be a bit overwhelming at the beginning . . . well, you'll soon get used to it). The saying 'it takes a village to bring up a baby' is actually a pretty accurate description.

MAKING CHANGES IN THE HOUSE – CREATING SPACE FOR YOUR BABY

Here's an exercise: grab a 2-kilogram bag of potatoes, cradle it in your arms and walk around your house pretending you're introducing your baby to his new home.

Point out mum and dad's bedroom, your study, the spare room where grandma and granddad stay . . . hey, hold on! Where's the sack of spuds going to sleep?

Well, you mentioned your study, didn't you? Guess what! You're looking at the new nursery, so start packing and get your stuff out of there!

Apart from finding room for the new addition to the family, you're going to need to look at how 'baby safe' your house is. Is it warm enough? Is it hygienic? Is the baby's room close enough to your normal living area so you'll be able to hear your child and get to her quickly?

While you're at it, take a look at those maintenance or repair tasks you've been putting off; you won't get much chance to sort them once the baby's at home!

Even more radical, you might actually have to renovate, rebuild, or even move to another, more child-friendly place altogether. You won't be alone; when you get to your antenatal class you might find that half the people in your group are refurbishing, redecorating or moving. It's just what happens when you suddenly need to make space for a baby. So don't put this off. And, if your budget will allow you to, you may want to consider paying a builder to make some changes.

23. 'I'm going as fast as I can!' Get started on any renovations well before the baby is born or you may find they never get done.

Babies are small, but they take up a heck of a lot of room! The new nursery, while it doesn't have to be huge, at least needs to accommodate a cot and some drawers for storage.

DAD TIP #21:

Don't wait until the eleventh hour to do your renovations. Start as soon as possible . . . like right NOW!

Other things to consider for the nursery include:

+ A changing table, with a storage shelf – highly recommended to avoid having to bend over to change nappies on the floor.
+ A wardrobe to hang clothes, or shelves for more storage (yes, you are going to need more storage).
+ A nursing chair. This is great for night feeds, as you don't need to take the baby out of the room.

So guys, you'll need to shift your wall planner and whiteboards. This is baby's room now, time for Winnie-the-Pooh friezes and Thomas the Tank Engine mobiles!

24. Your new life as a dad will be the biggest change you'll ever go through so start preparing yourself mentally early on.

CREATING SOME HEADSPACE FOR THE NEW ARRIVAL

Now is also a good time to mentally prepare for life with a baby.

Many guys don't realise that a baby will actually take up a lot of space in their already busy lives. It's easy to overlook, perhaps since you're not the one lugging around a 3-kilogram lump, that things are about to change big time. After all, during the pregnancy while the baby's inside your partner, it can seem as if there's still just the two of you. But as a first-time dad, you have no idea how much things are going to change once that neonate arrives.

The baby will require a lot of time and attention and as a good new-generation dad you'll need to make some emotional and physical sacrifices in order to accommodate this. The baby will also impact on your relationship with your partner. Again, it's very important beforehand to mentally prepare for this. A good way to start is by discussing with your partner what you think life will be like post-arrival, and perhaps agreeing on what parameters you'll set yourselves.

One of the hardest challenges is maintaining friendships with those pals of yours who don't have children. With the best will in the world you can swear to maintain contact, but chances are you'll end up going with the flow. Some of your friends might fade away because they just don't like babies. But also consider the possibility that they might have been trying to have one for years, unbeknown to you, and they may be finding the sight of your little bundle of joy hard to cope with. Be aware, too, that some of your friends might have suffered a miscarriage, or more than one, though you might not know it. The arrival of your little tyke could be too much for them, too.

If all that change sounds scary, one thing we can guarantee is that you'll both gain something that will expand to fill any space available, and that's love. The love you have with your partner isn't a limited commodity. Out of nowhere, you'll find a bonus amount will arrive with the delivery of your child and will grow as your child does.

Ahhh. Yes, very emotional. OK, let's come back down to earth . . .

ANIMALS AND BABIES IN THE HOUSE

Our pets are important to us, and often they have all the bragging rights, and free range of the place, pre-children.

We are their food source, their shelter from the storm, the fire lighters, the voices of calm and reassurance. We pamper them rotten every day and in return they offer us unconditional love.

But now what? A baby? In my territory? An intruder, an interloper – competition! Time for pets to have a union meeting and take stock.

Maybe you have a dog that just wants to lollop and dribble its way through life, smelling all the good stuff in the back yard and occasionally fetching and returning sticks to keep you happy – a good, loyal, keeper of the gate.

On the other hand, you might have a serious patch protector – cats, too, can draw boundary lines that even the dog respects and doesn't cross.

Cats miaow and purr a lot, but the saying is dogs have owners but cats have servants. They weren't given claws and split personalities for nothing and will quietly and effectively demand to be kept in the loop. If you don't do that, you may be surprised at just how sneaky a cat can be in reasserting its place in the scheme of things.

So the guardians of your empire need positive exposure to your new infant and plenty of reassurance. Once the realisation dawns that this is a permanent arrangement, that the newcomer is a precious, permanent part of the household – one of the crew – things should be fine. Until of course your infant is mobile, which is when your pets will let you know they don't particularly like being poked and prodded.

You need to be aware of those early interactions and responses. A sneaky nip might be a jealousy thing, but it is even more likely to be a gentle warning to your infant to keep hands off. Once the pets have added the name of your infant to their address book of acceptable humans, they will accept that the world isn't ending but just getting

a little more crowded. Their love (or in the case of the cat, tolerance) will also expand to cope.

Don't forget the simple courtesy rule. It's only right and proper that you advise all other household dwellers – the bird, goldfish, caterpillars, even the pet rocks – that there is a new kid on the block. This courtesy will offer them at least half a chance of avoiding being force-fed play dough or banana supreme with dust and ants *au naturel*, or being baptised in milk.

Some 'pet projects' you can undertake in the meantime:

+ Because pets have a highly developed sense of smell, start using the same lotions and powders that you'll use once the baby's arrived, so the pets can get used to them.
+ Consider taking the dog to canine obedience classes so he sits when you say sit, and stays when you want him to.

+ On arrival day, you hold the baby while your partner makes a fuss of the pet(s).
+ Remain standing, and don't allow the dog to lick your new baby. Keep him on a loose lead (the dog, that is), but a couple of metres away, and introduce the child slowly.
+ Compensate for the baby's demands on your time and energy by being extra fussy over your pets, so they know they're still loved.
+ Watch for any change of behaviour in your pet(s) – sulkiness, chasing tails, extra barking, changes in bodily functions, etc. These can indicate they're not coping well, in which case you might want to talk to an animal behaviourist.
+ Don't leave pets and the new baby alone together; always monitor the situation.
+ When the child is old enough to be fed in a highchair, make sure your dog knows it's not acceptable to jump up and put his paws on the highchair hoping for a tidbit. Maybe feed him at the same time.

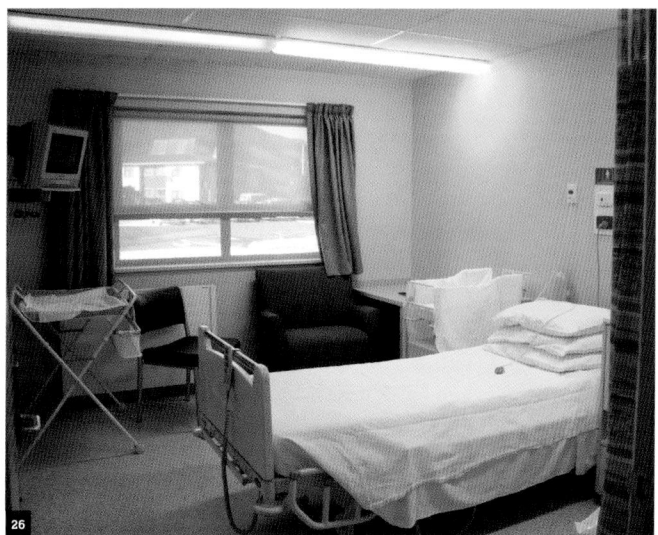

25. Pets are members of the family, too, and will need time to adjust to the new arrival.

26. A hospital tour is useful to take, and will include a look around typical birthing suite.

THE HOSPITAL TOUR

If you're planning to give birth in a hospital, one of the things to do beforehand is to take a hospital tour.

Don't worry: these are regular, informal events and you'll most likely be touring as part of a group of other parents-to-be. Even if you're not planning on having the baby at the hospital, you might find a tour useful as there is a real possibility of ending up there if there are any complications. You may also get to try out the laughing gas!

The hospital tour provides you with an opportunity to get to grips with essentials, such as:

+ Where to take your partner.
+ Where to park, or direct the taxi driver to drop you off.
+ How to get into the hospital after hours (and other safety procedures).
+ Where family can wait and what facilities are available.
+ What the birthing rooms and birthing suites look like.
+ What facilities are available to support different birth plans, e.g., spa baths for water births, etc.
+ What medical equipment is used and how

it works.
+ Whose responsibility it is to call family members and at what stage.

During the tour you might also be shown neonatal units or intensive care (IC) units, in case there are any complications. Typically you will also get a rundown on general availability and routines of hospital staff, specialists and outside caregivers.

There is one thing you need to remember for your hospital tour: ask lots of questions. Let's face it, you'll be meeting people who are involved in delivering babies every day, so make sure you come out satisfied that you know everything you wanted to know.

This is your chance to really find out without being under any kind of pressure, because once your partner is screaming her head off you probably won't be thinking 'I wonder what that thing over there does . . . I might just go and ask'.

You may actually get a taste of this (the screaming bit) from a woman in labour during your hospital tour. If it happens, remember to assure your partner that her birth experience will of course be absolutely pain-free and over within two hours (but don't sign anything).

THE HOSPITAL BAG

As with the baby's bag, this is not so much a fashion item as an essential piece of luggage for checking in to the hospital. So here is the DIYFather list of what to pack to take to the hospital.

For the mother:

- Clothes for labour, e.g., big T-shirt, nightie (possibly more than one).
- Nightie/PJs that open at the front (for feeding).
- Dressing gown and slippers.
- Toiletries.
- Maternity sanitary pads (lots) – these are different from ordinary pads. If you need to buy some, don't worry – you can't miss them. They're available from most supermarkets.
- Breast pads.
- Cream for sore nipples.
- Cotton underwear – dark colours are best. Apparently big knickers (granny knickers) are a plus for comfort.
- Maternity bras.
- Tissues.
- A hair tie (if she has long hair).
- Clothes to go home in/change of clothes.
- Magazines or books.
- Phone numbers of people to call.
- Music, aromatherapy, wheat packs, etc., for labour.
- Good-luck tokens – things that she wants to have around her while giving birth.
- Food and drinks (for immediately after the birth) – healthy breakfast/muesli bars are great and some isotonic sports drinks with lots of minerals.
- Bottled water (just take one bottle – you can refill it in the hospital . . . a lot of hospitals even have ice machines).

Note: Maternity wards tend to be quite warm (for obvious reasons), so wear light clothes that breathe.

DAD TIP #22:

Ask friends who recently gave birth (especially in the hospital you are planning to use) what they wish they'd had with them in hospital.

For the baby:

- Two (at least) singlets/onesies – kimono-style gowns (all newborn sizes).
- Cardigan/vest for on top.
- Several cloth nappies (even if you don't plan to use them – they are really useful for all sorts of wrapping and wiping).
- Disposable nappies (again, even if you don't plan to use them – they are practical at the beginning while you are still trying to get to grips with changing a newborn).
- Wipes (if possible, wet wipes in a container) . . . the first poo is like tar and difficult to get off with a dry wipe.
- Hand sanitisers (for you, your partner after handling/changing the baby, and for visitors before they touch the baby).
- Nappy rash cream (or equivalent, needs to be newborn safe) for after changing the baby/wiping her bottom.
- Outfit for taking baby home.
- Car seat/capsule (if you are planning to go home by taxi, make sure to tell them in advance that you are taking a baby and will need a seat for newborns).
- Head support for infant car seat.
- Blanket.
- A baby hat (soft material for newborns) – this has a vanity advantage in case of a ventouse birth (you'll see what we mean), but is also really good to keep your baby warm. Remember, babies lose most of their heat through the head.

DOMINIC:

As well as all the pyjamas, cooling leg gel, sports drinks and yada-yada that you'll need, don't forget some entertainment, as you may need to wait around doing nothing for ages. Take books, iPODs and favourite CDs (the hospital might loan you a ghetto-blaster), and treat your partner to the latest issues of her favourite glossy magazines. There's nothing like discussing new curtains to settle the nerves!

27. Never keep a girl waiting – especially if she needs to go to the hospital!

Note: While some hospitals can help out with clothes/nappies, as a general principle don't expect anything. Take everything you need so you won't be caught out.

For Dad (that's you!):

+ A change of clothes.
+ Bathing shorts, for when you're helping your partner in the shower, or in the event of a water birth.
+ Toiletries (soap, shampoo and conditioner, toothpaste and brush, deodorant, perfume etc.).
+ Energy/isotonic drinks, healthy snacks (muesli bars are ideal) and bottled water (one is enough).
+ Reading material (this book, of course!).
+ Phone numbers of people to call.
+ Music/iPods or small stereos if allowed.
+ Mobile phones (if allowed – check during the hospital tour) and phone chargers (mobile phone batteries that can outlast labour and the subsequent flurry of phone calls and texts have yet to be invented).
+ Camera/video camera plus extra batteries for the camera (just in case).

DAVE:
With our first child, my wife went into labour and the midwife came round to our house and told us we'd better get ourselves to the hospital. We had the bag all ready to go with the exception of drinks. My wife was pretty uncomfortable in the back of the car, out of her seat belt, leaning over the back seat. When I stopped at the petrol station round the corner from the hospital to get something to drink during the ordeal ahead, I got the first explosion of labour-related swearing. And in the end, the baby was born only an hour-and-a-half later, so we never used the drinks anyway . . .

DAD TIP #23:
Ask your partner to leave some essential items out for you to bring her in case she needs to stay in hospital a few extra days. You don't want to get into any fashion arguments with her when she's had the baby because the clothes you brought don't colour co-ordinate.

PREPARING FOR NON-HOSPITAL BIRTHS

Whether you intend to have one, or it just ends up happening that way, give some consideration to a home birth (or one that's sprung on you on the way to the hospital). Worried? Don't be.

The first thing to know is that home births, planned and unplanned, happen successfully every day around the world. The best thing you can do is have a chat with someone who has actually had a home birth. You can also contact organisations that help parents have successful home births at: www.homebirth.org.

Parents opting for a home birth typically point to the benefits of the relaxed environment of your own home. Of course the downside is that no matter where you are, there is a distance to be covered to get to the hospital if you have to.

What do you need for a home birth?

+ A midwife;
+ Sufficient space and a clear area for birthing;
+ Lots and lots of towels and hot water;
+ Support people to help;
+ A small inflatable pool for water births;
+ Emergency contact numbers close at hand.

To be on the safe side, have a bag of clean towels and container of water available in the car – you never know when you might need them.

ANTENATAL CLASSES AND COURSES

No matter whether you love or hate the idea of going to preparation courses and antenatal classes – we recommend you do. These courses are designed for mums and dads.

If you're keen to find out more about giving birth and what happens during the birth process – great! If you're reluctant to go along because you think they're a waste of time – suck it up and go anyway.

If nothing else it's a great test of how much you know, and usually a good opportunity to trade horror stories with other couples. But most importantly, think

of your partner – she probably won't want to go along on her own and, anyway, didn't you play a major role in this pregnancy in the first place?

Antenatal classes are mostly conducted over a period of weeks, usually in the evenings. However, these may put a strain on your already tight schedule (especially if you're trying to get the house ready for the baby). You may find in your area, or nearby, an antenatal class that only requires a weekend or two weekdays. Although these are longer than the evening sessions, they may be more suitable.

In the antenatal class a lot of focus, naturally enough, is on the mother and the coming baby. However, you are shown where you fit in during the whole pregnancy, birthing and early parenting role.

Many antenatal classes are starting to include special sections for fathers, normally led by a new father, where you get to ask questions of the newly graduated dad. Granted, these fathers may not be experts and may not be able to answer all your questions, but their experiences will speak volumes, and you can always save the hard questions for the antenatal facilitator.

STEF:
I was kind of anti antenatal classes but went along because of my partner. So I was wearing my 'they made me do it' T-shirt during the course. The course was mostly OK – but there was one session that stood out for me. This was when they separated the guys and the girls and we had a 'man' talk. Suddenly all sorts of things came out in a typically male way of sharing. That felt really great, and we still meet up as a group.

DOMINIC:
One particular piece of advice I recall from our excellent antenatal classes was on what to do if your baby had such a thick cold she couldn't breastfeed. 'There's only one thing you can do,' said the class leader. 'Suck the snot from her nostrils.' There was a collective 'Euw!' from us all, and touch wood, I've never yet had to put it into practice . . .

they made me do it

28. The T-shirt says it all really . . . though as much as I hate to admit it, antenatal classes proved useful in the end.

Things you can expect to be covered in an antenatal class are:

+ Decisions on bringing up your baby (which highlights whether you and your partner are even on the same page when it comes to raising and caring for a child).
+ What you are currently doing to support the mother (score some brownie points, guys, and start massaging your partner now).
+ The birth plan.
+ What happens during the birth (this normally comes with a video – graphic!).
+ Your role as a father and support partner.
+ Types of holds to support the mother while labouring.
+ Positions the mother can choose for giving birth.
+ The various drugs to assist with pain relief and their risks.
+ Intervention options, such as induction and forceps.
+ Hospital births and the options you get in the hospital, like having medical students present, or not. Note that if you choose to go with medical students, they are there for you, too; they will bring you refreshments and massage you and the mother. Value!
+ How to hold a baby correctly.

+ Changing a baby's nappy and the various nappy options now available.
+ Feeding: breast- and bottle-feeding.
+ Things you need for the baby: cots, lie-flat prams or buggies, baby monitors, etc.
+ Things to avoid, for the baby and her mother.
+ Baby first aid.

An antenatal class is an opportunity to ask lots of questions, and meet new people in the same situation. And there are normally plenty of reference resources available to borrow. So, if you haven't already done so, book in now.

Although antenatal classes are usually pretty comprehensive and provide you with a good knowledge base about what to expect from here on in (as well as providing reference material for those who want to know more), they're not the be-all and end-all when it comes to preparing for birth and babies.

They can sometimes be a tad academic or clinical, and may be biased towards certain options for birth plans and parenting styles. To put everything you hear into perspective, it's also a good idea to talk to others who have attended antenatal classes (preferably the ones you're about to attend), and who have had their baby.

Check with them about what they knew beforehand, what they got out of the classes, and how they rate them after having gone through the birth experience. Obviously every labour is different, so talk to a few people to get a range of feedback before you decide what's right for you.

Make some effort to get to know other couples in your class, especially those where it looks like the dad is going to be more than a bystander.

Antenatal classes tend to develop into 'coffee groups' once the classes are over, and it's likely you'll make some long-lasting and maybe significant friendships, as you're all facing the same stiff challenges together. You'll get to watch your babies develop and share the good and bad times together, and later, if these other couples are local, you might find them sending their kids to the same playcentres, kindergartens and schools.

To find out more about what to expect from antenatal groups, go to: www.DIYFather.com/groups.

DANA:
The only thing I remember from birthing class was the teacher's advice regarding the placenta: after the baby comes out, stay with him and don't stick around to watch the placenta come out next. Great advice!

ERIC:
Andrea wanted to attend an antenatal class. I was skeptical at first, thinking, I already have three children – what more could I possibly need to know? I figured it would be full of pregnant women, talking about things for mothers and nothing to do with the role of the father.

However, I'm glad I did go. What I found, apart from some very useful information, was an active focus on the role of the father. There was even an opportunity for the men to get together away from the women and have a frank man-to-man discussion. It's great to have the chance to meet other soon-to-be-fathers, too – everyone needs friends with things in common.

CHRIS:
At our second week of antenatal classes the instructor wheeled in a tank of nitrous oxide during her demonstration of the various kinds of pain relief. She produced a mask and asked us to pass it round for us to experience the delicious lightheaded feeling. And then the next week, despite having moved on to discussing the actual delivery, our teacher wheeled in the tank of NO2 again. But we did pain relief last week, we said. Oh yes, said our teacher, but this makes the classes far more interesting. And she passed round the mask again.

THE BABY SHOWER

A cool thing to do, especially if your partner likes surprises, is to organise a baby shower for her (in secret) with friends and family. It might be a good idea to test the water and find out if your partner likes this sort of thing though – otherwise your surprise baby shower might go down the drain quickly.

What is a baby shower, anyway? Well, it's like a celebration of the birth of the child, only in advance – a gathering to rejoice in the imminent arrival of your baby. Often it's done as a surprise for the mum, and you simply gather lots of your combined friends and family together, just as you would for a dinner party or barbecue. No big deal for a man to organise this, surely?

So use your partner's favourite party style with lots of food, flower arrangements, decorations (or not, depending on how fancy an occasion you want it to be) . . . whatever makes it special. You can either do this at your house, a conniving friend's house or, if your budget allows, maybe even a hotel or restaurant.

A great way of ensuring a successful baby shower, happy faces all round and brownie points for you for years to come, is to involve your partner's best friend. This is great for a number of reasons – they usually offer to do most of the organising, and they often have great ideas for what to do and who to invite (watch out for invitations to old friends from high school she hasn't seen for 10 years though!).

29. The baby shower – it's all about the parents, really.

29

If you're even smarter, you'll get everyone her best friend knows, and everyone you know, to help organise it. We recommend doing the baby shower in your own house; that way everyone else will come bringing food, balloons, etc., while you take your partner out to create a diversion. With luck you'll have to do very little but end up looking like the good guy if it goes well (and it will).

DARIAN:

We were given a nappy bag (made from plastic material) that carried the warning 'Do not place baby in this bag', and another that said 'Do not iron'. We were also given tiny baby flannels that warned 'This is not intended to be sleep wear'.

To recap:

+ Contact your partner's best friend (ideally, a control freak).
+ Compile a list of people to invite (she'll have a raft of people you've probably never heard of to add to your own list).
+ Organise a date and time and then arrange to take your partner out.
+ Your guests will arrive and take care of the rest.

30. Erm . . . not quite
what we meant by a
'dad shower'. . .

THE DAD SHOWER

The problem with baby showers is that traditionally the focus is on the soon-to-arrive baby and of course the star of the show, mum. This is great, and fair enough, no arguments from us. But you're going to be a dad, and this requires celebration of its own. So you need to get your best mate to organise a dad shower especially for you, a great event to mark your transition from man to father.

SCOTT:
Mine was organised by my friend Eric and held at a licensed bowling alley – almost like a stag night but without the stripper.

MATT:
Really? They have dad showers now? I got SCREWED!

It can be a bit like your stag or buck's night (perhaps without the stripper or the handcuffs), because hey, why should the women have all the fun?

So maybe meet at the pub or a bowling alley, have a few beers with some friends, and take all the ribbing they'll give you about sleepless nights and no more sex.

RICHARD:
Going out for a few beers with some mates for your dad shower is a nice way to celebrate such an event. It might also be the last time for a while that you can do that. During your evening out with the boys, share some uncensored parenthood experiences (good and bad) and pearls of wisdom.

It doesn't have to be a big thing, just something to launch you on the journey to fatherhood and especially the upcoming birth. Also, if your partner (or her control-freak friend) insists on an all-female baby shower, it gives you something to do. Make sure you tell all your friends that it's a long-standing tradition to give lots of valuable gifts to the father-to-be! Check out: www.dadshower.com for more on dad showers.

> **DANA:**
> I never had a dad shower. But if I ever did do one it would likely end up being something akin to a raunchy bachelor party. Truth be told, not much changed after being married, but it sure did once we had kids!

YOUR ROLE DURING LABOUR

Among the myriad things that need to be organised before the baby comes, don't forget to think about what you are actually going to do during the labour. Your antenatal class will have given you some ideas, but discuss with your partner what she expects you to do for her during labour.

Some things you can do include:

+ Coaching and encouraging her breathing.
+ Giving her back rubs and performing pressure-point massaging to relieve the pain.
+ Doing whatever you can to ensure she's as comfortable as possible.
+ Being the main communications point for family and friends who want to know what's going on.
+ Gatekeeping unwanted people out of the action.
+ Taking photos.
+ Remaining excited and upbeat even after eighteen-and-a-half hours' discomfort and still no sign of baby.
+ Trying to anticipate needs . . . and when that fails, taking orders.
+ Offering her your hand or two of your fingers to squeeze during contractions.

The role you can play as a new-generation father and partner is a varied one. It's only recently that fathers were allowed into the birthing suite, and it's only now that fathers are taking a more proactive approach – ensuring their role is recognised. So once more, man-up and be there for your partner.

Make sure she is well supported, and make sure you as a couple are supported also. Things can get pretty hectic during labour; sometimes the hospital staff have to look after several women giving birth at the same time and some of these women might have complications, which increases the pressure on the staff. Perhaps your partner will be one of those needing special treatment.

Whatever happens, it's important that you do your best to help your partner get what she wants. You have to carry the flag for her with nurses, doctors and specialists as she may not be in a position to stand up for herself, literally.

So while your father or granddad might reminisce about spending the day in the pub waiting for 'the phone call', you probably won't want to miss a minute of this huge opportunity to be part of something truly awesome.

> **DAVE:**
> The most magical moment of my life was delivering our third child. It had been quite a long labour after a complicated pregnancy, and we knew the specialist reasonably well by this stage. Just as the baby's head was starting to come out, the specialist turned to me and said, 'Do you want to deliver the baby?' I was gobsmacked and a bit scared, but I said, 'Sure, what do I do?' He replied, 'Just grab him here [and showed me where to hold on] and gently pull him out.' Moments later, I was holding my son. Telling the story now, I still feel shivers down my spine.

> **DEAN:**
> My wife's labour for our first baby lasted nearly 36 hours. The baby was just not coming through. When at last the midwife agreed to summon medical help, the suction equipment to pull the baby out failed (I think the wrong cup was attached to the tube). Eventually the baby was extracted by ventouse.

Note: If your partner's labour is not proceeding as it should, hospital staff may decide to use a ventouse to assist the birth. A ventouse is a vacuum device which can leave a funny lump on the baby's head but don't worry, this should disappear within hours or weeks at the most.

CHAPTER 4

SURVIVING BIRTH

Are you ready for the big day? If the honest answer is 'I don't think so', don't worry, you're one of about 99 per cent of pre-baby dads who don't feel prepared. Although it's said that 'nothing prepares you for the experience of childbirth', hopefully you've at least done a fair bit of work getting the house, nursery and the rest of the family ready for the big event. We've already outlined many practical things you can do which should make going through labour and arriving home (and living) with a newborn baby a lot easier to cope with. But there's always room for some last-minute stuff . . .

LAST-MINUTE PREPARATIONS

No matter how prepared you think you might be for the birth, there are bound to be some things you've overlooked.

Last-minute things to double check:

+ Make sure you've got all the important phone numbers handy or stored in your mobile phone.
+ Keep your mobile phone on you at all times and fully charged (charge it every day).
+ Arrange some cover at work, or wherever you're needed, so you can leave at a moment's notice if required.
+ Don't forget your camera or whatever you have decided to use to capture the big moment (take some extra batteries or a charger).
+ Line up your support person(s) and keep in regular contact with them.

So this is it – the last time either of you will be thinking 'me or you'. It's about to become 'the three of us' (or maybe more, if you're fortunate enough to have a multiple birth). Any time now the mum-to-be is going to undertake an exercise like no other.

And then it happens . . .

STEF:
People gave us some great tips for getting through labour, like, 'try to sleep as much as you can in advance'. Really? Nobody told us how to do that, though Raquel couldn't lie in the same position for more than half an hour and she had to go to the toilet every five minutes anyway. In the end we actually slept relatively little in the last few weeks before labour. In a weird kind of way it worked for us in that it 'trained' us to get by with four or five hours' sleep per night. That's not to say we weren't tired a lot of the time.

1. Keys, camera, wallet = check. Hospital bag in the boot = check. Hmmm . . . I think we're missing something . . .

2. And we have lift-off!

THE FINAL COUNTDOWN

All the waiting, the check-ups, the preparation, the anticipation . . . and then, suddenly, it's Game On. (See 'The DIYFather Murphy's Law for Babies' on p. 171 for information about the most likely time your partner will go into labour.)

Whenever it is, and whatever else is happening at the time, forget everything and focus exclusively on your partner until the baby arrives.

This is a fantastic time for dads, because you can really shine. While your partner has to prepare herself mentally and physically for the imminent birth, you can rise to the challenge and be a hero. It's a wonderful time for men because it's a very activity-oriented time, with lots of things to organise, whether it's calling a cab or running a bath in preparation for a home birth. Now is the opportunity for you to be at your positive best.

In all likelihood mum-to-be will be on an ascending scale of extreme discomfort and if it's her first child she may also be feeling very scared. At the very least she'll be anxious. So, as dad-to-be, even if you share that anxiety, it's time to show what you're made of. Try to stay calm, or at least act as though you are.

If the bravado and organisational skills don't come naturally, just follow your heart in being attentive, supportive, positive and reassuring – and do your very best to conceal your own worries or anxiety. Your partner's already trying to cope with all that and doesn't need an adult cot case in the room with her!

DARIAN:
While driving to the hospital my wife managed, between her contractions and heavy breathing, to make comments on which gear she thought I should be driving in.

3. Labour: It's hard work but well worth it in the end.

IT'S NOT CALLED 'LABOUR' FOR NOTHING . . .

In case nobody's mentioned it, giving birth can take a long time (especially the first time round), it can be very painful and typically involves a lot of blood. So what you need is patience, perseverance and something to calm your nerves and stomach.

If you have any doubts about your ability to cope in the delivery room or at the birth, wherever it happens to be, don't look! Just stay with your partner at the head end, stroking her brow and softly whispering encouragement and support (as much for yourself as her, probably).

On the other hand, it is an absolutely amazing event to witness, so don't count yourself out too easily. Birth isn't something you see every day.

Assuming you've done a bit of homework, you'll know the three stages of labour. Maybe you've even seen a birth video. What nothing can really prepare you for is what happens on the emotional level: the real experience of birth may affect you in many different ways.

So don't underestimate the labour process. It can be very draining emotionally for dads, to the point where you just want to go home and sleep for a few days. And you're not even the one giving birth!

Practical things you can help your partner with during labour include asking her:

+ If there's anything she wants you to do.
+ Does she feel comfortable in her current position. This question will only work during the early stages of labour.
+ If the room temperature is OK.
+ If she's thirsty, and offering to get her some water (ice cubes can be good).
+ Would she like some distractions – music, talking to her, telling her a story.
+ If she'd like you to just shut up for a while!

Call Me Dad!

In addition to the above:

+ Remind her of all the great things you are going to do when the baby is here.
+ Every now and then tell her she is doing a great job.
+ Start a log and record the time and all the events that are happening, e.g., start of contractions, dilation progress, drugs administered, baby's heartbeat, etc. You can use this later to create a birth journal or scrapbook.
+ Do not panic or stress at any time, for any reason.

DAD TIP #24:
We've all seen TV shows where the medical staff, midwife and husband are standing around saying, 'breathe, breathe!' To help your partner focus her breathing, hold a finger in front of her mouth and ask her to breathe so you can feel it on your finger. If she needs to breathe harder, move your finger further away (she won't notice!) and tell her you can't feel her breath. She'll try harder. It works.

So, in general, be as supportive and reassuring as possible. Tell her how much you love her, do your best to get reasonable answers to all her queries, and promise with real conviction to attend promptly to all those chores she remembers that need doing around the house.

Somewhere in the process don't forget to get something to eat and drink yourself. With all the attention on the mum-to-be it's easy to forget to look after yourself, but you need to stay fit and alert for as long as it takes.

If you're partner's OK with it, and at appropriate times, take a break every once in a while and get some fresh air. A few deep breaths outside will do wonders, and it's also a good time to mentally pinch yourself and say, 'Hey, I'm actually going to be a dad!'

Meanwhile, back in the birthing suite, don't take it too personally if, during labour, topics of conversation centre around the selfishness of men. This will probably be aimed at the male species generally, so you're able to share the blame with any man who enters the room: orderlies, other passing fathers-to-be, and particularly any male trainee doctor who wants to take a peek.

As we suggested previously, it can be fun to keep a labour log, i.e., what time did the waters break, when did the contractions start, when was she fully dilated, the exact birth time, and so on. You can also paste hospital memorabilia in there such as your baby's heart-monitor printout (or a photo of the screen – but check first that the electronics won't be upset by your digital camera). Perhaps even write down some thoughts . . . if nothing else it could help you write your father-of-the-bride/groom wedding speech later in life.

The DIYFather top-20 list of what not to say during labour:

+ How long d'you reckon before you'll be ready to have sex again?
+ Yeah, I know how you feel. I thought I had appendicitis once . . .
+ After this, shall we have more children?
+ Nothing's happening at the moment – I'll just go and watch the game.
+ Do you have to pull that face and make that noise? You look and sound constipated.
+ The nurses aren't too bad looking.
+ Can I try some of the drugs they are giving you?
+ Hell, I'm tired.
+ Another coffee anyone?
+ How long do you think we'll be here?
+ I think I can see the feet.
+ Does it hurt?
+ Do you think you will get bad stretch marks?
+ Man, you look terrible.
+ Honey, look, you made my hand bleed by digging your nails in.
+ I'm not sure I can go through with this.
+ Hey, baby, I just got a call from my old girlfriend.
+ Shall I go and get a takeaway pizza?
+ Any chance of going to the game with the lads on Saturday?
+ How about refinancing the house so we can build that gazebo?

RICHARD:
I found it was best not to continually ask, 'Are you OK?' Give her acupressure/massage – at least you feel like you are doing something and it might help a bit with the pain.

GETTING THE BEST FROM MIDWIVES AND HOSPITAL STAFF

If you have your own midwife, or you're provided with one by the hospital, let them get on with their job.

Midwives are great, they not only make things easier for the mum-to-be but they are able to say with complete authority the most important sentence you and your partner will hear during labour: 'Don't worry, this is quite normal.' They are often rewarded with a smile – albeit a pained one – from the mum-to-be, which is a good thing, even if it is at your expense.

Midwives are pivotal to your experience during labour, and whatever else you might have heard about them they are the ones who ultimately help you.

Some midwives can be like the movie matrons of old – with a robust attitude that says 'this is how it was always done, so this is how it will be'. However, while they are dealing with yet another birth, for you it's the first, and probably the most important event in your lives to date. Try to get along with your midwife, but also make sure you and your partner feel looked after, treated with professionalism and that your personal wishes are being taken into account.

If you have an obstetrician, make sure you ask them everything you want to know and are comfortable with the responses. If you don't understand something, ask for it to be explained in plain English.

In general, hospital staff tend to be very helpful: after all, they deal with women in labour and their nervous partners every day. However, if you suspect that something is seriously wrong with the service or support you are getting, don't put up with it. Again it is about making sure you are given a professional service. Don't sweat the small stuff, though – chances are you won't even remember once you are holding your newborn baby in your arms.

If you find yourself dealing with a particularly stressful situation or your partner is having a very difficult or drawn-out labour, check with hospital staff about the services available for fathers and relatives. Often there are quite a few support options.

SCOTT:
We had a couple of midwives before we found one we 'clicked' with. We stayed with her as long as possible. It's a very scary time, and having a midwife you can relate to and who doesn't stress the mother is a big thing, because if she is stressed then you will be, too. Our midwife in the end was great, lovely natured and with a great personality, because sometimes you just want to be light-hearted to take away the awkwardness.

DAD TIP #25:
Depending on how the hospital is organised, there may be times when your room or birthing suite is somewhat exposed to the corridor or other areas. Giving birth obviously involves quite a bit of 'exposure' anyway, but it's certainly not necessary for any passerby to witness what's going on. Check that your partner doesn't feel exposed more than necessary and if she does, find a way to give her some more privacy.

STEF:
After going through a 24-hour labour and no sleep for about 40 hours, we were SO relieved to finally have our little Noah with us and to have done it. All we wanted was to go to the maternity ward so that my wife and the baby could get some rest. Unfortunately the hospital was more concerned with having us fill in all the forms and writing birth reports. So it was another three hours after Noah was born before we were allowed into the maternity ward – I nearly lost it in those three hours as I was trying to get hospital staff to let us go. I still can't believe administration took priority over getting some well-deserved rest.

RICHARD:
The midwife ordered me to take my shirt off and give the baby a big hug, mess and all! Glad that I did as it was a special moment (bit of an understatement).

ERIC:
As our baby had turned breech, a C section was the only option. My other three children had had natural births, so I had no idea what a C section would look like. After the forms where signed, Andrea was wheeled into the operating theatre. First there was the epidural injection . . . but Andrea was having contractions and the baby was coming, ready or not, even if it was feet first!

It took what seemed like ages to get things sorted – it wasn't until a senior anaesthetist arrived that everything got back on track. I wasn't happy but kept it to myself for Andrea's sake. With Andrea on her back, tubes plugged into her, and a screen up near her face so she couldn't see what was happening (but not high enough to stop me watching), they cut into Andrea's abdomen. There wasn't as much blood as I thought there would be and it wasn't flowing out like in the movies and they weren't at all gentle. They pushed open the gap, moved things inside her out of the way, then continued cutting their way to the baby. Then the doctor reached in with his hands and, slowly but firmly, pulled the baby out. It's a girl! The first part of the baby that came out was her bottom. The rest came out quickly and before I knew it our little girl was being shown to her mother, then whisked away for cleaning, which was my job.

While Andrea was being put back together one layer at a time, I was cleaning a new baby. I'm a father again!

TRUSTING YOUR INSTINCTS
You should, of course, trust doctors, medical staff and midwives involved in delivering your baby. But this doesn't mean you should trust them blindly. We have come across stories from fathers who felt there was a tendency by hospital staff to pull the wool over their eyes, or it became obvious that something wasn't quite right with the birth and yet they, as the soon-to-be-fathers, were being kept out of the loop.

Sometimes the updates you get from various staff and specialists can seem to contradict each other, which of course does nothing to help your confidence levels.

When this happens (and only then), make sure you do whatever you can to get people to tell you the truth about what is going on. If information seems contradictory, ask medical staff to clarify what's going on. This is most important when things don't go to plan and procedures are suggested that you are either not familiar with or didn't want done. It is therefore important that you fully understand what is happening and remind medical staff of their obligation to explain things to you in a way you can understand. That's not to say you should get aggressive with them, just be firm and use your communication skills to the very best of your ability.

MATT:
One of the most sensible decisions we made about our son's birth was having back-up. For our big day we had support from my mother-in-law and one of my wife's best friends. Having them there made a huge difference. It meant there was always someone with the energy to rub my wife Tania's shoulders, it meant there was always someone with free hands to do the little jobs that come up, and it meant when I took a break after about nine hours I wasn't leaving Tania on her own.

We quickly got a good team atmosphere going and ultimately it was great being able to share our amazing experience with two people we love. A word of caution: don't ask someone to be your back-up unless you really want them to be there. Birth can be a pretty full-on experience for everyone involved and you don't want to go through it with someone you're not comfortable with.

Call Me Dad!

SCOTT:

Things for Renee didn't go as smoothly as we had hoped. We naively thought the inducement would happen and then by dinner time she would have delivered and we would be home by 8 pm. By 6 pm Renee was fully dilated (10 centimetres – enough for baby's head to come out), but Pyper decided she didn't want to come out and got 'stuck'. Renee tried for two hours to push her out, but to no avail.

We were moved to a basic operating theatre and they tried there for a little while but again to no effect. Then they decided to take Renee to the operating room to give her a C section, which stressed me out a lot, I didn't really want that for either Renee or Pyper; I was worried about them and just wanted both of them to be OK.

Like I've said before, I hate the sight of blood and gore and was relieved to be told to go to the waiting room, so I left her with her sister and was out the door! You're probably wondering why I was there at all! Truth is, the hospital does a lovely hot chocolate, and I didn't have much on that day anyhow. No, seriously, they came and got me after the epidural had been administered. It's hard to know how lots of women go through this more than once.

I remember going to the waiting room and thinking the worst, this was at 10.00 pm and by 10.41 pm they came out with Pyper. My instincts were very clouded but Pyper was delivered by forceps and in 41 minutes, and I was happy to learn they didn't have to do the C section in the end.

BEING THE HERO FOR YOUR PARTNER

Time to be the hero! Sounds like a great challenge, doesn't it? A bit like Obi-Wan Kenobi telling Luke Skywalker to 'use The Force'. But it's a lot harder than that. It's not enough just to think you're a hero – the idea is that your partner thinks you're a hero, based on the unlimited support you are able to offer her.

When your baby is born it might feel rather like a miracle: you helped create a little life and it's a part of you. It's easy to feel like a hero purely on the basis of that fact, which is further reinforced by the congratulations all round, repeated pats on the back and maybe even a politically incorrect cigar (well away from the baby, of course!).

But after all the celebrations are over and you find yourselves settling down to life with your new addition, you may find, in the months to come, that things don't always go according to plan. Sometimes, to be utterly honest, your baby is likely to drive you and your partner up the wall. After countless sleepless nights when no attempts to settle the baby seem to be working, that's when you need to step up and be a Superdad. Chances are your partner will be a lot more worried, tired and stressed out than you are, so put on your virtual cape, underpants on the outside and show that you're superhuman. It's a mindset rather than a specific action or task. You don't have to literally leap over tall buildings in a single bound, only metaphorically. Harness your strength and urge your partner to go back to sleep while you sort everything out. And by the way, even heroes cry sometimes.

4. Now is the time to put on your superhero cape and really step up for your partner, who at this point is likely to be even more tired than you are.

THE BIG MOMENT: BABY IS HERE!

5. Congratulations, you're a dad!

Typically, after some hours of hard labour, your baby finally enters the world and nothing else matters at that moment. The whole process of giving birth – the pain, the worries and the exhaustion – takes you on an emotional roller-coaster ride. Just go along with it, open yourself to the experience and let emotions come and go. If you feel like crying, cry; if you feel like laughing out loud, do that. If you feel absolutely nothing except stunned, don't beat yourself up about it – just stay in the moment.

Forget all your worries, fears, thoughts and anything else floating around in your head for this brief instant and just enjoy it.

You're nearing the point when you'll finally meet your baby, so it's once again time to man-up. Even if you don't like the sight of blood, few things beat the sheer wonder of childbirth.

Enjoy it to the maximum and do as much as you can for your partner. You might be asked to cut the umbilical cord – if you decide to do it, it may feel like an official way of welcoming the baby into the world and into your world. Send good wishes out into the universe as you do it and bless your baby's life.

DAD TIP #26:

If you decide to cut the umbilical cord, apply some good solid strength when you close the scissors as the cord can be surprisingly sturdy. You don't want a messy cut or to have to redo it a number of times. You're welcoming your child into the world, after all. Try to make it a memorable moment.

DANA:

When our son came out and was covered in this purplish, rubbery goo, my first honest-to-God reaction was, gee, if I was watching this in a movie, I'd have said it looked totally fake! Reality can be an amusing thing sometimes.

MATT:

During my darling wife's 12-hour ordeal it occurred to me our son's birth was more like a world-title fight than the beautiful, mystical, euphoric experience some might have you believe. Instead of rounds we had contractions and instead of a corner we had me sitting at the side of the bed. Apart from that, Tania reminded me a lot of a prizefighter, and she gave a knockout performance.

Looking back on our son's birth, it seems to me that this is a good way for a couple to approach the big event. You're a team, but she is the only one left battered, bleeding and bruised, which isn't to say your role isn't hugely important. Like Rocky's coach Mickey, you've got to rub her shoulders, tell her she is doing really well, give her an idea of how she is going, wipe her brow and not show any fear. But unlike Mickey, you're also there to kiss her and tell her how much you love her.

Even if you just find yourself saying 'you're doing really, really well, baby' over and over again, don't stop. Give it heaps. The more you can do to be involved without getting in the way, the better. In a lot of ways I reckon being a father starts the moment your partner's waters break, which means standing back and letting her do all the work isn't really an option.

THE AFTERMATH, ER, AFTERBIRTH

You will probably see (or, worse, smell), and hear staff talk about the placenta as your partner's body gets rid of it. You may get asked by hospital staff whether you would like to keep it or not. If you have a plan for what to do with it, great. If not, the hospital will dispose of it for you.

MIKE:

Our obstetrician made a point of showing the placenta to us and explaining what he was looking for, and asking us if we'd like to keep it. No, thanks!

Once the umbilical cord is cut there is usually a quick burst of activity. The baby and mum need to be checked to make sure they are both OK. For babies this is most commonly done using the APGAR score, established by checking the newborn baby on five criteria: activity, pulse, grimace, appearance, respiration. For each criterion a value of 0, 1 or 2 is assigned – giving a maximum score of 10.

The test is usually done twice, at one and five minutes after birth, and the scores are recorded on the birth chart. A low score for the first test generally means that the baby needs some extra attention, but it doesn't necessarily mean that there will be long-term problems.

If the score remains low at later tests your baby will probably be transferred to the neonatal unit (or if you're at home she will be taken to hospital urgently), and might require immediate medical attention.

In most cases, your baby will score above seven, which generally indicates that the baby is healthy. But watch what's going on and if you're wondering about something, ask. Don't forget your partner either – she will need you as well and this is the time to praise her for all her hard work and to tell her how well she's done!

Now comes the moment when you as brand-new parents get to hold your baby for the first time. This can feel very strange at first and you might experience a certain sense of helplessness. Don't worry about it – this is entirely normal. You'll be totally at ease in no time.

STEF:

I'm glad to say that our little man passed his first test in life with distinction: 9/10–10/10 – what a propeller-head!

MIKE:

The obstetrician asked if I'd like to cut the umbilical cord of my baby daughter. This took me by surprise as we hadn't discussed this option previously, but I figured it was a great opportunity. He showed me what to do, and as I cut the cord I said 'I hereby declare this baby open'. Silly thing to say, but I'm sure it will be dragged out for her 21st or wedding!

It's difficult to know what to do at first. A baby is not like a puppy: you don't just put it on the ground and watch it run around; it's a totally helpless little bundle, and at this stage is totally dependent on you. So just go with it and, if you haven't held someone else's baby before or been shown how, ask nursing staff or the midwife for help.

After all the hustle and bustle of the final moments of labour, you should now get some quiet time with your partner and baby. Even if it's just for a few minutes before you need to leave the birthing suite, or fill in forms, or whatever else requires your attention.

This is not a time to be embarrassed about the baby's appearance. Hospital staff or midwives will usually do their best to clean up the baby and make her look presentable, but newborns generally look quite wrinkled and exhausted – wouldn't you if you had just gone through the same experience?

So don't worry about any signs of blood left on your baby's head, or a bit of a rash on her skin. In most cases all of the icky bits will disappear over the next few days and you'll have a gorgeous-looking baby, just like you've always seen on TV.

Don't forget to take photos! They'll become the treasured memories of this never-to-be-repeated (at least not until your next child comes along) moment. It's their introduction to the big wide world and the beginning of a whole new chapter in your life, so it's worth capturing.

DEAN:

First thing I did when the baby was born, I shouted out, 'Oh my God, it's a baby,' and then cried my heart out. It was the most beautiful moment of my life and I've been fortunate enough to experience it twice.

SCOTT:

To me it was a roller-coaster ride, and once my sister-in-law brought Pyper out I held her and tears rolled down my face. I had a feeling that this was the most worthwhile thing I'd ever done in my life.

I couldn't take my eyes off her. I looked and re-looked at every single part of her little face – it felt like thousands of times – just staring at her like nothing I had ever encountered before. She looked so weak, helpless and defenceless – the natural protective instinct came over me and has stayed with me from that day to this and I know it will never leave. I made a promise to her that no matter what, I would always be there for her and I would always protect her.

Renee looked and felt like she had been through the ringer backwards, and I was glad that it was her, and not me! I wouldn't have been able to do for one minute what she did: I'm thankful for that, and proud of her.

It had been a long day, and it was going to be a long night. We waited with Pyper to see if she would take the skin test, which is laying her on top of Renee and then also seeing if she would bond with Renee.

I could tell Renee was excited, but also very tired and just wanted to sleep. I think she managed to get to bed at 1 am which was when I left to let them sleep.

Wow, what a long day it had been and we had a baby to show for it. With everything running through your mind when you go to bed, you wake up like a little kid on Christmas Day; you can't wait to get back there and see your little addition to the family.

6. The new arrival.

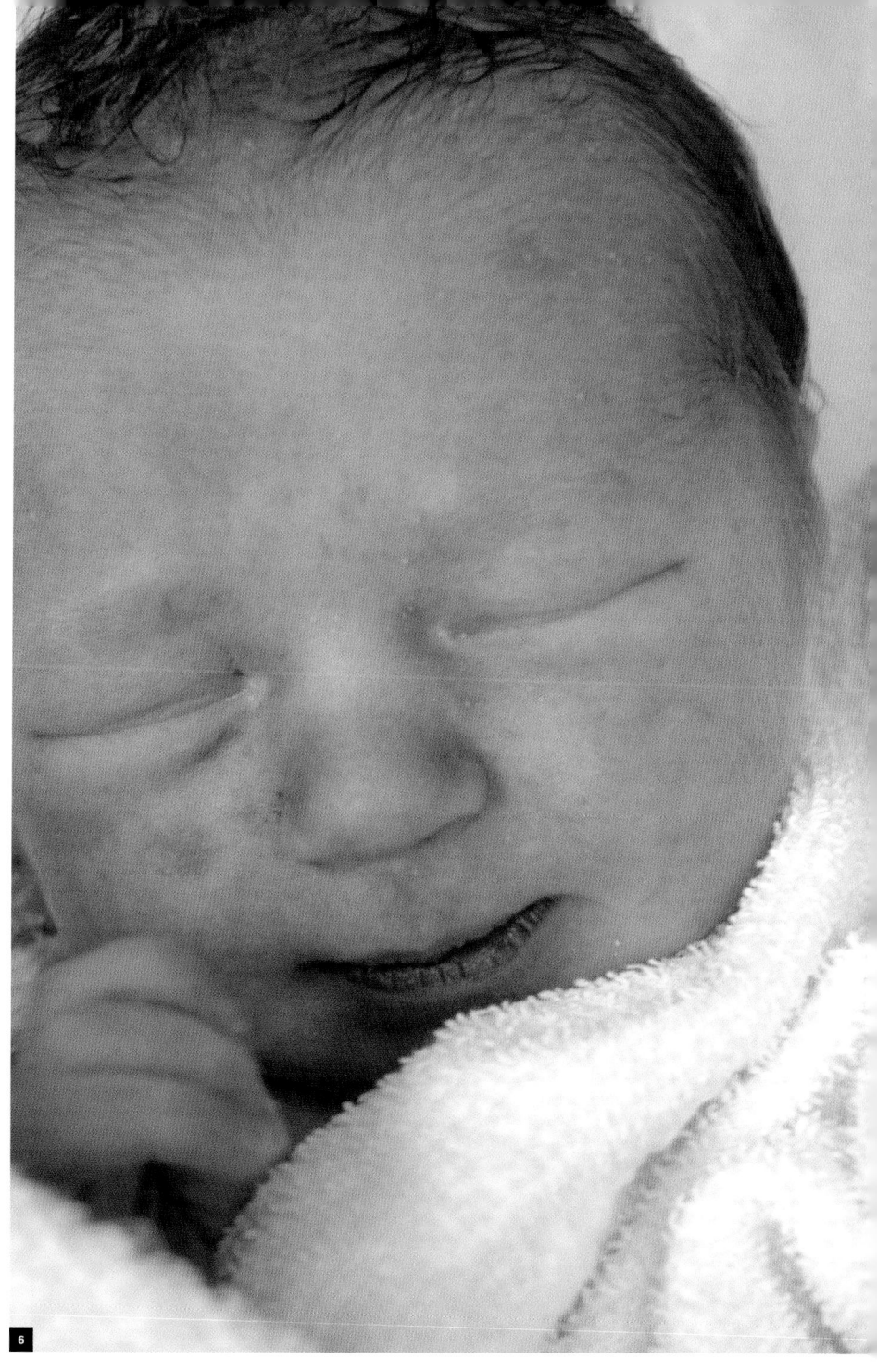

6

CHAPTER 5

LIFE AFTER BIRTH: THE DAYS AFTER

So now you're officially a dad! Feels great, doesn't it? Forget all the stress, exhaustion, embarrassment and feelings of inadequacy – your baby is finally with you and you now have the opportunity to reveal your inner Superdad! We did say that your special involvement doesn't stop after giving birth, didn't we?

Call Me Dad!

As always, stick to Rule One for being a dad – don't panic, or, rather, panic later. Remember, dealing with children is completely different to anything you've ever done before, and it takes a while to build confidence and get a feel for it.

In the first few days after the birth it's important to become comfortable with the basics of looking after a baby – feeding, sleeping, cleaning. The best way to learn is by using the total immersion method, i.e., just do it!

This is also the time when you find out that the catchphrase 'mums just know' might not be that accurate. It's true that pregnant and new mothers have inherent knowledge and skills that seem to come out of nowhere, but in many cases your partner has to learn the practical skills of looking after a baby the same way you do – by doing it.

While some mums take to it really well, don't be surprised or disappointed if your partner struggles at the beginning. This again is where you can be a Superdad by offering support and encouragement. After all, you're both learning, and if you support each other you will master the new skills quickly.

Don't forget the people around you – your family and friends. They've probably hung in there with you, so send them a message and share the good news with them. It's great living in the digital age – mobile phones with cameras and 'send to many' text messages and emails mean there's no excuse not to let the whole world know your good news! Make use of all the possibilities that technology offers us – or simply call one person and ask them to tell everyone else. You can also start your own baby blog, and maybe post the baby photos so that everyone can see them at their leisure.

MATT:
When you are at work, call to check in a couple of times a day. When you get home, don't act like your day was tougher than hers was – even if you're sure it was.

HANDLING A NEWBORN

One of the first things you are going to be faced with is the physical challenge of holding, carrying and 'putting down' a newborn baby. She'll look very fragile and it's easy to be worried about even touching her. But in general, babies, even neonates, are actually a lot more robust than they look. So get over the initial awkwardness or worries about touching her. Apart from anything else, she wants to be touched. Let's face it, she's had close physical contact and warmth inside your partner for the last nine months so she's not going to want to be abandoned now!

For handling newborns there is one very important rule to remember above all others, and that is: support your baby's neck. This is because her neck muscles are not able to support the weight of her head. In time, you will become aware of when she is able to hold up her own head (one of the first of many milestones), and you can also encourage her to do it. (See Chapter 6, 'Active Movement', p. 126.)

1. A dad at last: 'Hello baby, welcome to the world'.

2. It's important to always support a newborn baby's head.

3. A great way to hold your baby so she can see what's going on.

4. Another example of how to hold a newborn.

5. Hopefully the first breastfeed will go off without a hitch, but if its just not working, seek specialist advice.

She may be robust, but you must still always be gentle with your newborn baby. Most important, make sure she is in a safe and stable position at all times and that no matter what happens there is no chance she could fall, slide, tumble, or get knocked or hit by anything. A baby is born with a number of 'soft spots' (called fontanelles) in their skull which allow the head to pass through the birth canal. These eventually harden but it's important to be extra careful to protect and support the baby's head until the bones fuse.

Babies have very little spatial awareness at the beginning, and she won't be able to protect herself from anything falling on her. She also won't be strong enough to hold on to anything so if she starts to slide, she'll fall.

FEEDING

Let's start by assuming you've decided to go with breastfeeding. Cool, except that your partner might not have any milk. It can take several hours, or even days, until the first breast milk (colostrum) is available at the usual outlet. Availability aside, it can also take quite a while before mum and baby have developed a good customer relationship at said outlet.

Breastfeeding can be quite painful for mum at the beginning, too, and all the repeated attempts to get baby to latch

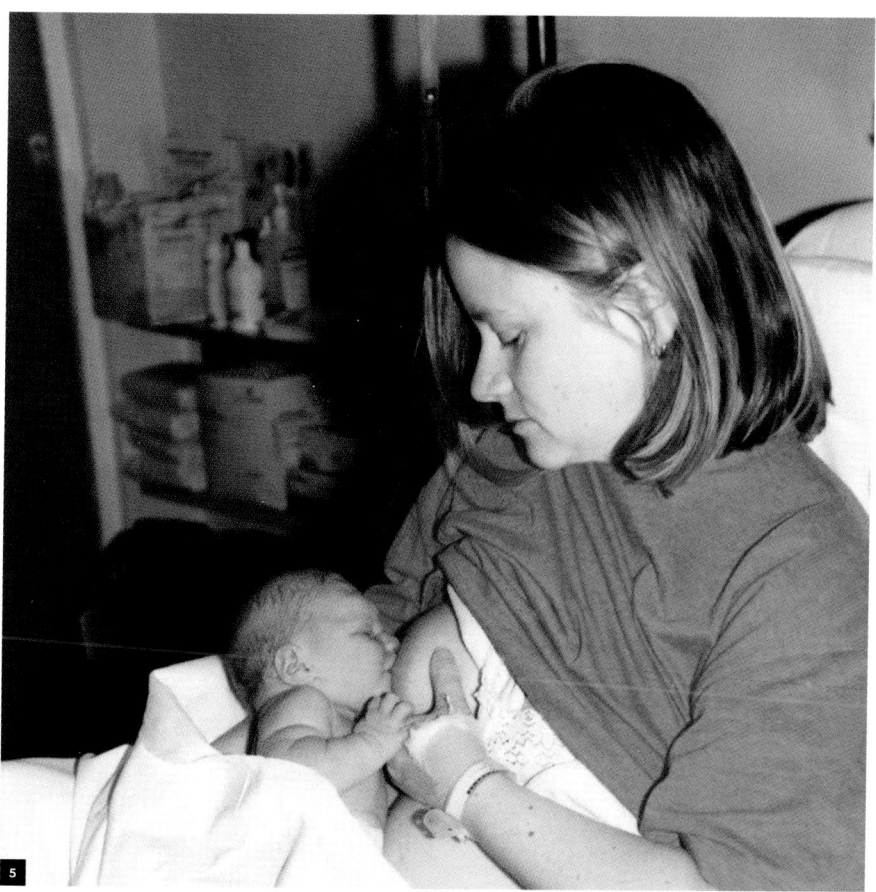

on (yes, that is the correct term) can further aggravate sore and sometimes cracked nipples.

Of course, the baby also has to learn how to breastfeed (well, he hasn't done this before either). He might have problems latching on or working out how to suck. Patience will usually do the trick, so do whatever you can to help your partner avoid stress. If need be, send people out of the room or find a quiet place for the new mother and child to feed. Babies sense when their mums are tense which can make them tense up also, further hindering the feeding process.

If things aren't going well, it's good for mum to have a break, so take the baby into a different room and look after him for a while. Then get them together again and encourage them to have another go. If you're really struggling and nothing helps, either ask for a lactation consultant (if you're still in hospital) or ask your midwife/caregiver to help you find a specialist. Generally these people are very good at helping you sort out feeding problems quickly.

Birth is a traumatic and exhausting experience for babies as well. It's important they get food as soon as possible, both to soothe them and to replenish energy resources.

With bottle-feeding, you've got one problem less in that there are no issues for your partner with sore nipples or the baby

6. Remember to place a cloth on your shoulder or lap before burping your baby!

not latching on properly. However, you might still experience feeding problems, so ask for help if things are not working out.

Whichever method you choose, it's important to make sure the baby gets several good feeds in the first few days. Midwives and caregivers will also regularly check feeding times, duration and sometimes even the baby's weight.

DAD TIP #27:
Start a baby journal right away. Record the time your baby has been feeding and for how long, record when the baby was asleep and when it had a full nappy. This will make it much easier to monitor progress. There are gadgets on the market to keep an electronic record of feeding and sleeping times, but pen and paper work just as well.

> **MATT:**
> When she's breastfeeding, for God's sake don't say anything about how much you miss having her boobs all to yourself. And don't moo. Ever.

BURPING
Burping is an essential part of the feeding ritual and a great technique for dads to master early on. Hey – it's really easy! It is important to burp your newborn baby after each feed, as a lot of air gets sucked in that needs to be released. At the beginning you need to help your baby release this air, but later on they will learn to burp by themselves, just like adults.

Burping is a fantastic dad activity in many ways. If your partner is breastfeeding, it's a great way to give her a break from holding the baby. It's also an excellent way to have some extra bonding time with your baby – you will be holding him very close to your body during the burping.

Getting your baby to burp requires a bit of know-how and lots of patience. Probably the most common way to burp a baby is to hold him so that his arms and head are against your shoulder. Keep his back straight and gently pat him on the back, as well as rubbing his back up and down. The patting and rubbing helps the tiny bubbles of air in your baby's stomach form a larger bubble, at which point the air will exit through his mouth. Many people sing or talk softly to their babies while burping them.

Sometimes you need to burp your baby mid-feed when you realise he has stopped feeding. Once burped, reward him by letting him continue feeding. If he's not keen on more feeding you'll probably want to give him a rest or even put him to bed for a nap, or for the night. If you are bottle-feeding, the recommendation is to burp after every 30 millilitres and at the end of feeding.

There are also other techniques you can try out, e.g., lay him flat on your lap, head down, tummy and hips on your thighs. Again, gently pad and rub his back.

DAD TIP # 28:
Before you start burping your baby, put a cloth nappy or towel on your shoulder or lap . . . that way you don't have to get changed when your baby spills a bit of excess feed, which happens frequently.

SILENT NIGHT?

Now that you are two plus baby, you'll develop a different understanding and appreciation of the meaning of sleep which will continue over the next few years. We recommend wearing your 'sleep is for the weak' T-shirt and smiling when you're tired. By the way, sleep issues tend to come back several times when your baby hits certain developmental milestones. For most babies, most problems are reasonably short-lived,

and there will come a time (even though you won't believe it when you're pacing up and down at three in the morning) that your child will sleep peacefully all night long.

But, to begin with . . .

THE FIRST NIGHT
Amazingly, there is a good chance that your first night with the baby will be great, mainly because the baby will be so knackered from the birth that she sleeps for many hours on end, allowing everyone else to get some much needed rest. If this is not the case for you, don't worry about it: you might as well get used to restless nights.

. . . AND BEYOND
Typically the second or third nights after the birth can be very challenging as the baby now demands full attention and will definitely let you know when he's hungry or unhappy about something. As you'll discover, babies are equipped with a perfect mechanism for letting you know exactly what they need:

What the baby wants to tell you:	How the baby tells you:
I'm still dealing with the after-effects of birth – my head hurts.	Cries a lot.
I'm hungry.	Cries a lot.
I'm tired but can't settle.	Cries.
I've got colic.	Cries a lot.
My nappy is full.	Cries.
I don't like all these people and noises.	Cries a lot.
I'm not comfortable in my current position.	Cries.
I'm too hot/too cold.	Cries.
Nothing is wrong.	Cries anyway.

If it's possible during the first few days, have some experienced people around (midwives, caregivers or other people who have had several children) so you can ask them for their opinion about why the baby is crying. In most cases you can settle the baby by feeding, by checking them over or giving them a cuddle.

You need to work out a simple routine for a typical 'quick check', e.g., check her nappy, temperature, when she last had something to eat and scan the environment. Is there anything that could be disturbing her – bright lights, loud noises, etc.?

Once you've gone through the basic checks (several times maybe), you need a bit of calm and patience. Babies can take quite a while to settle. If they don't want to feed or can't feed, give it a rest and try again after a while. If nothing seems to help and you've tried for an extended period (say, an hour) check with a midwife, caregiver or experienced parent. Again, in most cases your baby will be just fine, but it actually feels better to check with someone who has more experience even if it's just to calm your own nerves.

> **MATT:**
> When it's all a bit too much for your partner . . . repeat after me: 'You get some sleep tonight, honey, I'll get up to the baby when she cries.' Give her two nights of good, solid, uninterrupted sleep in a row. You'll be exhausted, but she'll be ready to take on the world for another couple of weeks.

FRONT, SIDE OR BACK?

There is an ongoing debate over the best sleeping position for babies. Most doctors tend to recommend babies sleep on their backs at the moment. Please note that these recommendations change every now and then as new scientific research becomes available. Check out www.changeforourchildren.co.nz for the latest information about SIDS (sudden infant death syndrome) or SUDI (sudden unexpected death in infancy). Until several years ago, doctors told parents to place babies on their stomachs to sleep.

In addition to placing the baby on her back, ensure her face is clear of sheets and blankets, as well as soft toys. Around her head should be a totally clear area. Tuck in any blankets you use as covers. Babies tend to wriggle at night – she shouldn't be able to pull blankets over her head accidentally. Make sure the blankets don't go further up than her waist.

Placing your baby as far down the cot as you can go helps reduce the risk of her wriggling under the sheets. This may look odd at first, but she will grow into the cot.

DAD TIP #29:
Ask your midwife or a trained healthcare professional to show you the technique of swaddling, which can't really be described sufficiently in words except to say it's a way of wrapping the baby tightly in a blanket like a parcel! This can help your baby settle into sleep more easily, as it aims to recreate the feeling of 'tight comfort' the baby experienced in the womb.

A WORD ABOUT FLAT-HEAD SYNDROME

What is flat-head syndrome? Basically it refers to a baby literally getting a flat head because she sleeps on her back over long periods of time. As the skull bones are still somewhat soft, they can be shaped by pressure. Flat-head syndrome is only cosmetic in nature and doesn't harm your baby's brain, but make sure you understand what it is and how it may affect your child.

Because back sleeping is recommended these days (see Front, Side or Back? above), over time your baby may develop a slightly flattened look to the back of his head. However, this will disappear after a couple of months as your little champ discovers how to move his head naturally while lying down.

If you want to assist this process with your newborn but also ensure that you reduce the risk of SIDS/SUDI as much as possible, always put your baby down on his back but turn his head to one side – only slightly and very gently. The next time he sleeps turn his head the other way. You only need to move his head a little bit so it doesn't rest exactly on the same spot.

7. Sleeping like a baby.

SCOTT:
The first night, holy smoke! We got home in the afternoon around three, and the place was as hot as the equator, so by the time 7.30 pm came around the baby was ready for bed. OK, here was the big test. Would she sleep?

A couple of hours later we decided that we'd go to bed, too, and see how the night would go. That was where the hopeful thoughts ended: she went ballistic, and I mean a screaming-type of crying – the sort where we got to the stage of, OK, I think I want to throw myself out of the top-storey window!

We tried cuddling her, bottles, holding, talking, etc., and even the cardinal sin of putting her into a Moses basket and then putting her into our room! Yep, one out of ten to us for effort.

We did everything possible that we could think of. Renee's mother was staying with us at the time, so it was a case of drawing on her knowledge to try and get Pyper settled. I think we expected too much, and really should have known that it wasn't going to be an easy ride.

She woke again during the night and then early in the morning. As far as sleeping routines go she was straight into it, there was no mucking around. We got her up around 6.30–7 am and swapped her swaddling clothes for day clothes, a way of letting her know that she wasn't going back to sleep straight away.

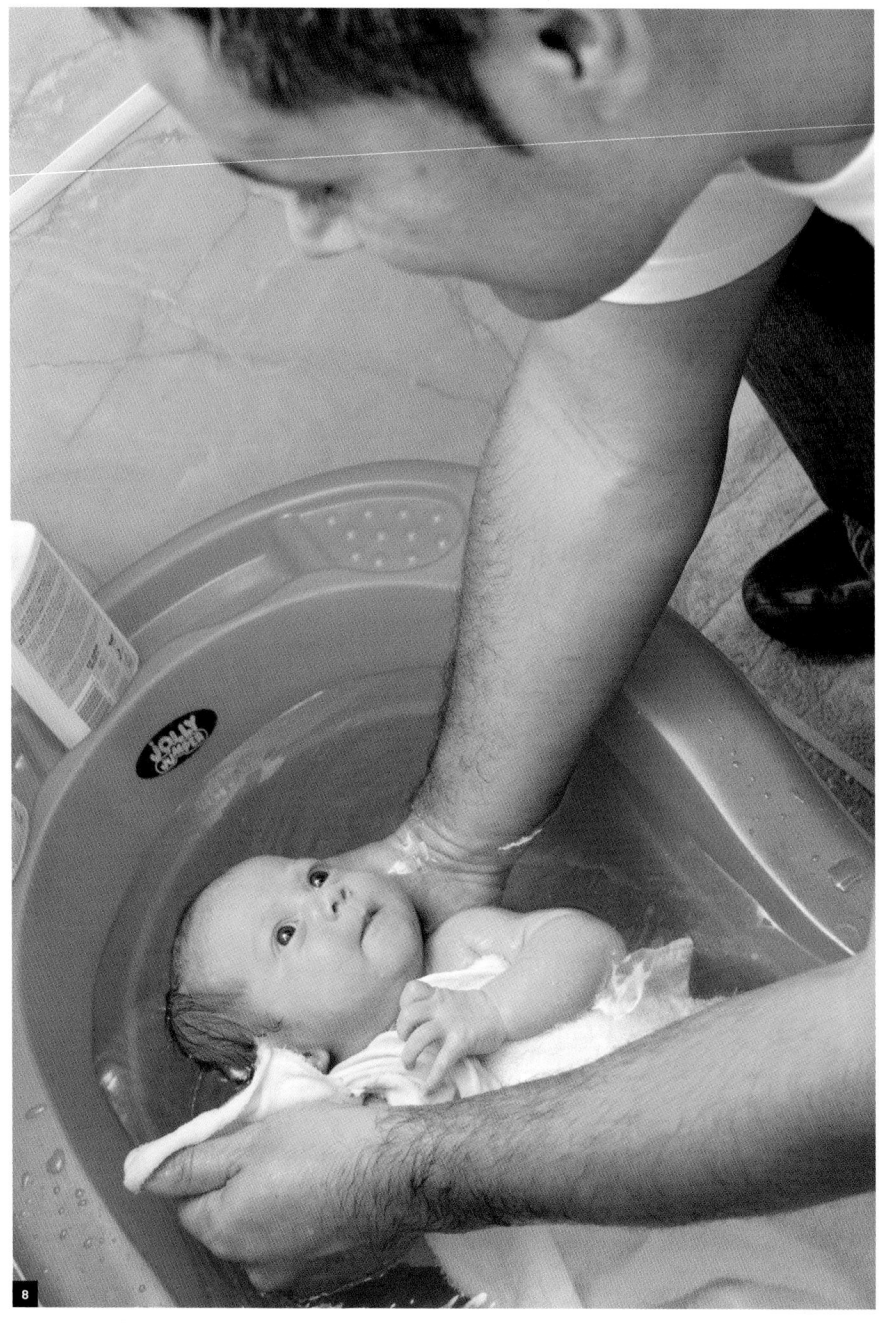

8. Bath-time with dad.

Call Me Dad!

DAD TIP #30:

Infants are programmed to wake up and call for more food or drink the second you close your eyes, whatever the time of day or night. So don't think you will be any smarter than the rest of us if this hasn't happened to you – yet!

Good sleep patterns will return for you about when your son or daughter leaves home! Until then, be grateful for any snooze you can snatch – anywhere, any time.

But, when your infant is sleeping, go and have a good long look at them. You'll never see anything so pure, so wonderful or so trusting. Remember that when you are having an off day – just go and take another peek. Cool, eh?

NEWBORN HYGIENE

Cleaning a baby may seem like a dirty job but someone's got to do it - so that someone might as well be you!

And you've got a cracker to start with! Called meconium, it's a baby's first poo. It literally looks and behaves like tar. Fortunately it usually doesn't smell much, but it can be quite tricky to get off. The great thing is, once you've cleaned meconium off your baby's bum you're qualified!

Over the next few days your baby's poo should turn bright orange-yellow, though nature has been kind in that it doesn't usually smell while your baby is still being bottle- or breastfed. Your baby might be an exception though - you never know.

Whatever happens, take it like a man and learn how to change your baby's nappies properly. Don't be afraid to ask others for help and get people to show you their tricks – there are definitely easy ways to change a baby.

DAD TIP #31:

Keep your fingernails trimmed. Apart from reducing the chances of scratching your little darling, it will save time and revulsion when cleaning infant excrement from under them!

LOOKING AFTER YOUR PARTNER

Now that your family unit has expanded, you are dutybound to look after both your infant and your partner, so where do you start?

For much of the time from now on, baby comes first, because it's the most vulnerable - especially at the beginning. So do whatever you can to look after the newest family member - don't just wait for your partner to ask you to help. When you've established that the baby is fine, your next thought should be about your partner.

In the first few days after the birth there are obviously many things to be done. Your partner will probably still feel pretty rough and, in the worst-case scenario, might even reject the baby, especially if the initial bonding hasn't been achieved. If this is your situation, seek help from your GP, midwife or another professional organisation.

By 'things to be done', we don't mean buying a bunch of flowers for your partner: there's more to it than that – but you knew that, of course. And anyway, friends and family will almost certainly have turned your home into a florist's shop by now.

Some of the very useful things you can do for your partner are:

+ Keep her well supplied with food and drink.
+ Ensure she has some pain relief to hand.
+ See that she's comfortable.
+ Take the baby out of the room every now and again to give her a break.
+ Take on an extra share of the chores at home.
+ Take time off from work to help out as much as possible at home while your partner is recovering.
+ Do more than your fair share of nappy changing whenever you are around, especially if the baby is being breastfed.
+ Manage the visitors and messages.
+ Encourage her to sleep and rest as often as she can.
+ Take care of the finances and bills.
+ Talk to her lots and let her know she is doing a great job as a mum.

ERIC:

Because Andrea had a C section, she was effectively out of action (including not being able to drive) for six weeks while recovering. Her mother stayed for the first three weeks, which was great. Really! Then I took the remaining time off work to take care of Andrea and Ava. Not that Andrea needed much care, she recovered quickly and well. I enjoyed looking after my new family: I made breakfast, lunch and some dinners. I did the cleaning and was more than happy to help with Ava as well, not that I could breastfeed her but I did take care of nappy duty and bathing . . . anything I could do to hold her. And I would spend hours just looking at Ava, even while she was sleeping.

THE BABY BLUES

No, this is not about starting your baby off on a career as a jazz musician. Experiencing a bit of a low immediately after giving birth, or a few weeks or months later, is very common. Sheer exhaustion and the radical change in lifestyle can be daunting. Fortunately, what is often referred to as the baby blues tends to go away after a few days. However, in some cases it may develop into postnatal depression (PND), which affects a significant number of parents. Yes, both parents – not just mums! Despite this, however, it is definitely new mums who are most susceptible to PND.

A number of risk factors have been identified which increase the likelihood of developing PND. So if your partner ticks any of the boxes below, be sure to keep a close eye on her following the birth.

Some risk factors for developing postnatal depression:

+ Past history of depression or other mental-health issues.
+ Limited support from family and friends.
+ Financial stresses.
+ Birth complications, such as caesarean delivery.

+ When the birth deviates wildly from the birth plan, e.g., had to deliver the baby in hospital with drugs instead of the natural home birth as planned.
+ Baby unwell or born with abnormalities.

If you suspect that you or your partner might be suffering from postnatal depression, it's important to spot it early so help can be sought. The first weeks after the birth are critical for parental bonding with the baby and PND can really interfere with this process. There is lots of support available though so don't be afraid to ask for help. Below are some of the key signs of postnatal depression. Sufferers might exhibit any combination of these as every case of PND manifests differently.

Symptoms of postnatal depression:

+ Not wanting to hold the baby or feeling detached.
+ Having negative thoughts about the baby.
+ Prolonged sadness/crying all the time.
+ Loss of interest and pleasure in usual activities.
+ Feeling irritable all the time.
+ Change in sleep patterns. (Obviously anyone with a new baby is going to have this symptom! However, people with PND often find they can't sleep even when the baby is settled as they are worrying so much about things.)
+ Loss of appetite.
+ Massively decreased energy, tiredness and fatigue.
+ Thoughts of worthlessness or guilt. Feeling like a bad parent.
+ Loss of concentration.
+ Extreme anxiety.

Outlook for PND sufferers

The good news is that the majority of sufferers have a complete recovery – but it's a good idea to seek help early. Without treatment, PND may last six months or more. With treatment, 70 to 80 per cent of sufferers will recover much sooner. So be aware of the signs and read up on it, or ask your healthcare provider or midwife for more information.

9. Mum, Dad, keep your eyes on the road please. Precious cargo in the back!

THE TRIP HOME

If you have chosen to give birth in a hospital you've hopefully also chosen a safe way of getting you all home.

Lots of hospitals won't allow parents to take their children home unless they have an approved safety restraint car seat, and they might even want to see it. This also goes for trips in a taxi, so if you call a cab ask if they have a car seat for a newborn baby. Better still, use the one you bought two months ago, yes?

That first drive home, especially if you're the one in the driver's seat, can be quite nerve-racking because you're aware for the whole journey that you've got this precious, helpless little bundle in the car. Every other motorist becomes a threat, and you might find yourself driving well under the speed limit!

DAD TIP #32:

A couple of months before your partner is due, buy or rent a car seat/capsule suitable for transporting your baby (see Chapter 3). Try it out before you need it – that is, for once in your life, read the instruction manual first and then install the seat in the car. You'll need to be adept at attaching it safely, so practise putting it in and taking it out a few times. There are lots of regulations about car seats and transporting infants. Make sure you are aware of them: unrestrained or inadequately restrained infants and children figure prominently in road death and injury statistics.

SCOTT

This was an interesting experience! We carefully put her in some warm clothes, and then carried her to the car looking like a little Eskimo. Being the middle of winter it was cold and raining!

We hadn't used the car seat before and we didn't have anyone knowledgeable to put it in. We carefully placed Pyper in her capsule and headed home, luckily for us only a 15-minute drive from the hospital. When we arrived we discovered that her capsule had loosened off, and since her neck couldn't support her head she'd slumped forward so that her chin was almost on her chest! We got a huge fright, though in fact she'd fallen asleep and was blissfully unaware of our panic. But it was a salutary experience for us: this wasn't the correct way to transport a precious little person. Time to go back to the manual!

DAD TIP #33:

Why not consider organising a nice welcome-home reception at the house? Perhaps a welcome-home banner, some balloons and, if it's not going to stress your partner too much, maybe some friends and family to greet the new family member.

10. A microwave steam steriliser for bottles.

It's a special event to arrive back home with a newborn baby. Yep – another 'Kodak moment'. Don't go overboard with the festivities, though – chances are you'll still be pretty knackered and the baby will need plenty of rest, too. It might be wise to check the idea out with your partner before you organise a welcoming committee. It might spoil the surprise, but if she really doesn't want any fuss made it will save you the effort and the risk of upsetting her. You can always have a celebration at a later date.

THE FIRST WEEK

After all the excitement of the last few days, now's the time that things will start to settle down as you and your baby get to know each other a bit better. Yep, the honeymoon phase with the baby has now subsided and your life as a family is about to kick off in earnest.

MORE ON CLEANING AND BABY HYGIENE
In case you haven't already worked it out, cleaning and hygiene take on a new significance with a newborn on the premises.

This is important for the baby while his immune system is developing. You and anyone who comes into contact with the little one will also need to be clean and germ-free before you handle him. It can be tough to keep others from touching the baby, but if someone isn't 100 per cent healthy, it might be better to ask them to refrain from holding him until they are fully recovered from sickness, just in case they pass on any nasty bugs.

It all starts with you by making sure you always wash your hands after handling food, waste, pets and, of course, after going to the toilet.

STERILISING
You need to know about sterilising and you will have to do it for about the first six months of your baby's life. There are lots of ways to sterilise baby bottles, but don't forget to buy bottle brushes to clean the bottles BEFORE you sterilise them. Any sterilisation method you use will not clean the bottle. It's really simple: the process of sterilisation makes already very clean bottles sterile.

The best and easiest method of sterilisation is done with heat and water,

Call Me Dad!

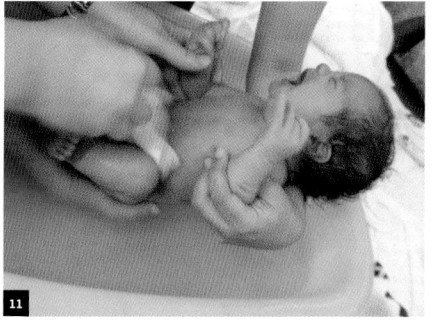

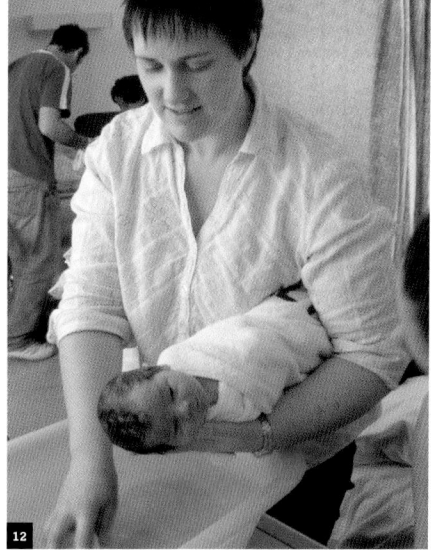

11. Keep your baby safe – get a firm grip.

12. Wash and dry the head first.

using steam and a microwave or boiling water in a pot on the stove. Microwave sterilising is done with a container that the baby-feeding equipment goes into (in pieces), with a little water. The container is sealed except for a small steam vent, heated in the microwave and left in the sterile container until ready for use. You can buy microwave sterilisers in most baby stores.

An alternative method to using a microwave is to boil the feeding equipment in a large pot. Double-check the manufacturer's guidelines on sterilising your feeding equipment, ideally before you bin the packaging.

There are also sterilising tablets available for baby-feeding equipment, which don't require heat. Again, read the instructions and follow them religiously. When it comes to sterilising feeding equipment you can't just go with 'good enough'.

The key thing to remember about sterilisation: as soon as you touch the bottle, teat or whatever, it is no longer sterile. That's why you need to wash your hands diligently prior to every handling of equipment used for feeding your baby.

BATHING

Bathing a newborn for the first time is an exciting, and possibly noisy, experience. In fact anything you do for the first time with the new family member will be exciting (and noisy, wet or messy). From here on her life will be full of firsts: the first smile, first giggle, first overflowing nappy, first word (or what you interpret as a word), first day at school, and then, later, the first boyfriend . . .

But one thing at a time. When bathing a newborn, don't fill her bath so that her little body is fully underwater; she doesn't need total immersion to get clean. Make sure you check the temperature of the water to ensure it's not too hot using the back of your elbow (for some reason the elbow makes a good temperature gauge), and skip the bubble bath for the first few months as the active ingredient that causes the bubbles could cause skin irritation or even an allergic reaction.

Make sure you have everything you need, such as a towel, fresh nappy and clean clothes, close at hand before you start the bathing process.

Use special baby soap and check that she's comfortable with the ingredients. Go for a plain soap first with as few additives,

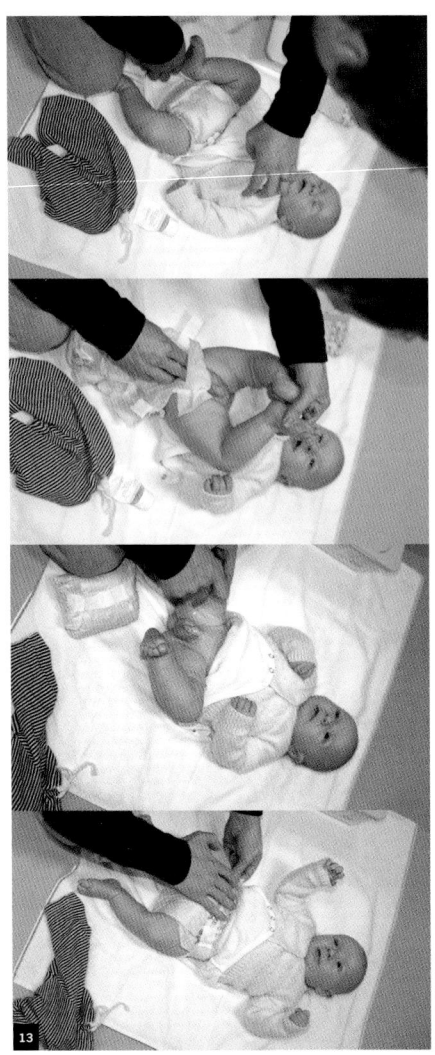

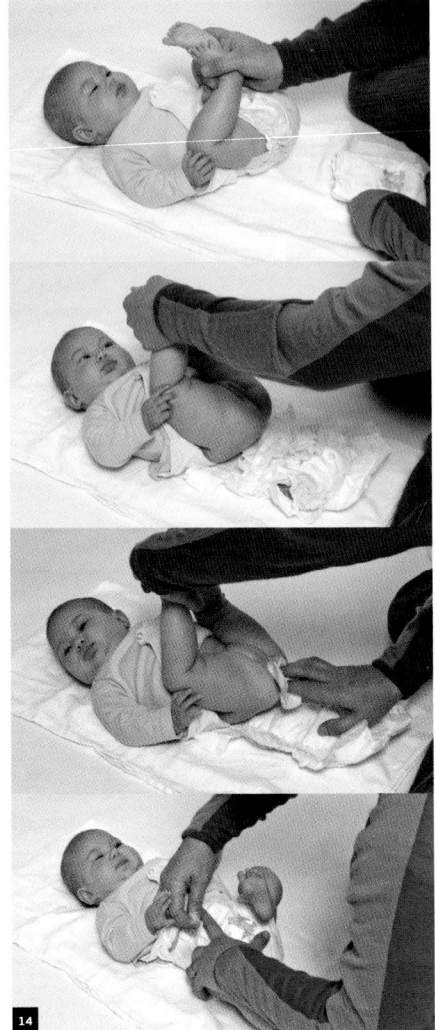

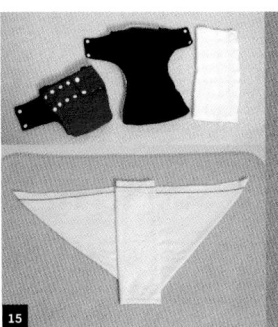

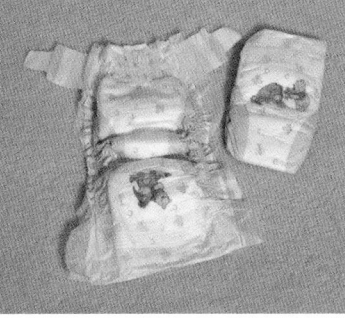

13. Golden rule to changing a boy. Tuck it down (or you might get a squirt!).

14. Golden rule to changing a girl. Wipe it down (front to back).

15. Different types of nappies (clockwise from top left): hybrid, disposable, cloth.

such as perfumes, as possible. Buy a soft hand cloth and, with a little soap and warm water, gently wash her whole body.

This is a great time to talk and coo to your child. Although she's spent nine months immersed in fluid, the noise of splashing, the echoes around the bathroom, the bright lights and so on can be a bit frightening. So your soft words of encouragement, explaining what you're doing as you wash your child, will help relax her and make bath time pleasurable for both of you.

Yes, we know she can't understand what you're saying, that's not the point!

How to bath the baby:

+ As usual, you need to support the baby's head, so get used to doing multiple things with one hand – your opportunity to show dexterity and multitasking!
+ Put your hand under his neck, so that you have your little finger and next finger supporting the shoulders and the remaining digits supporting his head, and with the other hand do the washing. If you're right-handed, use the left to support his head, vice versa for lefties.
+ Be particularly careful around the remaining bit of the baby's umbilical cord: avoid wetting it, or breaking it off prematurely (it will fall off when it's ready without your help).
+ Baby aside, ensure you're comfortable, and not putting a strain on your back, knees or arms. Elevate a baby bath on a table if it helps, making sure of course that it's secure and not going to slip off. A good thing to do is place a towel under the bath; it soaks up water, protects your table, and makes for an anti-slip surface.

    Note (hugely important): NEVER leave your baby unattended while in water.

DAD TIP #34:
When you are bathing your little champ, put some olive oil in the bath. It generally helps keep your baby's skin soft and also gets rid of any scabs on his skin or cradle cap on his head.

NAPPY CHANGING
Regardless of the type of nappies you use, the method of cleaning your baby hygienically is the same except for one thing: the sex of the baby. Cleaning a girl baby is different from cleaning a boy and, yes, it's because of 'the bits'.

Let's start with the basics:

+ Get into a comfortable position and use a baby changing table if you have one.
+ Have everything you need within arm's reach, and NEVER leave your baby unattended on an elevated surface!

You'll need:

+ Clean nappy.
+ Baby wipes (alcohol-free).
+ Baby powder and/or barrier cream (to keep baby dry).
+ Disposable change mat (if you're not at home).
+ A nappy bag (small plastic bag) to put the soiled nappy and wipes in.

How to change a nappy, step by step:

1. Before you remove the soiled nappy have a clean one already under the baby's bottom. (Alternatively, it might be wise to use a couple of sheets of budget paper towels to save wasting a clean nappy.)
2. Undo the soiled nappy and, as you remove it, wipe from the front to the back in one movement with the nappy in one hand, keeping the baby's bottom elevated by gently holding onto his ankles between the fingers of your other hand.
3. Skilfully(!) remove the soiled nappy in a tidy, rolled up bundle and set it aside. Ensure it is out of the baby's reach and away from where you might need to place your hands. Keep the baby's bottom elevated while you do this.
4. Take a wet cloth or wet wipe and, as you did with the nappy, start from the front and clean down. This is particularly important for baby girls: never clean from the back to the front with a girl as it

may cause an infection.

5. Once you're satisfied that your baby is clean and dry . . .
6. Apply some baby powder or barrier cream to the baby's genital area first followed by their bottom.
7. Wrap your baby's clean bottom in the fresh nappy (already under its bottom).
8. Place the baby in a safe place (stroller, buggy, cot, floor . . .).
9. Dispose of the nappy as per the manufacturer's instructions.
10. Wash your hands thoroughly in hot soapy water after each nappy change.

Note: If you have a baby boy, tuck his hose down while you change him or you might need to change his or your own clothes, too!

DAD TIP #35:
Babies quite often pee and/or poo within about three minutes of waking from a decent sleep, and if you go too 'Superdad' and change her instantly on waking, you may have a mess on your hands. Unless she's already soiled, wait a while before changing.

KEEPING AN EYE ON THE BABY
We have mentioned this before, and will keep mentioning it, because it's very important and that importance can be easy to underestimate. NEVER take your eye off, or move away from, your baby while she is on an elevated surface like a changing table. Babies tend to learn new things from one day to the next. Yesterday she wasn't able to roll – today she can. So don't take any chances.

If you have pets, ensure you have trained them to stay away from the change table, bassinette and cot; a water gun works as well as a stern 'no'. Pets just shouldn't be allowed near the baby's sleep or changing areas (this will assist your general hygiene around the baby).

WHEN TO SEEK HELP . . . INDICATORS
At some point, your baby will probably get sick. She is still building her immune system and it's only a matter of time. So don't worry too much, but make sure you can spot the signs. Unfortunately this can also be a major stress at the beginning – being able to spot whether your baby is sick, or just grumpy, tired or hungry. So, what are some of the indicators to watch out for?

+ Check if he is doing anything unusual, e.g., repeatedly tugging on his ear or rubbing a particular area.
+ Check for any unusual rashes, spots or skin discoloration.
+ Is he changed, fed and dry? If so and he just keeps crying or displays unusual behaviour check with a doctor, midwife or call a medical helpline.
+ Always check he is urinating, and how often. Dehydration at this age is very serious and needs to be checked.
+ What are his bowel movements like? If he has had diarrhoea for a couple of days and isn't getting any better, check with your doctor. Also if your baby hasn't had a poo for more than three days, check with a health professional.
+ Check his temperature and clothing. Is he perhaps too hot or cold?
+ Is he out of routine? Is he doing something out of character?

But whatever you do – don't panic. There are many reasons why any of the above could be happening even when your child is perfectly OK. Make sure you keep an eye on things, though. That's why keeping a log of feeding and sleeping times, soiled nappies and temperature is important because you'll be much better equipped if you do have to go to the doctor. They will ask for all this information. Sometimes the best you can do is go with your gut feeling – ultimately, you know your baby better than anyone. Trust your instincts! It can also help to stay with one GP who knows your baby well.

Remember, if you absolutely don't feel comfortable with what a doctor or health professional tells you, get a second opinion.

SCOTT:
Pyper was sick with gastroenteritis but looked happy and played as normal. The doctors thought we were paranoid but we knew we had a problem, and our regular GP knew we should keep pushing as well.

VISITORS

Having friends and relatives come over can be fun and stressful at the same time. Naturally you want to be a good host, but getting the place ready for visitors like you used to now you have a baby in the house is easier said than done.

Fortunately, friends and relatives will usually give you a few days' grace, knowing that you'll need time to get yourselves sorted. However, their patience can run out pretty quickly, and then the baby has to be presented.

Try to understand it from their point of view, too: they want to coo and aah at the new arrival and share your happiness, so roll with it and enjoy the extra attention when you show off your new baby. People aren't going to expect you to tidy the house and cook them a three-course meal, so don't worry too much.

Here are some DIYFather tips to make sure it all goes well:

+ Make sure your partner is ready and able to cope with people (other than your immediate family and close friends). She may feel a bit self-conscious about her body and looks – hardly surprising after what she's just been through, squeezing another human being out of her body!
+ Arrange people's visits so they suit your schedule (not theirs).
+ You might want to organise some specific visiting hours or visitor days so you avoid an endless and unpredictable stream of people coming every day.
+ Politely suggest that friends bring food and drinks so you don't have to spend too much time preparing – with luck you'll be able to feed off the leftovers for days!
+ Don't be afraid to cancel visits if things

aren't going according to plan or you've got a problem with the baby. Your baby should always comes first and your friends will surely understand and come another day.
+ Don't sweat the small stuff – if your house is not the well-ordered place it used to be, don't worry about it. The attention will be fully on the baby and certainly those of your friends who've had babies will know that it's really hard to keep a house tidy.

SCOTT:
What I tend to do is to just do things while they're there. Like, I will talk to a friend, feed Pyper and unpack the dishwasher, and just let them know that I have to carry on with the jobs otherwise they'd never get done.

So, you've got a few guests around, but unless your baby is asleep you can't just ignore her while you're being the host. It's a good thing to keep doing whatever needs to be done while still talking to your friends. Take them with you into the nursery and change the baby – you can do this and still hold a great conversation. Who said men can't multitask? They may also be interested to see you in your new role – a great time to show off your new dad skills!

On the other hand, those who've never had children or are baby-averse might not appreciate being invited to watch a soiled nappy being removed, so give them the option. You won't endear yourself to anyone by insisting they watch you perform!

STEF:
About 10 days after Noah was born we asked all our friends to come one afternoon. It was great – we had a fantastic afternoon with 20 people in the house. Noah didn't seem to mind and it was much easier to manage than constant visits over days and weeks. We also had help from close friends and family to prepare the 'afternoon with Noah'.

CHAPTER 6

THE FIRST THREE MONTHS

After a few weeks with a newborn baby in the house, you'll be starting to feel more confident in handling your little tiger. This is a great time to build on that confidence and consolidate your routine. It's important to feel some sense of normality is returning to your life albeit coupled with an element of randomness introduced by the little one – which only keeps it interesting!

1. A regular routine will help you, your partner, and your baby settle in to your new life.

Once you've survived the first few weeks with your baby, you'll find you're starting to formulate some routines that the baby is beginning to respond to. This is a very important part of ensuring your wee one is happy and well-adjusted.

THE NEW ROUTINE

A good place to start establishing a sense of normality to your lives is by adding structure to your day. This is mainly to help your baby settle, but you and your partner will also benefit from organising your lives around the baby's needs. It will help you keep track of everything that needs doing now you've got a baby in the family.

In the early stages, repetition and simple sequences of events help babies to gain a basic understanding of their environment and what life is all about. Research tells us that babies love to know 'what happens next', as it gives them a sense of security and stability. Because they have to learn so much, it's good for them to experience things happening over and over again, with predictable outcomes.

Although it can be hard to introduce a schedule at the beginning, the sooner you start the easier it will be.

Once again this is a Superdad opportunity, and you can shine with your organisational skills. It's really easy to do: just sit down with you partner and make a list of what you do on a typical day and when you do it. It's important to record things like sleep patterns, feeding times, play times and other events like bathing or outdoor activities.

In order for the routine to really benefit you and your baby, it's important to try to do things at roughly the same time each day, as much as possible. So whatever schedule you come up with, make it one that you know you can stick to. After a relatively short time you'll become aware of your baby anticipating the next item on the schedule, which is great! A schedule lets you manage your time and also helps your baby make sense of what must be a confusing world.

Here's an example of a routine for a one- to three-month-old:

7 am	Get baby up and feed her (if she wakes up earlier and is OK, leave her). After feeding, change her and interact.
8.30 am	Put baby back to bed.
11 am	Get baby up and feed her. After feeding, change her and interact, or take her for a walk.
1 pm	Put baby back to bed (change her if necessary).
3 pm	Get baby up and feed her. After feeding, change her and interact, or take her for a walk.
4.30 pm	One-hour nap.
5.30 pm	Get baby up and feed her. After feeding, give her a bath or shower.
7 pm	Get baby changed and put her to bed for the night.
9 pm	Wake up for night feed.

During the night a baby should be fed as and when required. As the baby is approaching three months, you should notice a reduction in the number of night feeds and a gradual increase in the duration of her sleep periods.

But remember, every baby is different, so if things don't work out as outlined here, don't worry. Introducing some sort of routine will most likely make your life easier, so give it a go, stick to it for several weeks, and then evaluate how things are going.

SCOTT:
When Pyper started sleeping through the night after eight or nine weeks, we really noticed how things changed for us, and we looked at some techniques for getting rid of the 9 pm feed. There were two nights in the following six months that she woke up crying. Other than that she slept through.

DOMINIC:
Some kids cry a lot, some don't. Our daughter pretty much cried constantly till she was four months old unless she was on the breast, or asleep. Friends and relatives told us she was probably a 'colicky baby', but we never could find two experts who agreed on exactly what colic was – wind, or an imbalance of gut flora, or something totally different. Or had we passed our stress on to her? Whatever it was, it eventually went away. Sometimes when you're in the thick of it, you have to keep repeating the mantra, 'This moment will pass.'

BASIC NECESSITIES OF LIFE: FOOD, WARMTH, CLOTHING (AND A WHOLE LOT MORE . . .)

No matter how you plan to manage your baby, pretty much everything will take longer and be more involved than you think. So our advice is simple, and it goes like this: be prepared, be very prepared!

At any time, your little one may throw up, fill the nappy, need a bottle or the breast, or want to be entertained, and if you don't have the appropriate clothes, drinks, nappies or toys on you, you'll find yourself in a pickle. Your baby will probably not appreciate this, and he'll let you and everyone around you know, very loudly!

So while it might sound a bit trite to say be prepared, do make sure you have just about everything you could possibly need on hand, particularly if you are to leave the house or plan to travel (see Chapter 7 [pp. 144–5] for advice on travelling with babies).

THE HEAT IS ON
Making sure your baby is comfortably warm, but not too warm, is an important part of looking after her for the first few weeks and months. A full-term baby can produce heat well, but is not so good at conserving it. If a baby's not adequately dressed, she needs to expend vital energy on keeping warm instead of growing. Also, babies at the right temperature tend to be more relaxed and calm. So being aware of your baby's temperature is very important, and knowing what sort of level you should be aiming for is a must.

For a quick check on your child's temperature, put your hands on her neck and see if it feels cold, hot or sweaty.

This gives you a rough idea of the baby's temperature, and is great for checking while she's asleep because you don't have to wake her up.

A more accurate method for taking temperature is to place a thermometer in your baby's armpit (this reads what is usually referred to as the axillary temperature). A normal reading is 36.1 to 36.5°C. If you want to go the extra mile, buy a digital infrared ear thermometer. They do all the work and can read the temperature without waking your baby (so long as you can get to her ear), and are also very accurate.

If you get temperature readings of over 37.5°C, your child might have a fever, typically as a result of an infection or illness. While fever itself is not an illness, it indicates that something might be going on in your baby's body, so get this checked. If you get continuous readings of more than 37.5°C, clothing or the room temperature are not likely to be the cause and you should definitely have your baby checked by a health professional as soon as possible.

CLOTHING AND WARMTH

So what does all of this mean for dressing your baby? A useful rule of thumb is that your baby should always wear one more layer than you've got on in the same environment, i.e., bedroom, other rooms, outdoors. A naked baby is comfortable in an atmosphere of around 30°C, so get into the habit of dressing them in two or three layers to keep warm enough in standard room temperatures of 18 to 20°C.

And when you're going outside, it's important to make sure your baby is dressed appropriately, with options to add or take off a layer as required. Always take some extra clothes in case it gets cold unexpectedly. Don't forget a woolly hat or similar for winter or cold-day outings, since babies lose a lot of body heat through the head. In summer, a hat (a different one!) is also essential for protection from harmful UV rays.

BABY MONITORS

Topping the list of gadgets for newborns is a baby monitor – a great little invention that enables you to hear coughing or crying when you're away from the baby's room.

As an alternative to mere walkie-talkie type models, you can also get sophisticated vital-sign monitoring stations – sometimes these are also referred to as 'angel-care monitors'. These more refined devices are installed in the cot and will alert you if your baby's breathing rhythm changes or his heartbeat stops.

> **SCOTT:**
> We were using an angel-care and a standard monitor. The angel-care monitor didn't really work that well, but the standard monitor did! We could hear everything, and I mean everything – it even tuned in to the people next door.
>
> I like the concept of baby monitors but I don't like relying on them, and this seems to happen a lot. We certainly did in the early months, but I think all you need is a good ear and to take the time to check on bubs.

MORE ON HYGIENE

Your baby's health is of paramount importance, so while getting the cleaning done and keeping the house tidy might be the last thing on your mind, it will make things easier and safer for you all if you do. Nothing makes your day more interesting than tripping over a toy or stepping in a full nappy.

Having a supply of clean and dry clothes for your baby is also important, so make your life easy by being Superdad again and organise the cleaning, tidying and washing in your house. You can do most of it inside an hour – it's no big deal.

A WORD ON CLOSE ENCOUNTERS WITH YOUR BABY

Skin-to-skin contact with your new baby is great for bonding and it's also great for the baby; she's kept warm against your skin, and learns about you through your smell, how you feel and the sound of your voice as you talk.

However, one of the hardest things you'll have to do is manage the contact your baby has with other people, especially if you know or suspect they might be unwell.

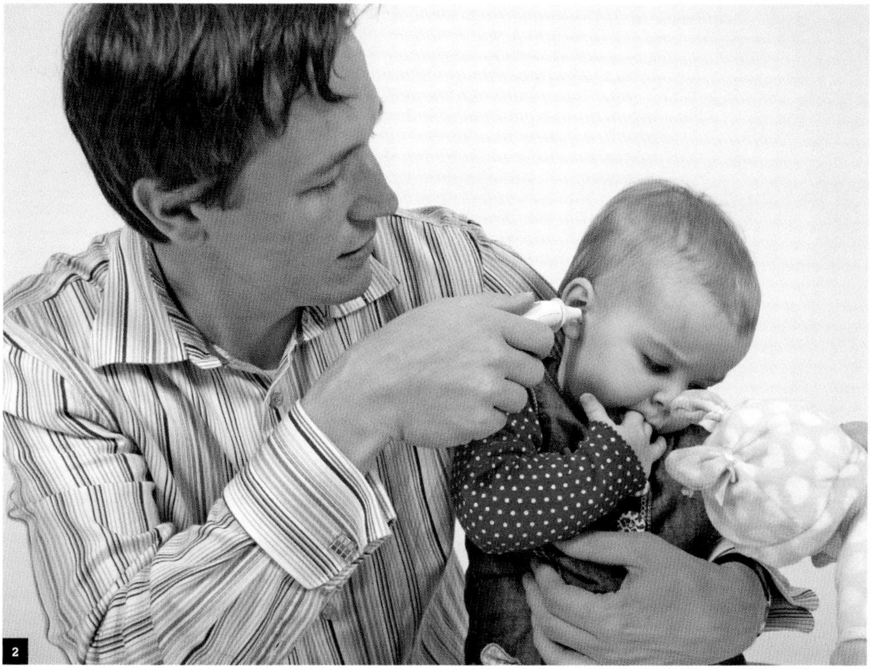

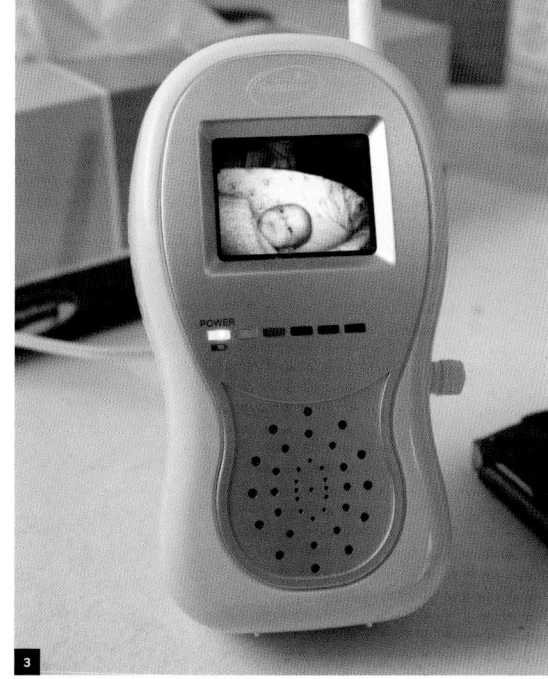

2. A digital thermometer: One of the quickest, easiest and most accurate ways to take your baby's temperature.

3. Video baby monitors are increasingly sophisticated. Some can even monitor your baby's vital signs.

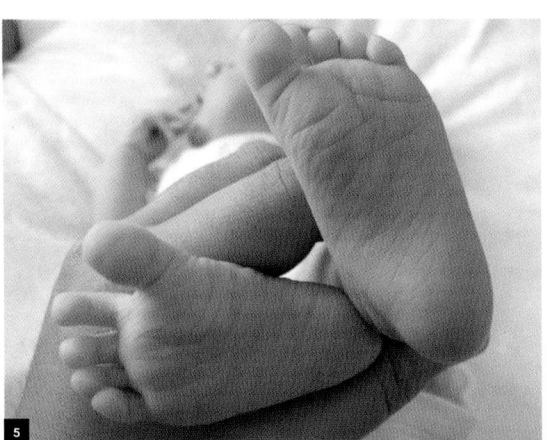

4. Skin-on-skin contact is great for the baby. It aids bonding and keeps her warm.

5. Just like every other part of your baby's body, your baby's toes and fingers are tiny – make sure you use special baby scissors for cutting her nails.

Call Me Dad!

In such cases you need a clear 'sorry, no touching' policy because your new baby's immune system is still in development, and they just don't have enough in-built resistance yet to protect them.

You might also have to manage people's desire to touch your baby if it's not acceptable in your culture to let that happen. Certain parts of the body, e.g., the baby's head, might be off-limits.

Of course there is a natural tendency for everyone to want to hold your baby and play with him, so control this as diplomatically as you can, providing appropriate protection for your child while still allowing him his share of adoration and people contact.

NINE-INCH NAILS

If there is one thing that grows even faster than your baby, it's your baby's fingernails and toenails. From a very early age you will probably notice they're razor sharp and grow like mad. So what do you do? You cut them, of course.

Easier said than done. Babies generally don't like having their nails cut, and with their fingers and toes being so small it's very difficult to make sure you ONLY cut the nail and nothing else. This requires a bit of skill, practice, patience and distraction (on the baby's part).

At the beginning it's really best to do this as a team effort. You need someone to hold and distract the baby while you do the cutting. Feeding is a good time to do this as the baby is generally focused on getting food in.

IMPORTANT: Make sure you get special baby scissors (they are either made of plastic or have very round edges everywhere). Don't ever use normal sharp and pointy scissors for adults as you never know when the baby might make a sudden move and injure herself.

STEF:
When Noah was about six months old, we were invited to a wedding – it was our first social event as a family and we were all looking forward to it. On the morning of the wedding, I was playing with him in bed and he suddenly lashed out and hit me in the eye. It had happened before, but this time the pain didn't go away and I could hardly see straight. I ended up at A&E and was told I had a 'corneal abrasion' – a scratch across the front part of my eye. Not pleasant, and needless to say the wedding was off (for us).

BARBER SHOP

If cutting people's hair is one of your life's unfulfilled ambitions, you're in for a treat when you have a kid. Why not have a go at cutting your baby's hair (assuming mum lets you – hey, it always grows back, so where's the harm?). Unless you have had some serious hairdresser training, DO NOT use actual scissors for this (way too dangerous). Instead, get a hair clipper. They are inexpensive and are pretty safe to use around babies. Most models come with snap-on attachment combs that determine the length of the hair left after the shave, i.e., 2 centimetres, 3 centimetres, etc.) The haircut is pretty simple – select the comb and shave your baby's head. As you get a little more confident you can experiment with different lengths on the side or back of the head. Come to think of it, perhaps this works best for boys – still, it's another great dad thing to do.

FOOD (THE BABY'S AND YOURS)

If you're breastfeeding you won't need to worry about preparing food for the baby for at least the first four months. Breast milk arrives fresh and at the right temperature, so no extra effort is needed.

There are a few exceptions, however. There are times when you need to be extra careful with feeding breast milk – for example, when the mother has mastitis and breastfeeding is painful. If mum expresses milk for later use, you need to obey the same rules as those who bottle-feed when it comes to hygiene.

If you freeze breast milk, don't keep it in the freezer for longer than a month. If you're ever in doubt about using frozen milk, don't use it.

DAD TIP #35:
Put sticky labels on the breast-milk containers for use in the freezer and write the date on them so you'll know how long the milk has been stored.

6. A girl can never start too soon!

When preparing food for a baby you have to be absolutely certain that everything that comes in contact with the food is extra clean (like hospital clean) and preferably sterile.

This is extremely important in the first three months while the baby is building up her resistance to all the bugs in the environment; you don't want her exposed to any unhygienic bottles or equipment. Make sure your own hands are spotless and that any surfaces that come into contact with feeding equipment are also extra clean.

Before you give the bottle to your baby it has to be the right temperature. There are many methods for checking the temperature if you don't have a food thermometer handy. An easy way is to use your lips or wrist – the liquid shouldn't feel hot (ideally the feed should be between 35 and 38°C). Practise getting a feel for the right temperature by guessing first and then checking with a thermometer.

YOU ARE WHAT YOU EAT
The first few months after the birth can be tough on you because your attention is nearly always on the baby. Although it can be difficult, it is important that you maintain a healthy and balanced

diet for yourselves, particularly if your partner is breastfeeding as the goodness (or not-so-goodness) in what you eat is passed on to the baby via the breast milk.

So isn't it great that catering is another area where you can shine as a dad?

If you know how to cook, you can really show off in the kitchen and reduce the family intake of takeaways and pre-prepared food. For nutritional value, you can't beat home-made food prepared with fresh seasonal ingredients – so, go for it!

What? You don't know how to cook? OK, ask your parents or friends for some simple recipes. Cooking is not rocket science – trial and error overcome pretty much everything – though persistence and common sense are great ingredients.

And cooking is definitely part of being a twenty-first-century dad, so if you haven't done so before, now is a good time to master a few simple dishes. You never know – you might actually enjoy it and move on to more sophisticated cooking, opening up a whole new world of culinary opportunities.

CLOTHING AND SHOE UPDATE

Once you've gone through the first few weeks of changing and dressing a baby, many of the things we said in earlier chapters will hopefully make sense to you.

You will probably appreciate closing mechanisms like Velcro (though not directly on baby's skin), domes or simple laces because they're much less messy than trying to undo a zipper crammed with leftover food and free-flowing infant bodily excretions. If you haven't experienced these difficulties yet, in time you'll see what we mean.

DAD TIP #36:

If you're in charge of buying clothes, don't forget to 'upsize' clothing. Apart from mushrooms and some bacteria, infants are arguably the fastest-growing thing on the planet and have been known to increase by a garment size a week. This is especially true if you haven't read the washing instructions and the warnings about shrinkage. Unfortunately these are generally found in the innermost recesses of a garment. As you'll notice, some kids' clothing is quite expensive so don't waste hard-earned money by accidentally downsizing that designer-label jumpsuit in the washing machine!

THE BABY WEARS PRADA?

Seeing as babies don't start walking until they are at least seven months old, the need for shoes (unlike knitted booties, which at least have warmth value) prior to this is pretty much nil. If you absolutely have to buy shoes for a newborn (or risk divorce) buy just one pair. This will save you a small fortune.

Later, when your child is mobile, you can buy more shoes, which will be useful if for no other reason than because one shoe will always be missing, or just out of reach behind the sofa or refrigerator.

Try to buy shoes a size too big so there's at least a chance they'll be useful for longer. You can always stuff them with cotton until they fit naturally (generally the day before your little treasure hurls one of them out of the partly open car window and under the oncoming 18-wheeler Mack truck).

DAD TIP #37:

Put your little champ on a piece of paper and draw around his feet. Cut out the outline and take with you when you are shopping for shoes. It's much easier to get a general idea of the fit before you actually try them on your baby. He may not be keen on trying dozens of shoes until you find a pair that fits.

DAD TIP #38:

When in doubt about anything to do with baby shoes, clothes (or almost anything else), ring the family expert: your mother. If she's not available, call your mother-in-law. They'll be only too happy to help.

OUT AND ABOUT

Your baby needs plenty of fresh air, especially during winter when the tendency is to stay inside. Spending time outdoors with your newborn is great, and a good opportunity to come out of the closet and shout, 'Look at me! I'm a dad!'

But before you leave the house, consider how long you're planning to be away. Is it just a five-minute breath of fresh air around the corner on the school playing field, or a three-hour expedition? If you're going to be away for longer than half an hour you should probably take the baby bag to avoid being caught out.

Here's the DIYFather checklist for the baby bag:

+ Fresh nappies.
+ Disposable changing mat.
+ Nappy-rash cream/powder.
+ Baby wipes.
+ Hand sanitiser.
+ Change of clothes (for the baby, and you if things go horribly wrong).
+ Food and fresh water for the baby.
+ A couple of small plastic bags (for soiled nappies and wipes if you can't dispose of them).

As comedian Billy Connolly once noted, there's no such thing as bad weather, only the wrong clothing. So the simple rule is to make sure your baby is adequately dressed at all times. If it's cold you need to make sure she's warm, if it's wet you need to keep her dry and when it's sunny make sure she doesn't get overheated or burnt.

Managing exposure to sunlight is particularly important because, while you obviously need to be extremely careful your little one doesn't get burnt, sunlight helps babies produce Vitamin D, which is necessary for bone, joint, muscle and neurological function.

Good sun-exposure management is:

+ Covering up your baby with light, airy clothing.
+ Using an infant sunscreen (check age limit – some are not recommended for newborns) for exposed areas including feet, neck, ears, face – and reapply on a regular basis.
+ Using a hat to cover his head and shade his face.
+ Avoiding middle-of-the-day exposure, usually from 11 am to 4 pm.
+ For older infants: protecting the eyes with baby sunglasses.

Call Me Dad!

7. Discovering different shapes and textures in the outdoors.

8. They're all mine! Toys are brilliant at stimulating the senses, but simple play with a parent can offer just as much.

DAD TIP #39:
Make sure all your containers and bottles are closed properly before you leave the house. Nothing worse than discovering that your nappy bag is now one large food container with a few extra ingredients like nappies, wipes and creams.

Many buggies and strollers are fitted with a sunshade to offer some relief from the light, but for those really sunny days you need the sun net. (You bought it when you got your stroller – remember?) If you notice some skin reddening after exposure to sunlight, or if your baby gets sunburnt, see a health professional ASAP.

DAD TIP #40:
Here's a tip for when you're out and about in the few months after the birth: Your partner's tummy may not shrink immediately, which can make her look like she's still pregnant for a while. So, if you're going to visit friends you've not seen for some time, and you're not taking the baby (because your mother's babysitting – isn't she great?), make sure you warn your friends WELL in advance that your partner's had the baby. There's nothing worse than her being asked when she's due, after she's given birth.

TOYS, TOYS (AND MORE TOYS)

This is definitely an area where you can benefit from the less-is-more approach.

While most toys appropriate for your baby's current age are probably useful and entertaining, few are absolutely essential. Many are quite expensive and don't offer as much enjoyment as simple interaction with a parent can. Your own performances (singing, making noises, talking and so on) can keep your child very happy at absolutely no cost other than time.

For the first three months there's a limit to what babies can do by themselves, anyway, and unfortunately it seems some toys are actually designed to distract babies so parents can do something else.

Most of the experiences offered by toys designed for newborns up to three months can be provided by items generally found in the house. The purpose of toys at this age is to expose babies to different textures, colours or sounds. You might come across Lamaze toys, in every imaginable size and style. They're generally good, not too expensive, and are among the more sensible choices at this age. Anything battery operated is definitely not essential, although you might want to try out a night light or musical mobile for the cot.

There's no doubting the importance

of stimulating your baby and helping him develop essential skills (see the Active Movement section at the end of this chapter, p.126), but some toys go overboard. Let's face it, your two-month-old baby won't learn to count from one to ten, or learn to play 'Twinkle, Twinkle Little Star' on a xylophone just yet. A good cuddly toy in soft, natural materials, and something like a rattle that makes a noise, will go a long way towards keeping him satisfied and stimulated.

DAD TIP #41:
A great way to control the number and cost of toys is to use a toy basket, adopting the philosophy that once it's full, that's enough. When you purchase or are given a new toy, make it a policy to give away an old toy that is no longer enjoyed or needed.

MAKING TIME FOR YOUR CHILD

Never underestimate how much your child will pick up from you, even in these early weeks and months.

Prepare to be amazed when your baby repeats one of your gestures, or has worked out how to do something without you consciously showing him. Be careful though, this parroting behaviour can extend to all sorts of things, some of which you might not be so thrilled about! Remember that 'first word' scene from *Meet the Fockers*?

Either way, it is absolutely key that you spend a lot of time with your child. Often it's about making time, not just fitting the baby in to the rest of your life. The rewards will be lifelong.

The more time you give your baby, the more he will learn and develop, and the more rewarding it will be for you. If you're a father who works to provide for the family, then take time out to look after your child and be part of his formative years.

On the schedule that you and your partner developed (yes, remember?), reserve a special time each day to spend with your baby. It's all too easy to get into the habit of fitting the baby in when it's convenient - so go out of your way to get involved, and stay involved, in your child's life. Apart from anything else, it takes the pressure off your partner so she doesn't have to come up with all the answers; it's not fair if only one parent has to make all the decisions all the time.

It's true that you might have to change the way you work, or reduce the number of hours you work, to spend more time with your child. So what? There's a saying that old people hardly ever wish they had spent more time at work, so do something about this now during these early, golden and vitally important developmental years – not when you're retired and your children have left home. Later, you won't believe just how short the baby stage was, how quickly it was over. Nothing speeds life up quite so much as a child growing up.

Above all, getting to know your child is a lot of fun. Babies have a way of making you forget everything else, and they bring a lot of laughter into your world. Every baby has a unique way of interacting with his parents - all the quirky things he does as he explores the world are wonderful (and sometimes hilarious) to observe.

9. 'It's a classic one, Dad. I think you'd like it.'

GENERAL HEALTH

Your baby deserves good health, but she can't manage that by herself. It's important that you both do whatever you can to ensure she remains healthy.

Looking after a sick baby can be very stressful, especially in these early weeks and months. You might not be able to avoid a common cold or other minor problems, but you can positively influence your baby's chances of avoiding serious illness.

Here are a few general guidelines:

+ Eat healthy and fresh food. If you can, continue with your exercise routines or whatever else you normally did to keep fit before baby came along. If you stay well, that's one less chance that your child will get sick.
+ Keep your house warm and dry at all times. When the baby is not in her room, open the windows and doors to let fresh air in.
+ Read up on the recommended immunisation schedule for babies. You need to fully understand the benefits and risks of the various vaccinations before you can make an informed decision. It's up to the parents to decide whether to follow the vaccination schedule, but most health organisations recommend immunisation.

+ Do whatever's necessary to reduce your baby's risk of exposure to cigarette smoke. If you smoke, consider giving up for the sake of your child's health. There's a ton of research showing that a smoke-free environment at home improves the general health of your child and reduces the risk of developing a whole host of health problems later in life. If you just cannot give up smoking, make sure you don't smoke anywhere near your child or inside the house. Inhaling second-hand smoke is linked to many serious medical problems and is considered one of the main risks for Sudden Infant Death Syndrome (see p. 125 for more information on SIDS).

GETTING SUPPORT

Life can be pretty tough, and sometimes lonely, for new parents.

Fortunately, parenting is an area where there's plenty of support available for just about everything. Besides friends and family there are literally dozens of support organisations, some of which you probably haven't even heard of. From dealing with very serious health issues, to casual meet-ups, to swapping parenting tips, and even to the loss of a child, there's support out there for everyone.

Support organisations can be formal or informal. Your GP or primary healthcare provider, or midwife, are great sources of information about where to go for professional support. They tend to keep lists of support organisations and often know who to contact for any given situation.

The idea of an informal support group is to link up with other fathers (or parents in general) to share concerns and frustrations, and to exchange ideas about ways of being a better parent. They're also an effective way to make friends and create a network of people around a common purpose.

If you attended an antenatal class, it won't be too difficult to get in touch with the other couples and organise a meeting. Sometimes this is a service offered by whoever is running the classes. You may also live in an area where someone has started a 'Parents in the Neighbourhood' (PIN) group, one option among many for setting up casual get-togethers with other parents.

And then of course there's the Web: with access to the Internet it's a great time to be a parent! The world's child-rearing experiences are there for you to tap into, and most support groups have a website. So if you can't find the group you're after, check out the Web. A great place to start is obviously our support group directory on www.DIYFather.com.

Finding a good support group can make all the difference – especially for us dads! Don't try to be the Lone Ranger; your child doesn't need a stressed parent who's trying to work things out all by himself. Ultimately it's about sharing information – so do your bit to learn from others, as well as help them. We live in the information age, after all.

If all else fails and you just can't find a support group, maybe you can start one yourself. Once you get going you'll be surprised how many people share a similar desire or need for the group you want to start. Create a website, put up a few flyers in the library or at the hospital. Most places won't mind putting up non-commercial notices, especially if they're aimed at helping others, as well as yourself.

DON'T FORGET YOUR PARTNER

Don't forget that your relationship with your partner still needs to be maintained. Be careful not to lose yourselves in the routine of parenting. Take some time out and go for walks together, which of course can be done with the baby in tow. Family and friends can provide heaven-sent opportunities for time out from the baby, too. Make it a regular occurrence to get out of the house together and enjoy each other's company (like you used to – remember?).

Reintroducing a bit of intimacy into your lives can be easier said than done. After a few months of living with a baby, you might have noticed that some things have changed:

+ It's possible you might have been put off having sex after going through the labour experience with your partner; all that pain, the screaming and the blood . . .
+ On the other hand, you might feel like having sex all the time but your partner might not be in the mood (or may still be experiencing pain).
+ If you do manage to get it on, you'll discover that babies have a cunning way of timing their crying.

If any of the above are true for you, all we can say is be patient, things will eventually get back to normal.

Despite the challenges, it is absolutely vital for your sanity and the future of your relationship that you spend some time alone with your partner – and make a conscious effort not to talk about the baby for a while!

THE END OF THE PROBATIONARY PERIOD

When your baby reaches the three-months-on-earth point you, too, will have reached a real milestone.

Some things will get easier after the third month – just in time for some new challenges (but more about that in the next chapter). Either way, hopefully you'll have managed to establish a routine of

10. If you can't find a
parent support group in
your area, start your own.

sorts: that's definitely the easiest way to organise all the additional chores you need to do, such as getting more baby food ready, cleaning the house, and putting four or five lots of clothing through the wash/dry/fold cycle every day while they're sleeping.

Talk to your child, even when they're so tiny that you can hardly find them in amongst the clothing. Warmth, security, clean clothes and a good feed on demand – that's pretty much all any of us needs in life, and it starts at this stage. An infant is really just training to be an adult. Think about it: how do you react when you aren't fed on time, don't have clean clothes and don't get enough sleep?

A WORD ABOUT SIDS

Sudden Infant Death Syndrome (SIDS) refers to the sudden and unexplained death of an apparently healthy infant during the first year of their life. It is also referred to as cot death or crib death. There is still relatively little known about the exact causes of

SIDS, and there is no proven method for preventing it. However, a number of studies have identified factors that may increase the risk of SIDS.

These include (during pregnancy):

+ Maternal nicotine use (cigarettes or patch).
+ Alcohol abuse.
+ Use of recreational drugs.
+ Being overweight.
+ Being under 20 at the time of giving birth.

Postnatal risks are identified as:

+ Low birth weight (especially less than 1.5 kilograms).
+ Exposure to tobacco smoke.
+ Excess clothing, excess bedding and overheating.
+ Births less than one year apart.

SIDS is one of the saddest topics you will come across around babies. It is beyond the scope of this book to cover it adequately. If you are worried about SIDS, or would like more information, we suggest you contact a local SIDS support organisation.

ACTIVE MOVEMENT – ZERO TO THREE MONTHS

Constantly looking for opportunities to help your child develop his full potential is just another part of being a Superdad. And guess what – it doesn't start when you take him to his first footie practice at age six. It starts from day one (or even before birth). So over the next three chapters we would like to offer you ideas about helping your child's development through playful physical activities and laying the foundations for the many amazing skills they will demonstrate in later years. It all starts now.

In order to provide you with the best advice in the interests of helping the development of our children, we've teamed up with a world-leading initiative called Active Movement, which was developed by SPARC (Sport and Recreation New Zealand). SPARC recognises that positive and appropriate early-movement experiences impact on the way infants, toddlers and young children learn, grow and participate in physical activity throughout their lives.

SO WHAT IS ACTIVE MOVEMENT?

Active Movement is about engaging in physical activity experiences which develop and enhance the emotional, social, cognitive and physiological growth of a child. Active Movement embodies the whole child. SPARC has developed the term to refer specifically to movement and physical activity in the early years of life.

Active Movement is essential for children's brain development. It strengthens the connections within the brain and body, and the development of these connections are vital for memory, sensory development and communication between the two sides of the brain, providing the foundation for all higher-level movement.

The connected development of the body and the brain mean that positive-movement experiences enable young children to grow through playfulness, and develop their imagination and the confidence and skills to participate in a world full of physical activities. As well as physical skills like eye, hand and foot coordination, physical movement impacts on children's cognitive abilities, the development of the senses, problem solving and spatial awareness.

WHAT DOES IT MEAN FOR ME?

What this means is that you as a parent have a unique opportunity to stimulate the development of your child by trying out a few simple ideas. You don't need any special equipment or training – all the activities are suitable for what will be available in the house, garden or park. Like many things you will do as a father, Active Movement is also a mindset you need to develop. Look for any opportunity to turn an everyday activity into a fun and safe game with your baby. Remember, some of the best learning takes place when you don't realise you are being taught – when you simply explore. You will also learn a lot about your baby when you engage with him fully. This is a unique opportunity for us dads to strengthen the bond with our children.

Below are some activities to try out. They are based on the fundamental movement patterns for confidence and competence in skills like jumping, running, catching, throwing and spinning your baby will need when she's older.

A key thing to remember is that babies develop in stages – until they have fully developed a particular stage they can't move on to the next one (for example, mastering gross motor skills must precede the development of fine ones). So it's the STAGE, not the AGE, that counts when you try these exercises. You will easily recognise what your child can and can't do (yet).

11

11. Simple activities like letting your baby watch leaves moving in the breeze will help develop their senses.

Activity ideas for zero to three months:

1. Sensory development

Park the baby's pram or buggy under a tree. This aids eye-tracking development as the baby looks at the leaves and watches their movement. Follow up by letting him experience the different textures of grass, sticks and leaves.

2. Baby massage

This activity involves gently stroking the baby while naming parts of the body and helps language development and body awareness.

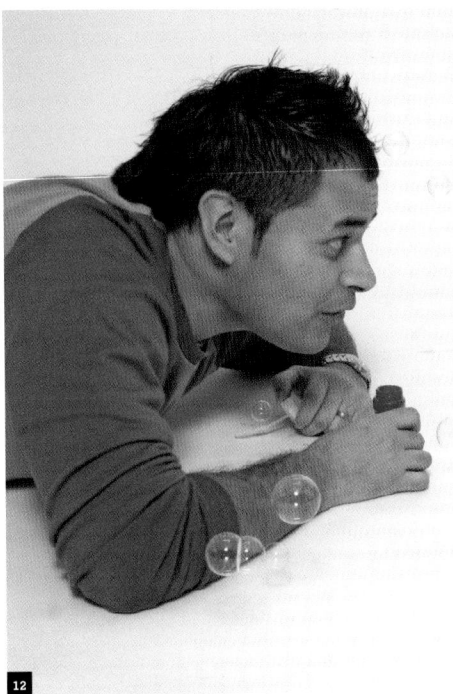
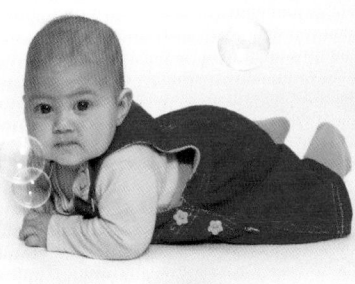

12

Why is massage good for you and your child?

+ It's a lovely way to relax with a baby or young child.
+ It helps children to feel welcome, loved and respected.
+ It soothes, relaxes and calms both of you, while also stimulating the baby's brain and sensory system.
+ It strengthens the baby's muscles.

3. Bubbles

Watching bubbles helps eye-tracking and upper-body development. You can also use bubbles in the bath: avoid the baby's face but allow bubbles to land on different parts of her body.

4. Swiss ball

Using a Swiss ball, place the baby on top (either on his tummy or his back) and gently roll him so that he is upside down, side to side, etc., while holding on to him.

Note: For more information about SPARC's Active Movement programme, or to download all brochures, visit: www.DIYFather.com/sparc www.sparc.org.nz.

12. Blowing bubbles is fun, keeps infants entertained and helps develop their eye-tracking skills.

13. Baby massage stimulates the brain and muscle development.

14. A Swiss ball can be fun and helps babies develop a sense of balance.

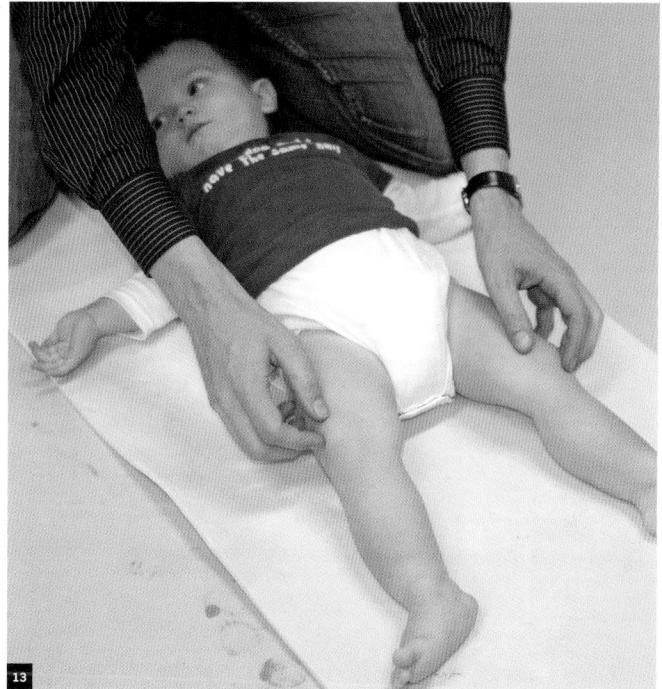

CHAPTER 7

THREE TO SIX MONTHS

Reaching the end of the first three months deserves a pat on the back. At this stage babies are beginning to look more like the ones you see in the ads and less like wrinkled monkeys. They're also a lot more resilient and are beginning to show signs of recognising people and places, as well as starting to interact with their environment.

Your little princess is now getting into some serious growth, and a certain relaxation takes over. Constant hovering to make sure she's breathing turns into constant hoovering as her regular sleep patterns become more defined, allowing you (finally!) to get the housework done. Yep, junior's now focused on the serious businesses of feeding and growing.

By now the chances are you'll have mastered the basics of looking after your baby – feeding, cleaning and handling her. Having fun? Good! And it gets even better over the next three months as your youngster learns lots of really cool things like being able to sit up, using her hands intentionally (grasping, flapping them around, and so on) and filling electronic hand-held devices with dribbly saliva.

1. Time to review what we know.

REVIEWING KEY DECISIONS

The three-month mark is a good point to review some of those key decisions you made and to ask yourselves, how are things working out? Does it still make sense to keep doing things the way you have done over the last three months, or is it time to change? This particularly applies to your daily routines, sleeping arrangements and feeding.

Reassessing your decisions ensures you're not blindly sticking to something that – although it worked earlier – might no longer be appropriate or necessary. Things change very quickly with a young baby, so review the way you're doing things every now and then.

ROUTINES

If you haven't established a daily routine, start doing so now; you'll all benefit from it.

As we've mentioned before, routines help your baby make sense of his environment and give a predictable rhythm to his existence. If he knows there is always a similar sequence to how the day unfolds it gives him a sense of comfort. He'll know what happens next and as a result will be able to prepare for it. A good example is that if your child knows the bath time–feeding–burping–bedtime–lights-out routine he should settle more easily at night.

If you've established a routine to your day you might now want to check whether it's still in line with the baby's evolving needs. For example, over time babies need less sleep during the day and more stimulation. Their feeding habits also change. If your routines have somehow become eroded along the way, now is a good time to get back on track and adjust them to the baby's needs.

The vast majority of behavioural issues at this young age (such as not going to sleep, not sleeping through the night and so on) can be influenced by the consistent use of routines. And speaking of sleep . . .

SLEEP

How is your baby sleeping at night? Is she sleeping through the night already (you lucky buggers!) or is she waking up frequently? How is she settling at bedtime? How are the night feeds going? Where does your baby sleep – in her cot, in your bed, or next to your bed? These are all things you need to look at when you want to get a feel for how well you are aligned to your original ideas about handling the baby.

Not happy? Well, you can change that. The great thing about babies is that no matter how ingrained you believe a habit is, you can change it, and most likely within two weeks. If you've had the baby sleeping in your room and now want to move her to the nursery, do it. The baby will find it strange at first and this period can be tough (for you and her), but after a few nights she should adapt and settle, providing you establish a bedtime routine in the nursery just as you'd previously done in your own room.

Sometimes babies change their sleeping habits by themselves. Often, though, if you want to encourage a particular change, e.g., reducing the number of night feeds or awake-periods, you have to actively do something about it. In many cases you may have to change things during the day, e.g., increase the number of feeds or change the timing of naps to affect how your baby sleeps at night.

DAD TIP #42:

To help your baby figure out the difference between day and night, make sure the nursery can be 'blacked-out'. It doesn't have to be pitch black, but it helps during summer months to reduce daylight in the mornings as well as the evenings.

FEEDING

By now you'll almost certainly have settled into a more or less defined feeding pattern and any initial problems should have been resolved. If you're breastfeeding it's sometimes difficult to tell just how much milk the baby's actually getting. Frequent weigh-ins to monitor his weight can definitely help.

You might now have to start topping-up feeds with either formula or expressed milk. Depending on how the breastfeeding is going, you might consider dropping completely and switching to bottle-feeds to ensure he is getting enough food. From month four onwards, look for signs from the baby that he's ready to start on solids.

THE ROUTINES THEY ARE A-CHANGIN'

You'll probably notice now that the baby's daily habits are changing. She's most likely spending more hours awake during the day and needing fewer night feeds (Yes! At last!).

Obviously this varies hugely from one baby to another – there's no set rule – so if yours is still sleeping during the day and waking at night, don't worry. Things will change. All you really need to do is check that the routine for your baby is in line with her needs.

Here is an example of a typical daily routine for a four- to five-month-old baby, but check with your midwife or healthcare professional for advice on developing a routine to suit your particular baby, especially her sleep patterns and feeding needs:

7 am	Get up – even if she wakes earlier, leave in cot/bed for as long as possible. First feed of the day.
7.30 am	Feed solid food as top-up (if ready for solids).
8.00 am	Awake period – time to engage/play/stimulate.
9.30 am	Morning nap. When starting to get tired, change nappy and put to bed.
11 am	Get up – second feed of the day.
11.30 am	Awake period – go for a walk or play.
1 pm	Midday nap. When starting to get tired, change nappy and put to bed.
3 pm	Get up – and if she wakes earlier, leave in cot/bed for as long as possible. Third feed of the day.
3.30 pm	Awake period – go for a walk or play/stimulate.
4.30 pm	Afternoon nap - one hour only.
5.30 pm	Get up/wake if necessary. Feed solids (if ready for solids).
6 pm	Evening routine – bath/shower, bedtime reading, stories, night routine.
7 pm	Final feed for the day (breast/bottle only). Put to bed for the night.
7.15 pm	Time to put your feet up and fall asleep in front of the telly!

Remember that you have to be flexible about your baby's routine. You should be working your day around him, rather than the other way round.

Since your baby will spend more hours awake during the day, think about how you're going to fill that time with activities. He needs plenty of fresh air, stimulation and also time to himself to work things out. But just leaving him with lots of toys on his own is certainly not the answer, and you have to put in some effort to engage with your baby.

THE FOOD REVOLUTION – INTRODUCING SOLIDS

At some point between months four and six your baby will be ready to start eating 'solids'. Surprisingly, solids are usually not very solid at all, and typically will be some form of baby-rice porridge or fruit mash.

Starting with solids is a great time for you, especially if your partner's been breastfeeding and you feel like you're missing out on the whole 'feeding the baby' experience. It means that you can now prepare meals for the baby and give them the appropriate food for the stage they're at.

Another thing to look forward to is that your baby's eating will get progressively more messy (until they're in high school, give or take).

Here's a list of clues that indicate your child might be ready for solids:

+ She is able to fully lift and support her head for long periods.
+ She starts putting things in her mouth and chews on them.
+ She looks at you while you eat or drink and mimics your chewing/eating.
+ She gives continuous feeding signals, i.e., it feels like you just can't give her enough milk.

Finding the right time to introduce solids is not an exact science. If in doubt, check with your midwife or healthcare professional. It might just be a case of trying it out. If your baby doesn't seem keen, wait for another couple of weeks and try again.

2. 'You call this a mess? Wait till I get a bit older!'

3. Try introducing your baby to different soft foods between the ages of four and six months to ensure he has a varied diet.

When you feel that solids time is near, here's a list of useful things to get in advance:

+ A good solid highchair (or feeding seat, which can be put on top of normal chairs).
+ A plastic floor mat (if you'd like to keep your carpet the way it is now).
+ Lots and lots of bibs (you can never have enough). Use big-sized bibs with a flexible bit that goes round the neck and closes with Velcro at the back (easier than tie-ups).
+ Baby-feeding spoons (these days you can get some fancy ones that change their colour if the baby food is too hot).
+ Drinking cups (especially those with a top and spout).

You also need to replace the teats of the bottles you're using. Your baby is now able to take more fluids at a time, and most teats for three- to six-month-olds have several holes instead of just one, enabling a greater flow of liquid.

Remember this eating solids thing is all new to junior, so you should introduce the new foods with a degree of excitement and optimism rather than being too cautious (which he'll possibly pick up on). And don't be afraid to eat some yourself with lots of 'Mmmm, that's lovely!' Let him know this food is really nice.

The great thing is that babies learn very quickly. So with sensible, careful steps your little champ will very soon be tucking into whatever you give him without question. This is a golden time where you can feed him good healthy stuff and he won't argue. Later, when he knows how to exercise discretion, you can expect some battles!

When you're introducing solids, don't hurry things: give your baby plenty of time and wait until he's swallowed what he has in his mouth before you cue up the next spoonful. And the cardinal rule for the first few months is: don't give him anything hot!

DAD TIP #43:
If you have a highchair, place it near your dinner table and have the baby around when you eat. Put on a 'show' for your baby of how humans (adults) actually eat. Give her a chance to observe you putting food in your mouth, chewing and swallowing. She's a natural copycat and will really get it after a while.

Typical starter foods (for the first few weeks after introducing solids) include:

+ Baby rice.
+ Mashed banana and apple (boiled).
+ Boiled carrots, potatoes and pumpkin.
+ Teething rusks.

Note: Don't add salt.

Concentrate on keeping the routine and the foods simple. Be patient and be sensible with their nutrition: there's a whole lifetime ahead of them to choose to eat badly, so give them a decent chance and stick to nutritious, healthy food appropriate for their developmental stage. To begin with, introduce one type of food at a time and give your baby the chance to get used to all the new flavours. Also, start giving them solids once a day at the very beginning. Gradually increase the number of solid feeds throughout the day.

DAD TIP #44:
You may be curious to try store-bought baby food yourself before you give it to baby. You may well find it bland but plain food is good for little ones whose taste buds are far more sensitive than ours.

> **SCOTT:**
> Introducing solids varies from baby to baby, possibly because some grow faster and/or their genetics call the shots. We found Pyper was still getting hungry towards the middle and end of the day, so we started off very cautiously and made sure we gave her just small amounts of mushed food, which included (and still does) vegetables such as carrots, beans, broccoli and potato – not all together, but we wanted to slowly introduce one food to her at a time. So it was carrots, then carrots and potato, then three or four items together. This worked well for us.

DAD TIP #45:
Have your camera ready! Introducing solids is a big developmental step and a superb photo opportunity. There's nothing like the expression on your baby's face as he tries certain foods for the first time.

Solids not only help babies grow, but the intake of more substantial food also enables them to sleep more easily. However, if you're not confident about developing a routine to introduce solids, talk to your midwife and perhaps childcare organisations. They should be able to help you out and might even offer useful guidelines for introducing solids.

Nutrition is a general subject, and needs adapting to be 'child-specific' because some children have special dietary requirements (and no, we're not talking about McDonalds for lunch on Fridays!). But at this tender age your child is something of a guinea pig, and you need to introduce foods one at a time, not only to see whether they react to something but also to give them time to get used to it, though we're not sure how anyone ever got used to Brussels sprouts.

Starting with solids doesn't mean you just suddenly stop breast- or bottle-feeding; your baby needs to be weaned off milk food slowly. As a rule it is recommended babies stay on breast milk or formula until they are about 12 months old.

> **STEF:**
> After the first three months we started giving Noah a few herbal teas in addition to water and breast milk – mainly fennel and chamomile. The fennel tea worked really well with digestive problems. Chamomile tea helped in calming him down in general.

DAD TIP #46:
Make sure you and your partner don't pass on your food likes and dislikes to your baby. Don't pull a face or make a disapproving sound when feeding the baby something you don't like yourself.

DON'T FORGET THE PAPERWORK

4. Babies come with their share of paperwork.

Like motor vehicles and most household appliances, babies also come with paperwork and you will have to register your baby one way or another, and perhaps even in multiple ways, soon after her birth. In some cases the hospital might forward birth records to the appropriate authorities on your behalf; you may discover, however, that you have to do this yourself. Make sure you obtain a birth report from the hospital or from your midwife to get your baby registered officially.

After that you'll be the proud owner of a birth certificate that records the name of your baby, her birth date, where she was born and other vital statistics. It's an important milestone, but guess what? More paperwork awaits!

Apart from registering your baby with the state and your church (if you belong to a certain faith), you will also need to add her to your health-insurance plan or register her with your primary healthcare organisation.

You will also need to give some thought to what will happen to your child if something happens to you and your partner, so speak to your solicitor about updating your will or creating one if you don't already have one. You might also want to consider appointing a guardian or two for your child, which is something you'll need to discuss with whomever you have in mind before you officially appoint them.

FINANCES AND INSURANCES

Money can be a major stress for new parents. In the first few months following your baby's arrival you're likely to find your finances screaming for attention. Whether, as is likely, you've dropped to one income, or stayed on two, the family's budget will have suddenly got a whole lot tighter.

Some of your new expenses will be capital investment, e.g., getting the room ready, buying a stroller and a car seat, while others are ongoing, e.g., nappies and other toiletries, baby clothes (which constantly need updating) and of course food. The costs can seem endless!

At some point, you'll have to plan for the future as well. You'll want to ensure your child has the most secure future possible. You'll want to be able to give him a head start in life. Wouldn't it be great if you could ensure that he doesn't end up with a crippling student loan? Or if you could help him out with a deposit on his first home?

Taking time right now to consider these future financial matters may seem like a low priority, especially when you have all this other stuff on the go (not to mention the current strain on the budget). But the reality is that there's no better time than right now to address these issues. So, should you start a savings plan for your child? Should you get medical insurance? Do you need life insurance? There are no right or wrong answers to these questions – it really depends on your personal circumstances – but you should at least ask the professionals for advice.

There are some great savings plans for education funds – from a standard bank savings account through to unit trusts. There are also good insurance products to protect your new family. In particular, you might want to consider income protection for the main breadwinner, especially if you've dropped down to one income. Ask yourselves, could you survive without that money coming in?

But insurance is quite complex and you need to get good advice before you make any decisions. Speak to your own insurance or financial adviser, if you have one.

SCOTT:
How can you relate to creation and death at the same time? I guess it's about making sure your little person is protected in the event that something happens to you and/or your partner. We updated our wills and made sure that Pyper had a guardian if we both died. She's also covered and will have adequate money available to her, though we stipulated that she wouldn't be eligible for this until around age 30, usually a time in your life where you're either struggling or still finding your feet. We thought a payout at age 20 might tempt her to buy a Ferrari and then have nothing to show for it by age 25!

MONEY TIPS FOR NEW FATHERS

1. Don't get life insurance for your baby

In our opinion there is no need for you to get life insurance for your baby at this stage, and if someone tries to sell it to you they're probably taking advantage of your emotions. The golden rule of life insurance is: take it out only if the loss of the insured person would have a financial impact on the surviving family members.

The main argument you might hear to justify insuring your child's life is to make sure they can get cover in the future. But this isn't a great argument. The chance of a healthy child developing a health issue that stays with her until she's an adult is not that high. What's more, unless you insure your child for a large sum from the beginning, the level of cover selected would probably be tiny compared with her needs in the future.

You may think you would need a break to grieve in the event of your baby dying. But in most cases you can only insure a child for quite a small amount. Also, if you have income protection and are unable to work because of grief or stress, the policy should pay for as long as you are genuinely unable to work (stress-related issues are common in income-protection claims). So, in a nutshell, make sure your existing plans are adequate rather than taking out any additional policies.

5. Babies can chew into your cashflow, but try not to let your own savings get too far offtrack.

2. Tailor life insurance to your situation

Congratulations, you're now financially responsible for someone other than yourself! So how much life insurance should you have? Once, you'd probably have been advised to multiply your annual salary by some magical number (some would say 10, others 15), which would give you an appropriate amount of cover.

That method was probably perfect – for the insurance agent. But as you can imagine, the results were not exactly tailored to each individual. Today, if you ask an adviser how much life insurance do I need, their answer should be: it depends.

You'll probably be asked to complete a questionnaire, or fact finder, to give your adviser a clear picture of you and your situation. The answer to the question should then also be pretty clear. It's not rocket science and no magical numbers are needed – your own situation will determine the life insurance sum that's right for you.

3. Work vs. stay-at-home (it's not just about salary)

Obviously more than just financial factors will determine who, or whether either of you, stays at home. On the financial side, don't just look at each salary; take into account any benefit packages, too. These can add up significantly, so look at which of them you need and the cost of not having them. Also, if you're weighing up returning to work, don't forget to factor in costs such as transport and day care.

4. Don't let your own retirement savings get sidetracked

You'll still want to retire one day – and that day is not getting any further away even if it might be the last thing on your mind just now! If you're considering taking a break from saving, plan now how you might be able to top up your savings later. If you're able to, just keep on saving.

You can still take advantage of benefit schemes that might be offered to young families. The key thing is to find out about them – so check the Web or speak to friends about what is available.

5. Find out about income protection

Since it's more likely, statistically speaking, that you'll become ill or injured than die unexpectedly, income-protection insurance is something that all parents ought to look into. And if the thought of relying on the state to support you and your family in the event that you become chronically ill or disabled worries you, it's even more important.

COOL THINGS YOU CAN DO WITH YOUR BABY THAT YOU COULDN'T DO BEFORE

Now that your baby is a little older you can do more with her, especially once she can start holding her own head up. Here's a loose collection of practical activities the two of you can do together.

BATHING

Put little animals (no not your dog . . . a rubber duck!) in the bath. If your baby takes to the water like that duck, you can also try pouring some water over her using a plastic cup or bowl.

DAD TIP #47:

Take your mobile phone into the bathroom and place it in a safe spot away from the water. This means that should anything happen you can call someone straight away but still stay with your baby.

SHOWERING WITH YOUR BABY

If you want to try something other than the usual baby bath, why not take your baby in the shower with you? It can be a lot of fun for the baby and for you. Obviously, you need to make sure your baby is safe, and keep an eye on her to see she is actually enjoying herself. If you do this instead of the usual bath, remember you're there to clean the baby, not yourself. Ask her mum to stay handy so that when you've finished washing baby, she can then safely take over and leave you to take care of yourself.

> **SCOTT:**
> I found that because I was home with her, I would rather give her a shower since it's faster. It also means that later, when she starts swimming lessons, hopefully she won't be scared of the water.

READING

Reading is a great way to get some extra bonding done with your child. It is a great 'winding down' activity, especially in the evenings to calm her down and prepare her for a good night's sleep.

There are tons of books for babies, and for this age you need to get some with lots of colours and shapes. Some of them have different textures for your baby to touch or pop-up shapes or figures to activate.

At about this stage you'll notice your baby responds really well to rhyme and repetition. This is great for stimulating brain development.

You might think she's not old enough for stories yet, but you'd be wrong; little kids love to hear the cadence of your voice as you read, and she'll love looking at the bright pictures as you talk about them. She won't always be the most rapt of audiences, and might occasionally try to eat the book, but she will like the experience.

DAD TIP #48:

Join the library. Buying lots of books for your baby can get very expensive (although they are designed for small people, it doesn't mean children's books only require a small budget). Most libraries are really good when it comes to resources for kids – so check them out before you splash out.

SINGING

'I don't do singing!' Actually, yes, you do – and you'll be amazed at just how self-confident you can get, crooning quietly to your little one to help him relax (especially when no-one else is home).

6

Call Me Dad!

6. Read to your baby whenever you can.

7. Take baby to the beach and watch her explore new sensations. You'll see the world with new eyes.

As with stories, it's the rhythm, the cadence, the simple sound of your voice he'll enjoy. No matter what your singing talent is like, he'll think you're cool and so long as it's got some soothing flow to it, junior won't care whether it's 'Twinkle, Twinkle Little Star' or 'I Can't Get No Satisfaction'. But even if he seems to really like rock songs, go easy on the Alice Cooper or Iron Maiden posters in the nursery!

WALKS

Going for walks on the beach or at the park and enjoying the environment is another great way to hang with your baby. Now that she's a bit older you can introduce her to all the weird and wonderful things there are to see when you are out and about.

Don't be afraid to get her or your hands dirty and show her what grass, sand or pebbles feel like on her hands and feet. The environment offers an endless source of materials, objects, sights and sounds to experience. This will engage and stimulate your little darling's five senses. It's great fun to watch how your baby reacts to all the different things she encounters during your walks together. She might also teach you to see the world with her eyes, which is a pretty special gift.

A WORD ON OVERSTIMULATION

Despite the importance of baby stimulation, at this tender age you need to take it a little bit easy with your baby. If you try to cram too much into the day and overload him with all the various forms of entertainment and stimulation we as adults are used to (TV, games, music in the background, phones, computers, etc.) it can be a bit overwhelming.

Over time this can manifest as restlessness, grumpy outbreaks or sleep difficulties. Singing nursery rhymes, using simple toys and playing together will go a long way. You don't need electronics!

8

ON THE ROAD AGAIN – BABY TRAVELS

Whether it's going to the shops or your first overseas holiday with the whole family, travel and transportation for your little one is very important. At this age he will probably sleep a lot while you're on the move, lulled into drowsiness by the motion of travel.

But you do need to consider and plan for the baby's needs, especially on long-distance car journeys. Frequent stops and regular feeds are essential. Check the manufacturer's instructions for your capsule on the maximum recommended time he should be in it. For most capsules, this is around two hours.

Travelling overseas can be a monumental project. You'll need to pack a separate bag (the biggest one) for your baby, and will basically need to take what feels like half the nursery with you! So, leave ample time for packing and think carefully about how you're going to meet all the baby's needs wherever you're going.

You also need to consider the journey itself, for example, how you'll feed and change the baby, where he can sleep and so on. And, of course, you'll need all the necessary travel documents organised and handy at all times. Finally, allow yourselves more time for

8. Precious cargo!

checking in. You'll have discovered by now that every trip takes longer than usual with a baby in tow.

BABY ON BOARD

With air travel, you'll need plenty of options to entertain her on the flight. All she knows is that you're all sitting down for an hour or three (or longer), with nothing special happening, and a lot of noise and activity (and strange people) around her. It doesn't make sense to her, so she'll need some comforting distractions.

It's possible to hold on to your stroller right up until boarding time. There is usually an announcement for people with babies to board before other passengers. At that point airline staff will take your stroller from you at the boarding counter, and load it into the plane for you. They will return it to you at your destination docking gate. A light but robust stroller is most convenient.

Take several bottles and food to give to your baby on the plane, but a note of caution: new regulations apply to carry-on liquids, aerosols and gels. These are typically limited to 100 millilitres each, and they must be packed in a sandwich-sized, clear, resealable plastic bag, separate from your toilet kit.

To help with adjusting for pressure differences during the flight, give your baby something to drink (or breastfeed her) as the plane takes off and just before landing (swallowing helps her ears to pop, which is important).

Waiting for the plane can also be a challenge. Little babies are not likely to be excited by the sheer experience of being in a plane. They don't know they're flying, so you need to treat them just as if you were at home in your living room.

If your plane's delayed or you have a long wait, take your little one around the block in the departure hall, looking at the shops or exploring the various facilities or departure gates. The idea is to try to tire her out so that she's ready for sleep when you board. Good luck!

If you have a choice of long-haul flights, it can be easier to opt for an overnight one if you can work it into your normal routine for the day.

Sea travel is not that much different: you still need to know how long you'll be travelling and ensure you've got everything you need for the journey. But it's easier than air travel because there's more space to move around (weather conditions allowing). At this young age there isn't anything you can give your baby for motion sickness, but chances are she'll be coping better than you, so don't worry too much.

If you can avoid it, don't travel alone with the baby. If you and your partner (or someone else) can share looking after her during the flight (or voyage) it will make things a lot easier. If you do have to travel alone with your baby, you'll need to keep an eye on her at all times (remember that film *Flight Plan*?) as well as attending to her every need. This will make it a very long and tiring journey.

DAD TIP #49:

You'll want to book a bulkhead seat for a long-haul flight to accommodate a bassinette for baby to sleep in. you'll also find the extra leg room is handy for nappy bags, blankets, etc.

NANNIES AND BABYSITTERS

At some point after the first three months, you may decide you're ready to employ a nanny or babysitter to take care of the baby. This is a huge step and will almost certainly be more difficult than you think. After all the hard work of bringing a baby into this world and looking after him, you are naturally very attached to him. Trusting someone else to look after him can be hard.

For precisely this reason it can be difficult to find a suitable person. You might want to start asking around in your wider family or circle of friends first because, ultimately, it always comes down to trust. Can you trust the person you are choosing to look after your child 100 per cent? The answer has to be 'yes'.

Another thing to consider is whether your babysitter has the necessary skills and experience. It's also a huge responsibility –

so first check out their experience, their references, and that they, too, are comfortable with it.

Next, it's a good idea to do a few trial runs and see how your baby reacts to the new help, and to check their hands-on skills while you're there. After a few sessions, if it all works out, you should feel confident to leave them in sole charge.

Tell your child minder as much as you can about your baby and any special needs or habits. Either way, make sure they know what to do if anything goes wrong. If there's a medical emergency, this means calling the emergency services even before contacting you.

THE WIDER FAMILY

Grandparents enrich a baby's life in so many ways – by playing and reading, by sharing life lessons and family history, by listening and lending advice, by providing stability to the family, and by offering emotional and spiritual (and financial!) support.

And with the issues facing both parents and grandparents today – such as differences in values and customs within the family, divorce, and perhaps a long-distance relationship – a grandparent's role in the child's life is more important, and more challenging, than ever.

So you'll be appreciated if you make a special effort to include your – and your partner's – parents in your family life. They will certainly appreciate being part of it and will likely offer to look after the baby, giving you some invaluable relief.

The other great thing about grandparents is that they've been there, seen it and done it. Grandparents are usually (naturally enough) a little more relaxed when it comes to dealing with the challenges of having a baby in the house. They will have their own way of interacting with the baby, and can offer him an alternative source of advice, comfort and love.

Some grandparents have also been known to spoil their grandchildren rotten – so be sure to explain how you want to bring your children up (diplomatically, of course!).

Advice will come thick and fast from grandparents, family and friends. Listen to their advice (especially from those who are parents), but you will of course remember that you are the parent, so do your own research, make informed decisions, and don't be afraid to follow your instincts.

CEREMONIES

If you haven't already done so, now might be a good time to think about some kind of ceremony to officially welcome the baby into the world or, if you are religious, into your faith. Even if you're not particularly spiritual, it's a great thing to consider. For example, you could hold a naming ceremony with all your friends around, or another ceremony involving those who've agreed to be your child's guardians.

Unfortunately, such ceremonies these days are sometimes seen as just another opportunity to acquire more useless presents for the nursery. Don't fall into that trap. Do some proper event management and add some real meaning to your ceremony!

SCOTT:
Recently, after a couple of wines, my wife told me that because I wasn't particularly religious and she was, we should have a naming ceremony instead of a christening. Now to be honest I'm not fussed on the whole thing, but what I was interested in was the whole modern equivalent to godparents – I'm not really sure what they are called. This means should daddy be a lazy, good-for-nothing drunk, with no future prospects, hopefully one of the godparent equivalents will step in and help him out with the lifestyle that he's become accustomed to! Hmmm, sounds great to me! Hopefully they won't read this and will be none the wiser!

9. It's important to encourage the development of relationships between your baby and members of your wider family.

10. A grand day out with granddad.

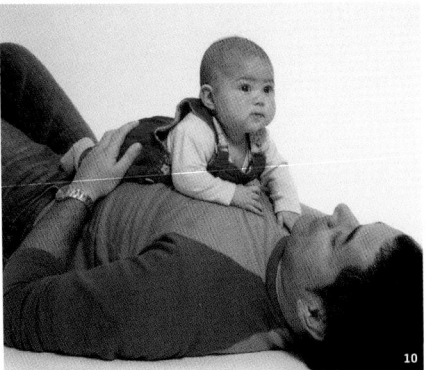

10

11

12

ACTIVE MOVEMENT –
THREE TO SIX MONTHS

After the first three months you will notice
amazing changes taking place in how your
baby interacts with the environment. By
now, many babies will be trying out facial
movements (yes, like smiling . . . isn't it just
fantastic when the little one smiles at you?),
focusing their eyes and discovering their
body parts. The following activities are
designed to support those developments
and stimulate further new skills.

DAD TIP #50:
Try making up your own words to existing
songs and rhymes, or try out different
languages if you know any.

1. Tummy time:
To encourage cross-line movement, place
toys just out of reach so she has to crawl
to reach them. And try the other activities
shown above.

2. Finger games:
For example, 'two little dicky-birds'. Finger-
puppets are great for this.

3. Singing songs:
Children are able to recognise and respond
to music right from birth. Accompany songs
with appropriate actions, for example
'Twinkle, Twinkle Little Star' and 'Round and
Round the Garden'. Doing this encourages
body awareness (where are my fingers and
hands?) and language development.

Call Me Dad!

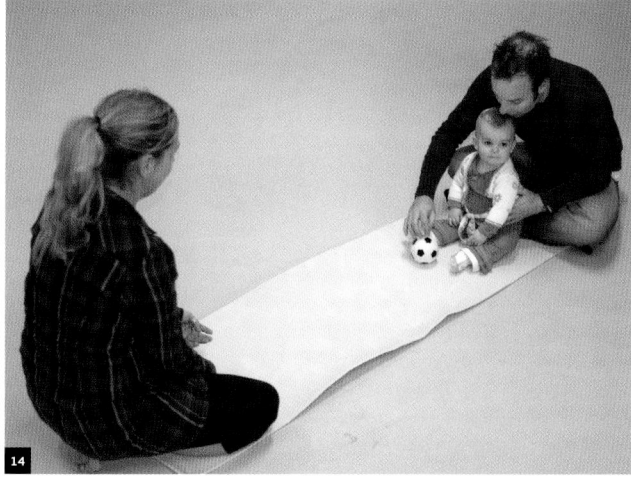

10-14. Stimulate your baby's development with simple activities such as finger games, playing 'catch', tummy time, singing and dancing.

Why music and singing are so important:

+ They generate an awareness of different emotions and feelings.
+ They encourage speech by repetition of words.
+ They teach basic concepts such as night, day, under, over, animals, rain, stairs, etc.
+ The child develops hand-eye coordination by tapping out beat from music.
+ The child improves memory skills by repeating favourite songs regularly.
+ The child develops timing skills, which help him to kick moving balls, throw and catch.

Here are some suitable songs which have lyrics that lend themselves to accompanying actions (you might even remember them from when you were pint-size!):

Incy, Wincy spider
Climbed up the waterspout
Down came the rain
And washed poor Incy out.
Out came the sun
And dried up all the rain

And Incy, Wincy spider
Went up the spout again.

Round and round the garden, goes the
*   teddy bear.*
One step, two steps, tickle under there.

4. Dance to music:

Do this while holding your baby. Remember to move slowly and turn both ways. Movements like swinging, spinning and rocking help develop your child's sense of balance. Her balance system starts to develop before birth and will continue to develop until adulthood.

Good balance is reinforced by having strong back and tummy muscles, so babies need constant activity to develop these areas. Good balance also helps your child to:

+ know how she fits into a space;
+ stay still when sitting, standing or lying;
+ develop eye movement and vision.

5. Catching:

Rolling a ball to your child, as well as being great fun, helps to develop coordination.

CHAPTER 8

SIX TO TWELVE MONTHS

The old saying that time flies when you're having fun is never truer than after the birth of your first child, although you may not fully appreciate the fun involved in getting your infant back to sleep at 3 am. So when your baby hits the six-month mark, you can marvel at the fact that you've been a dad for that long!

You're probably wondering where the last six months have gone! They flicked by as you were taking each day as it came, focusing on the next thing that needed doing. Take a moment to reflect on the last half year, and pat your partner, baby (gently) and yourself on the back for what you've achieved. Hopefully you'll come to the conclusion that you are the luckiest dad alive to have such a fantastic baby and partner. So, are you ready for number two yet? (Or three . . . or four?)

The next few months in your baby's development will continue to be action-packed – for you, that is. As your little champ gets the hang of eating solids and learns how to crawl, walk and talk, you'll have your hands full with things to do.

Your baby's demands for stimulation and interaction will also increase as she starts moving about, and communication will become two-way (verbal and non-verbal . . . you'll see what we mean by that). You'll notice how your little one goes through many changes – especially if you happen to be away for a week or so. Chances are that you'll find a different baby when you return (hopefully not literally – but you know what we mean!).

ROUTINES FOR BABIES AGED SIX TO TWELVE MONTHS

The daily routine for a six- to nine-month-old baby might look something like this:

7 am	Get up and have first feed of the day – start with solids, then top up with bottle/breast.
7.30 am	Awake period – time to engage/play/stimulate.
10.00 am	Morning nap. Get baby changed and put to bed.
11 am	Get up and give snacks (solids only).
11.30 am	Awake period – go for a walk or play.
12.30 pm	Lunch – feed solids, then top up with bottle/breast.
1 pm	Midday nap. Get baby changed and put to bed.
3 pm	Get baby up – even if he wakes earlier (leave in cot as long as possible). Afterwards give some snacks (solids only).
3.30 pm	Awake period – time to go for a walk, or play/stimulate.
5.30 pm	Dinner – feed solids only.
6 pm	Wind-down period – bath/shower, bedtime reading, stories, night routine.
7 pm	Final feed for the day (breast/bottle only). Put to bed for the night.
7.30 pm	Time finally for you to put your feet up and fall asleep in front of the telly (again!).

Towards the end of his first year your baby will probably change his sleep patterns again and gradually move to only one nap during the day. At that point, an example of the routine might look like this:

7 am	Get up, get changed and give first feed of the day – start with solids, then top up with bottle/breast.
7.30 am	Time to engage/play/stimulate.

10 am	Give some mid-morning snacks (solids only).
11.30 am	Lunch – feed solids, then top up with bottle/breast.
12.00	Midday nap. Get baby changed and put to bed.
2 pm	Get up, get changed and give some snacks (solids only).
2.30 pm	Time to go for a walk, or play/ stimulate.
4 pm	Give some mid-afternoon snacks (solids only).
5.30 pm	Dinner – feed solids only.
6 pm	Wind-down period – bath/shower, bedtime reading, stories, night routine.
7 pm	Final feed for the day (breast/ bottle only). Put to bed for the night.

When reducing breast/bottle-feeds, do so gradually over a couple of weeks. This allows time for your baby to adjust to the change. Doing this 'cold turkey' is not recommended.

SOME NEW CHALLENGES

Your baby's body is developing at a rapid pace, which can bring a lot of pleasure as well as some pain – for the baby and you. But don't panic: all these changes are normal and you're not being singled out for extra punishment!

I LIKE TO MOVE IT, MOVE IT

As your baby increasingly discovers her ability to move body parts, she will also take all the opportunities she can to practise doing so. In general this is great, as it helps her develop gross (meaning large, not horrible!) and then fine (smaller) motor skills. In some cases this can make your job as a parent more challenging. For example, when it comes to changing clothes or changing nappies, the newly discovered mobility really works against maintaining an orderly process.

Until now your baby mostly stayed where you put him and the movements of his arms and legs were easily controlled just by holding them firmly. From six months on you need to lift your game a bit, as your little champ will try to wriggle himself out of every situation that bores him, and being dressed is boring. So, too, is changing nappies, or clothes, which babies regard as utterly unimportant. You'll need to be more vigilant and skilful than before, and you'll need to use one of the Five Secrets of Parenting: Distraction. (See p. 19 for the other four secrets.)

Giving your baby something to do that makes a nappy change a more interesting event can work really well. Before you even start changing her, take a new toy or other suitable household item with you and give it to her to play with. You can even reserve some toys or items just for changing.

If you haven't already done so, you need to think a bit more carefully about where you change your baby. A changing table may no longer be safe as your baby's wriggling can easily get out of control, resulting in a fall. You don't want that to be even remotely possible – so think of alternatives that are safe – the floor, or on a bed (use a changing mat).

DAD TIP #51:
A cheap and cheerful distraction can be made by filling an empty transparent water bottle with washing-up liquid, water and some glitter. This budget 'lava lamp' shaker can keep babies entertained for a long time, as the liquid and glitter create interesting shapes and reflections. But you'll need to ensure the cap is screwed on tightly and there's no chance of the baby opening it and consuming the liquid. Best to use it only while you're changing the nappy and keep it well out of reach at other times (some babies can learn rather quickly to unscrew a cap).

Another thing you really have to do now is adjust the cot. As soon as your baby starts crawling and pulling himself up, you need to drop the bottom of the cot to the lower position so he can't climb out when he's standing. Do this sooner rather than later and don't underestimate your baby's ability to climb. Babies have been known to use toys in the cot as steps!

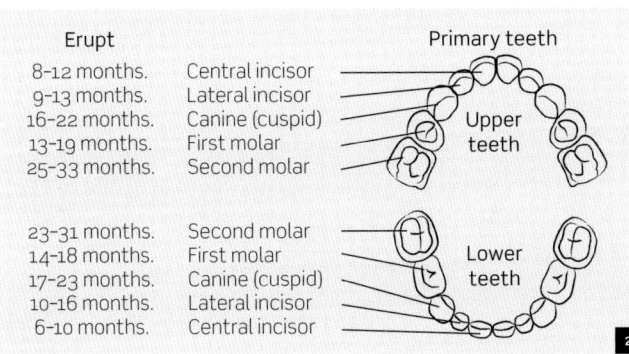

Erupt		Primary teeth
8–12 months.	Central incisor	
9–13 months.	Lateral incisor	
16–22 months.	Canine (cuspid)	Upper teeth
13–19 months.	First molar	
25–33 months.	Second molar	
23–31 months.	Second molar	
14–18 months.	First molar	Lower teeth
17–23 months.	Canine (cuspid)	
10–16 months.	Lateral incisor	
6–10 months.	Central incisor	

1. Show off those pearlers!

2. This diagram shows the average age at which each tooth comes through.

REALITY BITES

Your baby's first teeth should appear around month eight – although some little ones have been known to come into the world with a tooth or two already! But chances are you and your baby will have to go through teething. This invariably involves some pain (although we've heard stories of some babies not even noticing). Teething can turn sleep patterns and daily routines upside down as your little one tries to cope with a pain she certainly doesn't understand. As you'll probably know by now, the preferred coping method is to cry (as well as biting you or throwing things).

Excessive dribbling, reddening of the cheeks, a tendency to cling and general irritability are all things to watch for, but at your age you really shouldn't be showing any of these. So let's concentrate on the baby instead . . .

Signs of teething can indeed include a deluge of dribbling, ruddy cheeks and general grumpiness, as well as excessive biting. In extreme cases teething can also lead to inflammation of the gums, sinuses or ears (possibly accompanied by fever). If you suspect your baby has inflammation, see a doctor ASAP.

No matter what your baby's experience of teething, it's likely to make your parenting life even more interesting for a little while. Fortunately, teething generally happens in bursts – a few days of pain, then a few days back to normal – until finally the first tooth emerges. Aaah, cute!

But don't celebrate too soon, because this pattern will be repeated with many of the other teeth (apparently some teeth appear more easily than others). During the first year you'll most probably only have to deal with the central and lateral incisors (the cutting teeth, in the middle) which will be good training for when the more painful teeth come out (canines, and molars, for chewing).

Teething will possibly affect your feeding schedule. If you still breastfeed, get some bite rings – vital for mum during breastfeeds as your little precious is working out the difference between biting and sucking. Seriously, this can be a difficult period for both mum and baby. Help her educate the baby not to use his new teeth when latched on. One way is to remove the baby from the breast as soon as he starts biting. Keep him away for a few minutes before returning him to mum to finish the feed.

Some babies refuse to eat because their gums hurt and they're simply not interested in food. This phase generally passes when hunger overcomes pain – so there is no need to force your baby to eat. In fact you should never force your baby to eat as a general rule.

STEF:

Noah had an exceptionally hard time teething, perhaps because his teeth grow very slowly. Over a long period we had many difficult nights in a row, so naturally our energy levels got quite low. The amazing thing was that no matter how bad a night was, Noah always woke up in a good mood and greeted us with a huge grin (toothless at first). When you see your baby smile at you in this way you forget about all the frustration and sleep deprivation and you just melt. Nature's cunning way.

3. A teething ring filled with fluid is a worthwhile purchase for soothing teething babies.

Here are the DIYFather top-five hints for dealing with teething:

+ Buy some teething toys, e.g., teething rings – a variety of hard and soft ones.
+ Get some teething rusks – they're a great 'two-in-one' solution, providing both food and a semi-soft item to chew on.
+ Use teething gel – typically found in supermarkets or baby stores (but make sure it really is teething gel, the kind that's safe for babies).
+ You could even try an amber necklace – an alternative remedy, which baby wears during the day (take it off before they go to sleep). Amber is believed to reduce inflammations.
+ Give your baby some cold chamomile tea or chamomile powder (check your homeopathy store for this remedy). Do this during the day and especially in the evenings for a general calming and soothing effect.

DAD TIP #52:
Some babies like a 'cooling' sensation with their teething toys/rusks. So put them in the fridge (NOT the freezer) beforehand.

ILLNESSES – THE USUAL SUSPECTS
During the first year of your baby's life you might meet some of the usual suspects among childhood illnesses, as well as having to deal with the common cold or 'flu. Looking after a sick baby is no fun and can be heartbreaking at times as the little one looks so miserable.

So familiarise yourself with the common childhood illnesses, diseases and their symptoms. With foreknowledge you might be able to reduce their severity, and you can get appropriate treatment early.

Call Me Dad!

In any case, you should see a doctor if you suspect your child is coming down with something. www.DIYFather.com/health.

If you are the one going out to work, consider taking time off to help your partner look after the sick baby. Chances are you will be getting even less sleep than usual, and your immune system may have to do some extra work to fight off the bugs you're being exposed to, so take plenty of vitamins and boost your own immune system. There's nothing worse than having to look after your sick baby when you are ill yourself.

DAD TIP #53:
Check your own and your partner's vaccination records and find out whether you've been immunised against all the various childhood diseases, or whether you've had the illness yourself (you might have to check with your parents).

THE CRYING GAME
During the first year, a baby's favourite communication method is crying and they do it pretty well.

If crying goes on over an extended period, e.g., due to illness, or pains you can't do much about, it can become very stressful. You need to find rational and workable ways of dealing with this – the emphasis here is on YOU, on how you handle this, because there is only so much you can do to prevent your baby crying.

Have a look at the DIYFather list for coping with extended crying:

+ Take turns with your partner, and when you're not attending to the baby, go far enough away that you can't hear the crying.
+ Wear earplugs during the night when you know it's your partner's turn to look after the baby and you desperately need to catch up on your sleep.
+ Get some headphones that cancel out background noise (like the ones you can get for planes), and use them if you know the baby is being looked after.
+ Get some exercising done or leave the house for a short run – fresh air and physical activity are great stress busters.
+ Check with neighbours. It's amazing how the sound of a baby crying can carry.

One thing you might find effective in stopping the crying is to play music or 'white noise' (like switching on the vacuum cleaner) or sing to the baby. She may stop crying to focus on the noise or listen to you singing.

SLEEPING LIKE A BABY
As a result of the above changes, or for no apparent reason at all, your baby might alter his sleeping patterns. This can also happen as a result of your making adjustments to his daily, or nightly, routines (for example, if you're trying to reduce the number of night feeds he gets).

With so many changes happening it's not surprising that baby's sleeping patterns and habits will also change (if only he could let us know two weeks in advance!). This will probably make for some nocturnal surprises or difficulties in settling to sleep.

Baby sleep and how to influence it is the subject of numerous books, and there are an overwhelming number of theories, resources and sleep programmes available. There's a good reason for this – long-term sleep-deprived parents must be some of the most desperate beings in the universe. Consequently, they will go out of their way (or spend a fortune) looking for a solution.

It would be impossible to list all the various techniques and concepts here, and it's difficult even to make a recommendation as there's so much material available.

But if you are having problems getting your baby to sleep we suggest doing some online research, and speaking to other parents who have used a particular technique or programme you might be interested in before you try it. No matter what technique you choose, there's no gold-plated guarantee it will work, because every baby and every situation is different.

Also, the type of sleep programme you decide to try probably depends very much on your approach to parenting, e.g., 'control crying' might not be an option for you because you just can't bear to let your baby cry for extended periods.

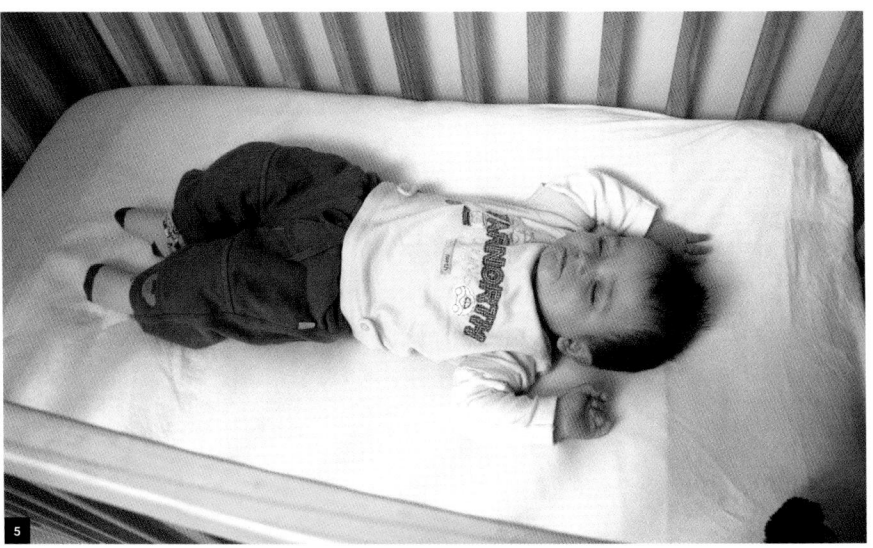

Call Me Dad!

MIKE:
Our first child went through a period of waking and crying in the night. We were advised to initiate a roster system whereby each of us (my wife and I) had a night on and a night off. That way, if it was my turn to get up and attend to the wailing, my wife could relax knowing it was being taken care of, and vice versa.

This didn't stop the crying (which turned out to be due to colic – it stopped on its own after 12 weeks, yawn) but at least it meant that each of us was only 50 per cent exhausted!

If you're really at the end of your tether, seek professional help from a local support organisation or your healthcare provider. To our knowledge, there are no 'magic pills' that doctors can prescribe for babies, although they might be able to help you in other ways.

You could also arrange for some temporary relief, like getting someone you trust to look after your baby for a night while you go somewhere where you can get a good night's rest. The world can look like a very different place after a decent sleep, especially if you haven't had one in a long time. www.DIYFather.com/sleep.

4. If you have a newborn who won't sleep through the night try an on/off roster system with your partner so both of you can get some sleep.

5. If only he could sleep so soundly through the night!

CHILD-PROOFING THE HOUSE

Newborns must find it frustrating being unable to move themselves about. There are all these new and tempting (if somewhat scary) things your baby can see but can't explore, because she's always too far away. So when she gets to the point where she can actually move her body, it's a hugely exciting time.

As a result she can look like she's got ants in her pants. Practising gross motor skills and developing the coordination required to move her body is an important part of her natural development. This may start as rocking back and forth on the spot, progressing to rolling, crawling and eventually walking.

At the first signs of this fantastic development taking place (typically around the six-month mark) your peaceful days of simply watching over your baby in one spot are over. If you haven't already done so, you'll need to child-proof your house pronto!

Child-proofing the house is another one of those great 'dad jobs'; once again, you can demonstrate to the world (and your family) what a cool dad you are. Child-proofing breaks down into the following general categories (you should check and deal with them all):

Furniture:
Walk through the entire house and check for anything that might be able to fall on top of your child: unstable furniture, doors they can open, drawers they can pull out, and so on. Fit baby locks to cupboards, and drawer protectors so she can't pull them out. If you have any unsecured furniture items (like a tall, thin CD rack) move them away temporarily. The same goes for anything precious or valuable at baby height.

Stairs/steps:
Although babies are pretty good at working out how to crawl up stairs, their spatial awareness hasn't fully developed yet. So you need to put gates in front of stairs and block access to steps.

Non-food items:

Anything that's not explicitly made for consumption by babies should be completely out of reach. The easiest way to do this is by moving them to 'higher ground', like a top shelf or cupboard. This is better than a lockable cupboard because one day you might forget to lock it. Typical substances/products this applies to are:

+ Just about every cleaning product in the house;
+ Pet food and litter;
+ Alcohol and spirits;
+ DIY and barbecue products (fire starters, paints, etc.).

Note: Most of the above are LETHAL, so it's absolutely essential you remove them from your baby's reach.

Garden/outdoors:

While it's important for your baby to spend time outdoors, at this age they aren't safe to do so on their own. There are numerous extra hazards in gardens, porches or other outdoor areas around the house. It is virtually impossible to create a safe area outside where babies and toddlers can play without adult supervision.

General hazards include:

+ Power sockets – buy some plug-in socket protector caps.
+ Cables – tuck them away safely or move to higher ground altogether. If he pulls on a cable he may expose a live wire and/or the device attached to it may fall on him.
+ Sharp items – any cutlery, knives, scissors, etc., which are not out of reach.
+ Heaters and fireplaces – you'll need safety shields around these.
+ Ovens and hobs – for obvious reasons. Keep your babies away from anything that's hot.
+ Dishwashers – keep door closed at all times. Babies might eat the rest of the dishwashing powder left in the compartment after the dishes are done.

Remember, babies have no concept of danger: to them everything invites exploration, so never allow them to play unsupervised. Neither do they have an appreciation of the value of things – however much you explain it to them through sign language, pointing or saying 'NO'.

Consider a play pen. These basically provide a confined safe area for your baby. Play pens can be a great relief for short periods when you just have to get something done and can't watch her. You know that in there, she's safe.

Child-proofing is an ongoing activity, because as your child develops she'll be able to access new dangers in the house and garden. So it's very important that you continue to check your house and property for anything that could be a hazard on a regular basis.

Having said all that, it's never too early to start educating your child about danger. If your child sees you touching a heater, for example, and wants to touch it as well, say firmly, but without shouting: 'No, that's dangerous.' You can also waggle your index finger as a warning signal. You'll be surprised at how much babies can pick up from gestures and your tone of voice.

DAD TIP #54:
A great way of checking that you've done a good job is to get down on your knees (and pray) . . . oh, and while you're doing that, crawl around your house. This will give you a similar perspective to your baby's. Check everything you can see and reach from down there, and remove or protect anything that's still unsafe.

DAD TIP #55:
Make sure you vacuum regularly and keep the floor particularly tidy. Babies have a habit of putting everything they find (and we mean everything) into their hungry little mouths. If they find stuff on the floor, it's not only unhygienic but also downright dangerous. Babies can choke on a button or peanut.

Make sure you spend some time making potential hazards around your home safe for your baby:

6. Fireplace with guard.

7. Gates over stairs.

8. Secure closing mechanism.

9. Door handle turned up.

10. Socket protector.

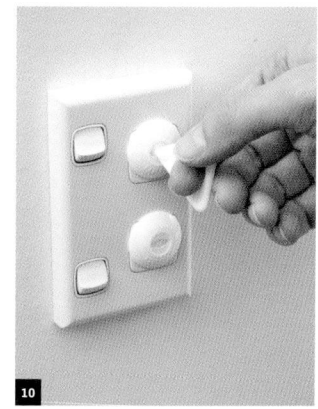

11

11. Mmmm . . . pegs.

12. Never underestimate the power of day-to-day household objects as endless sources of fascination for babies.

THE JOY OF EVERYDAY OBJECTS

When it comes to keeping your little one stimulated, you'll soon come to the realisation that:

+ The interest value of any toy is a few hours at the very most. No matter how excited your little darling is with his new toy at first, he'll find it utterly boring after a few hours.
+ New toys are expensive.
+ Anything battery-operated will get on your nerves after about five minutes and when the batteries run out you won't have any spares in the house (Murphy's Law – see more of these on page 171).

The good news is that for at least the first year of your baby's life there is a pretty good, cheap alternative to new toys. Here again is a chance for Superdad to shine, because you can turn everyday objects that are empty, broken or unused into toys.

Important: The key thing about using any household objects is to make sure they're safe for your child. Obviously don't use anything with sharp edges, detachable parts that could be swallowed, or anything painted with lead paint. So double-check that whatever you give him is safe. His natural curiosity will mean he'll bang the objects, put them in his mouth, and throw them, so they need to be robust (and not valuable!).

The DIYFather top-10 list of everyday objects that are bound to keep your baby stimulated:

+ Key rings.
+ Mobile phones (take the battery out).
+ TV/stereo remotes (take the battery out).
+ Vacuum cleaner (not plugged in).
+ A toiletry bag with old personal hygiene objects (toothbrushes, brushes, combs, etc.).
+ Computer keyboard.
+ A bag with coloured clothes pegs.
+ An old wallet with lots of old credit or business cards in it.
+ Large and empty cardboard boxes (to crawl through or hide under).
+ Empty shampoo/drinks bottles (which can be turned into rattles by filling with rice – but you have to make sure the tops are secure).

13. Cheap toys can be just as much fun, if not more so, than the expensive kind.

SIMPLE, CHEAP AND EFFECTIVE TOYS

Just as many everyday objects will entertain your child, we've also got some suggestions for simple and cheap toys for six- to twelve-month-olds. The great thing about these is that you can make most of them yourself. Alternatively, they are cheap to buy.

DIYFather top 10 simple and cheap toys for six- to twelve-month-olds:

+ Soap bubbles.
+ Finger/sock puppets.
+ Soft ball (tennis ball, small felt ball, toy football).
+ Mobile (no, not the phone . . . the thing you can hang or hold up, with lots of interesting objects attached to strings).
+ Alphabet mats with cut-out shapes for every letter and number.
+ Cardboard books.
+ Stack-up blocks.
+ Maracas (rumba shakers) and castanets.

LEAVING THEM WITH OTHERS

You might already have left your child with a babysitter or family member by now, but many parents don't like the idea of leaving their little precious with anyone until she's at least six months old.

That's not a bad thing, but sooner or later you'll want to go out as a couple and have some fun. The first time you do this is a big step, and don't be surprised if you find it difficult. It's important to get this right, for you, your partner and your child.

We've touched on babysitters in the previous chapter, but here's a reminder of some key things you and your partner should talk about before engaging the services of a childminder:

+ Does the babysitter have any experience, especially recent experience? How do you feel about leaving junior with your parents? It's probably many years since they babysat.
+ If the person is not family or a friend, what are their credentials and can you check their references?
+ Most important, do you trust them, and what is that trust based on?

Their intentions may be the best, but whoever is looking after your baby needs to understand that your child-rearing practices need to be maintained while you and your partner are away. This especially applies to:

+ Routines;
+ Feeding and special diets;
+ Sleeping and settling to sleep;
+ Your firm rules (such as no TV, no sweets, etc.); and
+ Anything else you're particular about.

There are some simple preparations you can make for this to work:

+ Arrange for the babysitter to come early, a good hour or so before you're due to leave, and – assuming they're not a family member the baby already knows – allow them to interact with your child while you're there so they get used to each other.
+ Leave your contact numbers (including emergency numbers) near the phone in clear sight. Draw the sitter's attention to them.
+ Tell the babysitter what procedure you'd like them to follow in the event of an emergency, so they're left in no doubt, and also what to do if for some reason they can't contact you, i.e., leave a family member's contact details, too.
+ Keep your phone on you at all times, switched on (to vibrate if you're going to a movie or show!).
+ Advise the babysitter where you'll be, and let them know when you expect to be home. Call them if the plan changes to say you'll be home later than expected.
+ Finally, make a conscious effort to take your mind off the baby (Hah! Good luck). If you've done all the background checks and preparations, your baby will be fine. It's a first difficult lesson in letting go, which will continue until your child leaves home, whenever that is!) But it's important for your own sanity to relax. If you're out with your partner for some 'us time', focus on her; that's why you organised the whole thing in the first place. Worrying about your baby achieves nothing. It certainly won't help your baby, and it might just ruin your outing.

REJOINING THE WORKFORCE

Returning to the workforce can be a nervous and exciting time for many parents, and it can also be a sad or frustrating time. There are many reasons why the primary caregiver might want to go back to work (financial, career options, interaction with other adults, etc.), but what do you do with your bundle of joy in the meantime?

If you don't have live-in care at home, then childcare/daycare or a nanny are your most likely options. But is it worth the cost, worry and hassle? It's an important question if your reason for returning to the workforce is financial, as childcare options typically don't come cheap. So you might find yourself working to pay for the care, which doesn't get you any further ahead financially. But it might meet other needs, such as retaining your position at work. Either way, you'll need to add up the numbers and do your homework before you go down the childcare path.

MONICA:

I was in a well-paid managerial position in a government department with a safe and secure job in an interesting environment. I enjoyed working with my colleagues, and I thoroughly enjoyed my job. When I got pregnant I thought, right, once the baby's born I'll take three months' parental leave and then return to work. Did I? No! I enjoyed my baby daughter so much that I just didn't want to go back to work! I resigned, and have absolutely no regrets about becoming a full-time mum.

Finding a childcare/daycare centre can be confusing; don't be tempted by the lowest price, look around, check various options and especially talk to people you know that have children in the centre you're considering. Many centres also offer try-out days where you can drop your child off (or hang around) to see how it goes. Certainly you should visit the premises of any centre you're considering to check out the environment and watch the staff at work. You'll soon get a feel for whether it's a well-run, safe and happy place for children.

DAD TIP #56:
It's common for childcare centres to have a waiting list, so if you're planning on getting your child into one, start investigating the options early.

What to look for in a childcare/daycare centre:

+ Safe location – is it in a safe neighbourhood/near a busy street?
+ Safe building – is it clean and child-safe (by regulation, it has to be)? Or is it old and rundown?
+ Is there a pleasant outdoor area available, with appropriate shelter from sun and rain?
+ Staff ratio – are there enough people to take care of the children at ALL TIMES?
+ Staff abilities – are they trained and qualified? There are strict regulations in place for operating childcare centres; don't be afraid to ask about staff qualifications.
+ How many children attend?
+ What are the centre's policies, e.g., about noise, behaviour, TV watching, sleeps, and so on? Do you agree with them?
+ What food and beverages do they give the children?
+ What is their incident history, and how long have they been registered with an official authority?
+ Can the dropping off and picking up of your child be organised safely and with relative ease?

If you decide to stay home and continue looking after your child but are worried about them not having the chance to interact with other babies, children or adults, early childcare/daycare centres are not the only options. You can also join (or start) a baby group or go along to some organised activities for babies.

COOL THINGS TO DO WITH BABIES AGED SIX TO TWELVE MONTHS

SIGN LANGUAGE

Baby signing is something that has really taken off in recent years and seems to be evolving all the time. Babies can learn to give signals from an early age, but signing typically starts when they are around eight months and their hand movements are more developed. It's important to realise signing 'lessons' are done in a spirit of fun rather than as a serious learning exercise. Every baby learns at her own pace and it is important that she doesn't feel rushed, otherwise both you and she will probably not enjoy it.

Why start with baby signing? Research tells us it helps develop their brains and gives them a method of simple communication with you. For many of their daily needs, e.g., 'I'm hungry', it decreases their frustration. It's a great dad activity and allows you to spend extra time playing and signing with your child. Signing is just one way of achieving a two-way communication with your baby, so you can be creative in your approach. It is just a fantastic moment though when you look into your baby's eyes and realise they understand a simple communication (and we're certain it's the same for your baby, who's probably feeling 'man, he FINALLY got it').

BABY SWIMMING

There are plenty of swimming centres that offer baby swimming. Introducing your baby to water can pay dividends later on when he needs to learn to swim, but can also be an excellent confidence builder, making your bathing (or showering) sessions easier and more fun. Whatever way you can find to expose your baby to water in a safe environment – do it. It's great for him to explore this natural element. No matter what you do, though, make sure your baby is ALWAYS SAFE in and near water. Never leave him unattended.

MUSIC FOR BABIES

Another great way to help your baby develop is to make music with him. Hopefully you will have already made use of the soothing effect of music by singing to your baby. As your baby gets older you can start introducing him to your favourite music.

You can also dance with him – either holding him or if he can already stand up, by holding his hands. As he gets older you can also get him to participate in the music by clapping hands or using simple percussion instruments, e.g., an empty box and a wooden spoon. Make sure you watch the volume levels as his hearing is a lot more sensitive than yours.

14. Introduce your baby to your music collection but remember, an infant's ear drums are pretty sensitive.

15. Though they may be wary at first, most babies soon come to love playing in the water.

16. Sign-language can be a wonderful communication tool for you and your baby before she starts to speak.

BABY GROUPS

Look in your local area for regular meet-ups with other parents or for special play groups/activity groups for babies. Your local library or community centre might run special groups that you can join. Don't be shy to ask to join existing groups, even if you are the only father in a mothers' group. If there aren't any groups in your area, just start one yourself – there are bound to be other parents who will join. If you start spreading the word or put a few flyers up, you'll probably get a group together very quickly.

Why is this so useful? It's great for your baby to interact with other babies, and good for you to network with other parents. You can find out what others are doing with their babies, discuss any issues that you might be experiencing, and generally swap ideas. It's also a great way to meet new people at a time in your life when it helps to have support.

BABY YOGA

No, this is not about having your baby hold herself in awkward positions. It is for you and mum to relax and bond with your baby, while taking care of your wellbeing. Your partner can benefit from postnatal yoga or baby yoga to alleviate common problems, such as back pain, weak pelvic-floor muscles, and other pains to do with lifting and feeding. You can benefit from baby yoga by spending that time with your baby, and doing simple exercises together that promote your and the baby's health. Not to mention a great way to relax and overcome the stress of rearing a baby.

It's also great for your baby to be in a public space with other adults and children, and to experience activities within groups. So, all up a great option for a fun and healthy pastime with your kid!

GETTING PREGNANT AGAIN

While it is apparently possible for your partner to get pregnant again six weeks after giving birth, would you want to? The answer could be a resounding 'yes!' if you've had a good run with your first baby, and you might be keen for more opportunities to apply your Superdad skills! Before you do, might we gently suggest you consider the following (with your partner):

Your partner's recovery:
Childbirth is very demanding on your partner's body, and every pregnancy is different. She might have had a good first pregnancy, but that doesn't mean the second one will be the same. Then again, if the first pregnancy was challenging, the second might be a breeze. The consensus among women seems to be that labour is usually quicker and easier the second time around. As for bringing up another baby – maybe you've had a blast with your first one, but the second one could be difficult. There's no way of forecasting.

Finances:
Now that you know how much your first child is costing you, make sure you have room in your budget for another one. If you were planning on your partner returning to work, then getting pregnant again needs serious consideration. On the other hand, if you have a second child of the same sex, you can save money with the hand-me-down clothes, plus you've already got toys.

Accommodation:
Can you accommodate another young member of the family, not only in your home but also your car? Sharing rooms can be challenging as a newborn and a toddler are on very different schedules and sleep patterns (later it's not so much of an issue). Transport-wise you can just about forget having any other passengers in the back seat. Your two babies might be small but their car seats aren't, and all their accessories and nappy bags take up space.

Energy (yours and your partner's):
Can you both handle it? This isn't an idle challenge but a genuine question to consider. So if you're tired now managing just one baby, you need to seriously examine your energy levels and your ability to cope, because having another will definitely put a lot more pressure on.

17. Baby yoga can mean fun and fitness for the whole family.

Time:

As with energy, do you have enough? What does your lifestyle look like now, and is there space for more elements? Let's face it, we already live in a time-precious age, so you want to be sure you can devote as much time to your second child as you did to the first. It's not a matter of giving your attention to whoever screams the loudest! (That might be you!)

Stress:

How are your stress levels? Is another child likely to bring either or both of you to breaking point? Not a healthy situation.

However, we don't want to sound like doom-and-gloom merchants. If you're both doing well from every point of view: physical recovery, money, accommodation, energy, time and you're coping with the stress, then why not have another baby? After all, it's just such a fantastic experience – isn't it? (Say 'Yes'!)

But if you're not doing well in any one of the areas we've listed above, it's probably better to hold off until you and your partner are on top of things (not winning-Lotto-on-top-of things, just where you know you need to be).

Another thing you might be wondering: what's the ideal age gap between kids? Well, how long is a piece of string? Ask 20 parents who've had two children and you'll get 20 different answers. If you're thinking of having another child as a playmate for the first, remember it doesn't automatically follow that they will play together.

But hey, don't let that get in the way! Whatever you choose to do, choose with your partner and love every minute of it.

18. Savour your baby's first birthday and reflect on the past year – you've reached a major milestone!

THE FIRST BIRTHDAY

The ultimate milestone (in terms of this book, anyway) is when your baby's first birthday arrives. This really calls for a celebration. There is obviously the birthday celebration you can put on for your baby, but there is also a more personal one for you and your partner. Both of you have managed to master doing something you have never done before. Congratulations! You are awesome. So take a moment and think of how you will celebrate with your partner.

OK, enough about you. Back to your baby. Here is the DIYFather list of ideas to celebrate your baby's first birthday:

+ Baby birthday party - invite lots of babies with their parents (perhaps people you've kept in touch with from your antenatal class or other courses).

+ Organise food for babies and prepare a suitable baby environment for them to really enjoy the day.

+ Make a photo album of top moments of the first 12 months. Use a robust album with laminated pages so your baby can play with it.

+ Create a small baby video starring your little champ. Keep it to less than five minutes as your baby may not be able to take more at this stage. For added fun, post it on youtube.com and share with friends and family.

+ Definitely TAKE THE DAY OFF WORK.

+ Make a toy for your baby (yes, MAKE – NOT BUY). You will know best what really gets your little champ going - things that make noise, things that have lots of colours and shapes, things with wheels, etc. Remember your DIY skills and let your imagination take over.

RICHARD:
We had a very small birthday party for the first birthday. We have since followed the rule that the number of invitations to children be the same number as the birthday we are celebrating, i.e., for her third birthday invite three friends (and their families).

FINDING YOUR FEET AS A DAD

There are countless studies on fathering, many of which find (or claim to find) that fathers need to be more actively engaged with their children. As a result there are many 'experts' (often women, for some reason) ready to tell men exactly how to do this. OK, it could be argued that females, as mothers, have an innate sense of parenting, but that doesn't mean dads can't find their own way through the thick mists of fatherhood.

Men and women each have a unique contribution to make to the rearing of their children. The key thing is not to try to turn them all out of the same mould. Which means, as a father you need to find your own style, as opposed to simply trying to copy what mothers do.

We believe that many men who are on the verge of becoming dads don't need ready-made concepts for how to be the best father, but rather reassurance that every man is already programmed to be a fantastic father. It's as much about confidence (and common sense) as it is about acquiring new knowledge.

So as we're nearing the end of the book, this is another encouragement to all fathers to be bold (and probably bald after a while), and find your own unique and beautiful fathering style.

THE DIYFATHER MURPHY'S LAW FOR BABIES

In case you haven't come across Murphy's Law yet, consider familiarising yourself with its basic premise: if anything can go wrong, it will. Knowing Murphy's Law will not help you in any particular situation, but it might help you see the irony in life in general, and to laugh at it (in a Monty Python, always look on the bright side of life, kind of way).

When it comes to babies, laughter is a much better response than anger for almost everything. So look through our top 10 list of Murphy's Laws for babies, and smile. After 12 months with a baby, you can surely come up with your own list as well:

+ Murphy's Law is spending ages trying to bottle-feed your baby, with her falling asleep on the bottle, dribbling it out of her mouth or pushing it away: by the time she finally gets into feeding, the bottle has run out.
+ If anything can go wrong, it will when the baby is nearby.
+ Your baby will damage anything in your possession in direct proportion to its value.
+ The law of selective digestion: the chance of your baby spilling milk is directly proportional to the cost of your shirt or the carpet.
+ The law of relativity: 10 minutes of handling a screaming baby is far longer than seeing her smile at you for 10 minutes during your lunch break.
+ No matter how long or how hard you shop for anything you need for the baby, after you've bought it, you'll find it on sale cheaper somewhere else.
+ When you bring the stroller, the baby will want to walk. When you forget the stroller, she will want to ride in it.
+ Your least stressful nappy-change occurs when you're alone with the baby. Your most stressful nappy-change always occurs when you're showing off your dad skills to someone you want to impress.
+ The likelihood that your baby decides to poo and pee increases when you are on your last clean nappy in the house, or with the value of the surface he is placed on.
+ The availability of daycare is inversely proportionate to how badly you need it.

END OF YEAR-ONE TEST – WHAT KIND OF PARENT ARE YOU?

At the end of your first year with a baby you will have developed your very own fathering style. Take our five-point quiz and see how you score!

1. Your one-year-old wakes in the night crying. Do you:

A. Rap on the wall, exhorting her to 'get over it'? (1 point)
B. Rap on your partner, suggesting she 'deal with it'? (2 points)
C. Get up immediately, rush into the bedroom and offer lullabies and confectionery? (3 points)
D. Wait a few minutes to see if the crying stops before going in to check/reassure? (4 points)
E. Wake refreshed the next morning? (5 points)

2. Your one-year-old wakes for the fourth time that night, the third night in a row. Do you:

A. Rush into her room and threaten her with dire punishment? (1 point)
B. Dig your partner in the ribs, reminding her that it was she who wanted a baby in the first place? (2 points)
C. Get up immediately, rush to the computer and Google-search sleep problems while your partner checks the baby? (3 points)
D. Take her into your own bed to cuddle and comfort her till she finally goes to sleep? (4 points)
E. Wake refreshed the next morning? (5 points)

3. Your toddler throws an almighty tantrum in the supermarket. Do you:

A. Smack him and look over your shoulder to see if anybody saw you? (1 point)
B. Crouch down next to him and spend the next 30 minutes explaining the ethics of displaying anger, from a liberal, rationalist, post-industrial perspective? (2 points)
C. Lie next to him on the floor and throw a tantrum yourself? (3 points)
D. Laugh while placing him back in the shopping trolley? (4 points)
E. Actually not notice till you find him lying on the floor on your second lap of the pet-food aisle? (5 points)

4. Your toddler poos on the kitchen floor. Do you:

A. Rub her nose in it? (1 point)
B. Point it out to your partner? (2 points)
C. Don surgical gown, gloves and nose peg before removing it with a long-handled shovel? (3 points)
D. Show her the proper place, in the toilet? (4 points)
E. Kick it under the stove? (5 points)

5. Your one-year-old son practises horseback riding on your dachshund. Do you:

A. Kick the dog for being near your baby? (1 point)
B. Get a bigger dog? (2 points)
C. Explain to him the importance of treating animals kindly? (3 points)
D. Call Animal Rescue? (4 points)
E. Join him? (5 points)

Add your scores from each part of the five-point quiz into one total to find where you stand on the parental spectrum:

<5 points: You can't count.

5-10 points: You need help. Your parenting is tense and volatile. Suggestions include: anger management, calming music, any meditation group that does not use recreational drugs.

11-15 points: Parenting style is perfectionist (not perfect), uptight with high expectations, though you do have your child's best interests at heart.

16-20 points: Parenting style is relaxed, undemanding, optimistic and fatalistic, though you do have your child's best interests at heart.

21-25 points: You need help. Your parenting is so relaxed you are virtually nonexistent. Suggestions include: bone-growth diet, team-building exercises, join the army.

>25 points: You can't count.

19

20

19. Crawling is great for developing your baby's motor skills.

20. Make a baby obstacle course and get her ready for the 2032 Olympics!

21. Reading proves even more useful as baby gets older, so keep it up. Try introducing another language, too, if you like.

ACTIVE MOVEMENT – SIX TO TWELVE MONTHS

After six months the speed of development accelerates even faster (can you believe it)? So now that your baby can roll around, use her hands and feet intentionally (yes, those kicks to your tummy are no accident) and make all sorts of funny noises (other than crying), she will pick up the pace again. Try the following activities, which are all great fun, and help your baby master the skills she is programmed to develop over the next six months.

ACTIVITY IDEAS FOR SIX TO TWELVE MONTHS

1. Crawling:
Get down on your knees and chase your baby around the room – let her chase you too! Even when your baby can walk already, crawling is still a great exercise for developing motor skills, and it's a lot of fun.

2. Challenge course:
Set up chairs with sheets to crawl under in the living room or outside on the lawn. Lay down cushions to jump over, ropes to walk along and balance, etc.

3. Hand/foot-eye co-ordination (good for sports training!):
Sit your baby on the floor. Hang a balloon (or another object that dangles) in front of him and use his hands/feet to pat the balloon. Hand/foot-eye co-ordination is great for sports training later in life.

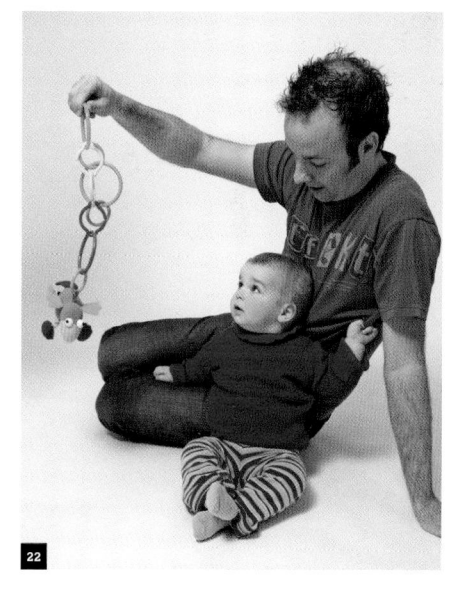

4. Language awareness:
When getting dressed, talk about the parts of the body that are being covered. Use names of body parts such as head, tummy, arms, legs and others that are not so commonly used (e.g., heel, ankle, thigh, spine, elbow).

5. Eye movement – eyes need to move, too!:
When reading to your baby, slowly point to different things in the picture at different places on the page. This encourages her eyes to move.

22. Dangling objects work hand-eye co-ordination.

CHAPTER 9

THE FIRST YEAR: LOOKING BACK

So you've made it to the first birthday. Congratulations! And what a year it has no doubt been. By now you'll most likely be familiar with that seemingly innate knowledge your baby has of what best stains clothing and how to leave indelible marks on the furniture. Relax! It's all part of the process.

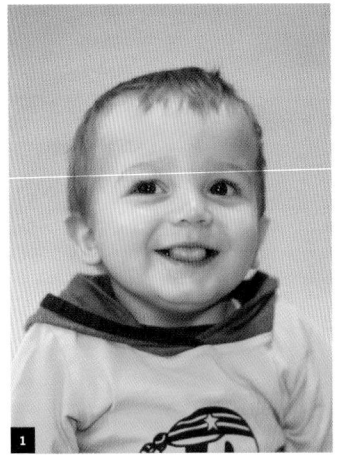

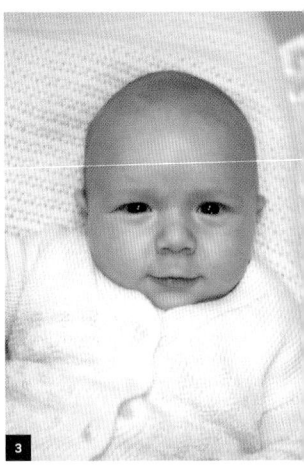
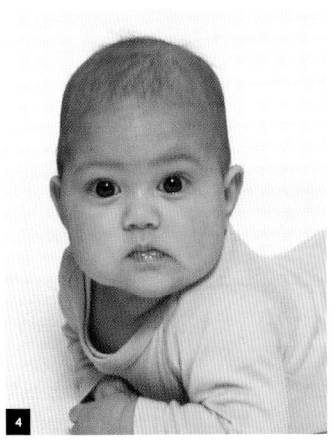

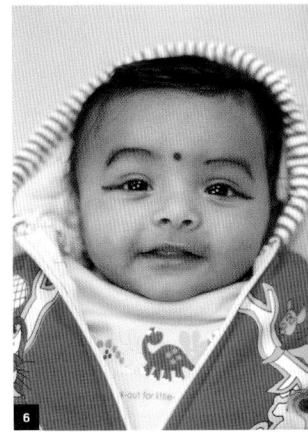

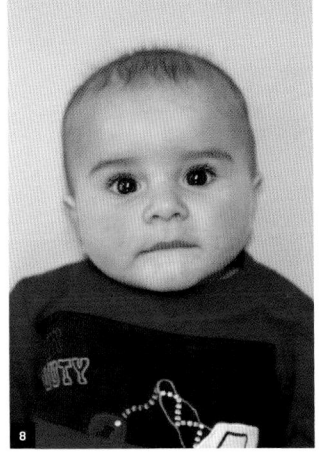

1. Noah
2. Reneé
3. Leo
4. Ava
5. Nicolás
6. Gauranga
7. Pyper
8. Daniel

This final chapter is about looking back over the first 12 months with your baby. We'd like to share some stories from dads, reflecting on the new and overwhelming experience they've been through, and what they would do differently if they knew then what they know now.

We'll also look at some more fun stuff for you to share with your developing child, and what to look forward to when looking after toddlers.

THE EXPERIENCE OF BEING A FATHER

STEPHEN:
It was so much more absorbing (of time, emotion and everything else) than I could ever have predicted.

BILL:
Becoming a dad for the first time is like being hit by a tornado. After I found out I was going to be a dad, I realised it was the end of my life being all about me. I would have a little dependant whom my life would now revolve around. It was time to become a family man and take on the responsibility of becoming a parent.

MATT:
Since becoming a father, I do worry quite a bit. I write letters to my daughter on a website called DearSpike.com. Like a lot of people who blog, my posts are categorised by topic. And one of the most frequent topics is 'worry', which is sort of funny because I've never considered myself to be someone who worries about anything much at all. I worry about our world – about what we're leaving for our children. I worry about the stupid wars we're fighting and the horrible ways we treat one another. I worry about the water and the air that we've polluted so horribly. I worry a lot about the world my daughter is growing up in, but I honestly don't worry much about my daughter herself. I'm so confident that she'll make the best of whatever world I leave for her.

STEF:
You cry and you laugh – it is a very emotional journey and I'm loving every minute of it. The stuff babies and toddlers do every day is actually quite funny, interesting or downright hilarious. Their behaviour can be pretty random at times and you often wonder how on earth they came up with something – but ultimately you just enjoy the unpredictability of it all.

ERIC:
The most powerful moment of my life, is holding my baby in my arms. I am my baby's provider, protector, teacher, entertainer and I give it all with my unconditional love, that is what it is to be a father.

DADS LOOK BACK

STEF:
The one thing I would do differently is to start a routine from day one, and be as strict as possible about timing when things happened. I think we really screwed this up and as a result made it much harder for Noah to settle, or even give him an idea of what his days should generally look like.

SCOTT:
Looking back, you think it's been the toughest part of your life, but damn, it's worth it. An old wise man once said to me, 'having children completes you'. At the time, Renee was pregnant and I thought that he was bloody mad, but after Pyper was born there was a feeling of completeness to my life like nothing else mattered. I now understood what he meant.

MATT:

I figured an antenatal class was a good idea. But three minutes into the first session, I wasn't so sure. Here's how it went: we all walked in, carrying pillows as instructed, then sat around and made small talk: When are you due? Oh, really? That's just a few days after us! What are you having? A baby. Wow, us too!

And then the instructor came in and had us introduce ourselves. 'Mums, I want you to tell me about what you love most about being pregnant. And dads, I want you to tell me what you hate most about it.' To our collective credit, most of the dads successfully dodged the question, although one poor sucker took the bait: 'I don't really like all the mood swings.' He wasn't at the second class.

The rest of the first class went more smoothly, though it ended with a rather awkward 'visualisation' exercise, kind of a semi-hypnotic activity where we all lay on the floor and the instructor took us on a hike through our minds: 'You're in a forest, and there's a stream of cool water, and up in the tree-tops there's a little squirrel . . .' In the right conditions – like after a yoga class with a bunch of open-minded, wholegrain-eating people vegging out on yoga mats – this might work. But not with a dozen uncomfortable pregnant women and an equal number of goofy dads lying in various states of discomfort on the floor of a hospital conference room with the smell of cafetaria food wafting in from next door.

The second session was better. For one thing, there were no visualisation exercises. Instead, we practiced positions, stretches and massages that will supposedly make labour more bearable for the mothers in our group. And the only dads who got hung this time around were the ones who hung themselves (like the guy who suggested we hold a contest to see which mother had the worst stretch marks.)

MORE ADVICE FOR EXPECTANT FATHERS

STEPHEN:

It's going to be the best experience you'll ever have.

CHRIS:

My advice for introducing babies to water:

1. Keep smiling: You don't want to give them a fear of water before they can even walk.

2. Keep watching: That way their head stays above water.

3. Keep cleaning: Seriously, newborn baby skin is prone to all sorts of rashes and flare-ups. This is an actual proper job you are being allowed to do! Best do it properly.

SCOTT:

This is the best time of your life, its all new, you have no idea, and your partner knows just as much as you do – nothing! It's a clean canvas and remember, there is no finish line and you can't make a mistake, all you can do is your best!

Make sure you take lots of photos, change lots of nappies, get vomited on lots – only then will you truly qualify as a DIYFather. Nothing can prepare you for fatherhood, except the acceptance that you are about to learn a lot.

Besides this book, we at DIYFather recommend you buy another book called *Save our Sleep*. It offers incredibly useful advice for establishing a routine that will help you and your baby sleep more regularly. You will never look back!

RICHARD:

The most useful present we got was two hours' free housework from a friend. It was a little weird to accept but I would have no qualms about accepting the same gift again!

MATT:

Give him the benefit of talking about his kid all the time for the first six months, because chances are that's the only thing he's going to be able to talk about. It's not that dads want to be like this. In fact, if you forced us to watch a videotape of ourselves, we'd probably be disgusted. But something happens when you have a kid and your brain shuts down and then it's all just nappies, nappies, nappies, baby food, breasts (but not like that!) and more nappies, blah blah blah!

Seriously, six months of patience is the absolute best present you can give a mate. Then, at the end of month six, buy him tickets to a football game and when you pick him up say, 'OK arsehole, we've talked about your kid for six months and that's great, but tonight we're going to talk about football, beer and breasts (but not like that!).'

RICHARD:

Take as much time as possible off work. I've been lucky both times to be able to be around a lot in the first six months. The early months I reckon will be the most draining time of your life – what with disrupted sleep, learning to look after a child, coping with unexpected problems, and so on.

Also, help your wife as much as possible – don't assume that because she is a woman she somehow automatically knows what to do. She has been experiencing huge changes in her life – hormonal, body shape, learning to breastfeed and suddenly having almost no time to herself. And spending time with your child now will help you develop a strong relationship later. You'll also miss less of those magic moments, like the first time he smiles, rolls over, pees on the carpet . . .

ERIC:

Don't forget your relationship: it was your relationship that came first and it is because of your relationship that you have a baby. You are not only just a father.

DEAN:

Make sure you take care of yourself by scheduling exercise. After you get over the initial sleep deprivation, it is possible to get out of bed three times a week at 5.30 am to exercise. I find it is the only time I can do it.

Where the baby's development is concerned, read to her straight away, and continue to read books that are just ahead of her level of comprehension so she'll be a little bit stretched.

STEF:

Get stuck in! Don't let overeager mums or other family members take control of everything with regard to your baby, causing you to feel more and more like an outsider. If need be, tell your partner or others that you want to be involved and, even if you are not doing things the same way they might do them, it doesn't mean it's wrong.

I think the best thing you can give a mate is your time and some practical advice (if he asks for it). Cook for the family, help in the garden, lend him stuff or ask how he's getting on. Even if he says no to everything it's still great for him to know that he can rely on you if need be.

MORE BABIES AND WHAT TO EXPECT FROM TODDLERS

RICHARD:

When I found out about baby number two I thought, I'm not ready for that! Exactly the same thought as when I found out about number one. I think my wife realised that I might be a little shocked so she broke the news by email (very twenty-first century).

STEPHEN:

When I found out about baby number two I felt delighted, but much more relaxed, and I probably enjoyed the actual birth experience more because of it.

BILL:

When my eldest son was born, it was like a huge rush of joy, excitement and exhilaration all at the same time. Becoming a dad for the second time, when my daughter was born four years later, was also exciting and still came with a rush of feeling, but it seemed more like a gift than a miracle to me. I felt very lucky to now have both a son and a daughter.

Twelve years later, becoming a dad again, well . . . Caleb arrived within 45 minutes of us realising his mum had gone into labour: I guess you could definitely call that a rush! He was born in our bedroom on a cold, wet winter's night. All went well, and I almost caught him as he popped out! I held him for about 30 minutes in total amazement and bonded with him just after he was born. I am now a SAHD (stay-at-home dad) and look after him during the day.

I have learnt so much becoming a dad again after 12 years, and want to learn more. I play an active part in my new son's early childhood and wish to give him as many opportunities as I can.

We learn when we have children later in life, the second or third time around, both from the things we've done right before and the mistakes we've made. Every baby also come with its own

challenges, ups and downs, surprises and routines, and generally just a busy, busy time!

DEAN:

A two-year-old is a very curious person, always experimenting, always exploring – he is, in fact, a scientist! And if you look at his activities in that way, it can change your perspective and allow creative ideas to emerge, making life easier for you and for him. I'd like to suggest an exercise to try. Just for one day, picture him not as a small child, but rather as a visiting scientist. He needs materials to use, time to do his research, and your assistance from time to time. If you had a visiting scientist at your house, wouldn't you feel curious too, and wouldn't you feel honoured to help however you could? That's exactly the right attitude to take with a busy toddler.

Unfortunately, society doesn't take that attitude, and we're led to believe that a two-year-old should behave like an adult. That's absurd and unrealistic of course, but nevertheless, it's what many people seem to expect.

Punishment doesn't work, and we need to look for more effective and positive alternatives. Sometimes it just takes a little imagination and a good understanding of your child's personality. When my son was two, he loved going to playgrounds, but never wanted to leave. This became a real problem for me, as it seemed impossible to prevent the tears and frustration at the end of an otherwise happy day. When I thought about what might make it easier, I remembered he loved racing me. The next time we left the playground, I asked if he wanted to race me to the car. He was happy with this solution.

The best advice I've ever been given about child-rearing is to use humour whenever possible. Also, remember: children do take our time. They take our energy. They take our love. But the more time and energy we give them now, the less they'll need in the future. And the more love they can give back.

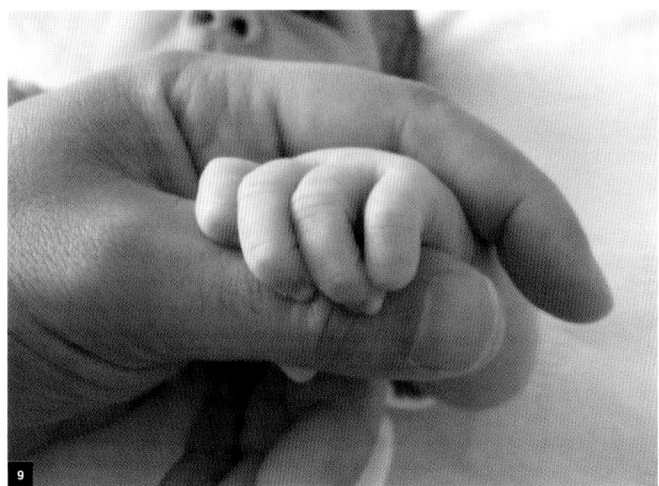

9. Your little miracle will continue to amaze you as he grows.

DEAN:
When I found out number two was on the way I was rapt, we both were. To be honest, before that we didn't really want a second child, as number one was so good. We only tried for a second baby so number one could have a playmate. Now we're so pleased we did.

SOME FINAL WORDS OF WISDOM

How do you get your baby to sleep?

RICHARD:
I originally put him in the Moses basket and rocked the basket on a rocking stool. The basket was much longer than the stool and rather unsteady, but it seemed to work . . . until the basket fell off the stool and the baby woke up rather suddenly.

I've also tried to perfect a method of putting a sleeping baby into his cot without waking him. The difficult bit is how to get your arm out from under him. I used to slide my left arm all the way up his back and his head until I held him mainly on my left arm. Then I'd gently slide my right arm out from under him until I was just holding his head. Success ratio – about 50%!

ERIC:
Establishing a routine has worked well for us, and Ava has slept through the night within a month of being home. Of course she will still occasionally wake during the night or earlier than usual.

DEAN:
We found having a routine is the most important thing, e.g., dinner, bath, feed, stories then bed.

STEF:
Get a good lullaby CD or songbook and play it or sing to your baby.

SCOTT:
Routine is the most important thing a little person can have, from the time they wake up to the time they go to bed, it's like being in the army. It's easy for me as a parent because I know when to feed her and when to put her down, etc. Playing with them also means they will fall asleep faster if you tire them out.

10-11. Fatherhood: the best and most challenging experience you'll ever have.

How did you get your baby to eat?

RICHARD:
Distraction, distraction, distraction. Initially we used a book, finger puppets, anything to make him forget he is strapped into a highchair and should be eating. Later on we would make up long-winded stories about helicopters, buses, planes, anything really to get him distracted enough to open his mouth. We also mixed up strange concoctions to disguise foods he wouldn't try. My favourite, i.e., most revolting, was yoghurt, banana and tuna! The aim being to get some protein into him. Eating in front of him also usually does the trick. After a minute he gets jealous and wants to try what we are eating.

SCOTT:
When they start eating solids trying to get them to eat anything can be a problem, so what we have found is, make sure you know what your baby likes in texture, what size they like their food and how you are going to feed it to them. I also give Pyper her own spoon so she thinks she is feeding herself and then I feed her in between her getting the food out of the bowl and into her mouth.

Tricks when changing your baby?

RICHARD:
1. Use a hairdryer for distraction – not sure if it's the noise or the warm air, but for months we put on the hairdryer every time we changed my son's nappy. If we didn't he screamed. How we came up with it I have no idea, but it worked!
2. Be prepared – have everything ready. And for boys, cover the cannon or you'll get wet.

DEAN:
If you are thinking about using eco-friendly nappies, just do it. We made the change when our second baby was about nine months, and wish we'd done it sooner. One thing's for sure – you don't have to think about going to the supermarket to buy nappies when they're on special.

SCOTT:
When they are a little bit older – around eight months plus – they wriggle and turn over and then also they try to run away while you're changing their nappy. Make sure you have the new nappy, cream and wipes at close range, then give them a book or their favourite toy to study and, hopefully, forget about being changed!

GLOSSARY

Afterbirth: The end result of the waste that comes out of the mother's body, and is usually made up of the amniotic sac, the placenta and the umbilical cord.

Amniotic fluid: The watery liquid surrounding and cushioning a growing foetus. It allows the foetus to move freely inside the walls of the uterus.

Amniocentesis: Also referred to as the amniotic-fluid test or AFT. A medical procedure used in prenatal diagnosis of genetic abnormalities and foetal infections, in which a small amount of amniotic fluid is extracted from the amnion or amniotic sac surrounding a developing foetus. The foetal DNA is then examined.

Braxton Hicks: Also known as false labour or practice contractions. These sporadic cramps are often felt during the second or third trimester of pregnancy.

Caesarean section (or C section): When the baby is delivered through surgery to the mother's abdomen often implemented if the baby is breech (upside-down) or shows any signs of distress during labour.

Cradle cap: A flaky, crusty, yellow-coloured skin rash that occurs on the scalp of newborn babies. Also known as seborrheic dermatitis, it is very common, is usually not itchy, and does not bother the baby.

Colic: A condition common in newborns whereby the baby cries incessantly without an obvious reason. One theory is that colic is due to abdominal pain caused by feeding, however, this has not been proven.

Colostrum: Also known as first milk or 'immune milk', it is a form of milk produced by the mammary glands in late pregnancy and the first few days after giving birth. Colostrum is high in carbohydrates, protein and antibodies and low in fat (as newborns may find fat difficult to digest).

Embryo: Your future baby is called an embryo from the moment of fertilisation until the end of the eighth week.

Epidural: The common shortened form of 'epidural anesthesia', a form of regional anaesthesia involving the injection of drugs through a catheter placed into the spinal column.

Foetus/fetus: The foetal stage starts in the ninth week after fertilisation, as your baby's major structures have formed, and lasts until birth.

Fontanelle: A soft part of an infant's skull that allows the head to pass through the birth canal. Fontanelles eventually harden, fusing the bones of the skull together.

Forceps: A handheld, hinged instrument (like giant scissors without blades) used for grasping and to assist the delivery of a baby in certain situations during labour.

Induction: A method of artificially or prematurely stimulating labour in a woman.

Nuchal-fold test: A non-invasive and painless procedure performed early on in the pregnancy, usually between 11 and 13 weeks. The test is used to determine the probability of having a baby with Down's syndrome or a similar condition.

Placenta: An organ that develops during pregnancy and functions as a gateway between the foetus and the mother.

Premenstrual Syndrome (PMS) or Premenstrual Tension (PMT): A collection of physical, psychological and emotional symptoms relating to a woman's menstrual cycle. The symptoms generally vanish after the menstrual flow starts, but may continue even after the flow has begun.

Postnatal: The period that starts immediately after the birth of a child and extends for about six weeks.

Premature: The birth of a baby before the standard period of pregnancy (also called 'full term') is completed.

Prenatal pregnancy: The carrying of one or more offspring inside the uterus, e.g., having twins or triplets.

SAHD (Stay-at-home dad): A male parent who is the main caregiver of the child(ren).

SIDS (Sudden Infant Death Syndrome): A syndrome marked by the symptoms of sudden and unexplained death of an apparently healthy infant aged one month to one year. Also known as cot death.

Ultrasound scan: An ultrasound-based diagnostic imaging technique used to visualise muscles and internal organs.

Umbilical cord: The connecting cord between the developing embryo or foetus and the placenta (also called birth cord).

INDEX

Page numbers in **bold** refer to illustrations.

A

accommodation, for more than one baby 168
active movement 126
    first three months 127-8, **128, 129**
    three to six months 148-9, **148, 149**
    six to twelve months 174-5, **174, 175**
afterbirth 87
age gap between children 169
air travel 145
alcohol 29, 30, 36, 125
amniocentesis 25, 34
animals 65-6
antenatal classes and courses 70-2, 124, 180
APGAR score 87

B

backpacks 55
babies
    bonding with 20, 101, 114
    first three months 111-29
    impact on your life 17-19, 65
    six to twelve months 151-75
    three to six months 131-49
babies, newborn
    bathing 105, 107
    bringing home from hospital 103-4
    dad's role 85, 93
    handling 93-4
    hygiene 100, 101, 104
baby blues 102
baby groups 168
baby showers 72
babysitters 145-6, 164-5
bags
    baby 56, 57, 120
    hospital 68-9
ball catching 149, **149**
bassinettes 52
bathing 105, 107, 141
baths 53
bedtime routine 133, 134, 152, 153, 183
bibs 136
birth
    dad's role during labour and birth 75, 79-82, 83, 85, 87-8
    last-minute preparations 78

birth certificates 138
birth plans 44-5
birthday, first 170-1, **170**
blood tests 34
bonding with your baby 20, 101, 114
booster car seats 54
bottle (formula) feeding 40, 95, 96, 97, 133, 137, 152, 153
    checking temperature of milk 118
bottles 55-6
    sterilising 104-5
Braxton Hicks contractions 34-5
breast pumps 56
breastfeeding 40, 95-5, 96, 97, 117, 133, 137, 152, 153
    after teething 155
    freezing breast milk 117
bubbles 128, **128**
buggies 57-60, 121
burping 96-7

C

Caesarian section 83, 102
capsules 54, 55, 103, 144
car journeys 144
car seats 54-5, 103
cars, family 47, 60
ceremonies 146
challenge course 174
chamomile tea 137, 156
changing tables 52, 64, 107, 153
childcare/daycare centres 46, 165
    what to look for 166
childproofing the house 159-60, **161**
clothes, babies'
    first three months 49-51, 119
    layers, for warmth 114
    what not to buy 62
    when going outdoors 114, 120
colic 97, 113, 159, 186
contact your baby has with other people 114, 117
cooking 118-19
cots 52-3, 153
crawling 174
crying 97-8, 99, 157
cups, drinking 136

D

dad/man showers 74-5
dads
    advice from other dads 180-1

end of year-one test 172–3
experience of being a father 179–180
feelings about having second baby 182
finding your feet as 171
five secrets of success 19, 153
involvement 10–11, 13, 32–3
mental preparation 65
readiness assessment test 13
stay-at-home 45–7
dancing to music 149, **149**
daycare centres, see childcare/daycare
centres
diet, parents 118–19, 123
distractions
to encourage eating 184
while dressing and changing babies 153,
185
DIYFather readiness assessment test 13
dressing 49, 119, 153, 185

E

education funds 139
exercise 27, 123, 157, 169, 181
eye movement 175

F

family 146
contacting after birth 93
support from 63, 78, 98, 99, 102, 123
visits from 109
fathers, see dads
feeding 118, 133
night feeds 64, 97, 113, 133, 157
schedules 113, 134, 152–3
see also breastfeeding; bottle (formula)
feeding; solids
finances 139–41, 168
finger games 148, **148**
fingernails, cutting 117
flat-head syndrome 98
food containers 55–6
foot/hand-eye coordination 174
forceps delivery 85
formula feeding, see bottle feeding
freezing food for use after birth 62
friends
contacting after birth 93
support from 63, 78, 102, 123
visits from 109
front packs 55
furniture, childproofing 159

G

godparents 146
grandparents 146, **147**
guardians 138, 146

H

hair cutting 117
hand/foot-eye coordination 174
hats 114 [check clothing page]
health 123; see also sickness
herbal teas 137, 156
highchairs 136
home births, preparation for 70
hospital bag, what to pack 68–9
hospital staff, getting the best from 82–3, 88
hospital tours 67
house renovations 63–4
hygiene
equipment for 53
first three months 114
food preparation 118
newborn babies 100, 101, 104

I

illness, see sickness
immune system 114, 157
immunisation 123, 157
income protection 139, 141
insurance 138, 139–40

J

journals
baby 96, 108
birth 81

L

labour
dad's role during labour and birth 75,
79–82, 83, 85, 86–8
list of what not to say during 81
lactation consultants 95
Lamaze toys 121
language awareness 174
libraries 141
life insurance 139–40
logs, see journals

M

massage 127–8
mastitis 117
meconium 101
midwives 33, 35, 70, 82–3, 88, 95, 96, 98,

134
monitors 114, 115
Moses baskets 52
Murphy's Law for babies 171
music 166, **167**

N

names, choosing 40, 43
naming ceremony 146
nannies 145-6, 165
nappies
    changing 101, 106, 107-8, 153, 185
    disposal 55, 56
    drying 56
    types 43-4, 106
newborn babies, see babies, newborn
night feeds 64, 97, 113, 133, 157
nuchal-fold test 25, 33-4
nursery 52-3, 63-4, 133
nursing chair 52, 64

O

obstetricians 33, 35-6, 82, 87, 88
outdoor areas around house, hazards in 160
outdoor trips 114, 120-1, **120**
overstimulation 143

P

parenting approaches 11-12
'Parents in the Neighbourhood' (PIN) groups
    124
partners, caring for and helping
    during first few days after birth 101-2, 181
    during labour and birth 75, 79-82, 83, 85, 87-8
    during pregnancy 27, 29-31
    maintaining relationship 124, **125,** 181
paternal leave 45
pets 65-6, 108
placenta 87
play pens 160
postnatal depression 102-3
pregnancy
    deciding to get pregnant again 168-9
    fathers being part of 31-3
    first feelings about 14-18
    first trimester 24-5
    helping your partner 27, 29-31
    problems and risks 36
    screenings and procedures 33-4
    second trimester 25-6
    telling others about 14, 16-17

things to be avoided or reduced 30
    third trimester 26
primary healthcare organisation, registering
    with 138
punishment 182

R

reading 141, **142**
registration of birth 138
retirement savings 140-1
routine
    first three months 112-13, 122, 179
    three to six months 133-4
    six to twelve months 152-3

S

safety
    childproofing the house 159-60, **161**
    on elevated surfaces 94, 108, 153
Sangenic 56
scissors 117
sea travel 145
sensory development 127
sex, during pregnancy 16, 37, 124
schedules, see routines
shoes **118,** 119
showering with your baby 141
sickness 108, 156-7; see also health
SIDS (sudden infant death syndrome) 98, 123, 125
sign language 166, **167**
singing 141, 143, 148-9, **148**
skin-on-skin contact 88, 114, **116**
sleep
    babies 97, 99, 113, 132, 133, 134, 152-3, 157, 159, 183-4
    parents 97, 98, 101
sleeping position for babies 98
smoking 30, 31, 36, 123, 125
solids 134, **135,** 136-7, 184
spoons, baby-feeding 136
Sport and Recreation New Zealand 126
stairs and steps, childproofing 159, **161**
stay-at-home dads 45-7
sterilising bottles 104-5
strollers 57-60, 121, 145
Sudden Infant Death Syndrome (SIDS) 98, 123, 125
sun exposure management 120, 121
support groups, informal 124, **125**
    baby groups 168
support organisations 123-4

support people, for birth 78, 83
swaddling 96, 98
swimming 166
Swiss ball 128, **129**

T
teething 155-6
temperature
    babies 113-14
    environment 114, 123
    formula liquid 118
thermometers 113-14, 115
time, spending with baby 122, 169
toddlers 182
toenails, cutting, 116, 117
toys
    everyday objects **162,** 163, **163**
    for newborns and first three months 53,
       62, 121-2
    six to twelve months 163-4
travelling with your baby **143,** 144-5, **144**
tummy time 148
20-week screening 34

U
ultrasound scans 24-5, 26, 33
umbilical cord, cutting 86-7, 88

V
ventouse birth 75
visitors 103-4, 109

W
walks 143
wills 138
workforce, rejoining 165
working vs staying at home 140

Y
yoga, baby 168, **169**

ACKNOWLEDGEMENTS

THANKS TO:

+ Our children Pyper, Nastassja, Christian, Amber, Ava and Noah for giving us the opportunity to be fathers in the first place!
+ Our partners Renee, Andrea and Raquel for their support and for putting up with all the baby talk.
+ Mike Bodnar for helping us turn our ideas into an actual book.
+ Alicja Skop for coordinating all the photo shoots and helping to pull it all together.
+ Karina Smith for her outstanding photographs and patience with us.
+ Special thanks to Mr Ussher for helping out with an emergency photo shoot.
+ Shelley Gilliver and the team at SPARC for their continuing support.
+ Tim Mahren Brown and The Campbell Institute for allowing us to temporarily take over their premises.
+ Dr Michel Sangalli for his help.
+ Baby Star in Newtown.
+ Yoga in Daily Life Centre, Wellington.
+ The various friends, family and children who have helped (or put up with our requests): Daniel, Dean, Leighton, Barbara, Amelie, Sally & Max, Kelly, Terry, Carolina R., Richard, Clara A., Tomás, Nicolás, Evan, Carolina C., Reneè, Ana, Dean, Daniel, Sanjay, Babita, Gauranga, Brent, Clara M., Mike, Victor, Ben, Leo, Gabriel Forsyth, Stu Forsyth and Lisa Reynolds.
+ The worldwide community of blogging (and non-blogging) dads who have sent in their stories: Matt Lawry, Gerry Browne, Matthew LaPlante, Richard Webster, Stephen Timperley, Dean Severinsen, Bill Wright, Darian Cairns-Cowan, Chris Guzzwell and Dana Glazer.

SPARC
ihi AOTEAROA
Sport & Recreation New Zealand
www.sparc.org.nz

Koringa Hihiko
ACTIVE
MOVEMENT